A Companion to Socrates

Blackwell Companions to Philosophy

This outstanding student reference series offers a comprehensive and authoritative survey of philosophy as a whole. Written by today's leading philosophers, each volume provides lucid and engaging coverage of the key figures, terms, topics, and problems of the field. Taken together, the volumes provide the ideal basis for course use, representing an unparalleled work of reference for students and specialists alike.

A Companion to Socrates

Edited by

Sara Ahbel-Rappe
and Rachana Kamtekar

BLACKWELL PUBLISHING
350 Main Street, Malden, MA 02148-5020, USA
9600 Garsington Road, Oxford OX4 2DQ, UK
550 Swanston Street, Carlton, Victoria 3053, Australia

The right of Sara Ahbel-Rappe and Rachana Kamtekar to be identified as the Authors of the
Editorial Material in this Work has been asserted in accordance with the UK Copyright, Designs,
and Patents Act 1988.

First published 2006 by Blackwell Publishing Ltd

1 2006

Library of Congress Cataloging-in-Publication Data

A companion to Socrates / edited by Sara Ahbel-Rappe and Rachana Kamtekar.
    p. cm. – (Blackwell companions to philosophy ; 34)
  Includes bibliographical references and index.
  ISBN-13: 978-1-4051-0863-8 (hardback : alk. paper)
  ISBN-10: 1-4051-0863-0 (hardback : alk. paper)   1. Socrates.   I. Ahbel-Rappe, Sara, 1960–
II. Kamtekar, Rachana, 1965–   III. Series.

  B317.C58 2006
  183′.2—dc22

                                                                        2005024158

A catalogue record for this title is available from the British Library.

Set in 10/12.5pt Photina
by Graphicraft Limited, Hong Kong
Printed and bound in the UK
by TJ International, Padstow, Cornwall

The publisher's policy is to use permanent paper from mills that operate a sustainable forestry
policy, and which has been manufactured from pulp processed using acid-free and elementary
chlorine-free practices. Furthermore, the publisher ensures that the text paper and cover board
used have met acceptable environmental accreditation standards.

For further information on
Blackwell Publishing, visit our website:
www.blackwellpublishing.com

This book is dedicated to the teachers all of us, contributors and editors alike, have shared, and to the memory of Gregory Vlastos.

Contents

Notes on Contributors

Sara Ahbel-Rappe is Associate Professor of Greek and Latin at the University of Michigan. She is the author of *Reading Neoplatonism* (2000), and a forthcoming translation of Damascius' *Doubts and Solutions Concerning First Principles.*

Ilai Alon was born in Jerusalem, where he received his academic education in Arabic language and literature. He specialized in medieval Arabic philosophy at Oxford. He is Associate Professor at Tel Aviv University, and has published on Socrates in Arabic literature, as well as a philosophical lexicon of al-Farabi. He is currently working on the institution of negotiations in Islam.

Hayden W. Ausland is Professor of Classics at the University of Montana. His publications on Plato include "On Reading Plato's Dialogues Mimetically," *American Journal of Philology* 118 (1997), 371–416.

Richard Bett is Professor of Philosophy and Classics, Johns Hopkins University. His publications include *Pyrrho, his Antecedents and his Legacy* (2000); Sextus Empiricus, *Against the Ethicists*, translated with introduction and commentary (1997); Sextus Empiricus, *Against the Logicians*, translated with introduction and notes (2005).

Tad Brennan is an Associate Professor of Philosophy and Classics at Northwestern University. He has written on all periods of Ancient Philosophy, from Presocratics to Neoplatonists. His books include *Ethics and Epistemology in Sextus Empiricus, The Stoic Life*, and *Simplicius on Epictetus' Encheiridion* (with Charles Brittain). He is currently writing a book on Plato's *Republic.*

Eric Brown, Associate Professor of Philosophy at Washington University in St. Louis, is the author of articles on many topics and figures in ancient philosophy, and of *Stoic Cosmopolitanism* (2006).

Mark Buchan is an Assistant Professor at Princeton University. He works and teaches mainly in Greek literature of the Archaic and Classical periods, with broader interests in literary theory, especially Marxist and psychoanalytic theory. He is the author of *The Limits of Heroism: Homer and the Ethics of Reading* (2004). He is currently working on a theoretical introduction to Homer's *Iliad*, as well as a series of essays on Greek tragedy. He is also the co-editor of a collection of essays on Lacan and Antiquity.

John Bussanich is Professor of Philosophy at the University of New Mexico. He is the author *The Relation of the One and Intellect in Plotinus* (1988) and of several papers on Plotinus, the later Neoplatonists, and on Plato's religious thought. He is currently preparing an anthology of translated Neoplatonic texts on mystical themes.

Louis-André Dorion has been Professor of Ancient Philosophy at the Université de Montréal since 1991. He has translated and commented on Aristotle's *Sophistical Refutations* (1995), and several of Plato's dialogues (*Laches and Euthyphro*, 1997; *Charmides and Lysis*, 2004), and he is currently working, in collaboration with Michele Bandini, on a new edition of Xenophon's *Memorabilia*, the first volume of which appeared in 2000 in the Budé collection.

Francisco J. Gonzalez is Chair of the Department of Philosophy and Religion at Skidmore College. He is the author of *Dialectic and Dialogue: Plato's Practice of Philosophical Inquiry* (1998) and editor of *The Third Way: New Directions in Platonic Studies* (1995). His publications also include a wide variety of articles on Plato, Aristotle, Heidegger, and contemporary hermeneutics. He has recently completed a book on Heidegger's interpretation and critique of Plato.

James Hankins, Professor of History at Harvard University, is the General Editor of the I Tatti Renaissance Library; his most recent book is *Humanism and Platonism in the Italian Renaissance*, 2 vols. (2003–4).

Richard Janko is Professor of Classical Studies and Chair of the Department of Classical Studies at the University of Michigan. He is the author of *Aristotle On Comedy*, *Aristotle: Poetics*, *The Iliad: A Commentary, Volume IV*, and *Philodemus: On Poems Book I*, and recently of articles on the Derveni papyrus and the Strasbourg papyrus of Empedocles.

Rachana Kamtekar is Assistant Professor of Philosophy at the University of Arizona. She previously taught at the University of Michigan and Williams College. Her research is primarily in the areas of ancient ethical and political philosophy. She is the author of several articles on Plato.

Richard Kraut is Charles and Emma Morrison Professor in the Humanities, and Professor of Philosophy and Classics, Northwestern University, Evanston, Illinois.

Kenneth Lapatin is a curator in the Department of Antiquities at the J. Paul Getty Museum. He is the author of numerous articles and reviews on various aspects of ancient art and culture, and their postantique reception, and five books: *Chryselephantine Statuary in the Ancient Mediterranean World* (2001); *Mysteries of the Snake Goddess: Art, Desire, and the Forging of History* (2002); *Ancient Greece: Art, Architecture, and History* (with M. Belozerskaya, 2004); *Seeing the Getty Villa* (2005); and *Guide to the Getty Villa* (2006).

Jonathan Lear is the John U. Nef Distinguished Service Professor at the Committee on Social Thought and the Department of Philosophy, the University of Chicago. His books include: *Aristotle and Logical Theory*; *Aristotle: The Desire to Understand*; *Love and Its Place in Nature: A Philosophical Interpretation of Freudian Psychoanalysis*; *Open Minded: Working Out the Logic of the Soul*; *Happiness, Death and the Remainder of Life*; *Therapeutic Action: An Earnest Plea for Irony*; and, most recently, *Freud*.

A. A. Long is Professor of Classics and Irving Stone Professor of Literature at the University of California, Berkeley. His books on ancient philosophy include *Stoic Studies* (1996) and *Epictetus: A Stoic and Socratic Guide to Life* (2002/2004), and he is also editor of *The Cambridge Companion to Early Greek Philosophy* (1999).

Daniel R. McLean teaches in the Department of Classics at the University of California, Los Angeles. He works in the field of Greek literature, and has published primarily on the reception of Socrates. This year, aided by a fellowship from the

Getty Research Institute, he will complete a volume examining how the literary and philosophical tradition has dealt with the complex problem of Socrates' body.

Avi Mintz is a doctoral candidate in the Philosophy and Education program at Teachers College, Columbia University, New York.

Paul Muench is a Ph.D. candidate at the University of Pittsburgh and will be Assistant Professor of Philosophy at the University of Montana beginning in 2006.

Debra Nails, Professor of Philosophy, Michigan State University, is author of *The People of Plato: A Prosopography of Plato and Other Socratics* (2002); *Agora, Academy, and the Conduct of Philosophy* (1995); and articles on Plato and on Spinoza.

James I. Porter is Professor of Greek, Latin and Comparative Literature at the University of Michigan. He is the author of *Nietzsche and the Philology of the Future* and of *The Invention of Dionysus: An Essay on The Birth of Tragedy*, and editor, most recently, of *Classical Pasts: The Classical Traditions of Greece and Rome*. His current projects include *The Material Sublime in Greek and Roman Aesthetics* and *Homer: The Very Idea*, a study in the production of the memory of Homer from antiquity to the present.

Susan Prince is Assistant Professor of Classics at University of Colorado, Boulder. She works on Greek thought and prose literature and is completing a book-length study of Antisthenes.

Christopher Rowe has translated and/or written commentaries on four Platonic dialogues (*Phaedrus, Phaedo, Symposium* and *Statesman*), and with Terry Penner has written a monograph on a fifth (*Plato's Lysis*, 2005). He edited *The Cambridge History of Greek and Roman Political Thought* (2000), with Malcolm Schofield, and *New Perspectives on Plato, Modern and Ancient* (2002) with Julia Annas. He is currently Professor of Greek at the University of Durham, UK.

George Rudebusch, who got his Ph.D. in 1982 from the University of Wisconsin, is Professor of Philosophy at Northern Arizona University and is the author of *Socrates, Pleasure, and Value* (1999).

Heda Segvic, formerly Assistant Professor of Philosophy, University of Pittsburgh, Pittsburgh, Pennsylvania.

Harold Tarrant is Professor of Classics at the University of Newcastle, Australia, and has published several books (most recently, *Plato's First Interpreters*, 2000, and *Recollecting Plato's Meno*, 2005) and numerous articles on Platonism in the ancient world. He is a Fellow of the Australian Academy of the Humanities.

Roslyn Weiss is the Clara H. Stewardson Professor of Philosophy and Chair of the Philosophy Department at Lehigh University. She has authored two books, *Socrates Dissatisfied: An Analysis of Plato's 'Crito'* (1998) and *Virtue in the Cave: Moral Inquiry in Plato's 'Meno'* (2001). A third, *The Socratic Paradox and Its Enemies*, is forthcoming in March 2006. She has also published numerous articles on ancient and medieval philosophy and on ethics.

Nicholas White is Professor of Philosophy at the University of California at Irvine and Professor Emeritus at the University of Michigan, and was formerly Presidential Professor at the University of Utah. He is the author of *Plato On Knowledge and Reality* (1976), *Individual and Conflict in Greek Ethics* (2002), and *A Brief History of Happiness* (2005).

Christian Wildberg is Professor of Classics at Princeton University. He teaches courses in Greek literature and classical philosophy.

Paul Woodruff is Darrell K. Royal Professor in Ethics and American Society at the University of Texas. His scholarly work deals with such subjects as Plato, Socrates, Protagoras, and ancient Pyrrhonism. He is the author of *Reverence: Renewing a Forgotten Virtue* (2001). His latest book is *First Democracy: The Challenge of an Ancient Idea* (2005). He has published a number of translations, widely used in college courses, of works by Plato, Sophocles, Thucydides, and Euripides.

Preface

We are living in the midst of a Socratic revival, both academic and broadly cultural. On the one hand, teaching by the Socratic method, Socratic counseling, and the trademark "Socrates Café" proliferate throughout the elementary schools and law schools, therapy offices, and cafés of North America (Phillips 2001, Marionoff 1999). On the other hand, scholarly works seek to discover the doctrinal commitments of the historical Socrates, the role of Socrates in Hellenistic philosophy, and the ideal of Socrates in such later thinkers as Montaigne, Kierkegaard, and Nietzsche.

Who was Socrates that he should have spawned such diverse offspring? Rather than venture a single answer, the essays in *A Companion to Socrates* investigate and exemplify the various ways in which versions of this question can be answered. Thus the essays examine the contexts in which Socrates himself lived and talked, and also the contexts in which he was studied and reinvented throughout history. To orient the reader, this preface aims to provide an etiology of the current state of the question in Socratic studies.

It was above all the path-breaking work of Gregory Vlastos, along with his students and associates (Vlastos 1991, Kraut 1984, Brickhouse and Smith 1994 and 2000, McPherran 1996, Irwin 1977 and 1995), which articulated a powerful thesis identifying the historical Socrates with the Socrates of Plato's early dialogues. Vlastos put the tools of analytic philosophy to use in the study of the philosophical views and arguments of Plato's early dialogues, and found in them arresting theses – that virtue is knowledge, that virtue is necessary for happiness, that it is better to suffer than to do injustice, that it is impossible to act contrary to knowledge of what is good, that piety is doing god's work – coupled with a mode of argumentation that was somehow to establish these truths but succeeded only in revealing to interlocutors that they too, like Socrates, were ignorant in the crucial matter of leading a good life. This framework, as we shall see shortly, has proved extremely productive.

The Socratic question of how to extract the historical Socrates from the various and conflicting literary representations of him had been given an influential formulation in the nineteenth century by Schleiermacher: how could so banal or ironic a figure as Socrates be the founder of Western philosophy? By demonstrating the philosophical interest of the Socrates of Plato's early dialogues, Vlastos had answered Schleiermacher's version of the question, but the question reappears in another guise: given that Plato, like Xenophon and the other Socratics, were writing in a literary genre well described as "biographical experiments" that aim at "capturing the potentialities rather than the realities of individual lives" (Momigliano 1993: 46), what hope is there for reconstructing the historical Socrates from these representations? The representations conflict at the most basic level: Socrates affirms and denies that the good is pleasure (Plato, *Gorgias* 495a–99b, but cf. *Protagoras* 351b–e, 354de); Socrates does and doesn't investigate questions of natural science (Aristophanes, *Clouds* 217–33; Aristotle, *Metaphysics* A.6.987b1–3; Xenophon, *Memorabilia* 1.1.11–16, 4.7.2–10; Plato, *Phaedo* 96d–99e, but cf. *Apology* 26de); Socrates disavows and avows having knowledge (Plato, *Apology* 21b–23b, *Theaetetus* 150cd, but cf. *Apology* 29b). So why suppose that the Socrates of Plato's early dialogues was the historical Socrates, rather than the Socrates of Xenophon's Socratic writings, or the Socrates of Aeschines, or Aristippus, or indeed of the hostile witness Aristophanes?

In one of the inspirations for this Companion, *The Socratic Movement*, Paul Vander Waerdt (1994: 3), having voiced his skepticism about the sources' ability to tell us much about the historical Socrates, suggests that these sources might be better used as guides to the thinking of their authors or for the recovery of philosophically brilliant portraits of Socrates. The portrait with which this volume opens is Plato's portrait of Socrates during the landmark events that ended his life: his defense when tried for impiety and corruption, his decision not to escape while awaiting the death sentence, and the serenity with which, facing death, he continued to philosophize. Debra Nails' "The Trial and Death of Socrates" uses the dramatically linked dialogues *Theaetetus–Euthyphro–Apology–Crito–Phaedo* to locate these events in their legal context and to reflect on Plato's contrasts between legalistic and true justice. One conclusion brought out by this contrast is that it was not malevolence but rather a failure to understand Socrates in the rushed atmosphere of the courtroom that was responsible for the Athenians' conviction of Socrates as guilty of "not recognizing the gods the city recognizes and . . . introducing into it new gods; and also corrupt[ing] the young" (Diogenes Laertius, *Lives of Eminent Philosophers* 2.40). This may have the ring of tragedy to our ears, but Christian Wildberg's "Socrates and Euripides" argues that there is no room for tragedy in Socrates' world, where it is better to suffer than to do injustice, and where death is no evil. Wildberg uses fragmentary material from fourth-century comedy, tragedy, and Socratic *logoi*, as well as anecdotes from later biographers, to create a body of evidence showing that Euripides and Socrates must have been intellectually engaged with one another; he goes on to problematize accounts of the character of their relationship based on Socratic themes in Euripides.

Was Socrates a sophist, as critics as old as Aristophanes and as new as Anytus and Meletus (Plato, *Apology* 18a–19d) claimed, but Socrates himself denied (19d, 20c, 21b, 22d)? If he was a sophist, what kind of sophist was he? It is now widely accepted that prior to Plato, the term "sophist" could describe any intellectual, and that it was Plato who turned it into a term of abuse. After surveying the use of the term in a range of fourth-century sources, Paul Woodruff's "Socrates Among the Sophists" suggests that Socrates' differences with the sophists are an insider's differences. For example, the sophist Protagoras teaches an art of speaking on both sides of an issue to determine what it is reasonable to believe (*eikos*) in the absence of knowledge – and not, as Plato suggests, always to affirm appearances over reality. Richard Janko's "Socrates the Freethinker" uses the relatively recently discovered Derveni Papyrus (authored, Janko argues, by Diagoras of Melos) and the thought of Diogenes of Apollonia to place Socrates in a group of reformation-style intellectuals who were replacing, sometimes by rejecting, sometimes by allegorizing, traditional stories about the gods with the idea of an exclusively good, and good-producing, god who was supreme. In the increasingly fundamentalist Athens of the fifth century, impiety trials against such intellectuals were not anomalous. Anthony Long, in "How Does Socrates' Divine Sign Communicate with Him?," turns to an essay by the Middle Platonist Plutarch (c. 50–120 CE), *On Socrates' Divine Sign*, to explore another dimension of Socrates' religious outlook: his experience of direct communication from his *daimonion*, which, Long argues, ought to be seen, along with Socrates' receptivity to its message, as at once divine and rational.

With the publication of Giannantoni's four-volume *Socratis et Socraticorum Reliquiae* (1990), which collects fragments attributable to members of the Socratic circle, came another great advance in Socratic scholarship. This collection makes possible the reconstruction of the philosophy of Socrates' associates such as the Cynic Antisthenes, the hedonist Aristippus, and others, as well as the comparative work on the writings of the self-styled Socratics of the fourth and third centuries advocated by Vander Waerdt (1994: 9–10). Susan Prince's "Socrates, Antisthenes, and the Cynics" and Louis-André Dorion's "Xenophon's Socrates" present us with two novel philosophical portraits. According to Prince, Antisthenes' Socrates took definition to be on the one hand central to language and knowledge, and on the other hand impossible, and Antisthenes concluded from this that contradiction is impossible. At the same time, Antisthenes' Socrates left ethics untheorized, as something embedded in a way of life, a community, and in the activity of interpretation. Dorion points out a number of differences between Plato's and Xenophon's Socrates, the most important of these being the importance Xenophon's Socrates accords to self-control with regard to bodily pleasures (*enkrateia*). Self-control is a precondition of virtue, for responsibility, freedom, justice, and the practice of dialectic all require the ability to resist the lure of pleasure, to overcome desires, to avoid the temptation to wrongdoing, and so on. Plato's Socrates, by contrast, gives this role to wisdom. What to make of this difference? A suggestive observation made by Dorion is that Xenophon's Socrates resembles other characters in Xenophon and Xenophon's ideal of himself more than he does Plato's Socrates.

The final essay in this section on sources, Ken Lapatin's richly illustrated "Picturing Socrates," traces the history of visual representations of Socrates, from antiquity's depiction of Socrates as a satyr or Silenus-figure, sometimes ennobled, to contemporary commercial images of Socrates.

The essays in the second section of Part I focus on Plato's Socrates, the Socrates brought to philosophy by Vlastos. A number of these essays explicitly or implicitly challenge Vlastos's account of Socrates' philosophy. Christopher Rowe's "Socrates in Plato's Dialogues" revisits the question of the difference between the Socrates of Plato's early and middle-late dialogues. Since Vlastos, this difference has been cast as a difference between a negative Socrates whose philosophical activity consists in refuting claims to knowledge or definitions, and a dogmatic Socrates who constructs elaborate theories, metaphysical and political. But Rowe argues that the only substantial difference is that the Socrates of the early dialogues holds that only the desire for the good and true or false beliefs about what is good can motivate action, whereas the Socrates of Plato's middle-late dialogues admits nonrational motivations as well (a difference which, Rowe acknowledges, ramifies enormously). The identification of distinctively Socratic philosophical positions and the attempt to render them, paradoxical as they appear, philosophically attractive occupy the next several essays in this section. Heda Segvic's "No One Errs Willingly: The Meaning of Socratic Intellectualism" develops a Socratic (and proto-Stoic) account of willing, a state that is at once volitional (we want the good) and cognitive (we can be said to want something when we know that it is good). George Rudebusch's "Socratic Love" asks whether, in addition to the needy love of the good just described, Socrates recognizes giving love and equality love, which Vlastos's (1981) "The Individual as an Object of Love in Plato" had faulted Socrates for neglecting. Rudebusch finds, in the *Lysis*, an argument to the effect that the good itself requites needy love with giving love – but no equality love. Another reply to Vlastos can be found in John Bussanich's "Socrates and Religious Experience." In his (1991) essay "Socratic Piety," Vlastos had argued that Socrates rejected the traditional Greek conception of the gods as powerful but amoral beings to be sacrificed to in exchange for favors, and put in its place a conception of gods as good and human beings as properly their assistants in benefiting human beings by caring for their souls; Socrates' lived piety consisted in a care of the soul which involved rational inquiry that would aid in the interpretation of the god's communications. Against this, Bussanich maintains that the role of rational inquiry, or philosophy, or dialectic, is to purify the mind of false (perhaps rationalistically derived) beliefs and admit to ignorance, so that knowledge born of religious experience can shine through. Finally, Rachana Kamtekar's "The Politics of Plato's Socrates" argues that Socrates combines a political discourse about the best constitution, traditionally used to justify a ruler's claim to the privilege of ruling, with the apolitical discourse of contemporary sophists, which characterizes ruling as a professional expertise, to argue that the sole basis for the evaluation of a ruler or form of rule is whether or not it accomplishes the professional goal of ruling, namely, the good of the ruled.

The last three essays in this section take up issues of the methods and goals of Socratic ethical inquiry. It is Plato who gave the world Socrates' most-quoted slogan, "The unexamined life is not worth living" (*Apology* 38a), and Richard Kraut's "The Examined Life" explains why Socrates should have thought the examination of one's values so necessary: our lives are more likely to go tragically wrong because we are shallow rather than because we are wicked (as does Euthyphro's); our values and thus the direction of our lives can become genuinely our own only once we have engaged in the kind of ethical inquiry that came to be called ethical philosophy. Plato's Socrates inquires into the goodness of the virtuous life, and the results are theoretical as well as practical commitments, such as the view that the virtues are forms of wisdom. But while one might have taken it as given that Socratic ethical inquiry took, *inter alia*, the form of investigating such questions as "what is piety?" (*Euthyphro*), "what is courage?" (*Laches*), "what is friendship?" (*Lysis*), Roslyn Weiss's "Socrates: Seeker or Preacher?" claims that in Plato's *Apology* Socrates describes his philosophical activity not in terms of a search for wisdom (such as answers to the "what is F?" question), but in terms of refuting others to show them their ignorance, which is the human condition, and to motivate them to inquiry, which cannot, however, make them any wiser. The contrasting positions taken by these two essays point to two fundamentally different conceptions of a philosopher that can be adopted by students of Socrates, even of Plato's Socrates: on the one hand, to be a philosopher is to adopt a certain mode of living and engaging (or not) with others, to which questioning is central; on the other hand, to be a philosopher is also to seek, evaluate, and even adopt certain determinate theoretical views – even if in a nondogmatic spirit, or for the sake of living well. Harold Tarrant's "Socratic Method and Socratic Truth" takes up the question, "what is the nature of the philosophical activity engaged in by Socrates?" Tarrant's project is to open up a question framed narrowly by Gregory Vlastos's (1983) "The Socratic Elenchus": how does Socrates' method (drawing out conflicts in a belief-set, according to Vlastos) achieve its goal (truth, according to Vlastos)? Tarrant conceives of Socrates' goal as not the discovery of true propositions, but rather "the refinement of belief *and* actions that spring from understanding one's role in the world." Because Protagoreanism, the ongoing availability of opposing arguments to any view, presented Socrates with an insurmountable obstacle to achieving the perspective-independent truth he would have liked, he contented himself with affirming as true statements the perspective-dependence of which does not invalidate them ("death is no evil for me"), disclaiming knowledge of universals. Tarrant proposes that the *Gorgias* introduces a new conception of truth and method according to which theories may be refuted, and may be true or false, independently of their advocates.

A second inspiration for this volume, pioneering work by Anthony Long (1988 and 2002), Julia Annas (1994), and Gisela Striker (1994), has shown that the figure of Socrates was central to the philosophical constructs of the Stoics and skeptics of the Hellenistic period. Significantly, it was less in virtue of their adopting philosophical precepts associated with Socrates than in virtue of their taking up Socrates' practices that these schools first claimed to be Socratic. Thus, when Plato's Academy took a skeptical turn in the third century BCE, its head, Arcesilaus (who led the Academy c. 273–242 BCE), seems to have invoked Socrates' practice of arguing *ad hominem* (using only the interlocutor's beliefs as premises) to negative conclusions, rather than his avowal of ignorance or his expressions of pessimism about our cognitive faculties (see Annas 1994, Cooper 2004). And Socrates' lifelong pursuit of wisdom and struggle against ignorance reappears in the skeptics' and Stoics' treatment of knowledge as immeasurably valuable and demanding, on the one hand, and rash assent as the greatest danger and source of all our troubles, on the other. The early Stoics relied more on Xenophon's Socrates than Plato's – arguably because Xenophon's Socrates lived on in the Cynics Antisthenes and Diogenes, whereas there was in sight no embodiment of Plato's Socrates (see Long 1988). Nevertheless, perhaps because Xenophon's Socrates was more unequivocally committed to doctrine – a teleological cosmology, self-mastery as the supreme virtue – than was Plato's, the Stoics could see their philosophical activity as consistently constructive and Socratic. But the Stoics also knew their Plato and seem to have developed new interpretations of Socratic precepts – such as that virtue is sufficient for happiness, that virtue is knowledge, and that other than virtue and vice, nothing is unconditionally good or bad – that survived Platonic criticisms (see Striker 1994 and Long 1988).

The essays in the last third of Part I take us to the Hellenistic period. Against the mainstream current according to which Stoicism is the most dogmatic of the Hellenistic schools, preserving or reformulating doctrines from Xenophon or Plato's early dialogues, Eric Brown's "Socrates in the Stoa" derives the Stoic paradoxes (e.g. virtue suffices for happiness; only the sage is free) from reflection on Socrates' way of life as a life spent in the search of knowledge, understood as a coherent set of psychological attitudes (the Stoics' "smooth flow of life"). Even the Stoics' departures from Socrates reveal a thoughtful engagement with his life: while Socrates practiced philosophy as his profession, to the exclusion of any other, but argued with anyone, be it humble Simon the Shoemaker or corrupt Critias of the Thirty, the Stoics appreciated the dangers of dialectic (see where it got Socrates) and took philosophy to be combinable with any profession. Tad Brennan's "Socrates and Epictetus" provokes us to consider how deep the Hellenistic imitation of Socrates really ran: could Epictetus only imitate the outer but not the inner Socrates, as is suggested by the difference between their dialectical performances? Was it the genius of Plato, unmatched by Arrian and indeed Xenophon, that gave Socrates depth? And what could explain the particular intensity and spitefulness of Socrates' irony – especially when, contrasting Socratic and Epictetan dialectic, we find it quite detachable from philosophical method? Finally, Richard Bett's "Socrates and Skepticism" examines the Academy's appropriation of Socrates as a proto-skeptic, from the headship of Arcesilaus into the time of Cicero (first century CE), and contrasts this with the "standoffish" attitude towards Socrates of the Pyrrhonist Sextus Empiricus (end of second century CE). Bett contests the Academic skeptics' interpretation of Socrates on the grounds that Socrates cannot have believed knowledge impossible since he spent his life seeking it, and offers an alternative account of Socrates' dialectical practices.

Leaving antiquity, we turn next to the medieval and Renaissance periods. Ilai Alon's essay takes us from the world of Greco-Roman antiquity, to the height of the Abbasid Caliphate in Baghdad. In the Arab world, Socrates comes into prominence with the translation movement of the ninth century; the philosopher al-Kindi wrote a number of treatises on Socrates, but the figure of Socrates had a widespread influence on medieval Arab culture as a whole, inspiring poets, and *hadith* scholars. Socrates captured the Muslim imagination as the sage *par excellence*, his martyrdom comparable to the philosophical martyrs of Islam, as for example the twelfth-century Platonist philosopher, Suhrawardi.

Although Socrates was familiar in the Latin West from Cicero and Apuleius, as well as Christian writers, it was (as in the parallel case of the Arabic Socrates) the translation work of Ficino in the Quattrocento that inspired a Socratic renaissance. Ficino made all of Plato available in Latin, and the Socratic writings of Xenophon were translated by Bessarion by mid-century. In James Hankins' essay, we meet another self-styled Socratic imitator in the person of none other than Marsilio Ficino, whose Socratic seminars in the city of Florence were designed to recapture the youth of Florence from those latter-day sophists who, according to Ficino, thrived in Italian universities. In the Humanist movement of the fourteenth century, Socrates became both moral preceptor in his Xenophontean guise, but also divine seer and holy man, a precursor to Christ.

Socrates' fortunes in the Renaissance continued to wax, and as French translations (see e.g. Le Roy's sixteenth-century translation of Plato's *Symposium*, which famously omitted the Alcibiades scene and was presented as a treatise on marriage) based on the work of the Italian Humanists brought the figure of Socrates into French culture, another Socratic revival was well on its way. Translations of Socratic lore exerted a powerful presence in the popular literature of early-modern France. Daniel McLean's essay discusses the theme of Socrates' private life as it appeared in the satiric works of Rabelais and others, where Socrates becomes, among other things, a hen-pecked bigamist or lecherous buffoon. The Socrates who lived in the comedies and bawdy letters as well as in narrative painting of the seventeenth and eighteenth centuries was rather a relic of a Roman-period Socrates, forged in traditions already obsessed with the anecdotal and the biographical (Seneca, Aulus Gellius, and Diogenes Laertius). It is this tradition that gives us the apparent familiarity that we enjoy today with Socrates' marital problems, even as it rehearsed what were ago-old questions concerning the moral integrity of Socrates' associations with youth. Ken Lapatin's essay, as mentioned above, documents the tremendous impact that Socrates' death in prison had on seventeenth-century French painting, with this theme again resonating with Christian sensibilities, just as it earlier had with Islamic. Yet the most important thinker to treat the figure of the dying Socrates in early-modern France was of course not a painter, but the essayist Montaigne (Nehamas 1998: 101–27), who mentions Socrates' name almost 60 times in his *Essays*. Montaigne's Socrates, especially the Socrates of his *On Physiognomy*, is a mixture of Xenophon's teacher of self-control, Plato's Silenus, and Montaigne himself. In offering the life of Socrates as a model and in hinting that he himself is a Socratic figure, Montaigne has Socrates invent an entirely new tradition in the early-modern period, which Nehamas called the art of living. How far this art of living extends into the nineteenth and twentieth centuries can be seen in the treatments of Kierkegaard, Nietzsche, and others. But this tradition is paralleled, as we shall see, by the researches of nineteenth-century philology. Together, Socrates, master of life and death, and the Socrates that comes under philological scrutiny, bring us into the twentieth century. Let us briefly explore these developments.

Perhaps the most influential predecessor of today's Socrates question, the question of how a seemingly ironic or at least philosophically banal figure came to be identified as the founder of Western philosophy, was Schleiermacher's 1815 lecture entitled "The Value of Socrates as a Philosopher." While previous centuries saw in the figure of Socrates many things – sage, martyr, founding hero of skepticism, Stoicism, Cynicism, even prophet Socrates' worth as a philosopher today is measured by an almost exclusive focus on the discovery of a Socratic doctrine worthy of the man. Prior to the nineteenth century, as we have seen, Socrates made his influence felt as a person, a philosophical ideal, even as an absence. All of this changes, not just with Schleiermacher's question, but also with the almost contemporaneous meditations of Hegel on the meaning of what he understood as the Socratic revolution in Greek thought.

As Nicholas White shows in his essay, Hegel's Socrates heralds the emergence of self-conscious *Geist* for the first time in the history of thought. This subjective principle demarcates the individual conscience as index of a new moral authority that supersedes the law of the state. The conflict between authority and individual, between state and self, repeats the emphasis on Socrates' death, on his struggle with convention; but at the same time, this Hegelian interpretation fueled the modern concern with Socrates' philosophy (as opposed to Socrates the person), as Socrates became, in the eyes of Hegel, the first philosopher to cultivate a self-conscious method. It remains to explain how these two different tendencies – one a subjectivity that becomes a new moral force, and the other a self-reflective method – are transmitted to the twentieth century and to its own version of Socratic philosophy.

In Hegel's emphasis on individual subjectivity as the essence of Socrates, there are distant echoes of Montaigne's notion of Socratic self-fashioning, and it was Kierkegaard who preserved this echo when he merged Hegel's subjectivity with his own interpretation of Socrates' negative irony. Kierkegaard's master's thesis, *On the Concept of Irony with Constant Reference to Socrates*, heralds a freedom-loving Socratic irony that functions to negate conventional values. Thus Kierkegaard claimed to discover in Socrates the radical freedom of his own existentialism. In this sense, one might be tempted to see Kierkegaard's appropriation of Socrates at a kind of crossroads between Socrates the thinker and Socrates the man. Muench's essay shows us that, on the one hand, Socrates' reputation as a dissembling social critic informed Kierkegaard's own role in Danish society. Indeed, Kierkegaard repeats the struggle between Socrates and the state religion through his ironic insistence that he, most devout of Christians, could not claim that he was a Christian.

James Porter's essay on Nietzsche's treatment of the Socrates question is richly suggestive of the enormous cultural complexity that Socrates had assumed by the time Nietzsche wrote. Nietzsche is aware of the power of the dying Socrates, before whom the youthful Plato prostrated himself, and notes the contradictions between the figure of a robust Socrates, full of life and passion, and the dreary rationalist, founder of all in Western culture that drains the vitality from life. Yet, according to Porter, Nietzsche's philological instincts lead him to posit the possibility that Socrates means so much that he cannot be separated from the fate of the Greek ideal as a whole.

Meanwhile, this ironic conception of Socrates emerges in new and hybrid ways in the twentieth century, in the work of Gregory Vlastos (*Socrates, Ironist and Moral Philosopher*) and of Alexander Nehamas (*The Art of Living*), both of whom present us with a Socratic philosophy that is thoroughly rooted in irony. For Vlastos, Socratic irony is relatively benign, bereft as it must be of any hint of deceit: Socrates speaks the truth by saying the opposite of what he means. For Nehamas, on the contrary, Socratic irony is not transparent, but is a complex amalgam of openness and concealment, designed to avoid the detection of any who do not merit the discernment of the real meaning of one's words (Nehamas 1998: 62). Both contesting and exploring the meaning of Socratic irony is a theme that connects several of the essays in the second part of this Companion. The essays by James Porter, Jonathan Lear, Tad Brennan, and Paul Muench are centrally occupied with the multiple meanings of irony that surface in the modern reception of the Socratic dialogues. Whether the irony of Socrates is transparent (Vlastos), concealing (Nehamas), part of the very peculiar identity of Socrates himself, as source and object of the Socratic tradition that he both invents and is invented by (Porter), or indeed a tragic but inherent part of the human condition (Lear), these essays seek to advance a discourse of irony. It might also be said that several of the essays in the Companion use the theme of ironic dissonance, whether that be realized, as in Kamtekar's essay on Socratic politics, as the distance between one's profession and one's realization of that profession; or (in Brennan's essay on Socrates and Epictetus) as the irony inherent in Socrates' profession of ignorance and great spitefulness toward those who claim to know; or between the desires of the self and the self-alienation implied by desire (as in Buchan's essay), to uncover some of the complexities of the Socratic persona.

Yet one of the greatest ironies that haunt would-be disciples of Socrates is precisely this tendency to imitate Socrates, or even to forge a Socrates that is an imitation of the disciple. Of course, Socrates himself was particularly concerned with Socrates, as we see him constantly struggling for self-knowledge (*Phaedrus* 229e). This call to absolute authenticity, or at least to the quest for authenticity, gives rise to another strain of Socratic philosophy, the tradition of Socratic self-examination. Jonathan Lear and Mark Buchan develop the Socratic theme of self-knowledge over against what might be called, for lack of a better word, a public fiction (whether that fiction is a mass or individual construction – both contests are displayed in the Socratic dialogues) in essays that cast Freudian and Lacanian psychoanalysis in the light of Socratic psychology.

For both Lear and Buchan, it is a question of how to use the ironic distance between the aspiration to selfhood and the limited autonomy that such an aspiration admits, to open up a space of self-reflection. Buchan works with Lacan's own appropriations of Plato's Socratic texts, especially the seminar on transference, thus presenting a Lacanian interpretation of Socrates' disavowal of knowledge. Lear, on the other hand, investigates a question that can rightfully be asked both of Socrates and Freudian psychoanalysis: how does talking about the soul actually change it? Thus it is not Freud's historical reception of Socrates that is of concern; for Lear, psychoanalysis actually is, or is at its best, a Socratic activity. Both essays call into question other interpretations of Socratic psychology and method by challenging the intellectualist tradition that sees no room for emotion in the teaching environment of the elenchus (as in Rowe's essay on Socrates in Plato).

The methodological Socrates has been in competition with the ironic Socrates, as we have seen, ever since Plato and Xenophon penned their biographies of the man who roamed the streets of Athens. Yet the methodological Socrates has come into his own now (on the connections between the analytic Socrates and the Hegelian Socrates see White), bolstered by yet another resurgence of Socratism, in the neo-Hegelian Socrates of Heidegger and of his student, H. G. Gadamer (Gonzalez). Gonzalez shows that the Socrates of Hegel has spawned its own avatars. They include a negative incarnation of Socrates in Heidegger's rejection of Socratic philosophy as too buried in discourse and thus excluding the more Platonic aspect of philosopher as visionary, as well as Gadamer's more idealistic appropriation of Socrates as forever asking questions that themselves become the goal and the way of the true philosopher.

In his discussion of the Socratic legacy in education, Avi Mintz shows that Socratic method is perhaps the most popular notion of Socrates today, versions of which abound in classrooms ranging from grade school to law school. The assumption that Socratic teaching is entirely or nearly entirely comprised by a specific technique of questioning to elicit the learner's innate understanding, or by engaging the learner in reasoning about beliefs that she already holds, gave rise to a whole educational movement that revolutionized American classrooms. Whether or not Socratic teaching can be reduced to the question of method alone, this rather more popular assumption again shows the power and significance of our modernist version of Socrates as methodological philosopher. Ausland's essay, which ends the volume by giving us a detailed account of Socrates scholarship in the nineteenth century, returns us to the Socrates question that began this Companion. Ausland shows that Vlastos's Socrates is a powerful combination of the Socratic ironist who on the one hand knows nothing, but on other hand is also an analytic philosopher, someone concerned above all with the question of method. At the same time, Ausland reminds us of another Socratic persona – that of the civic philosopher, bent on critical reformation of the body politic through the infusion of rationality into the life of power. This political tradition is exemplified by the work of Leo Strauss. Both of these traditions, Socrates the questioner and Socrates the reformer, have blossomed and borne fruit, as we have seen, not just in philosophical circles, but in political theory (Villa 2001), in law schools, and in everyday life.

If this preface were a map, we could now insert the phrase "YOU ARE HERE," in large red lettering. For we, in the twenty-first century, are in the midst of a Socratic revolution. Throughout its history, Socratic philosophy has interjected a dialogue between street philosophy and elite discourse, between individual autonomy and community norms, between scholars and zealots. Consequently, this Companion is offered to students of Socrates from all walks of life, to philosophers and to professional classicists, art historians and historians, and to just about everyone else who shares an interest in the questions that Socrates has provoked over the past two and a half millennia.

References

Annas, J. (1994). Plato the Skeptic. In Vander Waerdt (1994).

Brickhouse, T. and Smith, N. (2000). *The Philosophy of Socrates*. Boulder, CO: Westview Press.

—— (1994). *Plato's Socrates*. Oxford and New York: Oxford University.

Cooper, J. (2004). Arcesilaus: Socratic and skeptic. In *Knowledge, Nature and the Good*. Princeton: Princeton University Press.

Giannantoni, G. (1990). *Socratis et Socraticorum Reliquiae*. 4 vols. Naples: Bibliopolis.

Irwin, T. (1977). *Plato's Moral Theory*. Oxford: Clarendon Press.

—— (1995). *Plato's Ethics*. Oxford: Oxford University Press.

Long, A. A. (1988). Socrates in Hellenistic philosophy. *Classical Quarterly*, 38, 150–71. Reprinted in *Stoic Studies*. Cambridge: Cambridge University, 1996.

—— (2002). *Epictetus: A Stoic and Socratic Guide to Life*. Oxford: Clarendon Press.

Marionoff, L. (1999). *Plato! Not Prozac*. New York: Harper Collins.

McPherran, M. (1996). *The Religion of Socrates*. University Park, PA: Penn State Press.

Nehamas, A. (1998). *The Art of Living: Socratic Reflections from Plato to Foucault*. Berkeley: University of California Press.

Phillips, C. (2001). *Socrates Café: A Fresh Taste of Philosophy*. New York: Norton.

Porter, J. (2000a). *The Invention of Dionysus: An Essay on "The Birth of Tragedy."* Stanford: Stanford University Press.

—— (2000b). *Nietzsche and the Philology of the Future*. Stanford: Stanford University Press.

Strauss, L. (1960). *The City and the Man*. Chicago: University of Chicago Press.

Striker, G. (1994). Plato's Socrates and the Stoics. In Vander Waerdt (1994).

Vander Waerdt, P. A. (1994). *The Socratic Movement*. Ithaca and London: Cornell University Press.

Villa, D. (2001). *Socratic Citizenship*. Princeton: Princeton University Press.

Vlastos G. (1981). The individual as an object of love in Plato. In *Platonic Studies*. Princeton: Princeton University Press.

—— (1983). The Socratic elenchus. Reprinted with revisions in Vlastos (1991b).

—— (1991a). Socratic piety. In Vlastos (1991b).

—— (1991b). *Socrates, Ironist and Moral Philosopher*. Ithaca and London: Cornell University Press.

Acknowledgments

The editors would like to thank the University of Michigan's office of the Vice President for Research for generously funding the illustrations in this volume, along with the J. Paul Getty Foundation.

Our heartfelt thanks to Professor Stephen Menn, of McGill University, for the translation of Louis-André Dorion's essay into English, and for consultation on the volume as a whole.

Many thanks, as well, to Larry Dale Frye, Jr., University of Michigan, for his able proofreading, editing, and formatting of the entire volume.

Heda Segvic died in 2003. Wishing to include her voice in this collection, we reprint an edited version of an earlier paper by her. We would like to thank Myles Burnyeat and David Sedley for their help with this, and gratefully acknowledge the permission of Professor Burnyeat to print her article.

The editors also gratefully acknowledge the permission of *Kierkegaardiana* to print an edited version of Paul Muench's article.

Thanks to Dr. Nick Bellorini, Senior Editor at Blackwell Publishing, for his support and encouragement throughout.

Sara Ahbel-Rappe thanks the colleagues who participated in this book: her co-editor, Professor Rachana Kamtekar of the University of Arizona, Department of Philosophy; the Chair of the Department of Classical Studies at the University of Michigan, Richard Janko; and her colleagues in Classical Studies, James Porter and David Potter. She also thanks her partner, Karin.

Rachana Kamtekar thanks the many friends and colleagues who have contributed to this volume; the University of Arizona and Princeton University for support during the time the volume was put together; and Sara Ahbel-Rappe, for involving her in this project.

Part One

Socrates in Antiquity

Section I

Biography and Sources

1

The Trial and Death of Socrates

DEBRA NAILS

Athens, birthplace of democracy, executed the philosopher Socrates in the year 399 BCE for the crime of impiety (*asebeia*), i.e., irreverence toward the gods of the polis, which his accusers – Meletus, Anytus, and Lycon – had said was a corrupting influence on the young men who kept company with Socrates and imitated his behavior. But the city had been hearing complaints and jokes about Socrates for some thirty years by then. A popular comedian had in 414 added the term "to Socratize" (*sōkratein*) to the Athenian vocabulary, describing the conduct of long-haired youths who refused to bathe and carried sticks, affecting Spartan ways (Aristophanes, *Birds*, 1280–3). What was different in 399 was a wave of religious fundamentalism that brought with it a steep rise in the number of impiety cases in Athenian courts. Socrates, maintaining in his defense that he was not an atheist and that he had never willingly corrupted the young or indeed knowingly harmed anyone, was found guilty and went willingly to his execution against the exhortations and the plans of his companions, preferring death to the alternatives of desisting from philosophy or leaving his beloved polis to engage in philosophy elsewhere. Plato narrates the indictment, trial, and execution of Socrates in a series of five dialogues, the *Theaetetus*, *Euthyphro*, *Apology*, *Crito*, and *Phaedo*, set in the spring and summer of that year.

This singular event has been examined and reexamined ever since. There are other accounts,[1] but it is Plato's that has become philosophy's founding myth and that has immortalized Socrates in the popular imagination as a man of profound moral strength and intelligence – though also as a uniquely peculiar and inscrutable individual. When brought to trial, Socrates was 70 years old, married, the father of three sons ranging in age from 1 to 17, and poor; his net worth, including his house, was 5 *minae* (Xenophon, *Oeconomicus* 2.3.4–5), the equivalent of what a sophist might charge for a single course (*Apology* 20b9), and less than a skilled laborer could earn in a year and a half. He perished without publishing but having inspired his young companion Plato (424/3–347 BCE) and other men known as Socratics to compose dialogues and memoirs in which Socrates was featured. There were enough of these that Aristotle was later to refer to such Socratic works as a literary genre (*Poetics* 1447b11). What was it about democratic Athens in 399, its politics, religion, culture, laws, or courts – or about Socrates, or his accusers, or their charges – that might help explain what has appeared to so many as a great miscarriage of justice? In laying out some of the issues raised by Socrates' trial and death, I will follow the five dialogues mentioned above in relation to the legal thread through the events: summons, preliminary hearing, pretrial examination, evidentiary and penalty phases of the trial, imprisonment, and execution (Harrison 1971; MacDowell 1978).

Anyone who reads the five dialogues, amidst the telling of Socrates' final story, encounters indestructible philosophy – argumentation concerning being, knowing, and philosophical method.[2] So provocative and engaging are the extended philosophical passages in the *Theaetetus* and *Phaedo* that anyone inquiring into Socrates' trial and execution must make a conscious effort not to be distracted by brilliant arguments, not to be seduced away from the narrative line of Socrates' last days. That this should be so is Plato's ultimate defense of the philosopher, his highest tribute to Socrates and to the very idea of what it is to live the life of a philosopher: one's circumstances, no matter how dire, are never more than a backdrop for the conduct of philosophy.

Meletus' Summons and the Political Background

Several things had already happened when Socrates, the summons in his hand, greeted Theodorus in the spring of 399 (*Theaetetus* 143d1–2), and it is best to set them out in order.

Meletus of Pithus was Socrates' chief accuser. He was the son of a poet also named Meletus, but was himself "young and unknown" (*Euthyphro* 2b8).[3] To charge Socrates, a fellow-citizen, Meletus was obliged to summon him to appear at a preliminary hearing before the relevant magistrate, namely, the king-archon (*archōn basileus*), who had jurisdiction over both homicide and impiety. This Meletus did by composing a speech or document that stated the complaint and demanded that the defendant, Socrates, appear on a specified day. It was not necessary to put the summons in writing, or for the king-archon to agree in advance about the date of appearance, but at least four days had to be granted between the notification and the hearing.

Athenian public prosecutors, selected by lot and paid a *drachma* per day, had only narrow functions, so, when Meletus made his accusation, he became both plaintiff and prosecutor in Socrates' case. The summons had to be served on Socrates personally and preferably in public: active participation in Athens' extensive religious life was a civic obligation, thus to prosecute impiety was to act in the public interest. Any citizen could serve and, though it was not obligatory, could add his name to Meletus' document, if Meletus put his complaint in writing (as *Apology* 19b3–c1 implies he did). If a defendant could not be located, it may have been permissible to announce the summons in front of his house (as allowed some decades later); but the sanctity of Socrates' house could not be violated for that purpose. One or two witnesses accompanied Meletus in his search for Socrates, men who would later swear that the summons had been properly delivered. These may have been the two men who would be Meletus' advocates (*syn*goroi*) in the trial, Anytus of Euonymon, and Lycon of Thoricus, men of very different dispositions.[4]

Anytus was rich, having inherited a tanning factory from his self-made and admirable father (*Meno* 90a). Plato emphasizes his hatred of sophists at *Meno* 90b, 91c, and 92e. He was elected general by his tribe, and in 409 tried but failed because of storms to retake Pylos from the Spartans. Prosecuted for this failure, he escaped punishment by devising a new method of bribery for use with large juries that was later given the name *dekazein* and made a capital crime. In 404, he supported the government of the Thirty, but it soon banished him, whereupon he became a general for the exiled democrats (though his protection of an informer to the Thirty cast doubts on his loyalties). When the democracy was restored in 403, he became one of its leaders. Anytus served as a character witness in another of the impiety trials of 399, Andocides'. Xenophon calls Anytus' son a drunkard (Xenophon, *Apology* 31.1–4).

Lycon is known to us through an extended and sympathetic portrayal by Xenophon (in *Symposium*) who depicts him as the doting father of a devoted son, Autolycus, a victorious pancratist in 422 who was later executed by the Thirty. Lycon was a man of Socrates' generation who had become a democratic leader after the fall of the oligarchy of 411. In comedies, his foreign wife and his son are accused along with him of living extravagantly and beyond their means; he is accused with his son of drunkenness; but he alone is accused of treachery, betraying Naupactus to the Spartans in 405.

It is sometimes said that political animosity lay behind the impiety charges against Socrates, both because some of the men he was rumored to have corrupted were political leaders; and because, it has been claimed, he could not *legally* be charged with the political crime of subverting democracy (Stone 1988; cf. Burnyeat 1988). Although the labels "democracy" and "oligarchy" are ubiquitous, politics in Athens in the late fifth century resists reduction to a simple clash between broad-franchise democrats and narrow-franchise oligarchs for several reasons: many central figures changed sides, sometimes repeatedly; the oligarchies themselves varied in number (the 400, the 5000, the 30); clan and family interests as well as individual loyalties often cut across affiliation. During the long Peloponnesian War, from 431, Athens remained a democracy except for a brief period in 411. After a decisive Spartan victory in 404, however, the Assembly (*ekklēsia*) elected 30 men, three per tribe, to return the city to her predemocratic ancestral constitution. The Thirty quickly consolidated their power and wealth through executions and confiscations, driving supporters of the democracy into exile. After about 8 months of tyranny, in 403, the exiles retook the city in a bloody civil war, later driving the leaders of the Thirty and their supporters to Eleusis. An amnesty was negotiated with Spartan help that separated the two sides and made it illegal from 402 to bring charges against anyone on either side for crimes committed during the rule of the Thirty. Suspecting that the former oligarchs were hiring mercenaries, the democrats raided Eleusis in the early spring of 401 and killed all who were left. In the courts, from 400, the amnesty was observed for criminal charges, but residual hostility continued, and it was common to attack one's opponent for remaining in the city instead of joining the democrats in exile, as had Socrates' childhood friend Chaerephon (*Apology* 20e8–21a2). Socrates did remain in the city, but he opposed the Thirty – as his record shows – and there is no evidence that there was an underlying political motive in Socrates' case.

Upon receipt of the summons, to resume the narrative, Socrates enjoyed a citizen's right not to appear at the preliminary hearing, though Meletus' suit would then proceed uncontested to the pretrial examination stage. Even if charged with a murder, short of parricide, a citizen also had the right to voluntary exile from Athens, as the personified laws remind Socrates (*Crito* 52c3–6). Socrates exercised neither of those rights. Rather, he set out to enter a plea before the king-archon and stopped at a gymnasium on his way.

The *Theaetetus*: Trial and Death in Prospect

The *Theaetetus*, replete with references to Socrates' impending trial and execution,[5] opens the five-dialogue exploration of what it is to lead the examined life of a philosopher. Philosophy begins in wonder (*Theaetetus* 155d3) with the study of mathematical patterns, and, in Socrates' case, ends – if it ends – with his death as presented in the *Phaedo*. Although the *Theaetetus* stands first in Plato's narrative, it is rarely read in that context because of its overwhelming philosophical importance in distinguishing perceptions and true beliefs from *knowledge*.[6] Yet the Athenians' failure to make precisely these distinctions is crucial to what happened in 399. Why the polis executed Socrates comes starkly into focus four times in the dialogue, showing that – however well-intentioned – *the Athenians mistook their friend for their enemy and killed him*.

The first is a famous passage (*Theaetetus* 148e–151d) in which Socrates likens himself to his mother, Phaenarete, for both are midwives, she of bodies, he of minds. As she is beyond child-bearing age, he is beyond wisdom-bearing age. As she runs the risk of being confused with unjust and unscientific procurers when she practices her art, he runs the risk of being confused with sophists when he practices his (cf. 164c–d). Through Socrates' maieutic art, others "have themselves discovered many admirable things in themselves, and given birth to them" (150d6–8).[7] He admits he is considered strange and has a reputation for questioning others and making them suffer birth pains without proffering his own views; some men want to bite him when he disabuses them of the silliness they believe. As he draws the midwifery comparison, Socrates presages what he will later say in court: that his mission is compelled by the god; that he has a personal *daimonion* or spiritual monitor,[8] which here sometimes forbids his association with youths who return to him after choosing bad company; and that no god can wish evil to man – the denial of which serves as an example of "silliness." The gods acknowledged by the polis were those of the poets, gods who often wished, and even caused, evil; but Socrates acknowledged no such gods. Plato makes it easy to imagine Socrates playing into the hands of his accusers, for Socrates volunteers examples of youths whose corruption he could not prevent and says Homer's gods Oceanus and Tethys are really flux and motion (152e7–8, cf. 180d), that Homer's golden chain is the sun (153c9–d1).

A second perspective arises out of the discussion of Protagorean relativism. If knowledge is perception, then every juryman is "no worse in point of wisdom than anyone whatever, man or even god" (162c2–5; cf. majority opinion, 171a). Protagoras, impersonated by Socrates, says:

> about matters that concern the state, too – things which are admirable or dishonorable, just or unjust, in conformity with religion or not – it will hold that whatever sort of thing any state thinks to be, and lays down as, lawful for itself actually is, in strict truth, lawful for it (*Theaetetus* 172a1–b5; cf. 167c–d, 177c–d, *Protagoras* 320d–328d);

8

from which it follows that if Athens thinks it is just, then it *is* just for the city that it execute Socrates. But it is another matter entirely, Socrates objects, when one considers justice not judicially but legislatively, i.e., considers what laws *ought* to be enacted in the interest of the polis – for a polis can judge its own good incorrectly.

> whatever word it [the state] applies to it [the good], that's surely what a state aims at when it legislates, and it lays down all its laws, to the best of its ability and judgment, as being most useful for itself (*Theaetetus* 177e4–6; cf. 179a),

says Socrates. However, one state's decision may approximate the truth, actual justice, less well than another's, and the counselor-gadfly of one polis may be wiser than that of another (cf. 177d). The implication is that Socrates' execution could be legalistically just yet unjust in itself, unjust by nature, thereby raising two further issues pursued in the *Apology* and in the *Crito*: whether a citizen must obey an unjust law, and whether punishment is justifiable. If a polis unwillingly does wrong, it deserves instruction, not punishment – as Socrates replies to his Athenian jury (*Apology* 26a).

The third is the central section, well known as the philosophical digression (*Theaetetus* 172c–177c) comparing the practical man and the philosopher, corresponding to "two patterns set up in that which is."[9] The description of the philosopher shows why the polis would condemn him. In Athens, philosophers are completely misunderstood; they "look ridiculous when they go into the law courts" (172c4–6), and worse. The philosopher's inexperience in court is mistaken for stupidity, his inability to discredit others personally is ridiculed, his genuine amusement is taken for silliness; he thinks of rulers as livestock keepers, fails to value property, wealth, or noble ancestry; he is arrogant, ignorant, and incompetent (174c–175b). If such a man should violate the law as well, wouldn't it be right to kill him? Two further opinions Socrates expresses about the philosopher of the digression will feature in the undoing of Socrates himself: he studies natural science (173e–174a), and his gods are not those of the city (176b–c). For such a godlike man, "the fact is that it's only his body that's in the state, here on a visit" (173e2–5); he "ought to try to escape from here to there as quickly" as he can (176a8–b1).

Fourth and finally, while discussing whether knowledge is true judgment, Socrates asks Theaetetus whether a jury has knowledge when it has been persuaded to a true judgment by an orator or a skilled litigant (201a–c) – reflecting exactly Socrates' situation with his own jury. By the strict letter of the law, Socrates is guilty of not believing in the vengeful Olympian gods of the Athenians and the poets, thus his jury is persuaded to a true judgment by the orator Lycon and the skilled litigant Anytus, if not by the feckless Meletus. But the result is legalistic justice, not justice itself; it reflects a correct judgment, but not knowledge. As the digression puts it, the point is "to give up asking 'What injustice am I doing to you, or you to me?' in favor of the investigation of justice and injustice themselves" (*Theaetetus* 175c1–2).

The *Euthyphro* and Piety

The *Euthyphro*, on the nature of piety, takes place just before Socrates enters his plea before the king-archon. The diviner-priest, Euthyphro, a man in his mid-forties who will prove inept at grasping piety when Socrates questions him, nevertheless predicts impending events well, fearing that Meletus will harm "the very heart of the city by attempting to wrong" Socrates (3a7–8), and inferring that Socrates' spiritual monitor signals religious innovation "easily misrepresented to the crowd" (3b5–9). Socrates replies by zeroing in on the crux: the Athenians would not mind his spiritual monitor or his opinions if he were not imitated by the young (3c7–d2; cf. 2c–d); the reason he is a defendant, he says, is that he does not accept the poets' stories about the gods' wrongdoing, "and it is likely to be the reason why I shall be told I do wrong" (6a8–9). Socrates leaves no doubt that the quarrelling gods Athenians accept are not the ones he believes in: what he formulates as questions at 6b–c, he states unambiguously elsewhere: "we can state the truth like this. A god is by no means and in no way unjust, but as just as it's possible to be" (*Theaetetus* 176b8–c1). For Socrates, the gods agree perfectly in their goodness, justice, wisdom, etc., and could not come into conflict – something Euthyphro cannot accept.

But Socrates' insistence that what the Athenians are most concerned about is how the youths are affected introduces the topic of education that plays a role in the background. Athenian males of the propertied classes sought higher education in their late teens. Since success in democratic public life was enhanced by the ability to influence the citizenry in the Assembly and courts, many studied with rhetoricians to learn the latest techniques of effective public speaking. In the latter fifth century, however, new intellectual influences from abroad began making headway in Athens among the young: sophists and natural scientists. The former could outdo the ordinary rhetoricians by teaching new ideas about what constitutes a good life or a good state, and some of them taught logic-chopping and hair-splitting as well, to make "the worse into the stronger cause" (*Apology* 19b5–c1), encouraging the young to get ahead without regard for justice or even custom. Natural scientists too seemed a threat to social order, giving naturalistic explanations for natural phenomena, and were lampooned repeatedly in comedy. Over the years, as Athens suffered war, plague, loss of empire, and defeat, its citizenry became increasingly alarmed that the new learning was somehow to blame, and anti-intellectualism grew.

The Preliminary Hearing

Although the rough content of the summons is given by the conversation in the *Euthyphro*, how Socrates would later that day answer the charge at his preliminary hearing probably led to greater precision in the formulation of the charge itself. The preliminary hearing designated the official receipt of the case (*dikē*) by the king-archon who, in office for one year, would later preside at the pretrial examination and the trial. Meletus stated or handed over his complaint, and Socrates answered by entering his plea. The king-archon was authorized to refuse Meletus' case on technical procedural grounds, to redirect it to an arbitrator, or to accept it. If Socrates took substantive exception, challenged the admissibility of the charge in relation to existing law, he had the right at this preliminary stage to file a countersuit (*paragraphē*) that would have been heard first – but he did not. In the case of an oral or improperly written complaint, the king-archon rendered the charge in appropriate legal language, marking the official acceptance of the case, now an indictment in the modern sense. It was then published on whitened tablets in the agora and a date was set for the pretrial examination (*anakrisis*); from this point, word would have spread that old Socrates, that big-mouth, hair-splitting, long-time target of the comic poets, had been charged with impiety.

The indictment that we have – via Diogenes Laertius (2.40.3–7), who took it from Favorinus (second century CE), who said he saw it in the public archive, the Metroön – is so formulated that, taking both the *Euthyphro* passage and this one into account, a secondary literature has grown up over exactly how many separate charges Socrates faced:

> This indictment [*graphē*] is brought on oath by Meletus, son of Meletus, of Pithus, against Socrates, son of Sophroniscus, of Alopece: Socrates is guilty of not believing in the gods the city believes in, and of introducing other divinities [*daimonia*]; and he is guilty of corrupting the young. The penalty assessed is death.

Athenian law forbade impiety, and that is the single law Socrates is charged with breaking – in two ways (not believing . . . , introducing . . .), with one result: corruption of the young.

Narrowly and legalistically, the prosecution faced some obstacles: base individuals who could testify to Socrates' direct influence would be suspect as witnesses; the upright citizens who would have been convincing witnesses, Socrates' actual companions, would testify only to his piety and propriety (*Apology* 33d–34b). But the prosecution had the advantage that the charge of impiety was not limited to the period 403–399, for it was not a political crime; Meletus, Anytus, and Lycon had only to persuade the jury that Socrates had at some time in his long life been impious and, since some of Socrates' associates, whom he might be alleged to have corrupted, were already dead – Critias, Charmides, Alcibiades, and others associated with the particularly notorious sacrileges of 415 – the prosecution could cast aspersions without blatantly violating the law against hearsay evidence.[10] It is probably unwise to be too narrow or legalistic, however, for juries could be swayed by innuendo and fallacious argument, swept along by powerful orations. Besides, the king-archon's acceptance of the case is *prima facie* evidence that there was a case to be made.

The Pretrial Examination

The court fees normally assessed of a plaintiff at this point, to be reimbursed by the defendant if found guilty, were waived in Meletus' suit because impiety prosecutions were "in the public interest." Yet his action would not have been without risk: to discourage frivolous suits, Athenian law imposed a heavy fine on plaintiffs who failed to obtain at least one-fifth of the jury's votes, as Socrates points out (*Apology* 36a7–b2).

Unlike closely timed jury trials, pretrial examinations were occasions for questions to and by the litigants, including questions of one another, to make more precise the legal issues of a case so a verdict of guilt or acquittal would be more straightforward. It was no time for speeches. This procedure had become essential because of the susceptibility of juries to bribery and misrepresentation by speakers who deliberately and often skillfully interpreted laws to their own advantage. Originally intended to be a microcosm of the citizen body as a whole, juries were now manned by volunteers – the old, disabled, and poor – who needed the meager pay of three *obols*, half the *drachma* that an able-bodied man could earn for a day's work (cf. Aristophanes, *Wasps* 291–311). In 399, Athenian men age 30 or over were eligible to volunteer for jury service at the beginning of the archon year, in midsummer. Six thousand were impaneled, probably by lotteries for 600 from each tribe, to be deployed repeatedly in different configurations to the various civil and criminal courts throughout the year. When Socrates' trial took place at the approach of midsummer, the jurors were experienced if not jaded.

Also, unlike trials, the pretrial examinations could be adjourned and reconvened repeatedly – when, for example, one of the principal parties needed to collect information. If a litigant wished to delay proceedings for weeks or months, this was a rich opportunity. Magistrates could also use the pretrial examination to compel a litigant to reveal information. We do not know what went on at Socrates' pretrial examination, though his complaints at *Theaetetus* 172e acknowledge some constraints.

The Trial and Socrates' Defense: The *Apology*

Plato takes up the story again in the month of Thargelion (May–June) a month or two after Meletus' initial summons, when Socrates' trial occurred. Onlookers gathered along with the 500 or 501 jurors (*Apology* 25a)[11] for a trial that probably lasted most of the day, each side timed by the water clock. Plato does not provide Meletus' prosecutorial speech or those of Anytus and Lycon; or the names of witnesses called, if any (*Apology* 34a3–4 implies Meletus called none). *Apology* – the Greek "*apologia*" means "defense" – is not edited as are the court speeches of orators. For example, there are no indications in the Greek text after 35d8 and 38b9 that the two votes were taken; and there are no breaks after 21a8 or 34b5 for witnesses, although Socrates may in fact have called Chaerecrates or the seven named men. Also missing are speeches by Socrates' supporters; it is improbable that he had none, even if Plato does not name them.

It is sometimes said that Socrates was the first person in the West to be convicted for his beliefs – for a thought-crime or crime of conscience; and not believing in the gods of the Athenians is exactly that. In classical Athens, however, religion was a matter of public participation under law, regulated by a calendar of festivals in honor of a variety of deities, with new ones introduced from time to time. The polis used its revenues to maintain temples and shrines, and to finance festivals; it mandated consultation with Apollo's oracle at Delphi at times of important decisions or crises; generals conferred with seers before deploying troops; and the lottery system for selecting public officials left decisions to the gods. Prescribed dogma or articles of faith, however, were unknown, so compliance was measured by behavior; and it is very unlikely, based on extant Socratic works, that there would have been *behavior* to offer in evidence of Socrates' beliefs, e.g., neglecting sacrifices or prayers, for Socrates continues his religious observance through his dying day. Moreover, unlike the case of the acquitted

Anaxagoras a generation earlier (cf. *Apology* 26d6–e2), there were no writings to present as evidence of unorthodox beliefs.

Socrates divides the accusations against him into old and new, addressed in that order. He had a reputation fueled by several comic poets from about 429 that conflated him with both natural scientists and sophists, often emphasizing his egregious effect on the young:[12] he "busies himself studying things in the sky and below the earth" (*Apology* 19b5). The single case Socrates mentions explicitly in *Apology* is Aristophanes' *Clouds* (produced in 423, revised in 418). As clear as it is with hindsight that the *character* Socrates who introduces new gods, denies the old ones, and corrupts the young in the play is a composite of several different sophists, natural scientists, and philosophers (Dover 1968), the jury made no subtle distinctions. Besides, Aristophanes had made fresh attacks in *Birds* (in 414) and *Frogs* (in 405), both times emphasizing that the city's young men imitated Socrates. In the latter, the Socrates-imitators are accused of attacking the poets. Socrates says himself that the young men question and thereby anger their elders (*Apology* 23c2–d2). Though Socrates denies outright that he is a natural scientist, his familiarity with their investigations and his own natural-istic explanations make it no surprise that the jury could not tell the difference (e.g., *Theaetetus* 152e, 153c–d, 173e–174a; *Phaedo* 96a–100a). Those who had witnessed Socrates in philosophical conversation (*Apology* 19d1–7), his respondents becoming angry or confused, were not likely to have appreciated fine distinctions between philo-sophical inquiry and sophistry. Socrates' excuse for his strange behavior – the god makes me do it (20e–23b) – appears from the crowd's reaction only to have exacer-bated their misunderstanding.

Turning to the new charges, Socrates easily defeats Meletus in argument, demon-strating in turn that Meletus (1) has not thought deeply about the improvement and corruption of the young, (2) should have sought to instruct Socrates privately before hauling him into court, (3) confuses Socrates' views with those of Anaxagoras, and (4) holds incompatible theses: Socrates is an atheist; and Socrates introduces new divinities. Yet the very exhibition of Socratic questioning, coupled with Socrates' belit-tling of Meletus (26e6–27a7) may have boomeranged. The jury, riled again, may have found Socrates' tactics indistinguishable from those of sophists: they saw, but they did not understand. Socrates' relentless honesty, easily mistaken for arrogance, casts doubt on his every claim: he will do no wrong, even to avoid death; he is like Achilles; he has risked death in battle; he does not fear death; he will never cease to do philosophy, to examine himself and others, even for the promise of acquittal; he is god's greatest gift to the city; his accusers cannot harm him, and the jurors will harm themselves if they kill him.

A defendant is wise to refute what he can, and Socrates does address some of the evidence against him directly. (5) He admits he has had, since childhood, the spiritual monitor that Meletus ridicules, but he defends it. He attributes to it his inability to "yield to any man contrary to what is right, for fear of death, even if I should die at once for not yielding" (32a6–7), and offers two instances of his defiant behavior in proof of it: presiding (as *prytanis*) over the Council (*boulê*) in 406, he opposed the Assembly's unlawful denial of separate trials to six generals who were tried and executed as a group. As a citizen under the lawfully elected but corrupt government of the Thirty, he refused the order to seize a fellow citizen, a general allied with the

13

democrats in exile.[13] In both cases Socrates cites, crediting his spiritual monitor, the Athenians had later come around to Socrates' view. (6) He denies being anyone's teacher, receiving a fee for conversing, teaching or promising to teach, and is thus unwilling to answer for the conduct of others (33a–b). (7) The Athenian god Apollo ("the god"), he says, ordered him to question wise guys – which the youths of Athens enjoy (33c); and he says oracle-like that he believes in the gods "as none of my accusers do" (35d7).

(8) Socrates three times takes up the charge that he corrupts the young, twice in the same hypothetical way: "Either I do not corrupt the young or, if I do, it is unwillingly." If unwillingly, he says he should be instructed because "if I learn better, I shall cease to do what I am doing unwillingly" (25e6–26a4). Later: "if by saying this I corrupt the young, this advice must be harmful, but if anyone says that I give different advice, he is talking nonsense" (30b5–7). He also argues that many of his former and current young companions are present with their guardians, but that none of them have testified to his corrupting influence (33d–34b). Anytus had warned the jury that Socrates should perhaps not have been brought to trial but, since he was, must be executed or else the sons of the Athenians will "practice the teachings of Socrates and all be thoroughly corrupted" (29c3–5). Can this 70-year-old who insists he will continue to philosophize possibly yield to instruction? Socrates claims his advice is that the soul is more important than the body or wealth (30a–b), but there has also been testimony that he teaches the young to despise the gods of the city and to question their elders disrespectfully. Even Socrates could not blame the jury for finding him guilty, for it is mistaken about what is truly in the interest of the city (cf. *Theaetetus* 177d–e). So the gadfly is swatted. The verdict is guilty, and the trial passes into the penalty phase.

Socrates blames one of Athens' laws:

> If it were the law with us, as it is elsewhere, that a trial for life should not last one but many days, you would be convinced, but now it is not easy to dispel great slanders in a short time. (*Apology* 37a7–b2)

This isolated complaint in the *Apology* is supported by the running criticism of the court in the *Theaetetus* noted earlier, e.g., "is what's true to be determined by the length or shortness of a period of time?" (158d11–12; cf. *Gorgias* 455a). And it stands opposed to the remark of the personified laws that Socrates was "wronged not by us, the laws, but by men" (*Crito* 54c1).

Socrates goes on to describe himself as the city's benefactor; to maintain that he mistreats no one and thus deserves a reward, not punishment; to insist that he cannot and must not stop philosophizing, for "the unexamined life is not worth living" (*Apology* 38a5–6) – confirmation to some that incorrigible Socrates opposes the will of the city. In a last-minute capitulation to his friends, he offers to allow them to pay a fine of 30 *minae*, six times his net worth. He is sentenced to death and reflects that it may be a blessing: either a dreamless sleep, or an opportunity to converse in the underworld.

Socrates' trial was no evil conspiracy against an innocent, but something more profound and at the same time more tragic – a catastrophic mistake, a misunderstanding that could not be reconciled in the time allowed by the law.

The *Crito* and Socrates' Refusal to Escape

The day before Socrates' trial begun, the Athenians launched a ship to Delos, dedicated to Apollo and commemorating Theseus' legendary victory over the Minotaur (*Phaedo* 58a–b). During this annual event, Athenian law demanded exceptional purity, so no executions were allowed. Although the duration of the voyage varied with conditions, Xenophon says it took 31 days in 399 (*Memorabilia* 4.8.2); if correct, Socrates lived 30 days beyond his trial, into the month of Skirophorion (June–July 399). A day or two before the end, Socrates' childhood friend Crito – sleepless, distraught, depressed – visits Socrates in the prison, armed with arguments for why Socrates should escape before it is too late. Socrates replies that he "listens to nothing . . . but the argument that on reflection seems best" (*Crito* 46b4–6), whereupon a reflective conversation begins.

Socrates' argument that he must not escape is a continuation of his refrain from the *Apology* (28b, 29b, 32a, 32b, 37a, 37b) that he never willingly does wrong (*Crito* 49b–d). The principle is absolute. Wrongdoing, mistreating people, and injustice are the same, "in every way harmful and shameful to the wrongdoer" (49b5), never to be inflicted, not even in return for wrongdoing suffered (cf. *Theaetetus* 173a8), not even under threat of death (cf. *Apology* 32a), not even for one's family (*Crito* 54b3–4). Clearly Socrates cannot be morally consistent and inflict harm on Athens in return for harm endured, as Crito would prefer (50c1–3). Note, however, that although one should keep one's agreements (49e6–8) – one's social contract as it were – one cannot always keep all one's agreements at the same time. Socrates is right not to equate injustice with lawbreaking. We have already seen that (a) cities legislate their good to the best of their ability, but can be mistaken about what is in their interest, consequently establishing unjust laws; (b) Athens' law against impiety, insofar as it required acceptance of the quarreling, wrongdoing gods of the poets, was an unjust law; (c) orders from lawful governments to commit wrongdoing are not binding because they are unjust; and (d) Athens' one-day limit on all trials was an unjust law. Socrates had already found it necessary to violate the law of (b) when it conflicted with both his spiritual monitor and reason, and to disobey an order of type (c) when following it would have harmed someone else. Nevertheless, Socrates says he would be mistreating Athens to escape and must therefore remain in prison (49e9–50a3). To understand why that is so, we should take into account the argument of the *Theaetetus* and the *Apology* that (e) the correct response to unwilling wrongdoing is not punishment but wise counsel, instruction – the positive corollary to the negative principle of do-no-harm. When the laws tell Socrates to persuade or obey them (*Crito* 51b9–c1), they give a nod to this principle. Like keeping agreements, however, persuasion is not always possible and is thus subordinate to do-no-harm.

One might say Socrates should have attempted to persuade the Thirty, and perhaps he did, but that situation differed importantly: undermining a corrupt government by refusing to harm a good man was unlawful, but it was not unjust. In the present case, having already said that death may be a blessing, Socrates cannot point to a harm that would outweigh the harm he would be inflicting on the city if he now exiled himself unlawfully when he could earlier have left lawfully (52c3–6). In this case, the

15

laws are right to say that if Socrates destroys them, he will manifestly confirm the jury's judgment that he is a corrupter of the young (53b7–c3).

The impiety law Socrates violated is interesting in a different way. Whereas one can destroy laws by undermining them, one cannot *persuade* laws; one must rather persuade men. And that presents an insurmountable obstacle: in 410, a commission was established to inscribe all the laws, the Athenian Constitution, in stone on the walls of the king-archon's court. Just as the task was completed in 404, a series of calamities – Athens' defeat by Sparta, the establishment of the Thirty, then bitter civil war – persuaded the citizens that, however useful it was to have the newly inscribed laws readily available, those laws themselves had failed to prevent disastrous decisions over a generation of war in which the empire had been lost. When the democracy was restored in 403, a Board of Legislators (*nomothetai*) was instituted to write additional laws, assisted by the Council. A new legal era was proclaimed from the year 403/2, Ionic lettering replaced Attic for inscriptions, and a public archive was established so laws written on papyrus could be consulted and cited. From that year, only laws inscribed from 410 to 404, or from 403 at the behest of the new legislators, were valid; an official religious calendar was adopted and inscribed; and decrees of the Assembly and Council could no longer override laws (such as had enabled the six generals to be tried as a group over Socrates' objections).

However useful the reforms were, the Board was not a public institution seeking advice or holding hearings. Furthermore, it was a crime for anyone else even to propose a law or decree in conflict with the inscribed laws. Still, Socrates did what he could: he never shrank from discussing whether the gods were capable of evil and conflict. It is anachronistic to use the phrase "academic freedom" of the era before Plato had established the Academy, but what is denoted by the phrase owes its authority to Socrates' steadfast principle of following nothing but the argument that on reflection seemed best to him.

The Execution of Socrates in the *Phaedo*

Plato sets the final conversation and execution of Socrates in a metaphysically speculative, Pythagorean dialogue where intricately intertwined arguments, mythology, and Socratic biography have roles to play. The *Phaedo* is Plato's most dualistic dialogue, exploring the soul's troubled relationship with the body; and it is the only dialogue in which Plato's absence is explicitly remarked (59b10). What in the *Theaetetus* is Socrates' down-to-earth maieutic method, is in the *Phaedo* the soul's recollection of transcendent Forms. What in the *Theaetetus* is the philosopher's escape from the earthly mix of good and bad, is in *Phaedo* the soul's escape from the body.

Phaedo is, by custom, the dialogue most concerned with what it is to be a philosopher and to lead the life of philosophy – though in more rarefied air than when the rough Socrates practices his questioning techniques on anyone willing to be engaged by him. It is perhaps closer to the truth to say that the dialogue is about dying in philosophy, for the recurring image is of the soul's purification and final flight from the imprisoning body that distracts it with pleasures and pains, needs and desires,

16

throughout life. Phaedo tells the Pythagorean community at Phlius that – while Socrates' companions felt "an unaccustomed mixture of pleasure and pain at the same time . . . sometimes laughing, then weeping"[14] – the philosopher himself, on his last day of life, "appeared happy both in manner and words as he died nobly and without fear" (58e3–4), a proem sustained in the conversations about the soul that follow.

Without ever claiming certainty, and sometimes flatly denying he has it, Socrates wants to put his argument before his "judges," his friends: one who has spent a lifetime doing philosophy should face death cheerfully. He says, "other people do not realize that the one aim of those who practice philosophy in the proper manner is to practice for dying and death" (64a4–6) – which raises a laugh and Simmias' joke that people think "true philosophers are nearly dead" (64b4–6; cf. 65d, 80e). But the seriousness of the day's talk is plain when Simmias and Cebes have delivered themselves of arguments against the immortality of the soul, depressing everyone. Socrates rallies:

> If you take my advice, you will give but little thought to Socrates but much more to the truth. If you think that what I say is true, agree with me; if not, oppose it with every argument and take care that in my eagerness I do not deceive myself and you and, like a bee, leave my sting in you when I go. (*Phaedo* 91b8–c5)

Philosophical argument resumes. Near the end, Socrates breaks into a long story of the afterlife that "no sensible man would insist" were true, but where "Those who have purified themselves sufficiently by philosophy live in the future altogether without a body" (114c2–6).

In sharp contrast, realism dominates the opening and closing scenes in the prison. In the morning, Socrates visits with Xanthippe and their baby, and rubs his ankle where the bonds have been removed, speaking of pleasure and pain; the Eleven, prison officials chosen by lot, are already gone (59e–60b). Now, sometime in the afternoon and with the philosophical conversation ended, attention focuses again on the body. Socrates has no interest in whether his corpse is burned or buried, he says, but he wants to take a bath to save the women of his household from having to wash the corpse, then he meets with his family before rejoining his companions. The servant of the Eleven, a public slave, bids Socrates farewell by calling him "the noblest, the gentlest, and the best" (116c5–6), but cannot forbear weeping. The poisoner describes the physical effects of the poison, the *Conium maculatum* variety of hemlock (Bloch 2002). Socrates cheerfully takes the cup, "without a tremor or any change of feature or color" (117b3–5), and drinks. The emotions that have been threatening Socrates' companions now erupt violently – and are immediately checked by Socrates' shaming, "keep quiet and control yourselves" (117e2). The poison begins to work, and the poisoner follows its numbing progress from the feet to the belly – touching, testing, pressing Socrates' body. Socrates makes a last request of Crito. Presently, his body gives a jerk, after which his eyes are fixed. Crito closes them. Phaedo, the former slave, echoes the servant of the Eleven, ending the dialogue with an epithet for Socrates, "the best, . . . the wisest and the most upright" (118a16–17).

Notes

1 Xenophon is often cited, though he was not in Athens at the time: see discussions in Stone (1988), Brickhouse and Smith (1989: §§ 1–2), and McPherran (1996: *passim*); later accounts, mostly fragmentary, tell how Socrates was viewed in later centuries (see Brickhouse and Smith 2002, cited in Bloch).

2 Cf. allusions at, e.g., *Sophist* 216a–d, and *Statesman* 299b–300e, set dramatically when the indicted Socrates was at liberty pending trial.

3 *Euthyphro, Apology, Crito,* and *Phaedo* translated by G. M. A. Grube, revised by John Cooper.

4 Anytus appears in the works of 11 different contemporaneous authors (Nails 2002: 37–38), Lycon in 6 (Nails 2002: 188–89).

5 Litigation is a topic (172a–173b, 173c–d, 174c, 178e, 201a–c); but there are additional allusions to legal proceedings: (a) the *ad hoc* adoption of legalistic language (145c, 170d, 171d, 175d, 176d–e, 179b–c); (b) reminders about the time required by philosophy and limited by litigation (154e, 158d, 172c–e, 187d, 201a–b; cf. *Apology* 24a, 37b). Moreover, there are thematic ties to *Phaedo* (*Theaetetus* 144e–145a, 145c–d, 154c, 173e–174a, 176a–b, 205c).

6 By discussing *Theaetetus* in dramatic order, I make no claims about when it was written, though I reject the so-called developmental hypothesis that Plato's views evolved in some linear way: Plato tendered positions tentatively, leaving them open for revision, and returned to them repeatedly to address material for various purposes (Nails 1995: 219–31).

7 *Theaetetus* translated by John McDowell.

8 See *Republic* 496c4 (cf. 509c1), *Phaedrus* 242b9, *Euthydemus* 272e4, *Euthyphro* 3b5, *Apology* 31d1, 40a4, 41d6, and *Theaetetus* 151a4.

9 Thesleff (1967: 57–61) surveys three types of central section, arguing that Plato, like Pindar et al., occasionally sets a visionary speech at the center of a dialogue, e.g., the divided line passage in *Republic*. Blondell's (2002: 289–303) account of the digression notes the special role of the central section and cites more recent bibliography. The passage here shows, by the way, why Socrates would fit more comfortably in the primitive communal society of *Republic* 2 (369b–372d) than in even a purged Athens, though it is the latter that he loves (*Theaetetus* 143d).

10 Critias was a leader of the Thirty; Charmides was a member of the Piraeus Ten in the same period. The mutilation of herms and profanation of the mysteries is treated in Nails (2002: 17–20; s.v.v.); contemporaneous ancient sources are Thucydides 6.27–29, 6.53, 6.60–1; Andocides 1.11–1.70; inscriptions on *stelae* from the Eleusinium in Athens (*Inscriptiones Graecae* I 421–430); and Xenophon, *Hellenica* 1.4.13–21. Plutarch, *Alcibiades* 18–22; and Diodorus Siculus 13.2.2–4, 13.5.1–4, 13.69.2–3 may have used contemporaneous sources, no longer extant, in their much later accounts.

11 The round number 500 continues to appear in contemporaneous accounts long after we know 501 were employed to avoid ties.

12 See Nails (2002: 266–7) for Aristophanes, *Clouds*; *Birds* 1280–3, 1553, *Frogs* 1491–9 et al.; and for fragments of Callias' *Pedētae*, Teleclides, Amipsias' *Connus*, and Eupolis.

13 A more complete account appears in Nails (2002: 79–82), citing Xenophon, *Hellenica* 1.7.8–35; Diodorus Siculus, *Library of History* 13.98–103; and contemporary sources; cf. pseudo-Aristotle, *Athenian Polity* 34.1. The election and rule of the Thirty, with numerous ancient and contemporary sources, is at Nails (2002: 111–13). Leon of Salamis has an entry at Nails (2002: 185–6) with reference to Thucydides 5 and 8, *passim*; Xenophon, *Hellenica* 1 and 2, *passim*, especially 2.3.39–41; Andocides 1.94; Lysias 10, 13.44; Plato, Letter 7.324e–325a, and *Apology* 32c–d; and contemporary sources.

14   59a4–9. Considerable information about these companions is known. Of some 23 persons, only 2 are attested in the liturgical class, 5 or fewer are Athenian men under 30. There are 3 slaves and a (foreign) former slave, the illegitimate son of a rich man, 2 to 3 women, 3 children, and 6 foreigners, 1 of whom seems to have been wealthy (Nails 2002: xxxix; s.v.v.). The prison cell, which could not have held them all at once, has been unearthed (Camp 1992: 113–16).

References

Allen, R. E. (1984). *The Dialogues of Plato*. Vol. I. *Euthyphro, Apology, Crito, Meno, Gorgias, Menexenus*. New Haven and London: Yale University Press. Useful for its thoughtful commentaries, arguing that Socrates' foremost commitment was not to laws, but to a "single, self-consistent standard of justice, fixed in the nature of things" against which any set of laws must be measured.

Bloch, E. (2002). Hemlock poisoning and the death of Socrates: Did Plato tell the truth? In Thomas C. Brickhouse and Nicholas D. Smith (eds.), *The Trial and Execution of Socrates: Sources and Controversies* (pp. 255–78). New York and Oxford: Oxford University Press. Identifies *Conium maculatum* as the specific hemlock poison that produces the exact symptoms described by Plato in *Phaedo*.

Blondell, R. (2002). *The Play of Character in Plato's Dialogues*. Cambridge: Cambridge University Press. Provides a deeply moving treatment of the dramatic elements of the *Theaetetus*, and especially the digression, in chapter 5.

Brickhouse, T. C. and Smith, N. D. (1989). *Socrates on Trial*. Princeton: Princeton University Press. A watershed work on the arguments, historicity, and context of Plato's *Apology*, downplaying the role of politics in the miscarriage of justice that resulted in Socrates' conviction.

—— (1994). *Plato's Socrates*. New York: Oxford University Press. Argues that Socrates always obeys the law, which is always just, thus obeying an unjust law would not bring blame to Socrates but to the legislators and the law itself.

Burnyeat, M. F. (1988). Cracking the Socrates case. *New York Review of Books*, March 31, 1988, partially elaborated in The Impiety of Socrates (1998), *Ancient Philosophy* 17, 1–12. Finds Socrates guilty of not believing in the gods in which the city believes, amidst a masterful review of Stone (1988).

Camp, J. M. (1992). *The Athenian Agora: Excavations in the Heart of Classical Athens*. Corrected edition. London: Thames and Hudson Ltd. Includes line drawings and photographs of places and artifacts relevant to Socrates' last days.

Clay, D. (2000). *Platonic Questions: Dialogues with the Silent Philosopher*. University Park: Pennsylvania State University Press. Brilliant and idiosyncratic; develops the explicit allusions in the texts insightfully.

Cooper, J. M. (ed.) (1997). *Plato Complete Works*. Indianapolis and Cambridge: Hackett Publishing Company. Important not only for its widely-used translations, but for Cooper's sober and wide-ranging introduction.

Dover, K. J. (1968). *Aristophanes: Clouds*. Oxford: Clarendon Press. Describes the intellectual milieu in Athens in the late 420s, arguing that the Socrates of Aristophanes' play was a composite of foreign and local intellectuals.

Euben, J. P. (1997). *Corrupting Youth: Political Education, Democratic Culture, and Political Theory*. Princeton: Princeton University Press. An engaging essay on Socrates' role as educator within the democracy, drawing compelling parallels to contemporary culture-war debates.

Harrison, A. R. W. (1968, 1971). *The Law of Athens.* Volume I: *The Family and Property.* Volume II: *Procedure.* Oxford: Oxford University Press. Reissued 1998 by Hackett Publishing Co. with a foreword by Douglas M. MacDowell. Remains unsurpassed for the details of the issues that arise in connection with the trial and execution of Socrates.

Kraut, R. (1984). *Socrates and the State.* Princeton: Princeton University Press. Examines Socrates' attitude toward democracy, arguing that living an examined life would require Socrates, if he disobeyed a law, to persuade a court that he had been right to disobey.

MacDowell, D. M. (1978). *The Law in Classical Athens.* Ithaca: Cornell University Press. Essential for understanding the major changes in Athenian legal procedures at the end of the fifth and beginning of the fourth century.

Mackenzie, M. M. (1981). *Plato on Punishment.* Berkeley and Los Angeles: University of California Press. Authoritative, comprehensive source on its subject, thus important for the view of punishment Socrates alludes to in *Theaetetus* and articulates in *Apology*.

McPherran, M. L. (1996). *The Religion of Socrates.* University Park: Pennsylvania State University Press. Seeks the religion of the historical Socrates through an extensive survey of Greek religious practices, close readings of Socratic texts, and dialogue with Vlastos (1989).

Nails, Debra (1995). *Agora, Academy, and the Conduct of Philosophy.* Dordrecht: Kluwer Academic Publishers. In a study of Socratic and Platonic method, examines a variety of conflicting claims about Plato's philosophical development.

—— (2002). *The People of Plato: A Prosopography of Plato and Other Socratics.* Indianapolis and Cambridge: Hackett Publishing Co. Reference for information about the persons in the dialogues, their historical context, and evidence for dramatic dates.

Reeve, C. D. C. (1989). *Socrates in the "Apology": An Essay on Plato's Apology of Socrates.* Indianapolis and Cambridge: Hackett Publishing Co. Argues that the Socrates of the dialogue, having defended himself convincingly against the indictment, was unjustly convicted.

Stone, I. F. (1988). *The Trial of Socrates.* New York: Little, Brown and Co. Citing political reasons for Socrates' conviction, the great journalist pays tribute to Athenian democracy by telling, as he sees it, Athens' side of the Socrates story.

Thesleff, H. (1967). *Studies in the Styles of Plato.* Acta Philosophica Fennica. Helsinki: Suomalaisen kirjallisuuden kirjapaino. Handbook of Platonic composition technique, dialogue structure, comparative classification of styles.

Vlastos, G. (1983). The historical Socrates and Athenian democracy. *Political Theory,* 11, 495–516. Argues that Socrates preferred democracy to other forms of government but faulted men who misused democratic institutions for unjust ends.

—— (1989). Socratic piety. *Proceedings of the Boston Area Colloquium in Ancient Philosophy,* 5, 213–38. An influential paper taking the position that Socrates rationalized Athenian religion.

Weiss, R. (1998). *Socrates Dissatisfied: An Analysis of Plato's Crito.* New York and Oxford: Oxford University Press. Argues persuasively that the personified laws do not speak for Socrates, who follows the argument that seems best to him.

Woozley, A. D. (1979). *Law and Obedience: The Arguments of Plato's Crito.* Chapel Hill: University of North Carolina Press. Concludes disobedience to law would be permissible for Socrates only if the illegal action were itself intended to persuade.

2

Socrates and Euripides

CHRISTIAN WILDBERG

The Question and its Problems

Euripides (c. 485–406 BCE) was in his late twenties or early thirties when he first received a chorus and competed in the Great Festival of Dionysus. Socrates (469–399 BCE) was then, in the year 455, a mere boy of 14. Both were children of the generation of Athenians that had triumphed over the Persians at Marathon and Salamis. In 406, when Sophocles publicly mourned the death of his great rival, Socrates had still some seven years to live. By that time, the sociopolitical unity that had nourished and sustained Athens for most of the century had all but disintegrated; in the *Frogs*, written shortly after the death of Euripides and performed in 405, Aristophanes grapples in his own idiosyncratic way with the cultural disarray that had seized the city. Throughout his comedies, caricatures of both Socrates and Euripides feature prominently (though the two never appear together in the same play), and already in their lifetimes, as we shall see, these twin icons of the avant-garde of fifth-century Athens were closely associated with one another. Like the two different but complementary sides of a coin, the one symbolized a new and particularly obnoxious kind of eccentricity while the other was thought to sacrifice the traditional nomenclature of tragic drama to the aberrations of modern taste.

What, if any, was the actual relationship between Socrates and Euripides? Or rather, what can one possibly say about this supposed relationship without leaving behind more or less solid historical ground? Not a whole lot, it would seem. To be sure, it would be possible, and on obvious grounds quite reasonable, to reconfigure the question and to treat the subject matter before us on a purely literary level, mulling over the meaning and function of apparently Socratic motifs in Euripides' tragedies or the use of Euripidean lines in the narrative of a Socratic dialogue written by Plato. From a methodological standpoint, this would be a perfectly safe and perhaps even fruitful inquiry.[1] And to some extent the present argument will have to resort to precisely such an approach. But questions such as how Euripidean and Socratic motifs play out on a literary level cannot be our sole focus; the question reaches deeper and is, in consequence, much more difficult to answer. It goes *deeper* because it aims at the character of a particular *historical* relationship between two highly controversial intellectuals in fifth-century Athens. And it is much more *difficult* because neither Socrates

21

nor Euripides, nor anyone else for that matter, provided us with any hard biographical evidence concerning the private or professional lives of these two men. Euripides is permanently veiled behind his tragedies as their implied "author," and we are familiar with Socrates, if at all, only as a character in the philosophical "plays" of Plato – or as someone the Athenian general Xenophon remembered fondly. Needless to say, what Plato put into the mouth of Socrates decades after the latter's death may or (more likely) may not have anything to do with the historical Socrates, and what Euripides put into the mouth of any one of the characters may or (more likely) may not have anything to do with his own sentiments and beliefs. The same of course goes for Xenophon. Even if these literary productions contain the occasional historical nugget, the fact is that we have to admit, frustratingly, that we possess no good way of telling fact from fiction. And so, how can one ever hope to reconstruct a historical relationship that may (or may not) have occurred 24 centuries ago between two persons of whom we have absolutely no direct and reliable evidence?

The situation is not entirely hopeless, for even if we do not have any direct evidence of either historical person, it may still be the case that we have reasonably good evidence of the fact, intensity, and character of the intellectual bonds that constituted their relationship. And I believe that there is indeed, though admittedly scant, evidence of this kind, which I shall try to present and explore in the following pages.

But before this can be done, another formidable difficulty deserves to be mentioned, a difficulty that has more to do with us than with historical evidence, or lack thereof. For a modern interpreter, it is almost impossible to approach the question of "Socrates and Euripides" without considerable prejudice. In 1872, Friedrich Nietzsche placed a startling analysis of the relationship between Socrates and Euripides at the center of his provocative and extremely influential pamphlet *The Birth of Tragedy*. Bluntly put, it was Socrates' fault, according to Nietzsche, that Euripides' plays are so bad as tragedies. More than that, Socrates was to blame for the momentous cultural fact that the very genre of Attic tragic drama ceased to exist. Tragedy died at the hands of Socrates; Euripides was his henchman.[2]

Nietzsche's argument is shot through with seductive rhetoric and psychological speculation, and is moreover far from clear in every detail. To summarize his view briefly, Nietzsche contends that the "Kunstwerk" we refer to as "Attic drama" must be understood as the result of two competing impulses that shaped Greek artistic fecundity, one being the aesthetic drive towards measured and beautiful representation (the "Apollonian," as Nietzsche called it), the other impulse arising from the disturbing realization that human existence adds up to intolerable suffering; this impulse tends to express itself in the performance and experience of ecstatic music and dance (the "Dionysian"). Whereas the Dionysian moment acknowledges and somehow celebrates the terrifying abyss that threatens to devour human existence at any moment, the Apollonian artfully veils it in order to make life tolerable through the illusion of order and beauty. Attic drama, properly understood, originates, according to Nietzsche, from the pairing of just these two antagonistic and yet closely related moments; the powerfully disturbing beauty of tragedy arises precisely because the Apollonian scenes and images of the actions it depicts are painted on the baneful Dionysian abyss the chorus represents as their canvas.

Along came Socrates, and with him an entirely new perspective of the world. Socrates – rationalist, moralist, and optimist as he was – leads a life in denial of the Dionysian sentiment. For him, the abyss does not exist; the world is good, the gods are good, moral goodness is the key to happiness, and it can be found and secured by argument and reason. This optimism, Nietzsche declares, spelled the death of tragic drama; the genre withered away under the pen of no other than Euripides who wholeheartedly adopted Socratean rationalism, forging it into what Nietzsche calls an "aesthetic Socratism." If it was Socrates' maxim to equate goodness with rationality, Euripides' *oeuvre* espouses the (false) equation of rationality and beauty: only the consciously rational is beautiful. Euripides' tragedies are so shot through with clever rhetoric and dialectic, psychological insight, and ratiocinations that they ceased to be tragedies: they have already, according to Nietzsche, degenerated into the decadent genre of bourgeois stage-plays.

There is something that strikes one immediately as right about Nietzsche's dazzling analysis; one cannot help but admire the instinct that allowed Nietzsche to see the faultlines of cultural and ideological incompatibilities. To be sure, a person who firmly believes in reason and goodness and cheerfully downs the hemlock no longer lives in a tragic universe. The powerful rationality that guided Socrates' spirit transgressed the boundaries of the heroic world that typically frames Attic drama. A play that endears itself too much to the optimistic promises of reason must necessarily undermine the pessimistic trait that characterizes all tragedy. Still, what disturbs is Nietzsche's sweeping claim that makes the last great Attic tragedian the hangman of the genre, reducing him to little more than a tool of Socrates. Anyone who discusses the problem of Socrates and Euripides will want to avoid the Scylla of succumbing too readily to the prejudice Nietzsche tries to induce in his readers; but likewise, one should steer clear of the Charybdis of dismissing Nietzsche out of hand in a misguided attempt to defend Euripides against the charge. As if he needed defending.

Facts and Evidence

Everyone is entitled to their own opinion and interpretation, including Nietzsche, but not to their own facts. We must therefore turn to the facts and evidence that speak, directly or indirectly, to the relationship between Socrates and Euripides. First, a look at the broader picture.

The institution of the theater was undoubtedly of central cultural and intellectual concern in fifth-century Athens; the best minds competed for fame and glory in this genre, year after year facing a frightfully discerning and judgmental audience. Since we can claim with a great deal of confidence that Socrates was deeply influenced, in one way or another, by all kinds of contemporary intellectual currents like the sophists or more ponderous philosophical figures such as Anaxagoras, it seems a good wager to suppose that the culture of tragic discourse, with its representation of the human condition and the moral concerns it raises, might have been, to some extent at least, formative of Socrates' own thinking. It is furthermore reasonable to single out Euripides as presumably the most important figure in this regard, more so than, say, Aeschylus or Sophocles. There are not only the bare biographical facts that link

Socrates to Euripides in a privileged way: that they were approximately of the same age, that they lived in the same city in the most glorious time of her existence, witnessing both the delirium of her triumphs and the tremors of her decline. More importantly, both were prominent, even notorious, "public intellectuals"; one might call the one, as he has been, a philosophical tragedian,[3] the other, in view of his martyrdom for philosophy, a tragic philosopher, although presumably neither of them would have agreed to their respective labels. Much more than a figure like Sophocles, Euripides and Socrates were attuned to the culture of lively intellectual exchange that was shaped in the fifth century by the popularizing exploits of the sophists; both were heavily invested in that culture, with lives and livelihoods firmly rooted in the public sphere of ancient Athens, which they addressed for decade after decade in different contexts without ever leaving the city for any length of time. Only at the end of their lives does the one do what was strongly suggested to the other, to withdraw for good and to spend old age on foreign soil. In 408 or 407, a couple of years before his death, Euripides goes to Thessaly and then on to the court of Archelaus, King of Macedon, where he writes his last powerful tragedies. Socrates knew that his type of moral exhortation could not be expatriated in any easy way. It took him little trouble to persuade his friends that escaping from prison would not only be unreasonable and unjust, but also spell the end of his philosophic life.[4] During the roughly five decades they spent their active lives together in Athens, all the external parameters were firmly in place for a lively intellectual exchange just waiting to happen. Nietzsche was surely right in this general regard.

In the light of all these biographical parallels it is plausible to suppose that Euripides and Socrates knew of each other's intellectual commitments. It is safe to presume that Socrates saw the productions of Euripides performed on stage, either in Athens or the many smaller theaters that adorned the Attic town and villages. We do not even need to invoke the many ancient anecdotes that attest to this fact: according to Aelian, Socrates made a point of going to the theater *only* when Euripides competed.[5] Other anecdotes suggest that on those occasions he did not simply comport himself as a spectator who is content to be entertained; Socrates gets involved, as if the words spoken on stage were somehow addressed to him. According to Cicero, he called for an encore of particular lines,[6] using the very theater to make a spectacle of himself. In keeping with this anecdote a story of Diogenes relates: Socrates gets up and leaves the theater during the performance of the *Auge* because he disagrees with the content of a particular line.[7] One imagines large swaths of spectators momentarily turning their heads: a grim moment in the career of Euripides?

Even if the anecdotes just related are purely fictitious, it seems hard to imagine that the novelty and intensity of Euripides' plays would have not provoked a response from Socrates. And if that is true, it becomes even harder to imagine that Socrates' reaction to Euripides, whatever it may have been in and outside the theater, did not in some way rebound to affect the playwright. Perhaps this give and take of opinions happened quite naturally and casually: in another suggestive anecdote we encounter Socrates and Euripides as if they belonged to the same intellectual book-club: one day Euripides passed on the work of Heraclitus to Socrates, so the story goes, who read it and responded in mock-Heraclitean fashion: "What I understand is good; what I don't understand is also good – I think. But one would have to be a Delian diver."[8]

Whatever the specific value of this anecdote, we may take it as confirming the general picture outlined here. For at the time when this anecdote was alive (roughly the third century BCE), it was evidently part of common knowledge that Euripides and Socrates consorted with one another for the purpose of exchanging ideas. We don't ever hear of Socrates exchanging anything with Sophocles.

But there is even better evidence that firmly points in the same direction. The presumably first and oldest testimony we have of the historical Socrates, long before the time of Plato, stems from the Athenian comic poet Teleclides who competed in the middle of the fifth century and probably won his first victory in 446. And the very first thing we learn from him about Socrates is that he associated with Euripides! The fragment is quoted by Diogenes Laertius right at the beginning of his chapter on Socrates; the passage is worth citing in full, but not without drawing attention to the fact that some 600 years after the time of Socrates and Euripides (or whenever the *Lives* were written), Diogenes finds himself compelled to highlight the alleged relationship as the very first biographical fact about Socrates.[9] Diogenes writes:

> Socrates was the son of Sophroniscus, a statuary, and of Phaenarete, a midwife, as Plato says in the *Theaetetus*; he was a citizen of Athens, from the deme of Alopece. Some people believed that he helped Euripides write poetry; Mnesimachus[10] puts it as follows:
>
> > The *Phrygians,* that's a new play by Euripides;
> > Actually, Socrates puts on the firewood.
> > Again he says:
> > . . . Euripidean <tragedies?>, nailed up by Socrates.[11]
> > And Callias, in his *Captives*,[12] says:
> > A.: So why are *you*[13] so proud and all puffed up?
> > B.: That's my entitlement! Socrates is responsible for it.
> > And Aristophanes says in the *Clouds*:
> > He's the chap who writes the tragedies for Euripides,
> > Those wordy, clever ones.

Teleclides' joke about the *Phrygians,* which Socrates is said to have fired up with *phrygana,* sticks or faggots, operates on two levels; first, there is of course the linguistic level, because the word *phrygana* contains an obvious assonance to the plays' title. Secondly, the butt of the joke is Euripides, for the comic poet suggests that his colleague working in the tragic genre somehow needs a philosopher to "turn up the heat." Presumably in the same comedy he coins the hilarious word *sōkratogomphos,* "all nailed up by Socrates," perhaps a reprise of the earlier joke. If we suppose that the comedy of which these two fragments stem was performed sometime in the late 440s, then Socrates was only a young man in his late twenties and Euripides a well-known tragic poet in his early forties. It is remarkable that already at that time it must have rung true to the audience, at the very least, that these two men had something rather striking in common.

The joke must have come across rather well, for in the ensuing decades it turns into something like a comic *topos.* If the "person" addressed in the Callias[14] fragment of *The Captives (Pedētai,* performed in 429) is a Euripidean tragedy, which is a reasonable assumption, we get a joke very similar to Teleclides' jibe. And in the Aristophanes fragment, presumably from an earlier version of the *Clouds*, Strepsiades seems to ask after the man standing aloft high up in a basket, like a *deus ex machina* ready to be swung into action. He receives the answer: "He's the chap who writes the tragedies for Euripides, those wordy, clever ones." Finally, at the end of the *Frogs* (performed in 405), the butt of the joke is Euripides again; Aeschylus has just prevailed in the contest and the chorus explains what the problem with Euripides was (1491–9):

> It's a graceful thing *not* to sit
> Down with Socrates and chatter,
> Casting aside the art of music,
> Neglecting what's most important
> In the art of tragedy.
> Whiling away one's time
> With pompous arguments and outlines
> Is the mark of a man – gone mad.

Two things are noteworthy: first, the lines occur at the play's climactic finale; they are the very last words sung by the chorus, and the audience is supposed to be roaring with laughter at this point. It is unlikely that Aristophanes would have allowed himself to be flogging a dead horse. Second, in this latest variant of the joke, now at the expense of a deceased, Aristophanes ridicules Euripides no longer by insinuating that Socrates helped him write his poetry; rather, the charge is now that Euripides has neglected the tragic Muse and spent too much time in bad company. This somewhat mitigated charge may well be significant; if so, it would tie in nicely with our concluding assessment below.

Taken together, all this amounts to solid evidence that in the eyes of the Athenians Socrates and Euripides associated with one another over a long period of time, and that this association was regarded as close. What we are dealing with here are the echoes of an intellectual friendship that should be regarded not as a literary fabrication but as historical reality,[15] all the more so since old comedy is not even our only evidence. If we look towards the circle of minor Socratics, we find that Socrates' pupil Aeschines wrote dialogues in which Euripides appeared as interlocutor,[16] and Plato's younger brother Glaucon is said to have written a Socratic dialogue that bore the title *Euripides*.[17] The fact that Xenophon never mentions Euripides in his Socratic writings should not disturb us: his intellectual world offered little space for tragic poets.[18]

Unfortunately, we find little evidence in Plato to further corroborate this point, but given what Plato thought about the usefulness of tragic drama, this is perhaps not entirely surprising. Although Euripides is mentioned and quoted in Plato more times than Sophocles and Aeschylus taken together (Euripides 16 times; Sophocles 5 times; Aeschylus 9 times), there is only one passage in the entire *oeuvre* in which Plato has imagined a situation in which Socrates recites a Euripidean verse with approval (*Gorgias* 492a: "Who knows whether life does not mean being dead, and being dead life?"). In contrast to this, Euripides is roundly criticized in the eighth book of the *Republic* (568a) for saying that tyrants are wise on account of their association with wise men, and the same verse is extensively discussed in the presumably pseudo-Platonic *Theages* (125d–e).

The meager evidence in Plato should by no means shake our confidence in the historicity of the relationship between Socrates and Euripides. For there is also nothing in Plato's text that militates against the assumption that the two spent at least the occasional symposium together, talking deep into the night about their shared interests. At the end of the *Symposium*, at any rate, we see Socrates in some such situation, drinking and discussing with Euripides' colleagues Agathon and Aristophanes. Although the precise nature of the conversation got lost in the literary fog of inebriation, Socrates was, we are told, forcing his interlocutors to agree that their separate skills as tragedian and comedian respectively ought to be at the resource of one single poet. Just as the lovers in Aristophanes' speech in the same dialogue, each one of these two poets amounts to merely one half of an ideal whole. If we suppose that this famous episode about Socrates' valorization of the ideal tragicomedian is no pure invention on Plato's part but echoes a "true story" once told about Socrates (in which case it would be on a par with some other Socratic motifs in the *Symposium*), we might well speculate that Socrates may have had someone particular in mind who, in his opinion, was more of a poet than either one of his nearly spent drinking partners. After all, it was Euripides who could write powerfully crushing tragedies but also had, more than his great predecessors, the gift of the light touch.[19] Whatever the historical status of the scene, it seems that Euripides is brilliantly inscribed in it, tantalizingly present on account of his very absence.

If these considerations have made a strong case for the *historical reality* of an intellectual affiliation, we may now take the further step and ask whether there is also good evidence allowing us to make equally confident pronouncements about the *character* of this relationship? This question has two parts: first, how did Socrates react to Euripides? And second, how did Euripides react to Socrates? Now, for obvious reasons, we have little hope of making any progress on the former part of the question: the evidence is simply not available. But what about the second part? Looking at Euripides' plays, was he, as Nietzsche thought, a partisan of "aesthetic Socratism"? Can we go so far as to say that Socrates was the only person in the audience whose approval Euripides cared about, as Nietzsche also contended? Did Euripides appropriate Socratic concerns, or did he subtly reject the whole Socratic project?

Euripides' Socrates

In order to explore this sort of question we must examine the evidence we have in the plays of Euripides themselves, carefully avoiding, of course, the untenable hermeneutics of taking any given spoken line for authorial opinion. Two passages in particular have attracted the attention of scholars, especially since they seem to oppose Socratic thinking in fundamental respects and thereby, conveniently, helped to absolve Euripides from Nietzsche's accusations. First, there is the great monologue in the *Medea*, a play performed in 431. Medea agonizes over the decision whether or not to crown the act of her revenge with the murder of Jason's offspring, which are of course also her own children. With great psychological acumen Euripides portrays her internal conflict in which apparently different though not clearly distinct parts of her personality struggle to dominate her decision. One part of her knows perfectly well what would be good for

27

her and her children: escape, rescue, and survival; but another part is bent on triumphant revenge. In the end, she decides to commit infanticide – apparently against her better judgment. The monologue ends with the much-discussed verses 1078–80, which, ever since Bruno Snell (1948), have been taken to contradict the well-known Socratic position that reason harbors the strongest practical impulse.[20]

> And I know well what harm I am about to do;
> But stronger than my deliberations is my *thumos*,
> The cause of greatest harm to mortals.

Since we are not invited to think of Medea as an insane woman, and since the scene is conceived realistically enough, these lines seem to repudiate Socrates' counterintuitive thesis that no one acts against his or her better judgment; just as in the case of Plato much later, apparent akratic behavior is conceptualized by distinguishing competing internal motives that seem to belong to different parts of the soul. Medea is fully aware of the internal conflict of her emotional impulse on the one hand (her anger, *thumos*, and her indignation about Jason's disloyalty) and the counsels of reason on the other, the scruples about carrying out the evil deed (her *bouleumata*). In the end, she acknowledges that her *thumos* wins the upper hand, making her, on the philosophical account, an akratic person, who makes a terrible choice in spite of herself. Socrates, apparently, thought that this was impossible. One summary statement of his position can be found in the *Protagoras*:

> The many think something like this about knowledge (*epistēmē*); it is not powerful, it is no leader or ruler. They do not think of it as something like this. No: often, they think, knowledge is in a human being, but it is not knowledge that rules him, but something else – now anger, now pleasure, now pain, sometimes lust, often fear. They think of knowledge just as though they were thinking of a slave, dragged about by all the other things. Now, do you agree with this view of it, or do you consider that knowledge is something noble and able to govern man, and that whoever learns what is good and what is bad will never be swayed by anything to act otherwise than as knowledge bids, and that intelligence (*phronēsis*) is a sufficient helper for mankind?[21]

The opposition of reason and emotion (with one counseling towards goodness, the other towards evil) is of course much too simple a contrast to capture all the many considerations that flare up in Medea's mind at this point in the drama. There are at least two other considerations, both perfectly rational, that play into her deliberation. One is the consideration of what would be "right" in the larger scheme of divine justice, and here the verdict was, from the beginning of the play, "maximum penalty" for Jason. The other consideration is that her children, innocent but nevertheless implicated in her murder of Jason's new bride and the king, will never escape the Corinthians' vengeance. By killing the children herself, she effectively deprives the Corinthians of a retributive act of revenge on her.[22]

All this follows a perverse kind of logic, the tragic logic of a heroic age, to be sure, but what this logic effectively does is blunt the ostensibly anti-Socratic sting. For even if we suppose that these lines (1078–80), or the whole monologue for that matter, were written with Socrates' denial of *akrasia* in mind (which they might have been), it does not follow, for obvious reasons, that their author intended them to score against

Socrates. First of all, would the tirade of an irate woman "on the edge of a nervous breakdown" be the right medium effectively to reply to a philosophical argument? Would anyone in the audience (besides Socrates?) have understood the lines in this way?[23] And second, is it possible to concede without further argument that the claims of Medea's *thumos* are *entirely* irrational and not represent some kind of ratiocination, precisely those kinds of strangely compelling considerations and motifs that constitute a tragic plot? To be sure, just as almost everyone else in Athens, Euripides too most probably did not share Socrates rationalistic theory of action. What he seems to be taking issue with is not so much the claim that emotion never trumps reason but that reason is always capable of discerning and choosing the good. Is that something Socrates himself would have denied? Hardly, and the most we can say in this case is that Euripides seems to be taking a Socratic idea into account; or he may not be. Even if we assume he does, it remains quite unclear whether his "reaction" is one of approval or rejection. And so, the lines in question may or may not be related to Socrates; in either case they tell us nothing reliable whatsoever about the precise nature of the intellectual relationship between Socrates and Euripides.

The other and perhaps more promising text that is often mustered in this context is the monologue of Phaedra in the *Hippolytus*.[24] Phaedra has just confessed that she is in love with her stepson Hippolytus. The chorus has sung a song of lament, and now Phaedra addresses the members of the women in a monologue in which she also reflects quite generally on the motives of human action, 375–87:

> I have already pondered (*ephrontisa*) on other occasions in the night's long watches how the lives of mortals come to ruin. It seems to me that it is not due to the nature of their mind (*kata gnōmēs phusin*) that they do bad things – many people possess good sense. Rather, one must look at it this way: we know and understand (*epistametha kai gignōskomen*) what is noble, but we fail to carry it out, either because we are lazy, or because we prefer some other pleasure to the good.
>
> In life, there are many pleasures, and a lot of idle talk and idle time – what baneful delight! – as well as *aidōs* (reverence/scandal). This one is double, one is not bad, but the other a household's burden. If their significance were clear, the two would not be spelled in the same way.

Here we have the markers of philosophical "speak": understanding, the good, the mind's nature, the arrival at some conclusion after much thought, and laziness and pleasure as the antagonists to the good life. And here indeed, the position of Socrates (that knowledge is precisely not the kind of thing that will be dragged around by pleasures and other distractions, and that if people act in apparent contradiction to their better judgment, it is their judgment that is confused) – this position is quite explicitly rejected. Phaedra says that the particular nature of one's mind has little or nothing to do with one's actions; even those who know perfectly well what is noble and good fail to carry it out, either because they are lazy, or because they succumb to pleasures, of which, in life, there are many.

Most interpreters think that in this scene Euripides drapes himself in the mantle of the Athenian queen and, from the vantage point of the stage, publicly repudiates a view held by Socrates and his followers, whom we have to imagine sitting in the audience. In many ways, the conclusion seems to be inevitable that indeed the poet speaks in these lines to a specific part of the audience, those "in the know" and in equally general terms – or in "sketchy outline," as Aristophanes would disparagingly call it (*Frogs* 1496f.). Euripides may well be talking to a group of insiders. But is this aside to intellectual friends or foes clearly meant to be critical? All Euripides does is put the moral view of the many into the mouth of a character who belongs to the many – not from a social, but from a philosophical point of view. It is important to note that the monologue has a very specific function in the drama: it constitutes Phaedra as a *character* in *this* play. That is to say, it is part of the characterization of Phaedra that she now no longer simply succumbs to her passion by brazenly proposing to Hippolytus herself (as she did in the first *Hippolytus*); now she merely *ponders* the fact that this is the sort of thing people do: give in to passion against better knowledge. Phaedra is still ensnared in the trap Aphrodite has set for her and Hippolytus; but her reaction to this entrapment is a different one, one that was designed to be more palatable to the Athenian audience than the Phaedra of the first *Hippolytus*. I would be very surprised if the lines 375–87 of our play were one day to be found to have been part of its precursor.

Euripides is undoubtedly staging a scene Socrates would have something to say about. Phaedra's monologue is a provocation. But if it looks critical at first sight, it may in fact not be critical at all; questions of contextualization, dramatization, and characterization readily subvert any straightforward reading. What looks like anti-Socratean stage rhetoric can be destabilized too easily for us to count as reliable evidence for the poet's intellectual commitment. Does this mean that, all things considered, Euripides does, in the end, look more like a poet who, as Nietzsche supposed, squarely belongs to the Socratic circle?

I think not. Even though one could point, in a quite general way, to a number of points of contact and overlap between Euripidean drama and Socratic thinking (the common delight in the competition and confrontation of *logoi*, the provocation of the interlocutor or audience with "unfinished business," and possibly, as I myself have argued, a shared conception of what piety, properly understood, might be[25]) – all the same, these common features do not allow one to endorse Nietzsche's reconstruction of the relationship. For one thing is certain: there are a number of crucial Socratic concerns and ideas that have left no mark in Euripides' *oeuvre*. With Socrates, a new conception of the soul enters the world: the soul is no longer just the principle of life, but the most precious possession we have, the very center of our being, harboring the nature of our personality and the value of our character. The most important thing in the world, for Socrates, is the therapy of the soul; in Euripides, I find no trace of such a view.

Connected with this new conception of the soul is the Socratic view that it is better to suffer an injustice than to commit one. Again, no trace of this in Euripides. Was Euripides, moreover, of the optimistic opinion that a life founded on reason necessarily evolves into a good life? That the gods are good, and that they look upon humanity with benevolence? Socrates was apparently convinced of this, so much so that he was unable and unwilling to construe his conviction and execution as tragic fate. It was not even sad.

Although I cannot prove it, it seems to me that Euripides, just as most of his contemporaries, would have found views such as these rather baffling. Let us cast another glance at *Medea*. The heroine has been deeply offended in her role as wife and mother.

However, instead of preferring to suffer harm rather than to inflict harm, she takes the just punishment of Jason into her own hands, acting as if she were an agent of Zeus and the other Olympians who witnessed Jason's oath and betrayal. What she does is terrifying; what drives her is some deeply felt desire for revenge and retribution, a desire that surpasses the natural bond of a mother to her children. Like Heracles' thirteenth labor, the killing of her children is extreme, but it is not an act of madness. Rather, it is an act that is part and parcel of the inventory of the world we live in. What kind of world would it be in which the likes of Jason got away with perjury and betrayal, unpunished because "reason" prevented the victims of their crimes to follow the impulse of their feeling of outrage, and prevented them from exacting brutal punishment? Indeed, this would be a Socratic world, and Euripides seems to reject it vehemently. Or rather, he seems to state, plainly and simply, that *this* world is just not like *that*, neither now nor in mythic times; it would be a mistake to invest the world with optimistic clarity and goodness, for it is ambivalent, harsh, implacable, and above all tragic.

No doubt one could object that this is only a partial construal of Euripidean dramatic impressions, based on a reading of the *Medea*. Although one might perhaps be able (so the objection continues) to corroborate the tragic impression by referring to further plays such as the *Hecuba*, *Heracles*, or *Bacchae*, other plays are available to counterbalance this view. There are, after all, Euripidean plays that draw a more optimistic, perhaps even Socratic picture of human existence. Take for example the *Helen*, arguably Euripides' most philosophical play. Here the poet stages the opposition between appearance and reality and openly grapples with the question of right vs. might. Theoclymenus, the ruler of the Egyptian land where the real Helen found refuge during the Trojan War, wants to marry the beautiful Greek woman. The young ruler's father Proteus, at whose grave the action takes place, once promised the gods to keep Helen safe until the return of her legitimate husband. But now Proteus is dead, and with him, in some sense, the promise. The new ruler gives strict orders to inform him should Menelaus arrive, so that he may capture and kill him. When Menelaus does arrive *incognito*, only Theoclymenus' sister Theonoe, a virtually omniscient *femme sage* once called Eidō,[26] is aware of it (apart from Helen of course), and she soon faces the quandary whether to stand up for the just cause (that Helen and Menelaus be reunited according to Proteus' promise), or to look out for her own safety, to obey her brother, and to betray the couple.

Like Socrates, Theonoe is a figure of great moral awareness; like Socrates, she displays an impressive amount of autonomy, founded on superior moral and nonmoral knowledge; as in the case of Socrates, this sets her on a course of conflict with the interests of political power. Her moral position is, in the end, clear enough, but like Socrates she offers only passive resistance to injustice.[27] Striking similarities; but is Theonoe a Socratic figure? Emphatically not. All things considered, she is more of a Pythia, an oracular or priestly figure, the living extension of Proteus and her grandfather Nereus. She is mindful of her enormous power and open to supplication, but she does nothing to raise the level of moral awareness in her interlocutors; in the end, it is not she who reveals to her brother the error of his ways, but the *dei ex machina* Castor and Pollux. If a drama like the *Helen* cannot be harnessed to the yoke that supposedly ties Euripides firmly to Socrates, none can.

31

A Paradox and its Solution

Let us summarize the result of the discussion so far. A survey of the available evidence, even if it is taken *cum grano salis*, unequivocally suggests that Socrates and Euripides were well acquainted with one another, and acquainted to such a degree that their affiliation and apparent intellectual affinity became part of the humorous inventory of old comedy. Comedians repeatedly, and without much variation, poked fun at Euripides, charging him with idle Socratic chatter. There is little but nevertheless suggestive evidence in the Socratic literature of the fourth century that fits into this general picture, and later periods abound with anecdotes about Socrates' reactions to Euripidean plays and lines.

In a more specific way, scholars have pointed to passages in Euripides' plays that clearly resonate with Socratic concerns, though it remains fundamentally unclear if the poet wanted to provoke, endorse, or oppose the philosopher. Within the larger scheme of things one can point to certain common features such as the conception of piety mentioned above (understood as service to the gods, although Euripides seems less optimistic about the gods' benevolence), but other, central Socratic themes are absent from the Euripidean *corpus*. If one is honest, one has to admit that there is no hard evidence of a "significant influence" of one intellectual on the other, an influence that we could speak of, document, and describe on the basis of our literary evidence.

We are thus confronted with a paradox. The poet and the philosopher knew each other well, shared decades of their productive lives in the same city; but they did not, as far as we know and contrary to Nietzsche's allegations, influence one another in any clearly discernible way. This suggests that we know too little about the intellectual world Socrates and Euripides inhabited, and that we would be able to see the differences and convergences more clearly and distinctly if we were better informed. That may undoubtedly be the case, yet it seems to me that even on the basis of what little evidence we do have we are in a position to resolve the paradox and reveal it as a merely apparent one. More than that, one could even contend that the apparent paradox is itself an echo and a reflection of an actual state of affairs. For it seems that the apparently incongruent picture painted here stands to reason.

It stands to reason because it fits well to another apparent paradox, the fundamentally different and incompatible portrayal of Socrates in Plato and Xenophon. Already in the eighteenth century, Johann Gottfried von Herder wondered why it was that the figure of Socrates appears to us so differently in the two main sources that we have of his life and thought.[28] This has become a familiar crux, and it would be a mistake to downplay the differences or to attempt to harmonize the two accounts. Louis-André Dorion has recently given us an astonishing overview of the quantity and magnitude of the incompatibilities between the Platonic and the Xenophontic Socrates.[29] One vaguely attractive way to explain the discrepancy would be to point to the contingent historical fact that Xenophon, unlike Plato, was not part of the inner circle of Socratics. Herder, I think, had a better intuition, for he invokes the very nature of Socratic philosophizing itself as an explanation. Socrates was a much too dialectical and aporetic thinker to have indoctrinated the circle of his interlocutors with his own ideas and theories, if he had any. The fascinating dimension of Socratic philosophy is precisely this, that he understood himself as facilitator and trainer of his interlocutors' own minds; he was, in Herder's words, "only the midwife of their own intellectual Gestalt" ("nur die Hebamme ihrer eigenen Geistesgestalt"). Most probably, Socrates had indeed arrived at a number of moral truths, but the salient character of his philosophy was precisely not to propagate them, but to engage his interlocutors and to goad them on to search for respectable answers in the depths of their own souls, answers which they could refine and successfully defend in the back-and-forth of dialectical conversation.[30]

According to Herder, what Socrates did in the case of Xenophon and Plato was to bring out the character and convictions of their own minds, nothing more, nothing less; their testimonies of Socrates consequently tell us as much, and perhaps even more, about the respective authors than about Socrates. Returning to the question that concerns us here, it seems to me that the same could be said *mutatis mutandis* about Euripides, i.e. that the intellectual relationship between him and Socrates followed, and, if Herder is right, indeed *must* have followed a similar pattern. Of course Socrates helped Euripides write his tragedies, but not in the crude way imagined by old comedy. And of course, much like any other person who came into contact with him, Euripides recognized in Socrates his harshest critic; Euripides cared about Socrates' views, but not in the crude way imagined by Nietzsche. Euripides was much too independent an artist to simply allow his stage characters to affirm or deny Socratic, or anybody else's, theories and opinions. Rather, the Socratic influence on Euripides lies in the fact that Socrates, if he indeed interacted with Euripides to the level suggested by our sources, must have been to some extent the midwife of Euripides' own intellectual and artistic "Gestalt." There is, all things considered, no reason to agree with Nietzsche's wholesale condemnation of Euripides as a Socratic poet; and yet, it seems to be true to say that without Socrates we would not have Euripides – or at least not the one we do have.[31]

Notes

1. Sansone (1996) gives an excellent overview of the literary use of Euripides.
2. For a more detailed account of the figure of Socrates in Nietzsche, see James Porter's chapter 25 in the present volume.
3. Clement of Alexandria, *Miscellanies* 5.70.1, p.373 St. (= Nr 22 in Kovacs 1994).
4. *Crito* 53–54b.
5. Aelian, *Various History* 2.13 (= Nr. 18 in Kovacs 1994).
6. Cicero, *Tusculan Disputations* 4.63 (= Nr. 19 in Kovacs 1994).
7. See Diogenes Laertius, *Lives of Eminent Philosophers* 2.33. The line in question is found in the *Electra*, 379: "The best thing seems to be to let these things (i.e. false criteria of goodness such as upbringing, wealth, armament) alone." Either Diogenes erred in attributing the line to the *Auge*, or Euripides used the same line in different plays. In any case, in the context of the *Electra*, it is hard to see why Socrates should have taken issue with this verse.
8. Nr. 21 in Kovacs (1994). Diogenes Laertius was so fond of this anecdote that he relates it twice, in 2.22 (*Socrates*) and 9.12 (*Heraclitus*). According to Diogenes, the story was related by the Peripatetic Ariston of Ceos (third century BCE), and much later and differently by Seleucus Homericus, a grammarian of the early first century CE; the *bon-mot* that one would have to be a Delian diver to understand Heraclitus is variously attributed to Socrates and "one Crates."

9 Diogenes even thinks he knows the reason why Euripides and Socrates were so close: they both were pupils of Anaxagoras (Diogenes Laertius, *Lives of Eminent Philosophers* 2.19; 45).

10 Diogenes seems to be confusing Mnesimachus with Telecides; on the problem, see Patzer (1994) *ad loc.*

11 The two words *Euripidas sōkratogomphous* have been torn out of their syntax. A *gomphos* is a "nail" or "peg."

12 Performed in 429/8, around the time of the *Hippolytus.*

13 The addressed person is a woman as the adjective "proud" is feminine (*semnē*). Patzer (1994: 56) and Egli (2003) suggest that the addressee is either a personified Euripidean tragedy or Euripides himself in women's clothes.

14 The son of Lysimachus; cf. Egli (2003: 158).

15 Egli (2003: 162) arrives at the same conclusion when she suggests that the historical Socrates and Euripides most likely knew each other and in fact spoke with each other, presumably also about interesting philosophical doctrines and their consequences for an understanding of the divine.

16 See Patzer (1974).

17 Diogenes Laertius, *Lives of Eminent Philosophers* 2.124.

18 Xenophon hardly ever mentions Sophocles (twice: *Hellenica* 2.3.2; *Memorabilia* 1.4.3) and Aeschylus (once: *Symposium* 4.63) either.

19 On comic elements in tragedy, see B. Seidensticker (1982), *Palintonos Harmonia. Studien zu komischen Elementen in der griechischen Tragödie.* Göttingen: Vandenhoeck & Ruprecht, esp. ch. 5. In terms of wit and humor, Euripides' *Cyclops* (unfortunately the only extant satyr play we possess) compares well to any Aristophanic comedy.

20 Most recently by Egli (2003: 164–6).

21 *Protagoras* 352b–c. Other relevant passages are *Apology* 25d ff.; *Protagoras* 345e; *Gorgias* 488a; 509e. Cf. also Aristotle's discussion of Socrates' position on *akrasia* in *Nicomachean Ethics* 7.1–3.

22 Cf. *Medea* 790–7; 1060f.; 1234–9; 1301–5. The literature on how to interpret the *Medea* is vast and well beyond the scope of this chapter. For further discussion of the problem of Medea's motives, see e.g. Wildberg (2002: 37–61) with further references.

23 See Moline (1975), who makes the important point that anyone who credits Euripides with criticizing Socrates would have to show at the same time that some such criticism could have been grasped by the audience.

24 The play was performed in 428, just a few years after the *Medea.*

25 The basic idea is that piety must not exhaust itself in reverence, prayer, and sacrifice, but has to have an element of service rendered to the gods (*hypēresia*) at its center; see Wildberg (2002: esp. 102–9; 2003).

26 *Helen* 11; the name derives from the verb *eidenai*, to "know."

27 Theonoe refuses to help Menelaus and Helen, but she does not betray them either (1017–23). Compare Socrates' reaction when he was ordered by the Thirty to arrest and execute Leon of Salamis, 32c–d: although the order was unjust, Socrates refuses to arrest Leon, but he does nothing to help him. Another, albeit very tenuous parallel obtains between Socrates' worship of clouds in Aristophanes' play and Theonoe's ritual of purifying the ether (865–7). For an interpretation of that scene, cf. Wildberg (2002: 78; 87ff.)

28 See Herder's sketch in his "Outlines of a philosophy of the history of man" [Ideen zur Philosophie der Geschichte der Menschheit], published more than 200 years ago between 1784 and 1791, esp. III 13, 5.

29 See Dorion (2004: 95–113). After listing no less than 17 or 18 fundamental differences, Dorion concludes that the Xenophontic Socrates is without any doubt irreducible to the Platonic Socrates, and that their respective doctrines are irreconcilable.

30   This general assessment stands despite the fact that the specific notion of philosophic "midwifery" is probably not Socratic; see Burnyeat (1977).

31   It is my pleasure to thank Rachana Kamtekar, Sara Rappe, Louis-André Dorion, Lowell Edmunds, and Alexander Nehamas for comments on earlier drafts of this chapter. I also wish to thank Princeton's Institute for Advanced Study for a pleasurable and profitable sabbatical semester during which initial ideas on this topic indeed "advanced."

References

Alesse, F. (2004). Euripides and the Socratics. In V. Karasmanis (ed.), *Socrates 2400 Years Since His Death (399 B.C.–2001 A.D.)*. Delphi: European Cultural Centre of Delphi, 371–81.

Burnyeat, M. F. (1977). Socratic midwifery, Platonic inspiration. *Bulletin of the Institute for Classcial Studies*, 24, 7–16.

Dorion, L.-A. (2004). *Socrate*. Paris: Presses Universitaires de France.

Egli, F. (2003). *Euripides im Kontext zeitgenössischer intellektueller Strömungen. Analyse der Funktion philosophischer Themen in den Tragödien und Fragmenten*. Beiträge zur Altertumskunde vol. 189. Munich and Leipzig: K. G. Saur.

Irwin, T. H. (1983). Euripides and Socrates. *Classical Philology*, 78, 183–97.

Kannicht, R. (1969). *Euripides. Helena, herausgegeben und erklärt*. 2 vols. Heidelberg: C. Winter.

Kovacs, D. (1986). On Medea's great monologue (E. Med. 1021–80). *Classical Quarterly*, 36, 343–52.

—— (1994). *Euripidea*. Leiden, New York, Cologne: E. J. Brill.

Kullmann, W. (1986). Euripides' Verhältnis zur Philosophie. *Annales Universitatis Turkuensis*, B 174, 35–49.

Moline, J. (1975). Euripides, Socrates and virtue. *Hermes*, 103, 45–67.

Patzer, A. (1974). AISXINOU MILTIADHS. *Zeitschrift für Papyrologie und Epigraphik*, 14, 271–87.

—— (1994). Sokrates in den Fragmenten der attischen Komödie. In A. Bierl and P. v. Möllendorff (eds.), *Orchestra. Drama, Mythos, Bühne* (pp. 50–81). Stuttgart and Leipzig: Teubner.

—— (1998). Sokrates in der Tragödie. *Würzburger Jahrbücher für die Altertumswissenschaft, Neue Folge*, 22, 33–45.

Rosetti, L. (1992). Euripide e Socrate. In M. Montuori (ed.), *The Socratic Problem. The History, the Solutions* (pp. 379–83). Amsterdam.

Sansone, D. (1996). Plato and Euripides. *Illinois Classical Studies*, 21, 35–67.

Seidensticker, B. (1990). Euripides' *Medea* 1056–80, an interpolation? In M. Griffith & D. J. Mastronarde (eds.), *Cabinet of the Muses: Essays on Classical and Comparative Literature in Honor of Thomas G. Rosenmeyer* (pp. 89–102). Atlanta, GA: Scholars Press.

Snell, B. (1948). Das früheste Zeugnis über Sokrates. *Philologus*, 97, 125–34.

Wildberg, C. (2002). *Hyperesie und Epiphanie. Ein Versuch über die Bedeutung der Götter in den Dramen des Euripides*. Zetemata 109. Munich: C. H. Beck.

Wildberg, C. (2003). The rise and fall of the Socratic notion of piety. *Proceedings of the Boston Area Colloquium in Ancient Philosophy*, 18, 1–28.

3

Socrates Among the Sophists

PAUL WOODRUFF

Socrates died because a large panel of judges found against him by a small majority. Apparently, some of those judges were influenced by evidence that Socrates was a kind of sophist. They were not entirely wrong. Socrates was, in a way, a sophist, although not the kind that his worst critics made him out to be. But Socrates' defenders were not entirely right either.

Aristophanes' *Clouds* and works by Plato and Xenophon represent two sides in a debate, greatly extended in time, as to whether Socrates was a sophist. Aristophanes uses Socrates' name for the leader of his imaginary school of sophistic rhetoric and antireligious scientific inquiry, while Plato and Xenophon, probably starting after Socrates' death (over 20 years after Aristophanes' play was produced), guarded Socrates' memory on this score by showing him disputing with sophists in ways that underscore his differences from them.

This debate cannot produce a clear a winner, however, in its own terms. Neither side accurately depicts the historical Socrates with sufficient credibility for us to reach a verdict about the man who was condemned to drink hemlock in 399 BCE. All three authors wrote fiction. Aristophanes lets Socrates stand for teachers of much of the new learning, especially forensic rhetoric and natural science. Plato, by contrast, makes Socrates the extreme philosopher, aloof from science, rhetoric, literature, practical politics, and even from reciprocal friendships. His philosophical concerns range from ethics to epistemology and metaphysics, and some of the theories he expounds cannot have been taught by the historical Socrates, but must have been due to Plato. Xenophon's portrait of Socrates seems partially indebted to Plato's and, like Plato's, seems often to speak for interests and theories of the author. Lacking more authoritative sources, however, we will need to make the best use of these that we have. What Plato says about Socrates and the sophists is one thing; what he shows Socrates doing is another, and this will merit our attention in what follows.

Although the fiction of Plato and Xenophon is historical in a sense in which Aristophanes' is not, they are no more accurate than Aristophanes in their representation of the sophists or their teachings. What Aristophanes lampoons is some distance from what any sophist actually taught, while the boundaries Plato gives for the territory of sophists are artificial. Plato succeeded in defining the sophists as part of his project to show that Socrates was not one of them. We need to go behind these sources on both sides for a better understanding of the sophists if we are to judge the question whether Socrates could reasonably be classed with the sophists. I begin with the sophists, and will turn afterward to Socrates.

The Sophists[1]

Most of what students have been taught about the sophists is wrong, owing to Plato's one-sided representation of them, and the attractiveness, then and now, of identifying intellectual villains to provide contrast for the philosophers we admire. Accordingly, this section is a plea to look at the evidence more closely, at what Plato says, at the surviving texts, and at the considerable influence of sophists on writers such as Thucydides, Sophocles, and Euripides.

The teachers now known as sophists did not constitute a well-defined group at the time of Socrates. The earliest surviving use of the word *sophistes* is found in an ode of Pindar (*Isthmian* 5.28, 478 BCE), where it means "poet," and the remarks Plato provides Protagoras at *Protagoras* 316d ff., confirm that early poets could be considered sophists, although they did not use this word for themselves. In the context, Protagoras implies that Homer and Hesiod and Simonides acted as sophists in their role as educators, and indeed their poetry belongs to what we could aptly call the wisdom literature of ancient Greece.

The word *sophistes* is simply a masculine-ending noun formed from the adjective *sophos*, wise or clever. The adjective carries a double valence, as it sometimes suggests an admirable wisdom, and sometimes the sort of cleverness that can be devious and frightening. Such a double valence reflects the response of the Greeks to their own intellectual achievements, as we read in Sophocles' famous choral ode (exploiting the double valence of the word *deinos*): "Many wonders, many terrors, but none more wonderful or more terrible than a human being"; as the chorus goes on to show by examples, what is wonderful and terrible about human beings is the power they have through the inventiveness of the human mind (*Antigone* 332–75).

In the same way, the word *sophistes* must have had a double valence. Protagoras, in the passage cited above, says that he is the first to claim this title openly and with pride, suggesting both that he thinks a sophist is a good thing to be, and that there are those who would disagree. But this text already dates from well into the fourth century. In fifth-century usage, we find no breath of scandal attaching to the name until Aristophanes' *Clouds* (420 BCE). What this play satirizes is not an organized movement, but the confluence of a number of new streams of thinking that mark the fifth century as a period of extraordinary intellectual confidence and innovation. Taken together, these streams constitute what I will call *the new learning*. The major tributaries of the new learning are natural science (especially the secular approach to medicine), mathematics, social science (most notably theories about the origins of culture), ethics, political theory, and the art of words (which came to be known as rhetoric, but had a broader scope in this period).

Different thinkers of the period occupied themselves in different combinations of these. Gorgias, for example, probably devoted himself mainly to the art of words. Protagoras combined interests in the origins of culture with the art of words, and he may also have been a defender of democratic ideas. Antiphon did advanced work in mathematics, anticipating the calculus with his solution to the problem of squaring the circle; he also probably taught the art of words, argued that humans have a common nature, and actively agitated for the creation of a new oligarchy in Athens.[2] Hippias taught or claimed expertise in virtually every subject known at the time (*Lesser Hippias* 363d, 368b–e). All of these are now commonly called sophists.

The teachers now known as sophists do not have a great deal in common, but certain features are found in most of them:

1.1. Teaching for pay. Most sophists taught, at what we would call the level of higher education, for substantial fees, but Antiphon apparently made his money by writing speeches for others to deliver (*logography*), a new profession at the time. We are told that Protagoras amassed a considerable fortune by teaching, and Hippias (as shown in Plato) brags that he has done the same (*Greater Hippias* 282de).

1.2. Traveling. Most sophists traveled widely. They did so on business, to earn lecturing fees from around the Greek world, and probably also because many of them were interested in the variety to be found in different cultures. Antiphon again is an exception; he was an Athenian and seems to have worked at home. Protagoras and Hippias, by contrast, seem to have been in constant motion in the service of their lucrative business (*Greater Hippias* 282de).

1.3. Employing the art of words. Their one common attribute appears to have been their use of the art of words, but, since oral performance was the only way for them to teach, this is neither surprising nor, in itself, very interesting.

Sophists taught the art of balanced debate, with equally timed speeches on each side of a contentious issue, and this art is frequently displayed in tragic plays of the period, as in the balanced speeches offered each other by Creon and his son Haemon in Sophocles' *Antigone*. Thucydides employs the same art in his history, on several occasions. Now, if you know how to speak on either side of an issue equally persuasively, then (assuming that both sides cannot be right) you know how to give persuasive arguments on behalf of at least one position that is wrong. So the art of opposed speeches (*antikeimenoi logoi*) would seem to entail the art of winning an audience over to a false position. We shall see, however, that two speeches may collide over what is merely reasonable (*eikos* – see section 1.4 below), and that such cases are usually the subjects for the opposed speaking taught by sophists. In such a case, both sides may have equally reasonable cases to make, and the art involved in presenting both is innocent on the charge of telling plausible lies.

Aristotle says that Protagoras taught students how to make the weaker argument win in a debate (as Socrates is shown doing in the *Clouds*), and we are told by several sources that Protagoras taught people how to argue on both sides of any issue.[3] This is summed up in the oft-repeated claim that the sophists taught principally rhetoric, by which is usually meant the art of persuasive speech taken in isolation from the truth or content of speech. Recent scholars have argued, however, that this concept of rhetoric is due not to the sophists but to Plato, and although the matter remains under dispute, we must at least conclude that it is not clear that any sophist really had the concept of rhetoric that they are supposed to have taught.[4] Moreover, the Greek interest in public speaking in this period was not limited to persuasive speech in assemblies or law courts; Greek audiences were delighted by displays of speaking and debate, and these appear to have been a form of public entertainment.[5] Gorgias wrote famously in his *Encomium to Helen* that speech can have the power of a drug,[6] but playwrights and historians of the period, from Homer to Thucydides, almost always show artful speeches failing to persuade, owing to the popular suspicion of such clever displays.[7] Gorgias was widely admired for his fine style, and much imitated, but we have no reason to think his teaching affected the conduct of politics in Athens. Protagoras' interest in the art of words went beyond instruction in public speaking; he was interested in distinguishing kinds of speech acts and taught something under the title "the correctness of words" (apparently consistency and appropriate diction).[8]

1.4. Speaking without knowledge. Public speakers must often give speeches on subjects that are not known either to them or to anyone else. Policy issues, such as are debated in the Assembly, often hinge in what it is reasonable to expect (*eikos*). The outcome of a war, for example, cannot be known in advance, so that a decision on whether to go to war must rest on what is *eikos*. The same goes for some forensic issues; in the absence of an eye-witness, who would satisfy the conditions for having knowledge, a case at law would have to be decided on the basis of what is most reasonable.

Plato and Aristotle both make the complaint that sophists, especially Protagoras, prefer *eikos* to truth. *Eikos* is traditionally translated as "probability"; this translation dates to a time when the Latin-based word meant "believability," and is supported by the close affinity in ancient Greek usage between *eikos* and *pithanon*. Plato, however, understood *eikos* to mean a misleading facsimile of the truth – something that, although not true, could be mistaken for the truth. But studies of actual usage from the period show that *eikos* means what it is reasonable to believe in circumstances when the facts are not clearly known. In such cases, speeches on either side can be equally reasonable. Such, for example, are the speeches Thucydides reports to have been given by the two generals before the naval battle in the harbor at Syracuse (7.61–4, 66–8); the two forces were equal, and the two outcomes were equally probable. Indeed, the battle hung in the balance for an extraordinarily long time before a small, unexpected event started a cascade of troubles for the Athenians.

Prehistory, for example, must be a matter of *eikos*, as must the facts in a case without witnesses, or the future effects of policies under debate. The art of arguing on either side of an issue, with reference to *eikos*, was necessary to the procedure of adversary debate by which decisions were made in ancient Greece, even before democracy. I shall turn below to the likely connection between this sort of teaching and the good judgment that Protagoras offered to teach.

1.5. Promoting relativism. Sophists are often said to be relativists, but this general claim is not supported by the evidence. Relativism, simply defined, is the claim that the same sentence can be both true and false, in being true for one person and false for another. This is usually understood to be the claim that what I believe is true for me, while what you believe is true for you. The claim allows that contrary beliefs are in some sense true for different people.[9] Gorgias is probably not a relativist, because he seems to assert that no beliefs at all are true. Antiphon, who appeals to nature as a standard for criticizing law, cannot be a relativist, and the same would go for Callicles, who appeals to a natural standard of justice.

Protagoras, however, is a relativist according to the evidence of Plato's *Theaetetus* (which influenced later sources), but other evidence, even in Plato, tells a different story. Plato shows Protagoras in the *Protagoras* arguing in effect for a natural basis of the virtues of justice and reverence, on the grounds that they are necessary to human survival; groups of people without such virtues would have scattered and not been able to defend themselves, and the human race would have died out. Protagoras' implicit assumption is that if justice and reverence are present in a community, they will suffice to prevent the sort of divisiveness that tears a community apart. It would be preposterous to suppose that justice is whatever anyone thinks it is, and, at the same time, that justice is necessary to fend civil war away from any given community. Suppose, for example, that Thrasymachus gets to decide what justice is, so that justice is nothing but whatever benefits the ruler; then mechanisms for justice will not make society more stable, but more liable to division and even civil war. There must, on Protagoras' theory, at least be a pragmatic test for what counts as justice. Protagoras also had teachings about the correctness of words that are not compatible with relativism as defined above; he was prepared to criticize currently acceptable usage, but he would have no basis for this if he were a relativist regarding truth.

The good is another matter. Many sophists, however, seem to have made both the good and the beneficial relative to the beneficiary, as we saw above. Protagoras, for example, points out that olive oil is harmful to plants and the hair on most animals, but beneficial when applied to human hair and skin (*Protagoras* 334a–c). And Thrasymachus held that the justice that is beneficial to rulers is harmful to those over whom they rule (*Republic* 1.338c ff.); that is why he insists that Socrates say precisely what justice is, and not declare simply that justice is the beneficial (336d). By this he probably means that Socrates should specify, as Thrasymachus is about to do, who it is that benefits from justice if justice is beneficial.

1.6. Appealing to nature vs. convention. Some sophists drew a sharp dichotomy between convention (*nomos*) and nature (*phusis*). Earlier poetry and philosophy associated *phusis* with unchanging truth, and *nomos* with appearance or with the fluctuations of opinion. On the whole, when sophists make this distinction, they treat *nomos* with disdain and appeal to nature as a standard. Had they taken convention to be the standard, they would have been relativists, but they do not seem to have done so. No sophist, so far as we know, appeals to *nomos* to set aside a purported principle of nature, and a number of them go the other way.

Callicles (who may be Plato's invention) appeals to a law of nature as well as to natural justice in his argument against Socratic ethics (*Gorgias* 483a–484c). Hippias (again as represented in Plato) appeals to nature over *nomos* in his case for the kinship of educated people (*Protagoras* 337d–38b). Antiphon, in his *Truth*, argues for a common human nature, and may also be using nature as a standard by which to condemn human justice.[10] Protagoras evidently rejected conventional standards of linguistic usage; as an explicit prescriptivist he seems to have tried to follow a natural standard for the use of words (e.g., by insisting that "wrath" – a feminine word in Greek – should be masculine).[11]

1.7. Supporting democracy. Many of the teachers now known as sophists came from democratic cities, but not all, and not all were in favor of democracy. This is odd, because the public speaking (which many sophists taught) is especially valuable in democracies. Antiphon (probably the same man as the sophist) was executed for attempting to overthrow democracy in Athens, in spite of his plea that a seller of prepared speeches is an unlikely opponent of democracy.[12] Protagoras speaks in favor of democracy in Plato's dialogue of that name, but some scholars have doubted his sincerity, and others such as Thrasymachus and Callicles raise serious objections to the rule of law, widely recognized as an essential feature of democracy at the time.

1.8. Teaching virtue. The word "virtue," like "wisdom," has a range of uses. Normally, it can be used for any quality that one needs in order to be successful in some line of endeavor; accordingly, although it often has a clearly ethical meaning, it does not always do so. For Socrates, virtue is to the soul as health is to the body. That is what Socrates does not believe can be taught; not surprisingly, the qualities sophists claim to teach are rather different.

Gorgias evidently said that he never proposed to teach virtue, but a number of other sophists seem to have made just such a promise. Of these, Protagoras is preeminent; he announced that his main teaching concerned *euboulia*, good judgment (Plato's *Protagoras* 318d–319a), which Socrates understands to be expert knowledge (*technē*) of politics (319a). Protagoras accepts this understanding, and also follows Socrates when, without fanfare, he takes the *technē* of politics to be the same as virtue (*aretē*). This occurs during Socrates' argument that what Protagoras claims to teach cannot be taught (319a–320b). In a later, but related, context, Socrates implies that a sophist just is someone who proclaims himself a teacher of virtue (*Protagoras* 349a).

This is a more ambitious goal, however, than the one Protagoras advertised. His precise claim, as plausibly reported by Plato early in the dialogue, is to make each student better each day, by teaching him "good judgment [*euboulia*] about domestic matters, so that he may best manage his own household, and about political affairs, so that in the affairs of the city-state he may be most able (or perhaps most powerful) in action and in speech" (318a–319a). Good judgment is the ability to reason well without knowledge, and Protagoras probably thought he instilled this ability by teaching the art of words, insofar as this involved the judicious use of *eikos* (reasonable expectation).[13] Now no ability of this kind could be on Socrates' list of virtues, for the excellent reason that Socratic virtues are supposed to depend on knowledge, and good judgment is a desirable quality only when knowledge is absent (a point well made in the pseudo-Platonic dialogue *Sisyphus*).

1.9. Seeking natural explanations. Some sophists had some interests in natural science, but most of them concerned themselves more with social science, especially with theories of the origins of culture, and in this area they displaced the gods from their traditional role as source of the arts practiced by human beings.[14] But science of any kind had little appeal for most of the sophists.

As Aristophanes represents intellectuals in the *Clouds*, the same teachers promote both persuasive speaking and natural science, and the natural science they teach displaces the gods from their traditional roles in the explanation of natural phenomena. This is plainly presented as a threat to traditional religion.[15]

Some sophists worked in mathematics, and some may have dabbled in medicine.[16] Gorgias had an explanation for the kindling of fire by a prism (Diels and Kranz 5), as well as a physical account of color (4). But sophists were interested mainly in human matters; most attacks on traditional beliefs came from a different group of intellectuals. Protagoras declined to take a position on the gods (Diels and Kranz B.4), and none of the sophists can be identified with certainty as an atheist.[17]

41

Socrates

Socrates' defenders took pains to clear their hero on both of Aristophanes' charges, but, at the same time, they revealed a number of features that Socrates shares with sophists. Although Socrates is in a class by himself, he is more like a sophist such as Protagoras than he is like any other kind of intellectual figure of the period. Readers of this volume should be well prepared to support their own verdicts on the similarity of Socrates' positions to those of sophists. I will state my verdicts firmly, but I must admit at the start that most of them are controversial.

2.1. Teaching for fees. Socrates did not teach for fees. He denied doing so in his defense speech, and his enemies evidently did not contest the denial. Socrates was content to be poor; his threadbare style of living has been a kind of model for intellectuals ever since, from his immediate followers through Chaucer's Clerk of Oxenford to today's dressed-down professors.

2.2. Traveling. Socrates stayed at home, rarely venturing even beyond the city walls, except when he was on military service (*Phaedrus* 230d). Unlike some sophists, he had no interest in the variety of cultures, and, because he did not teach for fees, he had no need to travel. Moreover, the mission he took himself to have been given by the gods kept him in Athens (*Apology* 23b, 29d).

2.3. Employing the art of words. Socrates declines to take part in several aspects of public speaking as taught by sophists, but he engages actively in others.

Socrates will not accept long speeches from his partners in discussion (*Protagoras* 334cd, *Gorgias* 449b, 461e–462a). It follows that he will not take part in the balanced opposition of speeches taught by many sophists, and illustrated by poets and historians of the period (see 1.3 above). A playwright of the period who took on the subject of the *Crito* would have written it through a series of paired speeches, balanced as to length and strength of argument. Plato never writes such a scene. Crito is not capable of a full-dress argument, and Socrates does not need to give one in his own person; instead, he draws on a powerful tirade from the laws, which, he says with some irony, leaves him dumbstruck.

Even the *Symposium*, which opposes Socrates' speech to Agathon's, does not wear at that point the colors of adversary debate. Socrates first questions Agathon, leading him toward a change of position, and then delivers his speech, which is of a wholly different sort from Agathon's. And although the two speeches are opposed on the main points, the two speakers are not. Socrates speaks only, he says, for Diotima, whose teaching he remembers. This device shifts the authority of the speech away from Socrates and indeed outside of the debate altogether. The audience is not directed to hear both sides and decide for itself, as in a democratic debate, but to listen to an authority who is beyond the reach of debate.

Even in the short question-and-answer format that he prefers, Socrates does not look for the approval of an audience. Sometimes, as in the *Euthyphro*, he is alone with his partner; at other times, such as in the *Gorgias* and *Protagoras*, he has a substantial educated audience. But in no case does he look for agreement from anyone other than the partner he is questioning. He prefers an audience of one, and here too he differs from the sophists, who typically address large groups and teach their students to do the same.

Socrates' style of question and answer, however, does employ an art of words. His refutations are far too consistent to be the result of luck; Socrates knows how to take on any partner in debate and bring him down to defeat. Success in a wide range of cases is a sign of expert knowledge (*techne*) at work, and so many readers (like many of his partners) have believed that Socrates had an expert grasp of this use of words. He denies that he does so in a spirit of competition, however, and in this he differs from some sophists as Plato represents them (*Gorgias* 457c–58a).

We must not allow Socrates' criticism of public speaking to blind us to the evidence that he was himself an accomplished public speaker, at least as Plato represents him. Plato's *Apology* could be used to illustrate many of the oratorical devices taught in the period, starting from its elegant disclaimer of the art of speaking. In fact, this speech is more refined than any sophistic defense speech that has come down to us, although its rhetorical purpose is somewhat blurred by a tendency to insult its audience.

In other dialogues, too, we see Socrates employing the art of long speeches skillfully, although not in his own persona. The speech he imagines coming from the Laws in the *Crito* is very effective. So are the speech he attributes to Diotima in the *Symposium* and the speech he attributes to the cicadas in the *Phaedrus*. We should keep in mind that sophists often wrote speeches that they imagined to have been spoken by characters from myth or literature. Such are Gorgias' *Palamedes* and Hippias' speech of Nestor to Neoptolemus (*Greater Hippias* 286b). And most scholars now agree that the speeches in Thucydides are largely fictional, and that their brilliance owes something to the influence of the sophists. In short, Socrates' habit of fictionally attributing his speeches to others is nothing new; it places him squarely in the sophistic tradition. In this tradition, both Socrates and the sophists evade responsibility for what they say by these means.

2.4. Speaking without knowledge. Some sophists, eschewing appeals to expert knowledge, cultivate the art of speaking without knowledge (above, 1.4). Socrates disclaims expert knowledge (*Apology* 23b), and so, if he is to speak at all, he too must find a way to do so without expert knowledge. Socrates does speak without expert knowledge, and he appears to have developed a method for doing so without being mistaken too easily for an expert. So he is like the sophists in what he does (speaking without knowledge) but unlike them in trying to avoid the false appearance of authority.

Part of Socrates' criticism of the art of words, as taught by Gorgias, is that the art of words does not depend on knowing the truth about its subject matter (*Gorgias* 456b, 459b–e, 464b–65d). We have seen that some sophists taught the skillful use of arguments based on what is reasonable (*eikos*) when knowledge is not available. Now, Socrates understands *eikos* to mean what is plausible to a crowd (*Phaedrus* 273b), so that he likens the use of *eikos* to a system for pleasing a human audience (274a). In fact, the word refers to what is reasonable, and that is not always the same as what pleases a given audience. And although public speakers of the period do believe that adversary debate helps an audience to a conclusion about what is most reasonable, they do not seem to hold that what is reasonable can be determined by a vote. Otherwise, the concept of *eikos* would have been no use in supporting anthropological theories, in contexts where no vote is to be taken, such as those in Thucydides' *Archaeology* (1.2–20). So Socrates' criticism fails to strike the target of actual practice at the time.

From Socrates' criticism of the use of *eikos*, we would expect him to fall silent on subjects about which he disclaims knowledge, but Socrates sometimes discourses at great length, without having the knowledge he would need to do so with authority. Of course, the human situation is such that we must often make decisions without knowledge. Such is the case in the events recounted in the *Crito*: Socrates and Crito agree that they should listen only to experts, and not to the opinions of the crowd (48a). But then, in the absence of an expert on justice, they fall back on their own long-held beliefs about right and wrong (49a). Here (48e) and elsewhere, Socrates takes the agreement of his partner very seriously in the absence of expert knowledge (e.g. *Gorgias* 486e, ff.). What reason he might have had to do so I will not consider here. Socrates' style of question and answer, along with his habit of fictionally attributing his strongest theories to people not present, insulates him from the charge that he is wielding an authority which, as a non-expert, he does not have.

2.5. Promoting relativism. Socrates is not a relativist. Neither are most of the sophists. Still, Socrates marks a great difference between them. Sophists generally hold that when a virtue is beneficial, there may be something it benefits, and something it harms. Socrates reserves "beneficial" for an absolute use: if it is beneficial, really, it is beneficial without qualification.

As we have seen (1.5 above) the evidence is not convincing that any sophist was a relativist with regard to truth; that is, they did not in general assert that the same sentence could be true for one person and false for another. Many sophists, however, seem to have made both the good and the beneficial relative to the beneficiary, as we saw above, where I cited Protagoras' relativism regarding the good, and Thrasymachus' relativism regarding the beneficial. Both views seem reasonable; olive oil is good for some creatures and bad for others, and many policies do benefit one class of people while harming another.

Socrates does not seem to go along with either view. He pretends not to understand what Protagoras has said (*Protagoras* 334d); and he implies that he cannot see how to say what justice is without violating Thrasymachus' prohibition (*Republic* 1.337b). That prohibition, apparently, was against any definition of the form "justice is the beneficial" that does not specify precisely who it is to be beneficial for. So it appears that Socrates wishes to use words like "good" and "beneficial" without qualification. If a virtue such as justice is beneficial, Socrates believes, then it is beneficial for anyone who is affected by it, and no one – not even a criminal undergoing punishment – is harmed by justice (*Republic* 1.335b–d). Punishment is supposed to impart or strengthen virtue and thereby benefit the person punished, and, in general, the effect of any virtue on those it touches is to make them more virtuous, and that is a benefit. If this is Socrates' view, it goes beyond a rejection of relativism as usually understood, and ends with an affirmation of the use of value-words as complete or absolute predicates. In this, Socrates is markedly different from any sophist of whom we have knowledge.

2.6. Appealing to nature vs. convention. Socrates never appeals to convention in support of his views. Some of his partners do (Crito at 46c, ff., Polus at *Gorgias* 471e), but the view prevailing among sophists seems to have been that convention is a false tyrant, and that if there is a standard for judgment, it is natural (Callicles at *Gorgias* 483a, ff.). Socrates does not appeal to nature, however. His only appeal is to the opinion of an individual partner, one at a time, and in this he differs widely from the sophists we know about.

2.7. Supporting democracy. Some sophists did support democracy, and some did not, as we have seen. Socrates certainly did not, and he may have actively opposed it. How deeply he was engaged in the opposition to the democracy in Athens is matter for speculation. Antiphon (probably the sophist) was executed for his role in an oligarchic plot soon after the coup of 411, but Socrates was probably not so deeply engaged. He denies in the *Apology* that he took part in politics (31d, ff.), and he insists in the *Gorgias* (521d) that his practices in Athens take the true form of politics; by this, in context, he probably means that he alone undertakes the moral improvement of his fellow citizens.

2.8. Teaching virtue. We have seen that some sophists offered to teach virtue, and that what they meant by that is rather different from what Socrates would have meant, had he made the claim. The difference is owing to Socrates' theory of the soul as depending for its health on virtue. Nothing like that theory is found in any of the sophists.

Socrates never claims to know enough to teach virtue, and he would never charge a fee for what he says he does not know how to do. Still, he is a teacher of virtue in the most important way. He does not teach classes on the nature of virtue, nor does he promulgate definitions of the virtues. Nor does he offer training sessions for those who wish to become more virtuous. What Socrates does do is to exhort his fellow-citizens to take thought about acquiring virtue, and he shames those who do not respond (*Apology* 29d, ff.). This is a unique kind of teaching, unlike anything we know of the sophists.

2.9. Seeking natural explanations. Plato shows Socrates expressing an early interest in the explanation of natural events, which he soon abandoned (*Phaedo* 96a–99c), while never joining the rationalist project of providing natural explanations for events recorded in myth (*Phaedrus* 229d–30a). Xenophon attributes to Socrates what is probably the earliest known natural theology, an argument for the existence of the gods from observations of design in the physical world. But on the whole the evidence is unanimous: Socrates' passion is to work in the human world, and not to understand what human beings do, but to change it.

Notes

1 Much of the material in this section I have stated more fully in Woodruff (1997). For texts from or about sophists see Sprague (1972) and Gagarin and Woodruff (1995), hereafter cited as GW. For more detailed studies of sophists, see Guthrie (1971), Kerferd (1981).

2 Antiphon's identity. Some scholars hold that Antiphon the sophist was not identical to Antiphon the politician (Pendrick 2002); others hold that he was one and the same (Gagarin 2002). On the issues, see Woodruff (2004).

3 Aristotle *Rhetoric* 2.24, 1402a23, Diogenes Laertius, *Lives of Eminent Philosophers* 9.51.

4 Cole (1991), Schiappa (1990, 1999).

5 Gagarin (2001).

6 Gorgias, Helen 14 (Diels and Kranz B 11, GW 1, pp. 190–5).

7 Thucydides shows the demagogue Cleon only in defeat; Sophocles and Euripides never show a clever speaker in victory. Ancient literature shows no scene like Shakespeare's, in

which Marc Anthony wins over a hostile crowd by sheer force of rhetoric, or Henry V puts courage into a fading army.

8 Protagoras on the art of words: see the texts at GW 28–33 (pp. 188–9).

9 For a more elaborate discussion of the varieties of relativism, see Woodruff (1997); for the evidence that the sophists are not relativists, see Bett (1989).

10 Diels and Kranz 44. Interpretation of these matters is contested. See Woodruff (2004), and the books reviewed therein.

11 Aristotle, *Sophisticis Elenchis* 14, 173b17.

12 Antiphon's defense speech, GW 1, p. 219.

13 On the source of good judgment in the judicious use of *eikos*, see Woodruff (1994 and 1999).

14 Cole (1967).

15 Aristophanes' comic intent blurs the moral target; what he represents as traditional values (*dikaios logos*) seems equally debased. The hostility of the play to Socrates' teaching, however, cannot be missed.

16 The author of "On the Art," a medical text from the fifth century, was probably either a sophist dabbling in medicine or a medical doctor dabbling in arguments such as sophists used (Joel Mann, dissertation, 2005).

17 Kahn (1997).

References

Bett, R. (1989). The sophists and relativism. *Phronesis*, 34, 139–69.

Cole, T. (1967). *Democritus and the Sources of Greek Anthropology*. American Philological Association Monographs no. 25. New York: Oxford University Press, rpt. 1990.

—— (1991). *The Origins of Rhetoric in Ancient Greece*. Baltimore: Johns Hopkins University Press.

Diels, H. and Kranz, W. (1951). *Die Fragmente der Vorsokratiker*. [The Fragments of the Presocratics]. 6th ed. Berlin.

Farrar, C. (1988). *The Origins of Democratic Thinking: The Invention of Politics in Classical Athens*. Cambridge: Cambridge University Press.

Gagarin, M. (2001). Did the sophists aim to persuade? *Rhetorica*, 19, 275–91.

—— (2002). *Antiphon the Athenian: Oratory, Law, and Justice in the Age of the Sophists*. Austin: University of Texas Press.

Gagarin, M. and Woodruff, P. (eds.) (1995). *Early Greek Political Thought from Homer to the Sophists*. Cambridge: Cambridge University Press.

Grote, G. (1869). *A History of Greece*. 2nd ed. London.

Guthrie, W. K. C. (1971). *The Sophists*. Cambridge: Cambridge University Press.

Kahn, C. (1997). Greek religion and philosophy in the Sisyphus Fragment. *Phronesis*, 10, 247–62.

Kerferd, G. B. (1950). The first Greek sophists. *Classical Review*, 64, 8–10.

—— (1981). *The Sophistic Movement*. Cambridge: Cambridge University Press.

Mourelatos, A. P. D. M. (1987). Gorgias on the function of language. *Philosophical Topics*, 15, 135–70.

Pendrick, G. J. (2002). *Antiphon the Sophist*. Cambridge: Cambridge University Press.

Schiappa, E. (1990). Did Plato coin *rhētorikē? American Journal of Philology*, 111, 457–70.

—— (1999). *The Beginnings of Rhetoric in Ancient Greece*. New Haven: Yale University Press.

Segal, C. P. (1962). Gorgias and the psychology of the logos. *Harvard Studies in Classical Philology*, 66, 99–155.

Sprague, R. K. (1972). *The Older Sophists*. Columbia, SC: University of South Carolina Press.

Woodruff, P. (1994). *Eikos* and bad faith in the paired speeches of Thucydides. *Proceedings of the Boston Area Colloquium in Ancient Philosophy*, 10, 115–45.

—— (1997). Rhetoric and relativism: Protagoras and Gorgias. In A. A. Long (ed.), *Cambridge Companion to Early Greek Philosophy*. Cambridge: Cambridge University Press.

—— (1999). Paideia and good judgment. In D. M. Steiner (ed.), *Philosophy of Education. Volume 3 of the Proceedings of the Twentieth World Congress of Philosophy* (pp. 63–75). Charlottesville, VA: Philosophy Documentation Center.

—— (2004). Antiphons sophist and Athenian; a discussion of Michael Gagarin, *Antiphon the Athenian* and Gerard J. Pendrick, *Antiphon the Sophist*. *Oxford Studies in Ancient Philosophy*, April 2004, 323–36.

Yunis, H. (1996). *Taming Democracy: Models of Political Rhetoric in Classical Athens*. Ithaca, NY: Cornell University Press.

47

4

Socrates the Freethinker

RICHARD JANKO

A majority among the 500 Athenian jurors found Socrates guilty of the charge of impiety that was brought against him in 399 BCE, and even more of them sentenced him to death for it. Over the previous three decades scientists and intellectuals had begun to offer increasingly radical alternatives, which many people regarded as impious to traditional Greek religious beliefs. According to these scientists, there might be gods inside nature, but there was no room for the supernatural (Vlastos 2000: 56). Whether such arguments were advanced in speech or in writing, the Athenians repeatedly voted to punish their advocates with severe penalties, including death. This fierce reaction began with the outlawing of astronomy by the decree of Diopeithes and the exile of the physicist Anaxagoras in the later 430s BCE, and culminated with the execution of Socrates (Dodds 1951: 179–206). Whether or not Socrates had ever been one of these scientists, and whether or not he believed in the supernatural, as he clearly did, he was punished because many thought he was an "atheist" (*atheos*) in the Greek sense (Brickhouse and Smith 1989). This broad term included people who believed in new gods, in one god, or in no god at all. Socrates was indeed what we call a "freethinker," since he refused to submit his reason to the control of authority in matters of religious faith (Vlastos 2000: 60), yet he certainly believed in the divine. Even if we cannot establish beyond any doubt what he did believe, a new text from his time offers an answer to another vital question: what did many of the jurors think he believed, and why did such beliefs cause them so much outrage?

New Evidence for the Intellectuals' Challenge to Greek Religion

Socrates left no philosophical writings, but other intellectuals presented their arguments in written form. These, however, have largely perished. Only brief quotations survive of the treatise in which Protagoras expressed his controversial agnosticism about the gods and the terrors of Hades. There is still less of the work where Prodicus argued that gods were people who had been deified for benefits they had conferred upon the human race. However, in 1962 archaeologists excavating the remains of a funeral pyre at Derveni in Northern Greece found the remnant of a scroll of papyrus datable to about 330 BCE, part of which survived the flames. This scroll, known as the

Derveni papyrus, is a copy of a treatise written within Socrates' lifetime, as its style proves beyond any doubt. Many years after its discovery it remains unknown even to scholars, for several reasons. We obtained access to a complete text and translation only recently (Laks and Most 1997), and these were soon superseded (Janko 2002). The work has no indication of author or title. Its beginning is missing, and so are the lower parts of each of its 26 columns of writing. Above all, nothing we knew about early Greek thought had remotely prepared us for this treatise. Its contents are so bizarre that nobody could make head or tail of it until the whole text was available (Janko 1997; Laks 1997). The Athenians would have been even more appalled by it. For this treatise is the most important new evidence since the Renaissance for the intellectual and religious ferment which occurred in the Athens of Socrates' time. If rightly understood and put into its original context, it deserves to revolutionize our understanding.

Most of the Derveni text is an allegorical, pseudo-scientific interpretation of a poem about the creation of the world by the gods. Its author, whom I shall call "D." for convenience, indicates that this poem was used in mystery-cult; it was kept a strict secret throughout antiquity by the initiates who knew it. D. ascribes the poem to the mythical poet Orpheus, but it is likely to have been composed in about 550–500 BCE in Pythagorean circles. The Orphic poem narrated the history of the universe, showing how each generation of gods supplanted the previous one. It was full of shocking episodes: Zeus deposes his father Cronus and rapes his mother Rhea, committing, like Oedipus, the cardinal sins of Greek culture – yet doing so knowingly. Worse, Zeus swallows the Sky-god's penis which Cronus had chopped off, and thus engenders other gods (column 13). The god who dethrones his father is paralleled in Hesiod's poem *The Birth of the Gods*, which was fundamental to Greek religion; a god who swallows a penis appears in a Hittite religious text that is a thousand years older, the *Song of Kumarbi*. In short, these are traditional myths typical of ancient polytheism.

D. explains all these scandalous stories about the gods as an allegory for the latest scientific theories, according to which God is the same as Air, and Air is the divine Mind that runs the universe. If God is eternal, even the myth that He was "born" was a scandal in need of explanation (columns 16–17) (translations are mine unless stated, with square brackets for gaps in the text and round brackets for clarifications):

> [The next verse is] "Zeus was born first, Zeus of the shining bolt was last." [This verse makes clear that] Zeus existed before He was named; then He was named. For Air was pre-existent even before those things which now exist were put together, and He will always exist; for He did not come to be, but existed. Why (Zeus) was called "Air" has been revealed earlier (in my account). But He was thought to have been "born" because He was named "Zeus," as if He had not existed before. (Orpheus) said that (Air) will be "last" because He was named "Zeus," and this will continue to be His name so long as the things which now exist are put together in the same element (i.e. Air) in which they had been suspended when they were pre-existent. (Orpheus) reveals that the things that exist became such as they are on account of (Air), and, having come to be, are all in (Air) . . .

D.'s theories derive from two sources: first, the atomism of Leucippus, the earliest thinker to propose that the universe consists of atoms and void, and secondly, the molecular physics of Pericles' friend Anaxagoras, who was exiled by the Athenians for claiming that the sun is a red-hot stone bigger than half of Greece. D. also quotes the notoriously obscure earlier thinker Heraclitus of Ephesus. This treatise is about as strange as a book that argued, while citing Nietzsche, that the *Book of Mormon* is a coded account of Einstein's and Hawking's theories about the origin of the universe.

D.'s allegorical commentary on Orpheus' poem begins only in column 7. The preceding columns offer the key as to why he wrote his book. In them, he seems to veer crazily between disparate topics. In column 4, he cites Heraclitus' claim that the sun is only one foot across:

> Heraclitus, deeming our shared sensations important, rejects those which are individual. Speaking like an allegorist, he says: "the sun, in accord with its own nature, is in breadth the size of a human foot, and does not overshoot its limits: for if it steps outside its own breadth, the Erinyes (i.e. Furies), allies of Justice, will discover it."

In column 5, D. denounces the ignorance of the public, who doubt the traditional horror-stories about the terrors of Hades that their soul may face in the afterlife. They disbelieve them, he suggests, because they want to disbelieve them, but that is because they do not understand them, i.e. because they take them literally:

> . . . the terrors of Hades . . . ask an oracle . . . they ask an oracle . . . for them, we will enter the prophetic shrine to enquire, with regard to people who seek prophecies, whether it is permissible to disbelieve in the terrors of Hades. Why do they disbelieve? Since they do not understand dream-visions or any of the other realities, what sort of proofs would induce them to believe? For, since they are overcome by both error and pleasure as well, they do not learn or believe. Disbelief and ignorance are the same thing. For if they do not learn or comprehend, it is impossible for them to believe even if they see dream-visions.

In column 6, D. argues that the Athenian goddesses called the Eumenides (Furies) are really the souls of the angry dead. He thinks that the sacrifices used to placate them by magicians and by the initiates to the mysteries prove his claim:

> Prayers and sacrifices placate the souls. An incantation by *magoi* can dislodge daimons that become a hindrance; daimons that are a hindrance are vengeful souls. The *magoi* perform the sacrifice for this reason, as if they are paying a blood-price. Onto the offerings they pour water and milk, with both of which they also make drink-offerings. They sacrifice cakes which are countless and many-humped, because the souls too are countless. Initiates make a first sacrifice to the Eumenides in the same way as *magoi* do; for the Eumenides are souls. Hence someone who intends to sacrifice to the gods first [sacrifices] a chicken . . .

This is as bizarre as if one were to argue that the rite of Holy Communion proves that the air is full of transmigratory souls. Then there follows column 7 – the claim that Orpheus' poem is perfectly inoffensive, because he is speaking allegorically from beginning to end, and deliberately offering riddles which need to be decoded; these riddles are addressed only to a group of the elect, those who are "pure in hearing":

[I shall also prove that Orpheus composed a] hymn that tells of wholesome and lawful things. For he was speaking allegorically with his composition, and it was impossible (for him) to state the application of his words and what was meant. His composition is a strange one, riddling for people. But Orpheus did not want to tell them unbelievable riddles, but important things in riddles. In fact he is speaking allegorically from his very first word right through to his last, as he reveals even in the well-known verse. For when he orders them to "shut the doors" on their ears, he is stating that he is not making laws for most people, but teaching those who are pure in hearing.

The link between the peculiar series of topics in columns 4–7 is the need for interpretation. If people are to keep their faith, the rituals and holy texts must be interpreted. Whether it is the sacrifices of the *magoi* or those of the initiates, whether it is the obscure writings of Heraclitus or the shocking cosmogony of Orpheus, these things cannot be taken literally, but demand an allegorical interpretation, which D. is only too happy to supply.

D.'s interpretation of the poem is equally far-fetched. However, this causes him no embarrassment. As he catalogues the crimes of the successive rulers of the universe, explaining them all away by using allegory and etymology, he breaks off to insist once again on the importance of interpretation and the dangers of literalism. This is in column 20. Here he castigates the gullibility of initiates into the mysteries – not just state-sponsored ceremonies "in the cities" like those of Demeter at Eleusis, but especially private ones, into which one could be admitted on payment of a fee. Such initiates may expect the priests to tell them what the ritual means, but receive no explanation. D. implies that he knows better: he holds the key to the hidden meanings of the rites and the Orphic scriptures that went with them, whereas scandalous myths about the gods undermine people's faith if they are taken literally:

I am less amazed that those people who have performed the rites and been initiated in the cities do not comprehend them; for it is impossible to hear what is said and to learn it simultaneously. But those who have been initiated by someone who makes a profession of the rites are worthy of amazement and pity: amazement because, although they suppose, before they perform the rite, that they will have knowledge, they go away after they have performed it without gaining knowledge, and they make no further enquiries, as if they knew something about what they saw, heard or learned; and pity because it does not suffice them that they have wasted the fee which they paid beforehand, but they also go away bereft of their judgment too. Before they perform the rites, they expect to have knowledge; after they have performed them, they go away bereft even of their expectation. [For the sorcerors'] story appears to mean that Zeus [has intercourse] with his own mother . . . with his mother . . . but with his sister . . . when he saw . . . [The verses] "Zeus mounted her and begot Persuasion, Harmony and Heavenly Aphrodite" [mean that] . . . when neither the hot had come together with the hot nor the cold with the cold.

At the end of this extract D. is claiming, in typical fashion, that the story of how Zeus rapes his own mother and sister is an allegory for how the elements combined with each other in the primeval vortex. For D., fundamentalist interpretation, i.e. taking holy texts literally, is dangerous to religious faith, and allegorical interpretation is essential.

51

The Origins of Allegorical Interpretation

The allegorical approach was already a century old when D. wrote. By 500 BCE the epic poems of Homer and Hesiod had come to play a fundamental role in the teaching of literacy, and they had also become the basic text for Greek religion, as fundamental to it as the Bible to Judaism or the Koran to Islam. But the Greeks had no established clergy who saw it as their task to codify their holy texts or determine their meaning; in a very democratic fashion their interpretation was left up to everyone, including the poets. Difficult passages like the battle of the gods in Homer's *Iliad* 20–1, where the gods behave in an undignified way, subject to the basest of human passions, gave rise to the earliest recorded literary criticism. The philosopher and poet Xenophanes, the first Greek to advance the radical view that there was only one god and that he was good, attacked Homer and Hesiod for their portrayal of the gods (fr. 1.21–4 D.-K.):

> (At a banquet one must not) tell of the battles of the Titans or the Giants, nor those of the Centaurs, fictions of men of old, or their violent dissensions – there's nothing good in those – but (say) that God eternally has excellent foresight.

The earliest known allegorical interpretation was probably advanced in reply to Xenophanes. Theagenes, active in about 525 BCE, interpreted the battle of the gods as an allegory for the conflict between the physical elements in natural science, as a later source tells us:

> Homer does not tell appropriate stories about the gods. Against such a charge some offer a solution "from the diction," thinking that everything is an allegorical explanation of the nature of the elements, as in the confrontations of the gods . . . (They say) that he composes the battles by calling fire "Apollo," "Helios" and "Hephaestus," water "Poseidon" and "Scamander," the moon "Artemis," the air "Hera" and so on . . . Such is the type of defense "from the diction." It is very ancient, going back to Theagenes of Rhegium, who first wrote about Homer.

Theagenes presumably deduced that Hera stands for Air from an anagram of the letters of her name, HPA and AHP, in an early use of etymology.

The combination of allegory and etymology became common later in the fifth century. Several followers of Anaxagoras practiced both allegory and etymology in the 420s. Some claimed, in interpreting a verse of Orpheus, that Zeus was "mind" and Athena was "art" (George Syncellus, *Chronicle* p. 282.19 Dindorf). Anaxagoras' disciple Metrodorus interpreted the Homeric gods as allegories for the physical elements. An early Christian writer mocks this mercilessly (Tatian, *To the Greeks* 2.11):

> Metrodorus of Lampsacus in his book *On Homer* spoke very stupidly when he turned everything into an allegory. For he says that Hera, Athena and Zeus . . . are hypostases of nature and arrangements of elements.

Metrodorus also equated the Homeric heroes Agamemnon with the *aither*, Achilles with the sun, Helen with the earth, Paris with the air, and Hector with the moon

(Hesychius, Lexicon S.V. *Agamemnon*, and Philodemus, *On Poems* C cols. ii–iii Sbordone). Another follower, Diogenes of Apollonia, praised Homer "because he spoke about the divine not in myth but truthfully; for Homer thinks that Air is Zeus, since he says that Zeus knows everything" (fr. A8 D.-K.). Diogenes was active before 423 BCE, when Aristophanes caricatured his opinions in his comedy the *Clouds*, putting them into the mouth of Socrates. Diogenes thought that Air is omniscient, that Air is Mind, and that this divine Mind oversees the universe (fr. B5 D.-K.):

> It seems to me that what has intelligence is what people call Air, and that by this everyone is governed and that it rules over all things; for this very thing seems to me to be God, to have reached everything, to arrange everything and to be in everything.

The belief that Mind is God was shared by Diogenes, by the author of the Derveni treatise and, very possibly, by Socrates too, as we shall see.

"There Is Only One God and He Arranges Everything for the Best"

We have seen that, in the 420s BCE, followers of Anaxagoras claimed that their version of molecular physics could be found in the poetry of Homer when it was allegorically interpreted. The Derveni author does exactly the same, except that he transfers this approach to the sacred Orphic scripture. D. makes the following claims about the universe. Nothing is ever created or perishes, but only combines and separates; like is drawn to like. The universe is ordered by God, who is the same as Zeus, Mind, Air, Spirit, and holy Wisdom. The traditional gods are names for different stages in the evolution of the universe; for instance Cronus, Harmony, and Aphrodite are different names for the combining of things as like coalesces with like. Moreover, none of this makes sense unless D. also holds that there is only one God. This God, Air, pervades and controls everything in accord with the divine will. Indeed, God arranges everything in the best possible way to suit humankind, as columns 24–5 reveal:

> But (Orpheus) does not mean this when he states that (the moon) "shows"; for if he had meant this, he would not have stated that it "shows for many" but "for all" at once, both for those who farm the land and for sailors, showing them when they must sail, and the season for the former. For if the moon had not come into existence, people would not have found out the number of either the seasons or the winds . . .

> Each of (the bodies other than sun and moon) is suspended of necessity, so that they cannot join up with each other; for if it were otherwise, all those elements which have the same power as those from which the sun was put together would join up in a lump. If God had not desired the existence of those things which now exist, he would not have created a sun; but he created one that became of such a kind and dimension as is explained at the start of my account.

D.'s belief in only one God is monotheism; his claim that God is in everything is pantheism; and his faith that God has ordered everything for the good of the human race is teleology. His system combines the influences of the atomist Leucippus and the physicist Anaxagoras. This same combination of beliefs and influences recurs in the

53

writings of Diogenes of Apollonia. Diogenes decisively modified Anaxagoras' physics by giving Mind a teleological role, which Anaxagoras had not assigned to it when he described the workings of the universe in purely mechanistic terms.

When, in the later 430s BCE, an Athenian jury voted to send Anaxagoras into exile for impiety, it was on the ground that his materialist approach to astronomical research posed a threat to traditional religion. A few years later, it seems, another jury condemned Protagoras for impiety, although he had in fact only professed agnosticism: he had dared to publish a book which declared that he did not know whether or not there were gods. In response to such hostility, Anaxagoras' followers, including Diogenes, sought to reconcile the new science with traditional religious faith. Allegory was the main method by which they sought to do this. This response helped to provoke an even fiercer reaction on the Athenians' part. When we read that Diogenes "came close to danger in Athens" (Demetrius of Phalerum, in D.L. 9.57), we begin to see that this was part of the reaction which culminated in Socrates' execution.

Diagoras' Critique of the Mysteries and His Condemnation

Since Diogenes advocated this new combination of monotheism, pantheism, and teleology, I at first wondered whether he could himself have been the author of the Derveni text. But the fit with D.'s system of physics is imperfect, as Laks showed (1997: 130–2). Diogenes was a monist, i.e. he held that everything is a modification of a single primary substance, Air, which is thus immanent in everything. But D. was a pluralist, like Anaxagoras: he thought that everything exists independently of the Air, and that Air is both the space in which everything exists and a transcendent principle.

Another candidate for the authorship of D.'s treatise, Diagoras, sheds new light on Socrates' condemnation, since Diagoras too was condemned for impiety. In 415 BCE, eight years after the first performance of Aristophanes' *Clouds*, which ridicules Socrates and Diogenes, a witch-hunt erupted in Athens. Just when the Athenians were to embark on a catastrophic attempt to conquer Sicily, a place they could hardly locate on the map, they awoke to find that, in the night, all the statues of the god Hermes around the city had been smashed by unknown agents. In the ensuing panic, religious extremists attacked supposed offenders against the traditional religion who had allegedly mocked the Eleusinian mysteries. The Athenians' best admiral, Alcibiades, was a major target; he defected to the enemy, but many other citizens were tortured, condemned, and executed on the evidence of informers. This was done with the support of the priests of the mysteries at Eleusis, who had great power and prestige (Furley 1996).

In the same year or early in 414 the Athenians also condemned Diagoras of Melos for defaming the Eleusinian mysteries and deterring would-be initiates from taking part in the rites (T7–10 Winiarczyk). Diagoras was a lyric poet, progressive constitutionalist, and philosopher of the same age as Socrates (T1–5, 9A). An early Christian writer, well informed about the seamier side of pagan ritual and texts, says that Diagoras was condemned because he divulged the secrets of both the Orphic scriptures and the mysteries of Demeter at Eleusis (T27). Diagoras fled to a small town in the Peloponnese to escape the Athenians' wrath. Aristophanes includes two jokes about his escape in his play the *Birds* (1073, 1421), performed in the spring of 414.

54

Ancient sources list Diagoras among the "physicists" (*physikoi*) who speculated in their writings about the nature of the universe (T1–3). The fragments of his verse make a poet's typically vague references to "god," *daimon*, and destiny. This led one philosopher to deny that he wrote the "atheistic" prose treatise which also bore his name (T69). But another source says Diagoras had been a believer at first, only to lose his faith when someone who swore a false oath went unpunished by the gods; he then wrote a prose work presenting his views (T67).

In 399 BCE, the year of Socrates' condemnation, the prosecutor in another impiety trial reminded the Athenians of Diagoras' misdeeds ([Lysias] 6.17–18). He called the accused, Andocides, "far more impious than Diagoras; for Diagoras committed impiety in word against other people's holy rites and festivals, whereas the accused did so in deed against those of his own city," i.e. the Eleusinian mysteries. Since he claims that the accused "does not believe in gods," he clearly expects the jury to accept that Diagoras was an "atheist." As we saw, in using the term "atheist" (*atheos*) the Athenians did not distinguish between those who believed in new gods, different from those in which the city believed, only one god or no god at all. A century later the philosopher Epicurus gives us a vital detail about Diagoras' "atheism." He reports that Diagoras and other thinkers of the time altered the letters in the names of the traditional gods in order to deny their existence (Philodemus, *On Piety* I 518–41 Obbink):

> Epicurus criticized as quite mad those who abolish the gods from reality, as also in his *On Nature* book XII he criticizes Prodicus, Diagoras, Critias and others, saying they are insane, mad and like raving lunatics, bidding them not trouble or bother us. For they alter the letters in the names of the gods.

In other words, Prodicus, Diagoras, and Socrates' "pupil" Critias used etymology to explain away the existence of the gods, as Theagenes had done when he claimed that the goddess Hera is actually the air on the ground that "Hera" (HPA) is an anagram of the Greek word for "air" (AHP). Such an approach may seem trivial and absurd to us, but to the average Athenian it was gross blasphemy that endangered the safety of the state. For if gods did not exist, what power was there to uphold the sanctity of laws and contracts, which depended on people swearing by the gods to keep their promises?

Diagoras of Melos and the Faith of Socrates

Like Diagoras, Socrates was punished not for his deeds but "for his words," as an orator put it in 361/0 BCE (Hyperides fr. 55). It was not his behavior but his teachings that mattered. At his trial for impiety, Socrates was careful to distinguish between his faith in his inner divine voice (*daimonion*) and atheism as we understand it; nobody who knows all the historical sources, notably Plato and Xenophon, can question the depth of his faith in the divine. However, Aristophanes' comedies and Athenian law-court speeches show that most people confused belief in new gods with belief in no gods at all. As part of his initiation by Socrates into the mysteries of his Think-Tank, the bumpkin Strepsiades has learned that he must no longer swear oaths by Zeus. He tells his son Phidippides that he must now swear by Dinos ("Vortex"), because Dinos has supplanted Zeus (*Clouds* 828–30):

STREPSIADES: Dinos is king, now he's driven out Zeus . . .
PHIDIPPIDES: Who says so?
STREPSIADES: Socrates the Melian.

When Strepsiades says that "Socrates the Melian" taught him this, he equates the Athenian Socrates with Diagoras from Melos. In Aristophanes' joke Zeus is ousted by a new god whose name, Dinos, resembles that of Zeus etymologically, because Zeus' name often appears in Greek in the form Dios. However, this new god also represents the whirling "Vortex" of air which was thought to encompass the universe, i.e. a physical element. Aristophanes' joke, like D.'s treatise, combines a materialist explanation for the universe with a belief in God and reference to a divine succession. The reference to swearing oaths recalls the story of Diagoras' loss of faith. It does not of course follow from this joke that Diagoras was an atheist in the modern sense; "Dinos" is a new god and the physical element Air *at the same time*. Diagoras could well have believed that God is Air – because this is exactly what we find in the Derveni treatise!

The Derveni papyrus is, I believe, a copy of Diagoras' book which so enraged the Athenians that they decreed his assassination without trial. As Laks perceived (1997: 126), "the attack on religious obscurantism was made in the name of 'holiness'." By reinterpreting the Orphic cosmogony and mocking the Orphic initiates in column 20 of the text, Diagoras would have made his audiences question whether it was worth the trouble and expense of getting initiated. He would certainly have offended the priests who peddled salvation from the terrors of Hades (the topic of column 5) by offering initiation to those feeling in need of indulgence for their sins. They would have been furious that Diagoras divulged the sacred text of Orpheus in the process of offering his allegorical interpretation of it. The ultimate outrage would have been the allegory itself – the interpretation of the holy poem as a coded version of the latest physics, and the equation of God with a material element, Air. The priests at Eleusis too would have been angered by the mockery of public initiation in column 20 and the revelations about the initiates' sacrifices to the Eumenides, specifically Athenian deities, in column 6. The claim that the *daimones* and Eumenides are the souls of the dead would also have given offence.

We already knew about the backlash against the new physics from Plutarch's description (*Life of Nicias* 23.2–3):

> Men could not abide the natural philosophers (*physikoi*) and "astronomaniacs" (*meteoroleschai*), as they were then called, because they reduced the divine agency down to irrational causes, blind forces, and necessary incidents. Even Protagoras had to go into exile, Anaxagoras was with difficulty rescued from imprisonment by Pericles, and Socrates, although he had nothing whatever to do with such matters, nevertheless lost his life because of philosophy.   (trans. B. Perrin, adapted)

Scholars have often tried to minimize the Athenians' persecution of scientists and intellectuals, arguing that the trial of Socrates was an isolated case (Dover 1976;

Parker 1996: 199–217; Kraut 2000). But even if some of the evidence is contradictory or unreliable, more than enough remains to prove that there was an increasingly fierce anti-intellectual climate and that it was centered on "atheism." Any reader of the *Clouds* with a sense of humor, experience of persecution, or (best of all) both should find it hard not to take its final scene very seriously. We see Socrates' Think-Tank, the first university the world had seen, burned down with the thinkers inside. Aristophanes probably got the idea from a historically attested attack in about 454 on a meeting-house of the leaders of the Pythagorean sect at Croton in Southern Italy; most were burned alive (Kopff 1977 Van der Warden 1979: 217–21; Huffman 1993: 2–3). A few years later, the Athenians decreed the death of Diagoras.

Socrates Against the Poets

After Diagoras fled Athens, nobody had any reason to correct the Athenians' misapprehension about his beliefs. Although he was a theistic materialist, he remained a byword for "atheism." His case led other intellectuals to become both more cautious and more radical. It was not enough to explain away the scandalous myths of the poets by using the method of allegory and etymology employed by Metrodorus, Diogenes, and Diagoras. Instead, the role of traditional poetry both in education and in public and religious life needed to be challenged more fundamentally. This step was probably taken, following Xenophanes' precedent, by Socrates himself (McPherran 1996: 112–16, 289). His questioning of the poets is well attested by Plato (*Apology* 22a–c, *Protagoras* 340b–347a); indeed his chief accuser, Meletus, was "angry on behalf of the poets" (*Apology* 23e).

In his lost pamphlet *Accusation Against Socrates* published in 393/2 BCE, the rhetorician Polycrates celebrated Socrates' execution by putting a speech into the mouth of his second prosecutor, the politician Anytus. The later author Libanius still knew Polycrates' work and used it in a declamation which replies to it; he defends Socrates at length for criticizing the poets, showing that they had themselves advocated outrageous behavior (*Apology of Socrates* 62–126). Libanius also denies that Socrates resembled the "sophists" Anaxagoras, Protagoras, and Diagoras, with whom the Athenians were right to be angry (*Apology of Socrates* 154–5):

> Anaxagoras was justly imprisoned for his impiety regarding the sun and moon; you banished Protagoras fairly and appropriately for asking whether the gods exist or not; you were wise to promise a reward for the person who would kill Diagoras, since he mocked Eleusis and the ineffable mysteries; but who can say that there is a book or an argument about the gods by Socrates that is contrary to law? As you cannot show us one, Anytus, even if you cite a myriad of sophists who have been ruined you still do not convict Socrates.

This shows that Polycrates, and most probably Socrates' real prosecutors, did accuse him on these grounds. In the *Euthyphro* Plato makes Socrates meet Euthyphro, a religious fanatic, as the "young and ignorant" Meletus (2b) must have been. Euthyphro takes all the myths literally (6b–c), including the story that Zeus imprisoned his father Cronus (6a) and even more shocking events than that, which are not known to the

57

public (6b); he must mean the Orphic myths. He immediately assumes that Socrates is being prosecuted because of his belief in his *daimonion* (3b). But when he mentions the story that Zeus punished his father, Socrates asks whether he is himself being prosecuted for impiety because he finds tales of divine conflict distasteful (6a). He implies that he does find them so, that everyone should, and that this was indeed one explanation for the accusation. What would have offended most of the jurymen, however, was not criticism of the traditional myths in itself, which was practiced even by pious poets like Pindar, but their "atheistic" interpretation in terms of the new scientific materialism. Now that the Derveni treatise shows what such interpretations entailed, we need not continue to debate whether Socrates was condemned for challenging the myths or for his alleged atheism; by now many Athenians thought "atheism" went hand in hand with the reinterpretation of myth.

Socrates' successors continued his criticism of the poets. In 391 BCE his pupil Isocrates, in what he presents as a reply to Polycrates' praise of Busiris, was in fact replying to his attack on Socrates. Rejecting the claim that Socrates was guilty of impiety, he accuses the poets, and especially Orpheus, of being the ones who are truly guilty, because of the horrible myths which they recount: many poets were punished for what they said by suffering poverty, blindness, exile, or, in the case of Orpheus, being torn apart. Isocrates wants nothing to do with such myths or those who propagate them: "we shall consider both those who say such things, and those who believe them, to be equally guilty of impiety" (*Busiris* 38–40). Although he charges the poets, along with the wider public, with gross impiety for uttering and believing such stuff, he ignores allegorical interpretation as a possible solution to the problem. Plato went even further. In his *Republic*, where he calls for the censorship of the poetry used in education, he explicitly rejects allegory as a way out (3.378d–e):

> One must not admit into the city the imprisonment of Hera by her son and the ejection of Hephaestus by his father, when he was about to protect his mother from a beating, and battles among the gods such as Homer has composed – whether with allegorical interpretations or without them. For a young person is unable to judge what can have an allegorical interpretation and what cannot.

If Homer's poems are not censored as he recommends, then they should be entirely banned from the ideal state. At the end of the century Epicurus rejected the traditional *paideia* as vigorously as he rejected atheism (fr. 163; cf. fr. 117). Religion, philosophy, science, and the attack on the poets were by now inextricably linked.

The Religion of Socrates and His Condemnation

Socrates' own beliefs have been endlessly debated, and they could of course have changed during his long career. In his latter years, he famously claimed that he knew nothing except that he knew that he knew nothing. Aristophanes' *Clouds* alleges, as we have seen, that he held the views of Diogenes of Apollonia and of Diagoras of Melos. Even if this was false, people certainly believed it, as the evidence for Polycrates' pamphlet shows.

Socrates was condemned for many and varied reasons. He was hated by a powerful group of adversaries with different motives, and if he had not offered so unyielding a defense he might have been acquitted (Colaiaco 2001: 216–23). Some jurymen found him guilty on political grounds, even though this was illegal because of the recent amnesty. A later orator (Aeschines 1.73) says he was condemned because he had "educated" Plato's uncle Critias, the antidemocratic leader of the reign of terror by the Thirty Tyrants in 404–3 BCE; others, including Plato, felt the need to explain the fact that he had "educated" Alcibiades, who turned against Athens, came back, and left again (Plato depicts Alcibiades as impossible to teach). Plato once hints that the moderate politician Anytus, who could not have attacked him openly on political grounds, prosecuted him as a pro-Spartan follower of the oligarchs and a danger to the restored democracy, since his sophistical teachings corrupted the young (*Meno* 91c–92b). His critiques of democracy certainly contributed to this view (Kraut 2000: 15). Attack from behind the veil of religion was a good form of defense for some who had participated in the misdeeds of the Thirty Tyrants: thus one source (Andocides, *On the Mysteries* 94) alleges that the poet Meletus, who prosecuted him, was involved in the murder of Leon of Salamis under that régime, a crime in which Plato's Socrates openly states that he refused to take part (*Apology* 32c–d).

But others certainly felt threatened for religious reasons; thus Meletus charged him with introducing new gods that had not been approved by the city. According to Plato's *Apology*, when Socrates challenged him in court he modified his charge into an accusation of atheism in the modern sense, which Socrates easily refutes. According to both Plato and Xenophon, Socrates affirmed his belief in his "divine voice" (*daimonion*); one must recall that columns 3 and 6 of the Derveni treatise express belief in *daimones*, as does Socrates (Plato, *Apology* 27c). An attentive reader will notice, however, that Socrates never directly answers the charge that he believed in gods other than those in which the city believes (Burnyeat 1997; Colaiaco 2001: 26–30).

There should be no doubt that, despite his claim to know only that he knew nothing, Socrates had strong beliefs about the divine. According to Xenophon, he was a teleologist who held that god arranges everything for the best (*Mem.* 1.4, 4.3). According to Plato, when Meletus accuses Socrates of believing that the sun and moon are made of stone and earth, he replies that these are Anaxagoras' ideas, not his (*Apology* 26d–e). But in the *Phaedo* (97d–98a) Socrates says that he was once attracted to Anaxagoras' materialist thought, only to reject it precisely because it gave Mind no teleological role in the Universe. This is exactly the difference between Anaxagoras' views and those of his followers like Diogenes of Apollonia and the author of the Derveni papyrus, who both give Mind such a role. In Aristophanes' *Clouds* Diogenes' doctrines are the "mysteries" into which the comic poet's caricature of Socrates "initiates" his pupils. The evidence of the *Phaedo* and the *Clouds* strongly suggests that, at least during the 420s, Socrates himself was attracted to a teleological adaptation of the doctrines of Anaxagoras. Other sources report that Socrates was taught by a pupil of Anaxagoras called Archelaus (60A 3, 5, 7, D.-K.). The beliefs of Anaxagoras' followers, whether or not Socrates ever shared them, played a major part in his condemnation.

This new faith amounted to nothing less than belief in a new god, the divine Mind or Spirit that orders all things. This is very different from the traditional myths and poems about many different gods who could be in conflict with each other and who treated one another disgracefully. Since the Athenians counted as "atheists" both those who believed in new gods and those who believed in only one god, Anaxagoras' followers certainly fell into that category. One source says "Diagoras was a lyric poet who also introduced new gods, like Socrates" (schol. Ar. *Frogs* 320). Whether or not Socrates secretly shared this faith, the fact that he demanded a higher conception of the divine explains why he does not reply directly to Meletus' charge that he believed in gods other than those in which the city believed (McPherran 2000: 100–1). Plato makes the *Republic* begin with Socrates going to participate in a procession to celebrate the arrival of a new deity, the Thracian goddess Bendis, and the *Phaedo* ends with Socrates requiring the sacrifice of a cock to another newly introduced deity, Asclepius, as A. D'Angour pointed out to me. If the Athenians themselves could accept new gods, Plato implies, how could they accuse Socrates of impiety when he had only done the same?

The Dangers of Freethinking in Classical Athens

Diagoras' newly recovered treatise dates from the 420s BCE. This sensational text reveals exactly how, after the outlawing of research into astronomy in the 430s, spiritually inclined freethinkers tried to reconcile their new scientific understanding with the Greeks' traditional polytheistic religion, with its shocking myths and peculiar rites. Instead, some of them advocated not materialist atheism or even agnosticism (for which, respectively, Anaxagoras and Protagoras were condemned), but teleological monotheism, with a single god who is identical with Mind and Air (we might say "Spirit," i.e. "breath"), and who arranges everything for the best. Democritus confirms the contemporary appeal of this belief (fr. B30 D.-K.; "not" is my insertion):

> Among the intellectuals <not> a few stretch out their arms in the place which we Greeks now call "Air" and say "all things are called Zeus, and he knows all things and gives and takes them away, and he is king of all things."

These thinkers deemed their new belief compatible with the latest scientific theories and discoveries. Indeed, followers of Anaxagoras like Diogenes and Diagoras tried to prove this by applying the new techniques of allegory and etymology to the interpretation of holy texts like the poetry of Homer and Orpheus and of rituals like the Mysteries, arguing that they cannot be taken literally but convey scientific truth. But this attempt to reconcile the new science with traditional religion was so threatening to the religious establishment that it caused a fundamentalist backlash, when death sentences were passed first on Diagoras and then on Socrates.

Socrates' claim that he knew nothing except that he knew that he knew nothing proved insufficient to deflect the charge that he was teaching a new religion. After his execution his disciples had powerful reasons for concealing his real or alleged relation to such religious beliefs, and particularly so if they held similar beliefs themselves: they wanted to continue to teach in Athens without being convicted of impiety. Aristotle had to leave Athens when, in 322 BCE, the chief priest at Eleusis brought against him a charge of impiety (D.L. 5.5); Aristotle dryly observed that he would not let the Athenians sin against philosophy a second time (*Vit. Masc.* 41). Perhaps to protect themselves from such charges, philosophers after Socrates strongly condemned atheism in its modern sense. I cited above Epicurus' denunciation of Diagoras and other "atheists," even though he and his followers were often accused of atheism themselves. Plato's *Laws* prescribes savage punishments for atheists (10.907d–909d). However, by "atheists" he means those who deny that the universe is ruled by God or Mind (899c). His addition of "Mind" proves that, for him as for the followers of Anaxagoras, it was pious to believe that God is Mind.

The new text unveils nothing less than the Greek equivalent of the Reformation and Counter-Reformation. The fundamentalists' reaction had profound effects on the development of both science and philosophy. The brilliant scientific insights and investigations, notably atomic theory, begun by the pre-Socratic philosophers were halted, and no advance would be made in them until the seventeenth century. Meanwhile, the new monotheism of Anaxagoras' successors became the hidden faith of many intellectuals; its influence on the beliefs of such figures as Euripides, Antisthenes, Plato, Aristotle, the Stoics, the Gnostics, the Neoplatonists, and the more mainstream religious movements will turn out to have been enormous. Miraculous episodes in the history of thought, like fifth-century Athens, the Renaissance, or the Enlightenment, only occur when politics and religion let them happen. The fractured geography of Greece dictated that there be no strong central state; there was no organized clergy or church to regulate freedom of thought either. Most Greeks were free to think as they liked, and some of them did so, to remarkable effect. But under the pressures of military overambition and defeat, exaggerated fears, religious fundamentalism, and a constitution that granted the people unchecked power, the Athenians, proud inventors of democracy, halted scientific and philosophical progress by persecuting those whose ideas they judged to be dangerous, above all Socrates. Although his followers aptly punished them by making Athens into the greatest educational center of the ancient world, their intolerance still had disastrous consequences, because science and freethinking took 2,000 years to rediscover the paths to knowledge that the Greeks had first explored. By his death, Socrates signalled the moral of the story: legal limits to political and religious authority are vital to the intellectual progress of civilization.

References

Brickhouse, T. C. and Smith, N. D. (1989). *Socrates on Trial*. Oxford: Oxford University Press.

—— (2002). *The Trial and Execution of Socrates: Sources and Controversies*. New York and Oxford: Oxford University Press.

Burnyeat, M. (1997). The impiety of Socrates, *Ancient Philosophy*, 17, 1–12.

Dodds, E. R. (1951). *The Greeks and the Irrational*. Berkeley and Los Angeles: University of California Press.

Dover, K. J. (1976). The freedom of the intellectual in Greek society. *Talanta*, 7, 25–54; reprinted in *Collected Papers* (1988), vol. II, 135–58.

Furley, W. (1996). *Andokides and the Herms*. Bulletin of the Institute of Classical Studies Supplement 65. London: Institute of Classical Studies.

Huffman, C. A. (1993). *Philolaus of Croton*. Cambridge: Cambridge University Press.

Kopff, E. C. (1977). Was Socrates murdered? *Greek, Roman and Byzantine Studies*, 18, 113–22.

Kraut, R. (2000). Socrates, politics and religion. In Smith and Woodruff, pp. 12–23.

Janko, R. (1997). The physicist as hierophant: Aristophanes, Socrates and the authorship of the Derveni Papyrus. *Zeitschrift für Papyrologie und Epigraphik*, 118, 61–94.

—— (2001). The Derveni Papyrus (Diagoras of Melos, *Apopyrgizontes Logoi?*): a new translation. *Classical Philology*, 96, 1–32.

—— (2002). The Derveni Papyrus: an interim text. *Zeitschrift für Papyrologie und Epigraphik*, 141, 1–62.

—— (2003). God, science and Socrates. *Bulletin of the Institute of Classical Studies*, 46, 1–18.

Laks, A. (1997). Between religion and philosophy: the function of allegory in the Derveni Papyrus. *Phronesis*, 42, 121–43.

Laks, A. and Most, G. W. (eds.) (1997). *Studies on the Derveni Papyrus*. Oxford: Oxford University Press.

McPherran, M. L. (1996). *The Religion of Socrates*. University Park, PA: University of Pennsylvania Press.

—— (2000). Does Piety Pay?, in Smith and Woodruff, pp. 89–114.

Parker, R. (1996). Athenian religion: A history. In Smith and Woodruff, pp. 40–54, and in Brickhouse and Smith, pp. 145–61.

Smith, N. D. and Woodruff, P. (2000). *Reason and Religion in Socratic Philosophy*. Oxford: Oxford University Press.

Van Der Waerden, B. L. (1979). *Die Pythagoreer* [The Pythagoreans]. Zurich and Munich.

Vlastos, G. (2000). Socratic piety. In Smith and Woodruff, pp. 56–73.

Winiarczyk, M. (1981). *Diagorae Melii et Theodori Cyrenaei reliquiae* [The Remnants of Diagoras of Melos and Theodorus of Cyrene]. Leipzig: Teubner.

5

How Does Socrates' Divine Sign Communicate with Him?

A. A. LONG

One of the strangest features of Socrates' personality was his claim to frequently experience and instantly obey the warnings of a *daimonion* – a divine voice or sign – that came to him privately and unpredictably, when he was often about to perform some action. We can be certain that Socrates' claims to experience this divine visitation influenced his indictment for impiety or worshipping new, non-Athenian gods (Plato, *Euthyphro* 3b5; Xenophon, *Memorabilia* 1.1.2), and that it strongly contributed to the general sense of his being weird even among those who did not see him as a threat to religious tradition. In this chapter I want to ask what we should make of Socrates' daimonic experience and how it comports with his professed commitment to live a self-examined life – i.e. acting always and only on the basis of what he finds, on careful reflection, to be the best of reasons. Before discussing the divine sign or *daimonion*, I offer a few words of general orientation.

Socrates was raised in a polytheistic society whose religious practices were grounded in ritual, ceremony, and sacrifice. Divinities were believed, through their statues, to be visibly accessible by inhabiting the temples dedicated to them, and to deliver signs of their favor or disfavor through auspices, dreams, and oracles. Interpretation of such signs was the profession of priests and necromancers. Apollo's Delphic priestess was presumed to be directly inspired by the god and, as such, was quite exceptional. Ordinary persons, unlike Socrates, did not hear or expect to hear the voice of a divinity.

How did Socrates position himself in regard to traditional practices and beliefs? On the one hand, as we can see in Plato's dialogue *Euthyphro*, he was strongly opposed to an uncritical acceptance of mythology. Rather than take the gods to be a collection of erratic and competing superpowers, Socrates appears to have had a unitary (I don't mean monotheistic) conception of divinity as an always benevolent, truthful, authoritative, and wise agency.[1] In his conception of the divine, it never lies or cheats or acts for any purpose other than the best. How could Socrates be convinced of this conception, so radically different from that of his society in general? The answer seems to be – that he took divinity to operate according to the highest standards of rationality. If we, operating with our own intellects, could only figure out the right thing to do or to believe with compelling reasons, we would know what divinity itself approved.

On the other hand, Socrates was not so unremittingly rationalistic in his religious outlook as to reject traditional beliefs in divine communication through dreams and oracles. Plato represents him, at the beginning of the *Phaedo* (60e), as "making music" (composing poetry) in obedience to a type of dream he has often had, a dream he takes to have a divine origin; and in the *Apology* (21b) Socrates emphatically declares that his *reason* for going around Athens and interrogating people about their beliefs was to try to understand why the oracle to his friend Chaerephon had declared that no one was wiser than himself. The oracle puzzled Socrates, because he was convinced that he lacked authentic wisdom, but, rather than dismiss it, he supposed that the god could not lie, and therefore it was incumbent on him to uncover the oracle's obscure truth.

Perhaps Socrates treated reason and faith as independent sources of motivation, as many moderns do. Rather than endorse that presumption, which looks dangerously anachronistic in imputing to him a Christian, Judaic, or Islamic type of religious belief, we should start from the hypothesis that Socrates' rationality and religiosity were fully consistent with one another in his own eyes. Accordingly we would expect them to be completely implicated, the one with the other. That is to say, we would expect him to suppose that truths of reason are theologically sanctioned, and, equally, that theological sanctions are grounded in reason. The question I now come to, after these preliminaries, is what we should make of Socrates' divine sign and how we should interpret its way of communicating with him.

Over the last two decades Socrates' divine sign has attracted much scholarly attention. This is a welcome trend because few facts about the historical Socrates are better attested and more striking. Neither Plato nor Xenophon offers us much by way of psychological analysis of Socrates' daimonic visitations. These authors are consistent in describing the experience as the intermittent "voice" or "sign" from a god, and Plato sometimes has Socrates refer to it as "the customary divine sign" (*Euthydemus* 272e4; *Phaedrus* 242b9). His fullest account of it (*Apology* 31c–d) occurs in the context of Socrates' explaining to the jurors at his trial why he has lived a strictly private life:

> The reason for this is something you have heard me frequently mention in different places – namely, the fact that I experience something divine and daimonic, as Meletus has inscribed in his indictment, by way of mockery. It started in my childhood, the occurrence of a particular voice. Whenever it occurs, it always deters me from the course of action I was *intending* to engage in, but it never gives me positive advice. It is this that has opposed my practicing politics, and I think its doing so has been absolutely fine.

Socrates then gives his jurors an explicit justification for the correctness of the sign's warning him not to pursue a political life. The order of events is as follows: (1) Socrates thought he should enter politics; (2) the sign told him not to do so; (3) he obeyed the sign by refraining from politics; (4) retrospectively he figured out why the sign's prohibition was correct.

Typically, Plato has Socrates say that the opposition of the *daimonion* occurs immediately *after* he had formed an intention to do the opposite of what the divine voice subsequently prohibits. The implication is that Socrates is told not to do what he previously thought he had good reason to do. Note the emphasis on his checked intention in Plato, at *Phaedrus* 242b9 and *Euthydemus* 272e1. Note also, very importantly, that he takes the absence of the sign as giving him a positive endorsement of what he is doing (*Apology* 40a4).

According to Xenophon (*Memorabilia* 1.1.4), the divine sign gave Socrates explicitly positive as well as negative injunctions, and did so not only for himself but also for his friends. I shall say nothing about this difference from Plato's reports (setting aside the probably inauthentic *Theages* 128d1, according to which the sign gave Socrates admonitions concerning friends).[2]

Socrates, of course, was not unique in hearing prohibitive or prescriptive voices that impact the mind without the mediation of uttered speech. St. Paul and St. Joan are two powerful figures who also laid claim to have had such paranormal visitations. There must be a large psychological literature on such experiences. I have not made use of it, but I shall assume that in the saintly and Socratic instances we are not dealing with shamming, derangement, or simple self-deception. We should credit Socrates and the others with experiences that were not dream-like but palpable, vivid, and endowed with sufficient semantic content to be understood, or at least representable to consciousness, in ordinary language.

* * * *

Modern scholars differ in their assessments of Socrates' sign experience and its bearing or nonbearing on his professed devotion to rational inquiry. Before I outline this controversy, I need to make some clarifications. We can study Socrates' sign experience from three perspectives. First, by pursuing the clues that Plato and Xenophon offer us, we can ask, in a purely psychological and nonhistorical way, what kind of experience Socrates attributed to the divine sign's mediation, and how this experience impacted his consciousness. In other words, we can ask what was going on in Socrates' head, or what he experienced as going on in his head, when he described himself as hearing the daimonic voice. After all, Socrates was subject to the divine sign, or to what he described as such, irrespective of his own or Plato's understanding of how it impacted his mind.

Secondly, we can ask whether or how Socrates' reports of this experience and his responses to it cohere with the philosophical and theological commitments that, according to Plato, guided his life. Such commitments would include (1) his trust in the truth of the Delphic oracle, which initiated his testing the wisdom of his interlocutors; (2) his respect for dreams and other forms of divination; and (3) his practice of investigating the ethical beliefs of himself and other persons, motivated both by his own profession of ignorance concerning the exact truth pertaining to such things as justice and his conviction that it is better to be confuted of ignorance about such things than to think one knows them when one does not: i.e. Socrates' practice of elenctic argument by question and answer.

Thirdly, we can pursue a strictly historical inquiry into the cultural context pertaining to Socrates' daimonic experience; by which I mean both what Plato the author presumes that his readers will bring to the text in terms of their own theological and psychological outlook and also what other ancient thinkers like Plutarch made of that text. We today probably suppose that someone who claims to hear a divine voice is simply insane or seriously deluded. Yet, none of Socrates' contemporaries or later interpreters, apparently, took him to be mad, though they found him quite peculiar in this respect as in many other respects. Under this perspective, we can ask whether readers in antiquity supposed Socrates to be literally "out of his mind" when he claimed to have these experiences, or, rather, to be *in* his mind but not in it in a way that would be intersubjectively accessible to ordinary people.

In the next part of the chapter, I will focus on the second perspective – the coherence of Socrates' sign experience with his professed philosophical methodology – since it is this issue that has most concerned modern scholars. I shall then proceed to the first and third perspectives – Socrates' psychological and subjective experience and the cultural context – drawing on Plutarch's essay *On Socrates' Divine Sign*. At the end I shall try to bring all three of these perspectives together. The value of distinguishing them should become clearer as I outline the main points that have been debated between modern scholars.

According to Vlastos (1991), Socrates must have regarded the divine sign, just like dreams, as communicating to him, unlike elenctic argument by question and answer, through "extra-rational channels" (167). Vlastos supports his claim by citing *Apology* 33c. There Socrates says: "The practice of interrogating those who think they are wise, but actually are not, has been commanded to me, as I maintain, by the god through divinations and through dreams and every other means through which divine apportionment has ever commanded anyone to do anything." With this passage, which has as its context Socrates' response to the Delphic oracle, as reported to him by Chaerephon, Vlastos juxtaposes the following passage, spoken by Socrates to Crito (46b): "Not now for the first time, but always, I am the sort of man who is persuaded by nothing in me except the argument (*logos*) which appears to be the best when I reason about it."

Vlastos then asks whether we can make sense of the fact that, apparently, Socrates finds these two commitments – to follow argument wherever it may lead and to obey divine commands conveyed to him through extrarational channels – in perfect harmony. He responds that there is no conflict. In particular, we should not suppose that Socrates took the intimations of his *daimonion* to give him "a source of moral knowledge apart from reason and superior to it, yielding the certainty which is conspicuously lacking in the findings of his elenctic searches" (ibid.). Taking Socrates to view his sign experience in the way he assesses other instances of divination, where the diviner is "out of his mind," Vlastos (170–1) rejects the idea that Socrates took himself to have "two distinct systems of justified belief." There is no need to think that Socrates' commitments to obey the sign and to engage in the elenchus were in conflict, "because only by the use of his own critical reason can Socrates determine the true meaning of any of these signs." Thus, for Vlastos, it is exclusively the *Crito* passage that tells us how Socrates' conceived of reason – namely, that which can be submitted to *the strictly fallible procedure* of elenctic testing; much less, then, can Socrates have regarded the mere occurrences of the *daimonion* as rational and reliable sources of moral knowledge. All that he can get from the *daimonion* is "subjective reassurance," supplementary to but never capable of challenging his own reasoning (Vlastos, in Smith and Woodruff 2000: 191).

Mark McPherran (1996) follows Vlastos in characterizing the sign as an "extra-rational" phenomenon (189), and he goes part way towards Vlastos in proposing that, whenever possible, Socrates subjects the sign to "rational confirmation" (187). The sign, according to McPherran, does not provide Socrates with "expert" moral knowledge, but, contra Vlastos, we should view it as an "extra-rational" source "for the construction of particular moral knowledge claims that are themselves rationally grounded, if not wholly rational in origin" (191).[3] Unlike Vlastos, McPherran credits the sign with "sufficient epistemic significance to challenge the 'exclusive authority of secular reason'" (194). Not unfairly, he says that for Vlastos the sign is taken to be no more than a "hunch" (191).

My own sympathies are largely with McPherran. In particular, I agree with his writing (195) that Vlastos was not warranted in assimilating the status Socrates ascribes to his sign consciousness to the "out of the mind" condition he accords to dreams and other prophecies. Moreover, by calling the sign's effects on Socrates "reassurance," Vlastos reverses the order of events because the sign, when it occurs, does not reassure Socrates' about any of his prior beliefs but abruptly checks his prior intentions. What the divine sign gives to Socrates is not the kind of generalized true belief about moral concepts that Socrates sought by reasoning with his interlocutors, but intuitive certainty concerning the nonrectitude of a quite particular action he was contemplating. This intuitive certainty is something quite different from the full-blooded moral knowledge that Socrates consistently disclaimed having. Hence I don't think Vlastos need have worried about the sign's conflicting with Socrates' practice of the elenchus.

Even McPherran, however, concedes much too much to Vlastos in supposing that the sign should be called an "extra-rational" phenomenon. If, of course, we take the extrarational to include anything that has an allegedly divine source, or anything that is not established by discursive reasoning, that description would be correct. However, its correctness seems to me to be highly questionable, for at least two considerations, one historical and the other philosophical. The historical consideration – on which more later – is that the mature Plato believed, and very likely Socrates believed, that the divine voice is quintessentially rational and that human rationality is itself a divine gift. Indeed Xenophon has Socrates, in answer to a question about the *daimonion*, say that "the human soul partakes of divinity" (*Memorabilia* 4.3.14). The philosophical objection – on which also more later – is that the divine sign or voice appears to deliver messages with semantic, if not fully propositional, content. Indeed Vlastos accepts that the sign tells Socrates not to do this or that in Greek words he can understand (Smith and Woodruff 2000: 185).

You don't have to be a Wittgensteinian to regard semantic content or linguistic consciousness as the essence of rationality as such. Plato does not represent Socrates as taking the voice of the *daimonion* to be analogous to a mere hunch or feeling; rather, what it delivers to him is something of the form "Don't do what you had thought of doing," or, as Brickhouse and Smith say (1994: 195), "Stop here and now," or perhaps better than either of these formulations – to do justice to the fact that Socrates sometimes associates the sign with prophecy – we should hypothesize its form as that of a conditional: "If you do what you are minded on doing, you will not act rightly, or, you will fail to fare well." If Socrates was as committed to rationality as Vlastos proposes, it becomes very hard to see how he could honor this commitment unless he regarded the voice of the *daimonion*, which he always instantly obeys, as rationally sourced and grounded.

We may worry, as Vlastos does, if such an imperative or conditional is not accompanied by any formulated explanations; and we should distinguish (as Brickhouse and

Smith [1994: 194–5] carefully do) between Socrates' own ratiocinations and the peremptory voice of the *daimonion*. But it seems arbitrary to regard its prohibitions as simply falling within the domain of the extrarational, especially since Socrates has no difficulty, in many cases, in providing them with explicit reasons. I sympathize with Brickhouse and Smith, who say (1994: 193) "we must not simply assume that Socrates would consider the monitions of his *daimonion* as non-rational signs," and I equally sympathize with their allowing such monitions to count as giving him a reason to be persuaded of something.[4]

Thus far, then, I take myself to have confirmed my initial proposal that Socrates took his rationality and religiosity to be fully consistent with one another. What the perspective of Vlastos and his critics leaves quite undetermined, however, is the psychological nature of Socrates' divine sign experience and the channels of communication by which the divine voice reaches him. For suggestions about these matters I turn to the Platonist Plutarch, writing some 450 years later than Plato and Xenophon.

* * * *

In his work *On Socrates' Divine Sign*, Plutarch offers accounts of Socrates' experience that run the gamut from reductive rationalization to other-worldly revelation.[5] We are not obliged to find anything that Plutarch says authoritative since he was in no better position than we are to make sense of the divine sign. Nonetheless, Plutarch's essay is not only of great interest both historically and conceptually. It also anticipates the modern debate I have summarized concerning the question of whether Socrates' rationality and interrogative (or elenctic) practice are compatible with his according an independent authority to the divine sign.

Plutarch's essay is a long and complex work. Though much discussed from literary perspectives, its suggestions about Socrates' *daimonion* have been surprisingly neglected, especially by historians of philosophy.[6] Socrates' divine sign provides Plutarch with his essay's title, but this theme is actually ancillary to the work as a whole. Composed largely as a dialogue between numerous persons, including the Simmias of Plato's *Phaedo*, its main frame is a report at Athens of a Theban conspiracy that liberated the city from Spartan rule in 379 BCE. Soon after we first encounter the conspirators, they start to discuss mysterious findings at the excavation of a tomb. They then learn that an Italian Pythagorean is about to arrive, on a mission inspired by dreams and apparitions, to collect the remains of a certain Lysis from that person's tomb, "unless forbidden by some *daimonion* in the night" (579F).

On hearing this, one of the company, called Galaxidorus, protests about the prevalence of superstition and more especially about the tendency for prominent persons to give a bogus veneer of sanctity to what are, in reality, *their quite ordinary thoughts*. Authentic philosophy, he says, relies exclusively on reason for its ethical teaching. Witness Socrates' devotion to unadorned truth (580A–B).

To the objection that he is supporting Meletus' indictment against Socrates, Galaxidorus responds by saying that Socrates was no atheist. But, unlike the ravings of Pythagoras and Empedocles, he relied entirely on "sober reasoning." This rationalistic retort provokes his interlocutor to ask about Socrates' divine sign, which he claims to have observed giving a salutary warning to Socrates when he was engaged in discussion with Euthyphro (580C).

Galaxidorus responds scornfully (580F): "Do you really think that Socrates' *daimonion* had some special and extraordinary power?" He proposes that the sign, though quite trivial in itself, enabled Socrates to act in the context of matters too obscure for reason to decide, just as a sneeze or chance remark, in the case of a strong-minded person, may turn the balance of two equally strong opposing reasons.[7] On this account, Socrates' sign was no more than a hunch, supplementing his normal ratiocinations when he had to deal with matters intractable to them. We may call Galaxidorus a proto-Vlastos interpreter, inasmuch as he clearly takes the sign to be an extrarational phenomenon, though not necessarily a supernatural occurrence.

Not surprisingly, this highly reductive account of the sign is challenged, on the ground that it puts Socrates in the same position as ordinary people who, however, only resort to chance events when deciding between trivial alternatives (581F). Galaxidorus defends his claim, but he concedes the need to say why Socrates gave the sign such an exalted name. The basic point about the sign, he says, is not that Socrates was wrong to call it *daimonion* (rather than a sneeze), but that it was merely an instrument used by the sign-giver (582C). Galaxidorus now, apparently, accepts or concedes the sign's divine origin, but sticks to his claim that it presented itself as a mere hunch and not as a thought with semantic content. We may infer that he would have agreed with Vlastos that the sign demands from Socrates his own interpretation of its full meaning and truth value.

Galaxidorus does not leave matters there. He is ready to listen to Simmias, who is better informed about what people at Athens have said about Socrates' sign. After many pages, during which discussion returns to the conspiracy, Simmias gives his account (chapter 20) – not as a direct response to Galaxidorus, but as a report of a much earlier discussion concerning the sign that he had had with others, who purport to have included Socrates' immediate circle (588C–D).

* * * *

I will now summarize Simmias' account, point by point, and interpose my own comments.

1. Socrates, though he was asked to do so, offered no answer as to the essential nature of the sign: i.e. he was not known to have defined it (588B–C). But, in light of his regular dismissal of people's claims to have had visual encounters with the divine and his strong interest in those who claimed to hear a (special) voice, Simmias and his friends tentatively concluded as follows: Socrates' *daimonion* was not a vision, but the perception of a voice or the intuition (*noēsis*) of a discourse (*logos*) that made contact with him (*synaptomenos*) in a strange way (588C–D). The Greek words I have highlighted, or related forms of them, will be repeated throughout Simmias' account. There are three terms in Simmias' analysis: *logos*, which is the sign itself (or voice), its contact or conversation with Socrates, and his apprehension or intuition of its content or signification.

2. Next, Simmias explains the strangeness of the sign's communication with Socrates, on the presumption that he did not literally *hear* a divine voice. When dreaming, people may imagine they are hearing because they get semblances (*doxai*) and intuitions (*noeseis*) of certain discourses – i.e. without hearing actual utterances, dreamers get the sense of statements included in their dream experience. Ordinary people are too

distracted and emotional, when awake, to focus their minds on the significations (*dēloumenois*) that may be communicated to them "from superior powers," as they may be able to do during sleep. "But Socrates, thanks to his having a *nous* that was pure (*katharos*) and free from passion (*apathēs*), and to his minimalist involvement with his bodily needs, was easy to contact (*euaphēs*) and sufficiently sensitive (*leptos*) to respond immediately to what he experienced" (588D–E). Simmias conjectures that what Socrates experienced was a voiceless daimon's reason (*logos*) that made contact with his noetic faculty "just by its signification" (*dēloumenon*).[8]

I shall not pursue questions about Plutarch's sources for this account.[9] What I find chiefly interesting about it is its attempt to give a plausibly naturalistic inter-pretation to Socrates' sign experience, while also acknowledging its divine source. No doubt we want to interpolate the qualification, "what Socrates and Simmias take to be its divine source," and no doubt we also want to question the prèsumption concerning communicative superior powers. But neither Vlastos nor Galaxidorus ques-tions Socrates' good faith in such beliefs; and it would not be useful for us to do so. Socrates was notorious for his ascetic lifestyle, and we had better accept the fact that he, like other ascetics, was subject to certain paranormal experiences. It is quite reasonable for Simmias to credit Socrates with an exceptionally sensitive mentality and to look to it as an explanatory factor of his allegedly divine visitations. At the same time, Simmias does a good job in demystifying the psychological features of Socrates' experience. It had something in common with the way we get and apprehend voice-less statements in dreams, but with the difference that Socrates' sign could reach him when he was fully awake.

Simmias wisely refrains from speculating about what kind of semantic content the sign communicated to Socrates. He was no less wise, in my opinion, to refrain from asking how we should reconcile Socrates' obedience to the intermittent sign with his elenctic practice and disavowals of certain knowledge. It is better, in my opinion, to bracket those questions. Instead, we might do well to follow Galaxidorus in supposing that the sign manifested itself to Socrates in moments when he found himself seriously divided over the right course of action to follow (having second thoughts, as it were) or found himself checked in executing an intention, whether it was something as weighty as the question of entering political life or as marginal as that of crossing the Ilissus river (*Phaedrus* 242b9). (I do not understand why Vlastos was so insistent that Socrates' obedience to his sign messages must be subordinated to his elenctic attempts to establish the definitions of moral concepts; for he never appeals to the former in his practice of the latter.)

Simmias' story is helpful because it rejects the notion that the sign was a mere hunch. He credits it with semantic content, unlike Galaxidorus. Yet, far from seeing it as an extrarational source of information, he views it, as I would be inclined to do, as a fully intelligible and intelligent message, impinging directly on Socrates' intellect. We again will be inclined to say that the messenger must have been Socrates' subcon-scious or something purely internal to himself. Socrates, on the other hand, like the saints I have mentioned, presumably took its deliverances to have an authority and source that distinguished them from his ordinary states of consciousness.

Thus far I have outlined only the preamble of Simmias' account. I can deal more briefly with its sequel because it partly repeats the points already made. The fresh points that he makes are mainly of interest in underlining the rationality of the sign and the rationality of the mind receiving it.

3. In ordinary conversation, Simmias tells us, we are *constrained* to listen to the *logos* that we receive through our ears (588E). In the case of an exceptional individual, like Socrates, communication from the divine source occurs without constraint. Such a recipient's intellect is not impacted by vocalized sounds but simply "touched" by the thought that is being transmitted. Undisturbed by passion, the exceptional soul allows itself to be freely "relaxed or tensed" by the superior intellect's intervention.

Simmias offers homely physical analogies for the way a slight force can modify the motion of a large body. He then (or rather, Plutarch) draws on the famous model of the soul presented in Book I of Plato's *Laws* (644d–645b). There Plato invites us to model the soul on a puppet to which numerous strings are attached. The strings stand for our motivations (*pathē*), which tend to conflict with one another. One of these strings, and only one, is golden – the string of reasoning (*logismos*), adherence to which is equivalent to being guided by law. Because this string is gentle and not constraining, its guidance requires assistance, to prevent the other strings from dominating. That assistance, Plato seems to propose, must be something the whole self contributes if it has the appropriate structure; in which case we achieve self-mastery, the notion the puppet model is introduced to explicate.

Plutarch's direct or indirect dependence on this passage from the *Laws* is patent. He echoes Plato's terminology in his use of such words as *spaō*, *helkō*, and *neura*, and he has Simmias characterize the human soul as something strung with numerous cords, making it the most sensitive of instruments "if one contacts it according to reason (*logos*)" (588F), when, by getting a slight impulse (*rhopē*), the soul moves towards the intuited object (*noethen*). He echoes Plato's statement that the mind is the starting-point of passions and motivations (i.e. the lyre-like cords). But, instead of specifying Plato's golden cord of reasoning and its proper guidance of the soul, Simmias focuses on the soul cords' ability, as he has described them, to transmit motion to the entire embodied person.

Why does he do this? The answer, as we read on, is to consolidate his earlier claim concerning the human intellect's capacity to be readily contacted by what he calls "a superior intellect," without the mediation of spoken words. If an ordinary thought, without being voiced, can move our bodily mass, we should suppose, *a fortiori*, that the unvoiced thoughts and *logos* of divine beings can make direct contact with a person's soul and *logos*. With echoes of Aristotle's active intellect, Plutarch's Simmias likens this process to light generating a reflection (589B). Rather than regarding the divine beings' communications as too obscure to be accepted without interpretation, he treats them as being actually more luminous than thoughts expressed through nouns and verbs.[10]

As to the physics of divine communication, Simmias suggests that it is not essentially different from the way ordinary verbal sounds are transmitted (589C). In both cases air is the medium of transmission. The difference is that, in human intercommunication, the air has to be changed into language in order to convey thought to the listener. For divine beings and the recipients of their messages, the air is immediately charged with daimonic thoughts, and these convey their meaning directly.

Obviously, Simmias' account is replete with fantasy at this point. What is striking, nonetheless, is his effort to give a quasi-naturalistic interpretation to Socrates' sign experience. While acknowledging Socrates' exceptional mentality, he grounds his account in the general thesis that thoughts with semantic content can occur to people, not only without the mediation of spoken language but even without the mediation of sentence structure. The first claim is trivially true, whereas the second must be at least highly controversial. Still, unless we are in very logical positivistic moods, we surely want our psychology to accommodate mental states that we call inspiration or flashes of insight and intuition – meaningful thoughts that seem to come out of nowhere and are unlike our ordinary ways of formulating sentences in our heads and yet carry complete authority.

Perhaps Socrates' sign experience was like that. In any case, whatever we make of Simmias' account, it is salutary in its resistance to assessing Socrates' experience as something extrarational. He ends, very intriguingly, with an anecdote, supposedly illustrating the internal harmony that enabled Socrates to receive daimonic messages when he was awake. The story went that Socrates' father was told by an oracle to let the boy do "whatever came into his mind and not to constrain or divert his motivations but let them be," and simply pray to Zeus of the Agora and the Muses (589E). Simmias takes this anecdote to imply that Socrates "had a better guide for life within himself than countless teachers." Presumably the relevance of the oracle story to the prohibitive content of the *daimonion*'s Platonic messages is to be found in the statement that Socrates' father should refrain from diverting his son's motivations: if Socrates needs to rethink any of his intentions, he will do so for himself thanks to the *daimonion*.

Simmias' interpretation of the story may seem curious in light of his earlier account of the superior power's externality (*thurathen*, 589B). But in a certain sense, of course, Socrates was following himself in being obedient to his *daimonion*. The voice or sign that he claimed to experience was internal to him; what was external was its source, or was it?

Galaxidorus and Simmias assume so, as Socrates himself appears to have done. However, Plutarch's essay has a third suggestion to report – an oracular revelation to one Timarchus, who had sought to learn about the nature of Socrates' sign by incubating in a temple (590A–592E). Partly modeled on the myth with which Plato concludes the *Phaedo*, this passage also draws on the tripartite psychology Plato sets out at *Timaeus* 30a–d, where the rational faculty is called a *daimon*. By applying that conception to the elucidation of Socrates' sign, Plutarch implies that what Socrates obeyed, in adhering to his *daimonion*, was not a message from a quite independently existing divinity but his own *nous*. Socrates, we are to understand, thanks to his adherence to the rule of reason, has set his life under the direction of this *daimon*, which (inhabiting a bright star!) constitutes his suprasensible self.

Plutarch represents this account, which is packed with other-worldly motifs, as a myth, and seems to give his own credence to the more naturalistic explanation of Simmias (593A). I make just two comments on the mythical account. First, it shows that one ancient line of interpretation sought to bring Socrates' sign experience into line with Plato's mature psychology and eschatology. Though we would hardly follow suit, this approach should alert us to the fact that Socrates' culture, like that of the later Plutarch, invoked divinity much more readily than our Judeo-Christian outlook does in describing human beings and their attributes – witness the use of *daimonios* as a polite term of address.

Hence my second point. While the ancients certainly took Socrates' divine sign to be something remarkable, Socrates *was* remarkable and knew himself to be so; and what was remarkable, in Greek culture, typically fell within the divine domain. In order for us moderns to avoid both skepticism and credulity about his sign experience, we would do well to recognize that his accrediting it to a divinity need not imply that he himself regarded it as a supernatural or extrarational visitation with all the connotations we moderns naturally attach to such a claim.

* * * *

Finally, I should like to return to Vlastos and his insistence on minimizing the cognitive content and significance of the *daimonion*. My main point has been that, irrespective of history and cultural context, Vlastos imputes to Socrates an unduly restrictive understanding of what it means to act on the basis of a compelling reason. Plato gives us to suppose that the mere occurrence of the divine voice was a sufficient reason for Socrates to stop dead in his intended tracks. Can we make sense of that? I think we can, especially if we take note of the fact that Plato has placed the most striking references to the *daimonion* in the *Apology* – both its stopping Socrates from entering politics and its not opposing his defense speech.[11]

The Socrates of Plato's *Apology* is on trial for his life. He has experienced the *daimonion* ever since childhood. When it first occurred, presumably, it puzzled him, and he must have reflected a good deal on the occasions when it issued its admonitory voice. We can presume that he frequently asked himself why it visited him and inhibited his intentions on particular occasions, and what it was about those intentions that needed admonition. Gradually, through experience and questioning, he became convinced that its warnings were always completely on target. The certitude that he vested in the *daimonion* would thus be inductively warranted, like what we might call instant obedience to one's conscience or moral inhibition. It was not, like God commanding Abraham to sacrifice Isaac (Vlastos' example, Smith and Woodruff 2000: 197), a voice that came once out of the blue, but, as Plato says, a *customary* voice in which Socrates had learned through experience to place complete authority and truth, and thus to comport with his own conception of divinity. It did not provide him with reasons that could be formulated in terms of universalizable truths or categorical imperatives, binding on other persons. Rather, its *reliability for him* was what made it rational. It addressed Socrates in his own existential identity, giving him and only him, simply by its occurrence, both sufficiently certain intuition to refrain from what he had been minded to do and stimulus to figure out, as he often does, the rational grounds for its admonitions.

Notes

1   See Xenophon, *Memorabilia* 4.3.10–14; Plato, *Republic* 2.382e6.
2   For further texts that refer to Socrates' divine sign, see Plato, *Theaetetus* 151a3; *Republic* 6.496c4; *Alcibiades* 1.103a; and Xenophon, *Memorabilia* 1.11, 4.8,6; *Symposium* 8.5; *Apology* 4.4 and 13.6.

3 McPherran (1996: 188) refers to *Apology* 33c7–8, where Socrates says that his mission to engage in elenctic testing has been warranted "by the god and from prophecies and dreams and in every way by which a divine dispensation to do anything has been appointed to a human being to do," and adds that such commands are both "true and well-grounded (*euelencta*)." It may seem as if the divine sign must be included among such commands, but we should note that Socrates' statement explicitly refers to positive commands and not to any negative injunctions, which are the only province of the divine sign's work in Plato.

4 Space prevents me from giving more than a brief summary of the issues debated between Vlastos, McPherran, and Smith and Brickhouse. Smith and Woodruff (2000) includes the fascinating correspondence these scholars engaged in concerning Socrates and his *daimonion*.

5 The best text of this work is the Loeb edition of Einarson and De Lacy (1959).

6 Among the works I have consulted on *On the Divine Sign*, the most useful are Corlu (1970) and Babut (1988).

7 Plutarch was probably influenced by Xenophon, who says (*Memorabilia* 1.1.9) that Socrates recommended *learning* what is *accessible* to us, and seeking to discover what is not "clear" to humans through divination.

8 Cicero, *On Divination* 1.121, already makes the point about Socrates' purity of soul enabling him to experience his *daimonion* when awake. Whether via Plutarch, or some other source, Calcidius repeats the entire gist of Simmias' account in his *Timaeus* commentary; see Einarson and DeLacy (1959: 451n.).

9 For assessment of the conflicting proposals scholars have canvassed, see Corlu (1970: 57–9).

10 I am grateful to Michael White (who commented on my paper at a conference in the University of Arizona) for observing that Pietro Pomponazzi (late fifteenth/early sixteenth century) interpreted Aristotle's "active intellect" as an understanding in which "neither discursive thought nor composition nor any other sort of motion is lodged." On that view, with which, of course Plotinus would sympathize, it is not discursive or propositional information that represents the norm with respect to rationality.

11 I am grateful for discussion with Michael Morgan concerning the importance of Socrates' references to the *daimonion* in the context of the *Apology*.

References

Babut, D. (1988). Le part du rationalisme dans la religion de Plutarque: l'exemple du *De genio Socratis*. *Illinois Classical Studies*, 13(2), 383–408.

Brickhouse, T. C. and Smith, N. D. (1994). *Plato's Socrates*. Oxford: Oxford University Press.

Einarson, B. and De Lacy, P. (eds.) (1959). *Plutarch's Moralia VII*. Cambridge: Cambridge University Press.

McPherran, M. (1996). *The Religion of Socrates*. University Park, PA: University of Pennsylvania Press.

Plutarch (1970). *Le démon de Socrate* [The daemon of Socrates], trans. A. Corlu. Paris: Klincksieck.

Smith, N. and Woodruff, P. (eds.) (2000). *Reason and Religion in Socratic Philosophy*. Oxford: Oxford University Press.

Vlastos, G. (1991). *Socrates: Ironist and Moral Philosopher*. Cambridge: Cambridge University Press.

6

Socrates, Antisthenes, and the Cynics

SUSAN PRINCE

Socrates had many disciples other than Plato: this we know well. But when it comes to deriving useful insight from this fact, we are quick to declare impasse. We routinely translate the question of the real Socrates to the issue of surviving contemporary sources about Socrates and identify the complete literary texts of Aristophanes, Xenophon, and Aristotle as our possible avenues of access to an aplatonic Socrates. Aristophanes is dismissed as a comic parody, Xenophon is dismissed as banal and conventional, Aristotle is placed within the Academic tradition, and we turn back to Plato's dialogues as our only source of insight into why Socrates mattered and what made him the first moral philosopher. Since the work of Gregory Vlastos, we have further isolated some early Platonic dialogues as "Socratic" and have used them as our only good evidence for Socrates' work (but see Kahn 1996 and Vander Waerdt 1994).

In this chapter I will make a case for looking harder at the tradition of ancient Cynicism, and especially its forefather Antisthenes, for insight into Socratic moral philosophy in its original historical setting. Of the many Athenians who, we are told, associated with Socrates, a handful also wrote literature that attempted to portray Socrates in his activity of philosophy: the second book of Diogenes Laertius' *Lives of Eminent Philosophers* is in large measure a list of the authors of "Socratic dialogues" (*Sokratikoi logoi*) and their works. Although some of the titles are surely inventions of a Hellenistic tradition that tried to supply detail to the murky legends of some of the Socratics (such as Simmias and Cebes the two Thebans who discuss the nature of the soul in Plato's *Phaedo* 2.124–5), and some of the men named there might themselves be fictions (Simon the Shoemaker, 2.122, being the favorite object of this suspicion), we find named no fewer than 12 pupils of Socrates who wrote dialogues about him, often in rivalry with each other: Xenophon, Aeschines, Aristippus of Cyrene, Theodorus, Phaedo of Elis, Eucleides and Stilpo of Megara, Crito, Simon, Glaucon, Simmias, and Cebes. In addition to these, Plato and Antisthenes are treated elsewhere in Diogenes' book, since they founded continuing traditions of philosophical schools according to Diogenes' scheme. Of the fragmentary Socratics, whose remains have recently been made accessible in the four-volume edition of Gabriele Giannantoni, *Socratis et Socraticorum Reliquiae*[1] (hereafter *SSR*), both Aeschines and Aristippus left substantial material of philosophical interest. Both were seen as serious intellectuals in fourth-century Athens, and both have received some modern scholarly attention (see

Kahn and McKirahan in Vander Waerdt 1994). For Aeschines we have substantial fragments of dialogues in which we know Socrates was a character. But in the case of Antisthenes, we have both the best evidence overall and the most reason to believe that his thought was important.

We know that Antisthenes, like Plato, continued to develop in his thought after the death of Socrates, so that we cannot simply attribute any views of Antisthenes to the historical Socrates. But it is likely that Antisthenes, being older and probably closer personally to Socrates than was Plato, as well as probably quicker to "publish" after Socrates' execution and sooner to die, was a more conservative disciple. (These reasons are not to be confused with those standard in the eighteenth century for considering Xenophon to be our best witness to Socrates: Antisthenes was no uncritical reporter.) Just as we now debate what is Socratic in Plato, so we should also debate what is Socratic in Antisthenes. But at this stage in our progress on Antisthenes, his thought contributes to our picture in two main ways. Regarding language, definitions, know-ledge, and ontology (and thus, philosophy), it lets us complicate the history from Socrates to Plato to Aristotle which we presently reconstruct from Aristotle's state-ment at *Metaphysics* 987a29–b13, together with our readings of the Platonic and Aristotelian corpus (and sometimes, Xenophon, *Memorabilia* 4.6): Antisthenes accepted Socrates' position that definition was the core of language, and, potentially, of know-ledge; finding that definition of the ontologically required kind was impossible, he claimed that contradiction was also impossible, and that knowledge was related to language in only indirect and nontransparent ways. Regarding ethics, Antisthenes' work gives particular form to the ways Socratic ethics remained embedded in behavior and way of life, as well as in politics, use of language in community, and interpretation of nonphilosophical literature, especially Homer. What we can retrieve of Antisthenes' ethics in the abstract remains surprisingly untheorized (by contrast with, for example, the system of good and indifferent values traced by Long [1988: 164–71] to the Socrates inherited by the early Stoics), though we get clear intimations of a Socratic virtue ethics, in which all virtues are identical, almost, to knowledge. Although wisdom is the ultimate good for Antisthenes, his minimalist views on logic probably rule out *a priori* any theoretical discourse about wisdom or virtue.

From Antisthenes to the Cynics

Antisthenes of Athens (c. 445–365 BCE: see *SSR* vol. 4: 195–201), probably born of an Athenian father and a foreign mother, was about 25 years younger than Socrates, and thus one of his senior disciples (Plato and Xenophon, for example, were about 45 years younger than Socrates). Xenophon in the *Symposium* (esp. 4.57–64 and 8.4–6 = VA 13, 14) and *Memorabilia* (3.11.17 = VA 14) portrays Antisthenes as one of Socrates' most intimate companions and suggests that Socrates hands over uniquely to him his most valuable craft, helping to promote advantageous relationships within the city (*Symposium* 4.61). Though possibly born without citizenship after Pericles' restrictive law of 451/450, Antisthenes seems to have fought for Athens in battle in 424/3 BCE and may have gained citizenship at that time. He practiced a life of poverty, according to a speech he delivers in Xenophon's *Symposium* (4.34–45 = VA 82), although Xenophon's setting gives no indication that he is socially inferior to the other banqueters, and there are signs in that work and elsewhere that he associated with the wealthy figures in the circle of the sophist Gorgias.

Aristotle took interest in Antisthenes for his paradoxical views on language and logic: most famously, "It is impossible to contradict" (*Metaphysics* 1024b; *Topics* 104b = VA 152, 153), but also "It is impossible to define the essence" (*Metaphysics* 1043b = VA 150); and his most prominent legacy to later antiquity was his counterintuitive enunciation about the nature of virtue, which was sufficient for happiness, together with its relation to pleasure: "I would rather go mad than have pleasure" (Diogenes Laertius, *Lives of Eminent Philosophers* 6.3; twice in Sextus, and elsewhere = VA 122). Antisthenes' famous paradoxes are clearly extreme responses to Socratic questions, the pursuit of definition on the one hand and the claims about true happiness on the other. Although these extreme utterances have often led scholars to judge Antisthenes' thought as a reduction of Socrates' thought to a couple of its aspects, exaggerated out of proportion to the whole (see McKirahan's references in Vander Waerdt 1994), in other fragments Antisthenes addresses the same issues in ways incompatible with simple readings of the paradoxes (VA 149–59 on language, VA 111–15, 123–32 on pleasure). We see from the full set of evidence that Antisthenes probably did not believe in these paradoxes literally as stated, but delivered them to command attention for his real points, the futility of logical discourse and the counterintuitive path to happiness. More subtle Socratic features pop up throughout the surviving fragments of his once extensive written texts (some 63 titles in 10 volumes, according to Diogenes Laertius, *Lives of Eminent Philosophers* 6.15–18 = VA 41), even in the works on Homer's poems and Homeric characters that have been frequently divorced by scholars from his Socratic calling.

The Cynics, then, seem to have accepted the ideas behind Antisthenes' paradoxes – and perhaps his groundings for them – and applied them in practice as they lived out their "philosophy" of demonstrating virtue, rejecting the alternative claims of dominant culture, and calling others to do the same. Diogenes of Sinope (c. 412/403 to c. 324/321: see *SSR* vol. 4: 476) was for later writers (beginning already with Teles in the late third century BCE) the model Cynic, and in behavioral terms he was surely the original Cynic. The name "Cynic" itself, which is probably an adjective from the Greek word for "dog," was probably first applied to Diogenes (first attested in Aristotle, *Rhetoric* 1411a24–5 = VB184), although it is not impossible that "dog" was already a nickname for Antisthenes (Diogenes Laertius, *Lives of Eminent Philosophers* 6.13; see Goulet-Cazé in Branham and Goulet-Cazé 1996). An alternative ancient etymology derives "Cynic" from an Athenian gymnasium, the Cynosarges, where Antisthenes allegedly taught, but Antisthenes' teaching activities are obscure, and his institution of any type of "school" is unlikely (see Giannantoni in Goulet-Cazé and Goulet 1993). According to Hellenistic tradition, Diogenes was a pupil of Antisthenes, and this connection completed a five-generation chain of philosophical "succession" from Socrates through Antisthenes and Diogenes to the Cynic Crates of Thebes and then to Zeno of Citium, founder of the Stoa. Although the personal connection between Antisthenes and Diogenes has been disputed, largely on chronological grounds which would place Diogenes' expulsion from Sinope and arrival in Athens after Antisthenes' death (see most conveniently Dudley 1937: 2–3, who however dates Diogenes' arrival at 340, far too late), it is clear that Diogenes self-consciously modeled himself as a new Socrates, and so would have needed inspiration and information about Socrates from some source. There can be little doubt that Antisthenes was that source. Moreover, the chronological argument, developed from the dating of Sinopean coins and a recon- struction of the career of Diogenes' father, is itself feeble (Döring 1995: 126–34), and in short we are not compelled to reject the tradition that Diogenes learned about Socrates face-to-face from Antisthenes, even while a formal teacher-to-pupil relation- ship is unlikely. At the same time, our Hellenistic and post-Hellenistic sources, com- mitted to this line of succession (Mansfeld 1986), probably preserved aspects of Antisthenes' thought that are more proto-Cynic or proto-Stoic than we would have received through a disinterested tradition.

For Diogenes, and for the Cynics, Socrates was primarily a model of virtuous living and an outspoken voice of critique against an unreflective folk morality, perhaps in- creasingly obsessed with the false desires and pleasures of material affluence. Although for the Cynics language remained one tool for demonstrating beliefs and for convert- ing others, the notion that careful, transparent discourse leads to discovery of true propositions, axioms, or beliefs, which is fundamental to modern approaches to Socrates and indeed to the modern concept of "philosophy," is far divorced from the ancient Cynic tradition. Socraticism for them was a way of life, grounded indeed on some beliefs, but not identical to them. Language was used ironically, sarcastically, and often in parody of dominant discourse to challenge and change beliefs and behaviors, and its meaning was not equivalent to its face value. We can perceive a "philosophical" aspect of Cynicism in its mission to "deface the currency" of social conventions (Goulet-Cazé 1993), even if the surviving evidence allows us little understanding of the Cynics' conception or justification of the opposition between true virtue and the false conceits of culture. For the grounding arguments for the radical Cynic rejection of culture, as well as rejection of logic, we look to Antisthenes. Although our evidence there, too, is poor, we can find the missing arguments implied consistently in his fragments.

Antisthenes the Socratic

As the story goes (Diogenes Laertius, *Lives of Eminent Philosophers* 6.1–2 = VA 11–12), Antisthenes met Socrates as a mature man, after he had studied rhetoric with Gorgias and had taken on pupils of his own. In modern scholarship this narrative is supposed to render Antisthenes an impure Socratic, who already formed views and indeed composed some of his writings without regard for the Socratic project, and possibly in conflict with it (e.g. Rankin 1986). However, Diogenes' story also tells us that Antisthenes was converted to Socrates' side with complete fervor, such that he walked every day to Athens from his home in the Piraeus to converse with Socrates. If this story is historically true, and not the embellishment of a post-Platonic age that needed to explain how a "sophist" (as Antisthenes is called by another character at Xenophon, *Symposium* 4.4) could also be a Socratic, then it seems that such a great conversion would have affected Antisthenes' literary remains. We know little about the composi- tion, circulation, and purposes of prose texts in the time of Antisthenes, but it seems that after a significant conversion Antisthenes would hardly have authorized the circulation of any text that did not cohere fully to his Socratic values. Moreover, it was the execution of Socrates that stimulated the flurry of apologetic and protreptic literature among his followers, intended, respectively, to clear Socrates of the charges on which he was convicted and to cause readers to continue Socrates' mission by pursuing virtue and loving wisdom. Finally, although Antisthenes may have written for a purpose such as self-advertisement before the execution of Socrates, it is clear that all the texts, when read carefully, are part of the Socratic conversation. Being older than the other Socratics, Antisthenes retains intellectual marks of his pre-Socratic life: for example, his book title "Truth" (VA 41.32) had been used previously by the sophists Protagoras and Antiphon, and surely he intended the resonance to be recognized; his interest in rewriting philosophical myths for Heracles (VA 92–9) and in correct naming practice (VA 41.37–8, 160) recalls the sophist Prodicus. But this fact should help, rather than hinder, our use of Antisthenes to understand Socrates: after all, Aristophanes in *Clouds* confused Socrates with the sophists plausibly enough that the issue needed to be addressed at Socrates' trial. It is not that Antisthenes was oblivious to the difference between the sophists and Socrates: he is said to have attacked the sophists and Gorgias in particular (VA 203, 204), and the conversion story shows that the difference mattered to him. But Antisthenes can offer us a new view of the relationship between Socrates and the sophists, one that does not renounce Homer and the poets, rhetoric, or other traditional modes of moral discourse and education in the cause of philosophy, but appropriates them more subtly.

Antisthenes' reputation in the Hellenistic period, as reflected in the doxography in Diogenes Laertius, *Lives of Eminent Philosophers* 6.11–15, suggests that his primary interest was the ethics of the individual life: this had, after all, become the main concern of the Hellenistic philosophies, and some of the Stoics had promoted Antisthenes as their Socratic ancestor (Mansfeld 1986). Moreover, what is reported as Antisthenes' simple call to virtue appears sometimes as a call to simple virtue, in which education, for example, has no place (e.g. Sayre 1948, justified by Diognes Laertiues, *Lives of Eminent Philosophers* 6.11 = VA 134 and 6.103–4 = VA 161, 135). However, the catalogue of Antisthenes' writings preserved by Diogenes Laertius (6.15–18 = VA 41) and likely to be a more direct representation of his thought, tells a more complicated story. Unlike the information in the main text of Diogenes' "Life of Antisthenes," transmitted through several generations of biographers and doxographers, the book catalogue is arranged so carefully as to suggest the editorial work of a scholar with direct access to Antisthenes' texts and conversant with pre-Stoic, possibly Peripatetic, divisions of philosophy under which the texts could be classified (Patzer 1970: 107–63, developing an older perception). First, the "ethical" titles in the second and third volumes of this 10-volume edition are as much about law, constitution, justice, and success in social situations as about the good, bravery, freedom, and slavery (the last two being themselves social ideas, but probably of interest to Antisthenes, as to Plato, in reference to states of the soul). From the arrangement of titles, the double titles, and other evidence external to the catalogue, it seems that politics was primary to ethics, and not *vice versa*, as in Hellenistic philosophy. Second, the titles explicitly on ethics and politics (VA 41.13–24) are far outnumbered by titles concerned with language, dialogue, and literature, which occupy 5 of the 10 volumes: we find two groups of writings on so-called sophistic topics, public rhetoric in the first volume (VA 41.3–8) and

Homeric criticism in the eighth and ninth volumes (VA 41.49–66), and a third group, apparently more theoretical, on dialectic, questions and answers, contradiction, eristic, and so on, in the sixth and seventh volumes (VA 41.32–40, 46–7). The importance of language for Antisthenes, and its connection with ethics, is captured in Epictetus' pithy statement, "The beginning of education is the examination of names" (VA 160: see Brancacci 1990). Finally, Antisthenes' most famous titles on ethics, *Cyrus* and *Heracles* (in the fourth, fifth, and tenth volumes, VA 41.26–9,68–71), were not discussions *about* virtue, but fictional dialogues in which virtue was demonstrated through the mimesis or literary representation of virtuous (and possibly vicious) characters. This embedding of philosophical point into literary character and perhaps narrative suggests that Antisthenes, like Plato, expected his readers to use their judgment to discern virtue, not to be told directly what it was. In short, Antisthenes seems to have taken interest in politics, language, and literature alongside ethics, and indeed it seems that ethics was a special, advanced position in each of these prior realms. Nothing in this idea conflicts with our knowledge of Socrates from Plato and Xenophon, but from our modern vantage we tend to privilege statements about abstract ethics at the expense of the many passages in which the entanglements persist. Antisthenes, too, addressed ethics separately, as in his paradox, but the condensed overview of his thought available in this detailed and descriptive book list suggests that ethics was not simple or separable, but was actually everywhere.

Antisthenes on Language

Language, then, was one of Antisthenes' primary interests, but his view of its powers strayed from the course that led to Platonic Forms and Aristotelian logic and science. His overall view was that language was critically important at several levels, a most important constituent of the individual self as well as the main medium of social interaction, yet his most famous statements place limits on language. In these statements he is most likely attacking rivals, especially Plato, who were in the act of defining the sort of scientific discourse that would become the main tool of philosophy (especially in the *Theaetetus* and *Sophist*). Antisthenes was allegedly the first to define the Greek term "logos," the type of discourse that Plato and Aristotle closely associated with objective and infallible knowledge based on definitions and deductive arguments (Diogenes Laertius, *Lives of Eminent Philosophers* 6.3 = VA 151). But the particular definition of "logos" attributed to him seems a deliberate frustration of the very premise that the definitive logos can be constructed. The formulation preserved, "Logos is the <enunciation> revealing the 'what it is or was'," addresses the famous Socratic question, "What is it?" (i.e. courage and so on). Yet it uses a slippery verb, "reveal," which Gorgias had made problematic in his discussion of spoken or written words and their incapacity to "reveal" either reality or thoughts about reality (*On Not Being* 917a13, 980a19, b18); Aristotle, by contrast, would use the verb "signify" to name the relation between language and its meaning (*Topics* 101b). If "reveal" carries the weight it should in the wake of Gorgias, then Antisthenes is taking a strong stand suggestive of the position ultimately defended by Socrates in Plato's *Cratylus*, that the meaning of names is grounded by a relationship to reality, not by convention. However, the

80

reality revealed by the name is hardly a Platonic Form, as in the solution suggested in *Cratylus*: the temporal disjunction in Antisthenes' formulation, "what it is or was," seems to highlight the relevance of change and so rules out reference to timeless, absolute foundations of meaning, as Plato (and possibly Socrates) would have had it. We know from an oft-repeated anecdote that Antisthenes fully rejected Plato's theory of Forms (VA 149, also 147, 148). Finally, Alexander of Aphrodisias, the authoritative Aristotelian commentator of the late second century CE, commenting on Aristotle's own definition of definition at *Topics* 101b38 (VA 151), charges that Antisthenes admits more types of statement into his concept of definition than he should: that is, he allows predications that place the form (*eidos*) into a general class (*genos*) (such as "courage is a virtue") to count as "logos," whereas the definition of definition ought to state a criterion for those verbal formulations which capture the very form, or essence (*einai*), of the subject (i.e. what courage is). Although the details of Antisthenes' thoughts on these matters remain obscure, even a partial combination of these odd characteristics of Antisthenes' definition of definition derails the suitability of "logos" to be affiliated with a Platonic Form or to become a starting point for a science or scientific philosophy by the Aristotlean model. It is more likely that "logos," if it exists at all (Döring 1985 suggests that it does not), is a direct revelation or articulation of meaning in a relatively naive sense, which has a sort of reality in the language of a community, but not an unchanging reality.

The two famous Antisthenean paradoxes that interested Aristotle, "It is impossible to contradict, or almost even to speak falsely" (*Metaphysics* 1024b = VA 152, 153) and "It is impossible to define the essence" (*Metaphysics* 1043b = VA 150), are consequences of Antisthenes' basic refusal to accept that a thing (or, better, a concept: the Socratic question addressed itself to universal moral concepts) can be represented equivalently in language by any utterance other than its name: that is, no unique, authoritative paraphrase such as a definition is possible. Conversely – to make sense of the thesis against contradiction – he seems to have believed that every name carries its own reference, although it remains controversial what exactly was the object for that reference. Clearly some form of atomism is implied. However, scholars have usually assumed that reference was necessarily to a singular, possibly perceptible, thing (e.g. Caizzi 1964: 54), rather than to a class or type of thing, and this assumption has been the cause of many confusing expositions of Antisthenes' views. If each name refers uniquely and separately to its own part of reality, determined by the name's meaning, a sort of universal which is allowed to vary over time and perhaps in other ways, then contradiction in naming is impossible because disagreeing speakers are speaking in reference to different things (thus the explication of the late-antique commentators on Aristotle, VA 152, 153, echoing a paradox also familiar from Plato's dialogues, especially the *Euthydemus* and *Sophist*).

Those who would resolve the paradox point to two ways for doing so. Contradiction might well arise whenever the speakers agree on their subject, verbally at least, but attempt to make mutually exclusive predications of it, as Plato and later commentators such as Proclus explain: either the soul is immortal or it is not (see also Asclepius on Aristotle, *Metaphysics*, 1024b34 = VA153.28–9). Alternatively, contradiction can seem to arise when a linguistic term is predicated to a particular, nonlinguistic thing, as in the example "This is a horse" versus "This is not a horse." Antisthenes' position can meet the second objection (the speakers have different concepts of "horse") if not the first. But his position was probably intended to direct attention to a problem integral to the first objection, the conception of the propositional subject in itself: What is justice? What is a constitution? What is a leader? What is a soul? What is a god? The very possibility of a common reference by two different speakers is equated to their agreement in the meaning of a key term. This is, of course, the same sort of question raised by Socrates and addressed by Antisthenes' evasive definition of definition. If the speakers could ever reach agreement on these primary conceptual issues, saying things *about* justice and so on would be trivial, and the truth value of those claims might well be matters of fact.

The problem implies a close relation between language and belief about reality, and points to the advantages of having a language in close alignment with reality, even while it gives no apparent criterion for judging how one person's language is better than another's. We know from our copious evidence for the Cynic distinction between the wise and the foolish that there must have been some such criterion, if only in the Cynic's own intuitions. Antisthenes (and the Cynics) did not suffer from a general skepticism, relativism, or aporetic silence: most of our anecdotes illustrate the basic Cynic mission of educating others about true virtue and vice. Antisthenes thought that teaching through showing (see e.g. VA 103, 159) was effective, whereas arguing and refuting through tactics that depended on contradictions in language was more like becoming mad in reply to someone who was behaving madly (VA 174). Whereas Antisthenes' outlook on definition undermines the foundations of Aristotelian science, his denial of contradiction derails a dominant view of philosophical discourse, by which a principle of the possibility of contradiction must govern a context in which anything logical, and so true, can be asserted at all (*Theaetetus* 170e7–171c7; Aristotle, *Metaphysics* 1006a–9a). As the story goes (VA 148), Antisthenes' view was so fundamentally opposed to the view of his rival Plato that in response to Plato's claim that Antisthenes could not write about the impossibility of contradiction, Antisthenes produced the text he called *Sathon* (a diminutive term for the male member), using an indecent pun on Plato's name to show that the disagreement was not to be resolved through debate on Plato's terms, but reduced to a different practice of naming.

From Discourse to Ethics

Antisthenes did speak and write, of course, and he wrote about speaking, especially in situations of contest. In addition to book titles that refer to "antilogical" and "eristic" modes or content (VA 41.33, 34, 38, 46), Xenophon's *Symposium* depicts Antisthenes in the act of debate, and his sole surviving literary compositions, the *Ajax* and *Odysseus*, show fictional, Homeric characters engaged in a kind of debate over the nature of virtue. These examples seem to confirm the pessimism of the thesis against contradiction: discourse between differently minded people fails to persuade. Yet the fact that Antisthenes wrote profusely suggests that he intended his own written words to persuade. According to his near contemporary Theopompus, cited by Diogenes Laertius, he was "clever" with words and could "win over" through "harmonious conversation" anyone at all (VA 22). Socrates' praise of Antisthenes as a matchmaker in the city (*Symposium* 4.61–4 = VA) confirms this judgment. Both descriptions imply irrational devices, musical charm on the one hand and erotic charm (that is, manipulation of the erotic charm of others) on the other. What we have in *Ajax* and *Odysseus*, though, is not charming in any obvious way: scholars have long been puzzled over how to approach the speeches, and whether they even form a pair, and it is only recently that we have made progress (Rankin 1986; Eucken 1997). If Antisthenes' *Ajax* and *Odysseus* are typical of the kind of persuasion he aimed for in his literature, then it seems his messages were extremely indirect, requiring from the reader both emotional response and very careful thought beyond reception of the words or sentences themselves. To judge from these speeches (a tiny sample of Antisthenes' composition, but all we have), reading Antisthenes well was not like participating in an oral conversation, but required a sort of labor. Labor (*ponos*) and exercise (*askēsis*) were indeed aspects of his proto-Cynic ethics and program for self-improvement. When live conversation between differently minded people fails, as it apparently always does, the route of progress is education or improvement of the individual minds, and this takes place obliquely and experientially, not through exchange of literal propositions or analysis of their logic, but through an expansive engagement in the conceptual fields and verbal fictions of others, examining each name and considering its various meanings, seeing the worlds of others and considering how one might change or extend one's own field, and ultimately achieving a higher standard of discourse, whether in accuracy or in range. ("The beginning of education is the examination of names," VA 160.) This use of language to show rather than tell is continuous with the later Cynic interest in nondiscursive linguistic genres, whether literary fiction and parody (as in the work of Crates of Thebes, Bion of Borysthenes, Teles, Menippus, and possibly Diogenes of Sinope) or the oral diatribe. Although diatribe seems to tell and only to tell, in very high decibels, it is possible to understand the very blatancy of the message as a type of showing.

Antisthenes' rhetorical confrontation between the mythical characters Ajax and Odysseus (VA 53 and 54, probably referred to in the first volume of Diogenes' catalogue, VA 41.4–5) is not so much a contest for the arms of Achilles, as its mythical background implies, as a debate about virtue and the correct meaning of "virtue" and related terms from the vantages of opposed moral characters (Rankin 1986: 152–73). Scholars have been divided over whether or not the dispute has a winner, that is, whether we see just two incompatible views of virtue, or whether the eminently more appealing Odysseus is shown to be the better man. And, if Odysseus is better, it is unclear how his success and superiority in verbal power amount to superiority in ethical virtue. Ajax, who speaks first, subscribes to traditional ideas about military honor, which depend on physical achievement on the battlefield, transparency of intention in combat, and transparency of speech in representing historical events and intentions alike. Since his words and thoughts resonate with phrases and ideas attributed to Antisthenes in other fragments, it is clear that Ajax is meant to be sympathetic on some level. At the same time, his extreme adherence to traditional honor usurps any sense that he has an inner soul, that is, makes choices that diverge in any respect from what his culture instructs. Moreover, his inability to adapt to his circumstance, a competitive verbal debate, by amending his restrictive standards for the representative function of language ensures that he defeats himself pragmatically before Odysseus even speaks. Although he is only a literary fiction (and Antisthenes draws attention to this issue, VA 54.78–83), the contrast with the Odysseus character brings out his functional, and indeed his ethical, shortcomings. Odysseus, on the other hand, is adept at turning Ajax's points, and also his words, to the disadvantage of Ajax's position and toward his own success. Just as Odysseus used disguise in the Trojan War for a noble end, capturing the famous statue of Athena, the Palladium, and so securing victory for the Greeks, he uses language in nonliteral ways to reclaim from Ajax every value and symbolic prize Ajax has staked as his.

Although Odysseus might seem amoral in his use of cleverness and pursuit of victory, his view of self and community sets him above Ajax in a moral sense. Odysseus insists consistently that his performance in the Trojan War was always on behalf of the community of the Greeks, not himself individually. Ajax, on the other hand, even while he uses the first-person pronoun emphatically and often, has no concept of himself other than that given by his shame-based culture and no concept of the community other than its imperatives for individual behavior as represented in its traditional values. Whereas Ajax behaves according to the social code, Odysseus appropriates and manipulates social categories, especially those of the slave and beggar, to promote the real interests of society. This pair of texts, which is rich in nuance and bears careful reading, shows the pervasive effects of community on a character like Ajax: even as he attempts to perform as an excellent individual at the forefront of the community (fighting with his shield "alone" outside the battle line), he is almost a social artifact. It shows the superior individuality of Odysseus, who works within the terms of the community, but evaluates and redeploys those terms such that he has the true ethical space of choice and agency that could count as a real soul. Just as Socrates called others to know themselves by raising their consciousness about ethical concepts, and claimed that this knowledge was sufficient for virtue, so Odysseus criticizes Ajax' failures in self-knowledge, neglect of the psychic – or perhaps intellectual – components of "bravery" and "strength," and consequent failure in virtue. (Eucken 1997 emphasizes the similarities between Odysseus and Socrates as critic of those living an unexamined life.) As a pair, the characters are clearly examples of utter difference. At all levels their different "uses of words," to quote from an Antisthenean book title (VA 41.38) as well as the dictum in Epictetus (VA 160), correlate with, if they are not also identical to, their different degrees of intellectual power and, in a sense to be clarified further, ethical virtue.

Antisthenes adopts Odysseus again as an ideal figure in his discussion of the famous Homeric epithet *polutropos* ("of many turns") (VA 187), where the "wise" and "good" speaker or *rhetor* turns out to be the one who, by means of the *many turns* of words he holds in his mind, can *turn* the *many* with their diverse opinions toward one goal (the argument plays in punning ways with the various senses and references of "many" and "turn"). This discussion, like the speeches, has often been understood to yield a view of ethics too pragmatic to be Socratic, and so a relic of Antisthenes' sophistic youth. But a reconciliation with Socraticism is not hard to reach. Our disproportionately good evidence for Antisthenes' Odysseus character, by contrast with his Heracles and Cyrus characters, more famous in antiquity, or indeed the literary depictions of Socrates we know he produced (Panaetius in Diogenes Laertius, *Lives of Eminent Philosophers* 2.64 = IH 17: quite possibly Socrates was not his main literary character, as he was for Plato), probably skews our image of Antisthenes' views on ethical virtue, as opposed to the virtue of success typically represented by Odysseus in Greek litera-ture. Probably Odysseus represents an ideal for just one aspect of the wise man, his role as *rhetor*, whose function is to direct others toward the good rather than to be good himself. According to Xenophon (*Memorabilia* 4.6.15), Socrates called Homer's Odysseus an "infallible rhetor" because he could conduct arguments through the devices of people's beliefs. It is likely that in Antisthenes' view one needed to be good oneself before one could direct or rule others: this seems to be the view of the Socrates implied often by Xenophon and Plato (e.g. *Memorabilia* 3.6; *Alcibiades*). But in Antisthenes' writings the process of becoming good, as well as the nature of goodness in its full complexity, was exemplified by other characters, not Odysseus. We know that Antisthenes differentiated pure power, such as the power of cleverness that Hippias and Socrates discuss in the *Lesser Hippias* (which Plato probably wrote in response to Antisthenes' discussion of *polutropos*) from the sort of goodness that is equivalent to justice: the Antisthenes character in Xenophon's *Symposium* differentiates "virtue" and "justice" on the one hand, which are "indisputable," from wisdom and bravery on the other, which can be harmful to both friends and the city; only justice is absolutely good, mixed in no respect at all with injustice (*Symposium* 3.4). If Homer's Odysseus was beneficial to friends and the city (Antisthenes, like Socrates, makes it clear that he is interested in Homer's Odysseus, not the cruel Odysseus of Athenian tragedy), then he was probably also just, and this idea seems to be taken for granted rather than established as Antisthenes explores the way he uses his rhetorical power to (try to) benefit others. In the contest with Ajax, it is arguable that Odysseus' goal is more to convert Ajax from his rigid, shame-based moral view to virtue, and so save him from the suicide predetermined in the myth, than to win the contest for the arms. Insofar as he fails to benefit Ajax, Antisthenes' Odysseus might be a model not for success, but for a correctly constructed intention to benefit the interlocutor.

Technically, rhetoric was not the highest art for Antisthenes, but a second-best option for life in realistic circumstances. According to an anecdote preserved by Stobaeus (VA 173), Antisthenes recommended that a boy who was going to live with the gods should learn philosophy, whereas one who was going to live with humans should learn rhetoric. Similarly, in a fragment apparently from one of the *Heracles* texts (VA 96), Prometheus scolds Heracles with his care for human things: he will not become "perfect" until he learns the things "higher than human." Surely life with the gods was the superior form: many fragments of Antisthenes and the Cynics suggest that becoming *sophos* ("wise") is becoming like a god. Yet the order of presentation in Stobaeus' dictum makes rhetoric the climax and focus of the statement. The paradox, like the paradox Ajax fails to negotiate correctly, is that the individual, no matter how ethically perfect and near to the gods he might be, must still practice the art demanded by his circumstance in a community of imperfect – and often downright hostile, stupid, and wicked – companions. (Strong feelings about the life and execution of Socrates would be consistent with such an outlook.) Indeed, the speeches of Ajax and Odysseus, consistently with other evidence, suggest that Antisthenes' turn to a radical *autarkeia* ("self-sufficiency") – a clear precedent for a central value in all the Hellenistic philosophies – is driven by the prior assumption of a hostile social environment, perhaps stupid companions, and, above all, the powers of that social environment to compel conformity to its bad ways. One really does want to live with the gods, and makes great efforts to do so. But one must also live with humans, and it turns out that most of the surviving evidence for the Cynics is not their philosophy of ethical living, but the rhetoric that enables the virtuous man to live in, and try to deliver benefits to, the community. Life with the gods was a private matter, about which few traces have been preserved in the literary record.

Becoming Wise

In Xenophon's *Symposium* (4.34–44 = VA 82) Antisthenes delivers a long speech in praise of his "wealth," which turns out to be self-sufficient poverty. To need nothing is proper to the gods, as Diogenes of Sinope allegedly said (Diogenes Laertius, *Lives of Eminent Philosophers* 6.104 = VA 135; attributed also to Socrates at *Memorabilia* 1.6.10), and getting rid of certain desires is the negative side of Cynic freedom that is often understood as its central feature. The positive side of this freedom is, however, also clearly stated and justified in Antisthenes' speech, our earliest evidence for the Cynic rejection of society's material values. Antisthenes tells us that, without the concerns for luxury or satisfactions of the body beyond what is necessary, he has leisure for building the metaphorical wealth of his soul, by spending his days with Socrates. As we learn elsewhere (VA 163), becoming good requires exercise of the body with gymnastics and exercise of the soul with reason.

The self-sufficiency Antisthenes describes and justifies in his speech is economic. The financial terminology is clearly a metaphor for the ethical self, since "wealth" is used to signify on the one hand money and on the other, in what might be intended as a shocking displacement or revaluation, wisdom. Money is equated with the satisfaction of desires for food, drink, clothing, housing, and sex, those desires called the "pleasures of the body" in other Socratic texts. But, beyond the financial metaphor, we should take the economic or social terminology seriously. By Antisthenes' account, the desire for the pleasures money can buy has no absolute level of fulfillment; rather, the richest tyrants are still "poor" because they are never "filled up." The desire Antisthenes speaks of in his condemnation (*Symposium* 4.35–7) is not connected to particular needs or definite lacks, but a desire for more money, a purely symbolic good consisting in a share of social goods superior to that of one's companions, and the consequent power to control them and freedom from being controlled by them (hence the political paradigm of the tyrant). Thus the desire that concerns Antisthenes is a phenomenon of life in an economically interdependent society and, plausibly, even created by the fact of that society. Insofar as money might signify political power, we might see in this corrupted tyrant a frustrated citizen of the Athenian democracy, whose radical egalitarian ideology fails to distinguish "the bad" from "the good" (VA 71). Community creates desire for more because the pursuit of power within a community is an infinite quest for more. Since the pursuit is endless, engaging in the competition is a "difficult disease" (4.37), to which the solution is to fix a firm standard for the need for money. Only in formulating this escape from the disease does Antisthenes reduce the pursuit of money to the particular needs money serves, identifying his hunger, thirst, and need for warmth and comfortable sleep as standards for his food, drink, clothing, housing, and bedding (4.37–40). For sex, which apparently occurs as a less predictable need, availability or proximity (*to paron*) is the criterion for selecting a partner with minimal expenditure of effort or money. (Diogenes would notoriously eliminate even that need for social encounter by practicing masturbation.) All in all, Antisthenes finds economic freedom, symbolic for the freedom of the soul, by seceding from the economic system. When it comes to engaging with others on an intellectual basis, Socrates gives him "wealth" without weight or measure, and Antisthenes is able to share his "wealth" of wisdom with whomever wants it without envy or loss to himself (4.43), that is, without an economy. The argument he gives is surely a version of the core of the broader Cynic rejection of real society in all its guises, including also the political interactions of the city-state (about which Antisthenes elsewhere expresses his doubts: VA 68–78). The "negative" freedom from bodily, or expensive, desires as Antisthenes portrays it in this passage is a particular freedom, motivated by, first, the futility of seeking fulfillment for this type of desire and, second, the preference for the positive freedom to "see things most worth seeing and hear things most worth hearing and . . . to spend the day together in leisure with Socrates" (4.44. For other articulations of the *telos* or goal of Cynic freedom, see Goulet-Cazé 1993). This way of life, presumably, is the path to becoming wise, if it is not the life of wisdom already. If we hear little about this positive freedom from the later Cynics, it is because their efforts are consumed in using their freedom from society to demonstrate to others the existence of this path, one way to understand the famous Cynic "short cut" (Diogenes Laertius, *Lives of Eminent Philosophers* 6.104 = VA 135) to personal virtue.

In itself, personal virtue for Antisthenes and the Cynics remained in one sense a defense or power of resistance against external interference: thus Antisthenes privileges the idea of *ischus* ("strength") (in Diogenes Laertius' doxography, VA 134.4, and in his book titles on Heracles, VA 41.27 and 41.79), and becoming virtuous is building strength in various senses. Images of the wise soul living as if within his own imaginary "city walls" of reason are frequent (VA 107, 124, 134). But the idealization of Heracles and Cyrus, who were heroes because of their power to achieve, suggests that virtue had a positive nature also. Like the later Cynics, Antisthenes insisted that virtue could be learned (Diogenes Laertius, *Lives of Eminent Philosophers* 6.105 = VA 99), and the process of learning was the activity of *askēsis* ("exercise" or "practice") (VA 163), which necessarily involved large degrees of *ponos* ("toil" or "labor") (VA 85, 97, 113, 134). For Antisthenes, and perhaps Diogenes as well, this exercise and toil have at least three components, of which two are neatly juxtaposed as physical exercises, *gymnasia*, to train the body and mental exercises, *logoi*, to train the soul (VA 163, with Caizzi's emended text; Diogenes Laertius, *Lives of Eminent Philosophers* 6.70–1 = VB 291). In addition, Antisthenes seems to have recognized a third type of *ponos* that trains one's self-image or self-esteem: to suffer disrepute in popular opinion, which is of course untrained and corrupt, is itself a type of *ponos* that steers one towards virtue (VA 134.6–7, 88–90); at any rate the converse is true, as the praise of base flatterers is corrupting (VA 131). Physical training was surely the model case for *ponos* understood as good; athletic training was a firm part of Greek education since the dawn of our evidence, and especially since the broadening of the aristocracy in the archaic period. Our anecdotal evidence for Diogenes of Sinope emphasizes the physical

87

toils to which he would submit himself for the sake of hardening his soul toward indifference to external circumstances of bodily comfort (e.g., Diogenes Laertius, *Lives of Eminent Philosophers* 6.34), and Socrates is portrayed similarly by Xenophon, e.g. *Memorabilia* 1.2–6.

Although Antisthenes' discourse on controlling bodily comforts in the *Symposium* is consistent with the assumption that he, too, promoted physical *askēsis*, the bulk of our evidence suggests that the crucial exercise and toil in his view was intellectual. The soul was similar to the body, like an organ which became stronger in response to exertion outside its accustomed range of activity, not like a receptacle for beliefs, as in the famous images of the mind as a wax tablet or bird cage in Plato's *Theaetetus* 191–9. Nor was becoming good a mere turning or conversion, as in the image of Plato's soul turning its gaze upward in *Republic* 7. Thus the *logoi* were not propositions to be proven, understood in an instant of insight, or even retained, but activities to be undertaken as exercise, in analogy to gymnastics. From what we know of Antisthenes' actual activity – he talked with Socrates, talked with others, read texts, and wrote texts, including secondary texts about the primary ones – it would seem that his exercise in *logoi* was just reception and production of well-chosen verbal material, probably on the topic of the good life, together with the effort necessary to understand the concepts at stake. If, according to the discussion above, names and concepts rather than propositions are the main vehicles of truth and constituents of knowledge and wisdom in Antisthenes' views of language and epistemology, then the best way to develop a good grasp of truth was wide exposure to challenging uses of names. And for this reason, in addition to Athenian tradition, Homer made a good candidate for his studies. Standing at the beginning of Greek literature in the eighth century BCE, Homer was in many ways a foreign text by the fourth century, needful of comprehension also in the terms of Antisthenes' Socratic values. Thus, for example, Antisthenes reads Nestor's ability to lift a heavy cup in *Iliad* 11.636 as Homer's mode for saying that Nestor, like Socrates, could drink a lot of wine without being affected (VA 191: see further Pépin in Goulet and Goulet-Cazé 1993).

This conception of intellectual activity as toil, exercise, and training of the soul, rather than pursuit of knowledge in itself, illuminates Diogenes Laertius' famous summary of Antisthenes' ethical views at *Lives of the Philosophers* 6.11–12 (VA 134), especially regarding the intellectualism of virtue. Virtue is teachable (VA 134.2; also *Lives of Eminent Philosophers* 6.105 = VA 135.17) and, once gained, inalienable (VA 134.11; also *Lives of Eminent Philosophers* 6.105 = VA 135.18), except perhaps under the influence of others (*Lives of Eminent Philosophers* 6.103 = VA 161): these qualities are marks of intellectualism (Goulet-Cazé 1986: 141–2). The survival of achieved virtue without further exercise (implied in VA 161), makes Antisthenes' view more intellectualist than Xenophon's (*Memorabilia* 1.2.19). But virtue is, ultimately, a matter of deeds (*erga*), not of words or statements (*logoi*) (VA 134.4–5): that is, the activities and practices of engaging with words, on the analogy of physical gymnastics, is the matter of virtue, presumably its realm for operation and existence as well as its source. Correspondingly, when the virtuous man is described in Antisthenes' fragments, his essential virtue is identified as *phronēsis* (VA 41.69, 106, 132, 134.17), practical wisdom, about as often as he is called by the more purely intellectualist term *sophos* (or *sapiens* in Latin) (VA 54, 96, 187, 188, 192, and often in Diogenes Laertius, *Lives of Eminent Philosophers*). Most importantly for intellectualist ethics, though, this virtue falls short of identity or mutual entailment with happiness, an identity assumed in much post-Socratic ethical theory (Long 1988: 161, 164–71). Rather, virtue is almost self-sufficient (*autarkes*) for happiness (VA 134.3–4): that is, it needs nothing in addition except for "Socratic strength" (*Sokratikē ischus*). This Socratic strength, which probably refers to the strength of character Socrates exemplified rather than a strength that Antisthenes understood to be part of Socrates' theory about virtue (Goulet-Cazé 1986: 145), might be a name for the concept of the will that Aristotle found so lacking in Plato's accounts of Socratic intellectualism. Insofar as "strength" was a key feature in Antisthenes' portrayal of the virtue of Heracles (VA 41.27), where he apparently set it in parallel with *phronēsis* (so the book title at VA 41.69), Antisthenes might have gone some way toward incorporating a concept of will into ethical theory, even if his theory was expressed largely in the form of examples of fictional heroes.

Diogenes of Sinope, Defacer of the Currency

Whereas Antisthenes' arguments about *logos* were applied by the Cynics in their scorn for logic and embrace of nondiscursive linguistic modes, his views on virtue and pleasure were applied quite directly, and often in "rhetorical" exaggeration beyond their practical purposes, creating freedom for the pursuit of virtue and enacting this pursuit. According to one anecdote, "Diogenes used to say that he followed the example of the trainers of choruses, for they too set the note a little high, to ensure that the rest would hit the right note" (VB 266). Diogenes allegedly repudiated Antisthenes for being "too soft" (VB 584.8–10) and Socrates for living in too much luxury (VB 256): his only possession was his wallet for food (VB 158). But he apparently claimed a return to the emulation of Socrates, even if in this emulation he would be called "Socrates gone mad" (VB 59, attributed to Plato). Although Socrates and Diogenes become models in tandem for the wise man in later Stoicizing and Cynicizing authors, such as Epictetus and Dio Chrysostom, there is also an ancient sentiment that Cynicism is not continuous with Socraticism, presumably for its highly rhetorical character. Whereas Socrates was indifferent to poverty, the Cynic chose and embraced poverty. Whereas Socrates was ironic and bold, the Cynic was outrageously provocative and outspoken. Thus Clement and Epiphanius could say that Antisthenes "converted" from Socraticism to Cynicism (VA 107: Sayre 1948: 85).

For Diogenes, as for Antisthenes, we receive a story about the conversion to philosophy. In fact, we receive many stories about Diogenes, and stories and legends constitute virtually everything we receive (see Gerhard in Billerbeck 1991). But the story that captures the goal and spirit of his mission speaks of his act of "defacing the currency" (a quotation from his own text *Pordalus*, Diogenes Laertius, *Lives of Eminent Philosophers* 6.20 = VB 2). The Greek word for "currency" takes its root from the word for "custom" and in its particular form refers either to coined money or to the ways of culture. The word for "deface," too, is derived from the word for "stamping," which could be used literally in reference to misstamping the coinage or metaphorically in reference to restamping public custom in a new direction. Attached to this expression is a biographical story, attested earliest in the Stoic Diocles of Magnesia, late first century BCE, that Diogenes was forced into exile from his native city, Sinope, after either his father Hicesias or he himself was caught having defaced the currency, that is, devalued the coinage (Diogenes Laertius, *Lives of Eminent Philsophers* 6.20–1 and frequently = VB 2–4). It was, then, exile that made Diogenes a philosopher (VB 13), a paradoxical reward matched by the paradoxical punishment of the other citizens of Sinope, the condemnation to stay home (VB 11). This story may be literally true, or it may be a legend invented from the metaphor Diogenes used for his primary activity, defying the norms of society. At any rate, virtually every legend about Diogenes shows him defacing the currency, always in public, whether performing the things of Demeter (eating) or the things of Aphrodite (sex), and his shamelessness earned him the pejorative title "Dog," which he defaced into a compliment. In his writings (whose authenticity was doubted in antiquity) as well as his behavior he challenged the norms: in his *Republic* (*Politeia*) he apparently advocated incest and cannibalism, two of the strongest taboos of Greek culture. Surely this was for the effect of total challenge to the norms, not to cause people to eat their parents and mate with their kin (Döring 1995: 148). Coherently with the countercultural inclinations of Cynicism, women were apparently recognized as the equals of men regarding potential for virtue (Antisthenes states that the virtue of man and woman is the same, Diogenes Laertius, *Lives of Eminent Philosophers* 6.12 = VA 134.15), and, even while most references to women in the fragments address their sexual identities, Antisthenes' comments seem often intended to release women from these identities, and Hipparchia at least (late fourth century CE) became famous with her husband Crates for her provocative acts (*SSR* vol. 3: 577–9).

Because the Cynicism of Diogenes was inherently rhetorical and political, it was easy to divorce from the virtuous life that was allegedly its goal. Stoicism, it seems, inherited and developed the seriously moral aspect of Antisthenes' Socraticism, together with borrowings from the more technical Socratic schools, the Academy and Peripatos, and by the mid-Hellenistic period the "old" Cynicism had faded into literary activity, such as the satires of Menippus (Dudley 1937: 110–24). But Socrates and Antisthenes both were serious about politics, in the proto-Cynic sense of confronting others in the community and turning them to the pursuit of virtue. When under the Roman Empire Cynicism became relevant again, as a stance against power, Socrates if not so much Antisthenes could stand with Diogenes of Sinope as an emblem for both exhortation to virtue and the virtuous life itself.

Note

1   Second edition, Naples 1990: see bibliography. All fragments will be cited from this edition. The 1966 edition of Antisthenes' fragments by Decleva Caizzi remains valuable.

References

Billerbeck, M. (1991). *Die Kyniker in der modernen Forschung: Aufsätze mit Einführung und Bibliographie* [The Cynics in Modern Research: Essays with Introduction and Bibliography]. Amsterdam: B. R. Grüner. An anthology of important articles from 1851 to 1980, with a synthetic introduction by Billerbeck.

Brancacci, A. (1990). *Oikeios Logos. La filosofia del linguaggio di Antistene* [Proper Account. The Philosophy of Language of Antisthenes]. Naples: Bibliopolis. A detailed reconstruction of Antisthenes' theory of language and alleged dogmatism, with many speculative attributions from other ancient writers.

Branham, R. B. and Goulet-Cazé, M.-O. (eds.) (1996). *The Cynics. The Cynic Movement in Antiquity and its Legacy*. Berkeley, Los Angeles, and London: University of California Press. A collection of original essays (but with some translations from Goulet-Cazé and Goulet 1993) on Cynic, proto-Cynic, and neo-Cynic figures from the Scythians to modern times.

Caizzi, F. (1964). Antistene [Antisthenes]. *Studi Urbinati*, 38, 48–99. A ground-breaking overview of Antisthenes, covering his theory of logic and epistemology, his rhetoric and Homeric studies, and his image in Xenophon.

Decleva Caizzi, F. (1966). *Antisthenis Fragmenta* [Fragments of Antisthenes]. Milan: Istituto Editoriale Cisalpino. The first modern scholarly collection of the fragments of Antisthenes, with useful commentary; supplemented but not surpassed by Giannantoni's edition.

Döring, K. (1985). Antisthenes: Sophist oder Sokratiker? [Antisthenes: Sophist or Socratic?]. *Siculorum Gymnasium*, 38, 229–42. An interpretation of the epistemological and linguistic fragments that restores Antisthenes squarely to the Socratic tradition, against W. K. C. Guthrie's distinction between Antisthenes the sophist (in linguistic issues) and Antisthenes the Socratic (in ethical issues) posited in (1969) *A History of Greek Philosophy* V.3.

—— (1995). Diogenes und Antisthenes [Diogenes and Antisthenes]. *La Tradizione Socratica = Memorie dell' Instituto Italiano per gli Studi Filosofici* [The Socratic Tradition = Records of the Italian Institute for Philosophical Studies], 25, 125–50. A critique of the chronological and intellectual grounds for Dudley's separation of Antisthenes from Diogenes.

Dudley, D. R. (1937). *A History of Cynicism from Diogenes to the Sixth Century A.D.* Cambridge: Cambridge University Press. Reprinted (1980) Chicago: Ares. A dense and intelligent overview of ancient Cynicism, responsible for the modern separation of Antisthenes from the Cynics.

Eucken, C. (1997). Der schwache und der starke Logos des Antisthenes [The weak and the strong speech of Antisthenes]. *Hyperboreus*, 3, 251–72. A reading of Antisthenes' *Ajax* and *Odysseus* speeches as Socratic literature, in which Odysseus is similar to Socrates.

Giannanoni, G. (1990). *Socratis et Socraticorum Reliquiae* [The Remains of Socrates and the Socratics]. 4 vols. Naples: Bibliopolis. A comprehensive collection of the fragments of Socrates and his followers, including the older Cynics, with interpretive essays and summaries of important scholarship.

Goulet-Cazé, M.-O. (1986). *L'ascèse cynique: Un commentaire de Diogène Laërce VI 70–71* [The Cynic Practice: A Commentary on Diogenes Laertius 6.70–1]. Paris: J. Vrin. Exegesis and explanation of the serious core to the philosophy of Diogenes of Sinope.

Goulet-Cazé, M.-O. (1993). Le cynisme est-il une Philosophie? [Is cynicism a philosophy?]. In M. Dixsaut (ed.), *Contre Platon* [Against Plato], (pp. 273–313). Paris: J. Vrin. An examination of the likely reasons for ancient doubts that Cynicism was a philosophy, not just a way of life.

Goulet-Cazé, M.-O. and Goulet, R. (eds.) (1993). *Le cynisme ancien et ses prolongements: Actes du colloque international du CNRS, Paris 22–25 juillet 1991* [Ancient Cynicism and Its Continuations: Acts of the International Colloquium of the CNRS, Paris, July 22–5, 1991]. Paris: Presses Universitaires de France. A collection of original essays on Cynicism, its origins, reflections among the Romans, and modern reception; with Billerbeck, who renewed recent interest in the Cynics.

Kahn, C. H. (1996). *Plato and the Socratic Dialogue: The Philosophical Use of a Literary Form.* Cambridge, New York, and Melbourne: Cambridge University Press. An argument that all Plato's dialogues, early to late, constitute good and bad evidence for the historical Socrates: Plato's development as a writer and thinker cannot be equated with a fading loyalty to the historical Socrates.

Kerferd, G. B. (1981). *The Sophistic Movement*. Cambridge: Cambridge University Press. A stimulating account of the sophists taken on their own terms, without the lens of Plato's condemnation.

Long, A. A. (1988). Socrates in Hellenistic philosophy. *Classical Quarterly*, 38, 150–71. Reprinted in (1996) *Stoic Studies* (pp. 1–34). Cambridge: Cambridge University Press. An argument that strands in all major Hellenistic philosophies (skeptical, Epicurean, and Stoic) are descended from Socrates' thought and legacy.

Mansfeld, J. (1986). Diogenes Laertius on Stoic philosophy. *Elenchos*, 7, 295–382. An examination of Diogenes' likely sources for his history of the Stoa, with consideration of those sources for and against the claim that Stoicism is a development of Cynicism.

Patzer, A. (1970). *Antisthenes der Sokratiker: Das literarische Werk und die Philosophie, dargestellt am Katalog der Schriften* [Antisthenes the Socratic: The Literary Work and the Philosophy as Represented in the Catalogue of His Writings]. Diss. Heidelberg. A development of the important premise that the catalogue of Antisthenes' writings is the central evidence for his thought.

Rankin, H. D. (1986). *Anthisthenes [sic] Sokratikos*. Amsterdam: Adolf M. Hakkert. The best published overview of Antisthenes in English, but derivative of European scholarship and confusing on issues of logic and epistemology.

Vander Waerdt, P. A. (1994). *The Socratic Movement*. Ithaca and London: Cornell University Press. A collection of articles on the minor Socratics, who are taken as good witnesses to the philosophy of Socrates.

Vlastos, G. (1994). *Socratic Studies*. Cambridge: Cambridge University Press. A second collection (after 1991, *Socrates, Ironist and Moral Philosopher*) of articles on Socrates, including revisions of work that preceded the 1991 volume. Together these volumes are the most influential recent work on Socrates.

7

Xenophon's Socrates

LOUIS-ANDRÉ DORION
(TRANSLATED BY STEPHEN MENN,
MCGILL UNIVERSITY)

Xenophon and the Socratic Question

Of the many Socratic dialogues (*logoi Sōkratikoi*) written by Socrates' disciples, only those of Plato and Xenophon have come down to us in complete form; the others are preserved only in fragments. The chief interest of Xenophon's Socratic writings (the *Memorabilia, Symposium, Oeconomicus,* and *Apology*) is that they give us an alternative portrait of Socrates, the only complete portrait emerging from the Socratic circle that we are now in a position to contrast with Plato's. But if it turns out that Xenophon's Socrates (henceforth Socrates[X]) does not correspond to what we know of the historical Socrates, should we not then regard him as an impostor unworthy of our interest? Thus we cannot consider Socrates[X] without first taking a position on the so-called "Socratic question": that is, can we reconstruct the thought of the historical Socrates on the basis of the main surviving testimonies on him, those of Aristophanes, Plato, Xenophon and Aristotle? But the Socratic question, as it was debated from the time of Schleiermacher[1] to the beginning of the twentieth century, is not only an unsolvable problem – as is shown by the lack of any agreement – but also a pseudo-problem. If the *logoi Sōkratikoi* are works of fiction, allowing their authors considerable scope for invention not only in the setting but also in the ideas expressed by the characters including Socrates, then it seems hopeless to try to reconstruct the thought of the historical Socrates on the basis of the *logoi Sōkratikoi*. But if the Socratic question is doomed to remain an unsolvable (pseudo-)problem, we must draw the consequences; and one of the consequences is that there is no longer any obstacle to rehabilitating Xenophon's Socratic writings. The reasons that led to the eclipse of the *Memorabilia* and of Xenophon's other Socratic writings at the end of the nineteenth century are bound up with the Socratic question. In other words, if we examine the main criticisms which were brought against Xenophon's Socratic writings, and which resulted in the eclipse of these writings for most of the twentieth century, we will see that they were aimed above all at discrediting Xenophon's testimony in the context of a solution to the Socratic question. So if we set this question aside as a pseudo-problem, most of the criticisms of Xenophon's Socratic writings become irrelevant. Nonetheless, there is one criticism, and not a trivial one, which might survive the decline of the Socratic question. This criticism, going back to Schleiermacher's influential study (1818), argues that Xenophon was not a philosopher and that the properly philosophical interest of his Socratic writings is thin – so thin that it would be hard to understand Socrates' enormous philosophical posterity if he were merely the boring preacher depicted in the *Memorabilia*. This criticism has been taken up by all of Xenophon's detractors since the beginning of the nineteenth century, and recent writers still make use of it.[2] It is this criticism which underlies the summary judgment of those who declare that the only Socrates who counts on the philosophical level is Plato's (hence-forth Socrates[P]).[3] Shall we then banish Socrates[X] once and for all, as some writers openly advise?[4] The criticism which denies Socrates[X] the title of philosopher can how-ever be overcome by the following arguments:

a) The very fact that this criticism was never formulated before the beginning of the nineteenth century should provoke some reflection. What conception of philosophy does this criticism presuppose? Apparently one which sees philosophy as an essentially critical and speculative activity; so, since Xenophon's Socratic writings are not espe-cially critical or speculative, it is concluded, as if the inference were automatic, that they are of negligible philosophical interest. But if philosophy is understood as a way of life – and so the ancients understood it[5] – what right do we have to refuse the title of philosopher to Socrates[X], who strives to make his life and his *logoi* consistent,[6] and, above all, to make other people better?[7]

b) If Socrates[X] is not a philosopher, as is claimed on the basis of an anachronistic conception of philosophy, it would be hard to explain how he – Socrates[X], not just Socrates in general – could have had so much influence on many ancient authors, notably the Stoics, as is shown by the testimonies of Diogenes Laertius (7.2) and Sextus Empiricus (*Against the Professors* 9. 92–101), among others.

c) By no means all modern and contemporary philosophers have accepted Schleiermacher's criticism. Nietzsche, in particular, did not hide his admiration for the *Memorabilia*, calling it "the most attractive book of Greek literature":[8]

> Xenophon's *Memoribilia* give a truly faithful image [of Socrates], just as intelligent as their model; but one must understand how to read this book. The philologists at bottom believe that Socrates has nothing to tell them, and they get bored with reading it. Other people feel that this book both wounds you and makes you happy.[9]

Socrates[X] is certainly not as stimulating, subtle, or disconcerting a philosopher as his Platonic namesake, but that does not make him any less an authentic philosopher, in his aspiration to a self-sufficient life based on self-mastery.[10] This may be a conception of philosophy which has become alien to us, but that does not give us the right to deny that it is philosophy.

The Main Differences Between Socrates[X] and Socrates[P]

The interpreter of Xenophon's Socratic writings has two methods for bringing out the originality and distinctiveness of Socrates[X]. First, he can analyze in and of them-selves some philosophical positions peculiar to Socrates[X]; second, he can proceed to a comparative exegesis of Socratic themes that are shared by Xenophon and Plato. The aim of comparative exegesis is not to determine, with regard to some shared theme, which version is historically the more accurate, but rather to note the differences and to interpret them by seeing how they function, for Plato as well as Xenophon, in a philosophically coherent representation of the character of Socrates. In what follows I will try to illustrate these two exegetical methods: I will first[11] set out the philosophical position which is at the heart of Socrates[X]'s ethics and which sets him most clearly apart from his Platonic namesake, and then I will show[12] how this philosophical position forces Xenophon to rework at a fundamental level some Socratic themes which are also present in Plato. Socrates[X] cannot be reduced to Socrates[P], and there is no hope of harmonizing their doctrines. Those who claim otherwise are contenting themselves with surface agreements[13] that conceal deeper disagreements. For those who continue to doubt the distinctiveness of Socrates[X], here is a partial list of the main differences between the two Socrateses.[14]

1) Socrates[X], who never avows ignorance of any moral subject, is capable of defining the virtues,[15] while Socrates[P], who claims to be ignorant of the most important subjects, tries in vain to define the virtues. Thus Socrates[P] must always begin his quest anew, while Socrates[X] never gives the impression of being at a loss for an answer to any question he asks.

2) Socrates[X] openly acknowledges that he is a teacher and an educational expert,[16] while Socrates[P], who denies being anyone's teacher,[17] often represents himself as his interlocutor's student.[18]

3) Socrates[X] acknowledges that he does not himself practice politics, but forthrightly admits that he trains young people in politics;[19] while Socrates[P], who never acknowledges providing any such training, claims to be the only person who practices politics, in the sense that he is the only one who concerns himself with making his fellow-citizens better.[20]

4) For Socrates[X], politics is a *technē* like any other,[21] a mere technical competence which can be learned from a recognized teacher,[22] and not, as for Socrates[P], an architectonic moral wisdom, that is, a knowledge of good and evil which encompasses the different *technai*, setting the ends which they must each pursue for the good of the city.[23]

5) Socrates[X] attaches much importance to economics and to the conditions of material prosperity,[24] to which Socrates[P] is completely indifferent.[25]

6) Socrates[P] is very critical of the great Athenian leaders of his time, particularly Pericles and Themistocles.[26] Socrates[X], by contrast, treats them with the greatest respect.[27]

7) Socrates[X], quite sensitive to honor and fame, encourages those who aspire to honors.[28] Socrates[P] is himself alien to the pursuit of honors and recommends renouncing such ambitions.[29]

8) As many commentators have noted, Socrates[X] never displays the particular kind of irony characteristic of Socrates[P], which is closely bound up with his avowal of ignorance. Since Socrates[X] never avows ignorance, it is not surprising that he is not "ironic" in this way.

9) Self-knowledge consists, for Socrates[X], in recognizing the extent and limits of one's own *dunamis*, of what one is and is not technically capable of doing[30] – not in recognizing that the "self" is the soul and that one must therefore live with a view to the goods of the soul rather than to bodily or external goods.[31]

10) Socrates[X] thinks that virtue is the result of practice (*askēsis*),[32] and that one can lose it as soon as one ceases to practice,[33] while Socrates[P], who makes virtue a kind of knowledge,[34] seems never to recognize that one can lose it.

11) Inasmuch as physical strength is indispensable for the acquisition and practice of virtue, Socrates[X] gives much importance to the care of the body,[35] and, in contrast with Socrates[P], shows little interest in the care of the soul.[36]

12) Socrates[X] thinks, in accordance with tradition, that a man's virtue consists in helping his friends and harming his enemies;[37] Socrates[P], by contrast, maintains that one should never harm even one's enemies.[38]

13) Socrates[X] almost never uses the elenchus, and calls on a different kind of *logos* to make his companions better;[39] while Socrates[P], in the early dialogues, subjects most of his interlocutors to the elenchus.

14) While Socrates[P] is notorious for the "outrageousness" (*atopia*)[40] which so disconcerts his interlocutors, Socrates[X] is usually predictable and, with the exception of his first conversation with Euthydemus (*Memorabilia* 4.2), never leads his interlocutors into aporia.

15) Socrates[P] believes he has a mission from Delphic Apollo to live a philosophical life,[41] while Socrates[X], who professes no such mission, also does not see in the practice of philosophy (understood as examination of oneself and of others) an act of piety or of service to God.[42] His conception of piety is pretty much the traditional one.[43]

16) Socrates[X] has the benefit of the advice of a divine sign (*daimonion sēmeion*), which indicates to him what he and his friends should do or avoid.[44] In Plato, the divine sign never intervenes on behalf of Socrates' friends, and never indicates to Socrates himself what he should do, but makes itself known only to stop him from doing what he is about to do.[45] While Socrates[X] sees in the divine sign a means of divination like any other,[46] Socrates[P] makes it a special kind of divination, distinctive in being purely negative.[47]

17) Socrates[X] acknowledges that the gods have the power to harm human beings,[48] while Socrates[P] refuses to admit that the gods can ever be the cause of an evil.[49]

Socrates[X] and *Enkrateia*

But the main difference between the two Socrateses comes down to three characteristics which Xenophon presents at the beginning of *Memorabilia* 1.2, when he sets out to defend Socrates against the accusation of corrupting the young:

> It also seems extraordinary to me that any people should have been persuaded that Socrates had a bad influence upon young men. Besides what I have said already, he was in the first place the most self-disciplined of men (*pantōn anthrōpōn enkratestatos*) in respect of his sexual and other appetites; then he was most tolerant (*karterikōtatos*) of

cold and heat and hardships of all kinds; and finally he had so trained himself to be moderate in his requirements that he was very easily satisfied (*arkounta*) with very few possessions.[50]

The three qualities mentioned in this passage are *enkrateia* (self-mastery with regard to bodily pleasures), *karteria* (endurance of physical pain), and *autarkeia* (self-sufficiency). Xenophon frequently mentions these three qualities of Socrates in the rest of the *Memorabilia*,[51] and for good reason: this triad forms the core of Socratic ethics in Xenophon's writings. To see this, recall that Xenophon asserts that *enkrateia* is the foundation of virtue (1.5.4), i.e. the necessary condition of acquiring and practicing it. Immediately after asserting that *enkrateia* is the foundation of virtue, Socrates asks, "without it [*enkrateia*], who could either learn anything good or practise it to a degree worth mentioning?"[52] *Enkrateia* is thus the precondition for any learning or practice that may help in the development of virtue. Only once the soul is in full possession of itself, and masters the pleasures that press it to satisfy them,[53] does it meet all the conditions for becoming virtuous. Since acquiring virtue requires effort, dedication, and study,[54] and since the man who is the slave of his bodily pleasures will take no pleasure in this ascetic discipline, *enkrateia* is clearly a precondition for acquiring virtue.

The role of *enkrateia* is distinctive to the ethics of Socrates[X]. Socrates[P] gives it no such importance: he never presents self-mastery as the foundation of virtue, and even the term "*enkrateia*" is absent from the early dialogues; the *Charmides'* discussion of *sōphrosunē* is oddly silent on the traditional conception of *sōphrosunē* as a mastery of pleasures and desires. But one can hardly overestimate the role of *enkrateia* in the ethics of Socrates[X], who makes it the foundation of virtue and the source of all benefit or usefulness (*ōpheleia*). And to see the importance that Xenophon gives to usefulness, we need only recall that to defend Socrates against the charge of having injured the city and harmed the young people of his circle, Xenophon tries to show, on the contrary, how useful he was to his companions. Just this is Xenophon's aim in the *Memorabilia*: "in order to support my opinion that he benefited his companions, alike by actions that revealed his own character and by his conversation, I will set down what I recollect of these."[55] To give a clearer idea of the multiform usefulness of *enkrateia*, let us take stock of its many functions:

1) *Enkrateia* is indispensable for all who exercise power and occupy positions of responsibility.[56] Be it a mere slave responsible for the storehouses of an estate, or a leader responsible for the welfare of the city, whoever exercises power must absolutely be master of himself. Socrates is convinced that self-mastery is the precondition for governing anyone else: whoever aims at commanding people must at all costs be capable of resisting the lure of pleasure, for otherwise there is a danger that the promise of pleasure may warp his judgment and lead him to make decisions which will prove disastrous both to himself and to those for whom he is responsible.[57]

2) *Enkrateia* is the condition of freedom. If it is a prerequisite for acquiring virtue, and if people who have been reduced to slavery for economic or political reasons may nonetheless have access to *enkrateia* and to virtue, the worst slavery is necessarily that of the person who is enslaved to his passions and dominated by pleasure, since such a person does not have the freedom needed for the pursuit of the good and of virtue.[58]

3) *Enkrateia* is the condition of justice. The person who lacks *enkrateia* is constantly in need of money, because he is ever in search of means to satisfy his passions; so there is a danger that he will help himself to the goods of others to temporarily satisfy his cupidity. In Xenophon's *Apology*, Socrates explicitly connects his justice with the moderation of his desires:

> [W]ho is there in your knowledge that is less a slave to his bodily appetites than I am? Who in the world more free, for I accept neither gifts nor pay from any one? Whom would you with reason regard as more just than the one so reconciled to his present possessions as to want nothing beside that belongs to another?[59]

Contrariwise, the tyrant is unjust precisely because his lack of *enkrateia* impels him to seize and appropriate the goods of others.[60] In the *Memorabilia* (1.2.1–8), Xenophon invokes Socrates' *enkrateia* to refute the accusation of corrupting the young: how could he have treated them unjustly, given that he was a model of *enkrateia*, and that *enkrateia* is the foundation for all virtues including justice?

4) *Enkrateia* is the condition *sine qua non* of friendship (*philia*). As is illustrated by the story of Heracles at the crossroads,[61] the person who lacks *enkrateia* is incapable of forming a genuine *philia*, which would be beneficial both to himself and to his friends, because he treats others as a means, a mere instrument permitting him to satisfy his desires and obtain pleasure. This connection between *enkrateia* and friendship is expressly stated at *Memorabilia* 2.6.1, and is also implicitly present in the conversation between Socrates and Aristippus,[62] which serves precisely as the introduction to the long series of conversations devoted to *philia* (*Memorabilia* 2.1–10). It is striking that Aristippus and the woman who represents Vice in the story of Heracles at the crossroads both lack *enkrateia* and are both excluded, for precisely that reason, from their respective communities.[63] Genuine friendship is possible only between people who are virtuous and therefore masters of themselves. *Enkrateia* is also what allows one to fulfill the chief duty of friendship, which is to provide for the needs of a friend in difficulty. Given that the *enkratēs* person has limited needs and can be content with little, he will not hesitate to provide for the needs of a friend in difficulty; and inversely, the person who is not master of himself cannot count on genuine friends who will come to his help in case of need.[64]

5) *Enkrateia* is the condition of wealth and prosperity. If one does not succeed in mastering one's desires and limiting one's needs, notably those required to satisfy bodily pleasures, then money will inevitably be thrown away on the satisfaction of desires;[65] moreover, as the pursuit of pleasure prevents the *akratēs* person from devoting himself to money-making activities, he will always be short of money to satisfy the desires which leave him no respite. The widespread opinion that Socrates had no interest in economics arises doubtless from Plato's *Apology*, where Socrates openly acknowledges that he is poor[66] and that he has neglected his own affairs and the management of his household.[67] On these two points, Socrates[X] is sharply distinguished from his Platonic namesake: not only is he not poor, he cannot let himself say that he neglects *oikonomia* to any extent. Given the conception of wealth and poverty that Xenophon sets out in many passages, Socrates is not poor, because he has more than he needs. In the *Oeconomicus* (11.3), Socrates reacts very strongly against those who

regard him as poor: this reproach, he says, is the most unreasonable of all that have ever been brought against him. Since wealth is simply the excess of what one has over what one needs, one can be rich even if one has very little, as long as it is sufficient for one's needs. Wealth and poverty depend, not on the amount of money at one's disposal, but on limiting one's needs. Someone is poor if what he needs exceeds what he has,[68] however much that might be, while he is rich if what he has, however modest, fully suffices for his needs.[69] Xenophon sets out this relative conception of wealth and poverty in many passages, attributing it now to Antisthenes,[70] now to Hieron,[71] now to Socrates himself.[72] Unlike Plato, Xenophon could not say that Socrates neglects the management of his own affairs, without at the same time calling into question Socrates' ability to train future statesmen. Since Socrates[X] finds no discontinuity between the ability to manage the *oikos* well and the ability to administer the *polis* well, and since the former is indeed a precondition for the latter,[73] and since he prides himself on training future statesmen,[74] it follows in principle that he must be capable of training his young companions in domestic economy. And indeed he gives proof of his economic competence in *Memorabilia* 2.7.

6) More surprisingly, *enkrateia* is also the condition for practicing dialectic. By "dialectic," Socrates[X] means "the practice of meeting together for common deliberation, sorting, discussing (*dialegontas*) things after their kind (*kata genē*)."[75] Despite appearances, dialectic here is not the art of dichotomy illustrated in Plato's *Sophist* and *Statesman*, which divides classes successively in half in order to reach a definition, but rather an ability to bring a concept or an action under one of two great classes, good and evil. But the ability to distinguish good from evil, both in *logos* and in action, belongs only to those who are masters of themselves, because only in their case is there no danger that the lure of pleasure and the power of desire will lead them to take as good what is in reality an evil: "only the self-controlled (*tois enkratesi monois*) have power to consider the things that matter most, and, sorting them out after their kind (*dialegontas kata genē*), by word and deed alike to prefer the good and reject the evil."[76]

The importance of *enkrateia* also becomes clear in the plan that governs the sequence of conversations contained in the *Memorabilia*. For Socrates[X], a person's usefulness is grounded in *enkrateia*: this is what allows him to be useful to himself, and his usefulness then extends, thanks to his exercise of virtue, to his household, his friends, and finally his city and fellow-citizens. There are at least six passages in the *Memorabilia*[77] which clearly present *enkrateia* as the precondition of all usefulness, be it toward oneself or toward others (family, friends, city). A passage of Xenophon's *Apology* gives an excellent proof *a contrario* of Xenophon's conviction that the ability to be useful to oneself, one's friends, and the city is grounded in *enkrateia*. Commenting on Socrates' prophecy about Anytus' son, Xenophon says, "In saying this he was not mistaken: the young man, delighting in wine, never left off drinking night or day, and at last turned out worth nothing to his city, his friends, or himself."[78] It is thus on account of a lack of *enkrateia* that Anytus' son is prevented from being useful to himself, his friends, and the city. From usefulness to oneself, through usefulness to one's household and friends, to usefulness to the city, there is no break: these are all manifestations of one and the same disposition, *enkrateia*. There is good reason to think that one aim of the sequence of conversations from *Memorabilia* 1.3 to the end of Book 3 is to illustrate precisely this progressive extension of Socrates' usefulness, from the initial assertion of his main virtues (piety, self-sufficiency, *enkrateia*), through his own family and various of his friends, to his usefulness to the city as a whole. If Xenophon insists so strongly on the necessity of service to one's household, friends, and country,[79] should we not suppose that he wanted to illustrate just this progression of usefulness, extending in concentric circles from the individual to the whole city, in the case of Socrates? The plan of the *Memorabilia* is thus natural for Xenophon, corresponding perfectly to the successive stages of the development of usefulness, starting from its necessary grounding in *enkrateia*.

Reworking of Socratic Themes on the Basis of *Enkrateia*

It is only once we have brought to light the importance of *enkrateia* that we can really understand Xenophon's treatment of some Socratic themes which are also present in Plato. In other words, we can show how Xenophon reworks certain themes so that they fit coherently into his overall portrayal of Socrates, and so that they support the leading role of *enkrateia* in the ethics of his Socrates. Xenophon's reworking of certain themes is particularly clear in the cases of the Delphic oracle, the *basilikē tekhnē*, friendship, and *akrasia*.

The Delphic oracle

Faced with the diverging accounts of the Delphic oracle in the *Apologies* of Plato and Xenophon, we might hesitate between two interpretive choices: either we accept Plato's version in preference to Xenophon's,[80] for reasons which – we will have to admit – turn more on prejudice than on the possibility of deciding with certainty in favor of one version. Or else we keep both versions and, rather than disqualifying one in order to vindicate the other, we try to record their differences, and, above all, to interpret them in the context of the philosophical convictions of our two authors. According to Plato's account, the Pythia, in response to Chaerephon's question whether there is anyone wiser than Socrates, said that there is no one wiser than he (21a). In emphasizing Socrates' *sophia*, which consists in his recognition of his own ignorance, the Pythia's response expresses an essential trait of Socrates' character and of his ethics, as they are represented not just in Plato's *Apology* but in the early dialogues as a whole. Moreover, this particular form of *sophia* is directly connected to the practice of the elenchus, since one of the aims of the elenchus is to bring someone who wrongly imagines that he has knowledge to recognize his ignorance. Since Socrates[X]'s *sophia* does not consist in recognizing his own ignorance,[81] and since he does not usually practice the elenchus,[82] it is no surprise that Xenophon does not reproduce the response of the oracle as we find it in Plato's *Apology*, and still less the interpretation that Socrates[P] gives of it. In Xenophon's *Apology*, Socrates reports that the Pythia told Chaerephon "that no man was more free (*eleutheriōteron*) than I, or more just (*dikaioteron*), or more moderate (*sōphronesteron*)."[83] It is certainly remarkable that this response makes no mention of *sophia* – and this tends to confirm that *sophia* does not play as central a role in Xenophon as in Plato – but the choice of the three virtues that are mentioned is even more revealing, since it is entirely in accord with the preeminence Xenophon gives to mastery of one's pleasures and desires. The explanation that Socrates[X] spontaneously gives of this oracle shows that the three qualities in fact reduce to one, namely *sōphrosunē*, which in Xenophon is almost always synonymous with *enkrateia*.[84] In accordance with what we have already seen,[85] Socrates[X] presents moderation in pleasures and desires as the foundation of his perfect justice and unequalled freedom. The oracle's response is thus a kind of condensation of the main principles of the ethics that Socrates[X] incarnates, so that it is tempting to think that "Xenophon has reformulated Plato's account of the oracle's response in the service of his own understanding of Socratic ethics."[86]

The "kingly art" (basilikē tekhnē)

In the conversation on *enkrateia* at the beginning of Book 2 of the *Memorabilia*, Aristippus asks Socrates, "But how about those who are trained in the art of kingship (*tēn basilikēn tekhnēn*), Socrates, which you appear to identify with happiness? How are they better off than those whose sufferings are compulsory if they must bear hunger, thirst, cold, sleeplessness, and endure all these tortures willingly"?[87] The ability to endure hunger, thirst, cold, and fatigue shows that the *basilikē tekhnē* is closely connected with *enkrateia* (the ability to resist the lure of bodily pleasures) and *karteria* (the ability to tolerate physical pain). Whoever aims to command human beings must at all costs be capable of resisting the lure of pleasure and of tolerating pain, for if he is overcome by either of these, there is a danger that he will neglect his duty and his responsibilities. This is why, for Socrates[X], it is absolutely necessary to train future leaders to resist the lure of bodily pleasure (*enkrateia*) and to tolerate physical pain (*karteria*).[88]

The expression *basilikē tekhnē* occurs in only one other passage of Xenophon's Socratic writings, in Book IV of the *Memorabilia*, when Socrates is talking with Euthydemus:

> Surely Euthydemus, you don't covet the kind of excellence that makes good statesmen and managers, competent rulers and benefactors of themselves and mankind in general? – Yes, I do, answered Euthydemus, that kind of excellence I greatly desire. – Why, cried Socrates, it is the noblest kind of excellence (*tēs kallistēs aretēs*), the greatest of arts (*megistēs tekhnēs*) that you covet, for it belongs to kings and is dubbed "kingly" (*basilikē*).[89]

It emerges clearly from this passage and from all of Socrates' conversations with Euthydemus[90] that the *basilikē tekhnē* is a political competence founded on the individual's control over himself. It is precisely because it is related to *enkrateia* that the *basilikē tekhnē* is considered to be "the noblest kind of excellence." The person who possesses the kingly art is useful in the first place to himself, inasmuch as this art in making him master of himself guards him against making bad decisions under the influence of pleasure; he is then also useful to others, because his mastery over himself makes him capable of administering his household well and of leading others effectively.

101

Here we recognize Socrates[X]'s master-idea: it is *enkrateia* which guarantees at the same time a person's virtue, his ability to administer his own household, and his capacity for taking on political or military responsibilities. For Socrates[X], there is no discontinuity between one's control over oneself, virtuous relations with others, the profitable management of one's estate, and effective governance of human beings. Further on in Book IV, when Socrates has taken charge of Euthydemus' political and philosophical education, he restates, at the end of a chapter devoted to *enkrateia*, the close connection between self-mastery, ability to command, and happiness (4.5.11–12). This conception of the *basilikē tekhnē* essentially corresponds to the conviction that Socrates tries to communicate to Aristippus (2.1), that whoever aims to lead others must first master himself. Thus the kingly art should not be taken in an exclusively political sense – this would be to miss its ethical dimension, that it is first and foremost a mastery which someone exercises over himself. Conversely, it would be a mistake to present the *basilikē tekhnē* simply as the task of mastering oneself – that would be to cut off what for Socrates is its natural continuation, household and political *oikonomia*.

With these two uses of the expression *basilikē tekhnē* we may compare a passage of Plato's *Euthydemus* (291b–292c) which makes use several times of the same expression.[91] For Socrates[P], the kingly art is essentially a moral knowledge or wisdom (*sophia*), making no reference to *enkrateia*; not, as for Socrates[X], an ability to govern having self-mastery as its precondition. A comparative look at the *basilikē tekhnē* helps bring to light one of the main differences between the ethics of Socrates[X] and of his Platonic namesake: the *basilikē tekhnē* of the former is closely linked to *enkrateia*, while that of the latter gives *enkrateia* no role and is based instead on *sophia*.

The foundation of friendship

In Plato's *Lysis* (210b–c), Socrates presents Lysis with the choice of ruling or being ruled. But what puts someone in the position of ruler or ruled is wisdom (*sophia*): where one has knowledge, one commands others, but in areas in which one is ignorant, one is under another's command. Since knowledge or wisdom is the condition for being useful, whether to oneself or to others, it is also the condition for the formation of genuine friendship (cf. 210c–d). In the *Memorabilia*, Socrates presents Aristippus with the same choice of ruling or being ruled (2.1.1–20); but this time what makes the difference is self-mastery (*enkrateia*) and not knowledge: the person who rules himself can also rule others, while the person unable to master himself is condemned to be a slave to himself and to others. Given that self-mastery is at the source of all genuine usefulness, toward oneself or toward others, it is a prerequisite for the formation of a beneficial friendship (cf. 2.6.1). The parallel between these two texts is all the more striking in that both conversations serve as introductions to treatments of friendship. The difference we see in their treatments of the same theme – the choice of ruling or being ruled, and the conditions for the formation of friendship – is easily understood when we examine it in the light of the importance of *sophia* and *enkrateia* in Socrates' ethics according to the contrasting presentations of Plato and Xenophon. Inasmuch as Plato attributes to Socrates a decisively intellectualist ethics, which makes *sophia* the condition for acquiring and practicing virtue, it is no surprise that knowledge or wisdom plays a central role in the formation of friendship according to the *Lysis*, and that it is a condition *sine qua non* of the exercise of power. While Plato sees in knowledge or wisdom the foundation of virtue, the source of all genuine usefulness, and the condition of the exercise of power and of the formation of friendship, Xenophon attributes these functions to self-mastery; this is why they give different treatments of what is, at the outset, the same choice, to rule or to be ruled.

Akrasia

Both Socrates[X] and Socrates[P] maintain that a virtuous person who knows what is good will never act, under the influence of pleasure or of some other passion, contrary to his knowledge and his virtue.[92] However, if we consider the details of the arguments that they set out to support this conclusion, we will notice a number of differences. The most important concerns the role of *enkrateia*: while for Socrates[X] the impossibility of *akrasia* ultimately depends on the exercise of *enkrateia*,[93] Socrates[P] gives *enkrateia* no role, so that the impossibility of *akrasia* on the part of the virtuous person is explained purely by the presence of knowledge. In a revealing passage of Plato's *Protagoras*, Socrates says, "Nor is giving in to oneself anything other than error, nor controlling oneself anything other than wisdom."[94] In other words, self-mastery is not a disposition or ability independent of knowledge or wisdom, because it is simply a consequence of wisdom.[95] In these circumstances it is easy to understand why *enkrateia* as a distinct disposition is superfluous. The fact of being "overcome by pleasure" is due not to a lack of *enkrateia* but to the absence of wisdom or knowledge (357d–e). In the *Memorabilia*, by contrast, *enkrateia* is not only distinct from *sophia*, but in a sense prior to it, since it is the precondition for acquiring *sophia*.[96] Socrates[X] thus reverses Socrates[P]'s conception of the relations between *enkrateia* and *sophia*: while for Socrates[P] *enkrateia* is merely an effect of *sophia*, Socrates[X] thinks on the contrary that *enkrateia* precedes and is the precondition of *sophia*. It is thus no surprise that Socrates[X] attributes the impossibility of *akrasia* on the part of the virtuous person above all to the presence of *enkrateia* rather than to that of *sophia*. In the epilogue of the *Memorabilia*, where Xenophon gives a final retrospective praise of Socrates and prepares to take leave of his readers, he says that Socrates was "so self-controlled that he never chose the pleasanter rather than the better course,"[97] as if *enkrateia* alone were fully responsible for preventing *akrasia*.

This brief analysis of four Socratic themes shared by Plato and Xenophon has allowed us to note that on each occasion Socrates[X] gives to *enkrateia* the central role that Socrates[P] gives to *sophia*. The systematic character of the substitution of *enkrateia* for *sophia* leaves no room for doubt: Xenophon is seeking in this way to preserve the philosophical coherence of his portrait of Socrates, who is not only the incarnation *par excellence* of *enkrateia*, but also the tireless defender of an ethics that makes *enkrateia* the foundation of a virtuous life. We can thus see how unfairly reductive it is to represent Xenophon as a poor imitator of Plato: even on the assumption that he did borrow from Plato certain Socratic themes that they share, we must note that he has in each case reworked them to make them fit into his representation of Socrates.

Enkrateia and *Autarkeia*

Despite the importance of *enkrateia* in the ethics of Socrates[X], it is not an end in itself. *Enkrateia* is certainly indispensable, but as a means to something else, while *autarkeia* is a state desired for its own sake. Moreover, *enkrateia* is subordinated to *autarkeia* to the extent that it paves the way toward self-sufficiency. We can show that the members of the Socratic triad (*karteria, enkrateia, autarkeia*) are not all on the same footing, that there is a hierarchy among them: at *Memorabilia* 1.2.1 the first two members of the triad cooperate in order to bring about the third, *autarkeia*. This subordination of *enkrateia* and *karteria* to *autarkeia* is not obvious at 1.2.1, but it becomes quite clear in the conversation between Socrates and Antiphon (1.6). Let us recall the context. Antiphon blames Socrates for leading a miserable existence: he does not eat fancy food, he always wears the same rough cloak, he walks barefoot and does not have the money that would be needed to acquire pleasant things. In short, while (according to Antiphon) philosophy is supposed to be a school of happiness, Socrates is a master only of misery. But if Socrates has no money and demands no pay from his disciples, this is not – as Antiphon manages to insinuate – because his knowledge and wisdom have no value, but because he wants to keep his freedom to engage in conversation with interlocutors of his choosing. As is also shown in other passages,[98] Socrates' indifference to money is a consequence of his perfect *enkrateia*. Given that money serves mainly to acquire the goods demanded by the appetites, and given that Socrates has perfect mastery over his appetites, he will have little need for money. The frugality of his diet too does not mean that he has renounced pleasure, for the genuine pleasure of eating and drinking is not the artificial pleasure brought about by fancy expensive foods, but the natural pleasure resulting from the satisfaction of hunger and thirst, and a very simple diet is enough to allow him to "taste" this pleasure. As for clothing, here too it is not because he is poor that Socrates has only one cloak and that he goes barefoot. His dress is modest by choice: he has trained his body so well in enduring the pains of heat and cold and of the streets on which he walks barefoot that he has no need of sandals to protect his feet, and that a single cloak is sufficient for both summer and winter. If *autarkeia* is not a total absence of needs – which only the gods can have – but rather the ability to provide by oneself for one's own needs, we see better how, and how far, *enkrateia* and *karteria* pave the way for *autarkeia*. If we have many needs, we will have that much more difficulty in satisfying them all and in attaining the ideal of *autarkeia*. The role of *enkrateia* is precisely to master and to restrain the needs of the body (hunger, thirst, sexuality, sleep) which pull at us without respite. Analogously, *karteria* aims at hardening the body, making it more resistant and thereby also limiting its need for clothing to a strict minimum. Thus if we must train ourselves in *karteria* and *enkrateia*, it is in order to reach the state of self-sufficiency which clearly appears in this passage (1.6.4–10) as the crowning goal of Socrates' argument:

> You seem, Antiphon, to imagine that happiness consists in luxury and extravagance. But my belief is that to have no wants is divine; to have as few as possible comes next to the divine; and as that which is divine is supreme, so that which approaches nearest to its nature is nearest to the supreme.[99]

The priority of *autarkeia* over *enkrateia* is also confirmed by the fact that of these three virtues, only *autarkeia* is attributed to the gods. Since a god, unlike a human being, has no needs, a god is self-sufficient from the outset, so that it has no need to practice *enkrateia* to limits its needs, or *karteria* to tolerate extreme temperatures, to which it will not be exposed in the first place. Socrates^X's aspiration to self-sufficiency must be understood in the more general perspective of assimilation to god (*hōmoiōsis theō[i]*): since human beings aspire to happiness, and since a god gives us the model of a being who is both self-sufficient and happy, the philosophers in their search for happiness privilege ways of life which promise the highest degree of self-sufficiency to human beings. Here too Socrates^X can be contrasted with Socrates^P, since Plato never says or even suggests that his Socrates is self-sufficient. This is doubtless because the only self-sufficiency that would count in Plato's eyes is self-sufficiency with regard to knowledge and the good, not the self-sufficiency with regard to the material conditions of existence which Xenophon attributes to Socrates. And since Socrates^P is ignorant and constantly in search of the knowledge and virtue which would finally satisfy his aspiration to the good, he cannot be self-sufficient.

One Socrates and Many

Xenophon has sketched a portrait of the character of Socrates, and of the ethics he defends, which is perfectly uniform and coherent throughout the *Memorabilia*, *Symposium*, *Apology*, and *Oeconomicus*. Because there is no noticeable doctrinal evolution between these four texts, it does not much matter whether we know the chronological order of their composition. As is well known, this is not the case for Plato's dialogues, where we can find divergences, even contradictions, between the positions Plato attributes to Socrates in different dialogues, so that some scholars have gone so far as to maintain that the early dialogues represent a Socrates diametrically opposed to the Socrates of the middle dialogues.[100] Even within the early dialogues it is not always easy to reconstruct a single coherent Socratic doctrine. Now in Xenophon too we can in a certain sense identify several different Socrateses – not because Xenophon would like Plato have allowed himself, in the course of the development of his thought, to attribute to Socrates several incompatible philosophical positions, but rather because, in his other writings, notably the *Cyropaedia*, *Hiero*, *Agesilaus*, and *Constitution of the Lacedaemonians*, he attributes to other characters (Cyrus, Simonides, Agesilaus, and Lycurgus respectively) the same characteristics, virtues, and doctrines which Socrates incarnates in the four *logoi Sōkratikoi*. Is this indisputable kinship, between characters at first sight so different, to be attributed to the fact that Xenophon was so deeply and permanently marked by the imprint of Socrates that he has – as it were, in gratitude – attributed Socratic virtues to all of his heroes? Or has he instead drawn all his heroes, including Socrates, after one and the same model – himself? In that case the character of Socrates would be just one projection or avatar, among others, of an ideal whose features Xenophon has reproduced again and again in all his writings. However this may be, one thing is certain: the facts that Xenophon felt free to imagine different historical characters on Socrates' model, and that Plato attributed to the single character Socrates positions so divergent that the unity and coherence of this

105

character become problematic, are fully sufficient to show that the literary genres in which these texts of Plato and Xenophon are written allow their authors considerable scope for invention – so much so that it seems hopeless to search in them for what we will doubtless never find, the historical Socrates, securely beyond our grasp.

Notes

1. See Schleiermacher (1818) and Dorion (2001).
2. See Brickhouse and Smith (2000: 38, 42–3).
3. Thus it is said that Plato's Socrates is "in fact the only Socrates worth talking about" (Vlastos 1971: 2); that "it is only Plato's Socrates that is of major interest to the contemporary philosopher" (Santas 1979: x); that "as far as we are concerned, the Socrates of [Plato's] dialogues is the historical Socrates. He is certainly the only one who counts for the history of philosophy" (Kahn 1981: 319).
4. Thus Burnet (1914: 150): "It is really impossible to preserve Xenophon's Sokrates, even if he were worth preserving."
5. See Hadot (1995).
6. *Memorabilia* 1.2.18, 1.3.1, 1.5.6.
7. *Memorabilia* 1.4.1, 1.4.19, 1.5.1, 1.6.14, 1.7.1, 2.1.1, 4.3.1–2, 4.3.18, 4.4.25, 4.5.1, 4.8.7, 4.8.10–11.
8. Nietzsche (1967: vol. IV 3, 442); Posthumous fragment 41 [2] 1879.
9. Nietzsche (1967: vol. IV 2, 423); Posthumous fragment 18 [47] 1876: "whereas the Memorabilia of Xenophon presents a truly real portrait of Socrates, that one which is so witty, as was the object of a portrait; one must understand this book, however, in order to read it. The philologists basically believe that Socrates has nothing to say to them, and are thereby bored with it. Others feel that this book stabs at the same time that it flatters."
10. See below.
11. See below.
12. See below.
13. Like Luccioni (1953: 48–56).
14. Each of these points deserves a deeper analysis; here I am merely flagging the differences.
15. *Memorabilia* 1.1.16, 3.9, 4.6.
16. *Memorabilia* 1.6.13–14, 4.2.40, 4.3.1, 4.7.1; and Xenophon, *Apology* 20. See also *Memorabilia* 1.2.17–18, 1.2.31, 1.6.3, 2.6.30–2, 2.7.1.
17. Plato, *Apology* 19d and 33a.
18. *Euthyphro* 5a–b, *Greater Hippias* 286d–e, *Laches* 186a–187b.
19. *Memorabilia* 1.6.15, 4.3.1.
20. *Gorgias* 521d.
21. See, *inter alia*, *Memorabilia* 3.6–7.
22. See *Memorabilia* 4.2.2–7.
23. See *Charmides* 174b–c.
24. *Memorabilia* 2.7, 3.4.6–12, 3.6, 3.7.2, 4.6.14.
25. See below.
26. See *Gorgias* 503c–d and 517b–c.
27. See *Memorabilia* 2.6.13 and Xenophon, *Symposium* 8.39.
28. See *Memorabilia* 1.7.1, 3.3.13–14, 3.7.1, and so on.
29. *Gorgias* 526d, *Republic* 1 347b, *Phaedo* 82c.

30   See *Memorabilia* 1.7.4, 3.7, 4.2.25–9, and Dorion (2004).

31   This is the position defended by Socrates[p] in the *Alcibiades* 1 (129b–133d).

32   *Memorabilia* 1.2.19–23, 2.1.20, 2.1.28, 2.6.39, 3.3.6, 3.5.14, 3.9.1–3.

33   *Memorabilia* 1.2.19–24, 3.5.13.

34   *Protagoras* 349d–360e, *Laches* 194d.

35   *Memorabilia* 1.2.4, 3.12.

36   Plato, *Apology* 29e, *Alcibiades* 1 132c, *Charmides* 156d–157c, *Phaedo* 107c.

37   *Memorabilia* 2.1.28, 2.2.2, 2.3.14, 4.2.15–17.

38   *Crito* 49c–d, *Republic* 1 332d–336a.

39   See *Memorabilia* 1.4.1 and the commentary of Dorion (2000: cxxvi–cxliv).

40   See Plato *Symposium* 215a, 221d, *Gorgias* 494d, *Theaetetus* 149a, *Phaedrus* 229c.

41   Plato, *Apology* 29c–30b, 30d–e, 33b–c.

42   Plato, *Apology* 23b, 30a.

43   See *Memorabilia* 1.3.1, 4.3.16, 4.6.2–4.

44   *Memorabilia* 1.1.2–5, 1.4.15, 4.3.12, 4.8.1, Xenophon, *Apology* 12–13.

45   Plato, *Apology* 31d, 40a, *Euthydemus* 272e, *Phaedrus* 242b–c.

46   See *Memorabilia* 1.1.2–5, 1.4.15, 4.3.12, Xenophon, *Apology* 12–13, and Dorion (2003: 170–80).

47   See Plato, *Apology* 40a, *Phaedrus* 242c, and Dorion (2003: 183–8).

48   *Memorabilia* 1.4.16.

49   *Republic* 2 379b.

50   1.2.1 (trans. Tredennick and Waterfield).

51   For Socrates' *enkrateia*, see *Memorabilia* 1.2.14, 1.3.5–14, 1.5.1, 1.5.6, 1.6.8, 2.1, 3.14, 4.5.9, 4.8.11, Xenophon, *Apology* 16. For his *karteria*, cf. *Memorabilia* 1.6.6–7. For his *autarkeia*, see *Memorabilia* 1.2.14, 1.2.60, 1.6.10, 4.7.1, 4.8.11, Xenophon *Symposium* 4.43.

52   1.5.5 (trans. Tredennick and Waterfield).

53   Cf. *Memorabilia* 1.2.23: "it seems to me that every truly good thing needs to be exercised (*askēta*), and not least self-discipline; for the appetites that are implanted with the soul in the same body encourage it not to be self-disciplined, but to gratify both them and the body in the quickest possible way" (trans. Tredennick and Waterfield).

54   See *Memorabilia* 3.9.2–3.

55   1.3.1 (trans. Marchant). Socrates' usefulness is a real Leitmotiv (see, beside the passages mentioned in note above, *Memorabilia* 1.1.4, 1.2.2, 1.2.60–1, 1.7.5, 2.4.1, 2.5.1, 2.6.1, 2.7.1, 3.1.1, 3.6.1, 3.8.1, 3.10.1, 4.1.1, 4.4.1, 4.7.1, Xenophon, *Apology* 26 and 34).

56   *Memorabilia* 1.5.1, 2.1.1–7.

57   See also below.

58   *Memorabilia* 1.5.5, 4.5.2–6, *Oeconomicus* 1.17–23, Xenophon, *Apology* 16.

59   Xenophon, *Apology* 16 (trans. Todd).

60   *Memorabilia* 4.2.38.

61   *Memorabilia* 2.1.21–34.

62   *Memorabilia* 2.1.1–20.

63   See *Memorabilia* 2.1.13 (Aristippus) and 2.1.31 (Vice).

64   See *Oecononomicus* 2.8, *Memorabilia* 2.1.31.

65   See *Memorabilia* 1.2.22, 1.3.11, *Oeconomicus* 2.7.

66   Plato, *Apology* 23b–c, 31c, 36d.

67   Plato, *Apology* 31b and 36b.

68   As is the case for Critobulus (*Oeconomicus* 2.3–4).

69   As is the case for Socrates (*Memorabilia* 1.2.1, 1.3.5, 4.2.38–9).

70   Xenophon, *Symposium* 4.34–6.

71 *Hiero* 4.8–11.
72 *Oeconomicus* 2.2–10, *Memorabilia* 4.2.37–9.
73 *Memorabilia* 1.1.7, 3.4.6–12, 3.6.13–15, 4.1.2, 4.2.11, 4.5.10.
74 *Memorabilia* 1.2.17–18, 1.6.15, 2.1, 4.2, 4.3.1.
75 4.5.12 (trans. Marchant).
76 4.5.11 (trans. Marchant).
77 *Memorabilia* 1.6.9, 2.6.1, 2.1.19, 4.2.11, 4.5.3–6, 4.5.10.
78 Xenophon, *Apology* 31 (trans. Todd)
79 See *Memorabilia* 1.2.48, 1.6.9, 2.1.19, 2.1.28, 2.1.33, 2.6.25–6, 3.6.2, 3.6.4, 3.7.9, 3.12.4, 4.5.10, Xenophon, *Symposium* 3.4, 4.64, 8.38, *Oeconomicus* 4.3, 6.9, 11.8–10, 11.13, Xenophon, *Apology* 31.
80 Cf. Vlastos (1991: 288–9).
81 Cf. above.
82 Cf. above.
83 Xenophon, *Apology* 14 (trans. Todd) (slightly modified).
84 Cf., *inter alia*, *Memorabilia* 3.9.4.
85 Cf. above.
86 Vander Waerdt (1993: 39).
87 2.1.17 (trans. Marchant).
88 *Memorabilia* 2.1.1–7.
89 4.2.11 (trans. Marchant).
90 See *Memorabilia* 4.2–3 and 4.5–6.
91 See *Euthydemus* 291b5, 291c5, 291d7, 292a4, 292c4.
92 *Memorabilia* 3.9.4–5; *Protagoras* 352b–e, 355a–d, 358c–d.
93 Cf. Dorion (2003b).
94 358c (trans. Taylor).
95 Cf. also *Phaedrus* 237e.
96 See *Memorabilia* 4.5.6 and Dorion (2003b).
97 4.8.11 (trans. Marchant).
98 The sequence *enkrateia*/indifference to money appears three times in Book 1: 1.2.1–4 (*enkrateia*) and 1.2.5–7 (indifference to money); 1.5.1–5 (*enkrateia*) and 1.5.6 (indifference to money); 1.6.1–10 (*enkrateia*) and 1.6.11–14 (indifference to money). Cf. also Xenophon, *Apology* 16 where the same sequence appears.
99 1.6.10 (trans. Marchant).
100 Cf. Vlastos (1991: 45–80).

References

Brickhouse, T. C. and Smith, N. D. (2000). *The Philosophy of Socrates*. Boulder, CO: Westview Press.

Burnet, J. (1914). *Greek Philosophy: Thales to Plato*. London: Macmillan.

Dorion, L.-A. & Bandini, M. (2000). *Xénophon: Mémorables*. Tome I: Introduction et Livre I. (Introduction, traduction et notes par L.-A. Dorion; Histoire du texte et texte grec par M. Bandini.) Paris: Les Belles Lettres.

Dorion, L.-A. (2001). A l'origine de la question socratique et de la critique du témoignage de Xénophon: l'étude de Schleiermacher sur Socrate (1815). *Dionysius*, 19, 51–74.

—— (2003a). Socrate, le daimonion et la divination. In J. Laurent (ed.), *Les dieux de Platon* (pp. 169–92). Caen: Presses Universitaires.

—— (2003b). Akrasia et enkrateia dans les *Mémorables* de Xénophon. *Dialogue*, 42, 645–72.

—— (2004). Qu'est-ce que vivre en fonction de sa *dunamis?* Les deux réponses de Socrate dans les *Mémorables*. In *Les Etudes philosophiques: les écrits socratiques de Xénophon* (pp. 235–52). Paris: Presses Universitaires de France.

Hadot, P. (1995). *Philosophy as a Way of Life: Spiritual Exercises from Socrates to Foucault.* Oxford: Blackwell.

Kahn, C. H. (1981). Did Plato write Socratic dialogues? *Classical Quarterly,* 31, 305–20.

Luccioni, J. (1953). *Xénophon et le socratisme.* Paris.

Nietzsche, F. W. (1967). *Werke,* eds. Giorgio Colli and Mazzino Montinari. Berlin: de Gruyter.

Santas, G. (1979). *Socrates: Philosophy in Plato's Early Dialogues.* London: Routledge.

Schleiermacher, F. (1818). Ueber den Werth des Sokrates als Philosophen. In *Abhandlung der philosophischen Klasse der königlich preussichen Akademie aus den Jahren 1814–1815* (pp. 51–68).

Vander Waerdt, P. (1993). Socratic justice and self-sufficiency: The story of the Delphic oracle in Xenophon's *Apology of Socrates. Oxford Studies in Ancient Philosophy,* 11, 1–48.

Vlastos, G. (1971). The paradox of Socrates. In G. Vlastos (ed.), *The Philosophy of Socrates: A Collection of Critical Essays* (pp. 1–21). Garden City, NY: Anchor Books.

—— (1991). *Socrates: Ironist and Moral Philosopher.* Ithaca, NY: Cornell University Press.

8

Picturing Socrates

KENNETH LAPATIN

Because, in the disputations of Socrates, where he raises all manner of questions, makes assertions, and then demolishes them, it did not evidently appear what he held to be the chief good, every one took from these disputations what pleased him best.
–St. Augustine, *City of God* 8.3

Although Socrates is principally associated with the spoken word, he was born to the visual arts. His father, Sophroniskos, was a stone-worker (*lithourgos, marmorarius*), and he himself is reported to have worked as a sculptor early in life. Ancient literary sources report that he carved a group of the *Charites* (Graces) that stood at the entrance to the Athenian akropolis as well as an image of *Hermes Propylaios*. Attribution of actual surviving artworks to Socrates – just like words – remains highly problematic, of course, but multiple marble versions of both compositions are preserved. Their popularity in antiquity is likely the result of (mis)attribution to the philosopher, for Socrates was not a rare name; and homonymous craftsmen, among numerous others, are mentioned in ancient texts.[1]

If we cannot confidently identify any images *by* Socrates, we can readily recognize images *of* him, for descriptions of his physique and physiognomy by both his contemporaries and later writers emphasize his distinctiveness. Ancient authors agree that he did not possess the ideal beauty we tend to associate with Classical Greek males. Rather he was ugly: stocky, broad-shouldered, and pot-bellied. He was compared to a Silenos in that he had a thick neck, was bearded, balding, and had bulging eyes, a wide nose, open nostrils, a large mouth, and thick lips.[2] Hundreds of ancient portraits with such features have been recognized in diverse media: marble, bronze, terracotta, ivory and bone, engraved gemstones, clay seal impressions, wall-paintings, floor mosaics, and even coins.[3] Most of these depict only Socrates' head or bust, but sometimes he appears as a complete figure and occasionally he is represented with others. Each image, however, presents its own particular problems, and none of the surviving representations was made during the philosopher's lifetime. Postantique images, too, are plentiful, and although many of these are based on ancient prototypes and/or narratives, others are pure inventions. Nonetheless, in all cases, representations of Socrates are ideologically charged, serving the specific needs of those who commissioned and created them.

110

Ancient Portraits

Although Socrates himself lived in an age when posthumous – rather than contemporaneous – portraiture was the norm, we know of at least two images of him that were fashioned during his life. These do not survive, but were caricatures, of a sort, in the form of comedic masks worn by actors portraying Socrates in performances of Aristophanes' *Clouds* and Ameipsias' *Konnos*, both produced in Athens in 423 BCE. According to Aelian (*Varia Historia* 2.13), Socrates himself was in the audience of the former and stood to identify himself to foreigners who did not know who he was. This allowed audience members to compare the mask-maker's art to his actual visage. Fashioning a parodic image of Socrates would not have been difficult for mask-makers accustomed to producing convincing masks of satyrs (see fig. 8.1). Aelian, however, states explicitly that the mask-makers portrayed Socrates with an "excellent likeness." We cannot judge the accuracy of this evaluation today, but the physiognomic type, evident in contemporary depictions of satyrs in diverse media, was, as we shall see, clearly adapted by portraitists after Socrates' death.[4]

Ancient literary sources also preserve references to posthumous images of the philosopher:

Figure 8.1 Actor holding a mask for a satyr play. Detail of a volute krater by the Pronomos Painter from Ruvo, c. 400 BCE Naples, Museo Archeologico Nazionale 3240. Photo: after J. Charbonneaux, Classical Greek Art. London 1972, p. 274, fig. 315.

111

1) A fragmentary papyrus from the Villa dei Papiri at Herculaneum (*P. Herc.* 1021, col. 2, lines 13–17) preserves a passage of Philodemos of Gadara's so-called *Index Academicorum Herculanensis* derived from the fifth book of the *Atthis* of the fourth-century BCE Atthidographer Philochoros that, according to one recent reading, mentions an inscribed portrait (*eikon*) of Socrates by an otherwise unknown sculptor called Boutes (also the name of an Athenian hero).[5]

2) Diogenes Laertius (2.43) reports that the Athenians, out of remorse for having executed Socrates, honored him with a bronze statue (*chalkei eikoni etimēsan*) by the fourth-century BCE sculptor Lysippos that was placed in the Pompeion. Tertullian, writing in the late second century CE, slightly before Diogenes, gives a similar account (*Apologeticum* 14.8), but says that the Athenians dedicated a gold statue in a temple (*imaginem eius auream in templo collocarint*).

3) An ironic passage in Lucian (*Death of Peregrinos* 37), written in the mid-second century CE, suggests that Socrates in prison with his companions at his side was a common theme in ancient painting (and such scenes, as we shall see, were also popular in postantique art).

4) The sixth-century CE epigrammatist Joannes Barboukallos praises the painter of a wax (presumably encaustic) image of Socrates (*Greek Anthology* 16.327).

5) The fifth-century CE Athenian philosopher Marinos (*Proklos* 10) refers to the Sokrateion at Athens, a monument to the philosopher that was apparently located outside the Dipylon gate, near the Pompeion. No specific image is mentioned, but might this be the site of the golden (or gilded?) image mentioned by Tertullian (no. 2 above)? Or might Marinos be referring to the Pompeion?

There are three major challenges facing modern art historians who treat the ancient portraits of Socrates. First, to ascertain the relationship, if any, of the surviving portraits – and especially the well-preserved large-scale marble heads and herm busts (there are, alas, no life-size bodies that certainly represent Socrates) – to the images mentioned by the literary sources. Second, to determine what kinds of bodies these head types might have originally been attached to, for Greek portraits, unlike their Roman counterparts, usually relied heavily on body types, as well as facial features, to convey meaning. Third, to interpret how the complete portraits, so far as they can be reconstructed, were intended to be read by ancient viewers in their original contexts.

Since the early twentieth century, the surviving marble portrait heads have been divided into two types, prosaically called A and B. Both are thought to rely on lost bronze prototypes. (Some scholars recognize a third type, C, but most take this to be a variant of A.) The original of type A is usually considered to be earlier than that of type B, but both relative and absolute chronologies remain problematic.

Type A (fig. 8.2), with its round features, pug nose, and thin, receding hair, closely resembles the standard iconography of satyrs. That it actually depicts Socrates is clear from its resemblance to examples of type B that carry identifying inscriptions. Art historians have variously dated the origins of type A to the late fifth century BCE, the fourth century, and the Hellenistic period. Stylistic analysis suggests that the type was created in the first quarter of the fourth century, and many scholars have come to believe that Socrates' friends commissioned the lost bronze original soon after his death.[6]

Figure 8.2 Socrates, Type A. Roman marble copy after a lost Greek bronze original of c. 390–370 BCE (?). Naples, Museo Archeologico Nazionale 6129. Photo: Alinari/Art Resource, NY ART47708.

Type B (fig. 8.3) mitigates the ugly, satyresque features of type A into something more noble. Thus it is often associated with the portrait by Lysippos that Diogenes Laertius says the Athenians erected in the Pompeion (no. 2 above). Some scholars believe that the Athenian statesman Lykourgos commissioned this portrait for the Pompeion, for we know from other sources that he was responsible for a retrospective cultural program that included statues of other intellectual figures of Athens' past, such as Aeschylos, Sophokles, and Euridipes (see e.g. Zanker 1995: 57ff.). However, it has also been suggested that this "official" state portrait of Socrates, placed in the building where Athenian ephebes mustered for the Panathenaic and other official processions, was commissioned c. 318–17 BCE from Lysippos, a Sikyonian and the favorite sculptor of Alexander the Great, rather than from an Athenian artist, by the Macedonian client, Demetrios of Phaleron, who then ruled Athens (see Giuliana Calcani in Moreno et al. 1995: 256). Demetrios was a student of Aristotle and Theophrastos and composed *Socratic Dialogues* and an *Apology of Socrates.* Yet Diogenes Laertius' ascription of the Pompeion portrait to Lysippos has itself been called into question. Scholars (e.g. Voutiras 1994: 137ff., with previous bibliography) rightly cast doubt on the reliability of Diogenes' attribution, noting the author's reliance on literary *topoi*. For, as we have already noted with regard to images said to have been sculpted by Socrates himself, there is a common tendency to misattribute popular artworks to famous names.

113

Figure 8.3 Socrates, Type B. Roman marble copy after a lost Greek bronze original of c. 320 BCE (?). Malibu, J. Paul Getty Museum 82.AA.169. Photo: JPGM.

Whoever fashioned the prototypes of head types A and B, and whoever commissioned them, the body types that originally supported them are also the subject of debate. Were they seated or standing, life-like or idealized? Although no large-scale Socrates portraits survive with their bodies, we do have ancient statuettes, reliefs, and paintings. These depict the philosopher standing with an idealized physique (fig. 8.4) and with a pot belly (figs. 8.5, 8.6a, 8.6b), as well as seated (figs. 8.7 and 8.8). An eighteenth-century engraving by Georg Martin Preisler after a drawing by E. Bouchardon published in Antonio Francesco Gori's *Statuae Antiquae deorum et virorum illustrium* also depicts a Socrates head (resembling type B) on a seated body. The body of this statue survives in the Ny Carlsberg Glyptotek in Copenhagen, but it is far from certain that the now lost head was an original part of the composition, rather than a Renaissance restoration (see Richter 1965: 116; Frischer 1979: esp. 143–6). Indeed, the figure wears sandals, while Socrates famously went about Athens barefoot (on which see, e.g. McLean forthcoming). There is also little reliable evidence for the body associated with head type A, despite the attempts of scholars to identify one (see below). And it has even been suggested that the wording of the Herculaneum papyrus (*eikona prosopon chalkoun*) might denote a bronze bust or something resembling an *imago clipeata*, rather than a complete statue (Voutiras 1994; Speyer 2004).

In short, we have two head types (A and B), multiple body types (standing as well as seated), and two sculptors mentioned by ancient literary sources (Boutes and Lysippos).

Figure 8.4   Statuette of Socrates. Hellenistic marble replica (?) of a bronze original of c. 320 BCE (?), London, British Museum 1925.11–18.1. Photo: HIP/Art Resource, NY ART176240.

Figure 8.5   Socrates, Eros, and Diotima (?). Bronze appliqué from the Casa dei Capitelli Figurati in Pompeii. Naples, Museo Archeologico Nazionale. Photo: after F. Winter and E. Pernice, Hellenistishe Kunst in Pompeji, vol. 5. Berlin 1932, p. 49.

Figure 8.6a and 8.6b Terracotta statuette of Socrates. Malibu, J. Paul Getty Museum 75.AD.27. Photo: JPGM.

Figure 8.7 Socrates and Mnemosyne or a Muse (?). Side panel of a Roman marble sarcophagus, c. 160 CE. Paris, Louvre 475 c. Photo: Erich Lessing/Art Resource, NY ART79393.

Figure 8.8 Socrates seated on a bench. Roman wall painting from a private house at Ephesus, first century CE Ephesus Museum 1574. Photo: Erich Lessing/Art Resource, NY ART119414.

It is economical and attractive to combine these elements into two statues – an early fourth-century figure by Boutes dedicated by Socrates' friends in the Academy, and a later fourth-century figure, attributed to Lysippos, erected in the Pompeion (commissioned by Demetrios or the Athenian state under Lykourgos) – and later adaptations. This might well be the case. But we must also recognize that each and every point remains contentious. We have already noted the questionable attribution to Lysippos, and Voutiras (1994) has even suggested that the original of type B might actually be earlier than that of type A. The elements of the puzzle – heads, bodies, attributions, and dates – are rather like those of a child's flip-book that can be recombined in any number of ways.

Still, most scholars accept the traditional ascription of head type A to the early fourth century. In his interpretation of the lost original, Andrew Stewart attributes to its sculptor efforts similar to those ascribed to Socrates himself in his encounter with a physiognomist, reported by Phaedo of Elis in his now lost dialogue *Zopyros*, mentioned on two occasions by Cicero (*Tusc. Disp.* 4.37.80; *de Fato* 5.10, on which see especially McLean forthcoming b; note too that a bust of the type A Socrates portrait was discovered at Villa of Cicero in Tusculum: Richter 1965: 111, no. 3): "Most of the copies are so preoccupied with outer appearance that they seem completely to miss the true ethos of the man. Only a few intensify the expression by narrowing the eyes and drawing the lips tight, as if the philosopher were straining to conquer the satiric mask that the gods have allotted him" (Stewart 1990: 173). Indeed, Adamantios (I, 9) remarks on Socrates' "large and limpid eyes, expressive of his character," and other ancient authors discuss his extraordinary gaze.

Paul Zanker (1995: 32) takes this line of interpretation further, reading the facial features of type A as a challenge to the existing order: "In flouting the High Classical standard of beauty so blatantly, this face must have disturbed Socrates' contemporaries no less than his penetrating questions." Zanker sees the portrayal of later philosophers, such as Cynics, as "old and ugly or with unconventional appearance as an act of provocation," and retrojects a similar visual strategy onto Socrates' followers, to whom he, too, gives credit for commissioning type A: "The decision to adopt the comparison with Silenus for a portrait statue intended to celebrate the subject, presupposes a positive interpretation of the comparison, such as we do in fact find, in particular, in the speech of Alcibiades in Plato's symposium" (sic Zanker 1995: 34).

Zanker and others suggest that head type A might have originally been placed on a standing body, such as that represented in a small bronze furniture appliqué from Pompeii (fig. 8.5; there are further examples of the composition elsewhere).[7] Here, despite the himation and walking stick – standard attributes of the Athenian citizen with the leisure for long discussions in the Agora – the male figure is not depicted with an ideal, well-proportioned body, but rather as an ugly old man with sagging chest and pot belly. Whether this bronze relief truly reflects a late classical prototype is unclear: the female figure is modeled on the early Hellenistic Tyche of Antioch. Zanker (1995: 37–8) nonetheless suggests that with such a body the type A Socrates would appear as "the properly behaved citizen, but at the same time, as in the portrait head, with unmistakably ugly and deviant features." These features recall Silenos, who was not just a drunken follower of Dionysos, but a mythological creature, "separate from his breed," known for his wisdom and goodness, and as a teacher of young children.

Still, the association of the type A head with this body type remains tenuous, as does the ascription of the combination to an early portrait commissioned by Socrates' friends. Prior to Voutiras' (1994) reading of the sculptor's name as Boutes in the Herculaneum papyrus, type A was sometimes associated with the sculptor Silanion because of the realism associated with works of that artist and the fact that he is reported to have produced a portrait of Plato for the Mouseion of the Academy (Diogenes Laertius 3.25; see Zanker 1995: 38). In any case, the Silenos analogy has been seen

> as more than just pay[ing] homage to Socrates as the remarkable teacher; it presents a challenge as well. The deliberate visualization of ugliness represented, in the Athens of the early fourth century, a clash with the standards of kalokagathia. That is, a portrait like this questioned one of the fundamental values of the Classical polis. If the man whom the god at Delphi proclaimed the wisest of all could be as ugly as Silenus and still a good upstanding citizen, then this must imply that the statue's patron was casting doubt on that very system of values. We have to look at this statue of Socrates, with its fat belly and Silenus face, against the background of a city filled with perfectly proportioned and idealized human figures in marble and bronze embodying virtue and moral authority. . . . like a figure of a flute-playing Silenus . . . which, when you open it, contains a divine image . . . Socrates' body may be seen as an exemplar of [the precept], for the seemingly ugly form conceals the most perfect soul. The idea implies that the entire value system of

Athenian society is built upon mere appearance and deception, misled by its fiction of the eternal form of the body. (Zanker 1995: 38–9)

For McLean (forthcoming b), Plato's description of Socrates as a Silen that contains the greatest wonders is itself "a hybrid of the ridiculous and the serious, a generic, logical and philosophical amalgam whose anomalous nature serves as a metaphor for the role of the philosopher in society."

As attractive as this reconstruction and interpretation of the Socrates type A portrait may be, they must remain tentative, and so, too, are reconstructions and interpretations of type B, usually associated with the bronze statue Diogenes Laertius says Lysippos made for the Pompeion. Although the Pompeion has been excavated, and the lower courses of a statue base have been discovered in the peristyle at the south side of its propylon, scholars continue to debate whether the statue placed thereupon was standing or seated (Höpfner 1976: 106–7; Moreno 1984: 24–5; Voutiras 1994: 137ff.; Calcani in Moreno et al. 1995: 256). The type B head, in any case, seems to be a refinement of the satyr-like type A. In type B the round face of type A has been re-shaped, the provocative quality of the silen's mask toned down, the features idealized and assimilated to those of a mature citizen. Baldness has been reduced to the high forehead of an intellectual, and the hair is now long and curly. And the face is that of a noble old man. Although the attribution of the type to Lysippos is problematic, we might recall that, according to Plutarch (*de fortuna Alexandri* 2.2 [335B]), Alexander favored Lysippos because he "alone revealed his character through bronze and expressed his virtue through outward appearance."

The idealized standing figure preserved in a Hellenistic marble statuette from Alexandria, now in London (fig. 8.4), has been associated with type B, and a fragmentary terracotta of a similar figure was excavated near the state prison in the southwest corner of the Athenian Agora. Though resembling the overweight male on the bronze relief discussed above, this type seems to depict Socrates as a model citizen, balanced in a *contrapposto* pose, with a well-proportioned body, his himation carefully draped over his shoulder, the excess cloth held in both hands. As Zanker (1995: 60) notes, "These gestures, which seem so natural and insignificant, are in fact, to judge from [Classical Athenian] gravestones and votive reliefs, part of the extensive code of required behavior that carried moral connotations as well. Careful attention to the proper draping of the garment and handsome pattern of folds are an outward manifestation of the 'interior order' expected of the good citizen. In the pictorial vocabulary, such traits become symbols of moral worth, and, in the statue of Socrates, this connotation is particularly emphasized by the similar gesture of both hands." Stewart (1990: 188), moreover, suggests that the turn of the body indicates that the philosopher is engaged in dialogue, and what we are meant to see in this depiction is "the visionary Socrates of the *Republic* and later dialogues, no longer merely the ironical deflator of citizen and sophist, but the planner of the perfect state, the discover of Forms."

If the Pompeion statue was seated (see figs. 8.7 and 8.8), however, it would have to be interpreted somewhat differently: representing a teacher more than a citizen. It would also take its place at the front of a long series of seated philosopher portraits. Indeed, given that the Pompeion statue was located next to a bench within the building, a seated figure of Socrates might be seen as dramatically engaged in conversation

119

with its viewers. And given that the Pompeion served as a gathering place for Athenian ephebes, what could be more appropriate for the commemorative image of a great teacher? In fact, it seems to have been a seated image that inspired an ancient terracotta caricature of Socrates (inscribed), seated holding a scroll, apparently with the features of a monkey (see Bailey 1974)!

Socratic Narratives and Other Ancient Images

Both standing and seated figures of Socrates, as we have seen, not only appeared alone, but were also combined with other figures to create narratives. On the bronze appliqué from Pompeii (fig. 8.5), which was discovered in 1832 in the Casa dei Capitelli Figurati and was originally attached to a wooden chest, the standing male figure is placed opposite a seated woman, while a winged Eros stands between them. The pose of the woman, as noted above, is modeled on Eutychides of Sikyon's early third-century BCE *Tyche of Antioch*, and she has been interpreted variously as Diotima, Aspasia, and Aphrodite, while the male has been identified as Socrates. Schwarzmaier (1997), however, has recently argued that the seated woman is Aphrodite and the bearded male figure actually represents a satyr, rather than Socrates, based on his hairiness and the form of his ears, but the latter are difficult to distinguish and unfortunately are lost on an earlier and higher quality, but fragmentary version now in Malibu (JPGM 91.AC.64). The pose, meanwhile, is closely paralleled by draped terracotta figurines that clearly represent a philosopher, not a satyr (e.g., figs. 8.6a,b). Still, whether the multifigure scene is meant to illustrate *Symposium* 201d–212b or some other text, its erotic content is clear. Indeed, as McLean (forthcoming a) notes, Socrates' snub nose was, in the opinion of ancient physiognomists, a marker of lasciviousness.

Another "Socrates" with a woman on the short side of the mid second-century CE "Sarcophagus of the Muses" (fig. 8.7),[8] formerly in the collection of Cardinal Albani in Rome and now in Paris, must be interpreted differently, and not only on account of its context. The philosopher appears seated before an archway addressing a standing female. While this, too, might be Diotima or Aspasia, she is veiled and Eros is not present. The principal façade of the sarcophagus depicts the nine Muses, and the standing woman on the side may represent one of them, repeated, or their mother Mnemosyne, although Philosophia and Xanthippe have also been suggested. The iconography of the sarcophagus as a whole – with theater masks serving as corner *akroteria* and an Apolline griffin with a *patera* above the scene – indicates that the philosopher functions here as a representative of high culture, a fitting example of the *mousikos aner*, placed here to bestow cultural cachet upon the deceased. So too, it seems, does the depiction of the philosopher in a late first-century CE Roman painting from *cubiculum* 4 of the *villa rustica* of N. Popidius Florus in Boscoreale.[9] Here he holds a stylus(!) and appears in conversation with another standing woman, perhaps Diotima. (The pair is alternately interpreted as a cynic and a hetaira.) This painting originally adorned a black-walled room decorated in the third style of Roman painting; its other walls depicted delicate architectural elements, sacral-idyllic scenes, and Egyptianizing landscapes. One other figural panel was also found, but it was quite faded when discovered in 1906: it depicted a seated kithara player and a standing singer.

120

The owner of Terrace House 2 at Ephesos must have had a similar goal when, in the mid first-century CE, he commissioned a fine painting of Socrates (inscribed) seated against a red ground in a long narrow room (fig. 8.8). Here the half-draped philosopher sits on a bench supported by lion's paws. Figures of Muses also appear on the walls of this room. Apollo and the Muses are present elsewhere in the house as well, and in another room roundels painted in a very different style depict the busts of two venerable philosophers: they are inscribed *Sokrates Athenaios* and *Cheilon Lakedaimonios* (see Strocka 1977).

On ancient gemstones, meanwhile, the image of Socrates might have served either as an attribute of high culture, a sign of ethical identification, or, given the prevalence of the name (see note 1), merely as a personal insignia. It is also clear from ancient literary sources that portraits of historical figures on gems could have broader political significance. Indeed, we might imagine the representation of Socrates functioning as some sort of rebuke to state authority, as it occasionally did in the eighteenth century.[10]

When he was depicted in ancient floor mosaics Socrates clearly served as an attribute of high culture, for he was inserted into the ranks of the Seven Sages. In a third-century mosaic signed by Ampheion found in a suburb southeast of Baalbek (ancient Heliopolis), Socrates holds a place of honor at the top of the composition, above the muse Kalliope. In another floor mosaic at Apamaea he is centrally placed between six of the Seven and he alone is inscribed. At Cologne (fig. 8.9), meanwhile,

Figure 8.9 Socrates. Detail of a floor mosaic depicting wise men from Cologne, c. 375 CE Cologne, Römisch-Germanisches Museum, Inventar-Nr. M 1. Photo: Marburg Archive.

121

he appears with other philosophers in addition to the canonical Seven, but unlike the other portraits of Socrates, this inscribed mosaic depicts a bearded man with a full head of hair – it is an invention.[11]

Summary

Although more ancient images of Socrates survive than of most other Greek and Roman figures, and in multiple media, they are not without controversy. We can readily identify large-scale marble portraits based on descriptions and inscriptions, but significant information about the original statues – their complete poses, dates, sculptors, and patrons – remain elusive. What does seem clear, however, is that in the large-scale portraits Socrates was presented, first and foremost, as wise man, insightful if idiosyncratic. He may also have been represented as a model of the upstanding citizen, either by challenging or conforming to the ideals of the *polis*. For Roman elites, portrait busts of Socrates might decorate their libraries and gardens, and two double portraits of him combined with Plato and with Seneca are preserved. Depictions of Socrates in other media served diverse functions: wall paintings, floor mosaics, sarcophagus reliefs, and gemstones tended to associate their owners with the high culture of Classical Greece, either in a generalized way, or more specifically, these images could link individuals to some particular aspect of Socrates' teachings. Elements of criticism, parody, and burlesque were not absent, but these do not seem to have been nearly as prevalent as they became in later periods (see below). For despite appearing in many contexts, Socrates in antiquity was presented primarily as a culture hero.

Postantique Images

If mosaicists in the Roman provinces invented portraits of Socrates even though his iconography was well established through images as well as texts, what can be expected of artists in other cultures and in later periods? They seem to have fashioned images of the philosopher based on contemporary notions of the proper appearance of a wise man (at least until Raphael rediscovered Socrates' ancient iconography in the early sixteenth century), and they continued to employ his image in a variety of contexts to depict many of the same concepts as their ancient predecessors.

Socrates as Wise Man

As in ancient floor mosaics, Socrates appears with other sages in western medieval and early Renaissance art. A mid-twelfth-century edition of Boethius' Logica vetus now in Darmstadt (Hessische Landes- und Hochschulbibliothek, Inventar-Nr. Hs 2282; fig. 8.10), features him with Plato, Aristotle, and Adam flanking the crowned figure of Dialectic, who holds a serpent in one hand and a stemma of being in the other. Some 200 years later, Andrea di Bartolo employed a similar scheme to illustrate a poem by his father Bartolomeo on the Seven Arts and Seven Virtues, the so-called Panegyrique

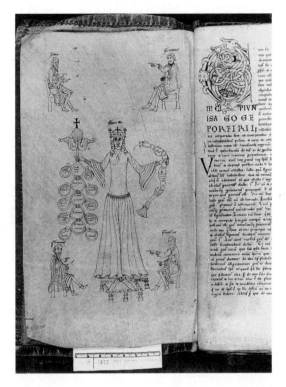

Figure 8.10 Socrates (lower left) with Plato, Aristotle, and Adam flanking the crowned figure of Dialectic. Boethius' Logica vetus, c. 1140. Darmstadt, Hessische Landes- und Hochschulbibliothek, Inventar-Nr. Hs 2282. Photo: Marburg Archive.

de Bruzio Visconti (Chantilly, Musée Condé ms. 599/1426, fol. 6v; fig. 8.11). Surrounding the personification of Philosophy, who contemplates celestial spheres inscribed with the names of the zodiacal signs, Plato, Aristotle, Socrates, and Seneca – wearing contemporary flowing robes and stylish hats – are enthroned in the corners of the page. To the lower left, Socrates, with long hair and a bushy beard, is inscribed, somewhat enigmatically, *Socrates stoycus, id est reprehensibilis vitiorum aliorum* ("Socrates the stoic, that is censuring [?] the vices of others"). Socrates also appears with other learned men in an early sixteenth-century southern Netherlandish tapestry (fig. 8.12). Here beneath the personification of Understanding, who blows a trumpet, Socrates stands to the far left of the uppermost register, among such ancient luminaries as Plato, Aristotle, Horace, and Galen, and Christian fathers, such as Saints Luke and Jerome.

Depictions of Socrates with other wise men are not limited to the West. A Persian illuminated manuscript from the *Khamsa* ("The Quintet") by Nizami Ganjavi, Nizam al-Din Abu Muhammad Ilyas ibn Yosuf (d. 1209) completed on May 19, 1510, also depicts a fictive Socrates among the Seven Sages at the feet of Iskandar (Alexander the Great) (New York, The Pierpont Morgan Library, Ms. M.471, f330). He wears eastern dress: intricately patterned flowing robes and a turban. Socrates and unnamed students appear in an early fourteenth-century Seljuk miniature of the Mukhtar al-Hikam

123

Figure 8.11 Socrates (lower left) with Plato, Aristotle, and Seneca flanking the figure of Philosophy. Bartolomeo da Bologna di Bartoli. Panegyrique de Bruzio Visconti. Fourteenth century. Chantilly, Musée Condé, Ms. 599/1426, fol. 6v. Photo: Giraudon/Art Resource, NY ART115886.

Figure 8.12 Socrates (left) and other wise men in an allegory of Learning. Tapestry, Southern Netherlandish, c. 1500–25. Photo: courtesy Getty Research Institute.

Figure 8.13 Socrates and two students. Miniature from al-Mubashshir ibn Fātik, Mukhtar al-Hikam ("The choicest maxims and best sayings"), early thirteenth century. Istanbul, Topkapi Palace Museum, Ms. Ahmet III, 3206. Photo: Giraudon/Art Resource, NY ART52590.

("The choicest maxims and best sayings") written by the Fatimid prince al-Mubashshir ibn Fātik in the eleventh century, now in Istanbul (fig. 8.13). Here the turbaned Socrates seems truer in spirit, if not in iconography, to the activities of a philosopher. He sits on a hillock, resting his head on his hand, as two of his students, who do wear cloaks draped over their patterned robes in a classical manner, appear to engage him in conversation.

Naturally, Socrates is often paired with Plato. The ancient double-headed herm featuring the philosophers was mentioned above. Circa 1250, Matthew Paris invented portraits of both philosophers for his fortune-telling book (Bodleian Library, Oxford, Ms. Ashmole 304; fig. 8.14). Not only did the artist have no ancient models on which to base his images of the ancient Athenians, but he also seems to have reversed their roles. Socrates, depicted in a flowing robe over a long-sleeved garment, and wearing a fanciful hat and shoes, is seated at a scriptorium holding pen and knife while Plato stands behind him, apparently dictating.[12] A fifteenth-century illuminated Netherlandish edition of St. Augustine's *City of God* (fig. 8.15; The Hague, MMW 10 A 11 365v), meanwhile, depicts a tale told by Cicero (*De Divinatione* 1.78) about the young Plato. In the center of the upper register, Plato's parents present their son to a beardless Socrates, who is seated at a lectern, wearing blue robes, a fur collar, and cap. To the right bees swarm around the infant philosopher, indicating that he will become

125

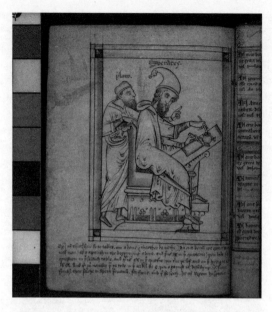

Figure 8.14 Socrates and Plato. Matthew Paris's fortune-telling book, c. 1250. Oxford, Bodleian Library, Ms. Ashmole 304. Photo: Bodleian Library.

Figure 8.15 The young Plato presented to Socrates (above). St. Augustine, *City of God* 8.4, fifteenth century. The Hague, Museum Meermanno-Westreenianum 10 A 11, fol. 365v. Photo: MMW.

famous for his honeyed words. Below, Plato, now adult, sits reading. The philosophy books on the table are labeled *Naturalis*, *Moralis*, and *Rationalis*.

Socrates appears in a number of other invented scenes. The *Schachzabelbuch of Konrad von Ammenhausen* produced in 1467 (Stuttgart, Württembergische Landesbibliothek, Inventar-Nr. Cod. poet. fol. 95v) depicts the philosopher absorbed in thought ignoring those around him. In early modern woodcuts such as those illustrating Hans Vintler's 1486 *Buch der Tugend* (Book of Virtue) Socrates embodies Age by playing hobby horse with his children, and the Perfection of Speech by teaching rhetoric alongside King Solomon. He also appears illustrating an episode related by Diogenes Laertius, dispensing advice about marriage (see further below). In all of these scenes he wears contemporary dress, albeit different in each one, and in the last he even sits enthroned, wearing a crown! Four years later, he is again depicted in contemporary dress in Anton Sorg's *Die Vier Angeltugenden* (The Four Cardinal Virtues), but significantly appears paired with Boethius. Here the significance seems to be similar to his earlier collocation with Seneca on an ancient herm, for all three were philosophical "martyrs."[13]

Socrates (inscribed) also appears engaged in intense discussion with sharp-taloned demons, who gesticulate emphatically, in a second illumination from the Netherlandish manuscript of Augustine's *City of God* mentioned above (The Hague, MMW 10 A 11, fol. 380v; fig. 8.16) illustrating chapter 8.14, in which Augustine discusses the three

Figure 8.16 Socrates discoursing with demons. St. Augustine, *City of God* 8.14, fifteenth century. The Hague, Museum Meermanno-Westreenianum 10 A 11, fol. 380v. Photo: MMW.

127

kinds of rational souls: those of the gods, of aerial demons, and of terrestrial men, focusing on the nature of Socrates' demon in particular. In the mid-sixteenth century, the Parmesian engraver Enea Vico, too, produced fantastic images of the philosopher. In one, Socrates' early and late lives seem to be combined: as he sits on the ground drinking from a cup (the attribute of a Cynic), wearing a short workman's tunic, he holds a compass and chisel, his mallet set down on the ground nearby. Before him is an unfinished statue (looking rather more like the ancient Socrates than the philosopher himself). Leaning against a tree in the background is a viol, alluding, apparently, to his taking up the lyre late in life (Diogenes Laertius 2.15). Elsewhere Vico depicts a young, thick-haired, beardless Socrates resisting the advances of a woman, a theme to which we will return below.[14]

Socrates was also grouped with cultural and political luminaries as a model to be emulated by Renaissance elites. In the mid-fifteenth century the French painter Jean Fouquet produced a fine drawing of Socrates among other great cultural figures of the past: Pindar, Artaxerxes, Gorgias, Esra, Empedokles, Zenon, and Nehemia (Berlin, Staatliche Museen zu Berlin – Preußischer Kulturbesitz, Kupferstichkabinett – Sammlung der Zeichnungen und Druckgraphik, 18–60 (N), KdZ 24599; fig. 8.17). Wearing only a green cloak, the philosopher, barefoot and beardless, but with a full

Figure 8.17 Socrates (middle left) and famous men. Jean Fouquet, c. 1450. Berlin, Staatliche Museen zu Berlin – Preußischer Kulturbesitz, Kupferstichkabinett – Sammlung der Zeichnungen und Druckgraphik, 18–60 (N), KdZ 24599.

Figure 8.18 Socrates (bottom row, second from left) beneath Prudence and Justice, with other notables from ancient history. Pietro Perugino (1448–1523). Perugia, Collegio del Cambio, Palazzo dei Priori (Comunale). Photo: Scala/Art Resource, NY ART135533.

head of hair, stands at the left end of the middle register, flipping the pages of a book. Another fictive portrait of Socrates, also identified by an inscription, appears in the company of other ancient notables in a lunette painted by Pietro Perugino for the Collegio del Cambio in Perugia's Palazzo dei Priori (1498–1500) (fig. 8.18). Dressed here as in the miniature, with a long beard, turban-like headdress, and mantle pinned to a long-sleeved undergarment, Socrates, with a book in his right hand, stands, the second figure from the left, beneath the personifications of Prudence and Justice (two of the four theological virtues). He stands alongside Fabius Maximus, Numa Pompilius, Marcus Furius Camillus, Pythagoras, and the Emperor Trajan, all of whose portraits are invented. Prudence herself is inscribed with a verse penned by the humanist Maturanzio that might equally well apply to Socrates: *Scrutari verum duceo, causasque latentes* ("I teach to search for truth and hidden causes").

The inscribed image of Socrates in an allegory of Virtue inlaid in the floor of the Duomo of Siena, designed by Pinturicchio in 1504 and executed in 1506, probably by Paolo Mannucci, is quite similar in appearance (fig. 8.19). The philosopher has a long beard, long-sleeved robe and mantle, and holds a book in his right hand. He also wears the turban of a Magus or an Old Testament prophet. The personification of Virtue, a beautiful young woman seated atop a mountainous island in the middle of the sea, offers him a palm branch, the symbol of victory. As a pendant to Socrates, the cynic philosopher Crates, who preached the virtues of poverty, dumps a basket of jewels into

129

Figure 8.19 Socrates (left) and Crates flank Virtue. Detail of the pavement of Duomo, Siena, designed by Pinturicchio in 1504 and executed in 1506. Photo: Scala/Art Resource, NY ART160656.

the sea. Meanwhile, a sixteenth-century fresco in the Trapeza of the Lavra monastery on Mount Athos includes the philosopher, crowned and holding a scroll, among other pagan philosophers who prophesied the coming of Christ in the lower register of a depiction of the Tree of Jesse.

These depictions of Socrates as a wise man, representing the earthly manifestation of a greater timeless abstraction personified elsewhere in the same scene, all owe something of the details of their iconography to the east, whether in the form of a magus or a biblical prophet. In the decorative scheme for the private library of Pope Julius II, which also features personified virtues in its uppermost register, Perugino's pupil, Raphael Sanzio, also presented Socrates among other ancient sages, but, for the first time, revived the philosopher's ancient iconography. Raphael invented the features of most of the historical figures in his *School of Athens*, painted in *Stanza della Segnatura* in the Vatican Palace between 1510 and 1512 – and famously provided many of them with the faces of his own contemporaries – but his Socrates re-assumes his ancient aspect: bald head, thin hair, pug nose, broad shoulders, portly body (fig. 8.20). This, of course, should come as no surprise, given Raphael's abiding antiquarian interests – in 1515 Julius' successor, Leo X, appointed him Prefect of Antiquities of Rome. The *School*

130

Figure 8.20 Socrates and his followers. Detail from Raphael Sanzio, *The School of Athens*. Stanza della Segnatura, Vatican City, c. 1510–12. Photo: Erich Lessing/Art Resource, NY ART120919.

of Athens predates by more than half a century the first published identification of ancient portraits of Socrates. Fulvio Ursini is usually credited with this, as multiple images of Socrates appear in his *Imagines et Elogia Virorum Illustrium* (Rome and Venice 1570, fig. 8.21). (Ursini's drawing of a statue of the philosopher holding a book roll has been considered an invention, but it may be related to a relief now in Naples, thought to derive from the Farnese Collection, in which a more heavily draped Socrates appears barefoot, holding a cup and walking stick, seated on a rock covered by a fawn's skin.[15]) A year earlier, however, Antoine Lafréry published in his *Illustrium vivorum ut extant in urbe expressi vultus* an engraving of an inscribed bust of Socrates with the legend "in amphiteatro Vaticano" (fig. 8.22). This bust may well have been the ancient model employed by Raphael, although others were present in Roman collections. In the *School of Athens* Raphael provided the ancient head type with a body in accordance with ancient authors' descriptions of Socrates. And not only does the appearance of Raphael's Socrates conform to that of ancient portrait busts and descriptions, but so too does the philosopher's action: he is gesturing emphatically with his fingers while haranguing his companions, who have been variously identified as Alcibiades, Xenophon, Aischines, Eukleides, Aratos, or, perhaps, Alexander.

131

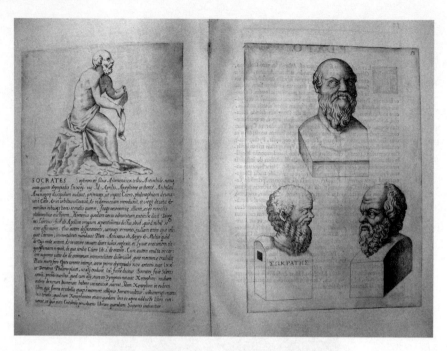

Figure 8.21 Statue and busts of Socrates. Fulvio Ursini, Imagines et elogia virorum illustrium et eruditor ex antiquis lapidibus et nomismatibus expressa cum annotationibus ex bibliotheca Fulvi Ursini. Rome 1570. Photo: courtesy Getty Research Institute.

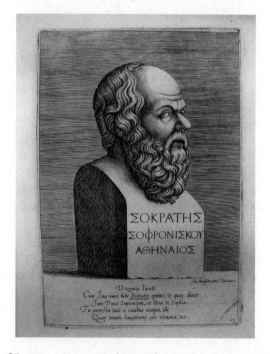

Figure 8.22 Bust of Socrates. Antoine Lafréry, Inlustrium virorum ut extant in urbe expressi vultus formis Antonii Lafreri. Rome 1569, pg. vi. Photo: courtesy Getty Research Institute.

Moralizing Tales

Socrates instructing his pupils was depicted by many artists, in many contexts, some generic, others more specific. An early Renaissance French edition of Valerius Maximus' *Facta et dicta memorabilia*, for example, includes an illumination of Socrates (inscribed), beardless, wearing an acorn cap and heavy, long-sleeved, blue robe lined with white fur, its *chaperon* (hood) pulled down over his shoulders (The Hague, KB, 66 B 13 fol. 184v; fig. 8.23). He sits at a bookstand in a cozy interior, rebuking Alcibiades, who, as Xanthippe explains, was found with the girl Mylon. This illustration accompanies Book 3, Chapter 4, which treats humble beginnings of great men, although the episode depicted has little to do directly with the text at hand, except insomuch as Valerius says Socrates examined "the deepest secrets of the human condition and the feelings that are hidden away in our hearts." In Book 7, Chapter 2, Ext. 1 of the same volume (fol. 321r) an episode also related by Diogenes Laertius (2.16) is represented: "The question was once put to him by a man whether he would advise him to marry or not? And he replied, 'Whichever you do, you will repent it'." Here a very different-looking, though still beardless Socrates, his response on the scroll he holds in his left hand, wears a long-sleeved violet robe, with ribbing at the shoulders, and a yellow sash, as well as a red and white cap. The youth, too, appears in contemporary dress.

Figure 8.23 Socrates, Alcibiades, Mylon, and Xanthippe. Valerius Maximus, Des faits et des paroles mémorables 3.4, fifteenth century. The Hague, Koninklijke Bibliotheek, 66 B 13 fol. 184v, Valerius Maximus 3.4. Photo: courtesy Anne Korteweg, Koninklijke Bibliotheek.

133

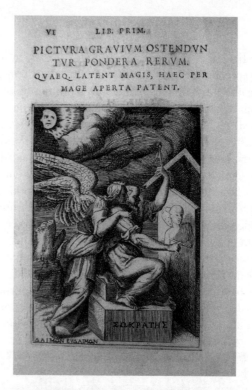

Figure 8.24 Socrates, his demon, and a stele. Giulio Bonasone in Achille Bocchi, Symbolicarum quaestionum de universo genere quas serio ludebat libri quinque. Bologna 1555, p. viii. Photo: courtesy Getty Research Institute.

Socrates is also depicted repeatedly in early modern emblem books. He appears several times in Achille Bocchi's *Symbolicarum Quaestionum de Universo Genere*, in engravings by Giulio Bonasone (1555, reprinted 1574). In an opening dedicated to Cardinal Alexander Farnese, Socrates crouches on a pedestal, his sleeves rolled up, sketching a preparatory drawing onto a stele (he holds a compass and square uncomfortably aloft in his left hand); his winged *daimon*, inscribed ?????? ????????? gazes over his shoulder (fig. 8.24). The link between Socrates' early career as a sculptor, his knack for elucidation, and the purpose of the emblem book are all manifested in the accompanying inscription: *Pictura gravium ostenduntur pondera rerum. Quaeq. latent magis, haec per mage aperta patent* ("The significance of weighty things is shown by a picture. Whatever is hidden deeper becomes more apparent"). Bonasone also depicted Socrates with Athena (inscribed Pallas), whose aegis lies on the ground (fig. 8.25). She leads *Pheme* (Fame, Reputation, or Rumor), whose hands are bound. The inscription above reads: *Compendiosa Fama quae, et pulcherrima talis, qualis haberi amabis esto* ("Advantageous Fame, although beautiful, be such that you want to be considered"). In a third representation of Socrates in this emblem book, the philosopher, wearing a cap and a long cape, kneels before the figure of the healing god Asklepios, offering him a cock (fig. 8.26). The Latin inscription *Quae sunt supra nos pertinere ad nos nihil* ("The things above us

134

Figure 8.25 Socrates, Minerva, and Fame. Giulio Bonasone in Achille Bocchi, *Symbolicarum quaestionum de universo genere quas serio ludebat libri quinque*. Bologna 1555, p. cxvii. Photo: courtesy Getty Research Institute.

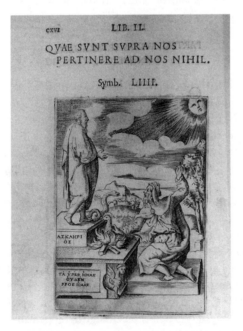

Figure 8.26 Socrates presents a cock to Asklepios. Giulio Bonasone in Achille Bocchi, *Symbolicarum quaestionum de universo genere quas serio ludebat libri quinque*. Bologna 1555, p. cxvi. Photo: courtesy Getty Research Institute.

135

Figure 8.27 Socrates and a mirror. Giulio Bonasone in Achille Bocchi, *Symbolicarum quaestionum de universo genere quas serio ludebat libri quinque.* Bologna 1555, p. cxxvi. Photo: courtesy Getty Research Institute.

have nothing to do with us") is repeated in Greek on the lower register of the god's pedestal, while the opposite page bears the title *Qui scire scit se nil, sapit* ("He who knows he knows nothing is wise"). Another image in this volume depicts Socrates seated at a table (with his back to a book, pen, and ink pot!) accompanied by an unidentified figure holding a mirror, whose protective wooden cover is half-opened (fig. 8.27).[16] The inscription is *En viva e speculo facies splendente refertur, hinc sapies, poterisq. Omnia dum ipse velis* ("Behold – a live face is splendidly transmitted from a mirror. You know this and you are able to do everything that you yourself want"). All of these images of Socrates, on some level, address the contrast between appearance and truth, and Socrates' ability to get to the core of matters. The episode with the mirror, moreover, was also depicted in Renaissance and later paintings, which, in keeping with Diogenes Laertius' more straightforward account (2.16), also included images of children: "He used to recommend young men to be constantly looking in the glass, in order that, if they were handsome, they might be worthy of their beauty; and if they were ugly, they might conceal their unsightly appearance by their accomplishments."[17] Domenico Fetti (1589–1624) set the scene in contemporary Venice (fig. 8.28), while Pier Francesco Mola (c. 1660) depicted Socrates in this narrative more closely following the ancient iconography of the balding philosopher.[18] The Spanish

Figure 8.28 Socrates instructing two pupils. Domenico Fetti, Florence, Uffizi. Photo: Scala/ Art Resource, NY ART118965.

painter Jusepe de Ribera, meanwhile, presented Socrates looking at himself in the mirror as part of a series of philosopher "portraits" created for the Duke of Alcala in the 1640s. His lost original is known today through later versions, copies, and prints, one of which was later engraved and labeled a self-portrait of Carravaggio (Darby 1948; Konecny 2003).

Another popular scene, not illustrated in antiquity apparently, illustrates an episode in the life of Socrates reported by Diogenes Laertius (2.17), Seneca (*de Constantia Sapientis* 18.6), Athenaios (*Deipnosophistai* 5.219b), and St. Jerome (*adv. Jovinianum* 1.48): Xanthippe dumps washing water over the head of Socrates (see McLean, ch. 22, this volume). The scene appears in the *Schachzabelbuch of Konrad von Ammenhausen* produced in 1467 (Stuttgart, Württembergische Landesbibliothek, Inventar-Nr. Cod. poet. fol. 285v; fig. 8.29), and is common in early printed emblem books. In the *Emblemata Horatiana* of Otto van Veen (1607, reprinted 1612 and 1684), Socrates, now with his ancient aspect, albeit wearing sandals, serves as the embodiment of "*Patienta, Victrix Malorom*" (fig. 8.30). He clutches his books and a scroll as his wife empties a pitcher down his back. Pigler (1938: 285–9) and others believe that composition draws visually on the iconography of Albrecht Dürer's depiction of *Job Castigated by His Wife* on a wing of the *The Jabach Altarpiece* of 1503–4 (Frankfurt, Städelsches Kunstinstitut 890), but recent scholarship suggests otherwise.[19] In any case, the episode is employed here

137

Figure 8.29 Socrates and Xanthippe. The Schachzabelbuch of Konrad von Ammenhausen, 1467. Stuttgart, Württembergische Landesbibliothek, Inventar-Nr. Cod. poet. 2, fol. 285v. Photo: Marburg Archive.

Figure 8.30 Socrates and Xanthippe. Otto van Veen, *Quinti Horatii Flacci Emblemata*. Antwerp 1612. Photo: courtesy Getty Research Institute.

138

PATIENTIA SOCRATIS.   33

In patientia veſtra poſsidebitis animas veſtras. Lucæ.21.

Figure 8.31 Socrates, Xanthippe, and Myrto. Laurens van Haecht Goidtsenhoven, *Mikrokosmos: Parvus Mundus*. Antwerp. 1579. Photo: courtesy Getty Research Institute.

to illustrate the ethical motto at the end of Horace's *Ode* I.24: *durum, sed levior fit patientia/quiquid corrigere est nefas* ("it is difficult, but whatever cannot be righted becomes bearable by patience"). If this is not a case of Socrates employed in the secularization, indeed, the classicization of a biblical exemplum, a similar scene, entitled "*Patientia Socratis*," appeared in Laurent van Haecht Goidtsenhoven's *Microkosmos* or *Parvus Mundus* (Antwerp 1579, reprinted 1600 and 1610) above a line from the Gospel of St. Luke (21.19): *In patientia vestra possidebitis animas vestras* ("In your patience you will possess your soul") (fig. 8.31). Here Xanthippe and Myrto together empty the pitcher on the head of the sleeping Socrates – and the text on the accompanying page departs from the ancient authors in identifying the liquid not as washing water (*nipteras*), but urine. In the background the two women go even further and give Socrates a beating. (This engraving also appears in J. van den Vondel's *Den Gulden Winckel der Kunstlievende Nederlanders* of 1613, reprinted 1718.) The episode was translated into painting by Cesar van Everdingen (1617–78), who did follow the ancient iconography, at least for the facial features of Socrates, who gazes unperturbed at the young Alcibiades, who, like a good aristocrat, is accompanied by a hunting dog,[20] and by Luca Giordano (1647–1705), who painted Xanthippe, finger to lips, sneaking up on Socrates as he sits at a table writing.

139

The Death of Socrates

In modern times, the most popular scene has been Socrates in prison with his disciples before, during, or after drinking hemlock. Lucian's allusion to ancient paintings of this episode was noted above, and it has been recognized, optimistically, on a single Etruscan gem,[21] but does not seem to have survived otherwise. Nonetheless, it is charmingly illustrated in the fifteenth-century Netherlandish edition of St. Augustine's *City of God* mentioned above (The Hague, MMW 10 A 11 362v; fig. 8.32): In the small pavilion to the upper left, a clean-shaven Socrates (inscribed), wearing a red hat and belted purple robe over a green undergarment, collapses behind a table strewn with books, having just drunk the hemlock from the goblet he still holds in his left hand. To the right his two accusers kneel before magistrates, pointing towards him, while in the foreground two bearded disciples and two women, presumably Xanthippe and Myrto, grieve emphatically. This scene, however, is not the focus of Augustine's text, which addresses Socrates' philosophy far more than his biography, but a noble death is more readily rendered into imagery than a philosophical practice.

From the seventeenth century, Socrates speaking with his disciples in prison, accepting, and drinking hemlock was regularly painted on a large scale or engraved for more widespread distribution. The scene was especially popular in France, where it

Figure 8.32 Death of Socrates. St. Augustine, *City of God* 8.3, fifteenth century. The Hague, Museum Meermanno-Westreenianum 10 A 11, fol. 362v. Photo: MMW.

Figure 8.33 *Death of Socrates*. François Boucher, c. 1761. Le Mans, Musée de Tessé, 1821. Photo: Marburg Archive.

was proposed as a moral exemplar by La Font de Saint-Yenne in *his Sentiments sur quelques overage de Pienture, Sculpture et gravure* in 1754, although it had been painted earlier on a large scale by Charles Alphonse Dufresnoy in 1650 (Florence, Palazzo Pitti). In 1762 the episode was adopted officially as the first classical theme set by the Academy in its annual student competition, although that same year a play entitled *The Death of Socrates* by Billardon de Sauvigne was closed by Paris police and censored before being produced the following year (Crow 1985: 200).

Among the many artists who produced such scenes the best known are François Boucher (fig. 8.33), Jacques-Louis David (fig. 8.34), Pierre Peyron, J. M. Moreau, Salvatore Rosa, Francois-Louis Joseph Watteau, Giovanni Paolo Panini, Angelica Kauffmann, Benjamin West, and Christoffer Wilhelm Eckersberg.[22] In Boucher's grisaille sketch, which never seems to have developed into a full-scale work, Socrates, beardless and sandaled, lies collapsed in baroque agony having drunk the hemlock: the empty cup lies on the ground in front of him. His distraught disciples swirl about, while three in the foreground apparently take note of his dying words.

David's painting of the scene has become the most famous. It was commissioned by the brothers Trudaine de Montigny, who were radical political reformers. Like other paintings by David, *The Death of Socrates* (a.k.a., *Socrates at the Moment of Grasping the Hemlock*) was meant to represent one who was unjustly condemned but willing to sacrifice himself for an abstract principle, in this case the immortality of the soul. The painting is based loosely on Plato's *Phaedo*, but David departed from that account and

141

Figure 8.34 *Death of Socrates*. Jacques-Louis David, 1787. New York, Metropolitan Museum of Art. Photo: author.

employed other sources as well. For example, the narrator of the *Phaedo* reports the strange feelings he and others present at Socrates' death experienced: that they both laughed and cried (59a5; see McLean forthcoming b). Such indeterminacy is not present in David's painting, however, which also relied on postantique descriptions, including works by the poet André Chenier and Denis Diderot's *Traité de la Poésie* of 1758, in which the death of Socrates is imagined as a series of affecting visual tableaux. Diderot argued that the essential meaning of Plato's dense metaphysical dialogue was best conveyed by a minimum of speech and maximum of pantomime. (Diderot, incidentally, signed his letters with seal representing the head of Socrates.)

David depicted Socrates as powerful and in full control of himself. He is mature, but muscular and physically vigorous: certainly younger than 70 years old. The figure at the foot of the bed, usually identified as Plato (who is famously absent from the *Phaedo*), represents a figure at a somewhat later stage of life. He is reportedly inspired by a passage in Samuel Richardson's *Clarissa*, but David also consulted the classical scholar Jean Félicissime Adry. "Plato" appears disconnected from the events taking place behind him, despite such realistic anchoring details as the inkpot, pen, and scroll abandoned on the floor. These lie next to Socrates' open shackles, a symbol of his release from worldly cares. On the bench to the right is a further, archaeological detail – the symbol of the Athenian state, Socrates' oppressor, taken from ancient coins.

As his family, to the far left, is led out of the cell, Socrates continues to speak, and his disciples, except "Plato" at the foot of the bed, swoon around him, giving in to emotionalism. Even the young executioner is moved and turns away. Yet as both he

142

and Socrates look in opposite directions, the lines of the composition lead to the cup of hemlock in the exact center of the painting. The total number of figures, 13, represents another departure from Plato's account, where there are more than 15 attendees (59b–c). Socrates plus 12 companions here are apparently intended to recall another martyr: Christ with his apostles. Indeed, for Diderot the example of Socrates showed that a high standard of morality could be achieved beyond the confines of Christianity, and David here seems to have adapted the composition of Poussin's *Sacraments*. Indeed, Socrates' raised hand echoes not only that of Plato in Raphael's *School of Athens*, but also that of Christ in Michelangelo's *Last Judgment*.

For David's contemporaries the painting also served as an allegory for recently abandoned attempts at reform, the dissolution of the Assembly of Notables in 1787, and the large number of political prisoners in the king's jails or in exile. Anticipating the Revolution, it gave expression to a new cult of civic virtues: self-sacrifice, devotion to duty, honesty, stoic austerity, and resistance to unjust authority. Thomas Jefferson was present at its unveiling, and admired it immensely. The printmaker and publisher John Boydell wrote to the painter Sir Joshua Reynolds that it was "the greatest effort of art since the Sistine Chapel and the stanze of Raphael. . . . This work would have done honour to Athens at the time of Pericles."

For David himself, moreover, the painting served as a weapon to unseat his rival, Peyron. Peyron had gained a royal commission for a *Socrates in Prison*, and David apparently proposed to paint the same subject for his private patrons in order to upstage him. "By comparison with David's version," writes Thomas Crow (1985: 244), "Peyron's is confused and incoherent. . . . Socrates' inflated, directionless gesture . . . floats above a diffuse array of grief-stricken poses; the crucial meeting of hand and cup is smothered in drapery. Put next to Peyron's, David's composition is all clarity and stately rhythms, weighting and unweighting the figural frieze as it reads from right to left, letting the massed emotions on the right side open dramatically into the suddenly released pose of the philosopher. The opposed vertical and horizontal gestures of Socrates anchor the scene securely around the moment of choice. The aching distance between cup and hand is the point of maximum narrative charge, which is gradually diminished and dispersed as one's attention moves to the left and finally back into the world beyond the cell."

Socrates' bravery in the face of death was also the subject of a group of bas-reliefs by Antonio Canova fashioned between 1789 and 1797. Canova apparently chose to explore Socrates' life in a series of studies he made for himself, rather than for any private patron or public display. He depicted scenes of Socrates nobly defending himself before his judges and base accusers, visible to the far left, apparently addressing the heavens above, rather than the mortals present (fig. 8.35); considerately sending his grieving family away from prison; preparing to drink hemlock in the presence of anguished disciples; and lying dead surrounded by mourning companions as Crito closes his eyes. These reliefs have been likened to "secular stations of the Cross" (Licht in Finn and Licht 1983: 252). In a fifth relief, fashioned by Canova after the others on the occasion of his election to the Accademia San Luca, but representing an earlier event in the life of the philosopher, Socrates valiantly defends Alcibiades at Potidea (fig. 8.36) – an important early episode rarely explored by artists. Here, in a composition of dynamic diagonals modeled on ancient battle reliefs, Canova presents not the philosophic or

143

Figure 8.35 Socrates defending himself before the judges. Antonio Canova, 1794. Possagno, Gipsoteca Canoviana. Photo: Witt Library, Courtauld Institute.

Figure 8.36 Socrates rescuing Alcibiades at Potidea. Antonio Canova, 1797. Possagno, Gipsoteca Canoviana. Photo: Witt Library, Courtauld Institute.

religious virtue of the other reliefs, but the martial heroism of Socrates – in a pose derived from the famous *Borghese Warrior* – who risks himself for a friend and his country.[23]

Socrates and the Erotic

Another relief attributed alternately to Canova and his Danish rival Bertel Thorvaldsen, but probably by neither, also depicts Socrates and Alcibiades (fig. 8.37). Now in the Kunsthalle, Bremen, this marble panel is on deposit from the German government, having been confiscated from its now unknown owner(s) by the National Socialist regime for Hitler's never realized art museum in Linz. It depicts a somewhat less glorious scene of the philosopher sternly "rescuing" his young protégé from the embrace of two female lovers. Carved in high relief, it is a masterpiece of foreshortened perspectives and psychological depiction – quite different from the related work of both Canova and Thorvaldsen, and more likely the work of the Italian neo-classical sculptor Lorenzo Bartolini (1777–1850).[24] Canova's pupil, Pompeo Marchesi, fashioned a plaster relief of the same scene, but with a third female figure and a much drier composition (Milan, Galleria d'Arte Moderna inv. 650; Musiari 2003: 22). With his hand on Alcibiades' shoulder, Socrates sympathetically escorts the head-hung youth away from the three ladies who, in various states of undress, seem saddened by his departure. Eighteenth-

Figure 8.37 Socrates fetching Alcibiades from the arms of his lovers. Lorenzo Bartolini (?). Marble. Bremen, Kunsthalle, Inv. Nr. 640-1981/6, Leihgabe der Bundesrepublik Deutschland 1981. Photo: courtesy A. Kreul, Kunsthalle, Bremen.

145

and nineteenth-century painters also depicted the philosopher turning Alcibiades from female pleasures.

This episode in Socrates' career, although apparently not specifically mentioned in any ancient source (and even contradicted by the ancient texts that describe the philosopher's educational visits to the homes of *hetairai*), also appeared in fifteenth-century manuscripts, as mentioned above, and Socrates himself was represented refusing the blandishments of women in sixteenth-century prints. Given that Socrates was condemned as a corruptor of youth, it is ironic that this theme was extremely popular. Its renewed popularity in early modern France and thereafter (see also McLean, ch. 22 this volume) seems to be attributable to a painting, now lost, by David's rival, Jean-François-Pierre Peyron. In 1776, the French academic painter François-André Vincent painted a pair of canvases depicting *Belisarius* and *Alcibiades Receiving Instruction from Socrates*, the latter depicted with his *daimon* (now Montpellier, Musée Fabre). Both paintings represented an "enlightened instructor of a youth destined for power" who also remains loyal to his country as a dutiful public servant, despite being grossly mistreated by the ruling regime (see Crow 1985: 198–200). Four years later, the king's superintendent of buildings, the compte d'Angiviller, commissioned two canvases from Peyron. One of them was to be a *Death of Socrates*, but Peyron chose instead to depict the *Funeral Rites of Miltiades*. For the second, d'Angiviller wrote to Joseph-Marie Vien, then director of the Académie de France à Rome: Peyron could choose the

Figure 8.38 Socrates, Eros, Alcibiades, and his lover. Martin Johann Schmidt, 1761. Vienna, private collection. Photo: Marburg Archive.

146

theme himself, but he would not be at all upset if it depicted some female nudes ("Je ne serois pas fâchét que l'un des deux fût un sujet où il y eût des fems, et nues, car il dessine bien.") And thus Peyron painted the first of two images of *Socrates Detaching Alcibiades from the Charms of Sensual Pleasure* (Rosenbert and van de Sandt 1983: 102, figs. 57–61; Campbell and Carlson 1993: 176–7). Peyron, however, was not the first to depict the scene. In 1761, Martin Johann Schmidt produced a charming sketch of Socrates apparently debating with Eros while Alcibiades embraces a shepherdess (fig. 8.38).

Meanwhile, by 1791 the episode had become a commonplace: Jean Baptiste Regnault (fig. 8.39) painted Socrates violently tearing Alcibiades from the richly appointed bed of his lovers (note the statue of Bacchus at the far left); and in 1815, Napoleon's brother-in-law and sometime lieutenant Joachim Murat commissioned Francesco Hayez to paint the same scene. The result (fig. 8.40), completed after the death of the patron, is a tamer but no less fleshy encounter, in which the clothed males appear to be engaged in philosophical discourse across the artfully posed, half-draped women. Jean-Léon Gérôme produced various versions of a more specific narrative: *Socrates Finding Alcibiades at Aspasia's House*, which is calmer still, though replete with archaeological detail (Socrates' sandals notwithstanding) derived largely, it seems, from the excavations of Pompeii and Herculaneum, though the figure Alcibiades seems to be based on Apollo in Raphael's *Parnassus*. All of these paintings – and contemporary tapestries depicting the same episode – feature no lack of female flesh, although their ostensible

Figure 8.39 Socrates drags Alcibiades from the arms of voluptuous pleasure. Jean Baptiste Regnault, 1791. Paris, Louvre. Photo: Erich Lessing/Art Resource, NY ART161621.

147

Figure 8.40 Socrates discovers Alcibiades in the women's quarters. Francesco Hayez (1815–19). Venice, Palazzo Papadopuli. Photo: Cameraphoto/Art Resource, NY ART163136.

message is the virtue of avoiding it.[25] This is a far cry from earlier images of Socrates engaged in philosophical discourse with enlightened women, such as the gilded bronze reliefs depicting the philosopher and Aspasia that decorate a pair of magnificent early eighteenth-century armoires by the master cabinet-maker André-Charles Boulle, once in the collection of William Beckford at Fonthill Abbey (Musée du Louvre OA 9518, c. 1710), or Friedrich Heinrich Füger's early nineteenth-century drawing of the same two figures, or perhaps Socrates and Timandre (Campbell and Carlson 1993: 302–3).

C. W. Eckersberg (1813–16), meanwhile, depicted Socrates alone with the comely Alcibiades, who patiently listens to the philosopher's explanations (fig. 8.41). A similar painting was executed by Jose Aparicio Inglada, a Spanish pupil of David.[26] (Thomas Crow's more recent analysis of David's *Death of Socrates* [1995: 92–102], moreover, addresses the sexualized charge of the ideal beauty of the young executioner, for which David was criticized by contemporaries.) A more blatant homoerotic valence appears in the German philosopher and librarian Friedrich Karl Forberg's *De Figura Veneris*, a sourcebook of ancient texts, with commentary in Latin, that treats a variety of sexual behaviors. First published as a supplement to Forberg's edition of Antonio Beccadelli's *Hermaphroditus* in 1824, it was translated into French under the title *Manuel d'érotologie classique* in 1882, and two years later 100 copies of a "literal English version" were privately printed in Manchester "for Viscount Julian Smithson and friends." One anonymous engraving (fig. 8.42) features an aroused Socrates approaching the sleeping

148

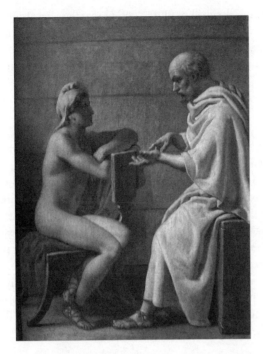

Figure 8.41 Socrates and Alcibiades. Christoffer Wilhelm Eckersberg, 1813–16. Copenhagen, Thorwaldsen Museum B212. Photo: author.

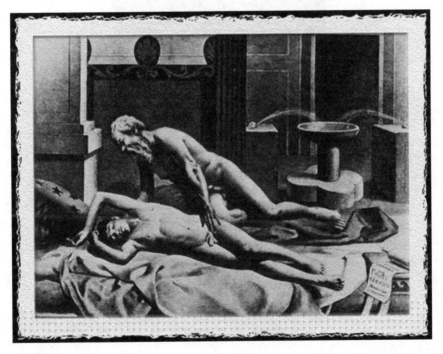

Figure 8.42 Socrates and Alcibiades. Friedrich Karl Forberg, *De Figura Veneris* (Manual of Classical Erotology). Manchester 1884. Photo: anonymous.

149

Alcibiades from behind. A scroll reading "*gnothi seauton*" lies draped over a stool in the foreground, while in the background is a fountain spraying from phallic jets. More recently, in S. Christiaenssens' 1994 *Alcibiades Dreaming of Socrates*, the roles are reversed, as the buff youth swoons over a bust of the bearded philosopher.[27]

Conclusion

To the images discussed above, numerous others might be added: Peter Paul Rubens, Pietro Testa, and Anselm Feuerbach all represented Socrates and his companions at Plato's *Symposium*; Joannes Sambucus and Asmus Jacob Carstens produced images of Socrates in a basket, derived from Aristophanes' *Clouds*; Honoré Daumier drew a caricature of the philosopher as an old man dancing while Aspasia stands beside him holding a fiddle; Eugène Delacroix painted *Socrates and his Daimon* in a spandrel of the library of the Assemblée Nationale de France in 1843 as part of a program appropriating philosophy (as well as other disciplines) on behalf of the state. Other images of the philosopher appear in tapestries ranging in date from the early sixteenth through the eighteenth centuries, and, as noted above, in early modern engraved gems, while the nineteenth-century Milanese sculptor Pietro Magni carved stately large-scale marble statues of the philosopher, to rave reviews (fig. 8.43).[28]

SOCRATES BY MAGNI.
International Exhibition, 1862.

Figure 8.43   Socrates. Monumental marble statue by Pietro Magni. Souvenir photograph from the International Exhibition, London, 1862.

Socrates' image has also been commercialized, appearing more recently on postage stamps, cigarette boxes, Chinese (!) silver coins, and *New Yorker* magazine covers.[29] A search on E-Bay turns up a number of statuettes, reliefs, prints, bookends, and even decanters available for purchase – in bronze, ceramic, plaster, resin, and "chalkware" – most far removed from the philosopher's ancient iconography.

Today, as in antiquity, the middle ages, the Renaissance, and beyond, representations of Socrates appear in a vast range of contexts – from the philosophical to the commercial, the personal to the political, the moralizing to the erotic. The multiplicity of these images and the varied uses to which they are put reflect the great influence of the philosopher and his continued versatility, despite the paradox of his ultimate inscrutability, for like his philosophy, Socrates' image seems capable of meaning all things to all people. There may be ample evidence for Socrates' appearance, but the truths that lie behind the representations remain elusive.

Acknowledgments

I am grateful to the editors and to B. Abott, M. Belozerskaya, A. Blanchard, D. Blank, D. Brafman, B. Brinkmann, R. Burnham, J. Daehner, C. Giviskos, C. Hess, M. Kjellman-Chapin, D. McLean, M. Meadow, C. Miner, D. Sider, and A. Stewart for discussion, references, and various insights. None of them, of course, are responsible for my errors. A. Blecksmith, H. Brandhorst, A. Korteweg, A. Kreul, P. Luijkx, and W. de Witt kindly provided assistance with and permissions for illustrations, the cost of which were kindly underwritten by the University of Michigan–Ann Arbor, and the J. Paul Getty Trust. I have not seen M. Trapp, "The Image of Socrates in Art from the Fifth Century BC to the Twentieth Century AD," in V. Karasmanis (ed.), *Year of Socrates: 2400 Years Since His Death (399 B.C.–2001 A.D.)*. Delphi: European Cultural Centre of Delphi, 2005.

Notes

1   For Sophroniskos and Socrates as stone-workers and sculptural works attributed to them in antiquity see Schol. Aristophanes *Clouds* 733; Diogenes Laertius 2.18–19; Pausanias 1.22.8; Valerius Maximus 3.4 ext. 1; Suidas s.v. *Sokrates*. For surviving ancient copies see, e.g., Lippold 1950: 112, pl. 35, no. 4; Palagia 1990. For homonymous craftsmen see Pliny, *N.H.* 35. 137, 36.32; Pausanias 9.25.3. Over 500 individuals named Sokrates are listed in the first three volumes of P. M. Fraser and E. Matthews (eds.), *A Lexicon of Greek Personal Names.* Oxford 1987–. See also *Enciclopedia dell'arte antica, classica e orientale 7.* Rome 1966. pp. 397–8, s.v. "Sokrates 1°" (W. Fuchs) and "Sokrates 2°" (P. Moreno).

2   E.g., Plato, *Symposion* 215a ff., 221d–222a, *Theaetetos* 143e; Xenophon, *Symposion* 2.19, 5.5–7; Cicero, *De Fato* 5; Sidonius Apollinaris, *Epistulae* 9.9.14, Lucian, *Dialogi mortuorum* 20, *Menippi et Aeaci* 417; Jerome, *adv. Jovinianum* 1.48. Of course, the descriptions of later authors might well have been influenced by portraits as well as earlier descriptions. It should also be noted that the character of Socrates in Aristophanes' *Clouds* is described as pale and scrawny, while other sources report that Socrates was overweight.

3   For convenient collections of the ancient visual evidence, see Richter 1965: 109–19; Richter 1984: 198–203; Schleiber et al. 1989; and Schefold 1997.

4   For Ameipsias' largely-lost *Konnos* see Diogenes Laertius 2.27. For late Classical satyr iconography see, e.g., Moreno 1995: 258–9, 328. For a later third-century mosaic from

Mytilene on Lesbos depicting Socrates, apparently as a dramatic character, see Charitonidis et al. 1970: 33–6 and note 11 below.

5 *P. Herc.* 1021, col. 2, lines 13–17: Voutiras 1994, esp. 146ff. I am grateful to D. Blank for examining the papyrus in Naples to confirm the plausibility of Voutiras' reading. A similar reading, identifying the sculptor as Sotes rather than Boutes, was postulated independently by Augustin Speyer who presented it at the 2004 annual meeting of the American Philological Association in San Francisco (Speyer 2004).

6 See Richter 1965: 112 for concise argumentation. The type is also treated by Stewart 1990, Zanker 1995, Schefold 1997, and, in greatest detail, Voutiras 1994.

7 Schwarzmaier 1997 is the most recent treatment.

8 Louvre 475 CA: Wegner 1966, no. 75.

9 Malibu, J. Paul Getty Museum 70.AG.91.

10 For gems depicting Socrates, see Richter 1965: 119. For possible uses and meanings of such gems, cf. Polybios 15.31.8; Athenaios, *Deipnosophistai* 5.212d–e. Compare, too, the fine carnelian intaglio depicting Demosthenes signed by the carver Apelles now in Malibu (JPGM 90.AM.13): dating to the late first century BCE, it may have served as the personal insignia of someone named Demosthenes; or been acquired by someone who hoped the magical properties of the stone and/or the image might improve his skill at speaking or his performance in court; or it could have been commissioned by someone who, like Cicero when composing his *Philippics*, looked to the earlier figure as a model for political and moral action. For Socrates in the eighteenth century see further below.

11 For these mosaics see, e.g., Richter 1965: 118; Richter 1984: 197–8. The inscribed mosaic depiction of Socrates from the House of Menander on Mytilene (see note 4 above) also seems to conform to the ancient iconography, although the philosopher holds a book roll and appears to wear sandals. Other mosaics from the house depict actors in Menander's plays, but the figures of Socrates and his pupils Simmias and Cebes do not appear to be masked and they are not known to have been characters in any of Menander's comedies. Thomas Gelzer cleverly suggested to Lilly Kahil that these figures might instead represent a performance of the *Sokratikoi logoi* that Aristotle (*Poetics* 1447b 10) mentions as common mimes without specific name.

12 For various interpretations of this scene see, e.g., Derrida 1987.

13 See Bartsch vol. 85, nos. 1486/50, 1486/132, 1486/202; vol. 87, no. 1490/383. For the double herm with Seneca, Berlin, Staatliche Museum 371, see Richter 1965: 114, no. 20.

14 Bartsch vol. 30, nos. 93 (316), 94 (317).

15 Naples, Museo Nazionale 1482/6697: see Darby 1948: 123–4, fig. 5, with bibliography. The provenance of the relief is uncertain. A handwritten card in the Museum photo archive states that it is from Pompeii. Darby's assertion that the relief shows Socrates holding a round mirror, rather than a cup, is unconvincing, although she is right to argue that this scene is too casual to be a depiction of Socrates drinking hemlock. The cup is a common attribute of a cynic. For the authenticity of Ursinus' statue see Frischer 1979: 143.

16 For another depiction of a similarly covered mirror, see P. Thorton, *The Italian Renaissance Interior 1400–1600* (New York: Abrams, 1991), fig. 270. I am grateful to Catherine Hess for this reference.

17 Cf. the common Renaissance interpretation of the mirror, e.g., Cesare Ripa, *Iconologia*, Padua 1611, p. 441: "Lo specchiarsi significa la cognitione di se medesimo, non potendo alcuno regolare le sue attioni, se I propri difetti non conosce."

18 Lugano, Museo Civico di Belle Arte: see Impelluso 2002, 318. For additional examples see Pigler 1974: 431.

19 See Brinkmann and Kemperdick 2005: 257–72, esp. 268–9.

20   Strasbourg, Musée des Beaux-Arts: see Pigler 1938; De Mirimonde 1974; McGrath 1977: 97–9; 1983: 232 esp. n. 21; Impelusso 2002: 317; McLean 2005.
21   Richter 1965: 119. See also note 15 for a relief in Naples.
22   For further examples see Pigler 1974: 432–33, and Rosenbert and van de Sandt 1983: figs. 105–17, 187–9, to which add: O. Ferraro; H. F. Gravelot; D. N. Chodowiecki; and V. Cambeceini.
23   Possagno, Gipsoteca Canoviana: Stefani 1990: 50–66.
24   Bremen, Kunsthalle Inv. Nr. 640-1981/6, Leihgabe der Bundesrepublik Deutschland 1981. For an early photograph of the piece at the Munich Central Collecting Point for recuperated artworks at the end of the Second World War, see the Lost Art Internet Database: www.lostart.de/recherche/einzelobjekt.php3?lang=english&einzel_id=219146. Its CCP number was Mü 13603 and according to its Property Card now in the National Archives in Washington its Linz number was 923. I am grateful to Jens Daehner for bringing this relief to my attention and to Andreas Kreul for permission to publish it. The attribution to Lorenzo Bartolini is Carolyn Miner's.
25   Gerome: Ackerman 2000: 53, 246–7, no. 131. See also the drawing of Étienne-Barhélémy Garnier in Campbell and Carter 1993: 206–7, no. 50, and the commentary on Peyron's drawing, p. 177.
26   See www.amis-musees-castres.asso.fr/GIF/Photos/Aparicio2.jpg
27   http://maple.cc.kcl.ac.uk/socrates/image/img/017christiaenssensalcib.jpg. See also Blanchard forthcoming.
28   See, e.g., McGrath 1983 and Ecker 1991. For Daumier and Delacroix see next note. For Fuger see Campbell and Carter 1993: pp. 302–3, no. 102.
29   Some of these are collected at http://maple.cc.kcl.ac.uk/socrates/image/. For additional images of Socrates, see, e.g., www.artres.com and www.groveart.com s.v. "Socrates."

References

Ackerman, G. M. (2000). *Jean-Léon Gérôme: Monographie revisée. Catalogue raisonné mis à jour.* Paris: ACR Édition.
Bailey, D. M. (1974). A caricature of Socrates. *American Journal of Archeology*, 78, 426.
Bartsch, A. von. (1978–). *The Illustrated Bartsch*, ed. W. L. Strauss. New York: Abaris.
Blanchard, A. J. L. (forthcoming). From *amor Socraticus* to *Socrates amoris*: Socrates and the formation of sexual identity in late Victorian Britain. In M. Trapp (ed.), *Socrates from Antiquity to the Enlightenment*. Aldershot: Ashgate.
Brinkmann, B. and Kemperdick, S. (2005). Deutsch Gemälde im Städel 1500–1550. Mainz am Rhein: Verlag Philipp von Zabern.
Campbell, R. J. and Carlson, V. (1993). *Visions of Antiquity: Neoclassical Figure Drawings*. Los Angeles: LACMA.
Charitonidis, S., Kahil, L., and Ginouvès, R. (1970). *Les Mosaïques de la Maison du Ménandré à Mytilène*. Bern: Vereinigung der Freunde Antiker Kunst (= *Antike Kunst Beihefte* 6).
Crow, T. E. (1985). *Painters and Public Life in Eighteenth-Century Paris*. New Haven and London: Yale University Press.
——. (1995). *Emulation: Making Artists for Revolutionary France*. New Haven and London: Yale University Press.
Darby, D. F. (1948). The wise man with a looking glass. *Art in America*, 36, 113–26.
De Mirimonde, A.-P. (1974). La genèse iconographique d'une oeuvre: Socrate, ses deux épouses et le jeune Alcibiade de César van Everdingen. *La Revue du Louvre*, 24, 101–4.

Derrida, J. (1987). *The Post Card: From Socrates to Freud and Beyond*, trans. A. Bass. Chicago: University of Chicago Press. (*La carte postale: de Socrate à Freud et au-delà*. Paris: Flammarion, 1980.)

Ecker, J. (1991). *Anselm Feuerbach: Leben und Werk. Kritischer Katalog der Gemälde, Ölskizzen und Ölstudien*. Munich: Hirmer.

Finn, D. and Licht, F. (1983). *Canova*. New York: Abeville.

Frischer, B. (1979). On reconstructing the portrait of Epicurus and identifying the Socrates of Lysippus. *California Studies in Classical Antiquity*, 12, 121–54.

Höpfner, E. (1976). *Das Pompeion und seine Nachfolgerbauten* (*Kerameikos* 10). Berlin: Walter de Gruyter & Co.

Impelluso, L. (2002). *Gods and Heroes in Art*. Los Angeles: J. Paul Getty Museum Press.

Konecny, L. (2003). Carravaggio's "self-portrait" by Ribera. *The Art Bulletin*, 85, 406.

Lang, M. L. (1978). *Socrates in the Agora* (Excavations of the Athenian Agora Picture Book No. 17). Princeton: American School of Classical Studies at Athens.

Lippold, G. (1950). *Die griechische Plastik. Handbüch der Archäologie im Rahmen des Handbuchs der Altertumwissenschaft* V.3.1. Munich: Beck.

McGrath, E. (1977). *Rubens: Subjects from History* (*Corpus Rubenianum Ludwig Burchard* pt. 13, 1). London: Harvey Miller.

——. (1983). The Drunken Alcibiades: Rubens' picture of Plato's *Symposium. Journal of the Warburg and Courtauld Institutes*, 46, 228–35.

McLean, D. R. (forthcoming a). The Socratic corpus: Socrates and physiognomy. In M. Trapp (ed.), *Socrates from Antiquity to the Enlightenment*. Aldershot: Ashgate.

——. (forthcoming b). *Refiguring Socrates*. Cambridge: Cambridge University Press.

Moreno, P. (1984). Argomenti lisipei. *Xenia: Semestrale di Antichità*, 8, 21–6.

——, et al. (1995). *Lisippo: L'Arte e la Fortuna*. Monza: Fabbri Editori.

Musiari, A., et al. (2003). *Pompeo Marchesi: ricerche sulla personalità e sull'opera*. Gavirate: Nicolini.

Palagia, O. (1990). A new relief of the Graces and the *Charites* of Socrates. In M. Geerard et al. (eds.), *Opes Atticae: Miscellanea philologica et historica Ramondo Bogaert et Hermanno Van Looy oblata* (pp. 347–56). The Hague: Uitgave van de Sint-Pietersabdig Steenbrugge Martinus Nijhoff International.

Pigler, A. (1938). Sokrates in der Kunst der Neuzeit. *Die Antike: Zeitschrift für Kunst und Kultur des klassischen Altertums*, 14, 281–94.

——. (1974). *Barockthemen: Eine Auswahl von Verzeichnissen zur Ikonographie des 17. und 18. Jahrhunderts*, 2nd ed. Budapest: Akadémiai Kiadó.

Richter, G. M. A. (1965). *Portraits of the Greeks*. Oxford: Phaidon Press.

——. (1984). *Portraits of the Greeks* (abridged and revised by R. R. R. Smith). London: Thames & Hudson.

Rosenbert, P. and van de Sandt, U. (1983). *Pierre Peyron 1744–1814*. Neuilly-sur-Seine: Arthena.

Schefold, K. (1997). *Die Bildnisse der antiken Dichter, Redner und Denker*, 2nd ed. Basel: Schwabe & Co.

Schleiber, I., et al. (1989). *Sokrates in der griechischen Bildniskunst: Sonderaustellung der Glyptothek und des Museums für Klassischer Bildwerke. 12 Juli bis 24 September 1989*. Munich: Staatliche Antikensammlungen und Glyptothek.

Schwarzmaier, A. (1997). Wirklich Socrates und Diotima? Eine neue Deutung zum Bildschmuck der Truhe aus der Casa dei Capitelli Figurati in Pompeji. *Archäologischer Anzeiger*, 79–96.

Speyer, A. (2004). Non-archaeological evidence for the earliest bust of Socrates? (abstract). www.apaclassics.org/AnnualMeeting/04mtg/abstract/Speyer.html

Stefani, O. (1990). *I rilievi del Canova*. Milan: Electa.

Stewart, A. (1990). *Greek Sculpture: An Exploration*. New Haven and London: Yale University Press.

154

Strocka, V. M. (1977). *Die Wandmalerei der Hanghäuser in Ephesos* (*Forschungen in Ephesos* 8). Vienna: Österreichischen Archäologishen Institut.

Voutiras, E. (1994). Sokrates in der Akademie: Die früheste bezeugte Philosophenstatue. *Mitteilungen des Deutschen Archäologischen Instituts, Athenische Abteilung*, 109, 133–61.

Wegner, M. (1966). *Die Musensarkophage* (*Die Antiken Sarkophagreliefs* V, 3). Berlin: Verlag Gebr. Mann.

Zanker, P. (1995). *The Mask of Socrates: The Image of the Intellectual in Antiquity*, trans. A. Shapiro. Berkeley and London: University of California Press. (*Die Maske des Sokrates: das Bild des Intellektuellen in der antiken Kunst*. Munich: C. H. Beck, 1995.)

Section II

Plato

9

Socrates in Plato's Dialogues

CHRISTOPHER ROWE

There is a character called "Socrates" who is the main speaker in most of Plato's dialogues (there is also a younger namesake of his who appears in a few). This Socrates has certain marked distinguishing features: he is drawn to beautiful young men and adolescent boys, while he himself is, by usual standards, remarkably ugly; he knows nothing, but can outsmart anyone he meets; in spite of saying he knows nothing, he goes on saying, and evidently believing, a number of extremely odd things ("no one goes wrong willingly," "all the virtues are one," "all desire is for the good," and so on); he specializes in question-and-answer, but is usually the questioner; he says he prefers short answers to his questions, and doesn't like long speeches, but will sometimes make long speeches himself; a divine voice sometimes stops him from doing things, but he finds the only justification for actions in philosophy (his kind of divine "inspiration" or "madness"); he can drink anyone under the table, but never gets drunk; he is courageous, hardy, typically goes barefoot; and so on. These features tend not to surface together, yet the descriptions of "Socrates" in different contexts, and the traits he exhibits in those contexts, overlap to such an extent that it is hard not to suppose that this is meant to be a single person, if a highly exceptional and extraordinary one (a person like the Socrates who appears in Aristophanes' comedies, and Xenophon's fiction and nonfiction).

And yet this same character, according to some contemporary Anglophone readings of the Platonic dialogues, has something of a split personality. In some, usually shorter dialogues, early ones according to the standard dating, he is saying things – so these contemporary readings assert – that are or resemble the things the historical Socrates said (if we can believe our other sources, and they are themselves independent of Plato and at least reasonably reliable: Aristotle is the most important). But at a certain point, generally taken to coincide with the beginning of something labeled the "middle" period of Plato's writing, "Socrates" starts talking – so the story goes – with a different voice: Plato's. That is to say, having spent some considerable time constructing variations on the master's themes, and presenting him as chief speaker, on the account in question the author Plato turned instead to using him as a mouthpiece for ideas that he – the master, Socrates – had never heard of: in particular, for the idea which has become emblematic of Platonism, that behind and beyond the perceptible world there exist certain eternal entities, "Forms," which explain and somehow ground the being of that world. Some continuity there might well be with originally Socratic ideas, but (according to the interpretation presently being described) the real Socrates himself has been left behind. He makes a bit of a comeback later on, in the *Theaetetus*, or – particularly – in the *Philebus*: here "Socrates" not only has the look and feel of his old self, but is dealing with the sort of subjects he used to deal with (*Philebus*: ethics and the good life), and in something like the sort of way he used to (*Theaetetus*: a discussion of several successive propositions, ending in impasse). But, so the story goes, these are exceptions to the general rule, and serve in a way to confirm it: that there is a trajectory, in Plato, that leads him away from his original source and inspiration. On one version of the story, indeed, Plato even comes to approve of Athens for killing off the old man: he becomes a constitutionalist, and as such has to disapprove of Socrates as a subversive – "no one must be wiser than the laws" (*Statesman* 299c6).

So runs one standard (Anglophone) account of Plato's handling of his "Socrates." I quote the late, influential Gregory Vlastos:

> In different segments of Plato's corpus two philosophers bear [the name "Socrates"]. The individual remains the same [i.e. has the same character, behavior, and looks?]. But in different dialogues he pursues philosophies so different that they could not have been depicted as cohabiting the same brain throughout unless it had been the brain of a schizophrenic. They are so diverse in content and method that they contrast as sharply with one another as with any third philosophy you care to mention, beginning with Aristotle's. (Vlastos 1991: 46)

The third of the sentences just cited is puzzling: ". . . could not have been depicted as cohabiting the same brain . . ." – yet they *are*, by Vlastos' own admission, "depicted as cohabiting the same brain." The only conclusion one can draw is that Vlastos supposes Plato's Socrates (the character) actually to have "the brain of a schizophrenic." This seems to expose the very implausibility of the type of interpretation in question. For how could it be that, having written numerous dialogues which – according to Vlastos and others – are written to defend, advance, even if necessary gently modify, Socrates' ideas (but presumably still get him at least roughly right), Plato should then proceed, in other dialogues, to traduce that very memory by putting things into "Socrates'" mouth that he never said, and actually run importantly contrary to what he said? Though Plato might have thought his own ideas were somehow legitimate extensions or corrections of Socrates', it scarcely looks credible that he should switch in this way from loyal reportage to inventive use of "Socrates" to front and present new, and non-Socratic, perspectives. On the standard interpretation Plato's *volte-face* is sudden and brutal: thus *Republic* Book 1 (on this interpretation) is a standard "Socratic" dialogue, but it is followed by nine books in which in many respects Plato strikes out on his own: the *Republic* is, in these books, the "middle" dialogue *par excellence*, with Forms – see above – at its heart. So Socrates is himself in the first book, but then suddenly becomes someone else (Plato), while retaining the same outward characteristics. (Vlastos, at 1991: 53, explains this sort of change in terms of "the dramatist's attachment to his protagonist": "as Plato changes, the philosophical persona of his Socrates is made to change, absorbing the writer's new convictions . . ." This too, however, seems to emphasize the problem rather than resolve it.)

160

At this point the natural response might be to say that after all the Socrates of the "early" dialogues is really an invention of Plato's, having real connections with the historical person, but at the same time essentially a literary and philosophical construct that serves Plato's own particular purposes. And that response is likely to be inherently attractive in any case, especially in an age like the present when, at least in literary studies, the notion of stable and discoverable truths is out of favor. (Especially so, of course, about people: could even *Socrates* know who the real Socrates was? Is it coherent to ask the real Socrates to stand up in the first place?) Such a perspective, although resisted by those who – perhaps reasonably enough – think Plato *the* chief source on Socrates, or at least on his philosophical thinking, is widely shared, and indeed would probably represent the fallback position of those numerous readers and interpreters of Plato who would prefer, for whatever reasons, not to engage with questions about the truthfulness or otherwise of Plato's treatment of Socrates. But the perspective in question is usually either combined with, or made redundant by, another common attitude towards the Socrates of the "Socratic" dialogues: that his forte is provocation rather than serious philosophical work, and that he is to be taken at his word when he says that he is no teacher. A typical Socratic dialogue ends in impasse (*aporia*); his paradoxical dicta in any case – so *this* view goes – make no sound philosophical sense, however effective they may be in stirring his interlocutors, and his readers, to philosophical reflection; and in general the "Socratic" dialogues fade into insignificance when compared with the works of Plato's "middle" (or "mature") and later periods. From this direction comes the caricature of Socratic method that survives in that modern academic phrase "Socratic questioning," by which is meant a kind of questioning that merely aims at getting clear about what the student or pupil thinks he or she is saying. A Socrates of this sort has no need of positions of his own, and if he has them they will surface only incidentally, as if to reassure us that he is a person of the right moral fiber to teach his students in the first place.

Seen from this angle, the "mature" Plato will only be doing what he was taught, and thinking for himself. (Plato *was* taught by Socrates – that is, he listened to him over long enough a period to be thoroughly captivated by him; everyone is agreed at least about that.) Nor do we have to worry any longer about the pupil putting the wrong words into his adored teacher's mouth, if the teacher had no very particular philosophy of his own, only a method and a few paradoxes, the latter including some with reassuringly modern liberal resonances ("it is no part of the just man to do harm to anyone," and so on). Plato himself, according to those who follow the line I am here describing, regards it as a requirement on any philosopher to review anything and everything he says, and shows every sign of following that policy himself. Thus the "Socrates" of a later dialogue like the *Parmenides*, which includes a thoroughgoing critique of, or reflection on, the very idea of Forms, will himself be nothing more than the archetypal philosopher, going through that very process of continual reflection and self-challenge that his counterpart in the "early" dialogues recommended (in fact the challenge comes from a friendly Parmenides, and Socrates is on the defensive; but no doubt both voices here are Plato's own). End of problem.

Reasonable though this response to our initial problem may appear to be, it depends, fatally, on underestimating the philosophical value, and indeed the philosophical content, of the dialogues labeled "early."[1] (To recall the initial problem: it was how to

161

explain the apparent shift, from the use – as many suppose – in some dialogues of the character "Socrates" to record or reflect on the historical Socrates' activity, to the use of him in others to represent un-Socratic, even anti-Socratic, ideas.) Or, to go back a further step, the response in question underestimates just how puzzling and peculiar those "early" dialogues can be. True, some are puzzling only in parts, and perhaps as soon as one has allowed that Socrates means to provoke, and probably has no definitive answers up his sleeve, they read comfortably enough: the *Euthyphro*, on "holiness" or "piety" (*eusebeia*, roughly a matter of having the right attitude towards the gods), and the *Laches*, on "manliness" (*andreia*) or courage, might be examples. The *Apology*, or *Defense of Socrates*, the one genuine part of the corpus not written in dialogue form, will certainly be another example of a Platonic work that one can read more or less straight through; another is the *Crito*, a kind of companion piece to the *Apology* that purports to give Socrates' reasons for refusing to escape from the jail where he is awaiting execution after his trial. But alongside these are other ("Socratic") dialogues that are likely to leave any modern reader feeling almost completely at sea. Here I cite what are probably the two outstanding examples: the *Lysis*, a series of bewildering arguments purporting to be about "friendship" (i.e. *philia*, a Greek term actually wide enough to include more or less any positive kind of human relationship, and in the dialogue treated as including human relationships with inanimate objects as well), and the *Charmides*, in which Socrates and others set out to say what *sōphrosunē* – "sound-mindedness" – is, but without once mentioning one of the things with which most contemporary Greeks would immediately have connected the term, i.e. self-control, or control over one's desires. A mere wish to provoke hardly seems a plausible explanation in these cases; and indeed Socrates' interlocutors in both dialogues are all, to a greater or lesser degree, caught up in the argument – *they* aren't merely provoked.

So let us suppose there is something else. It could in principle just be a matter of *bad arguments*, and this will be enough to satisfy anyone who wants to hurry on to the "mature" Plato. But then we seem to need to ask: just why so many bad arguments? Socrates seems capable of constructing good arguments elsewhere. More pressing still, what would be the point of writing down collections of bad arguments? Perhaps Plato is using fallacies to help train us philosophically (see Sprague 1962). Yet there is no sign in the text that the whole of the *Lysis*, or of the *Charmides*, is a *pis aller*: not just the interlocutors but Socrates himself seem to be caught up in the process of argument, as if they were going somewhere – even if, apparently, that turns out not to be the case. (There is in fact one moment near the end of the *Lysis* where Socrates has been taken as suggesting that everything that went before is "some kind of rubbish": see Smith Pangle 2002. But closer examination of the text shows that it is just one part of what Socrates, Lysis and Menexenus have been discussing that needs to be junked.) Or, to put it more positively, we are given every indication that, until the final impasse, everything has been going swimmingly.

To *begin* by supposing that an author – any author, but particularly a philosophical one – has made a mistake is generally, and rightly, regarded as bad policy. To find oneself in the position of supposing that a philosophical author, one known to understand a thing or two about arguments, has managed to string together a whole series of bad arguments ought to be plain embarrassing; or at least it is a state of affairs that calls for explanation. And here is one possible explanation – that there is more going on in dialogues like the *Lysis* and *Charmides* than is suspected by those modern interpreters who give up on them. In particular, there is more by way of *content*: the arguments, whether bad or good, revolve around a special way of seeing things: one that is reflected in those peculiar notions that Socrates keeps on expressing, i.e. "no one goes wrong willingly," "all the virtues are one," and so on.

But here we meet a problem that tends to point back in the direction of another version of the "two Socrateses" interpretation. The "special way of seeing things" that I refer to relates to the theory of action, or in other words, a particular theory about human motivation; and a theory that is generally regarded as faring rather badly when compared with the theory of the mature Plato. I quote from an influential paper by John Cooper:

> Everyone knows that in the *Republic* Plato advances the theory that the soul has three independent parts: reason, spirit and appetite, as they are usually called in English. Using this theory he constructs an account of the human virtues: each of the three parts of the soul has its own special role to play in a human being's life, and virtue, for us, consists in each of them playing its own role fully and in harmony with the others. Thus human virtue taken as a whole, according to the *Republic*, is a complex interrelationship among three separate psychological elements, each of which has its own indispensable contribution to make.
>
> Now this theory of virtue contrasts sharply with the Socratic theory found, for example, in the *Protagoras*.[2] According to the Socratic theory virtue is essentially a property of the intellect (and never mind what other parts of the soul there may be). That Plato in the *Republic* is self-consciously rejecting this Socratic theory is by now well accepted; and most philosophical readers no doubt agree that the *Republic*'s theory is a distinct improvement. Even if knowledge by itself does motivate action, as Socrates evidently though obscurely assumed, there are surely other motivating factors as well, and being virtuous must therefore partly consist in having these other factors, whatever they may be, in some special condition or other. After all, it will be agreed by all parties that to be virtuous is to have one's practical attitudes and dispositions – whatever it is that affects one's actions and the ways one is inclined to act – structured in some special way; the virtuous person's practical attitudes must be such as always to produce the (or a) virtuous and right action in the given circumstances. And if not only one's *thoughts* about what is good and bad, but also ways one *feels* about things (whether or not those are also ways one thinks about them) constitute practical attitudes affecting the ways one is inclined to act, then obviously virtue must be something more complex than the Socratic theory represents it as being. It must involve not just well-informed, correct thought about what is good and what bad for a person, but also certain specific states of feeling about these matters as well. From this perspective Plato's *Republic* theory can be seen as a stage in the progression from Socratic rationalism to the Aristotelian theory that moral virtue is an interfusion of reason and desire . . . (Cooper 1984: 3)

Thus, so far as Cooper's reading goes, even if there is content as well as argument in the "Socratic" dialogues, that content is philosophically rather less interesting than what we find in the *Republic* (and by implication in other post-*Republic* dialogues). Plato manages to get right, or more right, what the Socrates of the early dialogues – who is philosophically at least closely related to the historical person – got so obviously wrong.

163

Of course, in a way this deals at a single stroke with the original problem, at least in one very important area (the theory of action/motivation), i.e. how Plato the writer could move from memorializing his mentor to using him for his own purposes; after all, what greater service could he have done Socrates than by allowing him, finally, to *get things right philosophically?* How could Socrates, or anyone, object to being represented as saying things that were more nearly true than the things he actually said? The problem might still exist in other areas, on other topics; there the second, later Socrates would still be saying "unSocratic and antiSocratic" things (to use a phrase of Vlastos [1991: 3]), but at least in one major area, arguably the most important for Socrates, Plato's continuing to use Socrates even while departing from him would have turned out to be not only intelligible but thoroughly justifiable.

Here is what I believe is the crucial sentence in the passage cited from Cooper: "That Plato in the *Republic* is self-consciously rejecting this Socratic theory is by now well accepted; and most philosophical readers no doubt agree that the *Republic*'s theory is a distinct improvement." There is no gainsaying the main sense of the first claim made here: most serious modern readers of Plato would accept that the *Republic* is "self-consciously rejecting" *a* Socratic theory (if not quite the one Cooper describes: see below); and the second claim is certainly true – "most philosophical readers" would agree "that the *Republic*'s theory is a distinct improvement" over whatever theory it is "self-consciously" replacing. The expression "most *philosophical* readers" is no doubt meant to suggest that anyone who denies that the *Republic* theory is an improvement, and who is a philosopher, ought to reconsider his or her position. Whether or not Cooper is right about that, however, is a question that must wait on a clearer picture of what exactly it is that the Plato of the *Republic* is rejecting. If Socrates had espoused a theory of the sort Cooper attributes to him, it would be hard not to dismiss it summarily. But there is good reason to think Cooper's account of the Socratic theory to be defective. Christopher Taylor, for example, gives an importantly different account of the theory. The crucial difference is that the motivation of action, in Taylor's account of Socrates' theory, comes not from knowledge (or belief, or reason) but from *desire*:

> The basis of the theory is the combination of the conception of goodness as that property which guarantees overall success in life with the substantive thesis that what in fact guarantees that success is knowledge of what is best for the agent. This in turn rests on a single comprehensive theory of human motivation, namely, that the agent's conception of what is overall best for him – or herself (i.e. what best promotes *eudaimonia*). Overall success in life is sufficient to motivate action with a view to its own realization. This motivation *involves desire as well as belief* [italics added]; Socrates maintains (*Meno* 77c, 78b) that everyone desires good things, which in context has to be interpreted as the strong thesis that the desire for good is a standing motive, which requires to be focused in one direction or another via a conception of the overall good. Given that focus, desire is locked onto the target which is picked out by the conception, without the possibility of interference by conflicting desires. Hence all that is required for correct conduct is the correct focus, which has to be a correct conception of the agent's overall good. (Taylor 2000: 62–3)

From *this* kind of theory all of the Socratic paradoxes readily flow: virtue is knowledge (we'll get everything right if only we have knowledge: the good are the wise), all

164

the virtues are one (because they are the same thing as knowledge), and no one will go wrong willingly (only through ignorance). And this theory will, of course, be quite immune to Cooper's chief objection, because it does not make motivation a function of reason. It may be vulnerable to other objections, e.g. that it requires, counterintuitively, that even though we frequently go for things that are incompatible with our overall good, we never actually *desire* such things ("all desire is for the good"). In the *Nicomachean Ethics* (3.4), Aristotle scornfully rejects such a position, because, he says, it will turn out that what was wished for – why else would the agent have gone for it, if he didn't wish for it? – was not wished for after all; but then he would say that since his own assumptions are completely different, and he has no incentive to look to see how what he is rejecting might be developed in order to escape his objection. (While Aristotle does not explicitly attribute to Socrates the position he is criticizing, it goes well with the many other things that he does attribute to Socrates; and this seems reason enough – again, given that Aristotle is an independent witness – for us to consider treating it as authentically Socratic. As a matter of fact there seem to be only two people Aristotle could be referring to there in *Nicomachean Ethics* 3.4: either the historical Socrates, or the Socrates of certain Platonic dialogues; no one else that we know of held any position like the one described, or any position that implied it.)

There is no space here, either, for a discussion of how Socrates' theory might survive this assault of Aristotle's. It must suffice here to say that Socrates' theory *can* indeed survive it; furthermore, that Plato's Socrates argues at length and robustly – in the *Lysis* – for the position that it is in fact only the real good that we desire;[3] that just as this position leaves no room for our desiring bad things, i.e. things that are really bad for us, by the same token it leaves no room for irrational desires (if these are conceived of as blind passions, thrusting us towards – they care not what); that this explains the absence of the notion of self-control, or control over the appetites, from the analysis of *sōphrosunē* in the *Charmides* (what we *call* "self-control" rather requires a different analysis – that is, in terms of our beliefs); and that it also explains the fact that the Socrates of the *Symposium* – unlike the other speakers in the dialogue – manages to give a detailed account of the workings of romantic or sexual passion, *erōs*, exclusively in terms of desire for (the real) good.[4] It is, finally, *this* position – that we all desire the real good, and nothing else – which "the Plato of the *Republic* self-consciously rejects" (I recur to that long passage cited earlier from Cooper), i.e. in introducing the tripartite soul, because "appetite" at least is specifically said to be directed towards things irrespective of their goodness and badness. "Spirit," too, that other irrational part of the soul, has its own projects, even while being treated as the natural ally of the reasoning part. Only reason is directed towards the good – and that, it seems, only on condition that the two irrational parts allow it to function as it should.

Given what I have already said, it will be clear enough that I suppose it no easy thing to decide whether this new account of motivation is superior to the one it replaces, though it will certainly seem more familiar. However what matters more in the present context is to consider the consequences of the shift for our understanding of Plato's treatment of Socrates. Plato moves away from Socrates, at any rate in the explanation of action, and evidently because he thinks he can improve on him. Irrespective of whether or not it really is an improvement, Plato can surely justify having Socrates make the change, and reject his own earlier ideas; that is, just because he,

Plato, *thinks* it an improvement. That, after all, is what philosophers are supposed to do – change their position when they have been shown reason to do so; Socrates himself (Plato's Socrates) says as much (see e.g. *Crito* 49a–b). There are arguments in *Republic* 4 for the introduction of irrational parts of the soul, which Plato evidently thinks powerful. So what Socrates now says, after that, will be no more than what (Plato thinks) he should have said all along, and since he is committed to the truth, he could not reasonably object to having these new things put into his mouth.

Yet at the same time the consequences of the change are considerable. So great are they that Socrates really does in many respects cease to look like himself. If the way we behave is determined by our rational beliefs, then the only reliable way to change our behaviour – and Socrates always seems to be interested in *that* – will be to talk to us, rationally; that, plainly, is the way of the old Socrates, the Socrates of the "Socratic" dialogues (i.e. those that include a Socratic psychology). Nothing apart from talking and reasoning with us will be necessary, because there is nothing apart from what we think and believe that is even in principle capable of causing us to go wrong. If, on the other hand, even our settled beliefs about what it is best for us to do can be unsettled – and thwarted – by something else, then whoever wants to change the way we behave will have not merely to reason with us, but find a strategy to deal with that something else. The "something else," in this case, is represented by the irrational parts of the soul and their desires; and the question about how *these* are to be addressed, along with our rational selves, continually resurfaces in the *Republic* and other apparently post-*Republic* dialogues. Socrates, or his substitute as main speaker, turns away from the direct treatment of philosophical issues (in the company of individuals) to the question how the majority, "the many," are to be persuaded of the truth: in the *Phaedrus*, he describes and recommends a kind of philosophical rhetoric that offers different kinds of discourses to different kinds of souls, while in the *Statesman* the Visitor from Elea proposes that the masses need to be addressed through "storytelling" (*muthologia*) rather than by teaching; the *Republic* itself develops a program for mass education that depends on the controlled use of imaginative literature and other means in order to instill beliefs and dispositional attitudes in advance of, or even in place of, a genuine understanding of the truths that justify those beliefs and attitudes. What is at issue here is plainly a state-run educational system: it is a matter of the city or the state educating, or training, its citizens. One might think that a city run on Socratic lines would also need its education to be state-run, or at least state-sponsored. But Plato's Socrates, at any rate prior to the *Republic*, has no interest in politics, or political institutions, at all, except insofar as he is a citizen of the city of Athens, and subject to its laws; and *his* kind of education is one-on-one, or as near that as makes no difference. There is a real sense in which *political thinking itself* is "unSocratic," or at least any political thinking beyond a straightforward critique of political practice, or reflection on the "duties" of citizenship.[5]

Here we can be a little more precise. The Socrates of the (pre-*Republic*) *Gorgias* claims that he is – perhaps – the only true statesman alive (see *Gorgias* 521d–522a). His grounds are that he is the only person who tells people the truth about what is good for them; thus he is the only one who does what statesmen *ought* to do (but in fact do not). The point he is making relies on the fact that, in ordinary terms, he is about as far from being a statesman, a *politikos*, as one could get: paradoxically, he is claiming that in order to be what they claim to be, ordinary, so-called *politikoi* ought to be like him. (In fact, "*politikos*" was not a standard term for "politician"/statesman; Plato's choice of language here already reflects *his* view that statesmanship is a science.) And then the paradox is further increased by the fact that what Socrates does cannot, by its very nature, be done to the citizens as a body: dialectic, the process of question and answer typically represented in the "early" dialogues, cannot be carried on with more than a few. What the *Republic* and the *Statesman*, and by implication the *Phaedrus*, then supply is a means by which, after all, the truth can be brought into the lives of "the many." The legislator of the *Republic*, the true statesman of the *Statesman*, and the true orator of the *Phaedrus* in fact must all be philosophers; only they are making laws, devising educational curricula, or writing speeches and stories (or myths), instead of doing dialectic with beautiful young men.

These philosophers, it may be said, doing all these apparently non-Socratic things, do not look like Socrates at all. Plato seems to have distanced himself from Socrates in other ways too: though the *Republic* and other later dialogues use the question-and-answer style that characterizes most of their pre-*Republic* counterparts, the questions are more loaded, and the interlocutors generally contribute rather less than they did. So the dialogues are at least *less* Socratic, not just in terms of their content – of which there is far more that is positive and constructive, with *aporia*, impasse, occurring only rarely – but in the way that they are written. It is all too easy, then, to suppose that Plato has just *moved on*. This is the kind of reading of Plato that makes possible the interpretation of the *Statesman* to which I referred earlier, according to which he even came to approve of the Athenians for executing Socrates.

That interpretation, however, rests on a simple misreading of the argument of the *Statesman* (see Rowe 2001). The Plato of the *Statesman* remains as opposed to democracy as the Plato of the *Republic*, or of the *Protagoras*, and for exactly the same fundamental reason: that knowledge, especially knowledge about what is good and what is bad, is essential for governing, and that such knowledge is only accessible to the specialist, not to the layman. Since Plato has not found any source for this specialist expertise – so far as his argument goes, in any dialogue – except in or through philosophy, and Socrates is as a philosopher, Socrates is actually (still) the very *last* person whose execution Plato should be endorsing. True, Socrates goes on to the last protesting that he has no knowledge. Maybe Plato has in mind some other, non-Socratic philosophizing, which would have a hope of reaching some stable results; and maybe that is why, in his later period, he wheels in other main speakers in Socrates' place. What is certainly true is that these other speakers – the Visitor from Elea in the *Statesman* and *Sophist*, Timaeus in the *Timaeus*, the Visitor from Athens in the *Laws* – are by and large more assertive, less apologetic about making positive proposals on particular subjects than Socrates ever is. But except in the case of Timaeus, there is nothing in the actual processes of reflection exhibited by these speakers that marks them off from Socrates when he appears in the main role (Timaeus is a special case, and is identified as such: someone who attempts to reach truth by reflecting on perceptible reality). Rather the reverse: the *Phaedrus* makes Socrates himself a devotee of the very philosophical method that provides the skeleton of the argument of both the *Sophist* and *Statesman* ("collection and division"), while the Athenian Visitor in the *Laws* begins from the very same assumption about the purpose of the city-state, and of

167

statesmanship, that the Socrates of the *Protagoras* and *Gorgias* so eloquently asserts: namely that a city, and statesmen, exist for the purpose of making the citizens better people, i.e. of allowing them to live happier lives, ones that exhibit a true understanding of what is good and what bad (whether or not it is the people themselves, or only the statesman, who possesses that understanding).

We can go further. By and large the *Laws* has little to say about the philosophical underpinning of the proposed city of Magnesia; the Spartan and the Cretan who are the Athenian's interlocutors evidently do not have much of a head for deep thinking. But there is one place where Plato does after all seem to reveal his philosophical hand. This is in the last book of the dialogue, where the characters are discussing the operation and functions of the "nocturnal council," a kind of think-tank introduced to ensure that there is continuing reflection on the laws of the city, and that these remain as good as they can be. Discussion is envisaged as arising about the aim of legislation, which immediately turns into a little dialogue about the way in which the "virtues" or "excellences" (*aretai*) are, first, different from each other, and, second, the same – except that the Visitor suddenly seems to realize that Clinias the Cretan won't be up to contributing his part in the conversation, and goes on to something else. The significance of this little passage (961c–964b) is that precisely the same topic arose between Socrates and his opponent Protagoras in the *Protagoras*, in the context of a conversation that is fundamentally about how to educate young men for the political life. In other words, what appears to be driving the huge political project of the *Laws* is exactly the same kind of reflection that we find in the context of the supposedly apolitical Socrates of the early dialogues. In a sense, that project is precisely about bringing the insights of that Socrates to bear on the lives of the largest possible number – given that Socratic conversation as such can only go on between one or two, or a small number of people, whether they be the characters of an early dialogue or the members of the "nocturnal council."

But here is another striking fact. Despite having allowed that the human soul includes irrational drives that can interfere with the workings of reason, and push us in the direction of things that reason tells us are bad for us, the Plato of the *Laws* is still proposing that when we go wrong, and (e.g.) commit an injustice, we do so *involuntarily* (see 731c, 734b, 860d). In other words, even actions apparently caused by factors internal to ourselves can be, as we might put it, "against our will," or not wished for. (Especially for anyone fresh from reading Aristotle, this will be not just striking but shocking.) Even the worst tyrant, committing the worst acts conceivable, still does not *want* to do what he is doing. How so? Because, as Socrates always claimed, no one actually wants what is really bad for him (and doing the worst things is worst for the agent as well as the victim). The tyrant cannot see the truth about what he is doing; it is still, as Socrates always said, a question of intellectual error – even if, as the *Laws* implicitly claims, it is an error caused by internal factors: overblown desires of the wrong sorts. The Athenian of the *Laws* (he is probably Plato) is in one way deeply pessimistic: unless our education somehow makes us resistant to the siren calls of the irrational, we shall inevitably find ourselves – so he seems to suggest – exploring the depths of self-indulgence and injustice. And yet at the same time he retains more than a little of that beautiful Socratic optimism about human nature. A successful life *is*, in the end, a matter of our getting things right intellectually. Plato is evidently considerably less sanguine about the prospects for most people of their doing that for themselves. So in his view we shall need cities, and all the institutions of social control: an "education" system for the inculcation of the right beliefs, police, prisons, even capital punishment for those we cannot reform – if only, perhaps, because life is not long enough. (Socrates, for his part, as Plato seems to recognize, would prefer to do without such institutions: compare the simple community that he seems to prefer in the *Republic*, the one the more worldly Glaucon calls a "city of pigs.") But what will justify those institutions, or what in Plato's view will justify them, is a beautifully simple, Socratic truth, that we are as it were hard-wired for the good: the real good, and the best life achievable. We should not be misled by the apparently repressive, dictatorial nature of the regimes that Plato offers us by way of illustration, in the *Republic* and *Laws*, of what philosophical rule might look like. What is foundational for the whole is the claim that, one way or another, we need to get clear – intellectually – about the good and the bad (for us). One might just regret that Plato did not have more faith in our ability to do it for ourselves.

I conclude that in a very real sense, and despite all appearances, Plato remains deeply Socratic. His retention of Socrates as main speaker, except where – for various reasons – he needs someone else (not a know-nothing, anyway), is from that perspective entirely reasonable: this is a Socrates who not only looks the same, and sounds the same, but who for the most part is the same. It is just that at a certain point he is forced, by his author, to accept that our rational processes can be upset and interfered with by irrational factors that are just as much internal to us as our reason. But it is still our reason that makes us human (compare the image of the soul in *Republic* 9: part man, part lion, part many-headed monster). And no one – so Plato's Socrates goes on asserting – ever voluntarily accepted a worse life in preference to a better one; if anyone seems to do so, he or she is out of his of her mind, not seeing things straight.

A final question: is Plato's Socrates the real one? My own guess is that the kind of theory that Plato's Socrates uses and propounds (however indirectly) in the pre-*Republic* dialogues is the theory that the real Socrates was proposing, however much or little of it he succeeded in articulating. In fact, it does not matter how much that was, for in any case Plato articulated it for him. Until, that is, Plato's courage deserted him (as one might put it), and he began to concede to the standard view – standard for Greeks of the classical period as much as for us – that the human mind is a battleground between reason and passion.

Notes

1 The scare quotes reflect the fact that the traditional division between "early" and "middle" is no longer sustainable: so e.g. investigations seem to show that three of the dialogues usually claimed as "middle" (essentially because they contain Forms), i.e. *Phaedo*, *Cratylus*, and *Symposium*, actually belong with the early (earliest) group. (See further n. 4 below.) Those dialogues now usually labeled as "Socratic," i.e. especially those ending in impasse, are therefore – so far as we can tell – roughly synchronic with some "middle" ones. See Kahn (1996).

2 In a footnote, Cooper says that he follows "the by now conventional scholarly practice, according to which this character's central views are attributed to the historical Socrates." The "convention" he finds confirmed by Aristotle's treatment of Socrates, and in particular

of Socrates' handling of the virtues in the *Magna Moralia* and both *Nicomachean* and *Eudemian Ethics* (Cooper regards the *Magna Moralia* as Aristotle's; while his view is hardly universally shared, the treatise certainly reflects genuinely Aristotelian ideas).

3 For these claims, see Penner and Rowe (2005).

4 The *Symposium* is normally treated as a "middle," and so non-Socratic dialogue, on the grounds that it contains talk about Forms. Stylistically, however, the *Symposium* seems to belong in the same, early, group as the dialogues traditionally labeled as "Socratic" (see n. 1 above); and the account that Socrates – and the priestess Diotima, the fictional teacher he says he listened to – gives of human motivation is precisely parallel to the account he gives in the *Lysis*, even if it is less detailed. Aristotle and others have perhaps overestimated the difference that Forms make in the context of Socratic–Platonic philosophy: see Penner and Rowe (2005), and Rowe (forthcoming).

5 For another statement of some of the issues here, see Rowe (2003: 28–9).

References

Cooper, J. M. (1984). Plato's theory of human motivation. *History of Philosophy Quarterly*, 1, 3–21; reprinted in Cooper, *Reason and Emotion: Essays on Ancient Moral Psychology and Ethical Theory* (1999), 118–37. Princeton: Princeton University Press. On why Plato was right to abandon (Cooper's version of) Socratic moral psychology in favour of a tripartite soul, and in particular to identify a 'spirited' part/aspect of human nature.

Kahn, C. H. (1996). *Plato and the Socratic Dialogue: The Philosophical Use of a Literary Form*. Cambridge: Cambridge University Press. A moderately unitarian approach to Plato ("early" and "middle" dialogues only), which allows no room for a "Socratic" period.

Penner, T. and Rowe, C. [J.] (2005). *Plato's Lysis*. Cambridge: Cambridge University Press. A new and complete reading of the *Lysis*, with major consequences for the reading of Plato – texts and philosophy – as a whole.

Rowe, C. [J.] (2001). Killing Socrates: Plato's later thoughts on democracy. *Journal of Hellenic Studies*, 121, 63–76. Despite the implications of standard modern readings, Plato never came to approve of Athenian democracy for having Socrates killed off, and always remained a staunch opponent of democracy, as involving rule by the ignorant.

Rowe, C. [J.] (2003). Plato, Socrates and developmentalism. In N. Reshotko (ed.), *Desire, Identity and Existence: Essays in Honour of T. M. Penner*. Kelowna, BC: Academic. How Plato gave up on the Socratic theory of action; and the consequences of his thus giving up on Socrates.

Rowe, C. [J.] (forthcoming). What difference do forms make to Platonic epistemology?' In C. Gill (ed.), *Norms, Virtue, and Objectivity: Issues in Ancient and Modern Ethics*. Oxford: Oxford University Press. Answer: forms (Platonic ones) make considerably less difference than is often assumed, and was assumed by Aristotle.

Smith Pangle, L. (2001). Friendship and human neediness in Plato's *Lysis*. *Ancient Philosophy*, 21, 305–23. An attractive attempt to disentangle the argument of the *Lysis*, which nevertheless gives up too easily.

Sprague, R. K. (1962). *Plato's Use of Fallacy*. London: Routledge. Given (a) that Plato's arguments frequently involve fallacies, and (b) that he cannot have been unaware of the fact, why did he construct his arguments like that?

Taylor, C. C. W. (2000). *Socrates: A Very Short Introduction*. Oxford: Oxford University Press. A brilliant, (very) short introduction to different aspects of Socrates.

Vlastos, G. (1991). *Socrates: Ironist and Moral Philosopher*. Cambridge: Cambridge University Press. A highly influential book from the most influential modern writer on Plato's Socrates; not to be taken lightly, but its conclusions, and its starting-points, are less convincing than they have seemed to many.

10

No One Errs Willingly: The Meaning of Socratic Intellectualism

HEDA SEGVIC

The Western philosophical tradition is deeply indebted to the figure of Socrates. The question "How should one live?" has rightly been called "the Socratic question." Socrates' method of cross-examining his interlocutors has often been seen as a paradigmatic form of philosophical inquiry, and his own life as an epitome of the philosophical life. What philosophers and nonphilosophers alike have often found disappointing in Socrates is his intellectualism. A prominent complaint about Socratic intellectualism has been memorably recorded by Alexander Nehamas: "And George Grote both expressed the consensus of the ages and set the stage for modern attitudes toward Socrates when he attributed to him 'the error . . . of dwelling exclusively on the intellectual conditions of human conduct, and omitting to give proper attention to the emotional and volitional'."[1]

The complaints against Socratic intellectualism take two main forms. According to one line of criticism, Socrates ignores or overlooks – or at least vastly underestimates the importance of – the emotional, desiderative, and volitional sides of human nature, being too preoccupied with the intellect. The error attributed to Socrates by Grote belongs to this line of criticism. The second line of criticism does not charge Socrates with ignoring or marginalizing desires, emotions, and volitions, but rather with giving an inadequate, overly intellectualist account of them. These two lines of criticism have sometimes been combined, and sometimes confused. What they have in common is the thought that the desiderative, the emotional and the volitional are not given their due by Socrates.

I wish to challenge this understanding of Socrates. He holds that living a good life is a matter of living in accordance with a certain kind of knowledge. Since knowledge is an accomplishment of reason, the Socratic view is in some sense intellectualist or, perhaps more appropriately, rationalist. However, I argue that desiderative, emotional, and volitional propensities and attitudes are an integral part of the knowledge in which Socrates locates virtue. This undermines the more prevalent, first line of criticism. Towards the end of the chapter I address the second line of criticism and suggest a different overall understanding of Socratic intellectualism, one that centers on the view that every act of the human soul involves an act of reason. I work my way toward this understanding of Socratic intellectualism by looking into the role that volitions, emotions, and desires play in Socratic virtue.

171

A large part of this chapter deals with two Socratic theses. The first thesis, that no one errs willingly, has long been recognized as crucial to Socratic intellectualism; however, the precise meaning of this thesis has remained elusive. I argue that "willingly" is used here in a highly specific sense. The text which in my view offers the clue to the proper understanding of the No One Errs Willingly thesis is a passage in the *Gorgias* that has been much slandered in the literature on Socrates. The argument has often been thought confused, and the whole passage has sometimes been treated as a deliberate exaggeration on Socrates' part. I claim that the passage makes perfect sense, that Socrates intends it seriously, and that it plays a central role in the overall philosophical structure of the dialogue. I then turn to the second thesis, that *akrasia* – weakness of the will, as the Greek term is usually rendered – does not exist. I offer an interpretation of the denial of *akrasia* based on my analysis of the No One Errs Willingly thesis. The joint reading of the two theses leads to a perhaps surprising result. Certain kinds of wantings and volitional propensities are constituents of moral knowledge. The same can be shown for desiderative and emotional attitudes and propensities. Far from disregarding the volitional, desiderative, and emotional, Socrates attempts to build them into his account of virtue as knowledge. Furthermore, his remarks on wanting or willing, sketchy and conversational though they are, point – I argue – to a distinct notion of the will. If Socrates does have a concept of the will, this is the first appearance of a concept of the will in the Western philosophical tradition.

This interpretation shows that it is wrong to assume (as people have done since Aristotle) that Socrates ignores or marginalizes the desiderative and the emotional side of human nature, focusing solely on the intellectual side.

* * * *

Socrates claims that no one errs knowingly.[2] Why an intellectualist would make such a claim, we might think, is not so difficult to grasp. The intellectualist believes that when a person does what is morally wrong, that moral failure is due to an intellectual error. If only the person exercised his intellect well – if he knew better – he would not do what is wrong. Hence what we have to do in order to make people better – an intellectualist would have us think – is help them see how things really are; in particular, help them see what really is good or bad. I do not dispute that Socrates is a rationalist or intellectualist of some sort, or that a line of thought roughly corresponding to the one just sketched may be linked to his claim that no one errs knowingly. What I wish to emphasize is that in order to determine what kind of intellectualist he is, we must see how he conceives of the knowledge the absence of which he takes to be responsible for wrongdoing. I will argue that Socrates' conception of moral knowledge makes many of the objections traditionally lodged against his intellectualism unwarranted.

In addition to claiming that no one errs knowingly, Socrates also claims that no one errs willingly. Why does he make this latter claim? An answer to this question does not leap to one's eye from the pages of Plato's dialogues. One would expect that, if anywhere, an answer is to be found in the *Protagoras*, where Socrates argues at length for the view that *akrasia* does not exist, and where he also briefly formulates, and appears to endorse, the claim that no one errs willingly (*Protagoras* 345c4–e6; cf. 352a1–358d4). But the *Protagoras* is silent on what precisely the dictum "No one errs willingly" amounts to and how it is related to Socrates' denial of *akrasia*. Confronted with this silence, it is tempting to think that Socrates himself was in error. He must have thought, mistakenly, that "No one errs knowingly" implies "No one errs willingly." Those who recall Aristotle's discussion of voluntary and involuntary action in the *Nicomachean Ethics* and *Eudemian Ethics* may be especially inclined to think that Socrates simply made an error in passing from "knowingly" to "willingly."[3] [. . .][4]

* * * *

In Plato's *Protagoras*, Socrates introduces the thesis that no one errs willingly (at 345c4–e6) while presenting an analysis of a poem by Simonides. That no human being errs willingly is something, Socrates contends, that Simonides as a wise and educated person would surely have known. He proceeds to use this thought to guide his interpretation of Simonides, but he offers no gloss on the thesis itself. Although the *Protagoras* provides us with indispensable material for understanding Socrates' ethical outlook, and hence also for understanding the No One Errs Willingly thesis, a more direct clue to the meaning of this thesis comes from the *Gorgias*.

Our starting point should be *Gorgias* 466a4–468e2. In his exchange with Polus, Socrates declares that orators and tyrants do not do what they want to do (467b2, 466d8–e1), and that they have the least power of any in the city. Startled by this, Polus asks if it is not the case that orators, just like tyrants, kill anyone they want [. . .], and subject anyone they please [. . .] to expropriation or exile (466b11–c2). Socrates retorts that Polus has raised two questions rather than one (466c7, 466d5–6), and proceeds to draw a distinction between doing what one pleases, on the one hand, and doing what one wants, on the other (466d5–e2). Applying this distinction, Socrates now grants that orators and tyrants do "what they please" [. . .], at 467a3 and 467b8, or "what they take to be best" [. . .] at 467b3–4, but denies that they do what they want to do [. . .] (467b2, b6, 467a10; cp. 466d8–e1) – presumably when engaged in the actions mentioned: killing, expropriating, banishing. The passage makes it fairly clear why Socrates claims that orators and tyrants do not do what they want to do: what they do is not good, and one can only want those things that are good (see especially 468c2–7). But why should Socrates construe "wanting" in such a peculiar way? To answer this question, we should take a broader look at the matters discussed at 466–8.

Socrates' claim that neither orators nor tyrants do what they want to do is meant to be startling. What in common opinion distinguishes a tyrant from others is precisely the enormous power he has. As Polus had observed at 466b11–c2, the tyrant can put to death anyone he wants; he can dispossess or exile whomever he pleases. Thus he can visit what in common opinion are the worst of evils upon the head of anyone he wants.

Another bit of common lore is that having power consists in being able to do what one wants. Power is so understood by Socrates' interlocutors in the *Gorgias*, and Socrates raises no objection. What Gorgias and Polus add to the common view is the claim that orators are at least as powerful as tyrants, and probably more so (see esp. 452e1–8). This, of course, is advertisement on behalf of oratory by its practitioners or sympathizers. The advertisement nonetheless correctly identifies some of the aspirations, and some of the accomplishments, of oratory in the ancient world. Faced with Gorgias' and Polus' claims on behalf of oratory, Socrates does not take the obvious course, to reject as an exaggeration the claim that orators are so powerful. Rather, he takes the entirely nonobvious course of saying, first, that neither orators nor tyrants do what they want to do when they engage in the actions mentioned, and second, that they consequently have no great power in the cities. In making the transition from the first claim to the second, Socrates relies on the above-mentioned assumption about power: to have power is to be able to do what one wants to do; to have a lot of power is to be able to do much of what one wants to do. [. . .]

That doing what one pleases or what one sees fit [. . .] amounts to acting in accordance with one's opinion [. . .] is suggested in Greek by the very form of the words. [. . .] If doing what one pleases amounts to acting in accordance with one's *doxa*, opinion or belief, and there is, Socrates suggests, a sharp contrast between doing what one pleases and doing what one wants, it is not unreasonable to suppose that doing what one wants is linked with acting in accordance with one's *epistēmē*, knowledge. I shall defend the view that this is indeed so. In fact, I shall propose that wanting, as understood by Socrates in the present context, is even more intimately connected with knowledge than the phrase "acting in accordance with knowledge" might suggest. Before I do so, let me make some remarks about the appropriateness of bringing knowledge into the picture.

The contrast between *doxa*, opinion, and *epistēmē*, knowledge, is at the heart of the *Gorgias* as a whole. Socrates recoils from oratory, which he considers dangerous to the human soul. Oratory is dangerous because it enshrines mere *doxa*, opinion, and aims to convert it into [. . .] conviction, without regard for the truth of the opinion, hence *a fortiori* without regard for knowledge. [. . .] [C]onviction is what persuasion [. . .], if successful, leads to, and producing persuasion is the business of the orator. Following Gorgias' descriptions, Socrates characterizes the orator as [. . .] "a manufacturer of persuasion" (*Gorgias* 453a2). Socrates sees himself, by contrast, as concerned with knowledge, hence he keeps denouncing practices that systematically bypass this concern. The orator and the tyrant, each in his own way, stand accused by Socrates of being mired in such practices.

To say that doing as one pleases is to be understood as acting in accordance with one's opinion or belief, invites the question: an opinion or belief about what? Likewise for acting in accordance with one's knowledge. As far as opinion or belief is concerned, the very fact that Socrates treats [. . .] what pleases them (467a3, b8), as interchangeable with [. . .] what they think (believe, opine) is best (467b3–4), suggests an answer. The opinion is about what is best, or perhaps more generally about what is good, better, or best. Although I think that we can take our cue from the expressions Socrates uses, I do not mean to suggest that his understanding of these matters is determined by the peculiarities of certain Greek idioms. Socrates has philosophical reasons for seeing the matter this way – reasons which will emerge as we proceed. These reasons stand behind the form of words he uses.

My suggestion was that Socrates describes orators and tyrants as not doing what they want to do because in doing what they do they do not act in accordance with knowledge. [. . .] I propose the following, preliminary, characterization of the notion of wanting which Socrates relies on in the orators-and-tyrants passage: the agent wants to f just in case he desires to f taking f-ing to be the good or right thing to do (in the circumstances in question), and his f-ing (in those circumstances) is (or would be) good or right in the way he takes it to be. The point of glossing "good" as "right" is that wanting to do something, as wanting is understood here, does not merely involve a desire to f because f-ing is seen by the agent as having some goodness in it; the agent wants to f only if he desires to f seeing it as the right or correct thing to do.

Now this sort of wanting, which I shall call Socratic wanting or willing, is presumably still a desiderative state of some sort, in a broad sense of the word "desiderative." How can the ascription of a desiderative state to an agent possibly depend on the object of the desiderative state being in fact good? Whether an agent wants something, wishes for it, longs for it, and so on, depends on how he sees, or conceives of, the object of his wanting, wishing, or longing. Must we not leave open the possibility that the agent is wrong in his conception of the object desired, whatever the modality of his desire?

[. . .] The issue here is not whether generally speaking one can be mistaken about the object of one's desire. Of course, Socrates would agree that one can be. What is at issue is whether every kind of desire or volition that can be ascribed to a person is independent of the correctness of the person's conception of the object desired or wanted. A parallel may be of help here.

In claiming that orators and tyrants do not do what they want to do, Socrates is inviting us to think of wanting as a volitional state that is in some ways like perceiving. I do not perceive an object if I have some images; I perceive it only if my sensory impressions derive from the object itself in the right kind of way. Socratic volition is likewise a receptivity of the soul to a certain evaluative property of the object of volition, the property Socrates designates by the term "good." However, wanting is not sheer receptivity; it is mediated by a correct conception of the object of desire as the good or the right thing to do. Just as perception latches onto that aspect of reality that has an impact on our sensory apparatus, so Socratic volition latches onto a certain evaluative aspect of reality. Thus this kind of wanting can be correctly ascribed to the agent only if the object of his volition has the required evaluative property and the agent recognizes, and responds to, that property. We should call to mind again the relationship between belief and knowledge. Whereas having a belief consists in taking something to be true, knowing on Socrates' view is the secure grasp of truth. Likewise, Socrates seems to be suggesting, whereas desire involves believing that the object of desire is good,[5] wanting – the sort of wanting referred to in the *Gorgias* passage – implies knowing that the object of volition is good.

I can now offer a more precise characterization of Socratic wanting: I Socratically want to f just in case I want to f, recognizing that my f-ing (in the given circumstances) is the good or right thing to do. Thus I (Socratically) want to f only if my wanting to f is linked to my recognition of the goodness of f-ing; if it is a mere coincidence that I believe that f-ing is the right thing to do and that f-ing in fact is the right thing to do, my wanting to f is not Socratic wanting.

This characterization is meant to bring Socrates' notion closer to us, while staying reasonably close to his own idiom. Its drawback is that it unravels a unitary notion: Socratic wanting is meant to be, I think, both a volitional and a cognitive state. On the best reading, the wanting would be a volitional state in virtue of being a certain kind of cognitive state. Socrates has philosophical reasons for offering us this notion of

175

wanting. Before turning to them, let me make few remarks in defense of my interpretation of the orators-and-tyrants passage.

* * * *

[. . . It may be objected that] to understand the orators-and-tyrants passage one first has to settle the question whether Socrates uses the verb "to want" in a special sense. For, if he does not use it in a special sense, then it appears that his claim cannot possibly be true; but if he does use it in a special sense, then he and Polus are not speaking of the same thing; hence his disagreement with Polus, or with anyone who shares Polus' point of view, is not genuine.[6] The prevalent interpretation of the passage seems to be that Socrates does introduce a special sense of "wanting" in the passage under consideration, but that for this very reason his overall argument is marred by equivocation, and hence flawed.[7]

As Socrates uses the verb "to want" [. . .] in the orators-and-tyrants passage, a sentence saying that someone wants something is false if what the person is said to want is not good. When [. . . "want"] is used in this way, the sentence in question has truth conditions that are different from those that the sentence would have if [. . . "want"] were used as Polus uses it, and as presumably most Greeks of this time would use it. So Socrates does use the verb "to want" in a special way here. But from this it does not follow that he and Polus are speaking of different things, and hence cannot disagree. The notion of Socratic wanting is meant to express a truth about the underlying structure of human motivation. If we recognized this structure, Socrates appears to think we would see that the notion is legitimate and useful. Not everyone would agree with his picture of human motivation, and he can disagree with those who reject it.

Socrates is aware that his construal of "wanting" is not ordinary. When he introduces his distinction between doing what one wants, on the one hand, and doing what one pleases (*Gorgias* 466c9–467c4), he deliberately goes against Polus' prior implicit identification of the two. Socrates has quite a bit of explaining to do before it becomes clear what he means by his claim that Polus has raised two questions rather than one (466c7–e2). Nonetheless, he speaks as if Polus is in some way committed to the distinction, whether he realizes this or not. The very fact that Socrates proceeds to produce an argument, at 467c5–468e5, for the thesis that orators and tyrants do not do what they want to do, indicates that he does not take himself to be merely stipulating a new sense for the verb "to want." His argument starts from a more or less ordinary sense of "wanting." He begins by making claims about wanting that appear acceptable to Polus, as a person with commonsensical views about such matters, but somehow, at the end of the argument, Polus finds himself obliged to agree to the claim he had a little earlier labeled "outrageous" and "monstrous." So it seems that the not-exactly-ordinary construal of wanting Socrates proposes to Polus is meant to be connected with what Polus and others normally understand by "wanting."

At 468b1–4, Socrates formulates the following general claim about human motivation for action: "Therefore it is because we pursue what is good that we walk whenever we walk – thinking that it is better to walk – and, conversely, whenever we stand still it is for the sake of the same thing that we stand still, [namely, for the sake of]

176

what is good." Although Socrates does not mention desire (other than wanting) in the Gorgias passage, he presumably would not deny that desires move us to act. However, looking at actions in terms of desire, the same principle holds – that we do whatever we do because we pursue what we take to be good – since Socrates believes that people always desire what they take to be good.

For this understanding of desire, we should look at *Meno* 77b6–78b2. The argument in this passage is meant to bring Meno around to the view that everyone desires good things. Socrates puts the following question to Meno: "Do you assume that there are people who desire bad things [. . .] and others who desire good things [. . .]? Do you not think, my good man, that everyone desires good things?" (77b7–c2) Further below, the object of desire turns out to be what the person who desires takes to be good, not what as a matter of fact is good. As for those who at first appear to Meno to desire what is bad (77c2–3), Socrates argues that they desire what they do thinking [. . .] that it is good, and not recognizing [. . .] that it is bad (77c3–e4). Those who appear to desire what is bad are also described by Socrates as being ignorant about the object of their desire ([. . .], 77e1 and e2).

The object of desire according to the *Meno* passage is what people take to be good, whether or not their belief is correct. We should think of this as holding of all desiderative and volitional states: no one desires or wants a thing unless he takes it to be good. The sort of wanting Socrates invokes when he says that orators and tyrants do not do what they want to do is no exception; it fits entirely into the general theory of desire outlined at *Meno* 76–8. One does not Socratically want something without taking it to be good. But the notion of Socratic wanting is stronger, because the agent who Socratically wants to f does not merely take f-ing to be good; he recognizes f-ing to be good. Thus Socrates does not waver between two different accounts of desiderative and volitional states, unclear whether it is the good or the "apparent good" (that is to say, what people take to be good) that is the object of such states, as some have suggested. He has a unified view of desire that covers all its modalities, plus a special notion of a volitional or desiderative state that is also a cognitive state. Socrates does think that this sort of wanting in some way underlies all other desiderative and volitional states. This, however, is part of a substantive philosophical position, not the result of an elementary confusion. [. . .]

* * * *

The ostensible conclusion of the discussion between Socrates and Polus at *Gorgias* 466a9–468e5 is simply that orators and tyrants – when engaged in killing, expropriating, and banishing – do not do what they want to do (468e3–5; see also 468d6–7). But Socrates' concern is clearly with anyone who does [. . .] what is bad or wrong. Much later in the dialogue, at 509e2–7, he expressly formulates the conclusion of the argument in these wider terms. Talking now to Callicles, he refers back to his discussion with Polus. He says:

> Why don't you answer at least this question, Callicles? Do you think that Polus and I were rightly forced to agree in our previous discussion . . . that no one does what is unjust (or what is wrong) wanting to . . . but that all who do what is unjust (wrong) do so unwillingly . . . ? (*Gorgias* 509e2–7)

The conclusion of the discussion with Polus is now formulated as follows: no one who does what is wrong does so [. . .] wanting to. [. . . "wanting to"] is directly contrasted with [. . .], unwillingly, suggesting that we should construe [. . . "wanting to"] here as equivalent to [. . .] "willingly." If so, the conclusion of the orators-and-tyrants passage turns out to be the claim that no one errs willingly. For a more familiar wording of this claim, see *Protagoras* 345e1–2: [. . .], no human being errs willingly. The *Protagoras* passage reads in full:

> For [says Socrates] Simonides was not so uneducated . . . as to say that he praised whoever did nothing bad willingly . . . as if there were anyone who willingly did bad things. . . . I am pretty sure that none of the wise men thinks that any human being errs willingly . . . or willingly does anything shameful or bad. . . . They know well that all who do what is shameful or bad . . . do so unwillingly . . . (*Protagoras* 345d6–e4)

The Greek verb translated as "to err" [. . . *hamartanein*] ranges over a wide territory. It covers both doing wrong, in a moral sense, and simply going wrong, in the sense of making an error. This suits Socrates' purposes very well. We might try to capture the way in which *hamartanein* is suitable for his purposes by stating his position this way: no one commits injustice or does what is wrong willingly, but everyone who does wrong goes wrong. When wrongdoing is thought of as involving an error or mistake, it is easy to conclude that this is something one would not want to do. But however felicitous *hamartanein* may be for Socrates' purposes, he does not rely too heavily on the properties of this particular word.[8] When he suggests that Simonides was not so uneducated as to imply that a human being errs willingly, he may well be ironic, and in more than one way. Nonetheless, he associates a recognition that no one errs willingly with education and wisdom, thus treating it as something that requires insight.

* * * *

At *Gorgias* 509e2–7 Socrates gets Callicles to agree that no one does what is unjust or wrong wanting to, but that all those who do so do it unwillingly. The larger immediately relevant passage starts at 509c6. Socrates has been focusing his and Callicles' attention on two evils – the evil of suffering injustice [. . .], and the evil of doing it [. . .]. Now he raises the question of what it would take for us to save ourselves from falling into each of the two evils. In each case, he asks, is it [. . .] power, or [. . .] wish [. . .] that enables us to avoid the evil in question?

To avoid being treated unjustly, Socrates and Callicles quickly agree, one needs power (509d3–6). But what about doing what is unjust: is it [. . .] power or wish that saves us from this evil? Socrates permits Callicles to say that one needs power in this case as well (510a3–5) even though just a moment ago he had secured Callicles' agreement to the conclusion of the previous discussion with Polus, that no one does what is unjust [. . .] wanting to so do (509e5–7). Socrates intends Callicles to make the required connection between [. . . "wish" or "will"] and [. . . "wishing to" or "willingly"]. Like Polus before him, Callicles does not quite get Socrates' point. But Callicles is not entirely wrong in his answer, and this may be the reason why Socrates lets him off as he does. [. . . Wish] – as construed by Socrates – is sufficient for a person not to do what is unjust. But this [. . . wish], of course, is not merely a wish, but rather wanting or willing in the highly specific sense that Socrates had introduced in his

178

discussion with Polus, and reintroduced here in his discussion with Callicles. This kind of wanting or willing is (in a certain sense) power. Socrates' point is the following. To avoid becoming a victim of an unjust action, one needs power in the straightforward sense; indeed the power often needed is brute force. To avoid committing injustice, on the other hand, what a person needs is that his will be in a certain condition. When one's will is in this condition, one has all the power one needs, and all the power one can have, not to do what is unjust.

In speaking here of one's will being in a certain condition, I am of course relying on some more current notion of the will. There has been a long-standing dispute over the question whether the ancients had any notion of the will. Presumably, given the large number of widely different conceptions of the will that have emerged in Western philosophical thought since antiquity, the question is whether any of the ancient thinkers had a notion that is in some important way linked to one or more of these later notions. In his claim that orators and tyrants do not do what they want to do, as well as his claim that no one errs willingly, as I have interpreted these claims, Socrates introduces – apparently for the first time in Greek philosophical thought – a certain notion of the will, or something very much like a notion of the will. This notion of the will is in some ways peculiar. The [. . . "wish"] in question – the will, understood as I have suggested – prevents us from doing anything that is wrong. If so, this will – which is essentially the good will – cannot be weak. (This point is linked to Socrates' denial of *akrasia*, which I discuss below.) [. . .]

Power was also the main ground on which earlier in the dialogue the great orator Gorgias had defended and praised oratory. In arguing that orators are at least as powerful as tyrants, Gorgias was relying on the enormous and nearly universal appeal of power. Polus inherited his argument from Gorgias. Thus in discussing the tyrant's actions of killing, expropriation and banishing with Polus, Socrates is still addressing Gorgias' defense of oratory. Socrates now in response leaves his three interlocutors, Gorgias, Polus, and Callicles, with the following dilemma: either the power that enables a person to inflict what people consider to be the greatest evils on others is not good, and hence not something to be in the least admired, coveted, or envied; or else if power as such is good, orators and tyrants have none of it.

The notion that power as such is something good – clearly a notion that all three of his interlocutors are eager to push – undergoes a peculiar, deliberate, transformation at Socrates' hands. He in effect offers his interlocutors an option of choosing between two concepts of power. In both cases power is the ability to do as one wants. On the first concept, a person is powerful if he can do what he wants or desires, as the words "wants" or "desires" are usually understood. On the second concept, a person is powerful if he can do what he wants in the more special sense – in the sense of what I have called Socratic wanting. Socrates is not blind to the fact that this notion is a novelty to his interlocutors. What he wants is to recast the debate in a novel way. Gorgias, Polus, and Callicles may insist as much as they please that power, as they understand it, is good. They are simply wrong about this. Relying now on the second concept of power – the one that Socrates himself is pushing – virtue is power. To express Socrates' thought in a different way: a certain kind of knowledge, and a certain kind of will, are power.

* * * *

179

Socrates seems to propose his special notion of wanting – that of Socratic wanting – not as a notion we already have at work in our language, but rather as a notion that we occasionally grope for, and a notion that we need. We need it because it enables us to express something that is of relevance to all the willing, wishing, and desiring that we ordinarily do and ordinarily speak of.

The notion of Socratic wanting announces a certain ideal. There is nothing arbitrary, however, about this ideal. Desires and wants of all varieties are, as we would put it, intentional phenomena. They are directed toward something. In Socrates' view, they embody a certain direction of the soul: a striving of the soul for what is good, and the striving of the soul for its own good, or perhaps for the good proper to a human being. The ideal of wanting that he introduces in the orators-and-tyrants passage, and in its follow-up later in the *Gorgias* (509c6 ff.), is meant to embody the shape that this striving of the soul takes when the soul has gotten a grip on what the good that it is after in fact is. The Socrates of Plato's early dialogues does not often invoke human nature. But this is what we find him saying about it in the *Protagoras*:

> Now, no one goes willingly towards things that are bad ... or towards those one thinks ... are bad, nor is it in human nature ... so it seems, to want to go towards what one thinks is bad instead of to what is good. ... And when one is forced to choose between two bad things, no one chooses the greater if he is able to choose the lesser. (*Protagoras* 358c6–d4)

We, humans, are hardwired to seek our own good. What we want is, ultimately, to do well for ourselves. The striving for this condition of doing well, which Socrates calls "the good," is something that every human soul comes equipped with. Striving after the good is as basic to the soul as is its striving after the truth.

With regard to the considerations that impelled Socrates to introduce his special concept of wanting, it may be useful to quote a passage from outside what we consider Plato's Socratic writings, even if we do not, as we should not, treat it as evidence for the Socratic view:

> And isn't this also clear? In the case of just and beautiful things, many would accept things that are believed (reputed) to be so, even if they are in fact not so, and they do such things, acquire them, and get a reputation for doing and acquiring them.[9] But when it comes to good things, no one is content to acquire things that are believed to be so, but everyone seeks things that are in fact good and spurns mere belief. ... This, then, [sc. the good] is what every soul pursues and for the sake of which it does everything it does ... (*Republic* 505d5–e1)

Whatever special interpretation Plato might be putting in the *Republic* on the distinction between [...] things that are thought (opined, believed) to be good, on the one hand, and things that are good, on the other [...] there can be no doubt that the Socrates of the early dialogues is interested in a similar distinction: a distinction between what appears to be good, and what is good. Towards the end of the *Protagoras*, Socrates announces that it is the power of appearance [...] that makes us wander all over the place and regret our actions and choices (356d4–7). We mistakenly take for good things that in fact are not good, but merely appear to us to be so. If we had knowledge about what is good and bad, the appearing [. . .] would lose its grip over us ([. . .], 356d8); consequently, we would achieve peace of mind ([. . .], 356e1) and salvation in life ([. . .], 356d3; see also 356e2, e6, e8, and 357a6–7).

Furthermore, both the Socrates of the *Republic* and the Socrates of the *Protagoras* takes goodness to be an evaluative property of a special sort. No other question is of more importance to the business of living than the question: "Is this (what I am about to do, what I contemplate doing, what I am doing) really good?" We might believe that the action we are considering is admirable or useful; or that we shall be envied for it; or perhaps that it is in keeping with our outlook, although we shall be despised for it. But the nagging question always remains whether the action under consideration is really good; whether in acting as we do, we do good for ourselves. This concern is the driving force behind much ethical reflection. But it is a concern that is operative already at a prereflective level. What the nagging question brings out is that we aim – prereflectively no less than reflectively – not at what appears good, but at what is in fact good.

Thus the special, Socratic wanting is what wanting becomes when we have tracked down what we have been after all along. What we have been after all along – what our desiderative states are always tracking down – is where our well-being in the world lies.

* * * *

In saying that no one errs willingly Socrates has in mind, roughly, that no one does what is wrong recognizing it as wrong and wanting it as one wants things one recognizes to be good. We might find it helpful to put it this way: no one does what is wrong knowingly and willingly. But Socrates has no need to add "knowingly" to "willingly," since his claim that no one does what is wrong willingly implies that no one does it knowingly. If "willingly" is understood as I have suggested, the claim is clearly not that wrongdoing is involuntary in Aristotle's sense of the word (see *Nicomachean Ethics* 3.1). If one thinks that Socrates takes wrongdoing to be involuntary in Aristotle's sense of the word (or in something close enough to this sense), one will feel a need to explain how he came to embrace such a view. This, I think, is what gives rise to the mistaken belief that he infers that no one does what is wrong willingly from the idea that wrongdoing involves ignorance. He fails to realize – unlike Aristotle after him – that only certain kinds of ignorance concerning one's action make that action involuntary (cf. the second section above). On the reading I have proposed, Socrates' claim makes perfect sense; it does not reflect any such gross failure of judgment.

Special as the notion of Socratic wanting or willing is, it is a part of a larger disagreement with many of us. Socrates believes, for instance, that all who do what is wrong do so simply because they go wrong. Wrongdoers do not aim at something they recognize as wrong or bad; rather, they are misguided and ignorant about the nature of their action and its goal. Further, the thesis that no one errs willingly, as will transpire shortly, implies that *akrasia* is not possible. This is certainly not what many of us today think about weakness of the will, or what many people thought about *akrasia* in Socrates' own time.

We ought to start, however, with the position that Socrates takes himself to be denying when he rejects *akrasia*. At *Protagoras* 352d4–7, Plato formulates with some care the position that Socrates rejects:

> You [says Socrates to Protagoras] know that the many . . . are not going to be persuaded by us. They say that a lot of people . . . recognizing what is best . . . do not want to do it . . . when it is possible for them to do so . . . but do something else instead. . . .

The view that Socrates rejects – imputed to, and indeed put into the mouth of "the many" – is that a lot of people act against their recognition, that is to say, against their knowledge, of what is best. This I take to be Socrates' primary, or official, characterization of *akrasia*.

Nowadays weak-willed action is often characterized as action against one's better judgment – one's judgment of what, under the circumstances, is the better thing to do. When understood in this way, there is no reason why an *akratic* action could not in principle be a good thing to do, or at any rate better than the action which the agent (incorrectly) takes to be better. However, according to the characterization of *akrasia* which Socrates gives in the passage quoted, *akratic* action is by assumption wrong: the *akratic* agent does what is wrong knowing that it is wrong, considering or having considered a different course of action that is open to him, which he knows to be better or best. It is because Socrates construes *akrasia* in this way, and not merely as action against one's better judgment, that his denial of *akrasia* follows from his No One Errs Willingly thesis.

One important aspect of the official characterization of *akrasia* at *Protagoras* 352d4–7 has been generally overlooked. The many, Socrates says, claim that a lot of people, recognizing what is best, do not want to do it [. . .], when it is possible for them to do it, but do something else instead. Socrates invokes wanting here, and builds it into the characterization of *akrasia* offered by the many (see also [. . .] 355b2, [. . .] 358d2, and [. . .] 358e3). Thus the thesis he intends to deny is not just that one can fail to do what one recognizes is best, but more fully that an agent may recognize what is best and yet not want, or not be willing, to do it, and consequently, not do it. By contrast, we have to assume, Socrates contends that a person who knows what the right thing to do is, does want to do it, and other things being equal, will do it. (The more neutral word for wanting, [. . .], that Socrates uses here is appropriate since the position Socrates is denying is that of the many, who would not put their own point in terms of Socrates' special notion of wanting or willing. [. . .])

If Socrates uses "willingly" in a special way when he claims that no one errs willingly, to designate a volitional act that is also cognitive, does this not make his claim problematic? His concept of willing is not our concept. What can we do with such a peculiar concept? In response, I will match this question with another one. Socrates' rejection of *akrasia* amounts to the view that one cannot act against one's knowledge of what is best. Now the conception of knowledge that underlies this view should strike us as at least as peculiar as the concept of Socratic wanting. This is what Socrates has to say about the relevant kind of knowledge:

> Now, do you [Protagoras] too think that that is how things stand with it [sc. knowledge], or do you think that knowledge . . . is fine and such as to rule the person, and if someone

recognizes what is good and bad . . . he would not be overpowered by anything else so as to act otherwise than knowledge dictates, and wisdom . . . is sufficient to help the person? (*Protagoras* 352c2–7)

We no more share with Socrates his conception of *knowledge* than we share with him his conception of *wanting* or *willing*. But if this is so, should we regard his claim that no one errs willingly as more suspect than his claim that no one errs knowingly? As I pointed out in the beginning of this paper, the wanting or willing that the expression "willingly" refers to involves recognition of what is good or bad; it has now turned out that the knowledge of what is good and bad involves wanting that accords with the knowledge in question. Hence, one claim is as problematic or as unproblematic as the other; both claims stand or fall together. They should also be examined together.

[We have omitted sections 9–11 of the essay, on *akrasia* – eds.]

* * * *

The many take it that sometimes, driven by a desire or emotion, we act entirely against what our reason tells us is good, better, or best. Against this, Socrates holds that our actions themselves embody judgments of value. Our reason speaks in the very passion that drives us, even if reason does not speak in a way that is consonant with our remaining opinions or judgments. We take ourselves to be fragmented where we are not. Socrates sees the human soul as one and undivided. In taking the human soul to be unitary and undivided, he is ruling out the possibility that there is an irrational or nonrational part of our souls that is capable of motivating us to act entirely on its own. But the unity of the soul he envisages has a further significance: it ties inextricably together the practical side of our nature – the desiderative, the emotional and the volitional – with the supposedly nonpractical side of us, namely the side that forms judgments and possesses knowledge.

On Socrates' view, it is an inadequate conception of reason that lies at the bottom of the belief that *akrasia* exists. An inadequate and impoverished conception of reason might also lie behind certain misunderstandings of his position. Socratic intellectualism is often criticized as one-sided, because it does not do justice to the richness and complexity of our mental life. But on the account given here, the complexity and richness of our mental life, and of our nature, can remain untouched. Rather, Socrates' view might be that more of us goes into every state of our soul than we suspected; in some sense the whole power of the soul goes into every state of the soul. If our reason is at work in more places and in more ways than we might have thought, it should not be too surprising if it turned out to malfunction more often than expected. Specific malfunctionings of reason are also at the bottom of what people call *akrasia*.

One would expect that an intellectualist would propose an intellectual cure for an intellectual ailment. So, for instance, if virtue is knowledge, as Socrates appears to think, it might seem that all we need to do in order to instill virtue in those who lack it is instruct them about what virtue requires. But he never recommends such simple instruction; on the contrary, he insists that becoming virtuous involves much care and therapy of the soul. Reason is quite vulnerable. Susceptible to more maladies than we might have expected, it also requires more extensive and complicated care than expected. If we do not stick to the characterization of *akrasia* given in the *Protagoras*, we could concede that on Socrates' view humans are prone to a condition that might deserve to be labeled *akrasia*. The Greek word simply indicates weakness, and Socrates does take it that weakness of reason is displayed in the episodes usually considered *akratic*. What he presents as powerful – as not dragged about "like a slave" – is not reason as such, but knowledge, which is a stable overall condition of a well-functioning reason.

When Socrates describes virtue as knowledge, it is not just any kind of knowledge that he has in mind. Certain desires and feelings are part of the knowledge that virtue amounts to. In addition, Socratic volition as discussed above is part of moral knowledge. Socratic volition is an aspiration; it is part of an ideal of the good life. The virtuous person alone on Socrates' view does entirely what he wants to do. The virtuous person can do what he wants to do because the taking-to-be-good that his willing amounts to is itself a state of knowledge: it is an accurate grasp of what is in fact good. Being instructed on what one ought to want typically does not produce the desired wanting; this holds good for Socratic volition as much as it holds for volition as usually understood. Socrates would certainly agree with those who think that becoming good requires that one's whole soul be turned around. What he might disagree with is what happens in the process of turning the soul around. On his view, any change in the desiderative, volitional or emotional condition of the soul is itself a change in the condition of reason. [. . .]

Notes

1 Nehamas (1999: 27); the reference is to George Grote (1865: 399–400).
2 See *Protagoras* 352c2–7; also 358b6–c1.
3 John McDowell takes this view in his unpublished piece, "Irwin's Socrates and an alternative reading." The culprit, however, is ultimately Aristotle (cf. *Nicomachean Ethics* 3.1 and 3.4).
4 The "[. . .]" indicates where the original text has been edited to meet the constraints of space.
5 See *Meno* 76b6–78b2. I shall come to this passage below.
6 Terry Penner's 1991 interpretation of the passage is driven by an attempt to avoid the second horn of the dilemma.
7 For a statement of this view see Robin Waterfield's (1994: 142) note on *Gorgias* 468d. Cf. Terence Irwin (1979: 145–6) and Kevin McTighe (1984). The interpretation that seems to me closest to the truth is that of E. R. Dodds (1959).
8 From the point of view of this paper, the most useful discussion of *harmartia* is that of T. C. Stinton (1975 or 1990: 143–85).
9 Older English translations of this passage seem to me greatly preferable to the more recent ones, e.g. Spens (1763), Davies and Vaughan (1852). "*Kai dokein*" (see main text) is misconstrued by Lindsay (1935), Grube (1974) and Grube-Reeve (1992). Until they provide a parallel for their construal of *dokein*, the older translations must take precedence. The Grube-Reeve translation reads: "In the case of just and beautiful things, many people are content with what are believed to be so, even if they aren't really so, and they act, acquire, and *form their own beliefs* on that basis" (emphasis added).

References

Benson, H. (1992). *Essays on the Philosophy of Socrates*. Oxford: Oxford University Press.

Davidson, D. (1980). How is weakness of will possible? In *Essays on Actions and Events*. Oxford: Oxford University Press.

Davies, J. L. and Vaughan, D. J. (1935). *The Republic of Plato, Translated into English with an Analysis and Notes*. London: Macmillan.

Dodds, E. R. (1959). *Plato: Gorgias*. Edited with Commentary. Oxford: Clarendon Press.

Grote, G. (1865). *Plato and the Other Companions of Sokrates*. Vol. I. London: John Murray.

Grube, G. M. A. (1974). *Plato: Republic*. Indianapolis: Hackett Publishing.

—— and Reeve, C. D. C. (1992). *Plato: Republic*. Indianapolis: Hackett.

Irwin, T. (1979). *Plato: Gorgias*. Translation with Notes. Oxford: Clarendon Press.

Lindsay, A. D. (trans.) (1976). *The Republic of Plato*. London: Dent.

McDowell, J. (unpublished ms.). Irwin's Socrates and an alternative reading.

McTighe, K. (1984). Socrates on the desire for the good and the involuntariness of wrongdoing. *Phronesis*, 29, 193–236.

Nehamas, A. (1999). Socratic intellectualism. In Nehamas (ed.), *Virtues of Authenticity* (pp. 24–58). Princeton: Princeton University Press.

Penner, T. (1991). Desire and power in Socrates: the argument of *Gorgias* 466a–468e that orators and tyrants have no power in the city. *Apeiron*, 24(3), 147–202.

Santas, G. (1966). Plato's *Protagoras* and explanations of weakness. *Philosophical Review*, 75, 3–33.

Spens, H. (trans.) (1763). *The Republic of Plato*. Glasgow: R. and A. Foulis.

Stinton, T. C. W. (1975). *Hamartia* in Aristotle and Greek tragedy. *Classical Quarterly*, NS 25, 221–54. Reprinted in Stinton, *Collected Papers on Greek Tragedy*. Oxford: Clarendon Press, 1990.

Waterfield, R. (1994). *Plato's Gorgias*. Translation with Notes. Oxford: Oxford University Press.

Weiss, R. (1992). Killing, confiscating, and banishing at *Gorgias* 466–68. *Ancient Philosophy*, 12, 299–315.

11

Socratic Love

GEORGE RUDEBUSCH

Introduction

As the public saw him, Socrates taught his young followers – who clearly revered him – that the good will of loved ones was worthless if they did not have the expertise to produce a pay-off, and that they ought to replace sentimental attachments to family and loved ones with love for those able to make cold calculations of profit. Such doctrines would seem as heartless and shallow in Socrates' time as in our own. Ancient Greek, like contemporary English, had a variety of words for love, and we can find in Greek literature and philosophy examples and discussion of the ranges of human relations we refer to today as *love*: *needy* love (for example, in romantic or erotic love), *giving* love (as in parental love for children), and the *equality* love that can exist between best friends.

It is no surprise that Athenians ridiculed Socrates for his views. Aristophanes' popular comedy *The Clouds*, for example, satirizes Socrates on several grounds, but the climax – the point of highest comical absurdity – has one of Socrates' students repeatedly strike his father, justifying the beating with an argument that "to strike is to love" (line 1412). The parody is fair: Socrates says he is willing to let loved ones be destroyed, if only it make them "useful," in Plato's *Euthydemus* (285a7). It is no wonder that Socrates' words were made into formal charges against him at trial, including the charge that, Socrates making sons wiser than their fathers, sons may abuse their fathers, for Socrates' heartless arguments seemed to threaten the traditional authority of fathers over sons, an authority based upon procreativity not expertise. Socrates' proposal, in shock value, is analogous, in contemporary western society, to a proposal not merely granting legal standing to gay marriage but concomitantly denying the legal standing of heterosexual marriage!

It is likely that Socrates' words about love were the main reason he was found guilty and sentenced to death on the charge of corrupting the young. The other important charge brought against him at trial was that, like the new scientists of nature, he disparaged belief in the traditional gods. This charge was easy to refute, as both Xenophon and Plato record (Xenophon, *Memorabilia* 1.1; Plato, *Apology* 26b–28a). But neither Plato nor Xenophon deny that Socrates led his followers to these scandalous conclusions about love. Xenophon bluntly admits: "I know that he did say these things about fathers, family, and loved ones" (1.2.53). In Plato's *Apology* Socrates draws attention to the decades-old public perception produced by parodies such as Aristophanes' as being more likely to convict him than the actual courtroom charges (18a–19c), but instead of defending against the accusation based upon his scandalous account of love, he never mentions it.

In the *Lysis* (210b–d) Plato attributes the same account of love to Socrates as Xenophon and Aristophanes do. That account explains the two historically distinctive loves of Socrates' life, a *needy* love and a *giving* love. Socrates' greatest needy love was for the practical wisdom that enables a human being to live well, the only thing, according to Socrates, that was of unconditional importance: "For every man who knows not how to make use of his soul it is better to have his soul at rest and not to live, than to live acting according to his own caprice; but if it is necessary for him to live, it is better after all for such a one to spend his life as a slave rather than a free man."[1] In addition to Socrates' life-changing, needy love for wisdom – that is, *philosophy* – his greatest giving love was a religious benevolence towards other human beings. According to Socrates, God commanded him, as a philosopher, to convert nonphilosophers to the life of philosophy. Such conversions, Socrates believed, are unsurpassed among the goods one human being can give another.[2]

The *Lysis* gives us a picture of a Socrates defending precisely the scandalous doctrines for which the historical Socrates was put to death. There are other Platonic dialogues in which a character called Socrates speaks of love, at greatest length in the *Symposium* and *Phaedrus*. The *Symposium* describes the ultimate object of love as a mystically known, abstract Beauty, while the *Phaedrus* gives an image of the subject that loves as an everlasting, reincarnating chariot. These accounts, although to some extent consistent with the doctrines of the *Lysis*, are not direct defenses of the reported doctrines of the historical Socrates. The account of love Socrates elicits in the *Lysis*, unlike those of the *Symposium* and *Phaedrus*, is corroborated by Xenophon's report and Aristophanes' parody of Socrates. Scholars are probably justified in regarding the *Symposium* and the *Phaedrus* as more Platonic than Socratic.[3]

Leaving aside the transcendent Platonic accounts of love, one might ask why anyone would study the Socratic eccentricity of the *Lysis*. My answer is that Socrates, however unconventional, is likely to be right in his account of love. In this chapter I interpret and defend Socrates' account of love in the *Lysis*. I first show that Socrates explicitly states his doctrine of love in the *Lysis*, which is in terms of nothing but needy desire for beneficent wisdom. Next I show that this doctrine is identical with an implicit conclusion about love that Socrates also argues for in the *Lysis*. I call it an *implicit* conclusion because, although Socrates does not state it, his argument states the premises that entail it. The identity of the explicit doctrine with the implicit conclusion supports my interpretation of the *Lysis*. I provide further support for my interpretation by showing how it harmonizes at numerous points with related Socratic doctrines and arguments in other works by Plato and Xenophon.

Socrates' account has shocked many of our time as well as of his own. These are the scholars who attribute conventional conclusions about love to Socrates, despite the plain statement of the *Lysis*, the corroboration of Xenophon, and the explanation that the shocking account can provide of Socrates' unconventional life.[4] Although Socrates' account is indeed shocking, I defend it by showing the force of Socrates' reasoning and by replying to the main objections against it. The *standard* objection is that Socrates gives us an account only of needy love and ignores giving love, which leaves his account inadequate. This objection, I show, is based upon a misreading of the *Lysis*, which gives us an account of giving love as well as needy love. The *best* objection to the *Lysis* – it is Aristotle's objection – is that it ignores an important type of love, the equality love between best friends. Such love seems irreducible to either needy or giving love. This objection, unlike the traditional objection, is based upon an accurate reading of the text, and in reply I try to show how Socrates might plausibly explain equality love in terms of profound mutual needs.

Socrates' Explicit Doctrine of Love

In the *Lysis* Socrates speaks with Hippothales, a young man in love with the boy Lysis.[5] Socrates claims to have received from God the ability "to identify both the lover and beloved" (204c2). He speaks with apparent knowledge of the actions of those "wise in matters of such love" (206a1), and, when asked how "to win the love of boys" (206c3), modestly admits to having the ability "to demonstrate how to speak" (206c5–6) to win the love of such a boy. In that demonstration, with the boy Lysis, Socrates develops an explicit doctrine of what causes love, namely wisdom.

We should take this demonstration at face value to give us Socrates' account of love for the following reasons. First, as shown above, there are corroborating reports that Socrates was notorious for just such an account of love. Second, there is the evidence within Plato's *Lysis* itself. Socrates confidently gives the demonstration as a self-described expert on love. Lysis certainly takes it seriously: he gives it his closest attention, wants to recollect it as well as he can so that he can share it with Menexenus later, and will ask Socrates about any part of it that he might forget (211a–b). Socrates wants Lysis to take it seriously: he urges Lysis to recollect it as well as he can, to tell the whole of it clearly to Menexenus, and to ask him about any part of he might forget (211a–b). Moreover, within the demonstration, Lysis assents to Socrates only when Socrates' conclusions fit his own experience. Lysis disagrees with Socrates' suggestions when they strike him as contrary to his experience. For example, Lysis vigorously disagrees when Socrates tries to infer that Lysis' parents never stop him from doing what he pleases (207e8–9). Therefore, Lysis' assent within the demonstration is further evidence that he takes Socrates seriously and thus that Socrates seriously intends the demonstration and its conclusion. Hence it is an error to read frivolity or irony into this passage on the grounds that its conclusion is unconventional.

Socrates begins his demonstration with an unobjectionable inference and premise. The inference is that, since Lysis' father and mother "love him very much" (207d6), they therefore wish him "to be as happy as possible" (207d7). (Evidently this inference uses the word "love" in the sense of *giving* love. In the course of the *Lysis* Socrates switches back and forth between giving love and needy love, using the same terms – cognates of the Greek word *philon* – for both as if they were reciprocal and part of a single love relationship. As I show below, Socrates proves precisely this necessary reciprocity in his argument that love is requited.) Next the two agree to the premise that happiness requires that one be "free and able to do whatever one wants" (207e).

Given this sound inference and true premise, the two require an explanation of characteristic parental behavior: Lysis' parents do not let him do whatever he wants but prevent and subordinate his action to the will of others in the case of all his possessions, even in the case of his own body (208a–209a). Lysis' first explanation, that he is not old enough to be free to do what he wants, fails: for he is free in his actions with some possessions after all – in reading, writing, and lyre-playing (209a–b). They find a successful explanation why Lysis' parents give him freedom in some matters but not others: his parents allow him freedom insofar as he "has knowledge" (209c2).

Since Lysis' parents want to make him free and happy, not simply as a mule-carter, weaver, or lyre-player, but as a complete human being, they must make him wise not only at the skills of carting, weaving, or playing, but at the skill of living well as a human being. Socrates' argument supports this inference, and even though he does not explicitly draw it here, he does draw it elsewhere (*Euthyemus* 282a–b). The theme that the characteristic behavior of parents is to provide prudential wisdom to children is familiar in other Socratic dialogues (*Apology* 20a–c, *Laches* 185e–190b) and is explicit in a simile Socrates himself uses later in the *Lysis* as well: poets are like fathers insofar as they are "conductors of wisdom" (214a1–2, Loeb/Perseus trans.). The fact that Lysis lacks that prudential wisdom explains why his parents can at the same time be "eager to secure his happiness" (207e5) yet hinder and subordinate his actions as a human being. The function of parents – that is, what their giving-love consists in – is to give not carting, weaving, or playing skills, but prudential wisdom to their children.

Conventional thought might agree with Socrates' account so far, assuming that parental love explains why a parent gives freedom and control to a child who is wise. Socrates' next examples go beyond conventional thinking. Not just loving parents, but also neighbors, indifferent strangers, and even traditional enemies who are powerful rulers will give freedom and control to the wise. On the day when Lysis' father considers him to have greater expertise than himself, the father "will entrust" (209c5) the son with all that belongs to the father – as will Lysis' neighbor (209c–d). Heads of households are the same today, we must admit, in choosing those with whom they entrust their investment portfolios. Moreover, the Athenians "will entrust" (209d4) Lysis with what is theirs, when they consider him sufficiently intelligent. Today this remains the goal of democratic political systems. And the Great King of Persia, rather than his own firstborn son, heir of all Asia, "would entrust" (209d7–8) Lysis with, say, cooking or healing, if the king thought Lysis had a superior intelligence about these things. He would trust Lysis even to the extent of letting him throw fistfuls of salt into his stew or apply ashes to his own son's eyes, while not allowing his heir to put the least thing into the soup or touch his own eyes (209d–210a). Seasoning large pots of stew with fistfuls of salt is correct culinary technique, though not predictable by one ignorant of cooking (ancient salt was a malodorous, lumpy grit). Likewise wood ash, because of its antiseptic properties, was a common treatment at the time for eye infection, though it would be shocking to a nonexpert unfamiliar with the treatment. A contemporary parallel might be that the king would never permit his own son but would allow Lysis – if he were an expert dentist – to treat the son's toothache by putting a high-speed steel drill in his mouth.[6]

On the basis of these examples, the two agree that wisdom is the cause of love as well as power and freedom according to the following formulation. For clarity in

189

stating their formulation, I have lengthened brachylogies (marked with square brackets) and I use the upper-case letter "M" to refer to any *subject matter* of expertise (such as are given in Socrates' examples: chariot-racing, mule-carting, wool-working, reading, writing, lyre-playing, household management, civic governance, cooking, and healing) and lower-case letter "m" to refer to *any particular object known* by virtue of knowing M (such as particular chariots, mule carts, etc.). These schematic letters correspond in the text to Greek pronouns. Here then is the Socratic *Causal Role* for wisdom:

(CR) If we *are* wise (210b1, 210d1) in subject matter M,
    (i)   everyone will entrust their m's to us [for us to do whatever seems best to us] (210b1),
    (ii)   we shall do as we will with m's; no one will voluntarily impede us (210b2–4),
    (iii)   we shall be free with m's (210b4),
    (iv)   we shall rule over others in acting with m's (210b5),
    (v)   the m's shall be ours (210b5),
          – because (vi) we shall produce good with m's (210b5–6),
    (vii)   all will be lovers (*philoi*) of us with respect to m's (210d1),
    (viii)   all will be dependants belonging (*oikeioi*) to us about m's (210d2),
          – because (ix) we shall be useful and good [to everyone about m's] (210d2–3);
whereas, if we are *not* wise about m's (210b6),
    (~i)   no one shall entrust m's to us for us to do whatever seems best to us (210b6–7),
    (~ii)   [we shall not do as we will with m's]; all will impede us as far as they are able (210b7–c1),
    (~iii)   [we shall not be free with m's],
    (~iv)   we shall be subordinate to others in acting with m's (210c3),
    (~v)   the m's shall not be ours (210c3–4),
          – because (~vi) we shall produce no good from m's (210c4),
    (~vii)   no one will be lovers (*philoi*) of us about m's (210d3),
    (~viii) no one will be a dependant belonging to us about m's (210d4),
          – [because (~ix) we will not be useful and good to anyone about m's].

This formulation contains Socrates' explicit doctrine of the cause of love and friendship: if you are wise, your wisdom causes "all" – all, as I interpret it, who lack wisdom and recognize their lack – to become lovers of you in the sense of being needy dependants belonging to you.

As stated above, the Socratic doctrine CR is an unconventional and antitraditional view of love. On behalf of tradition, there are objections to CR. There is the *rhetoric objection*: CR depends not on my *being* wise, but on my *seeming* wise. Thus persuasive rhetoric may seem a better correlation with freedom, rulership, friendship, and ownership than wisdom. There is the *impotent knowledge objection*: CR depends upon wisdom being always capable of motivating the agent. But wisdom without the proper disposition of the less rational elements within the soul of the agent is impotent and unreliable. And there is the *good will objection*. CR depends upon wisdom being always good.

190

But wisdom in the absence of a good heart or morally good will does not seem good but rather neutral in its power to produce good and bad. The rhetoric, the impotent knowledge, and the good will objections are the three strongest objections to CR, and Socrates does not even mention them in the *Lysis*. But Socrates does consider these three objections elsewhere: the rhetoric objection in the *Gorgias*, the impotent knowledge objection in the *Protagoras* (352b–357b), and the good will objection in the *Meno* (77b–78c).[7]

Socrates' Implicit Conclusion about Love

Immediately following his demonstration with Lysis, Socrates is asked by Lysis for a favor, namely that Socrates make a second conversation with Menexenus, another boy of the same age as Lysis, and evidently Lysis' best friend. Socrates agrees, but says Lysis must join the conversation if Socrates needs help (211b). In this way the first demonstration is followed by a second, which provides an independent examination of love, an examination that ends in a puzzle rather than an explicit doctrine of love. I take it that Socrates, as one who knows how "to identify lover and beloved," is not himself puzzled but sets the puzzle as a test to his audience for pedagogic reasons.[8] Here I shall solve the puzzle and propose my solution as Socrates' implicit conclusion about love. It supports my solution that it makes the second account identical with the first, with their theses established by complementary methods: the first on the basis of illustrative examples, the second on theoretical considerations.

Socrates frames the second conversation with the question: "In what way does one become a friend of another?" (212a5–6) – in other words, what is the cause of friendship? The conversation first rules out that *the loving* – that is, "whenever one loves another" (212a8) – causes one or both parties to become a friend on the grounds that the loving need not be requited and that it is "irrational and impossible" (213b2–3) for a friend "to be friend to a nonfriend or enemy" (213c1–2). Second, the conversation rules out that likeness is the cause (214a–215a), on the grounds that, insofar as one is like another, one can render no benefit to that other. Third, it rules out that good can be friend to good – not insofar as they are like but insofar as they are good – on the grounds that insofar as one is good one has no need and hence no love of another (215a–c). Fourth, it rules out opposition as the cause of love on the grounds, already used, that it is impossible for one to be friend to a nonfriend or enemy (215c–216b).

These four arguments limit love to cases of either needing or conferring benefits – that is, to needy love or giving love – and, accordingly, Socrates will proceed to consider a model that provides both. He begins with the premise that there are three kinds of things: the good, the bad, and the neither good nor bad (the "NGNB," to use Reshotko's 2000 acronym). Socrates frequently makes this tripartite distinction in other dialogues.[9] From this premise and the preceding four results, by process of elimination, Socrates infers that "only the NGNB can be a friend, and only to the good" (216e7–217a2). Unlike the four previously rejected causal models of love, Socrates presents this model as an inference from a process of theoretical elimination. This model will never be refuted and is able to serve as the framework for Socrates as he develops his causal explanation of love in the remainder of the dialogue. In addition to its place in the structure of Socrates' argument, this model is in harmony with Socrates' doctrine in other dialogues that all desire is for the good.[10] The structure of the argument in the *Lysis* and the harmony of both premise and conclusion with other Socratic arguments indicate that this model is indeed Socrates' "favored hypothesis" (to use Santas's 1988: 84 expression).

The first causal explanation Socrates proposes for his model is that it is the *bad* that causes the NGNB to love the good. For example, he says, "a body on account of illness loves medical expertise" (217b3–4), where disease is a bad, medicine a benefit and thus good, and "a body, considered as a body, NGNB" (217b2–3). Socrates goes on to distinguish one sort of case, when illness is merely a "presence" (217b6) to a body so that it becomes needy but retains its status as NGNB, from another sort of case, when illness has so corrupted a body that it cannot profit from medicine and loses its status as NGNB, "having become bad" (217b6–7).

A problem Socrates notices with his model is that it does not distinguish intrinsically from extrinsically beloved objects. He gives three examples of extrinsically loved objects: (i) a sick man loves "a medical doctor for the sake of health" (218e4); (ii) a father loves an antidote, and the vessel that holds it, for the sake of his son who has drunk poison (219d–e); and (iii) silver and gold are loved for the sake of whatever they buy (220a). Socrates does not say, but his models illustrate, that this distinction applies to both needy and giving love. Socrates infers from the existence of any series of extrinsically beloved objects that it must end in an intrinsically beloved object, a "beginning" (219c6) or "first friend" (219d1). He recognizes that in ordinary language we call both extrinsic and intrinsic beloveds alike "loved ones" (220a7). The appearance of language notwithstanding, Socrates concludes that the only "real friend" (220b4) is the intrinsically beloved. (Socrates elicits the harmonizing thesis that we desire only the intrinsically good at *Gorgias* 468b–c.) One might have thought that the intrinsically valuable causes our love of and friendship for extrinsically valuable objects. By denying that extrinsically beloved objects are loved at all, Socrates has forestalled such an account. Socrates does not explicitly revise his model to state that the NGNB loves the *intrinsic* good only, on account of the presence of something bad, but his argument justifies such an interpretation.

There is a problem with the cause Socrates first proposed for his model, namely, that *bad things* cause the NGNB things to love the good. Socrates next explicitly rejects such a causal proposal on the grounds that (i) some desires are NGNB and would exist even if there were no bad things; (ii) what one desires, one loves; and (iii) if bad things were the cause of love, then if there were no bad things, there would be no love (221b–c). Premise (ii) of this argument states Socrates' new proposal for the "cause of love: desire" (221d3), and I therefore attribute to Socrates a revised model of love: the NGNB loves the good because it desires the good.

There remains another, potentially fatal problem facing this revised model of love. Socrates consistently discarded other causal models – namely the first, "loving," and the fourth, "opposition," as shown above – whenever they entailed the impossible result that there is love between friend and nonfriend. According to the revised model, the NGNB is a friend to the good – but will the good be a friend in return? If not, the NGNB would be a friend to a nonfriend, which would be fatal to the revised model.

192

Socrates does not explicitly raise this problem for his revised model, but his statement of the model is tentative (221d2, 221d6). In order to be consistent with his argument's assumptions, Socrates needs to establish that love will be requited according to this model. Hence, on my interpretation, it comes as no surprise that Socrates next establishes this very result. There is also, at the dramatic level, interest in this result. In context the boy Lysis is compelled to admit that he must requite the love of his lovers, including, it would seem, the pedophile Hippothales. But here as always in Plato the dramatic level of interest mirrors a theoretical level of inquiry.

The strategy of Socrates' argument to prove that love is requited is as follows. *Desire* is not a symmetric relation: A can desire B without B desiring A. But the relation of *belonging with* is symmetrical: if A belongs with B, obviously B belongs with A. Accordingly, from the postulate that desire is the cause of friendship, Socrates argues that, whenever there is *desire* and hence love and friendship, the cause of the desire is lack and *deprivation*. As a chess set can be deprived only of items that belong with it (the white queen, say, but not the queen of hearts), and as likewise a human family can be deprived only of family, not nonfamily members, so in general A can be deprived of B only if B belongs together with A (221d–e). Then, from the symmetry of belonging, Socrates draws the needed conclusion: if A loves B, B will love A (222a). In illustrating this argument, the chess set is my own interpretation, but the family membership illustration is implicit in Greek vocabulary: the noun *oikos* "household" or "family" is cognate with the adjective *oikeion* "belonging with" or "akin to." The English noun "family" has a similar slang cognate adjective, as in the expression, "He's family," meaning *He belongs with us* or *Treat him as our kin.*[11]

The love-requited argument removes the otherwise fatal problem with Socrates' model and justifies the following revised statement I make of it: if the NGNB A desires and hence loves the good B, then B will love and care for A. If we apply this model to human beings or human souls, who are as such NGNB, and supply Socrates' account of goodness as prudential wisdom, we get the same formulation as in the first account, stated in the Socratic doctrine CR(vii) and (ix) above: insofar as you are wise (= good), all who are not wise (= the NGNB) will be lovers of you, for you shall be useful and good to all (= you shall requite that needy love with beneficent care or giving love).

One might ask why the good requites the needy love of the NGNB.[12] Both premises of the Socratic answer to this question have already been stated in his first account. Prudential wisdom benefits the wise *by making them happy*, because (i) happiness consists in freely doing whatsoever one wishes (207e) and (ii) insofar as we are prudentially wise we shall do as we wish; no one will voluntarily impede us, we shall be free, rule over others, and possess their lives (= CR [ii]–[v] applied to the subject matter of prudence, namely human life). Corroborating passages in other dialogues where Socrates connects happiness to wise action are too numerous to cite; he precisely specifies that happiness is the correct use of what is NGNB at *Euthydemus* 282a. In the first book of the *Republic* Socrates elicits a functional account of the good man's beneficence to the man who is NGNB. According to that account, the function of the righteous or good human being is not to harm but to benefit others by making them more righteous (335a–d). In the same dialogue he elicits an account that makes the good man analogous to a craft worker, such that any expert, strictly so-called, does not seek his own advantage but the advantage of the object of his expertise (341c–342e).[13] It is no surprise that Socrates' gods, being wise, are beneficent (*Euthyphro* 15a, Xenophon, *Memorabilia* 4.3). There is a similar account in later, Platonic dialogues of needy love. This needy love is likewise transformed, when the need is met, into giving or creative love (*Symposium* 200a–e, 206e, 209b–c, 212a; likewise *Republic* VI, 490b). This connection of wisdom to beneficence explains why the creative god in the *Timaeus*, being good, is free of grudge and benevolent (29e, 41b).

Having developed his account of love, Socrates concludes the dialogue by testing the boys' understanding of the *oikeion* (that which *belongs* or is *akin*). This concluding passage has the logical form of three *disjunction eliminations*. A disjunction is a statement of alternatives: "a or b." In disjunction elimination one alternative is ruled out (*eliminated*) and the remaining possibility is inferred to be true.

The first disjunction is:

Either (a_1) there is or (b_1) there is not a difference between what is *oikeion* and what is alike (222b3–6).

Socrates eliminates alternative b_1 on the grounds that if it is true the *oikeion*, being alike, would be useless, leading as before to a failed model of friendship (222b6–c1).

The second disjunction is:

Either (a_2) the good is *oikeion* to all and bad *oikeion* to nothing or (b_2) good is *oikeion* to good; bad to bad; and what is neither good nor bad to what is neither good nor bad (222c3–7).

Socrates eliminates alternative b_2 by showing that if it is true, again "we have fallen into a previously rejected" model of friendship, making the bad be a friend to bad (222d1–3).

The third disjunction is:

Premise a_2 – that the good is *oikeion* to all and the bad to nothing – either (a_3) does not or (b_3) does entail that none are friendly with the good but the good (222d5–6).

When the boys choose alternative b_3, Socrates eliminates it by recalling that it is a model refuted earlier, impossibly making the good a friend only to the good (222d7–8).

Upon establishing the premises for these three disjunction eliminations, Socrates does not draw the conclusions but merely asks the boys: "What further use might the argument have?" (222e1). The boys cannot answer and the dialogue ends in perplexity. But it is only a tiny interpretive step to notice the consequences entailed by these three disjunction-elimination arguments:

(a_1) There is a difference between what is *oikeion* and what is like.
(a_2) The good is *oikeion* to all.
(a_3) The fact that the good is *oikeion* to all does not entail that none are friendly with the good but the good.

We find confirmation that Socrates accepts consequences a_1, a_2, and a_3 in his first, explicit doctrine of love, formulated above as CR (vii)–(ix), (~vii)–(~ix):

194

If you become wise, everyone will be your [needy] friend (*philon*) and belong (*oikeion*) to you; for you will be useful and good; if you do not become wise, no one – not even your father, mother, or other kin (*oikeioi*) – will be your friend (*philon*); for you will not be useful and good (210d1–4).

Accordingly, all are *oikeion* to the wise, which entails that (a$_2$) the good is *oikeion* to all, and hence that (a$_1$) the *oikeion* is different from likeness (since the good is not like all, in particular not like the NGNB nor the bad). Furthermore, all – that is all who lack wisdom and know their lack – are *philon* to the wise; hence some who are not good are friendly with the good; hence conclusion a$_3$ is also true.

The Main Objections to the Socratic Account

Before drawing my conclusion about Socratic love, I consider two objections. First is the standard contemporary objection to Socrates' account – by those who are not too shocked to take it at face value – that it reduces all friendship and love to needy love, ignores giving love, and thus is crude.[14] This objection fails since it is based upon a misreading of the text. Socrates, as I have shown, provides an account of giving love as well as needy love.[15] But readers ought nonetheless to worry that Socrates' account is incomplete. Although it explains both needy and giving love, it gives no account of *equality love* as a third type of love distinct from the giving and needy love in inequality relationships. I give credit to Aristotle for raising this second objection. Although he does not state it as an objection to the account in the *Lysis*, it is clear that he wrote his account of love and friendship, in which he emphasizes equality love as the only true friendship, with the *Lysis* in mind.[16]

Equality love, as we seem to experience it between "best friends," is a love such that neither friend's love is motivated by the need for goods or by a will to improve the other by bestowing goods: rather than getting or giving, the goal of both is *cooperation* in a shared life that in some sense requires an equality of character between the two friends. For example, in the *Euthydemus* Crito and Socrates engage to become, not students *of* each other, but students *together* (272c–d): their engagement as co-students, including the conversation in which they make the engagement, constitutes a part of their shared life as equality friends.

There are cases where an equality friend may also act as a giving teacher and therapist or as a needy student and client of another. For example, Crito at times takes it upon himself to admonish Socrates for being foolish (*Euthydemus* 304a–b) or unrighteous (*Crito* 45c), attempting to give to Socrates some of his own understanding and character. Such examples show that actual human beings are involved in relationships with each other that are compounds of both equality and inequality love, but they leave equality love distinct as a third type of love. If the character of the beloved becomes depraved, an equality love must end (as Aristotle points out, *Nicomachean Ethics* 9.3.3) although a giving love might begin. For example, the infidelity and betrayal that could end a best friend's equality love might mark the beginning of a therapist's giving love, where the therapist seeks to remedy the defects in the character of the client. Since equality love can exist only towards one of good or at

195

least satisfactory character, it is selective and thus distinct from giving love, which is beneficent to all (CR [vii]–[ix], discussed above). Since equality love does not try to acquire the character of the other, it is selective in a way that distinguishes it from needy love.

Socrates nowhere undertakes to analyze Crito's equality love for him, but before developing his theory of love in the *Lysis* he does emphasize the equality between the boyhood friends Lysis and Menexenus: neither one accepts the other as elder, nobler, more beautiful, or wealthier (207b–c). Although recognizing equality love pretheoretically in this passage, he nonetheless argues, as shown above, that not equality but desire for what is lacking must be the cause of love. Nowhere in the *Lysis* does Socrates state a need-based motivation for equality friendship.[17] However, in the *Protagoras*, Socrates proposes an equality friendship:

> Protagoras, do not suppose that I have any other desire in conversing with you than to examine the puzzles that occur to myself at each point. For I hold that there is a good deal in what Homer says – When two go together, one observes before the other – for somehow it makes all of us human beings more able to find solutions in every deed or word or thought; but whenever one conceives something alone, one has to go about searching until one discovers somebody to whom one can demonstrate it and with whom one can corroborate it. And I also have my reason for being glad to converse with you rather than with anyone else; it is that I regard you as the best at investigating in general any matters that a sensible man may be expected to examine, and virtue in particular.[18]

Socrates' proposal as lover here is needy: he needs to understand virtue. Socrates is proposing that Protagoras become his equal partner in an investigation, on the grounds that two can solve puzzles better than one, one seeing before the other and then validating the insight by demonstrating it to the other. Therefore, while Socrates is selective in choosing Protagoras as his investigative teammate for being "best at investigating," he is not proposing to become Protagoras' student in order to acquire Protagoras' character or knowledge. Thus this need-based partnership conforms to the selectivity criterion for equality friendship stated above.

When the mutual need that grounds the partnership is on the level of back-scratching, money-making, or game-playing, the resulting equality friendship is too superficial to be what human beings call true friendship. The relationship between best friends ought to survive the cessation of mutual itching, poverty, or interest in games. But there are more profound problem-solving partnerships involving moral character and conduct, such as raising a family together, where one may advise and consult on projects and test and respond in conversation. Such a partnership might well be the case, for example, with the relationship between Crito and Socrates as portrayed by Plato. It is not obvious that anything essential to equality friendship has been left out of such moral partnerships, with which one can provide an account of marriage and other true friendships having equality as a component. Yet such partnerships are motivated after all by need, indeed by the most enduring and profound needs that human beings experience, namely, for moral wisdom. Socrates' reduction of friendship to need is therefore defensible in the face of the equality-love objection.

Conclusion

The *Lysis* gives us an explicit doctrine and a complementary implicit conclusion about both needy and giving love. According to this account, all needy love, that is, all desire, is directed to and only to the intrinsically good. For human beings this good is nothing but prudential wisdom. A characteristic activity of this wisdom, an activity constituting the happiness of the wise, is to requite the needy love of others with giving love, a care that rules over and indeed owns the lives of the needy as it perfects them. The philosopher has needy love for wisdom. It is his destiny, as a human being and not a god, never to have this desire satisfied (*Apology* 23a), nor therefore to have divine wisdom and giving love. But there is a giving love appropriate to the philosopher, too, as a religious duty (*Apology* 23b, 37e) and as a consequence of his merely Socratic wisdom. The philosopher is surrounded by nonphilosophers, who are bad human beings, because they have the delusion that they possess prudential wisdom. The philosopher's duty is to convert bad human beings to NGNB, which is a lesser state of ignorance in which one is at least aware of not having prudential wisdom (*Lysis* 218a–b). A distinguishing feature of the Socratic dialogues is their portrayal of a Socrates trying in conversation to change the souls of those around him from bad to NGNB by converting them to philosophy. In the course of the *Lysis* Socrates tries to convert the boys Lysis and Menexenus in this very way. This Socratic activity is precisely his religious duty of beneficence to others and at the same time his "greatest conceivable happiness" (*Apology* 41c3–4). Yet insofar as Socrates accomplishes his Herculean labor of converting the bad to NGNB, his prospects for friendship are not over. For the NGNB continue to have needs, and to meet such needs Socrates will propose, as he did in the *Protagoras*, problem-solving partnerships between friends who seek to investigate together the nature of human excellence.

Acknowledgments

I thank Mark Budolphson, Rachana Kamtekar, Sara Ahbel-Rappe, Hope Rudebusch, and Mike Stallard for their advice on earlier drafts of this chapter.

Notes

1 *Clitophon* 408a–b.
2 *Apology* 29d–30a. See McPherran (1996) on Socrates' religion.
3 On a controversial distinction of dialogues between those where Socrates is a historical figure as opposed to a mouthpiece for Plato, see Penner (1992) and Irwin (1995: 3–16).
3 See for example Fraisse (1974: 129), Bolotin (1979: 89–90), Price (1989: 3), Osborne (1994: 58–9), and Bordt (1998: 132–140). Narcy (1997: 216) is an exception, recognizing Socratism in the account's shocking "reduction . . . of every value to *sophia*."
5 On the Greek cultural practice of pederasty, see Dover (1978) and Bordt (1998: 112–15).
6 See Rudebusch (2002) for further defense of these examples.
7 Rudebusch (1999: 21–3 and 27–30) defends Socrates' replies to the impotent knowledge and rhetoric objections.

8 On the advantages of this pedagogy, see Rudebusch (1999: 9–17).
9 On this tripartite distinction, see *Protagoras* 340c–344c, *Gorgias* 467e–468a, *Euthydemus* 281e, *Symposium* 180e–181a and 202a–b, and especially *Apology* 21c–23b, where Socrates must assume it in order to distinguish the three types of soul.
10 On all desire being for the good, see *Meno* 77b–78b, *Gorgias* 468a–b, 354c–475e, *Protagoras* 356b, *Symposium* 205e, and Xenophon, *Memorabilia* 4.2.10.
11 For discussion of this argument, see Rudebusch (2004).
12 Robinson (1986: 76 n. 23) asks this question.
13 On these passages see Rudebusch (2004).
14 Vlastos (1969) gives a widely-cited statement of this objection. Needy love is "utility love" in his terms.
15 Haden (1983) sees giving love as well as needy love in the imagery used in the *Lysis*.
16 Aristotle gives an account of friendship in *Nicomachean Ethics* 8–9. Price (1989: 9) gives reasons why Aristotle had the *Lysis* in mind as he wrote.
17 Bordt (1998) claims to find equality friendship in the *Lysis*. Rudebusch (2002) criticizes his finding.
18 *Protagoras* 348c–e. I adapted this translation from the Loeb series, online at perseus.tufts.edu.

References

Bolotin, D. (1979). *Plato's Dialogue on Friendship*. Ithaca: Cornell University Press. Commentary on the *Lysis*.

Bordt, M. (1998). *Platon, Lysis: Übersetzung und Kommentar* [Plato, *Lysis*: Translation and Commentary]. Göttingen: Vandenhoeck und Ruprecht. German, the most recent book-length treatment of the *Lysis*.

Dover, K. J. (1978). *Greek Homosexuality*. London: Duckworth. On Greek homosexuality and pederasty.

Fraisse, J.-C. (1974). *Philia: la notion d'amitié dans la philosophie antique* [Philia: the concept of friendship in ancient philosophy]. Paris: Vrin. French, on the *Lysis* and other ancient works.

Haden, J. (1983). Friendship in Plato's *Lysis*. *Review of Metaphysics*, 37, 327–56. On dramatic imagery reflecting needy and giving love in the *Lysis*.

Irwin, T. (1995). *Plato's Ethics*. Oxford: Oxford University Press. On ethical issues in and the distinction between Platonic and Socratic dialogues, including the *Lysis*.

McPherran, M. L. (1996). *The Religion of Socrates*. University Park: Pennsylvania State University Press. On Socrates' account of the virtue of piety, his own divine mission, and his revealed and natural theology.

Narcy, M. (1997). Le Socratisme du *Lysis* [The Socratism of the *Lysis*]. In G. Giannantoni and M. Narcy (eds.), *Lezioni Socratiche* [Socratic Readings] (pp. 207–33). Naples: Bibliopolis. On Socrates' explanation of love in terms of wisdom in the first account of the *Lysis*.

Nygren, Anders (1953). *Agapê and Eros*, trans. P. S. Watson. Philadelphia: Westminster. (Original work published in two volumes in 1930 and 1936.) Seminal historical survey of giving and needy love.

Osborne, C. (1994). *Eros Unveiled: Plato and the God of Love*. Oxford: Clarendon Press. Interpretation of love in Christian and Hellenistic authors as well as Plato.

Penner, T. M. I. (1992). Socrates and the early dialogues. In R. Kraut (ed.), *The Cambridge Companion to Plato* (pp. 121–69). Cambridge: Cambridge University Press. On the distinction between Platonic and Socratic dialogues with synopsis of Socratic ethics.

Price, A. W. (1989). *Love and Friendship in Plato and Aristotle*. Oxford: Clarendon Press. On the *Lysis, Symposium*, and *Phaedrus* and Aristotle's account of the equality and inequality friendships.

Reshotko, N. (2000). The good, the bad, and the neither good nor bad in Plato's *Lysis*. *Southern Journal of Philosophy*, 37, 251–62. On the tripartite distinction as it occurs in the *Lysis*.

Robinson, David B. (1986). Plato's *Lysis*: the structural problem. *Illinois Classical Studies*, 11, 63–83. More attentive to the force of argument within the *Lysis* than all earlier and most later studies.

Rudebusch, G. (1999). *Socrates, Pleasure, and Value*. Oxford: Oxford University Press. Interpretation of the Socratic account of pleasure and virtue as the chief good.

—— (2002). Review of Bordt (1998). *Ancient Philosophy*, 22, 177–80. Summary and evaluation of Bordt's interpretation.

—— (2004). True love is requited: The argument of *Lysis* 221d–222a. *Ancient Philosophy*, 24, 1–14. Detailed defense of the argument.

Santas, G. (1988). *Plato and Freud: Two Theories of Love*. Oxford: Blackwell. Comparison involves *Lysis* as well as other dialogues of Plato.

Soble, A. (1990). *The Structure of Love*. New Haven: Yale University Press. Analysis of love into two categories, the first, "erosic," including both needy and equality love, the second, "agapic," equivalent to giving love.

Vlastos, G. (1969). The individual as object of love in Plato. In G. Vlastos, *Platonic Studies* (pp. 3–34). Princeton: Princeton University Press. Seminal philosophical study of love in the *Lysis* and other dialogues by Plato.

12

Socrates and Religious Experience

JOHN BUSSANICH

For Plato it is hardly an exaggeration to say that philosophy begins with god and ends with god, who is the measure of all things (*Laws* 716). The search for wisdom and goodness is a response to the divine call to liken oneself to god as far as possible. In this chapter I shall explore how Plato expresses his religious experience and faith in the divine through the character of Socrates. Faith in this sense is neither blind nor irrational; rather it is the aspiration to live in terms of the transcendent and the ability to recognize the truth lying behind any expression or belief. The approach taken here represents a departure from the standard philosophical approach to Socrates' religion, according to which his religious beliefs are tested rationally in order to determine their truth-value and his experiences are metaphors of rational thought. Against this view I shall argue that Socrates' philosophical activity is not directed towards the justification of religious beliefs, but rather that his faith and religious experiences provide dialectical starting-points and specify his existential goals. The purpose of dialectic is to purify the mind of false beliefs and guide reflection towards the divine. From this perspective the "light of reason" shines not from the mind of a skeptic but from the eyes of a visionary Socrates. He is the successor to those philosophical mystics Parmenides and Empedocles, whose revelations crowned them as "divine men." Plato's Socrates also has direct access to the divine and generously imparts Orphic-Pythagorean teachings to his interlocutors, but they are not the intimates of esoteric circles. In order to transform minds fed on a deficient rationalist diet and swollen with the intellectual hubris and skepticism of the sophists, Plato's Socrates teaches with a wise ignorance which is the perfect medium for transmitting dreams, visions, and revelations.

The Servant of Apollo

Socrates' religious ideas are most readily accessible in the *Apology*, his speech responding to the charge of impiety. Meletus' indictment reads: "Socrates is guilty of not believing in the gods that the city believes in, and of introducing other new divinities; and he is guilty of corrupting the youth" (Diogenes Laertius, *Lives of Eminent Philosophers* 2.4). We have little reason to doubt that his religious beliefs were the main factor motivating the charges, political enmity notwithstanding, for his defense is aimed

200

directly against the charge of atheism. From the popular point of view Socrates' rejection of the literal reading of myth, his examination of beliefs in general, his moralized and unified conception of divinity, and his unusual religious experiences exhibited similarities to sophistic skepticism and scientific materialism (18bc). For Meletus (26bcd) each of these attitudes was sufficient to justify atheism. From the modern perspective the incoherence of an attack on Socrates for being a skeptic or materialist is remarkable enough, but it is also important to remember that Greeks lent greater weight to orthopraxis than to orthodoxy and both Xenophon (*Apology* 11–12; *Memorabilia* 1.1.1–2) and Plato testify to Socrates' practical piety. Socrates insists "I certainly do have altars; and I have shrines, both domestic and ancestral, and everything else of the kind, just like other Athenians."[1] Apollo, Zeus, and Athena are his "masters" (*Euthydemus* 302cd), but he rejects popular notions that the gods lie, steal, or desire sacrificial offerings in exchange for human petitions for external goods (*Euthyphro* 14c–15a; *Laws* 885b, 888c, 948c).

Socrates' conformity to traditional religious practice is compatible with a moralized theology and an inner-directed spirituality grounded in the philosophical cultivation of virtue. To Socrates' enemies, however, his orthopraxis seemed like a ruse. It is against these suspicions and the slanders they aroused that Socrates directs the story of the Delphic oracle. To quiet the jury's uproar at his admission that he possesses "human wisdom," Socrates responds "not as mine shall I tell the story which I'm going to tell, but I will refer it to a trustworthy source. As for my wisdom – whether I do actually have any and of what kind it may be – I shall call as witness before you the god at Delphi" (*Apology* 20e5–8). When asked by his childhood friend Chaerephon whether "any man was wiser than I . . . the Pythia replied that no one was wiser" (21a6–7).

> When I heard of this reply I asked myself: "Whatever does the god mean? What is his riddle? I am very conscious that I am not wise at all; what then does he mean by saying that I am the wisest? For surely he does not lie; it is not legitimate for him to do so." For a long time I was at a loss as to his meaning. (21b2–7)

Socrates is puzzled, but the immediate respect he shows for the oracle and Apollo its source refutes the atheism charge, at least for modern readers. Yet it is a puzzle why the oracle takes on such significance for him. In the public sphere, Apollo was associated with the foundation of temples and cults, regulating sacrifices and purification rites, and prophesying through seers (*Republic* 427bc; *Laws* 738bcd). Evidence of individual consultations survives in stories in which famous or wealthy people anticipate being identified by the oracle as the wisest or happiest but who are told that some unknown farmer has outstripped them (Reeve 1989: 31). Apollo's moral exhortations to humility and restraint were inscribed in the temple at Delphi: "know thyself," "hate hubris," "nothing in excess," etc. Moderation, awe towards the gods, recognizing the limits of human nature, and rejection of hubris comprise the core of this traditional piety. But Apollo's esoteric affiliations extend beyond popular piety. The popular Delphic theology emphasizes the gulf between gods and men, but for Orphic-Pythagoreans Apollo is also the god of healing, inner transformation, and divinization (*Cratylus* 405ab; Kingsley 1999: 84ff.). With an emphasis on Socrates' disavowal of divine wisdom and his embrace of epistemic modesty, scholarship has made Socrates a more philosophical and moralistic – but still a spokesman – for the traditional theology. But his visionary capacity and exceptional self-mastery, already evident in the "early" dialogues, suggest that a more radical, spiritual perspective stands behind this façade, one that should not be identified with the mystical visionary "Plato" of the "middle" dialogues. Before that gap is crossed it will first be necessary to connect Socratic with traditional divination.

Delphic oracles were communicated through the Pythia (from Python, the mythical snake slain by Apollo), an ordinary woman whose virginal body and unlettered mind were filled by Apollo. She sat at rest on a tripod; she was possessed, but not hysterical (Dodds 1951: 70). Vase paintings display her calmness (Latte 1940: 12). Inspired by Apollo, she entered a trance state and as a seer (*mantis*) delivered prophecies which were shaped and proclaimed by male priests (*prophētai*). But the Pythia herself determined the content through her mantic skill:

> It is customary to appoint interpreters (*prophētai*) as judges of inspired divinations (*manteia*). Some persons call them seers (*mantis*), being entirely ignorant of the fact that they (= *prophētai*) are expositors of utterances or visions expressed in riddles (*ainigma*), and are not to be called seers at all, but most precisely declarers (*prophētai*) of what the seers say. (*Timaeus* 72a6–b5)

Accordingly, Socrates first approaches the god's divination-riddle as an interpreter, but later in the *Apology*, and in other dialogues, Socrates is himself the *mantis*. Why does Plato invest Socrates with both functions? Are they altered when absorbed into the repertoire of the philosopher? On the one hand, Socrates observes that seers and prophets when inspired "say many fine things without any understanding of what they say" (*Apology* 22c1–3), but the Pythia and other seers do a lot of good when they are out of their minds, inspired with divine madness (*Phaedrus* 244ab; on poets: *Ion* 534bcd). Apparently, Socrates *is* in his right mind, but his psychology is hardly typical. At first simulating the virginal and receptive Pythia, Socrates is overcome with perplexity for a long time; only with great difficulty does he begin to inquire what the riddle means. Its claim that no man is wiser conflicts with his awareness of his own ignorance, so Socrates sets out to "refute" the prophecy by finding at least one person wiser than himself (*Apology* 21c1–2), in the process infecting others with his own perplexity.

But it is not a straightforward matter to refute riddling oracles, whose logic of ambiguity oscillates between concealment and unveiling. (Heraclitus fr. 93: "The lord whose oracle is at Delphi neither speaks out nor conceals, but gives a sign.") Neither the oracle's "no man is wiser" nor Socrates' self-reflexivity – "I am aware that I am not wise at all" (21b4–5), "what I didn't know I didn't think I knew" (21d7–8) – makes immediate sense. Initially, puzzling over the sign casts into doubt his awareness that he isn't wise, and then incites an urge for deeper self-knowledge: this desire is the aspiration for self-transcendence which ripples outwards and envelops others (Rappe 1995: 7).

The transforming potency of riddles is sometimes implanted in definitions: Socrates describes as riddles Critias' definition of temperance as "minding your own business" (*Charmides* 162a10, b4, 164de), the account of *philia* as "like is a friend to like" (*Lysis*

214de), and Simonides' account of justice as "giving what is owed" (*Republic* 332b). Riddles speak a divine dialect and provoke the desire to know, as in Aristophanes' profound meditation on Eros: "the soul of every lover longs for something else; his soul cannot say what it is, but like an oracle it has a sense of what it wants, and like an oracle it hides behind a riddle" (*Symposium* 192d1–3).

Does Socrates act impiously by testing the god's message? No. He insists that the god cannot lie: because the oracle comes from the god it must be true (*Republic* 382e). Indeed, like the god Socrates will speak only the truth (*Apology* 17b4–8, 20d5–6, 22b5–6, 24a4–5). He seeks out counterexamples to the oracle by examining those reputed to be wise and ends up confirming the truth he already accepts but doesn't fully understand. Because by its very nature a riddle says one thing and means another, Socratic dialectic is an act of unveiling which operates in the space it opens up between apparent and hidden meanings. Such testing of an oracle should not be read as the sort of straightforward refutation of false beliefs so familiar in elenctic arguments (21e4–5, 22a4). Insofar as his search for the oracle's unapparent truth exposes arrogant pretensions to wisdom, Socrates exemplifies the Apollonian prophetic and purificatory functions. Thus, he describes his therapeutic activity as "coming to the aid of the god" (23b6–7) and "service to the god" (23c1, 30a6–7), which has immensely benefited the city (30a7–b2, 38a1–3): "The people who are being examined . . . get angry at themselves, and become calmer toward others. They lose their inflated and rigid beliefs about themselves" (*Sophist* 230b8–c1; *Theaetetus* 210c1–4). Socratic elenctic therapy is a total assault on the ego, a radical depersonalization, which, combined with spiritual exercises, leads to the discovery of the true self (Rappe 1995: 15).

What further undermines the possibility that Socrates impiously challenges the oracle is the fact that he acts without opposition from his spiritual voice (the *daimonion*), which "has always opposed me in the smallest matters" (*Apology* 40a5–6). It is inconceivable that this infallible guide would remain silent at such a crucial moment, especially since the *daimonion* is itself the sign of Apollo (40b1). Despite these strong indications that Socrates acts piously, how can he believe that the oracle has imposed on him an obligation to philosophize? Now it is likely that Socrates was engaged in some sort of philosophical activity before Chaerephon's visit to Delphi, which most scholars date around or before 430 BCE, but in any case preceding the satirical portraits of Socrates by Aristophanes and Eupolis in the 420s. Socrates' reputation for wisdom must have prompted the latter's visit in the first place. The *Laches* (187d6–188a3) suggests that Socrates began his dialectical activity in early manhood, i.e. in the 440s (Stokes 1992: 53). And his admission "I am not wise at all" (*Apology* 21b3–4) shows the effects of long and rigorous self-examination. Regular interventions of the *daimonion*, the voice of which had accompanied Socrates since childhood (31d1–3), must also have deepened self-awareness. Moreover, he mentions the recurring dream always bidding him to practice the arts, i.e. philosophy (*Phaedo* 60e), as well as persistent divine incursions:

> But you can take it from me, I have been ordered by the god to do this, both in oracles and dreams, and in every other way that a divine manifestation has ever ordered a man to do anything. (*Apology* 33c4–8)

203

The standard view dates these experiences after the Delphic oracle, which is possible, but they would seem more plausibly to be related to Socrates' philosophizing beforehand. The early appearance of the *daimonion* indicates that Apollo had his arrows aimed at Socrates long before the oracle, so it is likely that Socrates' mantic powers, in the guise of "dreams and divinations," had begun to operate from an early age. Lacking clear evidence to the contrary, it makes less sense to assume that Socrates' various spiritual capacities were activated piecemeal after large intervals.

These points open up the possibility that the oracle propelled an already philosophically active Socrates into a more public and aggressive examination of those with a reputation for wisdom (21b–23b). Perhaps his post-oracle philosophizing eventually became formally elenctic – i.e. refuting an interlocutor's false beliefs by exposing their inconsistency with true beliefs – compared to an earlier protreptic phase. What is new is the zeal to exhort all to care for their souls: the god uses "my name as an example, as if he said: 'This man among you, mortals, is wisest who, like Socrates, understands that his wisdom is worthless.' So even now I continue this investigation as the god bade me" (23a8–b4). Though it cannot satisfy every doubt, such an approach is more plausible than the claims that the oracle led to Socrates' discovery that (a) his fellow Athenians were arrogant in their pretensions to knowledge of virtue; or (b) that Socrates had not been aware that he was specially qualified to test people; or (c) that he should practice philosophy at the expense of his own personal concerns (McPherran 1995: 222).

After the exchange with Meletus Socrates asserts that were he to disobey the oracle it would amount to atheism and fearing death, both egregious examples of thinking oneself wise when one is not (*Apology* 29a3–5). Eliminating the fear of death is an astonishing psychological achievement. I doubt that it arose simply from dialectical confirmation of the thesis that "no one is wiser." However mysterious it may seem to us, we must look to Socrates' exceptional intimacy with the divine as the grounds for his confidence, not simply his "intellectualism," as is commonly supposed. In order to diminish the strangeness of his devotion to the god, he draws an analogy between remaining at his post while on military duty for the city and under divine command: "the god ordered me . . . to live the life of a philosopher, to examine myself and others" (28e4–29a1). About his chastisement of Athenians for not caring sufficiently for wisdom, truth, or the best possible state of the soul (29e2–3) he says, "you should know that this is what the god orders me to do" (30a5). The religious connotations of this web of images involving warfare, guard-duty, and serving one's commander are rooted in Orphic-Pythagorean tradition. The *Phaedo* invokes "the language of the mysteries, that we men are in a kind of *prison*" (*phroura* also means "guard-duty," 62b2–4) and that "the gods care for us and that men are one of their possessions (*ktēma*)" (62b7–8; *Laws* 902b8). The *Laws* explicitly likens the gods to commanders of armies and identifies them as allies: "gods and spirits are fighting on our side, the gods and spirits whose chattels (*ktēma*) we are" (906a6–7). At our best we humans are servants and slaves of demanding but benevolent masters, like puppets (644d) and toys (803c) of the gods. The Athenian excuses his remark that being like puppets humans are "hardly real at all," explaining that "I was looking away toward the god and speaking under the influence of that experience (*pathos*)" (804b7–8, tr. Pangle). The accent falls on a kind of mantic or religious experience (*pathos*) as the source of this insight. It hardly matters, I think, that Socrates is absent from the *Laws*, perhaps Plato's last dialogue, since these points about spiritual psychology apply also to the Socratic piety found in the so-called "early" and "middle" dialogues. The insignificance of human affairs, the duty to serve benevolent gods, and the relentless pursuit of wisdom are espoused in the *Apology* and *Phaedo* by someone intimate with the divine (*Phaedo* 63b7; *Laws* 902c2):

> That I am the kind of person to be a gift of the god to the city you might realize from the fact that it does not seem like human nature for me to have neglected all my own affairs and to have tolerated this neglect now for so many years while I was always concerned with you, approaching each one of you like a father or an elder brother to persuade you to care for virtue. (*Apology* 31a9–b5)

Precisely by ignoring his own interests and displaying the friendship of a close relative Socrates channels divine benevolence into human care for the good.

Socrates' account of his service to Apollo in the *Apology* is consistent with the *Euthyphro*'s constructive accounts of piety as service to the gods who use us as their servants to achieve excellent aims (*Euthyphro* 13e10–11; McPherran 1995: 54; Brickhouse and Smith 1994: 65–7). In the elenctic dialogues Socrates' service comprises protreptic exhortations to virtue combined with doxastic and emotional purification. His intermediate position between men and gods is charted more fully in dialogues with a metaphysical perspective. He is like Eros the *daimon* (*Symposium* 202de), or the young gods who assist the Demiurge in creating living things (*Timaeus* 41a–d). Paradoxically, however, Socrates reproduces in himself divine friendliness and dominance in extending benevolent care through giving orders (*Symposium* 216e7–a2) and arguing coercively (Blondell 2002: 121, 194). He promotes the god's moralizing agenda by going to war with the city and its values. Apollo's direct channel to Socrates, the *daimonion*, keeps him out of politics, the life-blood of the city (*Apology* 31d).

> I was attached to this city by the god – though it seems a ridiculous thing to say – as upon a great and noble horse which was somewhat sluggish because of its size and needing to be woken up by a kind of gadfly. It is to fulfill some such function that I believe the god has placed me in the city. I never cease to rouse each and every one of you, to persuade and reproach you all day long and everywhere I find myself in your company. (30e2–31a1)

This radical intervention is a call to self-transcendence, an awakening to the true self, not simply a warning about the evils of hubris. In Plato's portrait of Socrates the pious servant becomes the moral hero whose "wanderings" (like those of Odysseus) and "labors" (like those of Heracles) are undertaken to find the god "irrefutable" (22a6–7). In likening Socratic dialectic to the labors of Heracles (*Euthydemus* 297b–98e, *Phaedo* 89c, *Cratylus* 398d), Plato invokes the divine heritage of the hero and his ultimate divinization (Sophocles, *Philoctetes* 1419–20) and, esoterically, the Pythagorean appropriation of Heracles as spiritual hero (Detienne 1996: 126; Kingsley 1995: 257–60). These intimations of immortality in the *Apology* emerge from the shadows when the theme of initiation into the Bacchic mysteries appears at *Meno* 81bcd, and in the opening section of the *Phaedo* where Socrates appears as another Theseus, the conqueror of the Minotaur and savior of the Athenians (*Phaedo* 58abc). As Theseus was saved by Apollo, so does Socrates become prophetic like the swans, his fellow servants of Apollo (85b). As an initiate into the mysteries, he is confident that he will commune with good gods in a blissful realm after death (63b, 69c, 81a, 108c, 111b, 114bc), which he faces with serene confidence in both the *Phaedo* and *Apology* (41cd). In the *Phaedo* this confidence is inspired by the prophetic power coming from Apollo (84e–85b) and the Orphic tale of the afterlife (107d ff.). In the *Apology* the silence of the *daimonion*, the sign of Apollo, convinces him that his death is a good thing (40bc), especially if the second alternative, keeping company with just gods and questioning traditional heroes, turns out to be true (40e–41c).

The *Daimonion*

Gregory Vlastos characterized Socrates' *daimonion* as "the gravest of the difficulties we all have to face in our effort to make sense of Socrates." In the *Euthyphro* Meletus' charge of "making new gods" refers to Socrates' recurring divine sign (3ab), whose scope is broad and appearances frequent. In the *Euthydemus* the voice tells Socrates not to leave the Lyceum, just before two sophists appear and debate begins (272e–273a; cf. *Theages* 129b; *Theaetetus* 150e1 ff.). The *daimonion*'s interventions might appear to be random, but normally they indicate that the god has work for Socrates. The providential reading is justified by the famous accounts in the *Apology*:

A. I have a divine or spiritual sign which Meletus has ridiculed in his deposition. This began when I was a child. It is a voice, and whenever it speaks it turns me away from something I am about to do, but it never encourages me to do anything. This is what has prevented me from taking part in public affairs, and I think it was quite right to prevent me. (31d2–6; *Theages* 128d)

B. A surprising thing has happened to me, jurymen . . . At all previous times my familiar prophetic power, my spiritual manifestation, frequently opposed me, even in small matters, when I was about to do something wrong, but now that, as you can see for yourselves, I was faced with what one might think, and what is generally thought to be, the worst of evils, the sign of the god has not opposed me, either when I left home at dawn, or when I came into court, or at any time that I was about to say something during my speech. Yet in other talks it often held me back in the middle of my speaking, but now it has opposed no word or deed of mine. What do I think is the reason for this? I will tell you. What has happened to me may well be a good thing, and those of us who believe death to be an evil are certainly mistaken. I have convincing proof of this, for it is impossible that my familiar sign did not oppose me if I was not about to do what was right. (40a2–c2)

Socrates' "familiar prophetic power" (*mantikē*), the "sign of the god" perceptible only to him, marks his intimacy with the divine, which aroused the envy and hatred of his accusers (Xenophon, *Apology* 14). When he encountered the Pythia's oracle, Socrates was the interpreter; the *daimonion* makes Socrates himself a seer. But unlike diviners and poets (*Ion* 534d), Socrates does not seem possessed or "out of his mind"; and the *daimonion* may speak anytime during Socrates' everyday waking life, not only in extraordinary circumstances or withdrawn in meditation. Although he does not test the authenticity of each daimonic event, Socrates can inductively confirm the benefit of the *daimonion*'s interventions. The good results which it helps bring about, and the bad ones it prevents, are not necessarily moral, e.g. in the *Euthydemus* episode. However, the final sentence of Text B might warrant a moral reading, in which case the *daimonion*'s keeping Socrates out of politics prevents him from committing moral evils. Nevertheless, it might only imply that the god kept him alive to continue his elenctic service, as occurred when he disobeyed illegal actions ordered by both oligarchic and democratic regimes (32a–e). If the *daimonion* represents a necessary condition for Socrates to act justly, then he would be just as dependent on the *daimonion* as the poets are on "divine manifestation" (*theia moira*) to compose sublime poetry (*Ion* 542a). But Socrates' references to "divine manifestation" (*theia moira*) in his life and in others' (*Apology* 33c, *Phaedo* 58e; *Meno* 99e–100a; *Republic* 492e) must include a commitment to divine goodness. This is why he is totally certain when he asserts that he wrongs no one (*Apology* 37a4, b3) and that he makes Athenians happy (36e1).

Why does Socrates place such trust in the *daimonion* and in other divine commands? Because, it has been argued, his belief in the goodness of the gods – which is supposedly subject to constant revision (Reeve 1989: 70) – has been justified by elenctic testing. This puts the cart before the horse. Socrates does not argue for the goodness of the gods; and when he asks for evidence of any harm which might have been caused by his questioning, he aims to justify the validity of the *daimonion*'s activities to the jury, *not* to himself (*Apology* 32a–e, 33de). Moreover, the "convincing proof" that death is not an evil (40c1) is based on daimonic silence, but it is not subject to elenctic confirmation. The point is driven home with this strong assertion: "What has happened to me now has not happened of itself, but it is clear to me that it was better for me to die and to escape from trouble. That is why my divine sign did not oppose me at any point" (41d3–6; Brickhouse and Smith 1989: 238–57). In none of these cases, nor in his response to the oracle, does Socrates aim to justify rationally communications from the gods (contra McPherran 1995: 188–9). Rather, he seeks to understand the experiences which in themselves are self-authenticating and to explain them to others who might be persuaded by his account.

Additional clarity on the workings of the *daimonion* emerges in the episode when Socrates impiously ascribed evils to the divinity Love:

> Just as I was about to cross the river, the familiar divine sign came to me which, whenever it occurs, holds me back from something I am about to do. I thought I heard a voice coming from this very spot, forbidding me to leave until I made atonement for some offense against the gods. In effect, you see, I am a seer, and though I am not particularly good at it, still . . . I am good enough for my own purposes. I recognize my offense clearly now. In fact, the soul too, my friend, is itself a sort of seer (*mantikon*); that's why almost from the beginning of my speech, I was disturbed by a very uneasy feeling. (*Phaedrus* 242b8–c8)

In his first speech Socrates has done something wrong by stating falsehoods about a god, who must be good, for which "offense" he must purify himself (242e–243a). Note how easily Socrates distills positive content from the *daimonion*'s bare opposition. He draws out the purificatory implications of Apollo's apotreptic intervention when an uneasy feeling rises from the mantic spirit within him to meet the voice of the god.

Socrates' "normal" awareness is overcome by the suprarational divinity and a nonrational feeling. There is no indication that Socrates judges his experiences of the divine inadequate because they contain no rational explanations, or simply because they depend on transcendent beings, or are nonteachable or nontransferable to others (McPherran 1995: 199).

The *daimonion* is better understood in the context of Diotima's teaching in the *Symposium*, where the seer reveals to Socrates that *daimones* are messengers who convey prayers and sacrifices from men to gods, and commands and gifts from gods to men.

> Through them all divination passes, through the art of priests in sacrifice and ritual, in enchantment, prophecy, and magic. Gods do not mix with men; they mingle and converse with us through spirits instead, whether we are awake or asleep. He who is wise in any of these ways is a man of the spirit (*daimonios*). (202e4–203a4)

Daimonic wisdom enables one to be a self-aware channel of divine power. The daimonic man is in fact the philosopher to whom Eros is likened (204b): Eros, the offspring of Poverty and Plenty, is a "magician, sorcerer and sophist, philosophizing all through his life" (203d6–7), who gives birth to beautiful things in conversation (210d, 212a). The philosopher's erotic skill is an expression of his daimonic, magical nature. The one subject Socrates knows (*erōtika*) he learned from Diotima (177e1, 210d5; *Lysis* 204c and *Phaedrus* 257a; *Theages* 128b; Xenophon, *Memorabilia* 4.1.2). Given the mantic source of this knowledge, it is natural for the *daimonion* to oversee Socrates' erotic involvements. An intense and clever hunter (*Symposium* 203d5), "the lover of inquiry must follow his beloved wherever it may lead him" (*Euthyphro* 14c4–5). Socrates' unique philosophical eroticism shapes the famous midwife metaphor presented in the *Theaetetus*, where the *daimonion* guides him in selecting pupils:

> God compels me to attend the travail of others, but has forbidden me to procreate. So I am not in any sense a wise man . . . But with those who associate with me it is different. . . . all whom God permits are seen to make progress – a progress which is amazing both to other people and to themselves. And yet it is clear that this is not due to anything they have learned from me; it is that they discover within themselves a multitude of beautiful things. (150c–7–d8)

Socrates assists at the birth of beliefs by means of incantations and judges their authenticity (*Theaetetus* 157c9; *Charmides* 156d ff., 175e, 176b; *Meno* 80a). Sometimes a pupil leaves Socrates before he should, mixes with bad company, then wishes to return: "in some cases, the divine sign that visits me forbids me to associate with them; in others, it permits me and they then begin again to make progress" (*Theaetetus* 151a3–5).

Besides the receptivity of the interlocutor, progress in dialectical inquiry therefore depends on divine guidance, Socrates' physical presence, and even on his *eros* for a pupil, as happens with Alcibiades, whom Socrates was the first to fall in love with (*Alcibiades* I 103a). Initially, not "human causes" but the *daimonion* (103a5–6) and the god (105d3–6) opposed his speaking with Alcibiades, but later the god (*theos*) told him to (105e6–106a2). "Answer my questions, Alcibiades. If you do that, then, god willing, if we are to trust in my divination (*manteia*), you and I will be in a better state" (127e4–6). The *Theages* seems to identify the *daimonion* with the god; it endows both entities with an active role in guiding Socrates' interactions (*Theages* 129e–130a); and it attributes power (*dunamis*) to the *daimonion* (*Theages* 129e1; *Alcibiades* I 105e5). It also adds a unique feature: Aristides insists that he makes greater progress the closer he comes to Socrates – in the same house, in the same room, looking at Socrates, sitting next to and, most of all, touching him (130de). The *daimonion*'s activities in the *Theages* and *Alcibiades* I have convinced many scholars that these magical, primitive, and popular elements are decisive signs of inauthenticity (cf. Joyal 2000: 82–99, 121–30). Addressing this controversy is beyond the scope of this essay, but it seems to me that some scholars arbitrarily impose consistency and constraints on the variety of divine interventions countenanced by Plato. The crucial point is that he clearly makes Socrates susceptible to both apotreptic and protreptic divine interventions.

Other Varieties of Religious Experience

Aristides' attempt to acquire wisdom by touching Socrates is ridiculed as miraculous and superstitious. Besides a few unanalogous passages from Homer and the tragedians, the only "popular" examples of spiritual touching cited by skeptics come from the Gospels (Tarrant 1958; cf. Mark 5:27–30 [uncited]), where a woman touches Jesus in order to draw on his healing power (*dunamis*). Alcibiades is also struck by Socrates' "amazing power" (*dunamis*, *Symposium* 216c7), laments his own fall from goodness when Socrates is absent (216b), and recounts how he tried to seduce him (217a–219d), throwing "his arms around this truly superhuman (*daimonios*) and amazing man" (219c1 tr. Rowe).

The episode at the beginning of the *Symposium* shows us a Socrates prone to supernatural experiences. Aristodemus reports that Socrates fell behind on the way to the party and stood in a porch. Agathon impatiently wanted him brought in, but Aristodemus advised against it: "It's one of his habits, you know; every now and then he just goes off like that and stands motionless, wherever he happens to be. I'm sure he'll come in very soon, so don't disturb him; let him be" (175b2–5). When he arrived Agathon says: "Socrates, come lie down next to me. Who knows, if I touch you, I may catch a bit of the wisdom that came to you under my neighbor's porch. It's clear you've seen the light. If you hadn't, you'd still be standing there." Socrates playfully rebuffs him: "How wonderful it would be, dear Agathon, if the foolish were filled with wisdom simply by touching the wise. If only wisdom were like water, which always flows from a full cup into an empty one when we connect them with a piece of yarn" (175d1–9). But this banter is not completely in jest, for the concrete anticipates the transcendent: Plato uses the same verb (*haptesthai*) for Agathon's touching Socrates and for the mind grasping the truth in Diotima's revelation (212a5), as well as for its grasping being through *erōs* (*Republic* 490b3–4). Of course, Socrates doesn't actually believe Agathon can acquire wisdom in this "magical" manner, but this little episode is significant nonetheless. (1) Agathon believes (and so do Aristides and Alcibiades) that Socrates possesses daimonic power (*dunamis*, *Symposium* 218e2) and that physical contact would enhance his wisdom. (2) His state of absorption on the porch is the source of Socrates' irresistible charisma and his wisdom, which Agathon wants a piece of. (3) "Touching" or "grasping" characterize both the immediate, nonlinguistic, and suprarational mingling of soul and truth and the spiritually erotic connectivity between master and pupil.

In his encomium of Socrates Alcibiades recounts that at Potidaea (432 BCE) Socrates astonished his fellow soldiers by standing in the same spot "lost in thought" from sunrise to sunrise. On the second morning "he said his prayers to the sun and went away" (220d4–5; on Pythagorean identifications of sun/Helios = Apollo, Burkert 1972: 149–50). Most scholars see these episodes as involving nothing more than intense thinking, a view which strains credulity and which is belied by the physical circumstances. The fact that Socrates stood motionless in the snow for 24 hours, without suffering any harm, is a clear signal that Socrates' mind and his *body* were in an altered state. In light of his spiritual experiences – his dreams and daimonic interventions – it is more reasonable to think that Socrates had entered a meditative trance of complete detachment from normal sensory awareness and indeed the normal self (for shamanic analogies, Dodds 1951: 140ff.; on Dionysian ecstasy, Morgan 1990: 93ff.). Recall the calmness of the Pythia and the rational ecstasy associated with Apollo (Kingsley 1999: 79ff.).

Socrates also struck Alcibiades as extraordinary even when he was not rapt in mystic trances. During the retreat from Delium (424) Socrates seemed to Alcibiades "remarkably more composed than Laches. But when I looked again I couldn't get your words, Aristophanes, out of my mind: in the midst of battle he was making his way exactly as he does around town 'swaggering and casting his eyes this way and that' [*Clouds* 362], observing his friends and his enemies in the same calm way" (*Symposium* 221a7– b4). This calmness seems to have been distinctive of Socrates: Alcibiades is amazed by his detachment from sexual advances (219bc) and from both lack and surfeit of food or drink (219e–220a). To explain this behavior as a result of "rational control" is an oversimplification. Plato fills Alcibiades' narrative with the words "amazing," "strange," and "supernatural" – leaving readers in no doubt about Socrates' rare spiritual attainments. Socrates' self-mastery seems to transcend restraint and control (*Laws* 710a, 875cd; *Phaedo* 69a). It is like that attributed to the virtuous man at peace with himself (*Republic* 443d), "a virtue of self without self, the virtue of the empty and mindless peace that belongs to the fully mindful and enlightened sage" (Kosman 1983: 216).

Paradoxically, the picture of a calm and detached Socrates is combined with the Marsyas whose words cast a spell and intoxicate Alcibiades (215b–e), leading him to describe Socrates as a Corybant and surrogate for the god Dionysus. Later he invokes the madness and Bacchic frenzy of philosophy (218b4), akin to the highest kind of madness in the *Phaedrus*, whereby initiation and possession are identified with the mind's contact with pure being (*Phaedrus* 249cde, 250bc). The point cannot be developed here, but I believe that the divine inspiration and suprarational noetic intuition celebrated in the *Phaedrus* (and other ascent passages) are Plato's attempts to represent imaginatively Socrates' trances. However, to call them "experiences" is misleading, in the sense that Plato envisions realms beyond an individual's subjectivity, an impersonal state of consciousness identified with pure being and truth.

Complementary to the possessed Socrates of the *Symposium* and *Phaedrus'* perfectly initiated lover is the philosopher of the *Theaetetus* digression who "should make all haste to escape from earth to heaven; and escape means becoming as like God as possible; and a man becomes like God when he becomes just and pure, with understanding (*phronēsis*)" (176a9–b2; Laws 792d).

> Only his body lives and sleeps in the city. His mind, having come to the conclusion that all these things are of little or no account, spurns them and pursues its winged way, as Pindar says [fr. 292], throughout the universe, "in the deeps below the earth" and "in the heights above the heaven"; geometrizing upon earth, measuring its surfaces, astronomizing in the heavens, tracking down by every path the entire nature of each whole among the things that are, and never condescending to what lies near at hand. (173e2–174a2; *Phaedrus* 249d1)

This is a quasi-shamanistic picture of the philosopher, as the Pindar quotation indicates (cf. Empedocles fr. 134.4 on "holy mind traversing the entire universe with swift thoughts"). This human aspiration to divine status cannot be achieved by discursive reasoning and rational control of the passions alone; the practice of spiritual exercises, which purify and calm the mind, are necessary to make it receptive to divine revelations. Plato appropriates the language and stages of the popular Eleusinian mysteries in order to characterize the transcendent visions in the *Symposium* (210a–212a) and *Phaedrus* (250bc). Yet far more internally significant are the meditative practices of Orphic-Pythagorean esotericism. In the *Phaedo* Socrates explains that the virtues purify and wisdom itself is purification (69c1–2). Inner purification is far more difficult, and rare, than ritual purification, for "many carry the thyrsus but the Bacchants are few" (69c8–d1). Plato embellishes the Orphic-Pythagorean path with his own metaphysical vision. The philosopher touches reality "using pure thought alone" (66a1); through purification "we shall know all that is pure, which is presumably the truth, for it is not permitted to the impure to touch the pure" (67a8–b2). Pure knowledge follows "a path to guide us out of our confusion" (66b2–3): the practice of meditative withdrawal from the body and external things and concentration on the inner reality of the soul (64e5–6, 65c7–9, 66a, 81bc). The primary goal of these spiritual exercises is not to establish the truth of soul–body dualism or to promote extreme asceticism as an end in itself, but rather to effect a radical transformation of consciousness. Purification means "to separate the soul as far as possible from the body and accustom it to gather itself and collect itself out of every part of the body" (67c6–8; *Republic* 611bc).

> When the soul investigates by itself it passes into the realm of what is pure, ever existing, immortal and unchanging, and being akin to this, it always stays with it whenever it is by itself and can do so; it ceases to stray and remains in the same state while it *touches* things of the same kind, and its experience (*pathēma*) then is what is called wisdom (*phronēsis*). (*Phaedo* 79d1–7)

We encounter here the same concrete (touching) and affective (experience) language to characterize the nondiscursive grasp of the truth discussed earlier.

Calmness again appears as a distinctive effect of this inner concentration on the soul as the true self (see Gocer 1999). The peacefulness of the *Crito*'s (44ab) opening scene emanates from Socrates' unconscious: he experiences a prophetic dream of a white lady who assures his arrival in fair Phthia (Achilles' home, literally "the place of

211

dying"). The unnamed lady may be Persephone, the goddess of the underworld (McPherran 2003: 82–3), who played a pivotal role in south Italian Pythagorean traditions. The Pythagorean practice of silence, incubatory dreaming, and communion with divinities have shaped this presentation of Socrates (Burkert 1972: 112–13, 154–61; Kingsley 1999: 173–83). After drinking the hemlock Socrates remarks: "I am told one should die in good-omened silence. So keep quiet and control yourselves" (*Phaedo* 117e2). This is the consummation of the meditative silencing of the mind which is a necessary precondition for "contemplating the true, the divine" (*Phaedo* 84a7–8). Plato provides one glimpse of this procedure:

> I suppose that someone who is healthy and moderate with himself goes to sleep only after having roused his rational part and feasted it on fine arguments and speculations, and having attained to clear self-consciousness; second, he neither starves nor feasts his appetites, so that they will slumber and not disturb his best part with either their pleasure or their pain, but they'll leave it alone, pure and by itself, to get on with its investigations, to yearn after and perceive something in the past or present or future that it doesn't know. He's also calmed down his passionate part and doesn't go to bed in an emotionally disturbed state because he's been angry with someone. And when he has quieted these two parts and aroused the third, in which reason (*logistikon*) resides, and so takes his rest, you know that it is then that he best grasps the truth and that the visions that appear in his dreams are least lawless. (*Republic* 571d6–572b1)

The detachment of the soul or intellect from the body during sleep was widely known in archaic and classical times (Dodds 1951: 143ff.); and the reference to "past, present or future" is traditional in Orphic-Pythagorean shamanism (Detienne 1996: 207 n. 94; Bolton 1962: 156–67). Plato closely links his psychological theory and self-awareness to otherworldly visions of the truth. The visionary capacity attributed here to "reason" is a reminder of the transcendent source of Platonic reason. It is, in reality, the power transmitted to the soul-puppet via the golden and sacred chord controlled by divinity (*Laws* 644e–645a).

As the symbolic vehicle of these diverse functions, the figure of Socrates represents Plato's refashioning of the Orphic-Pythagorean "divine man" (*theios* or *daimonios anēr*), the inquirer who serves Apollo in the agora by chiding his fellow citizens "for not caring for nor giving thought to wisdom or truth, or the best possible state of your soul" (*Apology* 29d9–e3, cf. also 30a7–9, 36c5–7, 39d8). In *Alcibiades* I this care for the self aims at knowledge of one's soul, the ideal self (129a–130c). The highest stage of self-knowledge is the realization of oneself as a purified mind in communion with being (*Republic* 611b–612a): "Now we ought to think of the most sovereign part of our soul as god's gift to us, given to be our guiding spirit (*daimon*)" (*Timaeus* 90a2–4). Socratic perfectionism begins with the Delphic demand to know one's limits but culminates in a suprarational awareness of the self as godlike.

Notes

1   All quotations from Plato's writings are taken from Plato, *Complete Works* (1997), with occasional alterations to sharpen the sense.

References

Blondell, R. (2002). *The Play of Character in Plato's Dialogues*. Cambridge: Cambridge University Press.

Bolton, J. D. P. (1962). *Aristeas of Proconnesus*. Oxford: Oxford University Press.

Brickhouse, T. C. and Smith, N. D. (1989). *Socrates on Trial*. Princeton: Princeton University Press.

—— (1994). *Plato's Socrates*. Oxford and New York: Oxford University Press.

Burkert, W. (1972). *Lore and Science in Ancient Pythagoreanism*. Cambridge, MA: Harvard University Press.

Detienne, M. (1996). *The Masters of Truth in Archaic Greece*. New York: Zone Books.

Dodds, E. R. (1951). *The Greeks and the Irrational*. Berkeley: University of California Press.

Joyal, M. (2000). *The Platonic Theages: An Introduction, Commentary and Critical Edition*. Stuttgart: Franz Steiner Verlag.

Gocer, A. (1999). *Hesuchia*, a metaphysical principle in Plato's moral psychology. In M. McPherran (ed.), *Recognition, Remembrance and Reality: New Essays on Plato's Metaphysics and Epistemology* (pp. 17–36). Kelowna: Academic Printing & Publishing.

Kingsley, P. (1995). *Ancient Philosophy, Mystery and Magic*. Oxford: Oxford University Press.

—— (1999). *In the Dark Places of Wisdom*. Inverness: Golden Sufi Center.

Kosman, L. A. (1983). Charmides' first definition: sophrosyne as quietness. In J. Anton and G. Kustas (eds.), *Essays on Ancient Greek Philosophy II* (pp. 203–16). Albany: SUNY Press.

Latte, K. (1940). The coming of the Pythia. *Harvard Theological Review*, 33, 9–18.

McPherran, M. (1996). *The Religion of Socrates*. University Park, PA: Penn State University Press.

—— (2003). Socrates, Crito, and their debt to Asclepius. *Ancient Philosophy*, 33, 71–92.

Morgan, M. (1990). *Platonic Piety*. New Haven and London: Yale University Press.

Plato (1997). *Complete Works*. Edited with an introduction by John M. Cooper. Indianapolis: Hackett Publishing.

Rappe, Sara. (1995). Socrates and self-knowledge. *Apeiron*, 28, 1–24.

Reeve, C. D. C. (1989). *Socrates in the Apology*. Indianapolis: Hackett Publishing.

Stokes, M. (1992). Socrates' mission. In B. Gower and M. Stokes (eds.), *Socratic Questions* (pp. 26–81). London: Routledge.

Tarrant, D. (1958). The touch of Socrates. *Classical Quarterly*, 8, 95–8.

Further Reading

McPherran, M. (1996). *The Religion of Socrates*. University Park, PA: Penn State University Press. (The most comprehensive study of the religion of Socrates in the early dialogues.)

Morgan, M. (1990). *Platonic Piety*. New Haven: Yale University Press. (The best study of Plato's religious thought and experience.)

13

The Politics of Plato's Socrates

RACHANA KAMTEKAR

Examining in this way what would be the virtue of a good leader, he [Socrates] stripped away all the other qualities but left this remaining: to make whomever one leads happy.

–Xenophon, *Memorabilia* 3.2.4

Introduction

Modern readers of Plato find it easier to admire Socrates as an exemplary citizen in relation to his *polis* than as a political philosopher. As a citizen, Socrates refused to obey the orders of a violent and unscrupulous regime to arrest a fellow citizen for execution (*Apology* 32ce); he was the sole member of the Council to oppose the illegal mass trial of the generals who had failed to rescue the survivors of the Battle of Arginusae (*Apology* 32bc); he openly criticized his city's government, and was willing to die for his principles – do no injustice (*Apology* 32ce; *Crito* 49ab); obey the god's command to philosophize even if the cost of doing so is death at the hands of your city (*Apology* 29d, 38a); abide by the decision your city makes concerning you even if it is unfavorable to you (*Crito* 50a–53a).[1] On the other hand, the reasoning Socrates provides for abiding by the city's decision – that not doing so would constitute an attempt to destroy the law; that since the laws are like a citizen's parents, it is not permissible to retaliate against them; that by remaining in the city and not expressing dissatisfaction with its laws the citizen agrees to obey those laws – fails to recognize reasonable limits on what a city may require of its citizens. And the leitmotif of Socrates' political thought – the criticism of democracy as rule by the ignorant (*Crito* 44d; *Protagoras* 319bd; *Gorgias* 454e–55a, 459a–61c) in the pursuit of desire-gratification (*Gorgias* 502e–503d, 521e–22a) resulting in the corruption of the citizens (*Gorgias* 515d–17c) – seems to be based on an implausibly low estimate of most people's capacity for political judgment and an implausibly high estimate of the specialized knowledge required for politics. Finally, there is no avoiding Karl Popper's criticism that Plato mistook the fundamental question of politics to be "who shall rule the state?" and ignored the far more important question of how to design institutions so as to check the abuses of political power,[2] a matter which greatly occupied Athenian democratic practice and thought.

214

In these circumstances, it is tempting to distinguish the exemplary individual Socrates from the theorist Plato. Popper himself excuses the historical Socrates (who survives in Plato's *Apology* and *Crito*) for neglecting the issue of checks on political power on the grounds that because of his "emphasis upon the human side of the political problem, he could not take much interest in institutional reform."[3] According to Popper, Socrates was engaged with the Athenian democracy critically but constructively, attempting to reform its (usually oligarchic-leaning) political elites by forcing them to think critically. By contrast, Popper argues, Plato betrayed the legacy of Socrates by having him speak on behalf of an antidemocratic constitution in the *Republic* (1962: 189–97).[4] More recently, Terry Penner has argued that Socrates' intellectualist moral psychology commits him to the view that only the nonpolitical activity of engaging with one's fellow-citizens in philosophical dialogue can benefit them.[5] Socrates' response to politics is, on this view, to "change the subject" – that is, to try to reform the characters of the politically ambitious young men with whom he interacted. And this project of moral reform through critical conversation must soften Socrates' attitude towards democracy. As Richard Kraut puts it, Socrates "thinks that the many will always rule badly, and he would prefer a society of moral experts [in this regard he is as authoritarian as Plato]. But he sees little hope for anything better than democracy, and he values the intellectual freedom provided by this political system."[6]

Approaching Socrates' politics as politics in some extraordinary sense, consisting of critical and oppositional activity focused on individual intellectual transformation, has the advantage of reconciling Socrates' claim that he does not participate in politics (*Apology* 31d) with his claim that he alone of all the Athenians undertakes the true political expertise and engages in political affairs (*Gorgias* 521d): there is a sense, a special Socratic sense, in which Socrates' moral engagement with individuals is political; yet this is not politics in the ordinary sense at all.[7] But while there is something to this conception of Socrates, if criticism and the attempted moral transformation of individuals were the whole of Socrates' contribution to politics, it would be hard to see why courses in political theory or the history of political philosophy should, as they commonly do, begin with the Socrates of the "early dialogues." Surely the more plausible beginning would be Plato's *Republic*, which both describes an ideal constitution including the details of an educational system for moral cultivation and systematically criticizes other actual and ideal constitution-types.

Leo Strauss wrote that Socrates was "the founder of political philosophy."[8] The present chapter attempts to show in what sense this is true – and it will be for rather different reasons than Strauss thought (see the section below). In brief, the argument is that Plato's Socrates[9] transforms the traditional "who should rule?" question by yoking its consideration to the idea that ruling is a profession; Socrates thereby introduces a nonpartisan basis from which to discuss that question. In section two of the chapter, I sketch the ancestry of the "who should rule?" question in Socrates' predecessors and identify two justifications they offer for the privilege of ruling. In the third section, I argue that Socrates' contribution to this debate develops out of his internal criticism of a quite separate discourse, that of the advertisements, made by contemporary sophists and orators, for a new professional education in politics. These figures professionalize political rule in the sense that they describe it as an activity in which success can be achieved by mastery of the skills that may be acquired by studying with them. Socrates accepts their characterization of political rule as a profession, and uses this characterization to insist that success in this profession consists in improving the citizens – rather than in any personal advantage of the ruler. Thus (although the teachers of the political profession are not eager to admit it) the professionalization of political rule has implications for the constitutional debate because it entails a certain account of what correct rule is, and what its goal is. Socrates' criticism of the professional discourse results in a novel and nonpartisan basis for answering the question "who should rule?," but it does so by replacing a prevalent conception of political rule as a privilege, the claim to which demands justification, with a conception of political rule as a profession, in which the claim to expertise demands a show of credentials. Referring the debate about who should rule to a discussion of what skills the job of ruling requires not only inaugurates nonpartisan evaluation of political regimes, it also invalidates some considerations previously given in support of certain partisan answers. I discuss these results of Socrates' reconceptualization of the question "who should rule?" in the fourth section.

The Constitutional Debate

In Plato's *Laws*, the Athenian lists seven bases on which people may claim to be worthy to rule others: that they are their ancestors, that they are of higher birth, that they are older, that they are masters and the others slaves, that they are stronger, that they are wise and the others ignorant, and finally, that having been chosen by lot, they are favored by the gods and fortune (690ac). Readers of Plato will associate the sixth claim, of the wise to rule the ignorant, with Socrates. But just how does Socrates argue that the wise should rule the ignorant? To understand Socrates' contribution to the debate about who should rule, we need first to get a sense of the shape of the debate before Socrates. (The first evidence that Socrates is concerned with the question "who should rule?" may be in the *Crito*, where the Laws remind Socrates he has always praised Crete and Sparta for being well governed [53a], but this may have been praise for the conformity of behavior in Crete and Sparta to Cretan and Spartan law, rather than for the laws themselves.)

Herodotus puts in the mouths of sixth-century Persian nobles who have lately seized power a debate about which form of government – democracy (the rule of many), oligarchy (the rule of a few), or tyranny (the rule of one man) – they should choose (the discussion is a little anachronistic because it refers to fifth-century Athenian institutions like the selection of officials by lot and public examinations for officials). The argument for the superiority of democracy to tyranny is that there are no checks on a tyrant, the result of which is that the tyrant becomes arrogant and commits many atrocities; by contrast, democracy's institutions allow no one that kind of power; instead, in a democracy, all citizens are equal before the law. The argument for the superiority of oligarchy adds to the criticisms of tyranny criticisms of democracy: democracy puts in power ignorant men who are even more arrogant than a tyrant; oligarchy, on the other hand, puts the best men (present company included) in power, and the best men will produce the best policies. The argument for the superiority of tyranny adds to the criticisms of democracy criticisms of oligarchy: oligarchy leads to feuding and bloodshed; further, conflicts within oligarchies and democracies lead to tyranny anyway; finally, if the tyrant is the best, then nothing is better than his government (*Histories* 3.80–2). Herodotus may have taken these arguments from a sophistic source, perhaps Protagoras, who is said to have written a *Peri Politeias* (Diogenes Laertius, *Lives of Eminent Philsophers* 9.55) and whose *Antilogikai* is said by Aristoxenus to have been the source of Plato's *Republic* (3.38). (The Herodotus passage's exhaustive rehearsal of all arguments on all sides supports the attribution to Protagoras' *Antilogikai*.)

Common to debates about who should rule is the view that ruling is a privilege the possession of which has to be justified; those who would rule have to show themselves to deserve the privilege of ruling – either in exchange for something they provide or because they are simply worthy of ruling. The giving of justifications for ruling may even precede any debate about or contestation of any leader's claim to rule. For instance, Homer's Sarpedon gives a general justification of elite privilege when he explains that aristocrats have the privileges that they do (and common people don't) because they fight where the battle is fiercest (*Iliad* 12.310–21). The suggestion is that the courage of the aristocrats is both intrinsically good and valuable to the community.

Two kinds of considerations in support of the different forms of government inform the debate as to who should rule. One consideration is the *protection of the citizens* – so just as democracy promises protection from the whims of one who would place himself above the law; the tyrant too is described as a guardian of the people, whose rule preserves them from the violence of faction and feud. A second consideration is that *the ruling individual or group be "the best."* This consideration might be expressed in terms of divine right, as in Homer, by Zeus' gift of the scepter to the king (*Iliad* 2.100, cf. 7.412, 9.96). Even though these two considerations – providing protection and being superior – usually go together in actual arguments, as long as the content of the superiority is not simply superiority in providing protection, they are quite separate considerations.

The pseudo-Xenophon *Constitution of the Athenians* is one text that distinguishes superiority in protecting the citizens from some other kind of superiority. The author disapproves of the Athenian constitution because the Athenians prefer the well-being of the inferior at the expense of the superior (*chrēstoi*) (1.1). But he also suggests that it is just for the (inferior) common people to have more than the nobility, on the grounds that it is the common people – that is, the navy rather than the hoplites – who defend Athens (1.2). So his point of view seems to be that it would be best if the intrinsically superior on the one hand had more, and on the other hand, did more by way of protecting Athens. However, since they don't protect Athens, justice doesn't demand that they have more; rather, it demands that those who actually protect Athens have more. Still, despite their failure to protect Athens, the "superior" surpass the common people by their many intrinsic merits: they have the least injustice, the most self-restraint and concern for good things (1.5). The Athenians (i.e. common Athenians), for their part, can tell who's superior and who's inferior, but they prefer the inferior because the inferior are more useful to them (2.19).

The most remarkable instance of the view that intrinsic superiority entitles one to rule is of course Callicles' speech in Plato's *Gorgias*, which characterizes as "nature's justice" the rule by the superior (482e–84c). Although Callicles does not explicitly oppose the condition in which the stronger and more capable have a greater share to the condition in which the common good is achieved (he opposes it instead to the condition in which all have a "fair share"), his examples of the superiors who by nature's justice have a greater share are conquerors, raiders, and lions. And the reason the lion is king of the animals is not that he protects them.

Callicles' is obviously an extreme position, but it is evidence that a party's intrinsic superiority could be taken as by itself a reason for that party to rule. This may be the sentiment in, for example, Democritus' pronouncements that it is by nature fitting for the superior to rule (Diels-Kranz 267), that it is hard to be ruled by an inferior (49), and that it is proper to yield to a law or a ruler or someone wiser (47). Alongside this belief in a reason for the superior to rule, Democritus remarks that poverty under democracy is preferable to prosperity under a dictator to the same extent as freedom is preferable to slavery (251); perhaps the thought is that democracy at least limits the extent of an inferior's power over one. That Democritus is no Calliclean is shown by his advice that his audience not try to acquire power for themselves contrary to the common good (252).

The other consideration in favor of a kind of rule – that it protects the people – is more widely used, and there is usually more to be said about just how a ruler/rule of that kind can or will protect the people. So, for example, in Thucydides' account of the debate at Syracuse (*History of the Peloponnesian War* 6.39), the oligarchs contend that the wealthy are best able to rule because they are the least tempted to take the city's money for themselves and the democrats counter that the "*dēmos*" whose interests are served by democracy includes all the citizens, and that all citizens in a democracy have a fair share – by contrast with the oligarchy, in which the dangers, but not the profits, are shared.

I have documented the use of and emphasized the distinctness of these two considerations in favor of someone's or some group's rule in order to bring out Socrates' distinctive contribution to the debate. By contrast, Leo Strauss argues that the question "who should rule?" arises naturally out of the politically engaged stance of the classical political philosopher, and the answer "the best should rule" arises equally naturally and prephilosophically, and needing the philosopher only to spell out its implications and defend it against objections by "bad or perplexed men."[10] But this account assumes that "rule by the best" is not a controversial ideal. Yet the interpretation of "best" is seen to be a matter of contention in Thucydides' Syracusan debate. And the democrats in Herodotus' constitutional debate do not even try to claim on behalf of democracy that the *dēmos* are the best.

In the constitutional debate, the alternatives for rule – by the many (the poor), the few (the rich or historically rich), or one man – are idealizations of actual constitutions. It is not as if Socrates can argue in favor of rule by the wise by pointing to or idealizing some existing constitution in which the wise rule. Yet to make a case for rule by the wise, it would seem necessary to address the claims to rule of the wealthy, the nobly born, the military, and so on. In the *Republic*, when Plato does describe and argue for the superiority of a constitution in which the wise rule, he helps himself to the conception of a ruler who is motivated to rule because his ruling is necessary rather than because ruling is something fine or good (347cd, 520e–21a) and whose rule is justified by his qualifications. There has been a quiet revolution between the idea of rule as privilege, claim to which requires justification, and this idea of rule as a job the performance of which calls for certain qualifications. The question "who should rule?" has come to depend on the question "what does the job of ruling demand?" In the next section, I argue that Socrates takes the conception of ruling as a job requiring certain skills from contemporary sophists, but that he argues that determining what the requisite skill is depends on the answer to the question "what is the goal of ruling?"

Professionalizing Political Rule

In all likelihood Socrates takes over the idea that political rule is a job requiring certain skills from some of his older contemporaries. Plato includes among these Protagoras, who claimed to teach "sound deliberation (*euboulia*), both in domestic matters – how best to manage one's household, and in public affairs – how to realize one's maximum potential for success in political debate and action" (*Protagoras* 319a),[11] and Gorgias, who claimed to teach rhetoric, "the ability to persuade by speeches judges in a law court, councilors in a council meeting, and assemblymen in an assembly or in any other political gathering that might take place" (*Gorgias* 452e) which produces "freedom for humankind itself and . . . the source of rule over others in one's own city" (452d). Both Protagoras and Gorgias characterize politics as a field in which one can excel when one has achieved the mastery over the skills (deliberation, rhetoric) that they teach.

Before we delve into Socrates' engagement with the sophists and orators, a word about what they were doing in Athens. The demand for sophists and orators seems to have arisen with two changes in Athenian circumstances in the fifth century which made traditional elites' claim to political power and prior political skills obsolete: democracy and empire. If the vote of the *dēmos* was required for a politician's plan to carry, it was no longer enough to be a great general; the politician had to be able to speak persuasively to the assembled *dēmos*, and since he did not have a common culture and education with them, he had to learn what appealed to them in particular. In addition, Athens' new status as an imperial power complicated its affairs and this, combined with the requirement that any issue be decided by the Assembly in a single day, created a demand for politicians who could devote themselves to mastering Athenian political affairs. Plato's contemporary Isocrates expresses one kind of response to the complexity of Athens' affairs when he denies the possibility of scientific knowledge (*epistēmē*) of "what we should do or what we should say" and instead upholds the importance to the politician of "insight" (*phronēsis*) and the ability "by his powers of conjecture (*tais doxais*) to arrive generally at the best course" (Isocrates, *Antidosis* c. 271[12]). But however desirable mastery of political affairs or good judgment may have been in a politician, the democratic system made the ability to speak persuasively not just a desideratum but a necessity.[13]

In this context, "professionalizing" political rule amounts to claiming that there is a body of knowledge, sufficiently wide in scope and precise in formulation, upon the learning of which the would-be political leader should expect success. Describing a new discipline as a *technē* (profession, craft, art) or *epistēmē* (science) is a way of claiming for it a status possessed by better-established practices like medicine. That status derives in part from the professional's ability to bring about a valued result (such as health) on the basis of some understanding of the factors involved (rather than by luck). (I have chosen the term "profession" to translate *technē* rather than the more usual "craft" or "art" for several reasons. First, in English, "craft" sounds as if it refers to something one does with one's hands and "art" to something in the fine arts, perhaps as opposed to the sciences, whereas *technē* has none of these connotations; like the *technai* about which there are disputes, such as medicine and politics, a profession is thought to have an important intellectual component. Second, in contemporary English "professional" has normative connotations that seem to resonate with those of *technē*: people speak today of professional standards and professional [or unprofessional] behavior.)[14]

I mean this to be a minimalist account of what is entailed by calling the subject one practices or teaches a *technē*, and I want a minimalist account because it seems to me that more substantial accounts reflect controversial innovations by Socrates (and other fifth-century intellectuals) to which we will want to pay special attention. So, for example, Aristotle characterizes a *technē* as involving knowledge of universals, by contrast with experience (*empeiria*) or knowledge of particulars; as involving knowledge of causes; and as teachable (*Metaphysics* 1.1). But these may be peculiarly Socratic emphases (on the contrast with experience, and on knowledge of universals and causes, see e.g. *Gorgias* 464c–65a; on teachability, *Protagoras* 319be, 361ac). Aristotle's characterization is quite different from that of the late fifth-century Hippocratic *On Ancient Medicine*, according to which medicine's claim to be a science rests on its answering a need, having a starting point and longstanding method for discovery and being explicable to laypersons (2). While this text also insists on medicine's having a precise and complete understanding of causes and their effects on the body (20), it insists that these are found out by experience, which allows distinctive causes to be investigated by the method of difference – by contrast with causal and explanatory principles that derive from a more general physical investigation. Again, Socrates' insistent demand that any claimant to a *technē* specify its product (*ergon*) (*Gorgias* 447d–54b; *Protagoras* 318a–19a; *Euthydemus* 288e–92d; *Cleitophon* 409bd) builds on what must have been a widespread expectation that a professional could name or point to the beneficial product he had on offer, but it goes beyond that expectation in demanding that the professional give an account of this product. After all, a doctor might be expected to tell his patient the symptoms of his disease and of his cure, but it is not reasonable to expect him to give a nonexpert an explanation of how the disease produces the symptoms, or how the treatment effects the cure, or of what health is, particularly in any given case. (However, Socrates is himself subjected to this higher standard of giving an account of the product of a craft when Thrasymachus demands that he say what the just [which Socrates has been treating as the product of the *technē* of justice, *Republic* 332d ff.] is without saying that it is the advantageous or beneficial and so on [*Republic* 336cd; cf. *Cleitophon* 409cd].)

In his conversations with the sophists and orators, Socrates accepts the formal claim that expert knowledge in politics brings about good political results. His questions focus on the content of the expert knowledge they profess (What is it about? What is the evidence that they really have it?), on their conception of good political results (Are these really good? If not, what are the good results to be brought about by political rule?) and on the relationship between the two (Does their expertise really have the results they claim it does? Or what sort of expert knowledge would it take to bring about these results, or genuinely good results?). So, for example, in the *Gorgias*, Socrates counters Gorgias' claim that rhetoric is an expertise which produces the good political result of enhanced social and political power for the orator-politician (452de) by pointing out that however rhetoric achieves its effects, it is not through any knowledge of the matters of justice and injustice about which it makes speeches (459ae, 461b), and that even if it enables the orator-politician to visit evil upon anyone he wishes, it does not enable him to bring about any good for himself or anyone else (466b–68e). So rhetoric fails to be political expertise on two counts: it lacks knowledge of central political matters (the just and unjust), and it fails to bring about any genuine good.

The sophists and orators contemporary with Socrates cannot have welcomed his agreement with their claim that expert knowledge in politics brings about good political results. For Socrates not only agrees with them that expert knowledge brings about successful political rule, but also adds that only those with expert knowledge are qualified to (thus should, or may) rule. Sophists and orators like Gorgias, Protagoras, and Thrasymachus, noncitizens in Athens, would have shied away from being seen as telling the Athenians how they should run their city; they claimed only to be helping aspirants to political power within the existing constitution, thereby allowing their professional training to be equally attractive to partisans of democracy and oligarchy. Socrates, on the other hand, was centrally in the business of evaluating ways of living, both individual and communal. Further, while the need to attract students led sophists and orators to allow the conception of successful political rule to depend on the would-be student's conception of success or advantage, Socrates' insistence on a substantive account of the (goods) produced by successful political rule brought into the limelight the difficulties of making recommendations without any views on what is non-instrumentally good.

In *Republic* 1, Plato points out both the common ground and the differences between Socrates and a contemporary sophist, Thrasymachus. It is Thrasymachus who introduces the idea of a professional expertise of ruling which enables its possessor, insofar as he is a professional, to rule unerringly (340c–41b). Socrates accepts the idea that there is a profession of ruling; he disagrees with Thrasymachus, however, about the goal of this profession. According to Thrasymachus, the professional ruler rules to his own advantage. But the introduction of the idea of a professional ruler opens up other dimensions of the profession of ruling. Socrates argues, by analogy with the other professions, that a profession's goal is always the improvement of that over which it has power. He seems to be reasoning: if [as you Thrasymachus maintain] ruling is a profession, then [you must concede that] its product is like that of other professions, and the product of any other profession is the improvement of that over which it has jurisdiction. For example, the doctor in the precise sense is so called because he treats the sick, the healing of the sick being the advantage which the profession of medicine is directed towards (341cd, 342c). He generalizes, "No kind of knowledge seeks or orders what is advantageous to itself . . . but what is advantageous to the weaker, which is subject to it" (342cd; Grube-Reeve, trans.). If political rule is rule over

221

citizens, then its goal must be their betterment, not the ruler's. In the *Gorgias*, Socrates announces that he himself is a practitioner of the political profession (521d), perhaps the only one. If improving citizens is the goal of the political professional, then, since Socrates' protreptic and elenctic activities have that goal, he can reasonably count himself a political professional.

In this argument, Socrates claims that the professions "by nature" aim at the betterment of whatever they have jurisdiction over; for example, medicine was discovered to remedy the deficiencies of the human body (341de). This seems a deliberate departure from the common line of thought that the professions were discovered for the benefit of mankind: Protagoras' myth gives us many other examples of the deficiencies to remedy which Prometheus and Zeus gave humans the various professions (*Protagoras* 321c–22d). The common line is, although initially more plausible, perhaps more vulnerable to misuse than Socrates'. If we specify the goal of a profession by the benefits it gives us humans – saying with Thrasymachus that the goal of shepherding is surely not the welfare of the sheep but rather the production of the meat and wool the sheep provide for the shepherd's benefit (343b) – then it is open to someone to specify the goal of another profession by the benefits it gives some one subgroup of humans, perhaps even by exploiting another subgroup. (Thrasymachus' choice of an example is particularly striking, given the standard characterization of the ruler as a shepherd [e.g. Homer, *Iliad* 2.243; Xenophon, *Memorabilia* 3.2.1; Aristotle, *Nicomachean Ethics* 8.11, 1161a12–15; criticized at *Statesman* 267c ff.].) Safer, then, to look for an internal connection between a profession and its goal. And to specify the internal connection when we also have to determine the goal, it makes sense to turn to the other professions as models, on the assumption that the professions resemble each other. Resemblance between the professions seems to be the basis of Socrates' argument that injustice isn't an expertise and the unjust person isn't clever or good because the unjust try to outdo each other whereas experts only try to outdo nonexperts, not other experts (349a–50c).

Socrates' conception of the relationship between a profession and its goal is stronger than might be thought. Socrates does not claim that in no circumstance can it ever benefit the practitioner of a profession to practice his profession (a view which, as long as he wants to treat justice as a profession, would deliver him right into the hands of Thrasymachus, who claims that justice is another's good [343c]). He only claims that benefiting its practitioner is not the goal of any profession. Benefit to the practitioner might be an incidental result of the profession; it might be the result of practicing the profession, perhaps in a given social context: doctors might get monetary payment, recognition, or gratitude for practicing medicine, but the goal of medicine remains healing. Similarly, rulers may get wages, honors, or they may only avoid the "penalty" of having worse people than themselves ruling (347ad), but it will not do to confuse the job of ruling with any of these socially mediated consequences. But that is just what people who think of ruling as a privilege, like Thrasymachus, do.

Socrates' answer to the question "what is the goal of the job of ruling?" converges with one answer to the question "who should rule?": the goal of the job of ruling is the benefit of the ruled; that individual or group should rule who is best qualified to benefit the ruled.[15] We saw above that advocates of democracy, oligarchy, and tyranny all claim to benefit the ruled – so Socrates is hardly being controversial by claiming that political rule aims at the benefit of the ruled. Rather, he is showing that the sophists, who would prefer to remain silent on the "who should rule?" question, are committed by the very notion of a profession of ruling to the answer "he who best fulfills the goal of ruling" – for any profession has action-guiding norms which are structured by the profession's goal(s).

Socrates' use of the notion of a profession deprives Thrasymachus of the respectability associated with being a professional practitioner or teacher – insofar as Thrasymachus himself pursues the injustice he praises (343c–44c). If one's motive for engaging in a profession conflicts with the goal of that profession, one's claim to be a professional of that sort is invalidated. Not everyone will care about this loss, and this marks the limits of the normative force of the notion of a profession. Anyone who can swallow the loss of prestige that goes with having to take a position that says, "I don't care about being a professional, I just want my own advantage," will need a deeper response than Socrates gives to Thrasymachus. (On this point, it is worth noting that while Thrasymachus is unmoved by Socrates' argument that someone who uses his power to benefit himself rather than those he rules is, contrary to Thrasymachus, no expert ruler, he sweats and blushes when Socrates argues that the unjust person is neither clever nor good.) It is perhaps in recognition of this need for a deeper argument that from *Republic* 2 on, Plato takes on the more fundamental question of why it is better to be just rather than unjust.

Consequences for Political Thought

One consequence of defining ruling as a profession aimed at benefiting citizens and using this definition to answer the question "who should rule?" is that it provides a position from which to criticize existing regimes without becoming an ally of any of the parties vying for power – in the particular case of Socrates' criticism of the Athenian democracy, of the oligarchs. So although Socrates' criticism of democracy as rule by a foolish mob resembles the criticism of the oligarchs, because Socrates ties the content of the wisdom that could qualify someone to rule so closely to the job of ruling, and because he defines the job of ruling in terms of its goal of improving the citizens, he cannot but be a critic of oligarchy, tyranny, and the like, as well. Rulers in existing oligarchies and tyrannies are no less ignorant, and so no less incapable of improving the citizens, than the *dēmos*.

For Plato, himself disillusioned with the injustice of successive political regimes in Athens (*Seventh Letter* 324b–26b), it would have been important to find a kind of political criticism that did not play into partisan hands. Plato certainly portrays Socrates as a nonpartisan individual: the *Apology* carefully balances Socrates' opposition to both democratic injustice against his refusal to participate in oligarchic injustice (32bc and 32ce). Further, among Socrates' associates are Critias, one of the Thirty Tyrants who terrorized Athens after coming to power in 404, and his cousin Charmides, appointed by the Thirty to govern the Piraeus; but Socrates' longtime friend Chaerephon, who was told by the Delphic oracle of Socrates' wisdom, and who was lampooned by Aristophanes for "Socratizing," was an ardent enough democrat to go into exile in 404. While we might find it unsettling that Socrates should have associated with both kinds of people, perhaps he found partisan political affiliations none too deep given the example of his beloved Alcibiades, who, after having been an Athenian general, defected to Sparta, then worked for the Persians, but was subsequently forgiven and welcomed back by democratic Athens.[16]

It may be objected that the position from which to criticize existing regimes provided by the sophistic professionalization of ruling is redundant because the very considerations raised in favor of one kind of rule or another – that the rule secures some common good, or that it puts in power the intrinsically superior who deserve to rule – can themselves be given nonpartisan readings. But possibility is not history, and we do not see nonpartisan evaluations of forms of rule prior to Socrates. The *Theaetetus* opposes speech in the service of personal and political interests to speech that seeks the truth about justice and injustice (173ae, 175cd). It is of course contentious to treat these as mutually exclusive kinds of speech – after all, interested speeches from different perspectives could conceivably further an inquiry into the truth – but the distinction between partisan and nonpartisan political speech is useful. Prior to Socrates, debates about who should rule are partisan: although the parties offer arguments which can in principle be detached from the partisan point of view advancing them – oligarchic or democratic or monarchic – in practice they are never so detached, and there are no instances of a neutral investigation of the question from some agreed-upon starting point. Perhaps it is the hope of a debate in which each party gives the strongest arguments in favor of its view and against the alternatives that the winner will not only seem best to all concerned but will also be best, objectively. But even in this case, the process leading to agreement involves the parties *qua* partisans of some or other arrangement, rather than *qua* investigators who begin with objective or even just shared principles. Further, we should not underestimate the conceptual breakthrough required to go from dealing with political issues only in partisan argument and dealing with them disinterestedly. Alongside the attitudinal difference between partisan and disinterested, significant conceptual resources have been developed in the tradition of political philosophy since Socrates (the idea of aggregation, the impartial spectator, the technique of universalization). My claim here is that the idea of political rule as a profession is the conceptual resource that Socrates uses to engage in nonpartisan evaluation.

A second consequence of Socrates' professionalizing political rule is the invalidation of one of the considerations given in support of answers to the "who should rule?" question; namely, that the superior, just in virtue of being superior, deserve to rule. In the *Gorgias*, Callicles says that nature's justice demands that the superior rule over and have more than the inferior (which they may accomplish by force) (488b). Although Callicles identifies the superior, the better and the stronger, he does not believe that these qualities are constituted by having power, as the many do in Athens (488d–89b); rather, his idea is that some people are intrinsically superior and for that reason deserve to rule and have more; at Socrates' suggestion, he identifies the superior with the more intelligent (489ce).

Callicles' invocation of nature shows him to be committed to an ideal of justice different from Socrates', and so Socrates needs to show him what is wrong with that ideal of justice. The obvious way for Socrates to do this would be to question Callicles:

why does superior wisdom justify having more? Or, alternatively, what is the connection between ruling and having more?

However, instead of raising these challenges, Socrates seems to grant Callicles the point that superior wisdom (about some F) justifies having more (of F) – but, Socrates adds, this must be in order to facilitate proper use (of F). So, Socrates asks Callicles, if you think that the more intelligent should have more, then should the doctor, the one who is more intelligent about food and drink, have more food and drink than the others, or should he be given the job of distributing food and drink to everyone including himself, on the basis of their strength or weakness (which determines how much food they need)? (490ce).

At first sight, it seems as if Socrates is just not hearing the normative claim in Callicles' words, that the superior or more intelligent deserve to rule over and have more than the others. Socrates speaks as if the only thing that follows from greater intelligence is entitlement to manage whatever the intelligence is about.

In his commentary, Irwin writes,

> Here and in 490e Socrates does not seem to distinguish "have more," *pleon echein*, and "take more" or "outdo," *pleonektein*; cf. 483c. But "getting the advantage," *pleonektein*, 491a, seems to be the result of getting a larger quantity, *pleon echein*. Perhaps Socrates argues: superior wisdom gives no claim to have more, *pleon echein*, and therefore, contrary to Callicles, it gives no claim to advantage, *pleonektein*.[17]

However, if we assume that Socrates (unlike Callicles) does distinguish having more (i.e. having the charge of more) and taking more (i.e. more than one's share, for oneself), then we can take Socrates at his word: superior wisdom justifies having more of what one is wise about (because one can use it properly); it does not, however, justify taking more of it for oneself (*ou pleonektēteon*, 490c4). The idea that wisdom justifies possession because it enables correct use is very close to the idea that most things ordinarily thought to be good are only good if accompanied by wisdom, because only wisdom reliably enables the correct use required for such things to benefit us (*Euthydemus* 280c–82b).

Socrates challenges Callicles' claim that intrinsic superiority entitles anyone to taking more of anything for himself not by defending some other ground for privilege than intrinsic superiority, but instead, by embracing the idea that intellectual superiority of some kind is relevant to ruling, and treating it as the basis for assigning responsibilities, just as the doctor's knowledge of the body dictates that he perform the task of assigning food and drink to bodies in accordance with what they need.

I do not think this recasting of Callicles' idea is partisan. It does not favor any of the traditional political regimes or parties. And it raises the excellent question what on earth intrinsic superiority has to do with ruling unless it is superiority at ruling. This question is a pressing question for Callicles in a way that it is not for Thrasymachus, for Callicles believes that it is nature's justice – that is, really just – for the superior to rule and take more, whereas Thrasymachus makes no claim about what is just by nature, contenting himself with an exposé of existing societies' conceptions of justice as a front for norms that in reality benefit the rulers, and a critique of adherence to these norms as contrary to subjects' self-interest.

Conceiving of ruling as a profession rather than a privilege leaves a number of questions unanswered. Even if only the professionally qualified can do the job of ruling (i.e. really do the job, so that its goal is achieved), are professional qualifications sufficient to entitle someone to rule? (In the *Lysis*, Socrates suggests the answer is yes, 209d.) And if rule by the professionally qualified alone counts as political rule, what else must be in place to require the professionally qualified to rule? Finally, if ruling is not a privilege or prize, how is a ruler to be compensated? Plato takes up these questions in the main books of the *Republic*, where detaching jobs from the privileges that usually go along with them frees him to imagine a distribution of social goods which – instead of only compensating citizens for their contribution – enables people to do their jobs and to enjoy whatever goods they can.[18]

I'd like to return, finally, to the Popperian complaint that Plato's Socrates misguidedly focuses on the question of sovereignty or "who shall rule the state?" to the neglect of the question of how to design political institutions to check the abuses of political power. I hope to have shown why his thought has the focus it does. It is not that he (or Plato) subscribed to a theory of unchecked sovereignty, nor that he (or Plato) was obsessed with (re)establishing hierarchies. Rather, it is that his far more intellectually radical project of transforming the conception of ruling from privilege to profession, and spelling out the normative implications of ruling being a profession, provides a new basis for answering the question of sovereignty.[19]

Notes

1   But see Vlastos (1994) for a criticism of Socrates as a political actor.
2   Popper (1962: 120–1). Note that in the *Laws*, Plato does address the issue of checks on political power.
3   Popper (1962: 191).
4   Cf. Grote (1875: III.240).
5   Penner (2000).
6   Kraut (1984: 244). By contrast, Kraut argues, Plato found this same freedom horrifying (277).
7   An exception is Brown (2000), who attributes to Socrates cosmopolitan rather than local (polis-wide) commitments. However, in Brown's own expression, the cosmopolitan commitments are part of Socrates "extraordinary" politics of investigating along with anyone, citizen or foreigner (*Apology* 23b). My focus here is on Socrates' ordinary, i.e. polis-restricted, politics.
8   Strauss (1989: 76).
9   I focus on Plato's Socrates in works from the *Apology* through *Republic* 1 not out of a firm conviction that their Socrates represents Socrates' own teachings rather than Plato's views, but because I find in them a significant development in political thought that risks being overshadowed by the constructive project beginning with *Republic* 2.
10 Strauss (1989: 68–9).
11 Lombardo and Bell, trans. This, and all translations of Plato, are from Cooper and Hutchinson (1997).
12 Norlin (1928–54).
13 Ober (1989) and Connor (1992).
14 For discussion of Socrates' use of the notion of *technē* see Irwin (1977).

15 Cf. Parry (1996: 22–3), who says that if Socrates had the notion of legitimacy, he would have said that the legitimate ruler cannot just improve rulers but must improve the ruled.
16 For more on Socrates' associates, see Nails (2002).
17 Irwin (1979) *ad loc.*
18 I discuss the *Republic's* principles for distributing social burdens and benefits in Kamtekar (2001).
19 For comments on this paper, I'm very grateful to Steve Gardiner and to the audience of the (2005) Arizona Ancient Philosophy Colloquium on The Socratic Legacy.

References

Brown, E. (2000). Socrates the cosmopolitan. *Stanford Agora: An Online Journal of Legal Perspectives*, 1, 74–87. http://agora.stanford.edu/agora/libArticles/brown/brown.pdf.

Connor, W. R. (1992). *The New Politicians of Fifth Century Athens*. Indianapolis: Hackett.

Cooper, J. and Hutchinson, D. (1997). *The Complete Works of Plato*. Indianapolis: Hackett.

Gagarin, M. and Woodruff, P. (1995). *Early Greek Political Thought from Homer to the Sophists*. Cambridge: Cambridge University Press.

Grote, G. (1875). *Plato and the Other Companions of Sokrates*. London: John Murray.

Irwin, T. (1977). *Plato's Moral Theory*. Oxford: Clarendon Press.

——. (1979). *Plato: Gorgias*. Oxford: Clarendon Press.

Kamtekar, R. (2001). Social justice and happiness in the *Republic*: Plato's two principles. *History of Political Thought*, 22(2), 189–220.

Kraut, R. (1984). *Socrates and the State*. Princeton: Princeton University Press.

Nails, D. (2002). *The People of Plato: A Prosopography of Plato and Other Socratics*. Indianapolis: Hackett.

Norlin, G. (1928–54). *Isocrates*. 2 vols. London: Heinemann.

Ober, J. (1989). *Mass and Elite in Democratic Athens: Rhetoric, Ideology, and the Power of the People*. Princeton: Princeton University Press.

Parry, R. (1996). *Plato's Craft of Justice*. Albany: SUNY Press.

Penner, T. (2000). Socrates. In C. Rowe and M. Schofield (eds.), *The Cambridge History of Greek and Roman Political Thought* (pp. 164–89). Cambridge: Cambridge University Press.

Popper, K. (1962). *The Open Society and Its Enemies, vol. 1: The Spell of Plato*. Princeton: Princeton University Press.

Strauss, L. (1989). *An Introduction to Political Philosophy*, ed. Hilail Gildin. Detroit: Wayne State University Press.

Vlastos, G. (1994). Socrates and Vietnam. In Myles Burnyeat (ed.), *Socratic Studies*. Cambridge: Cambridge University Press.

Wright, M. R. (1988). The origins of political theory. *Polis*, 7(2), 75–104.

14

The Examined Life

RICHARD KRAUT

The Examined Life Examined

"The unexamined life is not worth living" (*Apology* 38a5–6). That familiar statement of Socrates, perhaps the most provocative ever uttered by a philosopher, encapsulates the essence of his philosophy and his way of life. Socrates presents himself – or, rather, Plato presents him – as the embodiment of an examined life. To see what such a life demands of us, we must look to the example Socrates sets, as this is captured on Plato's page. That demand can either inspire or repel us – precisely the effects Socrates had on his contemporaries. The fascination and nobility of his ideal would be diminished, had he said that the unexamined life is one lifestyle among many, something we should choose only if we feel so inclined. At the same time, there seems to be something absurdly demanding, perhaps even a contemptible severity, in Socrates' insistence that we all live as he lived. In any society, at most a few can spend all of their days in ethical discussion, as Socrates did. Do all of the others really lead worthless lives? Does Socrates have good reasons for criticizing the way so large a portion of humankind conduct themselves? And in any case, what value can an examined life have, if only a few people devote themselves to it, and they have as little impact on the lives of their contemporaries as Socrates did? For that matter, precisely what is so good about an examined life, for someone who is able to live it? Even if we *all* could manage it, why should any of us even try?

Few, if any, moral philosophers working in the academies of today would endorse Socrates' dictum. What can be demanded of us, they would say, is that we refrain from injuring others in egregious ways (murder, assault, theft); that we go some way (exactly how far is a matter of dispute) towards benefiting at least a few others; that we be honest, just, kind, tolerant; that we do what is morally right because it is right, not as a strategy for achieving nonmoral ends. They would say that ethical discussions of the sort Socrates engaged in with his fellow citizens is a worthwhile pursuit (it is, after all, somewhat like what these philosophers do for a living); but, they would add, it is not necessary or even desirable that *everyone* engage in the sort of abstract ethical inquiry that absorbed Socrates. Certainly, they would say, it is not a necessary feature of a good person that he or she live an examined life. One becomes a good person, in their opinion, in ways that are obvious to anyone who has common sense: by being properly trained, in one's early years, to recognize what is morally right, and to want to do what is right because it is right. One needs to become adept in the use and application of such words as "ought," "right," "good," "just," "honest." But to do that, we need not, as Socrates supposed, enter the abstract and difficult domain of moral philosophy, asking ourselves and each other such questions as "what is courage?," "what is justice?," "what is it to be a friend?" What we need, instead, is to acquire the social and emotional skills that allow us to recognize what is morally right and to want to do what is morally right with a good heart. Socrates, according to this way of thinking, was simply mistaken in supposing that being a good person consists, wholly or partially, in being a good moral philosopher.

Not everyone agrees, however, that the Socratic call to the examined life can so easily be rejected. During a large portion of the modern period, his call to self-examination earned him a place close to that of Christ and other religious leaders who were regarded as the great moral paradigms of human existence. Benjamin Jowett, the principal translator of Plato in the late nineteenth century, told his students at Oxford, "The two biographies about which we are most deeply interested (though not to the same degree) are those of Christ and Socrates."[1] Such comparisons continue into the twentieth century: Socrates is treated as a "paradigmatic individual" (along with Buddha, Confucius, and Christ) by the existentialist writer, Karl Jaspers (1962). But in the early years of the twenty-first century, academic moral philosophy is not struggling to come to terms with Socrates (as it is with Aristotle, Hume, Kant, Nietzsche, and Sidgwick) – rather it has passed him by.

The Socratic thesis that an unexamined life is not worth living, I would like to suggest, is neither easy to accept nor to reject. The case for rejecting it has just been sketched. In what follows, I explain what it means to live such a life, and why Socrates thinks we must do so.

Plato's *Apology*

The place to begin such an inquiry is with Socrates himself – or, rather, with Socrates as he is presented to us in Plato's *Apology*, where the words, "the unexamined life is not worth living," are uttered. When Socrates makes this statement, the jury has already found him guilty, and must decide what punishment to impose. Meletus, one of the prosecutors, has proposed that he be put to death, and it is Socrates' prerogative to propose an alternative punishment. He asks: should he ask to be exiled, and then, when he moves to some other city, give up his way of practicing philosophy? His response is that he cannot, because giving up philosophy would be disobedient to the god. He then adds: "If I say that this is the greatest good for a human being – to have discussions every day about virtue and the other things about which you hear me conversing and examining myself and others – and that the unexamined life is not worth living for a human being, you will be still less persuaded by what I say" (38a1–6). Socrates then proposes a monetary fine, but the jury decides that he should be put to death.

But *why* should every human being lead an examined life? Socrates makes no effort, at this or any other point in his defense speech, to answer that question. He links his call to the examined life to the further claim that discussing virtue is a great good – but that too is a thesis that receives no defense in Plato's *Apology*. We should not be surprised that Socrates offers no argument for these claims. He is, after all, not giving a philosophical lecture, but defending himself against the charges against him, by trying to show that his way of life was undertaken with the best of motives and with no ill effects. His audience does not care whether or not it can be *shown* that the best sort of life is an examined life; it wants to know what it should do with someone with ideas like these.

Suppose we assume that wisdom is the greatest good a human being can possess. And suppose we also accept Socrates' claim that his ethical conversations have brought him closer to wisdom than any other human being has come. Those premises will secure the conclusion that there is great value in Socratic inquiry, but they are as open to challenge as their conclusion. Why *should* we take wisdom to be the greatest good? And why suppose that this virtue consists, even partly, by the kind of abstract ethical inquiry Socrates engages in? It seems plausible to say instead that there are many different kinds of wisdom, and that although the sophistication acquired through a study of moral philosophy is perhaps one of them, it cannot be assumed to be more valuable than all other forms of wisdom. Socratic inquiry may improve one's philosophical skills – but does it make one a better person? Does it enhance one's ability to act well? Plato's *Apology* does not answer these questions, and is not designed to do so.

Not Worth Living

We will therefore have to turn to other works of Plato, and ask whether they give us a better understanding of why Socrates thinks the unexamined life is not worth living. But before moving away from the *Apology*, we should pause to make sure we understand what that Socratic dictum means.

One of its terms – *anexetastos* ("unexamined") – creates no difficulty. *Exetazein* means "to examine, inquire, scrutinize, test, prove." It and its cognate noun, *exetasis*, are the words Socrates frequently uses to describe what he does in his conversations with others. A life to which the cognate adjective, *anexetastos*, applies is one that has not been subjected to the kind of ethical examination Socrates conducts.

But the other important term in Socrates' dictum – *biōtos* – requires closer examination. Consider "worth living," the phrase that has long been the standard translation, at least since Jowett. When we say of someone that his life, at a certain time, is not worth living, we mean that he is no better off going on living than he would be were he to die. Ideally, the time at which death should come is the time when it ceases to be worth living. Accordingly, if someone's life has *never*, at any point, been worth living, then at any time in his life it would have been good for him to die.

If we understand Socrates to mean that all unexamined lives should be put in this category, then we are attributing to him an extremely harsh attitude towards his fellow citizens. If he rescues them from danger (as he presumably does, when he fights in battle), he thinks he does them no good. One has to wonder: why does he think that he should lift a finger for them?

A life that is not worth living is not merely a bad life: it is one so lacking in value that it would be best for the person living it to die. There is no reason to attribute to Socrates the thesis that unexamined lives are at that depth of misery. For *biōtos* does not have to mean "worth living"; it can also be translated "to be lived." So understood, Socrates' dictum should be formulated: "The unexamined is not to be lived." That does not have to mean that it should be terminated; rather, it can be taken to mean that one should not live that way. If one *is* living that way, one must make a change – not because death would be better, but because a much better kind of life is possible.

It is Socrates' mission to convince his fellow citizens that by living unexamined lives, they are missing the greatest good there is, and that they must therefore change their lives. It is no part of his mission to convince them that they are so badly off that they would be better off dead. (What would be the point of trying to prove that to them?) I propose, therefore, that we scrap the standard translation, and that we take Plato's Greek at *Apology* 38a5–6 to mean: "no human being should live an unexamined life." We need not fear that, by interpreting Socrates in this way, we are turning his philosophy into a tepid piece of advice. The thesis that every human being should be engaged in ongoing Socratic inquiry is one of the boldest claims ever made by a philosopher. Once one has given that thesis a full airing, there would be no philosophical or practical point to having a further discussion about whether those who do not live by this rule would be better off dead.

One other point about Socrates' meaning should be emphasized: he holds that ethical inquiry is a process that one should undertake throughout one's life, not merely for some brief period. One cannot live up to his demand by spending a half year asking the questions he asks, then turning to other matters, and never revisiting such issues. For the call to the examined life is linked to the thesis that the greatest good for a human being is "to have discussions every day about virtue" and other ethical matters (*Apology* 38a3). We should recognize how audacious a claim this is. We should expect Socrates to give us reasons to accept it.

The Socratic Dialogues

Where are we to turn for his arguments? Nearly all of Plato's dialogues contain an interlocutor – typically he is the dominant speaker – named Socrates. But some scholars hold that in certain portions of some of these dialogues, the conversation of "Socrates" gives us a roughly accurate portrait of the historical figure of that name; whereas in others, "Socrates" becomes a mouthpiece for Plato, whose philosophy, though greatly influenced by that of the historical Socrates, also differs significantly from it.[2]

That is the approach to be followed in this essay. The thesis that no human being should live an unexamined life is very likely to have been at the heart of Socrates' philosophy, but it is not a position that Plato himself endorsed – or, at any rate, he did not embrace it throughout his philosophical career. To see this, we need only consider the division of the ideal city depicted in the *Republic* into three classes: philosophers, soldiers, and workers. It is the philosophers who can be said to live an examined life: they are the ones who are trained to ask and answer the sorts of questions that exercised Socrates. The soldiers and workers, by contrast, live unreflectively and accept the laws and decisions of the rulers. It is the job of the rulers, and no one else, to be wise about practical matters. So, the Socrates of the *Republic* rejects the thesis that every human being should lead an examined life.

What are we to say about this conflict between the *Apology* and *Republic*? One hypothesis – an implausible one, I believe – is that this discrepancy reflects a reversal in Plato's own thinking. According to this interpretation, when Plato has Socrates say, in the *Apology*, that one should live an examined life, he, Plato, is inserting his own philosophy into Socrates' speech. But that is not a credible way of thinking about the relationship between Socrates and Plato. There is no reason to doubt that the historical Socrates engaged many of his contemporaries in discussions about virtue, that his doing so aroused considerable hostility, and that he nonetheless persisted because he thought there is great value in such questioning. It does not matter whether the historical Socrates uttered the very words about the unexamined life that we have in our Greek text. What cannot be plausibly denied is that the great value of an examined life is an assumption central to the life and thought of the historical Socrates. As we have seen, that guiding idea is significantly modified by the principal interlocutor of the *Republic*. The most plausible explanation of this discrepancy, I would like to suggest, is this: as Plato reflected on the central message of his teacher, he came to the conclusion that it has a more limited application than Socrates realized. Yes, says Plato, the examined life is the best available to a human being; but it is not good for everyone to try to live it. Let a small number live that way, and let the rest be guided by them.

When we realize that Plato was inspired by Socrates but moved beyond him, it becomes tempting to study his dialogues by putting each of them into one of two categories: first, those in which the conversation centers around themes and uses ideas that are likely to have belonged to the historical Socrates; second, those that are more fully dominated by ideas that are likely to have been Platonic modifications of or departures from Socrates. No doubt, Plato injected, in some way or other, his own thinking into everything he wrote; it is unlikely that a philosopher of his brilliance and originality would ever have been content to be a passive recorder of someone else's words. Even so, it can be helpful to sort his compositions into groups, based on their affinities to or dissimilarities from each other. The ones that have come to be called "Socratic" are relatively short, almost exclusively ethical in focus, exploratory, and simple in structure. They are devoted primarily to the destruction of bad ideas or the demonstration of the limitations of the interlocutors; they contain positive ideas as well, but these ideas are not developed at length, and they are never integrated with metaphysical and epistemological material. That is an apt characterization of such works as the *Laches*, *Charmides*, *Euthyphro*, *Crito*, *Protagoras*, *Hippias Minor*, *Hippias Major*, *Lysis*, and *Gorgias*. In these dialogues, Plato's thinking travels more or less within the confines first mapped by his teacher. Socrates, as Plato presents him in the *Apology*, shows no interest in any topic other than the improvement of human life. He is, at least during his mature years, an ethical philosopher, not a metaphysician, or epistemologist, or scientist. This hypothesis is confirmed by Aristotle: Socrates, he says (*Metaphysics* I.6 987b1–2), concerned himself only with ethics, and did not examine the world of nature.

Many dialogues have a rather different character. They are of greater length, the doctrines they propose or examine are therefore more fully elaborated, and their ethical content (when they have any) is interwoven in complex ways with metaphysical and epistemological material. That is an apt description of the *Phaedo, Cratylus, Republic, Phaedrus, Parmenides, Theaetetus, Sophist, Statesman*, and *Timaeus*. The division of Plato's works into these categories does not demand that we place each dialogue into only one of them. Some – the *Meno* and *Euthydemus*, for example – contain some parts that have the character of Socratic dialogues, and others that make them resemble the second, less Socratic group.

It is likely that most of the Socratic dialogues were written earlier in Plato's career, when the influence of Socrates was strongest; but that leaves open the possibility that he continued to write a few such dialogues at the same time that he was working on his lengthier metaphysical-epistemological-ethical works. He may have regarded some of the Socratic dialogues as excellent ways to prepare his readers for the more complex works he was preparing at the same time. That would explain why some of them – the *Lysis* and *Charmides*, for example – contain material suggestive of ideas more fully worked out in the longer and more complex dialogues.

We are now equipped to return to our main theme. The dictum that no one should lead an unexamined life belongs to the philosophy of the historical Socrates, not that of Plato. We want to know what arguments Socrates gives for that thesis, but we do not find them in Plato's *Apology*. Where then are we to look? The best place, we now see, is among the Socratic dialogues, for here Plato's philosophizing is more Socratic in character – more fully dominated by ethical concerns, less tied to other philosophical projects – than it is elsewhere.

As we will now see, this strategy produces worthwhile results: we do receive, in these dialogues, a deeper understanding of Socrates' reasons for thinking that the ethical discussions he provokes are of the greatest importance. These Socratic works can be read as illustrations of what goes wrong when one does not examine one's life with sufficient care and intelligence.

A Survey of Unexamined Lives

Euthyphro takes himself to be an expert about religious matters. In the dialogue named after him, he is bringing a suit against his own father, whom he takes to be responsible for the death of a man who worked on his family's property. To prosecute one's own father is an extreme measure, and was so regarded by Euthyphro's contemporaries. Euthyphro nonetheless thinks that he has a religious duty to do so. Perhaps he is right about this – but is he in any position to make this decision? Does he have any basis for answering questions about which actions are religious duties?

What Socrates discovers, during the course of his interrogation of Euthyphro, is that he has given no serious thought to this matter, or to any other general questions about the nature of piety. Euthyphro is a clear example of someone who lives an unexamined life (even though he regards himself as an expert on questions of piety), and the dialogue named after him reveals how grave are the consequences of his neglect of philosophical matters. His religious life will almost certainly go badly, unless he has the great fortune to make accurate guesses throughout his life about what his religious duties are. If, as seems plausible, it is impious for him to bring murder charges against his own father in this case, then he is already making a horrible mistake, without recognizing that he is doing so.

One simple lesson that emerges from this dialogue is that lack of attention to philosophical questions about ethics will have disastrous consequences for the quality of the life one is leading. Euthyphro is about to commit a wrong of the worst sort, not because he is selfish, or power-hungry, or greedy, but because he is dim, dull, shallow. Because he has no intellectual curiosity, no interest in reflecting philosophically about ethical questions, he lacks and will never acquire even the beginnings of a systematic and general understanding of the ethical terms he uses. No doubt, he learned from his parents how to use the word *hosiotēs* ("piety") and many other terms that have normative import. But the education one receives in one's childhood takes one only so far; it does not by itself enable one to make good decisions with the normative vocabulary one has acquired.

The Socratic dialogues present another example of a man embarked upon a morally dubious mission: Crito, in the dialogue that bears his name, proposes to free Socrates from prison by bribing his jailors. One of Crito's reasons for offering to help Socrates escape is that he is ashamed of how they will look: many people think that in this situation Socrates' friends should use their resources to help him escape, and if they make no effort to do so, they will all look like cowards (45e–46a). Remarkably, although Crito has been a devoted follower of Socrates for many years, Socrates has not yet been able to free him from his slavish dependency on what others think of him. Socrates has to insist upon a point that he has made to Crito many times: the foremost consideration in any decision must be the justice or injustice of what one does – not the impression one will create in others. One of the lessons of the dialogue is that political decisions – for example, the question whether to accept punishment, even when it is unjust – must be based on a general theory about how a citizen should treat his city. Until one sets aside the influence of popular opinion, and works out a theory of civic duties, one is very likely to go badly astray in political matters. Luckily, Crito happens to have come under the influence of Socrates; on his own, he will be the slave of his desire to present a manly appearance. Euthyphro, by contrast, pays no attention to his public image, and has nothing to guide him but his own unreflective and unreliable sense of confidence about religious matters. Each in his own way lives an unexamined life.

There would be no objection to giving serious consideration to popular opinion about ethical matters, if the populace whose opinions serve as one's guide really had made a thoughtful study of questions of right and wrong, good and bad, justice and injustice (*Crito* 47b). But suppose one does find someone who has undertaken such a study – someone who claims to have thought long and hard about moral matters, and to have become an expert in this area. That is precisely the situation described at the beginning of Plato's *Protagoras*: the famous sophist who gives the dialogue its name has come to Athens, and Hippocrates asks Socrates to accompany him, as he goes to meet the famous visitor and to enroll as his student. Socrates warns him: do not entrust something as precious as your soul to someone who may not be the expert he claims to be (313a–c). Hippocrates feels an urgent need to go beyond the moral education he has received from his parents as a child, and he is right to do so. He hungers for moral knowledge, but in order to acquire it, he must have some basis for deciding whether someone who claims to teach it really has the knowledge he professes to have. What Socrates' conversation with Hippocrates implies is that one must never surrender one's own critical intelligence by putting one's education entirely into the hands of someone else. One should test the claims of those who profess to have moral knowledge, but to do this successfully and reliably, one must educate oneself and decide, by one's own lights, which moral propositions to accept. That leaves open the possibility that some people really are moral experts, and that they can be of great service to others, by discussing moral matters with them. But the possibility that there might be such people does not obviate the need for all of us to live examined lives; unless we do so, we risk putting ourselves in the hands of people who will do us great harm.

Even those who admire and associate with Socrates are not thereby inoculated from going badly astray. Charmides and Critias, who are interrogated by Socrates in the *Charmides*, evidently did not profit from their conversations with him (they were among the despised Thirty Tyrants who ruled Athens from 404 to 403 BCE), nor did Alcibiades, who betrayed Athens in the later years of the Peloponnesian War. (The dialogue named after him, though perhaps not written by Plato, repays careful study; as does the portrait Plato draws of him at *Symposium* 212c–223d.) Alcibiades, as he is depicted in Plato's *Symposium*, confesses that he was always made to feel ashamed of his way of life, when he was in the presence of Socrates (216b–c), but even so, he could not bring himself to take philosophy seriously. Charmides, Critias, and Alcibiades provide further examples of unexamined lives and of the difficulties we can find ourselves in, when we do not devote ourselves to ethical inquiry. If people like Crito and Euthyphro do not become great wrongdoers, as Critias, Charmides, and Alcibiades did, that is through sheer good fortune.

The eponymous interlocutor of Plato's *Ion* provides us with a remarkable example of someone who surrenders his rational faculties and becomes the vessel for the thoughts and emotions of someone else. Ion is a rhapsode – a professional reciter and interpreter of Homer. But he confesses that he does not have knowledge of the subjects that Homer writes about; rather, he says that the thoughts of Homer are breathed into his soul, and through him, into the souls of his listeners. This chain of inspiration, Socrates suggests, begins with the muse who inspires the poet: the writer of verse sets aside his intelligence in order to receive the influence of the god, the rhapsode is in turn inspired by the poetry he reads, and the members of the audience who listen to the recitation of the rhapsode also surrender their minds and become possessed by the beauty of what they hear (533d–35a). To the extent that lovers of poetry lead their lives under its influence, and do not critically examine the ideas it contains, they are (like Hippocrates) handing over their lives to the governance of others. If they are lucky, the opinions of the poets who inspire them are true, and they will have surrendered themselves to a good guide. But that is no way to live one's life.

Plato's *Gorgias* examines another mode of surrendering one's soul uncritically to the influence of others. Success in Athenian political life requires one to do whatever appeals to the crowd (502e, 513b–c): one must seek the approval of large numbers, and one's speeches must be designed to please them. One becomes like a pastry cook who chooses ingredients solely on the basis of the pleasures of the palate but not the health of the eater. Callicles, the last and most audacious of Socrates' three conversational partners, criticizes the two earlier interlocutors, Gorgias and Polus, for having answered Socrates in a way that shows their unwillingness to say something that they would be ashamed of: they don't themselves believe all that they say, but answer in the way that is expected of them (482c–e).

The idea that people have a superficial allegiance to what they say in public – that they present a false self to others in their daily social intercourse – is taken up again in Book II of the *Republic*, when Glaucon claims that most people, when given the chance to make themselves invisible (through possession of the ring of Gyges), would engage in wrongdoing, even though in public they condemn such wrongdoing. In their daily intercourse with others, they hide behind a false self, a mask used as a device for getting what they want. Not only do they fail to ask themselves what they should want – what is worth wanting – but they also give others a false impression of which desires they have and which they lack. They have no true self – a self of one's own devising, developed through critical self-inquiry – and so what is hidden by their social mask is nothing they have made themselves, but a passive imitation of others. That unflattering portrait of the common man derives from Plato's reflections on the difference between living as Socrates lived and living an unexamined life.

There is, however, one passage in the Socratic dialogues that attributes to ordinary people a definite criterion for deciding how to act, one that accords perfectly with their desires. In Plato's *Protagoras*, Socrates holds that most people base their decisions solely on future pleasures and pains (352b–56c). They regard pleasure and pain as the two most powerful forces in human life, and they treat pleasure as the only good thing, pain the only bad thing. Accordingly, when they decline to pursue a pleasure, or willingly accept what is painful, that is only because they make a reasoned calculation that the alternative they choose brings them the greatest amount of pleasure in the future, or the smallest amount of pain. Socrates does not attack this criterion for decision-making in *Protagoras*; all of his efforts, in this dialogue, are devoted to showing that someone who makes decisions in this way should agree that knowledge – that is, knowledge of future pleasures and pains – is the decisive factor in human life, and that we are incapable of choosing a course of action that conflicts with what we know to be best. But it is striking that here Socrates attributes to ordinary people something his interlocutors do not possess: a criterion for making decisions, and one that it is adopted because it is an authentic expression of what one wants.

However, it would be madness to suppose that one's life will go well merely because one has some authentic criterion for decision-making. It has to be the right criterion, and so one must ask oneself what reason there is for thinking that pleasure and pain should play this all-important role in one's life. That is not a question that many ordinary people ask themselves. Their outlook, as Socrates characterizes it, is a kind of emotionalism: they think that knowledge is not an important influence on human life, in comparison with desires, fears, love, pleasure, and pain. That attitude keeps them from reflecting about what their aims should be. Even if knowledge of such matters is possible, they think it would have little influence on their actions. And so they surrender themselves to their desire for pleasure and their aversion to pain. The only kind of practical thinking they think worthwhile is deliberation about how to get the best mix of these goods. Whether there is some better way of making decisions, whether some pleasures have a badness that is not reducible to their effect on future pleasures and pains – these are questions they do not ask. They are therefore taking an enormous risk, like so many of Socrates' interlocutors: if the quantity of pleasure and pain one experiences is not, on its own, an unerring guide to decision-making – if other sorts of things are also good and bad – then most people will fare very poorly.

"Most People Are Other People"

One way to appreciate the force of Socrates' demand that we live examined lives is to consider a similar sentiment found in Oscar Wilde's *De Profundis*: "Most people," he writes, "are other people. Their thoughts are someone else's opinions, their lives a mimicry, their passions a quotation." One might protest, against Wilde: Why should my opinions *not* also be the opinions of others? Is it so terrible if what I believe is also what someone else believes? If the proposition I believe is true, then what objection can be made to my believing it – should I stop doing so, merely because someone else believes the same proposition?

Wilde is getting at something important, but only if we take him to be saying that it is a defect never to form or to abandon a critical intelligence – an ability to evaluate ideas – and merely to accept, unthinkingly, what others say, what they do, the way they feel. It is a grave flaw to want to become like another person, if this is merely an unreflective imitative response, and not accompanied by an evaluation of whether that person is admirable and therefore worthy of imitation. If I love a painting, it should be because I see it with my own eyes and respond to it with genuine emotion, generated from my own appreciation of what is good about it. That others love it should incline me to suppose that there is something there to be appreciated; but if I do not see it and respond to it with my own recognition and emotion, then I am not getting from it what they get (assuming that their reaction to the painting is neither misguided nor inauthentic). The same point applies not only to painting but to the way we react to the ideas that other people have about what is good and bad. If we merely imitate what they think and do, without evaluating them as people and assessing the quality of their ideas we confront the world with minds that are not of our own making. We are, in effect, other people, and have no true self.

Alcibiades says about Socrates: no other human being is or has ever been like him (*Symposium* 221c). But although Socrates' call to the examined life is a rejection of unthinking imitation, it is not a demand that we become unusual, merely for the sake of being unusual. Nor does Socrates hold that acting from motives that are genuinely one's own is the sole criterion by which we should evaluate decisions – although, as we have seen, he does criticize those who act only out of a sense of shame and a fear of looking bad in the eyes of others. The examined life is to be led because there are standards of correct action that we know all too little about; as a result of our ignorance, our lives are not nearly as good as they should be. The correct standards must be discovered through our own efforts, and recognized as correct by our own lights. But if we ever make those discoveries, then, in that respect, we will all be alike.

237

The thesis that we should not live unexamined lives is not meant to stand by itself, as a proposition whose truth shines forth on its own. Rather, it is best seen as resting on a picture of human development and human nature: human beings are naturally attracted to pleasure and averse to pain. They seek power and status, and the wealth that brings power, status, and pleasure. It is no accident that these were the dominant values of Athens (*Apology* 29d–e); they are the dominant values of nearly every human community. Although every child who receives a moral education learns how to communicate with others by using such common normative terms as "good," "just," and "shameful," that education leaves enormous gaps in their moral understanding, and these gaps have to be filled by further inquiry; for the conception they have, as they emerge from childhood, of justice and goodness, is still rudimentary. The limited education they receive has to compete with powerful psychological forces – for pleasure, power, and status – that so often guide human actions. Those who rightly feel the need for further education all too often have no idea how to meet that need: they deliver their minds to people who are impressive in some manifest but superficial way – because of the beauty of their verses, or their great fame and power. Or they simply give in, unreflectively, to psychological forces, and turn their powerful desire for pleasure and aversion to pain into the sole standards of right action.

The great value of an examined life is that it is the only reliable way to root out errors that have taken hold of one's mind because of defects in one's education, and to fill the enormous gaps in one's conception of what is good, just, and fine. Socrates conceives of it as a process that never comes to an end. No matter how much progress one has made in one's moral understanding, there is more to be learned, and so further philosophical discussions of virtue and other normative topics will always be needed. That is a way of thinking about science that has become commonplace. The sciences, as we now think of them, perpetually move from one problem to another, for each solution gives rise to new areas of research. Socrates, we might say, seeks a science of ethics. It is not something that puts an end to all normative questions, by answering them once and for all. No matter how much of it we learn, there will be an ongoing need to learn more, and perhaps even to revise our old ideas in the light of new ones. Those who make progress towards this ever-receding goal achieve a greater intellectual depth, and become less prone to making serious errors about how to live their lives.

Virtue, Knowledge, and Good Will

That is why we should live examined lives. But that is not the only point Socrates insists upon. He says that we should also strive to be good people – to be just, courageous, *sōphrōn* ("restrained," "self-controlled," "moderate," "temperate"), and to possess all of the other virtues. Do these injunctions have anything to do with each other, or are they separate tasks – perhaps even tasks that might interfere with each other? Socrates argues, in the *Protagoras*, that they form a unity; they are all aspects of a single project, and therefore, properly understood, cannot conflict. The unity of the virtues is revealed by the fact that they are all related in various ways to the search for and acquisition of knowledge or wisdom. In order to have any virtue, one has to act well in a certain sphere of human life: to be courageous, for example, one must be able to face what is fearful, and to handle one's fear in the right way. But to do that, one must ask oneself which aspects of one's environment and of human life one should fear. Is death, for example, genuinely bad, and should we fear its approach? That is not a question our childhood moral training by itself equips us to answer. It can be answered only by someone who examines his life and asks which things are genuinely harmful and therefore to be feared. That task, in turn, cannot be successfully pursued unless one has an understanding of what is *good* for human beings; knowledge of what is bad and knowledge of what is good are not two independent studies. So genuine courage (as opposed to a willingness to undertake risks, however foolish) cannot be separated from philosophical inquiry of the sort Socrates undertakes.

The same argument applies to any quality that is a genuine virtue: it must be a good quality for someone to have, and its goodness can be recognized only through ethical inquiry. The virtues are not acquired at an early stage of life, a stage at which we have no genuine understanding of life's proper aims; but much later, when and if we acquire a better understanding of what we should be aiming at, and how to achieve it. That is what Socrates is getting at, when he proposes, in the *Protagoras*, that the virtues are forms of wisdom or knowledge. That does not commit him to the conclusion that someone who has the virtues will feel no emotions. A courageous person will be afraid of what should be feared, and a restrained person will experience pleasures in the appropriate way. But these emotional reactions will flow from their understanding of what should be felt on each occasion. Any childish emotions we have (surely everyone has felt these – and not only in childhood) will have to be eliminated and replaced by justified feelings.

In the *Meno*, Socrates argues in the following way for the thesis that virtue is a form of knowledge (87e–89a). Consider anything that is generally thought to be good, other than virtue: for example, health, or beauty, or strength. These advantages may in fact be good, on balance and over the long run; but certainly there can be occasions when it might, on balance, be disadvantageous to be healthy, or beautiful, or strong. A strong and healthy person, for example, might overestimate his strength and fitness, and take on a task that leads to his death. A boy's good looks might lead others to treat him in a way that harms his intellectual development. Whether these apparent goods really are good depends on how they are used, and knowledge of how to use them well is not a skill that necessarily accompanies them. To know how to use these assets, so that one really benefits from them, is a matter that requires some examination and practice. The same can be said of mental qualities that are generally assets, but which, in certain circumstances, can be disadvantageous. According to Socrates, the factor that makes the difference between a good and a bad use of one's assets is wisdom – the knowledge of how to use these things well. (For a similar argument, see *Euthydemus* 278d–82a.)

His argument resembles one that Kant uses in the opening pages of the *Groundwork of the Metaphysics of Morals*. He begins: "Nothing in the world – indeed nothing even beyond the world – can possibly be conceived which could be called good without qualification except a good will." And he supports this by enumeration: such qualities of mind as intelligence, judgment, and courage, however good they may be on many occasions, will be harmful "if the will, which is to make use of these gifts of nature . . . is

239

not good." So too for the gifts of fortune – power, riches, honor, health, contentment. They make for "pride and arrogance, if there is not a good will to correct their influence on the mind." Kant concludes that nothing but the good will has "intrinsic unconditional worth."[3] There is no time when good willing is inappropriate or harmful.

But Kant's opening remarks, however similar to Socrates' ideas in the *Meno*, do not lead him to the conclusion that it is part of being a good person to engage in ethical inquiry – to participate in conversations every day, as Socrates did, about what virtue is. Kant believes that ordinary moral agents do not need help from philosophy in order to apply normative concepts to particular circumstances; they need only guard against the corruption of their motives by nonmoral incentives. An adult of sound mind will recognize where the path of duty lies. What requires extraordinary effort is not knowing how to behave, but behaving with the proper kind of motivation, for one's willingness to do what one ought must be powerful enough to serve as one's sole motive, and to overcome all competing motives. Perfecting one's soul, for Kant, is a matter of purifying one's heart rather than philosophically training one's mind. Like Socrates, he makes something internal to the soul central to all value – but it is something that involves no sophisticated and abstract reflection. These two philosophers are alike only in their devaluation of what lies outside the soul.

Following Kant's lead, one of the most influential moral philosophers of the twentieth century, W. D. Ross, holds that anyone who possesses an educated person's moral sensibility is capable of putting together a complete list of duties and a complete list of things that are good or bad.[4] The project that requires philosophical skill and care is that of understanding what it is for something to be a duty, or to be good, but this enterprise has nothing to teach ordinary educated adults about how they should lead their lives. What is difficult in practical matters, he thinks, is knowing what to do when duties conflict, or when good and bad things are so closely balanced that no single alternative is clearly superior to any other. What to do, in these situations, depends on the details of each circumstance, and abstract ethical theory can say nothing useful to guide the moral consciousness of ordinary people.

In one respect, utilitarianism – the thesis that our sole duty is to maximize the good – is closer to Socratic philosophy than is Kantianism. For utilitarianism takes a revisionary attitude towards the common-sense moral framework that children learn from their parents and their community. Children are usually not taught to produce as much good as they possibly can. The goals set before them are necessarily far more modest, and often the morality they learn consists in an assortment of rules: do not hit, do not lie, do not take what is not yours, be helpful to your brothers and sisters, respect your elders. The main ideas of utilitarianism – that the well-being of the whole world should be one's focus, and that one should be willing to do harm whenever that produces the greatest balance of good over harm – are ones that most utilitarians have arrived at only by reading philosophy and having conversations with teachers, students, and friends. In order to become a utilitarian, one must go through a period of self-examination: one must ask whether one really thinks that this policy of doing maximal good by doing some harm is an improvement over one that adheres to the far more complex network of rules that are widely accepted. One must also ask oneself the all-important question: what is in fact good?

240

But in another respect, utilitarianism is very far from endorsing Socrates' call to the examined life. For, as we have seen, that injunction is based on the idea that having "discussions every day about virtue" and other such topics is the greatest good for a human being. Socrates thinks that the main subjects of ethical conversation can never be exhausted; the major problems of ethical life can never be solved, once and for all, because every step forward in understanding will bring new questions with it. That is an idea that utilitarians vehemently reject. They think of the utilitarian formula as something that can never be improved upon. Once one has learned what is good, they assume, there is no need to continue thinking about it: one should simply produce as much of it as possible, and that is not a practice that requires or profits from ongoing philosophical inquiry. We may need to confer with each other about what the effect of our actions is likely to be; but we do not need to keep talking about ethics.

The Socratic Character of Ancient Ethics

The major moral philosophers of antiquity side with Socrates about at least this much: they hold that if philosophical ideas – based on systematic and abstract reflection, and advancing beyond the common morality we learn as children – do not, in some way, inform one's thinking, then one is very likely to live very badly, and to do great damage to others. Above all, they think, one must arrive at an understanding, far beyond that of a child, of what is good. That is the principal concept of Greek ethics, and the Socratic dialogues lay the groundwork for its centrality, by showing the impossibility of understanding what virtue is without understanding what is good or bad. (*Laches* and *Charmides* are particularly important to this project.) The highest kind of knowledge, Plato holds in the *Republic*, is knowledge of the Form of the good – and it takes many years of scientific training to acquire it. The student of ethics, Aristotle says, is embarked on the project of trying to become a better person, and in order to do so, he must come to a better understanding of the chief good of human life. Like an archer aiming at a target, he will be better able to hit his mark – living and making choices as he should – after having come to see, through philosophical argument, what his mark really is (*Nicomachean Ethics* I.2). The Epicureans identify the good with something obvious and universally acceptable: pleasure; but they hold that pleasures differ enormously in kind and value, and that only philosophical reflection can establish which kinds are best for us to pursue. The Stoics hold that only an appreciation for the teleological structure of the universe can help us rid ourselves of the childish emotions that undermine our well-being. Pyrrhonian Skeptics are uniquely Socratic: they pride themselves on being the only philosophical school that continues to engage in ongoing intellectual inquiry, after the fashion of Socrates, and eschewing all settled opinions.

For all of these thinkers and schools of antiquity, it is only systematic and abstract thinking that can reveal what is central to the proper conduct of our lives. If we make our decisions only with the aid of the ready-to-hand materials that are available, without reflection, to any adult, we will go badly astray. These followers of Socrates believe that we must adopt one or other of these two courses: we must (as Plato says) leave it

241

to a small number of experts to refine and systematize our normative vocabulary, and devise ways by which their theories will seep into the moral consciousness of ordinary people; or (as Socrates himself says) we must each go through this process, as best we can, on our own. One way or the other, we will err in the application of normative terms to our daily decisions, unless those terms are shaped by conscious reflection on their proper use – that is, by philosophical theory.

Notes

1   Quoted from Turner (1981: 265).
2   See for example Vlastos (1991) and Penner (1992).
3   Quoted from the translation of Lewis White Beck (1959).
4   See Ross (1930: esp. p. 40).

References

Jaspers, K. (1962). *Socrates, Buddha, Confucius, Jesus: The Paradigmatic Individuals*. New York: Harcourt, Brace & World.

Kant, I. (1959). *Foundations of the Metaphysics of Morals*. Trans. with an introduction by Lewis White Beck. Indianapolis: Library of Liberal Arts.

Penner, T. (1992). Socrates and the early dialogues. In R. Kraut (ed.), *The Cambridge Companion to Plato*. Cambridge: Cambridge University Press.

Ross, W. D. (1930). *The Right and the Good*. Oxford: Clarendon Press.

Turner, Frank M. (1981). *The Greek Heritage in Victorian Britain*. New Haven: Yale University Press.

Vlastos, G. (1991). *Socrates: Ironist and Moral Philosopher*. Cambridge: Cambridge University Press.

Wilde, O. (1905). *De Profundis*. London: Methuen.

Suggestions for Further Reading

Brickhouse, T. C. and Smith, N. D. (1994). *Plato's Socrates*. New York: Oxford University Press.

—— (2000). *The Philosophy of Socrates*. Boulder, CO: Westview Press.

Guthrie, W. K. C. (1969). *A History of Greek Philosophy*. Vol. 3. Cambridge: Cambridge University Press.

Irwin, T. (1995). *Plato's Ethics*. New York: Oxford University Press.

Kahn, C. H. (1996). *Plato and the Socratic Dialogue: The Philosophical Use of a Literary Form*. Cambridge: Cambridge University Press.

Reeve. C. D. C. (1989). *Socrates in the Apology*. Indianapolis: Hackett.

Santas, G. X. (1979). *Socrates: Philosophy in Plato's Early Dialogues*. London: Routledge & Kegan Paul.

Taylor, C. C. W. (1998). *Socrates*. Oxford: Oxford University Press.

15

Socrates: Seeker or Preacher?

ROSLYN WEISS

The first thing that is likely to come to mind when one considers the nature of Socratic moral inquiry in Plato's dialogues is the seemingly ubiquitous "What is *x*?" question. Aristotle, in the *Metaphysics*, affirms the centrality of this question for Socrates: "Socrates made the moral virtues his business (*tas ēthikas aretas pragmateuomenou*), and was the first to seek to define them [each] as a whole (*katholou*) . . . he reasonably sought what it is (*to ti esti*)" (*Metaphysics* XIII.iv.1078b17–30). Socrates typically proposes that the "What is *x*?" question be investigated together by him and his interlocutor and even asks, not infrequently, that the interlocutor enlighten him with respect to it. It is indeed this question in its various permutations that launches the conversation in many of the dialogues: "What is holiness?" in the *Euthyphro*; "What is temperance?" in the *Charmides*; "What is friendship?" in the *Lysis*; "What is courage?" in the *Laches*; "What is rhetoric?" in the *Gorgias*; "What is virtue?" in the *Meno*; "What is beauty?" in the *Greater Hippias*; "What is justice?" in *Republic* I. Moreover, the question's weight and importance are amplified by the frequently expressed Socratic insistence that one cannot know anything *about* the *x* in question (or in some cases that one cannot recognize instances of the *x* in question) until one has an adequate definition of it – an insistence that has come to be known as the "Priority of Definition principle."[1] Surely it is in the "What is *x*?" question, if anywhere, that Socratic moral inquiry is to be found.

Remarkably, however, nowhere in the *Apology* does Socrates make reference to an interest in definitional questions or include "inquiring together" among his activities. Moreover, there is no trace in the *Apology* of the Priority of Definition principle. Yet, if Socratic moral inquiry is to be understood as joint searches for answers to "What is *x*?" questions, is it not odd that the *Apology* makes no mention of them? After all, what Plato gives his readers in the *Apology* is a glimpse into Socrates' *self*-understanding, that is, into Socrates' own understanding both of himself and of his mission. In this way, Plato equips his readers with the lens through which he would have them view the Socrates of the other dialogues and the Socratic practice of philosophy depicted in them. Without the *Apology* Plato's readers would have scant hope of understanding just what it is that Socrates is doing in the other dialogues. If the *Apology*, then, does not accord the "What is *x*?" question a position of prominence, is this not a reason to doubt its centrality to the Socratic philosophic project? Indeed, insofar as the *Apology*

243

constitutes Socrates' defense of himself against charges that could well result in his execution, what possible explanation could there be for Socrates' failure to cast his philosophic activity in a positive light – to characterize it as joint inquiry with others into moral truth and as a way of learning from others and together with them – other than that this is not what he actually does?

Moral Inquiry and Ignorance in the *Apology*

The Socrates depicted in the *Apology* is, alas, not a man whose aim is to attain wisdom either from others or with them. He is not engaged in the theoretical pursuit of definition, nor does he insist that one cannot know anything about justice, for example, or recognize instances of it, until one has arrived at a perfectly adequate definition of it. Instead, the Socrates of the *Apology* directs all of his activities *at* people and their views. He is a man with rather specific and pressing practical goals: to change what people care about, to get them to recognize their ignorance concerning the most important things (*ta megista*, *Apology* 22d7), that is, concerning moral matters,[2] and to encourage them to live both the just and the examined life. Indeed, Socrates famously maintains that "the unexamined life is not worth living (*biōtos*) for a human being" (*Apology* 38a5–6).

Socrates' confidence concerning the decisive value of the examined life for human beings derives from his conception of what it is to be human. In the *Apology* Socrates identifies ignorance of *ta megista* as a (or perhaps even as *the*) critical feature of human nature. Of his own ignorance Socrates is well aware (*Apology* 21b); of the ignorance at the heart of the human condition he quickly becomes aware. He comes to interpret the Oracle's proclamation that no one is wiser than he as a revelation of universal human ignorance with respect to what matters. "That one of you, O human beings, is wisest," Socrates takes the Oracle to be asserting, "who, *like* Socrates, has become cognizant that in truth he is worth nothing with respect to wisdom" (*Apology* 23b). Indeed this point is given even further explication at *Lysis* 218a, where the philosopher is someone who *has* ignorance but nevertheless is not actually ignorant, that is, he has not become his ignorance. What distinguishes the person who has ignorance but is not quite ignorant from the person who *is* ignorant is that the former, but not the latter, is still able to see his own ignorance. Those whose ignorance has, as it were, seeped into their very identity are blind to their own ignorance and hence egregiously stupid and wicked. Thus according to the Oracle as Socrates understands it, its message is not that Socrates *happens* to be wisest (such that at least theoretically someone else might be found who is wiser still), but rather that he (or his name) serves only as a pattern or paradigm (*paradeigma*) for the very height of human wisdom, the wisdom that recognizes its radical deficiency.

Socrates does not and cannot, then, believe that any merely human human being will be wise with a wisdom greater than his. No merely human human being will know anything of importance; the very best among them will know that they don't know. Sophists, therefore, who think they can "educate human beings" and make them noble and good are woefully mistaken.[3] And since, generally speaking, it is those who have the biggest reputations for wisdom who prove to be the most sorely lacking (*Apology* 22a), what better way can Socrates serve the god than by showing those who seem wise to themselves and to others, but not to him, that they are indeed not wise (*Apology* 23b)?

Exhortation, Refutation, and Examination

According to Socrates' account in the *Apology* of his divine mission, it comprises what appear to be three distinct practices: (1) exhortation, (2) refutation, and (3) examination. Let us consider the nature of each of these activities individually, in turn, and then see how they are related to each other and to the activity Socrates in the *Apology* calls "philosophizing."

Exhortation

Socrates is, by his own admission, a preacher. Daily he exhorts (*parakeleuesthai* – *Apology* 29d5) others to abandon the pursuit of power, prestige, and wealth, and to make the turn to virtue. (See also 36c.) He nags and annoys, relentlessly urging those who indulge in these worthless pursuits to mend their ways. He is nothing short of a divinely dispatched pest, who, as he describes it, "does not stop settling down everywhere upon you the whole day" (31a1).[4]

Among the terms that Socrates uses in connection with his activity of exhortation are "persuade" (*peithō*), "reproach" (*oneidizē*), and "counsel" (*sumbouleuō*). He goes around, he says, doing nothing but "persuading" young and old not to care for body and money but for the best condition of the soul (30a–b). He engages in the business of others, privately, as a father or older brother might, "persuading" them to care for virtue (31b). He "persuades" each person to put care for himself before care for his things (36c). Socrates will "reproach" anyone who claims to care for virtue but does not really possess it – whether young or old, foreigner or townsman – admonishing him for regarding the things worth the most as least important and the paltrier things as more important (30a). He "persuades" and "reproaches" each Athenian, "settling down everywhere upon you the whole day" (30e–31a). And he assures his condemners that they are quite mistaken if they think that by killing him they will prevent someone else from "reproaching" them (39d). He also asks that his condemners "reproach" his sons after his death if they do not care about the things they should and if they suppose they are worth more than they are (41e). He "counsels" these things in private but he offers no public counsel (31c), and declares that if he has "counseled" badly and thereby corrupted any young people, they themselves should have come forward to accuse him when they got older (33d).

Central to the activities of exhortation, persuasion, reproaching, and offering counsel is the matter of what people care about. When Socrates exhorts, persuades, reproaches, or counsels what he asks of people is that they care rightly, that they get their priorities straight and, in particular, that they reorder their current *mis*guided cares and priorities.

245

Refutation

Socrates speaks several times in the *Apology* of his practice of *elenchein* (see 23a5, 29e5, 39d1), a method of testing that involves cross-examination or refutation. In his attempt to disabuse pretenders to knowledge or pretenders to virtue of their illegitimate confidence in their own wisdom, and thereby to clear away one obstacle to the pursuit of genuine wisdom, Socrates subjects such self-styled "experts" to elenchus. Swiftly and surely he reduces his interlocutors to *aporia*, the inevitable perplexity and inconclusiveness that result when an unreflective individual is challenged by a skilled questioner.

Elenchus is not, however, a direct method for discovering truth. Socrates' own moral views do not seem to arise out of elenchus; the proof of their truth resides, if anywhere, in the failure of his opponents' views to survive the elenchus, or in the invariably ridiculous showing made by them in elenctic exchanges with him (*Gorgias* 509a).[5] Indeed, strictly speaking, not only is no opinion proved true by way of elenchus, but no opinion is proved false, either. What happens in elenctic exchange is that the interlocutor's asserted view generates a contradiction when either it itself or propositions it logically entails are taken in conjunction with other propositions to which Socrates secures the interlocutor's assent. It is only when the propositions to which the interlocutor agrees and which yield the contradiction of his original view are, as a matter of fact, true, however, that the interlocutor's view will have been proved to be, as a matter of fact, false. Although elenchus does not, then, refute the interlocutor's view except in this provisional way, that is, contingent upon the truth of the propositions to which he consents, nevertheless there is a sense in which the interlocutor is himself always refuted in elenchus: insofar as he is shown to be unable to sustain his view without contradiction, he forfeits his warrant to hold it.

For the sake of shaming the shameless among his interlocutors and of deflating their bloated self-images, Socrates will use against them any premises that they will accept and any argument – sound or not, valid or not – that will persuade them. He need not endorse the premises of his own arguments nor does he feel constrained to construct only arguments that are logically impeccable. We note that in distancing himself from the Sophists in the *Apology* Socrates never denies that he makes the weaker argument the stronger – even though that accusation figures prominently in the old charges against him as he conceives them (18b–c). He denies only that he teaches professionally, that is, that he takes money for whatever it is that he does (19d–e).

Examination

Socrates most often describes his philosophic activity as examining (*exetazein*) himself and others. The life devoid of this sort of critical reflection, "the unexamined life" (*ho anexetastos bios*), is, as he declares, an unlivable one. It seems that this activity is equivalent for Socrates to philosophy itself. He rejects the disparaging sense that his first set of accusers attach to "philosophizing" – the sense in which what it involves is investigating "the things aloft and under the earth" and "not believing in gods" and "making the weaker argument the stronger" (23d) – and puts in its place a philosophizing that entails "examining myself and others" (28d).

246

What is the relationship among exhortation, refutation, and examination? If examination is, at it seems to be, synonymous with philosophizing, and if philosophizing as the way of life to which Socrates is committed encompasses the practices of exhortation and refutation, it would seem that both exhortation and refutation should be in some way forms of examination. Indeed, we find refutation linked to examination, and exhortation linked directly to "philosophizing." At *Apology* 22e–23a, Socrates speaks of the "examination" from which he has incurred many hatreds, and then glosses that "examination" as "refuting someone else." And again at 29e4–5 he declares that if someone claims to care for virtue he will not let him go but will "examine him and refute him" (29e4–5). At 29d4–5 he says that he will not stop "philosophizing and exhorting you." (I take the *kai* here to be epexegetical.)

Although these linkages between examination and refutation and between exhortation and philosophizing tend to diminish the distinctiveness of these practices, nevertheless, the differences among them are hardly negligible. Exhortation, as we have seen, is an activity in which Socrates addresses people directly and reproaches them concerning what they care about or advises them on what they ought to care about. Here is an example of Socratic exhortation (29d7–e3):

> Best of men, you are an Athenian, from the city that is greatest and best reputed for wisdom and strength: are you not ashamed that you care for having as much money as possible, and reputation, and honor, and that you neither care for nor give thought to prudence, and truth, and how your soul will be the best possible?

Here is another (30b2–4):

> Not from money does virtue come, but from virtue do money and all the other good things become good for human beings, both privately and publicly.[6]

In neither of these instances is there anything remotely resembling refutation. For one thing, whereas refutation proceeds by question-and-answer, exhortation is just a harangue. For another, exhortation is not exercised upon one's views but upon one's allegiances. Nor does preaching seem to qualify as any kind of examination or philosophizing. Yet, Socrates seems to so regard it.

And what about refutation? Is refutation so clearly a kind of examination or philosophizing? Examination, we recall, has two dimensions: it encompasses not only examination of others but also examination of oneself. Refutation, by contrast, seems to have but one: although it can unproblematically be assimilated to examination as directed against others, how can it be practiced on oneself? Yet Socrates twice pairs refutation with examination.

Since it is undeniable that Socrates regards both exhortation and refutation as examination or philosophizing, is it possible, perhaps, that despite their differences these enterprises are closer to one another than they appear? Yet how can preaching and *self*-examination be associated with refutation?

One interesting fact to bear in mind as we consider the possibility that preaching and even self-examination might turn out to be in some way closely related to refutation is that there are no instances of direct exhortation in any of Plato's dialogues

247

outside the *Apology*, nor is there anywhere in Plato anything that obviously qualifies as Socrates' examination of himself. With respect to exhortation, what we see in the other dialogues is Socrates asking questions; we never see him preaching. Whatever admonishment he gives his interlocutors, whatever moral lessons he would have them learn, he transmits indirectly through raising doubts about their views. Indeed, even when he sermonizes, his sermons are summaries of conclusions that emerged from elenctic exchange (see, e.g. *Gorgias* 478e–479e; 506c–509c), conclusions that always remain open to question (see, e.g. *Gorgias* 480e; 509a–c). And with respect to self-examination, what we never witness in the other dialogues is Socrates or anyone else subjecting Socrates' beliefs to scrutiny. The activity we do see depicted in the dialogues is Socrates' refutation – of others. Are we to assume, then, that the practices of exhortation and self-examination are things that Plato wants his readers to know that Socrates engages in (and therefore tells us about in the *Apology*) but then for some reason simply chooses not to depict him thusly in the dialogues, or are we to think that they are somehow embedded in the activity of refutation that Plato does show us?

Let us see first how the gap between self-examination and refutation might be narrowed. Examination, like refutation, is an activity performed on someone. The term derives its broader philosophical sense from a more-narrow military one. Used rarely in Plato, its source lies in fifth- and fourth-century military activity and service, specifically in the notion of the review, examination, or mustering of troops.[7] By examining others what Socrates does is hold them up to scrutiny. And the way he does this is by elenchus.

Elenchus, then, targets others. It is not a method that operates on oneself. Nevertheless, self-examination is parasitic upon elenchus, upon elenchus as practiced on others. In investigating the views of others (e.g. Polus's view in the *Gorgias* that suffering injustice is worse than doing it), Socrates' own opinions (e.g. his view that doing injustice is worse than suffering it) are strengthened (though, theoretically at least, they might have been weakened). What Socrates finds as a result of testing others is that his own opinions are the ones that remain standing. Even Socrates' assertions that his opinions wander (*Euthyphro* 11b) or that he "cannot agree with myself" and is "always changing my opinion" (*Lesser Hippias* 37b–c) or that he is "absurd" (*Protagoras* 361a) are not, contra Kraut (1984: 287 n. 64), truly admissions of perplexity: they are, instead, a description of what happens to Socrates' opinions in *elenchoi* that proceed from premises that his interlocutors – but not he – endorse. Indeed, Socrates makes it unquestionably clear in the *Crito* at 49a–d and in the *Gorgias* at 482a–b that his own beliefs do not shift. Hence, by means of elenctic exchange, unlike the opposing views that are embraced by Socrates' interlocutors, his own views appear *less* absurd after examination than before (*Gorgias* 509a). It is even likely that as a result of the frequent testing of others Socrates thinks himself justified in regarding his beliefs as true: indeed, at *Gorgias* 472b, he chides Polus for trying to "banish me from my property, the truth." Self-examination, then, is not a separate process from refutation. It is its byproduct.

Let us consider now how exhortation might be connected to refutation. As we have seen, the two practices seem not at all alike. Nevertheless, perhaps what we are meant to infer from the total absence of instances of exhortation in all dialogues except the *Apology* is that the didactic dressings-down of people that are recounted in the *Apology* are not to be taken as literal representations of what Socrates did. They are to be taken instead as explicit articulations of the messages implicit in Socratic refutation. If the diatribes that Socrates describes in the *Apology* are just the moral lessons that he means for his interlocutors to derive from his refutation of them, then exhortations and reprimands would count as examination and philosophy. As long as the messages are not delivered explicitly but are left to be inferred by the interlocutor from dialogical exchanges, as long as they are posed as questions and presented as something to think about, there is no need to set them apart from "philosophizing." Rather than suppose, then, that Socrates actually says to some hapless Athenian whom he corners, "Are you not ashamed that you care for having as much money as possible, and reputation, and honor, and that you neither care for nor give thought to prudence, and truth, and how your soul will be the best possible?," we should understand that this is the sort of reproach that is *implicit* in the elenctic exchange Socrates might have had with him. Moreover, it should be noted that Socrates explicit exhortations in the *Apology* do nothing to undermine this point: since Socrates is facing a corruption charge it stands to reason that at his trial he would spell out his moral messages even if in his daily practice he expects them to be inferred. In his daily practice, though not at his trial, his purpose is to urge his interlocutors to think.

If this is right, then Socrates engages in just one activity: refutation. It is refutation that Socrates regards as his divine mission. Through refutation Socrates exhorts his interlocutors; through refutation he examines not only their views but his own. With respect to his interlocutors, Socrates engages in refutation in order to win them over to the life of virtue and philosophy. It is refutation with which he fights for their souls. He challenges those who are either complacent or overconfident in their moral beliefs and attempts to discredit the views of those who would champion injustice. The *Apology* compares him to a gadfly (30a). And it uses military metaphors to characterize his activities: he remains at the post at which the god stationed him, risking his life in the examination of himself and others (28d–29a); furthermore, he "fights for the just" (32a1). Military metaphors appear in other dialogues as well: Socrates "will fight all-out, in word and deed," for the worth of searching for what is not yet known (*Meno* 86b–c); he "rallies the retreating and defeated [troops]" to combat misology (*Phaedo* 89a) and "fights back" to defeat the argument of Simmias and Cebes (89c); he believes that "we all must be lovers of victory in regard to knowing what is true and what is false as regards the things we are talking about" (*Gorgias* 505c).[8] If Socrates is a fighter, then refutation is his weapon. Elenchus is Socrates' way of combating his interlocutors' arrogance, wickedness, and foolishness.[9] Indeed, it is a weapon with many uses: it (1) lays bare not only their beliefs but also their souls; (2) exposes their ignorance; (3) shatters their views; and (4) shames them. It is because refutation bestows all these benefits that Socrates regards what he does as the greatest benefaction (*tōn megistōn euergesian*, *Apology* 36c4).[10] It may also be interesting to note that these are the very benefits that Socrates would have his condemners bestow on his own children if they grow up with their priorities askew and if their reputations outstrip their worth: "when my sons grow up, punish them, men, and pain them in the very same way I pained you, if they seem to you to care for money or anything else before virtue. And if they are reputed to be something when they are nothing, reproach them just as I did you: tell them that they do not care for the things they should, and that they suppose they are something when they are worth nothing. And if you do these things, we will have been treated justly by you, both I myself and my sons" (41e–42a). For Socrates to do justice is to confer benefit as to do injustice is to confer harm.

With respect to himself, Socrates engages in refutation for entirely different reasons. For, unlike his interlocutors, Socrates is already aware that he is ignorant and so is not in need of having his ignorance exposed. He also knows himself and what he believes and so does not need to have his own self and his own beliefs uncovered. His views are good and noble ones, so he has no need to be refuted or shamed.

How Socrates has reached his good and noble beliefs is, unfortunately, hidden from view. Plato, it seems, would have us assume that Socrates' beliefs were largely already formed and were already the subject of admiration at least by some (by Chaerephon at least) before Chaerephon's visit to the Oracle, that is, before Socrates took up his divine mission. But regardless of how his beliefs were acquired they are *secured* through his refutations of others. Although philosophy as we see Socrates practice it in the dialogues is, for the most part, something he practices on others and for the benefit of others, nevertheless, as Socrates suggests in the *Protagoras* (331c, 333c), it is in examining others that he examines himself. Refutation is the practice through which Socrates confirms for himself the superiority and truth of his own views.

Socratic elenctic exchanges are not, then, occasions of moral *discovery* for Socrates.[11] He brings to these conversations a set of beliefs to which he is firmly committed.[12] That is not to say that under no circumstances would he change his mind: after all, he knows he doesn't have wisdom about *ta megista*.[13] But it *is* to say that the circumstances under which he would change his mind would be rare indeed. For a person who has, as Socrates has, identified the most basic truths – such as that the soul is more important than the body and that really living well is better than merely seeming to – and who has then diligently sought to keep his other beliefs consistent with these, it is hardly likely that he will easily renounce his hard-won beliefs. Because he has made the effort to get to the fundamental truths and to keep his beliefs consistent with them, his beliefs are not likely to run away like the untethered statues of Daedalus (see *Meno* 97e) at the first sign of a contrary point of view.[14] Moreover, by not taking money from anyone and by staying out of politics, Socrates buys himself the luxury of having to please no one: unlike the orator whose views must shift with the shifting winds of public opinion (*Gorgias* 490e10–11) or with the whims of the tyrant in power (510a), Socrates is beholden to no one. And, most importantly, Socrates has a well-ordered soul. He is thus less vulnerable to those other persistent threats to the stability of one's moral beliefs: emotion and appetite. What is there that could tempt Socrates to relinquish his steadfast commitment to justice? Why, not even the threat of death itself.

Inquiry – Not Teaching

Despite refutation's versatility it does not count for Socrates as teaching. To be a teacher one must be an expert, an *epistēmōn*, concerning human and political virtue. Yet it is precisely this that no one can be. The height of human wisdom is, as we saw, the recognition of one's ignorance with respect to *ta megista*.

Yet, why is human wisdom with respect to *ta megista* limited in this way? Why can there not be a trainer of human beings who can make human beings noble and good in human virtue like the *Apology*'s trainers of foals and calves can make foals and calves noble and good in foal-and-calf virtue (20a–b)? Why can there not be a reliable dispenser of advice on matters of right and wrong "before whom we must be ashamed and whom we must fear more than all others" (*Crito* 47d)?

One reason is, as the foal-and-calf analogy suggests, that an expert on human virtue would have to stand to human beings as a trainer of foals and calves stands to foals and calves. In other words, what would be required for the comparable training of human beings is a *god's*-eye perspective. Yet in order for a human being to have such a perspective would he not have to be a god – or like one? A doctor treats our bodies, but who but a god can prescribe for our souls?

Second, in almost all other human enterprises but the moral one, there is in principle a final and decisive way to arrive at solutions and to recognize success: there are tests, standards. Yet in moral matters, there are no such tests or standards. As Socrates points out in the *Euthyphro* (7b–c), if the gods dispute about number, weight, or measure, they will not dispute for long. But if they dispute for long, it will be because their dispute is about moral matters: right and wrong, good and bad, noble and base. There is in moral matters no counting, no scale, no yardstick. Without any fairly clear-cut way to measure, there can be no knowledge. And where there is no knowledge there can be no teachers. We do, to be sure, have reason to guide us; but, in moral matters, the premises upon which reason operates are just people's opinions. Reason can deliver coherence, but can it guarantee the truth of our premises?

In the absence of moral instruction, the best we can do is talk – to each other. The kind of philosophy that Socrates recommends is lateral – not hierarchical. We examine each other and ourselves. We test opinions against other opinions. In the process, it is hoped, some opinions will emerge as better and others as worse, some sets of beliefs as more coherent and others as less so.

If Socrates recommends the *life* of examination of oneself and others as best, that can only be because moral inquiry is a life-long enterprise. Indeed, an enterprise that does not culminate in knowledge is an enterprise that cannot ever end. Elenchus provides no tether strong enough to secure moral beliefs permanently. One can never be certain that tomorrow will not bring a new and devastatingly powerful argument that will cast doubt on an opinion held today. In life, and even in death (see *Apology* 40e–41c), the best a human being can do is to keep challenging and testing his own views in light of others.

Even though moral knowledge will not be attained, the love of wisdom remains the driving force behind moral inquiry. There are many things that we will never know – the nature of the gods, what happens after death, what the soul is and whether it survives our death – but these are all, like the matter of what the best life is for a human being, things that the more philosophical among us nevertheless deeply desire to know, yearn to know, and *strive* to know. These are things that we make every effort to be right about, things that, if we think hard enough, we might actually *be* right about. It is not impossible that we will attain truth. But even if we do, we will never know.

The "What is *x?*" Question

Let us return at long last to the "What is *x?*" question. If the Socrates of the *Apology* has no interest in definitions of moral (or other) terms but engages primarily in refutation, why, then, we may ask, is the Socrates of the other dialogues fairly obsessed with them? The solution to this puzzle lies in the essentially instrumental nature of the "What is *x?*" question. For Socrates, definition is not an end in itself. Like so much else that Socrates does in conversation with his interlocutors, the "What is *x?*" question is tactical, strategic. It quite effectively loosens the tongues of Socrates' interlocutors. They do not feel threatened, at least initially, by the seemingly innocuous definitional questions that Socrates poses. The "What is *x?*" question encourages them to venture answers that reveal much about themselves: not only about what they believe, but about how conventional or radical they are, how cautious or bold, how diffident or pompous, how well- or ill-intentioned. Most often what they reveal is their ineptitude and the shallowness of their thinking. It is the "What is *x?*" question through which Socrates is able, in accordance with the god, to demonstrate that the interlocutor doesn't know and doesn't care. Young or old, cooperative or resistant, there is scarcely an interlocutor in the bunch who deeply cares about *ta megista*. They may care about being great but for the most part they don't seem to care about being good. And yet, as Euben (1990: 206) puts it, for Socrates, "being great becomes being good, courage becomes the willingness to suffer injustice rather than commit it, and the purpose of life is not to conquer Syracuse, avenge one's friends, build an empire, or leave monuments behind but to conquer tyrannical impulses [and] harm no one."

Of course, the "What is *x?*" question does more than merely expose Socrates' interlocutors as people who don't know and don't care. The "What is *x?*" question affords Socrates the opportunity to suggest alternatives to his interlocutor's answers. It provides a way for Socrates to introduce new ways of thinking about things. For although Socrates surely wants to get his interlocutors to think, that is not all he wants. Like a preacher, Socrates wants to get them to think rightly. It is not enough for him that Euthyphro think about holiness; it is imperative that he think about it differently from how he had been thinking about it, that he improve his thinking about it. It is not enough that Polus think about whether power is really the greatest thing; he needs to think that it isn't. At the core of Socratic moral inquiry, then, is Socrates' attempt to get his interlocutors to think as he does. What makes what he does philosophy is that he attempts to do so by asking questions and presenting arguments. As he says: "this even happens to be the greatest good for a human being – to construct arguments (*tous logous poieisthai*) every day about virtue and the other things about which you hear me conversing and examining both myself and others" (*Apology* 38a2–5).

Notes

1 See *Euthyphro* 7b–e; *Laches* 190d; *Greater Hippias* 26c; *Gorgias* 448e, 463c; *Meno* 71b; *Republic* 1.354b–c. For scholarly discussion of this principle, see e.g. Santas (1972); Beversluis (1974); Nehamas (1975); Burnyeat (1977); Irwin (1977); Vlastos (1985); Benson (1990).

2   Cf. *Gorgias* 527e1–3, where the expression, "the most important things," *tōn megistōn*, refers to the question of which way of life is the best one, *ho tropos aristos tou biou*.

3   See *Apology* 20b9–c1.

4   Translations from the *Apology* rely heavily on West and West (1984), but are frequently modified.

5   See Kahn (1992: 246–8).

6   In this translation I follow Burnet (1924: 124). See also Burnyeat (2003).

7   See Burnet's note (1924: 96) on *Apology* 22e6. Also see Goldman (2004: 3).

8   The same idea is expressed in *Laws* 5.731a by the Athenian stranger: "Let all of us be lovers of victory when it comes to virtue, but without envy."

9   See *Protagoras* 333c.

10 See *Gorgias* 506c1–3.

11 See Polansky (1985: 257 n. 15): "The early dialogues seem to show us a Socrates confirming his moral doctrines to others rather than developing his moral doctrines for himself."

12 See *Republic* 1.337e.

13 That there is a difference between belief, even when true, and even when held with great confidence, on the one hand, and knowledge, on the other, is one of the very few things Socrates would claim to know (*Meno* 98b3–5).

14 See *Meno* 97d–e.

References

Benson, H. H. (1990). The priority of definition and the Socratic elenchus. *Oxford Studies in Ancient Philosophy*, 8, 10–65.

Beversluis, J. (1974). Socratic definition. *American Philosophical Quarterly*, 11, 331–6.

Bloom, A. (trans.) (1968). *The Republic of Plato*. NY: Basic Books.

Blundell, M. W. (1992). Character and meaning in Plato's *Hippias Minor*. *Oxford Studies in Ancient Philosophy*, suppl. vol., 131–72.

Burnet, J. (ed.) (1924). *Plato: Euthyphro, Apology, Crito*. Oxford: Clarendon Press.

Burnyeat, M. F. (1977). Examples in epistemology: Socrates, Theaetetus, and G. E. Moore. *Philosophy*, 52, 381–98.

—— (2003). *Apology* 30B 2–4: Socrates, money, and the grammar of *gignesthai*. *Journal of Hellenic Studies*, 23, 1–25.

Euben, P. (1990). *The Tragedy of Political Theory: The Road not Taken*. Princeton: Princeton University Press.

Goldman, H. (2004). Reexamining the "examined life" in Plato's *Apology of Socrates*. *The Philosophical Forum*, 35, 1–33.

Irwin, T. (1977). *Plato's Moral Theory*. Oxford: Clarendon Press.

Kahn, C. (1992). Vlastos's Socrates. *Phronesis*, 37, 233–58.

Kraut, R. (1984). *Socrates and the State*. Princeton: Princeton University Press.

Nehamas, A. (1975). Confusing universals and particulars in Plato's dialogues. *Review of Metaphysics*, 26, 287–306.

Polansky, R. M. (1985). Professor Vlastos's analysis of Socratic elenchus. *Oxford Studies in Ancient Philosophy*, 3, 247–59.

Santas, G. (1972). The Socratic fallacy. *Journal of the History of Philosophy*, 10, 124–41.

Vlastos, G. (1983). The Socratic elenchus. *Oxford Studies in Ancient Philosophy*, 1, 27–58.

—— (1985). Socrates' disavowal of knowledge. *Philosophical Quarterly*, 35, 1–31.

West, T. G. and West, G. S. (trans.) (1984). *Four Texts on Socrates: Plato's "Euthypro," "Apology," and "Crito" and Aristophanes' "Clouds."* Ithaca, NY: Cornell University Press.

16

Socratic Method and Socratic Truth

HAROLD TARRANT

Introduction

Readers of the early dialogues of Plato may soon feel that his Socrates[1] proceeds methodically towards the ultimate embarrassment of his verbal wrestling-partners. Several recurrent tactics are easily identified, giving credence to claims that Socrates has a method.[2] As Aristotle saw, he demanded universal definitions and he employed *epagōgē*.[3] He elicited from an interlocutor whose belief he would question certain other beliefs, seemingly more fundamental, entailing the contradiction of the original belief.[4] He flattered, hassled, cajoled, and criticized. He employed his own recurrent themes, presented in a positive light, so as to undermine others. More fundamentally, he pursued philosophy neither in solitary meditation, nor out among the masses, but on a one-to-one basis,[5] following an argument through with one individual at a time, as if the nature of philosophy demanded that it be practiced dialogically.

These recurrent features suggest that Socrates had methods, and most assume that one core methodical activity can properly he called *elenchos*.[6] But then there is considerable confusion as to what this *elenchos* is for, though methods should relate directly to goals. Some forget to ask what Socrates' method is for early enough.[7] To be preoccupied with discovering method, and ask its purpose as an afterthought, lulls us into assuming that Socrates has the same goals as a modern moral philosopher. Though both aim to offer a critique of rival theories and to advance human understanding, nevertheless Socrates' own prescientific age used concepts of knowledge, truth, and error that differed from ours. Hence one of the most persistent problems of Socratic studies is whether Plato's Socrates has methods for discovering some truth, or only for refuting an opponent. In the latter case, can a single thesis finally be revealed as false, or does Socrates merely establish that one out of many theses is wrong? For showing that it is not the case that (P and Q and R) is scarcely as significant as showing ~P. So what, if anything, does Socrates' method discover?

One response is to suggest that, as Socrates' method is so intensely *personal*,[8] it makes little sense that the primary aim is to establish by argument any particular proposition P, or its negation. Indeed Walsdorf (2003: 295) has recently claimed that Socrates "does not understand what makes ethical propositions true." Might the personal method mean that Socrates is concerned simply to improve the moral character of interlocutors, making morality the goal rather than truth?[9] That Socrates' ultimate concern was *excellence* seems clear from the request that he makes at the end of the *Apology* about his own sons, which is not about remedying ignorance. He asks friends to pester them with reproaches if they put material things before excellence, or exaggerate their own importance (41e). This agrees well with his description of his own personal services to the community at 29d–30b, in the course of which he scrutinizes (*exetazein*) and puts to the test (*elenchein*) their *claims to care for excellence*.

However, Socrates was not simply a moral reformer. His moral service involves confronting people with the *reality* of their situation rather than the image they cultivate. He is closely associated, in the *Protagoras* and elsewhere,[10] with the thesis that moral error stems from mistaken belief, a thesis requiring Socrates to leave the interlocutor closer to the truth. He belittles Protagoras' claim that his pupils show daily improvement by observing that any new knowledge is somehow an improvement for its recipients (318b). Indifference to the truth is not something to be associated with any version of "Socrates," from Aristophanes' *Clouds* on. His method is indeed directed towards individuals, but it aims to improve their understanding.[11] The reason why it seems not simply to be concerned with proving or disproving propositions is that propositions at that time were not conceived of as dwelling in isolation, capable of being spelled out in sentences across the pages of a philosopher's text and examined independently for their truth or falsehood.[12] They dwelt only in the beliefs or claims of individuals – from whom they were not readily divorced. For moral beliefs were intimately related to kinds of life, and exposing belief systems entailed the exposure of flaws in people's very lives. A friend of Socrates, like Nicias at *Laches* 187e–188b, well appreciates how Socrates' questions were ultimately transformed into an examination of one's own life.

So we must realize that Socrates aims at both epistemological and moral advances,[13] primarily for his interlocutor, secondarily for himself. Somehow in-depth questioning must lead towards *both* the refinement of belief *and* actions that spring from understanding one's role in the world. We today may doubt the links between the moral critic, the moral behavior of his "pupil," and an increase in the latter's happiness. Much is said in Plato's dialogues that questions them too, but in Plato's simplest exposition of Socratic philosophy, where Socrates instructs Cleinias, it is some kind of behavioral knowledge or wisdom that guarantees proper employment of our assets and so offers us well-being (*Euthydemus* 279d–282a). Furthermore, Socrates encourages us to believe that this knowledge may somehow be taught (282c). It was one of the great hopes of the age, promoted by Protagoras, that teaching could secure for citizens the kind of life they craved for – in which excellence guaranteed their well-being.

Protagoras also left an epistemological legacy, an optimistic one for self-confident individuals, which emphasized that judgment depended ultimately on us, and that each of our perspectives was valid. We judged things as they stood in relation to ourselves, not in isolation. Differences in opinion were natural, since we all related to things differently, and they did not undermine the validity of either of the "conflicting" views: each individual saw things as they were *for that individual*. Still, just as the sick person's sensations are inferior, so morally inferior individuals have undesirable perspectives on moral issues.[14] Protagoras offered hope that the well-adjusted individual, standing in a healthy relation to the world, would indeed offer excellent leadership –

255

and that the healthy community, which shared perceptions molded by such leaders and saw issues as one, would achieve new prosperity. Even so, a central plank of Protagoras' message was that there were two arguments on every issue.[15] Such arguments would surface in law-courts and assemblies, and were integral to the debate necessary to ensure that the state made "healthy" decisions. While Aristophanes' *Clouds* never directly links Socrates with Protagoras, the plot depends upon the Protagorean theme that opposite arguments are always available. They are personified and housed within Socrates' establishment, though treated impartially by Socrates himself. Neither is simply true or false, and either might be persuasive. This encourages us to answer the question "How did Socrates respond to the epistemological challenge of Protagoras?" Our answer will help understand why Socrates conducts investigations as he does in Plato.

The rift between Socrates' profession of ignorance on many issues, and his personal certainty on others, led Vlastos to postulate a *limited* knowledge derived from Socratic *elenchos*,[16] i.e. from his scrutiny of a person's beliefs. An alternative is to see it alongside the fact that Socrates has no answer to Protagoras' insistence that humans can only view objects and issues from a limited perspective, *even though he sought for a truth that was independent of perspective*. Hence he is more likely to make strong affirmations and denials in cases where it seems enough to judge "what is so for him," than when universal answers are required. His method of philosophizing via question and answer helped to remedy the limitations of perspective on these wider issues, so that truth might emerge more fully in collaboration with others.[17] For his personal religious experience (*Apology* 33c) entailed that he differed deeply from Protagoras regarding a higher wisdom among the gods, so he resisted the notion that humans could be the *final* measure. That divine knowledge did exist, and was able to direct human conduct, seemed to him obvious. Such guidance offered the hope of acting rightly under the influence of knowledge, even where we cannot know for ourselves.[18]

I now approach the interaction of Socratic method and Socratic epistemology from various perspectives: those of refutation, proof, midwifery, and the actual knowledge claims that "Socrates" makes in the *Apology* and elsewhere. Since conventional wisdom affirms that Socrates may be approached through the so-called early dialogues of Plato, I draw my evidence largely from what are commonly regarded as such. While I believe in no canon of "early Socratic dialogues," we must here beware of using distinctive features of Plato's own epistemology. Though chronology is not of major concern to me, one quasi-chronological theme will recur. The arguments with Callicles in the *Gorgias* agree poorly with other traditionally early material, and must be discounted as a "source" for Socrates. Since Socrates' method is conventionally called *elenchos*, and refutation is (a) the major acknowledged goal of *elenchos*[19] and (b) the usual result of Socrates' activity, I shall begin here.

Who or What is Refuted?

A: POLUS: Well this claim is yet more difficult than the previous one to refute, Socrates.

SOCRATES: No Polus, it's impossible – for what's true is never refuted.

(Gorgias 473b8–11)[20]

B: [Socrates:]   That's how clever the two have become at combat in arguments and at refuting what's said at any given time, regardless of whether it's true or false.

(*Euthydemus* 272a7–b1)

These two passages employ the same terminology for "refute," *exelenchein* in B and in Polus' part of A, while *elenchein* is used by Socrates in A, and must be understood in the same sense as the compound verb. Yet what is denied in A, that what's true can be refuted, is seriously entertained in B. There are no howls from Crito, Socrates' worthy interlocutor in passage B, that only what's false can be refuted. And yet these two dialogues are usually considered close in date and "Socraticity." What does this tell us about the concept of refutation employed here? Does the Greek notion of refutation not imply the falsehood of some proposition that has been put forward? Does it tell us about the concept of truth itself? Or should we assume that "Socrates" in B is being so scornful that his words make no pretence of honesty?

So what is it that normally gets refuted? Is it a statement or a proposition, or is it rather a person making a statement whose inadequacy is exposed? Normally it is the *person*, for out of about 90 examples of the relevant verbs, only a handful have something else as their object (in some cases after negatives or implied negatives, as something *not* to be refuted):

Dialogue	Object of refutation
Apology 21c1	Delphic oracle
Phaedo 85c5	doctrine
Charmides 166e2	the *logos*
Euthydemus 272a8	things said
Euthydemus 286e2	an account not involving falsehood
Euthydemus 286e6	an account not involving falsehood
Euthydemus 287c1	the last argument
Euthydemus 288e5	the value of gold
Protagoras 331d1	the *logos*
Protagoras 331e1	the parts of the face
Protagoras 347e7	the meaning of a poet
Gorgias 473b9	a *logos*
Gorgias 473b11	truth
Gorgias 473d2	a *logos*
Gorgias 482b2	philosophy
Gorgias 497b7	trifles (internal accusative)
Gorgias 527b3	other *logoi*

This list can be shortened. The Delphic oracle is thought of in personal terms. Several other cases are poorly translated "refute," including the *Phaedo* and *Charmides* examples (roughly "put to the test"). The first example in the *Euthydemus* is B above, and the last means "expose." The first example in the *Protagoras* means "put to the test," the second tends to mean "expose," and the third "properly put to the test." Clearly, however, *logoi* are something easily thought of as open to refutation in both *Euthydemus* and *Gorgias*, in the latter perhaps under the influence of oratorical uses of the term.[21] Up to nine examples of *logoi* being tested or refuted compare with 74 cases of persons being tested or refuted overall, making it clear that *elenchos, qua* process of refutation, is primarily aimed at persons, and less commonly thought of as refuting something said.

On examining *Euthydemus* 286e–288a we see how controversial the idea of refuting a claim can be. The sophist brothers maintain, in the tradition of Protagoras and others (286c), that making false claims is impossible. It is Socrates' assumption here that where there is no false claim there is no possibility of refutation either (286e). Socrates asks, in response to Dionysodorus' invitation to try and refute him, whether refutation is possible without anybody making a false claim. Euthydemus says that it is not, and seems to question whether Dionysodorus had issued an invitation to refute at all. By 287e Socrates is prepared to affirm that if he has not made a mistake, then Dionysodorus will not refute what he says. Undoubtedly the reader is meant to feel instinctively, like Ctesippus (288a–b), that Socrates is correct, and that refutation must involve error. But even this passage does not support the idea that propositions can be refuted in isolation, for their truth is not considered in isolation from the individual making a claim. Consider the following:

286c: Is this possible on your account, to refute without somebody making a false claim?

287e: If I wasn't making a mistake, you will not refute, even though you are wise, ...

The presence of the person making the claim is seen as crucial for a process of refutation. Cannot some claim, considered in abstract, be true or false then? Plato was perhaps pondering this very question as he wrote this very passage. Socrates had asked at 287c about the meaning of a phrase, using the verb *noein* (have sense, think, or intend). Dionysodorus induces Socrates to admit that it is only animate things that have sense, and then that phrases are inanimate. So Socrates must have mistakenly supposed that a phrase could have sense – or had he (287e)? Socrates does not actually mind, for if he was wrong, then so is the theory that one cannot get things wrong, whereas, if he was right, then nobody has refuted him.

As usual in the *Euthydemus*, the puzzles are there for readers to reflect on, not so that they may be solved. Is it illegitimate to speak of what *sense* a phrase has, or what it means? Do words have significance on their own, regardless of who uses them and how? The *Euthydemus* recognizes that utterances may be ambiguous, so that contradictory statements may both be valid in *some* sense, something made clear in Socrates' discussion of the first two sophisms (277e–278b). Here he speaks of the way in which *people* use the term *manthanein* for both "learn" and "understand," so that the meaning of any phrase employing the term depends on the particular sense in which an individual *intended* it. The reason why it can be used by the sophists to produce a radical dilemma is that they themselves do not actually *mean* the term in one sense rather than another.[22] The sophists offer practical proof that words and phrases do not, taken alone, have signification. But if they don't have their own sense, or intention, or meaning, then *words* are never refuted, only the people who employ them. For sure, *somebody's* words can be refuted, but only insofar as that person means something by them.[23]

But does the *Gorgias* – in particular the six references noted above – agree with the concept of truth in the *Euthydemus*? Is the idea of refutation applied simply to propositions, or is it even here linked to *what a person means*? I take the three cases at 473b–d together. At 473b9 (quoted above) Polus affirms, with considerable sarcasm, that Socrates' last claim is more difficult to refute than the previous one. Following this, it is evident that Socrates, when he responds that "what is true is never refuted," is *both* affirming the truth of his own claim (that those who escape punishment are the most unfortunate), *and* claiming that this makes it impossible to refute.

At d2 Polus discusses the difficulty, or lack of it, in refuting his own amplification of Socrates' claims. One can imagine much the same claims being made about the assertions of a legal opponent, and indeed Polus' techniques are derived from rhetorical practice (471e). Socrates now systematically attacks those techniques, denying that refutation, *in respect of the truth* (471e7–472a1, cf. 472b6), results from appeals to many witnesses (471e–472c), the use of scare-tactics and scornful laughter (473d–e), or putting a matter to a vote (474a). For Polus, *elenchos* here aims to *shame* a person rather than disprove a thesis. In developing his own rival criteria for *elenchos*, Socrates is not denying the personal nature of the process or the shame, but in this kind of debate one's defeat is shameful *by association with false claims*. One is refuted when one realizes that one cannot consistently maintain all one's claims. So, although *elenchos* tests claims, these claims remain firmly linked with people.

Let us move on to the remaining passages in this dialogue where *logoi* or something similar are the objects of *elenchos*. In this case we have three widely separated passages from the discussion with Callicles. The first of these (482b2) is unusual, in that Philosophy is personified: she is the beloved[24] of Socrates. So Socrates' invitation to Callicles to refute her is *in a sense* an invitation to refute what philosophy keeps *saying*. Even so, Philosophy can scarcely have some personal meaning with which the bare words of a statement are fleshed out. We are now approaching the notion of testing propositions in isolation from their fallible human sponsors.

The second passage (497b7) scarcely needs attention,[25] but the third (527b3) is more interesting, and definitely concerns the refutations of theories. In the midst of so many *logoi*, when all the others are refuted, only this *logos* [that one should avoid committing injustice rather than receiving it] is unmoved. The figures who promoted these *logoi*, Callicles, Gorgias, and Polus, have just been mentioned, but the remarkable thing is that Socrates himself does not actually feature in this context between 527a8 and c4. The rivals here really are viewed as theories, not as persons. Indeed Socrates is keen to share his theory with Callicles, as 527c4–e7 shows. At the end of the *Gorgias* these *logoi* are like recipes for rival lives, and they are beyond their proponents' control. They are patterns of happiness and unhappiness of which the *Theaetetus* will speak (176e–177a), better associated with a mature Plato.

This new tendency to divorce the theory from the speaker, a tendency that removes a major reason for writing dialogues between clearly delineated characters proposing theories relative to their situations, results in a new approach to the conduct of argument. No longer needing to refute a *person*, Socrates is prepared after 505d to conduct the argument by supplying his own answers. We have left behind what is usually termed Socratic *elenchos*, and the end of the *Gorgias* sees a transition towards having theories rather than people refuted. The theories, it might seem, can themselves take on the qualities "true" and "false" irrespective of their proponents, though Plato still seems reluctant to make this next step. It is noteworthy that, after acknowledging that the myth might be despised if something better and truer could be found, 527a6–8, the close of the dialogue fails to use any words that are irrevocably linked to truth and falsehood. The final criticism of the way of Callicles is that it is "worthless" (e7), not that it is false.

There is then some reason for holding the belief that Plato has moved, in the arguments with Callicles, to doing something that cannot readily be associated with his earlier Socrates – to seeing statements or theories in the abstract as legitimate objects of refutation. That in turn would require that words should have meaning in isolation from those who utter them. One can point to two likely consequences of such a development: first, Plato wishes to consider the nature of this truth or falsehood that belong to words alone; second, Plato no longer needs to depict verbal encounters between rivals, but prefers cooperative investigation of whether the claims are true. The former happens in the *Cratylus*, the latter in the *Phaedo* and most of the *Republic*.

Can Propositions Be Proven?

"SOCRATES: Is it not shown that what was said was true?
POLUS: Apparently."

(Gorgias 479e8–9)

These words have appeared to some to indicate a claim of secure proof by Socrates to which Polus agrees.[26] This is a major justification for seeking a Socratic method that brings Socrates to conclusions he knows elenctically, i.e. to the highest degree humanly possible.[27] One could translate the verb rendered as "shown" (*apodeiknumi*) as either "proven" or "demonstrated," thus promising knowledge-giving Socratic methods. But can the word mean all that is assumed? Let us examine this verb, and its noun *apodeixis*, in works traditionally thought to precede *Republic* 2. The speaker's identity is important, as we are expecting anything with a close bearing on Socrates' method to come from Socrates himself. Of 45 occurrences of the relevant vocabulary, 20 involved speakers other than Socrates, 11 of these being the Pythagorizing interlocutors of the *Phaedo*, who use this vocabulary in the context of logical proof more readily than does Socrates (a ratio of 2 or 2.5 to 1)! What this means for the Pythagorean part of Plato's heritage can only be guessed at. Of the 25 times they are spoken by Socrates only nine cases were *obviously* concerned with the establishment of something by logic: *Alcibiades* 1 130c5; *Gorgias* 479e8; *Phaedo* 77c6, 77d4, 105e8; *Protagoras* 357b7, 357c1, 359d5, 361b1.

These results are problematic for those who would see the Socratic *elenchos* as something that can terminate in *apodeixis*. The authenticity of the *Alcibiades* 1 remains disputed, and the thesis supposedly demonstrated here is the identity of a person with their soul – remarkably close to that of the *Phaedo*, from which other examples come. The *Phaedo* in turn is usually acknowledged to be employing the methods of the mature Plato, not of Socrates, and it is in any case the interlocutors who use this vocabulary more readily. The largest number of examples actually come from the final pages of the *Protagoras*. This is where Plato's "Socrates" is often assumed to have been arguing in a strictly *ad hominem* fashion – without concern for demonstrating the truth – yet the first three cases refer to aspects of these arguments. The first two actually concern the need for Socrates *and* Protagoras to show the masses what "being worsted by pleasure" actually is. While this is achieved through reasoning, we are dealing less with "proof" than with "pointing out." In the third example from this sequence Socrates is only using the verb in response to Protagoras' use of it two lines earlier, and saying "If it has been *correctly* demonstrated . . . " If the verb really implied conclusive proof, then "correctly" would seem redundant. The final example refers back to Socrates' main endeavors, in *trying to show* that all the virtues are one. Furthermore, just as Socrates chooses to use the verb at 359c in answer to Protagoras, the same could be said of the dialogue as a whole. It had been introduced by Protagoras at 323c–325b, where it was a verb for what he "shows" by a combination of argument and evidence. It implied evidence for a thesis being argued, but not that this thesis was "true" in such a way that there could be no valid contrary opinion – for that could not be expected in Plato's depiction of the author of the relativist claims in *Truth*. He cannot be talking of the absolute truth or falsehood of statements or theories considered in isolation from those who sponsor them. Nothing prevents us from taking Socrates' use of this vocabulary later in the dialogue roughly in Protagoras' sense – implying an explanation of one's valid belief and of why this is so for oneself.

So when one asks what sense the verb has at *Gorgias* 479e8 one should consider the following possibilities:

1. That it foreshadows a strong, possibly Pythagorean sense found in the *Phaedo*.
2. That it is used only to imply an explanation of Socrates' valid case (for believing that the unjust man is less happy than the man who is treated unjustly, and still less so if he avoids punishment).
3. That it is used in a sense determined by the use that Polus would make of it.

The second explanation surely deserves to be dismissed. Socrates is not making a mere Protagorean truth claim here. He is not claiming to have demonstrated the validity of thesis T from his own perspective; but to have demonstrated that T is true. The claim transcends the perspective of an individual observer. The third explanation is just possible, for, though Polus has only used the verb once at 470d2, this was when the debate over injustice was taking shape. Hence it is possible that Socrates' use of the verb is intended to recall Polus'. However, that cannot guarantee that the concept of *apodeixis* is the same for both speakers, for while Socrates responds to Polus' use of *elenchos*, he insists that his concept has significant differences (471d–e, etc.). In this case, too, Polus thinks *observable facts* can demonstrate his position, while Socrates' claim to have demonstrated his view rests on argument.

We concluded section 1 with the observation that *elenchos* in the arguments with Callicles has passed beyond the exposure of *human* flaws, and involves determining which *theories* can be revealed to be flawed. Similarly we are likely to conclude that *apodeixis* at the end of the argument with Polus, a page and a half before the entry of Callicles, takes on a comparable new sense, similarly concerned with truth itself rather than with people's qualifications as truth-speakers. First, however, one should look at one remaining interesting use of the verb late in the *Gorgias* at 527b1, where it is claimed that Gorgias, Polus, and Callicles have *been unable to demonstrate* that one should live any other life but the one advocated by Socrates. The negative makes the sense of the verb difficult to judge, but it must be a different use from that of Polus at 470d: Socrates means "you were unable to establish by argument," and their failure to demonstrate this is clearly being attributed to the extreme improbability of their thesis rather than their intellectual capacity, for they have just been described as the cleverest of the Greeks. They had the credentials for challenging Socrates' thesis but they failed. Socrates invites us to draw the conclusion that their failure arises from the impregnable truth of his thesis, not from his own intellectual capacity.

What Is There That a Midwife Can Know Elenctically?

". . . and they do not believe that I do this out of benevolence, being far from recognizing that no god is malevolent towards humans, so neither do I do any such thing out of malevolence, but that it is utterly unlawful for me either to go along with a falsehood or to bury the truth."

Here the "Socrates" of the *Theaetetus* (151c7–d3) explains the misunderstanding that brings his elenctic practices unpopularity. It cannot seriously misrepresent the historical Socrates, however late this dialogue is, for Plato has passed beyond such methods, and it is Socrates who is unpopular for the exposure of interlocutors through question and answer. There is an implication that Socrates can recognize both truth and falsehood while he operates, paradoxical when compared with his denial of any wisdom of his own (150c8–d2). Can Socrates, although devoid of higher knowledge, "know elenctically"[28] matters arising from interrogation: either that the interlocutor's initial claim had been false, or that the conjunction of this claim and additional premises is false?[29]

On one reading of divine law's prohibition in the passage cited, Socrates cannot ignore the falsehood of the conjunction of P, T, and U, after this becomes clear in interrogation. So Socrates would be suspending judgment while questioning, then bringing the falsehood of the interlocutor's combined position to light once there is a realization of what the argument has shown. He learns as a result of this very *elenchos*, and thus acquires elenctic knowledge. In this case discerning true claims seems impossible. On another reading Socrates recognizes true and false claims at the beginning[30] and reveals their status during interrogation. This would mean that the truth-value of such claims is something he knows, yet, since he has not personally *discovered* anything (150c–d), he does not know *through himself*. Can he somehow know these things *through another* then, or through his wide experience of what *others* have realized in earlier conversation with him? Could such knowledge be what he brings to bear in deciding which of an interlocutor's claims he should resist. If Socrates recognizes, say, that "courage = endurance" is false, then he already knows the truth on the very matter concerning which he claims to seek the truth, and his profession of ignorance seems misleading. Yet if he does not know the truth of any premises or evidence he employs, then his proud claim that he does not offend divine law by agreeing with falsehood or quarreling with truth seems hollow.

Why is it left ambiguous whether Socrates is able to sense the truth or falsehood of a claim initially, or whether this only emerges at the end? Why is he so confident of how he will respond to truths and falsehoods, yet so keen to dismiss knowledge of his own? We must not risk obscuring the nature of Socratic "midwifery by importing alien assumptions here, and two fundamentals must be corrected before we understand this passage. One is the assumption that Socrates must *consciously* recognize the truth or falsehood of the theory whether at the start or at the conclusion. What Socrates must do is to feel instinctively that an answer requires investigation, or that the conclusion speaks against the answer's being correct, not that he should know this. Constantly a god is implicated in his activity (150c8, d4, d8, 210c7),[31] the god acts through him, and his motivation and the god's cannot differ (151d1). Socrates is thus a divine agent of inquiry, as in the *Apology*, so that his response can be attributed to divine knowledge rather than to his own human knowledge. This is why the restriction on Socrates' allowing falsehoods or hiding truths is determined by *themis* (151d3), a divine code of practice.

The second mistake is our slipping into a modern conception of truth. As long as one persists in asking about the truth and falsehood *of propositions* then one will get no further. Theaetetus' "offspring" cannot be seen in abstract, but are peculiarly his. His first "offspring" at 151e is like an individual artist's sketch of what knowledge is, to which increasing detail can be added if required. It is more picture-like than book-like. Moreover that offspring cannot belong to Socrates, just as a mother's child cannot be the midwife's. If a collection of propositions were to fail examination by Socrates, then Socrates would know that there was a falsehood there quite as much as the interlocutor, and this "knowledge-that-not" would be demonstrated to the interlocutor and to Socrates simultaneously, or possibly to Socrates a little earlier. The knowledge would arise for both, thanks largely to Socrates' efforts, so why should it not be his own quite as much as another's? If the test could reveal that a proposition were true, then Socrates would know that too. Socrates' tests, however, are tests of the individual youth's theory, and his evaluation of it is not actually billed as knowledge at all, but as opinion, for at 151c the verb *hēgeisthai* ("consider") is used rather than a verb of recognition. His whole art, rather like early medicine as then conceived, can be thought of as guided by the divine wisdom of a god, but he himself cannot "know" either what is so absolutely or what is so for others, only what is so for himself. About things beyond his own self he can only opine.

What Is There To Be Known in the *Apology*?

The most famous claim of Socrates is that he knows that he knows nothing (*Apology* 22e–23b). Awareness concerning one's own ignorance is termed human wisdom (20d8), while it is allowed that well-known sophists may have a wisdom greater than human (e1). The nature of divine wisdom remains unclear, except as found in Apollo's knowledge that human wisdom is worth little or nothing (23a5–6). Socrates' human wisdom is evidenced again at 29a–b, where he knows his ignorance about whether death is bad (cf. 37b). Here, however, something positive that Socrates does know is contrasted with this ignorance, and it can hardly be a careless lapse into everyday language. Socrates *knows* that to disobey a superior is wrong (29b). He knows it so well that he will die rather than disobey Apollo.

At first sight we appear to be confronted with an absolute truth that Socrates does know. But he doesn't claim that this knowledge is exclusive, but speaks as if most of the jury knows this too. In these circumstances we should not be justified in turning this into a universal moral truth that Socrates knows. Rather he realizes that such disobedience is *bad for him*, and he expects others to realize that it is *bad for them* too. This is personal knowledge, of a kind that anyone was expected to know *relative to their own situation*, as is Socrates' awareness of his own ignorance. Both are part of his own experience, where one's own experience and nobody else's is a valid judge of how things are; he speaks with authority as if declaring that the wind blows cool to him. While he could be lying, he cannot have misread the situation as it affects him.

Plato is careful in the *Apology* to make Socrates claim enough to explain his convictions, without damaging his disavowal of knowledge on an important class of things we generally suppose we know. Besides 29b, there is another claim to know about values at 37b7–8, where Socrates questions the sense of proposing penalties that he *knows* to be evil in preference to death, which might possibly be good. Once again, nothing is said in his explanation (37b8–e2) about how those penalties would affect anybody other than himself. He speaks from *his own perspective*. Against this limited *knowledge* of values that Socrates claims in the *Apology*, there are a host of examples where he boldly states his view on moral matters, but uses only verbs implying impressions, opinions, or belief.[32]

The same caution is used in matters concerning the divine. He believed and adopted the view that Apollo was instructing him to philosophize (*ōiēthēn te kai hypelabon*: 28e5); and he makes the assumption that his divine sign's failure to appear to him prior to, or during, his court speech means that what has happened is for the best (*hypolambanō*: 40b6). This last assumption is a strong one, because the evidence (*tekmērion*: c1) clearly seems very compelling to him, and lengthy reasoning follows (40c–41c) to show how it is not improbable. If Socrates now becomes confident that death is good, then this is wholly dependent on trust in the supernatural – the divine has not opposed him on the day of his trial. Socrates is able to conclude by induction, based upon past experience (33c, 40a), that the divine unstintingly shares its knowledge of good and evil with him; but his induction is a matter of faith, not knowledge. Socrates *has access to* privileged divine knowledge, but does not possess it for himself. This makes him extremely confident of his own future, but he can only judge his own situation, not that of others. Whether his death will be better than the life of those he addresses remains *unclear* to all except god (*adēlon*: 42a2).

What Is There To Be Known in the Other Early Dialogues?

Is the care with which Plato has Socrates use claims to know something in the *Apology* matched elsewhere in the early dialogues? I examined words for "I know"[33] put into the mouth of "Socrates" in relevant works. I shall delay consideration of the arguments with Callicles.

There is one example of Socrates claiming to know something largely from experience of himself. This is *Lesser Hippias* 372d2: "And I'm well aware of this, that it's my fault, because I'm the type that I am . . ." (cf. *Apology* 21b4–5). Three examples from the *Greater Hippias* are from self-experience provided only that the *alter ego* is another side of Socrates himself. The experience of other people is the source of widespread claims to know something about the interlocutors,[34] and likewise of several claims to know about people more widely.[35] Another category of knowledge concerns matters of Socrates' memory,[36] and at *Meno* 91d2 his claim to know about Protagoras' financial success comes from collective Athenian memory. All these knowledge claims derive from acquaintance with everyday matters, and are unremarkable, even for a systematic doubter.

Two cases seem more problematic. In the *Protagoras* (360e8–361a3) we meet what could be construed as a claim to know something by logic, taking the form: "I know that *x* would most easily become clear if *y* did first." If Socrates is claiming to know the interconnectedness of two things, weakness of will and the teachability of virtue, this claim sounds somewhat technical, but it still falls short of a pronouncement on cause and effect. Socrates' general experience of philosophic investigation might give him good reason to make this claim, and it seems unnecessary to suppose that any concept of abstract truth is present. *Meno* 98b2–5 shows Socrates inclined to claim knowledge that there is a difference between right opinion and knowledge. The context is such that the claim must have been carefully thought through by the author. This knowledge could perhaps be the product of Socrates' general awareness of human intellectual conditions, including his own. In particular, it could be the product of his thinking his own experience through. And it should be added that the claim is made with a certain amount of diffidence. So we still lack proof that Socrates makes claims that are not dependent on experience, and there are no claims to the sort of moral knowledge that Socrates seeks.

Yet the *Gorgias* is once again interesting. There is no use of "I know" without the negative in the arguments with Gorgias and Polus. Only in the arguments with Callicles does Socrates claim to *know* anything, and the first of these examples is wholly unusual. However, let us first of all acknowledge the extent to which even here Socrates conforms to his normal practice. One finds a claim to historical knowledge based on his own experience of Pericles (515e10), and similar claims to a knowledge of Callicles' associates based on hearsay (487c). One finds an experience-based claim to know about what an interlocutor will say (512d1), or about any future prosecutor of Socrates being corrupt (*poneros*: 521c9); the latter, however, seems to involve a significant element of *moral* certainty. Similarly Socrates claims to know the sort of fate he would suffer if he were brought to court (522b3), and it is the kind that the doctor would suffer if prosecuted by the fancy cook. Such a claim could be partly based upon experience, but Socrates would scarcely have any experience about doctors being prosecuted by cooks, or about how he will fare himself. Similarly a claim at 522d8 that he knows he will bear death easily (if he dies for lack of flattering oratory) seems arrogant and overconfident. He has not yet been in this situation, and the element of sheer prophecy seems to be outweighing the self-experience element.

265

But what of 486e5–6:

Well I know that whatever you may agree with me on, concerning the opinions my soul adopts, this is directly the truth itself.

The claim is essentially a claim to know a foolproof test of moral truth. It may not be a claim to know moral truths, but it is a claim to have the method for verification. The claim is subsequently justified in terms of Callicles having all the qualities required of a dialectical opponent. He does not lack intelligence, or bravado, or sincerity. Thus agreement between Callicles and Socrates will be the final indication of truth (487e7). What concept of truth is being employed here then? Is it more than something's being correct from a given perspective, so that it actually reflects objective reality regardless? In my view it has begun to be just that, but is it because Socrates and Callicles approach the issues from opposite perspectives *and still reach agreement* (on some points at least), or because objective truth is now seen as being more accessible than before? Since Callicles cannot finally be won over, the latter alternative seems to me more plausible.

One should not leave the *Gorgias* without briefly glancing at the passage that speaks of his earlier conclusions on justice being fixed by "iron and adamantine arguments" (508e). This does not, apparently, mean that the conclusions are unequivocally true, but that the contrary view cannot credibly be put unless Callicles, or somebody still more forthright, "unties" them. The arguments, then, leave no room for a different perspective. However, Socrates still affirms that he does not know the true position, though he never met anybody able to successfully argue the contrary view (509a). So he assumes that his own view reflects reality. This is the passage that gives the most credibility to the view that Socrates has "elenctic knowledge" that shows him, through his own experience in argument, positions that are indefensible. It is supported by 527a–b, but not by other relevant dialogues, for only now have we met the final test of a Socratic thesis: the best qualified interlocutors, who are least likely to agree.

Truth at the End of the *Gorgias*

The arguments with Callicles, including Socrates' summing up of the argument with Polus at 479d–481b, stand out with regard to the truth-content of Socratic refutation, demonstration, and knowledge. Theories rather than individuals become the objects of examination (509a, etc.); demonstration reflects the truth of the claim rather than the strengths of its adherents (479e; 527b); and Socrates' knowledge-claims go beyond matters of simple personal experience (486e5, 522b3, d8).

Observe the increased regularity of truth-related vocabulary after 478d over what went before. The adverb "truly" (*alēthōs*) occurs seven times in the work, with its first occurrence at 482c. "In truth" (*tēi alētheiāi*) occurs in Gorgias' words at 452d5, but Socrates only uses it at 509b5, 514e3, and 520b2.[37] Other cases of the noun "truth" occur nine times in the *Gorgias*,[38] only twice in the earlier conversations (459e8, 472a1). "In reality" (*tōi onti*) is employed only with Callicles, eight times by Socrates.[39] The comparative "truer," incompatible with Protagorean epistemology (*Theaetetus* 167b4), otherwise absent from "early" Plato, occurs at 493d4 and 527a8.[40] So there

266

is a significant increase in truth-related terminology late in the *Gorgias*, beyond what can be explained by changing subject-matter. This vocabulary of truth or reality tends to accompany passages that distinguish what's really good pursued by true arts from the apparent good pursued by false arts. Socrates can speak of genuine rhetoric, real care of the body, really making people good, and true political craft (517a5, e5, 520d6, 521d7); his final message concerns true rather than apparent goodness (526d6, 527d1). The underlying theory had been part of the dialogue since 464b, but the language of truth had not appeared there.[41]

Partly under the influence of Callicles' distinction between convention and nature, the *Gorgias* shifts its focus significantly towards the distinction between appearance and reality as Plato moves towards the final vindication of justice. What concept of reality, or nature, or truth, influences Plato here? It seems clear that he seeks nothing less than how things are in the real world, beyond any individual or otherwise re-stricted perspective. The interlocutor has been selected so as to justify an expectation that this truth will come to light.

So *in reality (tōi onti)* your agreement with me already marks the *finishing line of the truth (telos . . . tēs alētheias)*.

(*Gorgias* 487e6–7)

With Gorgias and Polus, Plato was content to demonstrate Socrates' superiority, to raise difficulties with the former, and to refute the latter in the manner that his rude-ness demands. With Callicles, whose perspective counterbalances his own, Socrates engages in a quest for objective truth. The constraints of Protagorean theory are over-come. The arguments with Callicles, like those of the *Phaedo* and the *Republic*, aim at real answers. The radical nature of this plan is easily lost on us today, for we have forgotten the spell that Protagoras had cast.

Conclusion

The world of ancient philosophy was stunned by Vlastos' great article on the Socratic *elenchos*, in part because it seemed to show how Socrates' method might be regarded as a truth-giving process. It postulated two underlying epistemological assumptions by which it worked:[42]

A. Whoever has a false moral belief will always have at the same time true beliefs entailing the negation of that false belief.
B. The set of elenctically tested moral beliefs held by Socrates at any given time is consistent.

A explains why the process worked at all: error could always be refuted from within. B was thought to explain why Socrates could pick the faulty premise from a group that were inconsistent, and it closely involves the idea of elenctic knowledge.

Others have observed that the very problem Vlastos' B was supposed to solve is a problem arising almost exclusively from the *Gorgias*.[43] Of the Platonic passages used by

Vlastos as testimonia T4, T5, T8, T15, T17–18, and T20–4 (477e–478a, 472c–d, 500b, 473e, 472b–c, 479e, 472b, 474a, 474b, and 482a–b) derive from the *Gorgias*, with T20 (479e) and T24 (482a–c) playing especially important roles.[44] The later pages play an even greater role in Vlastos' 1985 account of Socratic knowledge, including T6 (509a), T9 (505e), T12 (486e), T16 (512b), and crucially T28–30 (508e–509a, 479e, 505e–506a). As Vlastos' seminal article was taking place, totally unrelated work was published in Finland by Thesleff and New Zealand by myself, arguing that the *Gorgias* is a dialogue given a later revision.[45] *Inter alia*, revision involved the addition of the arguments with Callicles. The *Gorgias* may thus be inconsistent in itself, owing to separate chronological layers. In that case Vlastos' problem would be illusory.

Rejection of a dual date for the *Gorgias* cannot avoid the fact that it is a problematic work for anybody examining Socrates' method. The evidence usually points less to a method than to an empirically acquired routine. In the *Gorgias*' terms that would make it a *tribē* or *empeiria* rather than a *technē* (463b4, 501a–b).[46] Plato cannot have Socrates' activity classed as a *tribē* since it would then aim at an interlocutor's pleasure rather than his good (464d, 501a–b); for that reason Socrates must be the practitioner of a true *technē* (521d–e). Yet to qualify as a *technē* Socratic investigation would have to be able to *give an account* of the therapeutic procedures it applies (465a, 501a), something never previously offered. The Socratic art of correction thus becomes virtually the *technical* counterpart of the routine of rhetoric, and it aims at what is truly good for the interlocutor. That is why Plato must give Socratic interrogation an account of itself in the *Gorgias* in particular, contrasting its methodology with Polus' "routine," and linking it with the *genuine* benefit the interlocutor.

Yet Vlastos is not refuted! His claim A remains attractive, and I think insightful. His claim B would be unnecessary, though not necessarily mistaken. Socratic conversations were indeed a way of comparing one's own perspective on issues with those of others, so that aberrant perceptions are ultimately recognized as aberrant. Not only do they not cohere with the perceptions of others, but they do not cohere with one's other beliefs either. Because the capacity to make moral judgments does indeed reside in human beings, the recognition and removal of what is "sick" or aberrant is all that is required for moral and cognitive health. If Socrates trusts his own moral health, then he can have reasonable confidence that his perspective on moral issues does not suffer from the same distortion that he often notes in others. If this confidence is to be called "elenctic knowledge" so be it. The purpose of this chapter has been to show that no method of establishing the truth of propositions is involved. Which leads me to commend with reservations another of Vlastos' theories. Plato's more "Socratic" Socrates is no epistemologist.[47] He cannot be an epistemologist in our sense of the term since his concept of truth is so radically different.

Notes

1   The "Socrates" of whom I write is intended for the most part to reflect the historical Socrates, but the evidence that I shall draw on is that of Plato's dialogues: any, in fact, that try to communicate to us something of the Socrates that Plato had known. However, I avoid postulating any period of Platonic development in which every position sponsored by

Socrates reflects the "doctrines" of the historical Socrates. Rather I am moderately confident that Plato tried, wherever his other purposes allowed, to depict a Socrates who *behaved* like the historical figure, and *spoke* like that figure too. This behavior and this speech were often used to promote a distinctly Platonic agenda, but Socrates remained a recognizable character, not just a mouthpiece, in every dialogue in which he takes a major role – except perhaps the *Philebus*.

2   Most assume this much to be so. Brickhouse and Smith at least go so far as to find nothing that corresponds to the description "the Socratic *elenchos*," (2002: 147). Walsdorf (2003: 297–308), denies that Socrates has a "method" rather than a "manner or style" (298) of pursuing definitions; he also denies that Socrates has a theory of definition.

3   *Metaphysics* 178b27–30; *epagōgē* is usually translated "induction," but does not match the modern concept; see Vlastos (1991: 267), Robinson (1953: 33).

4   For this pattern see McPherran (2002: 242), who claims that this contradiction may then be claimed by Socrates to refute the original belief; Benson (1995, cf. 2002: 106), believes that what Socrates seeks to show is that the interlocutor did not have the knowledge that he supposed.

5   For Benson (2002: 107 n. 17), it is always *ad hominem* in the sense that it is always aimed at a specific individual.

6   I argue against this assumption, sometimes preferring the term *exetasis*, Tarrant (2000 and 2002). Others have made similar points about the failure of the term to match any use of Socrates.

7   Carpenter and Polansky (2002) deduce that there is a great variety in the *elenchos* (i.e. Socrates' method) from the variety of its aims, but even they, insofar as they work within a tradition, are starting from some assumptions about method itself.

8   This is the case even in Aristophanes *Clouds*, 478–86, where he can only work upon Strepsiades if he knows his individual characteristics, and where we never hear, let alone see, of anything like group teaching.

9   This view might perhaps be associated with Brickhouse and Smith (1994: 12–14), though it is not clear to me whether they consider the examination of persons vastly more important than that of the truth, or whether they are rather offering a corrective of previous assumptions.

10 That one's degree of goodness matches one level of cognition is regarded as a recurrent theme of Socratic conversation by Nicias at *Laches* 194d1–2.

11 For Socrates' desire to promote knowledge see Benson (2002: 108–13).

12 I do not offer an example of a modern scholar who claims this, but believe that the characteristic practices of much of modern literature do indeed encourage such an assumption.

13 Cf. Renaud (2002: 195) denies that there can be "a clean separation between the purely logical and the ethical functions of the elenchus."

14 I draw unashamedly on the speech attributed to Protagoras at *Theaetetus* 166a–168c, especially 167a–c, where the interpretation of Protagoras is unlikely to be historically perfect, but where we may very well be seeing how Socrates and Plato had understood the sophist's legacy.

15 Diogenes Laertius, *Lives of Eminent Philosophers* 9.51 = Diels-Kranz 80 B6a, but the idea clearly lurks behind Aristophanes' *Clouds*, and makes an important appearance in Euripides *Antiope* also (fr. 89), a play particularly conscious of the new intellectualism.

16 Vlastos (1985 and 1994: 39–66).

17 Blondell (2002: 49) sees the commitment to dialogue as "an assertion of human plurality"; I suggest that the need to allow for human plurality is itself grounded in epistemology.

18 For recent treatment of the cases where Socrates professes to know ethical truths see Walsdorf (2004), which contains a pertinent survey of earlier attempts to explain them.

Walsdorf regards attempt to offer a coherent explanation of Socrates' cases of (assumed) knowledge or ignorance across "early" dialogues as naive.

19 See Carpenter and Polansky (2002: 89): "Refutation is merely one of the functions, though a most crucial one, since all of the other purposes may be accomplished through refutation."

20 I note that Lesher (2002: 26) suggests that this passage and *Protagoras* 344b are the earliest in which *elenchos* has an unmistakable refutational sense, but care is needed.

21 See Tarrant (2002: 69); and for rhetorical features of Socrates' methods see Ausland (2002).

22 Brickhouse and Smith (2002: 153) suggest that the sophists may actually operate with the same "doxastic constraint" as Socrates (i.e. need the interlocutor to answer in accordance with his belief), but it is clear that they, unlike Socrates, have no commitment to exploring propositions in the sense in which they are meant, nor do they mean anything themselves by them (cf. 286d–e).

23 It seems obvious that the *Sophist* does have an account of true and false *logoi* that allows truth and falsehood to be independent of the intentions of a speaker, 261c–263d. Socrates does not himself intend to indicate anything by stating "Theaetetus flies," but it is false *per se* regardless of the absence of intention to say anything about Theaetetus at all.

24 Though the noun for philosophy is of course feminine, the word used at 482a4 is *ta paidika*, in theory neuter, but regularly indicating a junior male partner.

25 I take the "little things" that look like the object as properly an *internal* accusative.

26 Vlastos (1994: 19, 45, 59).

27 See Vlastos (1983 [T20] and [1985] T29).

28 For the concept of elenctic knowledge, as something falling short of certain knowledge, see Vlastos (1985 and 1994: 56–61); I think Vlastos' view is attractive, but misses the mark on the precise nature of a knowledge that is less than divine.

29 That the initial claim (p) is refuted is affirmed by the "constructivist" position on the *elenchos*, and it follows that Socrates will know ~p thereby. "Nonconstructivists" see Socrates learning only that the conjunction of p and the further premises t and u is false. Even the nonconstructivist position seems incompatible with the concept of truth that on my view precedes the later pages of the *Gorgias*. For Socrates ought on their view to be able to claim "I know that not (p + t + u)," where p, t, and u are propositions that have abstract meaning, whereas on my view all that he know is that this interlocutor cannot simultaneously defend *claims* p, t, and u.

30 On the "pre-elenctic" belief that an interlocutor's view needs testing, see Carvalho (2002).

31 There might be a subtle hint in "God help my saying so" (151b4), that Socrates' brilliant guesses as to a young man's intellectual needs are themselves the result of divine inspiration.

32 *dokei*: 28d8, 34e3, 35b9; *oi(o)mai*: 30a5, c4, d4, c9; cf. 32c1, 38e2; *hēgoumai*: 35c8; *pepeismai*: 37a5, b2.

33 *gignōskein, eidenai, epistasthai, syneidenai*. Past tenses ("I knew") have been considered also.

34 *Alcibiades* 1 104c4, 105c7, 106e4, 110a10, 112a10; *Euthdemus* 272d3, 295d1, 297d8, 302a5, 303e7; *Euthphro* 15d8; *Laches* 192c5; *Lysis* 204b7; *Meno* 80c1; *Protagoras* 335a9 (total 15).

35 *Crito* 49d2; *Euthdemus* 303d2, d4; *Meno* 80c3; *Protagoras* 356c2 (total 5).

36 *Euthdemus* 292a2, a5, and memory of a poem at *Protagoras* 339b5.

37 Also used by Callicles at 492b4, c3.

38 Callicles uses it at 482e4, Socrates elsewhere.

39 487e6, 492d4, 493a1, 495b8, 517e5, 520d6, 526d6, 527d1. Callicles uses it at 482e3.

40 Only interlocutors use the superlative: *Laches* 193e3 (Laches), *Cratylus* 435e5 and 438c1 (Cratylus), and *Lesser Hippias* 364e8 (Hippias).

41 One might blame "Callicles" for part of the increase (482c5, e3, e4, 487a–d), but he cannot explain everything.

42 Pp. 57–8; in Vlastos (1994: 27–8).

43 Kraut (1983), Benson (1995: 48 n. 11).

44 Numbering differs slightly in the revision of 1994.

45 Thesleff (1982), Tarrant (1982). I have discovered a further stylistic feature that makes it highly unlikely that the arguments with Callicles were penned immediately following the arguments with Gorgias and Polus (1994: 118 n. 28), and Thesleff revisits his similar theory at the 2004 Symposium Platonicum at Würzburg.

46 Walsdorf (2003: 297 with n. 107) sees the implications of Socrates' requirements for a *technē* in a similar context.

47 Vlastos (1991: 47 etc.).

References

Ausland, Hayden W. (2002). Forensic characteristics of Socratic argumentation. In Scott (2002), pp. 36–60.

Benson, Hugh H. (1995). The dissolution of the problem of the elenchus. *Oxford Studies in Ancient Philosophy*, 13, 45–112.

—— (2002). Problems with Socratic method. In Scott (2002), pp. 101–13.

Blondell, Ruby (2002). *The Play of Character in Plato's Dialogues*. Cambridge: Cambridge University Press.

Brickhouse, Thomas C. and Smith, Nicholas D. (1994). *Plato's Socrates*. Oxford: Oxford University Press.

—— and —— (2002). The Socratic *elenchos*? In Scott (2002), pp. 145–57.

Carpenter, Michelle and Polansky, Ronald M. (2002). Variety of Socratic elenchi. In Scott (2002), pp. 89–100.

Carvalho, John M. (2002). Certainty and consistency in the Socratic elenchus. In Scott (2002), pp. 266–80.

Kraut, Richard (1983). Comments on Gregory Vlastos, "The Socratic elenchus." *Oxford Studies in Ancient Philosophy*, 1, 59–70.

Lesher, James H. (2002). Parmenidean *elenchus*. In Scott (2002), pp. 19–35.

Renaud, François (2002). Humbling as upbring: The ethical dimension of the elenchus in the *Lysis*. In Scott (2002), pp. 183–98.

Robinson, Richard (1953). *Plato's Earlier Dialectic*. Oxford: Oxford University Press.

Scott, Gary A. (ed.) (2002). *Does Socrates have a Method?* University Park, PA: Pennsylvania University Press.

Tarrant, Harold (1982). The composition of Plato's *Gorgias*. Prudentia, 14, 3–22.

—— (1994). The *Hippias Major* and Socratic views on pleasure. In Paul A. Vander Waerdt (ed.), *The Socratic Movement* (pp. 107–26). Ithaca, NY: Cornell University Press.

—— (2000). Naming Socratic interrogation in the *Charmides*. In L. Brisson and T. M. Robinson (eds.), *Plato: Euthydemus, Lysis, Charmides* (pp. 251–8). Proceedings of the V. Symposium Platonicum (Selected Papers), Sankt Augustin. Academia Verlag.

—— (2002). *Elenchos* and *exetasis*: capturing the purpose of Socratic interrogation. In Scott (2002), pp. 61–77.

Thesleff, Holger (1982). *Studies in Platonic Chronology*. Helsinki: Societas Scientiarum Fennica.

Vlastos, Gregory (1983). The Socratic elenchus. *Oxford Studies in Ancient Philosophy*, 1, 27–58.

—— (1985). Socrates' disavowal of knowledge. *Philosophical Quarterly*, 35, 1–31.

—— (1991). *Socrates: Ironist and Moral Philosopher*. Cambridge: Cambridge University Press.

—— (1994). *Socratic Studies*, ed. M. Burnyeat. Cambridge: Cambridge University Press.

Walsdorf, David (2003). Socrates' pursuit of definitions. *Phronesis*, 48, 271–312.

—— (2004). Socrates' avowals of knowledge. *Phronesis*, 49, 75–142.

Section III

Hellenistic Philosophy

17

Socrates in the Stoa

ERIC BROWN

According to Diogenes Laertius' *Lives of Eminent Philosophers*, an unbroken chain of teachers and pupils links Socrates to the earliest Stoics (1.15). The founder of Stoicism, Zeno of Citium, is said to have studied with Crates (6.105 and 7.2), who is supposed to have absorbed Cynicism from Diogenes of Sinope (6.85 and 87), and Diogenes, in turn, reportedly earned the label "Cynic" under the influence of Antisthenes (6.21), who is called a follower of Socrates (6.2). Ancient philosophical biographies show a fondness for teacher–pupil successions of this sort, and historical facts did not always get in the way. Nevertheless, there is no doubt about the point that motivates this particular succession: Socrates influenced Stoicism profoundly.

Stoics manifested their debt to Socrates in two distinctive ways. First, Stoics embrace paradoxical doctrines in the style of Socrates, and indeed, they embrace many of Socrates' own paradoxes. Cicero saw this clearly, averring that "most of the surprising so-called *paradoxa* of the Stoics are Socratic" (*Academics* 2.136). When Cicero wrote *Stoic Paradoxes* to show how his rhetorical skill could make the paradoxes of the Stoa plausible to a general audience, he concentrated on six of the "most Socratic" (4) theses: only the fine is good, virtue suffices for happiness, vicious actions are equal and virtuous actions are equal, everyone who is not a sage is insane, only the sage is free, and only the sage is rich. Cicero's purposes do not include explaining the Socratic provenance of these paradoxes, and many scholars today would balk at his list. No one denies that paradoxical doctrines link Socrates to the Stoics, but most scholars prefer to attribute different paradoxes to both Socrates and the Stoics: no one does wrong willingly and all virtue is one.

A second way in which the Stoics pledge allegiance to Socrates is by invoking him as an example to imitate. Seneca, Musonius Rufus, Epictetus, and Marcus Aurelius – all prominent Stoics in the time of the Roman Empire – do this. (None did this more than Epictetus; see the next chapter.) The record is less clear for earlier Greek Stoics, whose writing is almost all lost. The evidence of interest in Socrates is perfectly clear: the second head of the school, Cleanthes (331–232 BCE) cites Socrates for the view that advantage is not severed from what is just (Clement, *Stoicorum Veterum Fragmenta* 1.558); the obscure third-century BCE Stoics Zeno of Sidon and Theon of Antiochia each wrote an *Apology of Socrates* (Suda s.v. = SSR I C 505); another third-century

BCE Stoic named Sphaerus wrote a work titled *On Lycurgus and Socrates* in three books (Diogenes Laertius, *Lives of Eminent Philosophers* VII 178); Antipater of Tarsus, a second-century BCE head of the school, invoked Socrates in his book *On Anger* (Athenaeus, *Stoicorum Veterum Fragmenta* 3.65: Antipater) and collected Socrates' remarkable divinations (Cicero, *On Divination* 1.123); and Panaetius (185–109 BCE) defended Socrates from the charges of bigamy frequently made by Peripatetics (Plutarch, Aristides 335c–d = fr. 152 van Straaten). Still, it is not clear how much of this evidence shows that Socrates was taken to be an example worth imitating. It is not nearly as clear as the evidence for the much later Roman Stoics, or even for Posidonius (c. 135 to c. 50 BCE), who numbered Socrates alongside Diogenes the Cynic and the proto-Cynic Antisthenes among those who had made progress (Diogenes Laertius, *Lives of Eminent Philosophers* VII 91 = fr. 29 Edelstein-Kidd).

From the relative silence of the historical record, one might infer that the earliest Stoics did not invoke Socrates as an example. But arguments from silence, rarely powerful, are especially weak when the record is meager. Moreover, early Greek Stoics share the commitments that do lead later Roman Stoics to invoke Socrates as an example. For instance: the third Stoic scholarch, Chrysippus of Soli (280–206 BCE), like Seneca (c. 1–65 CE), wrote "protreptic" works to encourage a philosophical way of life, and also like Seneca, he applied himself to the part of ethics "concerning appropriate actions, recommendations and warnings" (Diogenes Laertius, *Lives of Eminent Philosophers* 7.84; cf. Sextus Empiricus, *Against the Professors* 7.12) that Stoics called the "paraenetic" or "perceptive" part (Seneca, *Moral Epistles* 95.1: *parainetikos topos* or *pars praeceptiva*, from Greek and Latin words for "rule"). But Chrysippus, again like Seneca, recognized the limited value of rules in encouraging progress toward a fully philosophical way of life, and it seems that he, still like Seneca, endorsed the political life of a king in part because of the value that a king could have as an example for citizens to imitate. So it is quite easy to suppose that Chrysippus and his fellow Greek Stoics in the third century BCE agreed with the later Stoics (Seneca, *On Tranquility of Spirit* 5.2, *On Kindness* V 6.1–7) and the rest that Socrates was a model worth imitating. At the very least, it is far easier than imagining who else an early Stoic might have proposed, and Socrates was widely thought (by, e.g., Xenophon, *Memorabilia* 1.2.2–3) to have improved others' lives by serving as an example for them to imitate. So although skepticism about early Stoic invocation of Socrates as an exemplar is possible, it seems more prudent to suppose that even the earliest Stoics manifested their Socratic inheritance in two ways.

A Stoic, however, might well find something wrong with distinguishing these two ways, for it is unlikely that any Stoic encountered the Socratic paradoxes as a matter of theory, entirely cut off from Socrates' own life. After all, Socrates did not commit any of his theorizing about the paradoxes to writing, and the writings about Socrates portray him in action and thereby connect what he says (including his paradoxes) with his way of life. This suggests that reflection on what Socrates did led the Stoics to hold him up as an example to imitate and to endorse the Socratic paradoxes. So understood, there is just one inheritance, the gift of Socrates' way of life.

On this way of looking at things, there is also something wrong with scouring particular texts to distinguish between the Stoic paradoxes that "really are" Socratic and those that are not. The question for each of the paradoxes is "Did the Stoics arrive at this by reflecting on what Socrates did?" Unfortunately, this question cannot be answered by looking at the Stoic writings. In part, this is due to the paucity of early Stoic writings, and in part, it is due to the kind of evidence we have for Stoic views, since we do not possess much of any Stoic's intellectual autobiography. Still, we can answer the related question, Could the Stoics have arrived easily at their paradoxes by reflecting on what Socrates did? We can do this by reflecting for ourselves on what Socrates did and by testing how easily these reflections point in the direction of Stoic paradoxes.

This is the task of this chapter. I will demonstrate how reflection on Socrates' way of life leads not only to the so-called "prudential paradox" (no one does wrong willingly) and the unity of virtue but also to the six theses that Cicero highlights. Then, to test my hypothesis, I will also consider the ways in which the Stoics qualified their enthusiasm for Socrates' life, and I will argue that these qualifications, too, can be connected to deep reflection on what Socrates did. My primary aim is to explain the Stoics' Socratic inheritance. But I also hope to vindicate Cicero against the current scholars and to cast new light on Socrates. I pin these hopes on a simple fact: the way Socrates lived expresses philosophical commitments that are there to be articulated by anyone who examines his life, whether Socrates himself, or Plato, or Antisthenes, or a Stoic. This is why the question of which paradoxes are Socratic cannot be settled by reference to what Socrates managed to see upon self-examination, much less by reference to what some character called Socrates says in someone else's dialogue. And it is why Stoicism enlarges our awareness not just of what philosophy can be, but also of what Socrates, the Greek and Roman ancients' philosopher *par excellence*, was.

From Socrates' Life to Stoic Paradoxes

The stories about Socrates reveal a single central commitment: to examine lives, his own and others'. He sought to examine lives himself, and he exhorted others to do so, as well. Reflection on this commitment leads easily to the Stoa if we note four further features of Socrates' way of life.

First, Socrates preferred to examine lives by question-and-answer. He did not typically offer long speeches with worked-out theories for others to accept or reject; instead, he asked others questions about their commitments. This characteristic method inspired the genre of Socratic dialogues, and it hardly escaped the Stoics' notice. Book 3 of Chrysippus' *On Dialectic*, for example, insists that question-and-answer argument was important to many previous philosophers, including and "especially" Socrates (Plutarch, *Stoic Refutations* 1045f–1046a).

Although this feature of Socrates' life does not lead immediately to Stoic paradox, it does suggest three important points. First, because Socrates asks questions with the aim of examining lives, he has good reason to focus his queries on the commitments that affect the shape of those lives. And so he apparently did: in the surviving Socratic dialogues, he targets the "most important things," asking about how to live. The Stoics should notice this, too, but it is available to them to disagree with Socrates about what things count as most important, about what commitments are essential to living. As we shall see, many Stoics did disagree with Socrates on this score.

277

Second, if Socrates expected his method to be able to deliver a full examination, he must have thought that (at least) the fundamental moving and shaping attitudes of one's life are (at least potentially) accessible to one. Socrates is less often depicted reflecting on this point, but he was surely committed to it. For if dialectic is sufficient to examine a life, either there are no inaccessibly unconscious drives, or they make no significant difference to life. Of course, Socrates can concede that at least some people are sometimes unable to recognize some of their commitments. Indeed, he can say of them what we might: that they are in denial. But he can also and must insist that their failure to know themselves does not preclude the possibility of self-knowledge. So a Socratic does not yet have to outrage all common sense. But outrage is coming, for the accessibility of our motivating attitudes is crucial to the paradox that no one errs willingly.

Finally, Socrates' commitment to examining lives suggests that there is something good, in general, about examining one's life and, in particular, about engaging in question-and-answer to examine one's life. (Why else would he be so committed to it?) Unsurprisingly, then, Socrates is regularly portrayed avowing the deep importance of the examined life. But this point raises a question: What exactly is the good that Socrates' dialectical examination offers?

To answer this question, we should introduce a second feature of Socrates' examinations, namely, their results. These are typically negative: Socrates regularly shows that the examined person did not have a consistent set of commitments. Sometimes, however, negative results are good. In this case, it is plausible that identifying bad things is good – it at least makes the avoidance or elimination of bad things easier – and plausible that inconsistencies in one's commitments about how to live are bad. Inconsistency in one's commitments is bad in at least two ways. First, inconsistency undermines justification. If, for example, Euthyphro has inconsistent attitudes about piety, then he cannot justify prosecuting his father against the charge that the prosecution is impious. Second, inconsistency threatens the smooth flow of one's life. In part, this second problem piggybacks on the first. Imagine that other people object to something that I want to do. If I cannot justify my desired course of action, then how smooth will my life be? Surely it will not be smooth if I have to bend others to my aims, or be bent by them. Nor is opting for fraud in place of force a guarantee of calm waters ahead. Nor can I easily quit human society to duck the whole problem, for even if the practical difficulties of solo life were easily surmountable, it is likely that I want to live with some other human beings, and so the mere temptation to leave would be just another manifestation of my inconsistency. As this already suggests, inconsistency threatens not just a socially smooth life, but also a psychologically smooth one, but the psychological difficulties of inconsistency extend far beyond any social problems. If I have inconsistent attitudes about how much coffee I should drink, for example, then I am subject to psychological conflict, and I cannot satisfy all my attitudes about coffee (and temperance and nutrition and the rest). There will be dissatisfactions – bumps – in my experience of life.

Zeno of Citium and his followers characterized the human good as a smooth flow of life (Stobaeus II 7.6e 77, 20–1 Wachsmuth; cf. Diogenes Laertius, *Lives of Eminent Philosophers* 7.88 and Sextus Empiricus, *Against the Professors* 11.30), and so these considerations are very close to central Stoic doctrines. But we need a third feature of

Socrates' life to reach the eight paradoxes highlighted above. So let us notice that Socrates examined others not just for the negative result of uncovering inconsistency. He also aimed for a positive result: he sought wisdom or knowledge. If we notice this fact – and who could fail to notice it while characterizing Socrates as a lover of wisdom – and if we take Socrates to be a model, then we must think that his dialectical work can, at least in principle, lead to knowledge. Nor is this is an unreasonable thought. We have already seen that Socratic examination can reach all of one's primary motivating commitments and can bring inconsistencies to light. So dialectic can at least minimize inconsistencies in one's motivating attitudes. In fact, it can do more. Socrates typically exposed inconsistencies by questioning the inferential relations among the examinee's commitments. So any set of commitments that survives Socratic dialectic must exhibit not only mere consistency but also some measure of coherence. We can make sense of how Socratic dialectic aims at knowledge by conceiving of knowledge in terms of coherent psychological commitments.

The Stoics did conceive knowledge as a coherent set of psychological attitudes. They say that knowledge is a "cognitive grasp" (katalēpsis) or a system of cognitive grasps (also called an "art" or "expertise," i.e., technē) that is "stable, firm, and unshakeable by reason or argument (logos)" (Stobaeus II 7.5l 73, 19–74, 1; Diogenes Laertius, Lives of Eminent Philosophers 7.47; Sextus Empiricus, Against the Professors VII 151; Pseudo-Galen, Stoicorum Veterum Fragmenta 2.93; Philo, ibid. 2.95; and cf. Cicero, Academics 1.41–2, who attributes this account of knowledge to Zeno). Central to this definition is the idea that one who knows cannot be forced in a dialectical argument to give up something that he takes himself to know and cannot be led by a dialectical argument to assent to anything that contradicts with what he takes himself to know. The Stoic conception of knowledge neatly expresses the positive aim of surviving Socratic dialectic.

It also raises difficult questions because it seems clear enough to many philosophers that a person could have a coherent set of false beliefs. The evidence suggests that Socrates himself did not worry about this objection, for it appears that Socrates did not concern himself with what knowledge is. Perhaps he just assumed that we have enough common sense to retain at least some true beliefs that would guarantee the truth of all the commitments in a fully coherent set. Those whom Socrates influenced developed different ways of bolstering this assumption. Plato, for example, at least entertained the thought that our souls are naturally geared to the truth by their disembodied experiences before our lifetimes. The Stoics, by contrast, insisted that we are naturally situated in such a way that at least some of our experiences of the world are veridical; they insist that someone who knows has not only perfect mastery of dialectical arguments but also perfect reliability in assent to sense-impressions.

But the finer points of these epistemological reflections on the Socratic way of life are unnecessary to explain the Stoic paradoxes. Once a Stoic embraces psychological coherence as the positive goal of Socratic examination, four of the eight paradoxes are near to hand. Since psychological coherence is knowledge, those who have incoherent (inconsistent or underdeveloped) commitments are ignorant. It also seems reasonable that virtue or excellence characterizes those who know and vice or defect characterizes those who are ignorant. Does this mean that excellence characterizes everything that a knower does, and vice characterizes everything that an ignorant person does?

279

Yes, if we recall the accessibility of motivating attitudes. The person who knows has no conflicting attitudes, conscious or not. So when she judges that such-and-such is excellent to do in these circumstances, she has no motivation to conflict with doing such-and-such. There is no way to explain how a virtuous person could fail to do what she judges to be excellent. And since the virtuous have knowledge, this result means that the excellent cannot fail to do what is, in fact, excellent. On the other hand, the person who is ignorant is doomed to act in defective ways. Even if he does something that is describable in the same terms as what the excellent person would do, we nevertheless cannot say that the ignorant person does something excellent because the excellence of an action depends upon the reasons for which it is done, and the ignorant person's reasons are defective.

We are now playing with paradoxes. First, note that all excellent actions are excellent by virtue of the agent's whole coherent psychology. Actions are not just or temperate by virtue of some limited set of judgments or affective conditions: the same full set of attitudes makes this action just and that action temperate. So the conditions that cause just and temperate actions – justice and temperance, respectively – are the same coherent state of the soul. This is the paradox of the unity of virtue. The paradox need not imply that there are no distinctions among the virtues. A Stoic can and some did distinguish by saying that some judgments (or "theorems") are primary in just actions and others primary in temperate actions (Diogenes Laertius, *Lives of Eminent Philosophers* 7.125–6; Stobaeus II 7.5b5 63, 6–25 Wachsmuth). But there was controversy over this point (see Schofield 1984). The third-century BCE renegade Ariston of Chios denied that a coherent psychology would make judgments in the form of "general theorems" about value (Seneca, *Moral Epistles* 89.13 and 94.2; and Sextus Empiricus, *Against the Professors* 7.12), and so he also denied that there are grounds to distinguish among the virtues, except in relation (e.g., Diogenes Laertius, *Lives of Eminent Philosophers* 7.161). He urged a more radical understanding of the thesis that virtue is one. This seems to have been a dispute about how to understand the Socratic point that the virtues are all one and the same; similar disputes occasioned by Ariston will be considered below.

Next, recall the point that actions done from psychological coherence are virtuous and actions done without psychological coherence are vicious, and add the assumption that there are no degrees of coherence. (This new assumption is reasonable enough: either one's psychology is in harmony or it is not.) We now can say that all virtuous actions are equally virtuous and all vicious actions are equally vicious, and this gives a point to the paradox that all vicious actions are equal and all virtuous actions are equal. As with the unity of virtue, this paradox is compatible with some distinctions. A Stoic can admit that there are grounds for praising some virtuous actions more than others or for blaming some vicious actions more than others (Cicero, *On Ends* 3.48; cf. *Stoic Paradoxes* 20). Indeed, a Stoic should admit this insofar as the commitments that are built into a coherent psychology will themselves generally prefer some virtuous actions to others and will generally prefer to restrain some vicious actions more than others. The Stoic will insist, however, that all virtuous actions are equally virtuous and all vicious actions are equally vicious.

Another of Cicero's paradoxes follows if we add the reasonable assumption that psychological coherence is a model of health. For now we can say that everyone who fails to be wise will fall short of the standard for mental health, and that gives us reason to say that everyone who fails to be wise is insane. Again, the paradox can be understood in a way that renders it false. The Stoics are not saying that a lack of wisdom is indistinguishable from, say, paranoid schizophrenia. They are simply drawing out a Socratic lesson in a particularly pointed way.

Finally, since excellent actions are all and only those done by the knowing and vicious actions are all and only those done by the ignorant, no one does wrong knowingly, and this sustains the prudential paradox that no one does wrong willingly. Again, though, there is potential confusion. The Stoic does not maintain that wrongdoing is always involuntary or free from blame. Rather, the Stoic insists that someone who knows what she is doing would never do wrong. By putting the point in terms of "willingness," the Stoics invite the confusion, but they are nevertheless drawing attention to a perfectly natural sense of acting willingly, the sense in which everyone wills to act while knowing what one is doing. Nor are the Stoics simply sliding from a quotidian sense of "knowing what one is doing" to a demanding sense. When we act from ignorance, we act from an incoherent psychology: we have conflicting or underdeveloped attitudes. But no one wants conflicting or underdeveloped attitudes, at least not as such. When we act, we will to do what we do, and not to undermine or undersupport it. But on the Stoics' Socratic analysis, wrong actions cannot be willed in this wholehearted, integrated way.

Four of the Stoic paradoxes have now emerged from reflection on the Socratic way of life, and in particular from reflection on knowledge as the psychological coherence sought by Socrates' examinations. The remaining four paradoxes depend upon reflection on a fourth feature of Socrates' life: his zealous commitment to examining lives. It is a standard part of the picture of Socrates that he was on a mission. He did not let other interests get in the way, and he did not back down when his examinations discomfited those around him, not even when he faced death. This should suggest to a Stoic reflecting on Socrates' life that there is nothing comparable to the activity of examining lives, nothing for which one might trade it. The Stoic might naturally express this by saying that only philosophical activity is good, that everything else has at best an incomparably different kind of value. But this thought needs to be brought together with our earlier reflections on knowledge and excellence. Surely the philosophical activity that is good is not done from ignorance but from knowledge: it is excellent, virtuous activity. And so the Stoic is led to the thought that only virtuous activity is good.

This introduces another paradox: only the fine is good. Stoics refine this thought by insisting that only virtue itself is, strictly speaking, good, since only virtue has the causal power of benefiting. On this view, virtuous actions, virtuous persons, and virtuous collections of persons (cities, say) are good in a looser sense because virtue benefits through them (Stobaeus II 7.5d 69, 17–70, 3; Sextus Empiricus, *Against the Professors* 11.25–6; and the textually problematic Diogenes Laertius, *Lives of Eminent Philosophers* 7.94). This paradox, too, can lead to misunderstanding. For if only virtue is good, one might think that there is no reason to go for things like health and wealth. Indeed, Stoics maintain that such things are not by themselves beneficial for us; rather, the excellent use of them is beneficial, and the foolish use of them is harmful. So they as opposed to their use – are indifferent to our flourishing. But that is not to say that

281

they are entirely indifferent to us: according to most Stoics – Ariston of Chios is the prominent exception – health, wealth, and the like naturally stimulate us to pursue them. Similarly, other people who are not virtuous are indifferent to our flourishing, but not entirely indifferent to us, since we are naturally stimulated to care for other human beings. Still, the Stoics do not consider health, wealth, and the concerns of others to be goods under another name. When a Stoic goes for health or seeks to help her brother, she is merely preferring health and merely preferring to see her brother aided. She does not see any good in health or in her brother's condition, and she will not be troubled if she fails to achieve health or help for her brother. Her true aim is to go for health or seek to help her brother virtuously. Her natural inclinations for health, wealth, the concerns of others, and the rest are sensitive to the circumstances, and when she chooses the best action available to her, she locates her good in nothing but choosing the best action available to her in the circumstances.

Two more paradoxes enter as consequences of the Stoic sage's perfect grasp of what is good. First, only the sage is free. Deep attraction to things other than one's own virtue leave one enslaved to fortune, and even imperfect apprehension that only virtue is good leaves one vulnerable because one's imperfect judgments are weak and "shakable." But the sage is truly free of fortune's effects. Of course, this freedom that the sage enjoys does not guarantee political freedom, or even freedom from chattel slavery; the Stoics thought that even a chattel slave could and should philosophize (Philo, *Stoicorum Veterum Fragmenta* 3.352 and Lactantius 3.253 with Athenaeus, ibid. 3.353). Second, only the sage is rich. Because the sage alone enjoys what is genuinely good, the sage alone has real wealth, real accumulated value. Of course, the sage's wealth does not guarantee a large amount of money; the Stoics, unlike so many other Greek philosophers, do not think that one has to be financially well-off to live well.

Finally, the exclusive goodness of virtue leads to the paradox that virtue suffices for happiness. Happiness is just the name for a life lived well with enjoyment of goods. But for the Stoics, there are no goods except for virtue, and so there is nothing to living well with enjoyment of goods except living virtuously.

Taking Exception with Socrates

Reflection on Socrates' way of life leads to Cicero's six Stoic paradoxes and the two frequently mentioned by modern scholars. In fact, the connections between Socrates' way of life and fundamental tenets of Stoicism are so deep that one might wonder why the Stoics did not recommend living exactly as Socrates did. Before closing, then, I will consider three ways in which Stoics qualified their enthusiasm for Socrates.

One charge of disagreement needs to be quieted, however. It is reported that the Stoics call irony a trait of the worthless, and not of the sage (Stobaeus II 7.11m 108, 12–13 Wachsmuth = *Stoicorum Veterum Fragmenta* 3.630), and it might be thought that they are thereby disparaging the irony that is prominent in Plato's portrait of Socrates. This is not the case. The standard Greek meaning of "being ironical" (*eirōneuesthai*) is deception, and the Stoics can reject deception without disparaging Socratic irony, which gently mocks and riddles without intending to deceive. In fact, the Stoics had better not be disparaging Socratic irony, since their paradoxes preserve a measure of it: the paradoxes are gently mocking expressions – "only the sage is rich," after all – that pose riddles without being intended to deceive.

There are real disagreements with Socrates, though. First, according to the standard picture, Socrates worked in the agora, out in the open, and was willing to question anyone, Athenian or foreigner, young or old. Stoic response to this was complex. On the one hand, Socrates' openness to examining all sorts of people shows a love of humanity (cf. *Euthyphro* 3d), and the Stoics embrace Socrates' cosmopolitan commitment to benefiting (that is, examining) foreigners alongside compatriots. In *On Lives*, for example, Chrysippus suggests that the sage will engage in politics if circumstances permit, but that he will not limit himself to politics in his homeland if he can better serve human beings abroad as a political advisor (see Brown forthcoming: ch. 7). Later Stoics Musonius (fr. 9 [That Exile is No Evil] 42, 1–2 Hense = Stobaeus III 40.9 749, 2–3 Hense) and Epictetus (*Discourses* 1.9.1) and the Stoicizing *Tusculan Disputations* of Cicero (5.108) and the *On Exile* of Plutarch (600f–601a) make the Socratic provenance of this cosmopolitanism explicit. On the other hand, Socrates' willingness to examine anyone reflects the assumption that dialectical examinations pose no significant risks, and the Stoics reject this as reckless. Like Plato (*Republic* 537e–539a), who thinks that dialectic is too dangerous to be shared with the young, Chrysippus recommends that teachers of Stoic philosophy exercise caution in introducing opposing points of view (Plutarch, *Stoic Refutations* 1036de). The underlying thought seems to be that young people are so easily misled that they should not be exposed to full philosophical activity at a young age. But this disagreement with Socrates is readily explained by reflection on Socrates' life. The fate of Socrates and some of his followers should be enough to cause one to rethink the wisdom of fully extending philosophical activity to the young. Here the Stoics are disagreeing with Socrates, but respecting some lessons of his life.

Second, Socrates lives as though philosophy were a special kind of career, exclusive of other careers like cobblery and ordinary politics. Socrates' philosophical life is not a life of withdrawn contemplation as it is for Plato, Aristotle, and Epicurus – indeed, it is, according to Plato's *Gorgias* (521d), engaged in politics – but it is, like the contemplative life, separate from other possible careers. Stoics reject this feature of the Socratic way of life, too, for they insist that living philosophically is compatible with any situation in life. As I have already noted, Stoics think that even a chattel slave can and should philosophize. Nevertheless, the conception that informs this disagreement may nonetheless be rooted in a reflection on Socrates' way of life – indeed, one may very well extract from the inclusivity of his inquiries a commitment that is not evident in the way he seems to regard his own activity as a specialized career. Socrates dedicates himself full-time to dialectical examinations – he is willing to examine cobblers and the like, in the hope that a cobbler might know more than he about the most important matters. So although Socrates' way of life by itself gives the impression of a special sort of career apart from the need to make money, the way he extends his mission might still suggest something more in accordance with the Stoic picture.

Finally, on the standard account, Socrates had a narrow conception of the important matters that one must examine. He ignored not just the question about what knowledge is but also questions about the natural world (Plato, *Apology* 19b–d; Xenophon, *Memorabilia* 1.1.11–16; Aristotle, *Metaphysics* A 6 987b1–2; etc.). Many

283

Stoics, including the early heads of the school, rejected this; they held that one needed to understand the way the natural world is to have knowledge, i.e., psychological coherence. On their view, physics, logic, and ethics are unified just as justice, temperance, courage, and wisdom are.

But here, too, we have a disagreement with Socrates that shows deep engagement with him. First, there were Stoics, especially Ariston of Chios, who opposed the teaching of the scholarchs. Ariston rejected the study of the natural world in Socratic terms by saying that it is beyond us human beings (Diogenes Laertius, *Lives of Eminent Philosophers* 6.103 and 7.160; Seneca, *Moral Epistles* 89.13 and 94.2; Sextus Empricus, *Against the Professors* 7.12; Stobaeus II 1.24 8, 13–18 Wachsmuth). Second, at least one of the scholarchs insisted that Socrates did have cosmological views. Zeno of Citium evidently connected the basic doctrines of Stoic cosmology to Socrates by relying on the one portrait of Socrates displaying views about the nature of the cosmos (Xenophon, *Memorabilia* 1.4.5–18 and 4.3.2–18; see Cicero, *On the Nature of the Gods* 2.18 and Sextus Empiricus, *Against the Professors* 9.101 with DeFilippo and Mitsis 1994). So the Stoics disagree about whether any of them are disagreeing with Socrates. Their contest over whether the good life requires knowledge of the cosmos is also a contest over who Socrates was, and this vividly exhibits in one small part the development of Stoicism out of reflection on Socrates' manner of living.

References

Alesse, F. (2000). *La Stoa e la Tradizione Socratica* [The Stoa and the Socratic Tradition]. Naples: Bibliopolis.

Brown, E. (2000). Socrates the cosmopolitan. *Stanford Agora: An Online Journal of Legal Studies*, 1, 77–84.

—— (forthcoming). *Stoic Cosmopolitanism*. Cambridge: Cambridge University Press.

DeFilippo, J. G. and Mitsis, P. T. (1994). Socrates and Stoic natural law. In Paul A. Vander Waerdt (ed.), *The Socratic Movement* (pp. 252–71). Ithaca, NY: Cornell University Press.

Long, A. A. (1988). Socrates in Hellenistic philosophy. *Classical Quarterly*, 38, 150–71.

Schofield, M. (1984). Ariston of Chios and the unity of virtue. *Ancient Philosophy*, 4, 83–95.

Striker, G. (1994). Plato's Socrates and the Stoics. In Paul A. Vander Waerdt (ed.), *The Socratic Movement* (pp. 241–51). Ithaca, NY: Cornell University Press.

18

Socrates and Epictetus

TAD BRENNAN

Introduction

Epictetus was a celebrated Stoic philosopher of the Roman Imperial era. His precise dates of birth and death are not known, but the years 60 CE and 130 CE cannot be far off the mark. Born into slavery, he spent his youth as a slave in a powerful Roman household, and was freed only as a late teen or young adult. He became the student of Musonius Rufus, a Stoic philosopher who came from Roman nobility, but taught in Greek, as Epictetus did. He was exiled from Rome by the emperor Domitian, and lived the rest of his life in the Greek city of Nicopolis.

The parallels between Socrates and Epictetus are striking: the following biographical précis could apply to either.

> A brilliant and celebrated talker, he wrote nothing. Nearly everything we know of him comes from the writings of a devoted student who depicted him in conversation with others. There are, at the same time, so many contemporary references to him from independent sources that there can be no doubt that he was an historical figure, and that he must have been roughly as the student portrayed him. He was notorious for his poverty and for the simplicity of his life. Young men were attracted to his evident moral integrity; his courage, honesty, modesty, and good cheer. His philosophical activities incurred official displeasure, which ended his philosophical career in his home city. A man of deep piety and unimpeachable moral rectitude, he was nevertheless possessed of a salty, mocking, and plebeian sense of humor, that derived some of its effectiveness from its ability to shock. When he spoke with important people, he would prod them to examine their lives, and dismantle their pretensions. The theme of his every sermon was virtue; he spoke almost exclusively about ethics, and the physical and logical aspects of philosophy he relegated to a distant second place in the curriculum.

The similarities between Socrates and Epictetus are made even more striking because of the similarities between the students who wrote their biographical records. In the case of Epictetus, the student in question was Arrian – Lucius Flavius Arrianus – a Roman noble who seems to have conceived early in life a plan to be the new Xenophon, and devoted his career to producing literary works that would parallel the earlier figure's output. Thus he wrote a treatise on hunting with dogs, to match Xenophon's

Cynegeticus, a history of Alexander's wars, to match the *Anabasis*, and finally, to match Xenophon's *Memorabilia*, he wrote the *Discourses of Epictetus*, in which he recorded conversations between Epictetus and the students and visitors at his school. Even though we have lost half of the eight volumes that Arrian wrote, we still have in the four surviving volumes of the *Discourses* an unparalleled source for our knowledge of later Stoicism and later philosophy in general, as well as a valuable source for the social history of philosophy and pedagogy in the early Imperial era.

This chapter juxtaposes Socrates and Epictetus for two reasons: to use Socrates to deepen our understanding of Epictetus, and to use Epictetus to deepen our understanding of Socrates. It is the second of these that will be of more central interest to readers of this volume. We can learn something about the legacy and afterlife of Socrates by seeing his impact on Epictetus. We can also gauge something of Socrates' greatness by seeing how easy it was to imitate the outer man, and how hard it was to reproduce the vital element of genius.

Epictetus seems to have invoked Socrates' name and fate on a daily basis; he quotes or refers to Socrates more than to any other figure, even more than the leaders of the Stoic school to which he belonged, and clearly models his own life and ways on the ways and life of Socrates. Where Socrates had been condemned to death, Epictetus was condemned to exile; where Socrates endured battle and discomfort, Epictetus endured slavery and torture; where Socrates drew his examples from common-place cobblers and carpenters, Epictetus drew his from low-brow diversions like dice and ball-games. Socrates was content with his single cloak, and Epictetus made do with the commonest kind of earthenware lamp.

The trouble is that it is so easy to copy Socrates' Silenic exterior, and so difficult to copy his divine internal essence – indeed, it is difficult and controversial, as the present volume should amply attest, even to say what that divine internal essence is. Epictetus himself was well aware of the general problem, and he explicitly cautions against copying the exterior garb of the Cynics (themselves avidly copying Socrates) without copying their internal psychic disposition, which he takes to be the thing of real value in the Cynic way of life (3.22). Epictetus did succeed in recapturing some parts of Socrates' internal disposition, but not the parts that might first suggest themselves. I shall argue this case by looking at two points of resemblance where Epictetus licenses Socratic trademarks: his use of the elenchus, and his use of irony.

The Elenchus

Elenctic refutations can be found in the *Discourses*, as can an interest in definitions. But several things have changed.

The legacy of Stoic empiricism has led to a new rationale for how dialectical encounters with ordinary people can lead to philosophical results. Why think that there is any truth in that idle and popular reservoir of opinions, the common man on the street? Plato had answered this question via the doctrine of Recollection. The Stoics answered it by appeal to the doctrine of preconceptions (*prolēpseis*, singular *prolēpsis*). Preconceptions are concepts of natural features in the world, such as "human being" or "water," which all of us are guaranteed to acquire by natural processes, if our sensory faculties are unimpaired. Even though we are born with our minds like a blank sheet of paper, as the Stoics tell us, throughout our childhood we receive innumerable perceptual impressions, for instance the perceptions of particular human beings. Through the accumulation of these impressions we develop a concept of human being that is both accurate in its outlines and also adequate to allow us to proceed philosophically; it has everything needed for a full understanding of human beings, once dialectical refinement has purged it of unclarities and accretions. Among the preconceptions that we acquire naturally in this way, the Stoics claimed, are the concepts of goodness, virtue, and the other central issues in ethics, derived from our perceptual observations of human affairs. The preconceptions are the raw material for elenctic inquiry, and their emergence into a fully articulated, philosophically refined system of philosophical concepts is inquiry's goal. Here is Epictetus' methodological reflection on this point:

> Preconceptions are common to all human beings, and one preconception does not conflict with another. For who among us does not assert that "the good is advantageous and choiceworthy," and that "we ought to follow and pursue it in every circumstance"? And who among us does not assert that "justice is a fine and fitting thing"? Where then does the conflict come in? It concerns the application of these preconceptions to particulars, when one person says "he did well; he is courageous," and the other says, "what? He acted like a mad-man!" There it is; the source of interpersonal conflict for human beings.... What then is it to acquire an education? It means to learn how to apply the natural preconceptions to particular cases, in the way that corresponds to nature. (1.22.1–4, 9)

So far so good; Stoicism seems to have provided an epistemological framework that can make possible a Socratic search for wisdom through dialectic, under the description "learning to apply the preconceptions to the particulars." But in practice, the Epictetan results differ from Socrates' accomplishments in even the shortest Platonic dialogues. The difference seems to lie both in the complexity of the elenctic structures that each dialectician employs, and also in the complexity of the underlying object of search.

Differences of Structure

Epictetan arguments are invariably short and unconnected. Whether the negative argument of refutation or the positive argument of doctrinal exposition, Epictetus never seems to construct extended chains of distant points, nor do we ever see him use multiple elenchi in concert. The texture, surprise, and brilliance of a Socratic refutation comes in part from his habit of eliciting some harmless-sounding concession from an interlocutor at an early juncture, letting it sit idle and unmentioned for some minutes, and then combining it at the last moment with some other concessions that jointly demolish the interlocutor's views. By contrast, an Epictetan destructive argument never needs to assemble more than a few premises; sometimes he simply elicits the interlocutor's assent straight away. And the elenctic stages are not strongly marked as they are in Plato.

287

Consider the typical 3.1.1–9, in which Epictetus sets out to convince a young man that beauty consists in virtue. Epictetus secures his agreement to the following propositions:

1) For each species (dogs, horses, and humans taken for induction) some members are beautiful and some are ugly.
2) A member is beautiful when in the state that most corresponds to its nature;
3) each species has a different nature
4) so the states that constitute beauty will be different for each species
5) but the same thing, generically speaking, will make each species beautiful
6) and this factor that is generically the same will be *aretē*, i.e. the *aretē* of each species (again by induction on horses and dogs)
7) when we praise humans dispassionately (*dikha pathous*) we praise the just, temperate, and self-controlled rather than their opposites
8) thus you will make yourself beautiful when and only when you make yourself just, temperate, etc.

If we are impressed by the use of induction from cases, the animal examples, the question and answer, the securing of agreement, then we may cast it as an elenchus, whose target for refutation was something like "human beauty consists in fine hair and costly adornments." But the interlocutor does not state that claim at the beginning of the passage (it seems instead to be inferred from his appearance), and Epictetus takes no pains to spell out its negation at the end.

This is not to deny that Epictetus sometimes employs straightforward *ad hominem* refutations of an interlocutor's position, i.e. the canonical Socratic refutation. But the difference in what they make of such refutations shows, I think, why it was always a mistake to single out the elenchus in Socratic method. Most of Plato's Socratic dialogues have a structure that extends far beyond the set-piece elenchus that has dominated discussions of Socratic methodology. Far more happens than the mere eliciting of premises for p and not p. To say that it is the elenchus that characterizes Socratic philosophizing is rather like saying that it is the melody that characterizes Bach's compositions: it encourages us to focus at the wrong level of compositional complexity. Of course Socrates used elenchi, just as Bach used melodies, but the better question is to ask, of any given refutation, what is Socrates using it for? Is he using it, as at *Euthyphro* 8b8–d2 merely to nudge his interlocutor away from an *ignoratio elenchi*? Is he using it, as at *Republic* 1 338c in order to request a clearer formulation of a proposal? Or is Socrates using a complicated system of refutations in order to sketch out a complex positive doctrine?

Consider the *Protagoras*, for instance. If we look for the elenchus, we can find it: Protagoras makes some claims about the virtues and then is shown, in a series of brief exchanges, that he is committed to the opposite of these claims. But to characterize the dialogue in this way is to miss the fact that Socrates constructs an argumentative architectonic that incorporates a half-dozen brief refutations, and dozens of pages of text. It is not an unstructured string of unrelated refutations; what Socrates does is to demonstrate the equivalence of the five virtues by constructing four pair-wise equivalence-proofs (in fact he must offer two proofs of the final pair-wise equivalence between courage and wisdom, because Protagoras balks at his first attempt). And in a virtuoso feat of theorem-proving, each of the proofs he constructs turns on a different trick; none of them uses the same device twice. Or consider in the *Gorgias* the lengthy and complex refutation of Callicles' claim that pleasure is the good, stretching from 492 to his capitulation at 499, involving at least three distinguishable elenctic movements, each employing a different and complementary argumentative strategy (from 494b to 495c a direct attempt to find pleasures that Callicles will agree are bad; from 495c to 497d an argument based on an analysis of change between opposites; from 497e to 499b an argument from an analysis of "presence" or property-inherence). Notice how each of these different elenchi are related to fundamental issues about nonethical matters – the analysis of pleasure, change and inherence – that Socrates will develop into topics in their own right in other dialogues; these themes and melodic motifs are briefly sounded here, but will be more fully orchestrated elsewhere. This kind of complexity is not uncommon in Socratic elenchi, but there is nothing like it in Epictetus.

Differences of Object

In Epictetus, the task of securing agreement to the preconception is far too easy, and the preconceptions which people are shown to possess are far too thin and informationally impoverished when compared to the Forms that Socrates wishes to find. This is the second problem with Epictetan elenchus.

There is a great gulf between trifling propositions like "just things are to be done" or "the good is advantageous" and the fine-grained, particularist knowledge of how such preconceptions are to be applied to particular cases. And this fine-grained, particularist knowledge is intrinsically uncongenial to discursive verbal analysis of the set-piece elenctic style: there's simply not a lot to say about it, whether one has it or not. The adept, who has the Aristotelian eye, cannot provide useful antecedent formulations of his method; the struggling beginner would better spend his time attempting to judge cases under expert guidance. There is no middle ground of articulable discursive theory that would allow us to talk our way from an initial grasp of the preconceptions up to a detailed knowledge of how they apply to cases.

The excitement in reading Plato's Socratic dialogues comes from the sense that we are exploring and mapping that middle ground: we are searching for some knowledge that can be elicited from ordinary speakers, but will be surprising, substantive, and contentful. It will start from our common stock of preconceptions, but show us new and unsuspected connections between disparate concepts and beliefs, and will give us, if we can pursue it to its conclusion, such a clear grasp of ethical truth that we will be able to solve individual cases with certainty and ease.

Take, for example, the *Euthyphro*. Socrates wants to find an account of piety that has two features: first, it is the sort of thing that we could acquire by means of Socratic question and answer, right here and now, if Euthyphro will only persist and not abandon the search. Second, it is the sort of thing whose possession, once acquired, will allow us to "look upon it, and using it as model, say that any action of yours or another's that is of that kind is pious and if it is not of that kind that it is not pious"

(*Euthyphro* 6e). Any action. Merely by possessing that account, we will be able to judge every possible particular case that could arise, down to the finest differences of detail.

The Form, even here in the *Euthyphro*, has this double aspect; it resembles a concept so far as its means of discovery go, but in its informational density, in its richness of detail, it more closely resembles a perceptible particular. It's as though a game of twenty questions could lead to the answer "box turtle," and then by winning that game I could come into instant possession of a real flesh-and-blood box turtle that I could examine and study to the level of microscopic detail, to learn about box turtles in every particular. That, it seems to me, is Socrates' goal, even in the earliest Platonic depictions of him, even before the *Meno* has introduced the doctrine of Recollection that could make this more plausible (since it is not implausible that a conceptually slender verbal guessing-game could remind me of the whereabouts of an informationally dense perceptible particular that I have merely misplaced).

This goal affects how we understand dialectical defeats. When Laches proposes that courage is holding one's position in battle, Socrates reminds him that sometimes it is equally courageous to retreat (*Laches* 190–1). This counterexample is taken, by all participants, as evidence that Laches' proposal is a failure, and that Laches does not know what courage is; he just isn't seeing it. The definition's failure is taken as an occasion for further talk, further research, further discussion, directed towards developing a more adequate account of courage.

But when we talk with Epictetus, the fact that a case fails to fit with an interlocutor's proposal is no longer taken to undermine the interlocutor's possession of a definition, nor does it provide a spur to further discussion. Instead, the Epictetan analysis will say that Laches is in full possession of the "preconception" of courage – he has all of the thin-blooded, conceptual content there is to be had in such a thing – but that he failed to apply it properly to the case at hand. What is needed is more training, more habituation, more repetition of precepts.

We might put the point anachronistically by saying that Epictetus seems to have lost confidence in the possibility of a synthetic *a priori*, the possibility that the pure exercise of rationality can lead to astounding discoveries. Pure philosophizing, of the Socratic question-and-answer type, can now produce nothing more than analytic truisms, uncontroversially acceptable to the virtuous and the vicious alike. Differences in moral character are the result of years of nondialectical training; exercising one's ability to resist temptations ("starting from the smallest things . . ."), drilling oneself in saws and slogans ("say over to yourself . . . ," "have ready to hand . . ."), and training one's appetites to resist the temptation of drinking cold water on a hot day.

This picture of ethical knowledge – that it consists largely in the nonrational habituation of our desires and emotions – is familiar from Aristotle, and many people find it more plausible as a view of ethics than the view I am attributing to Socrates. Many people will find Epictetus' more empiricist understanding of conceptual content more plausible as an account of rationality, too. My point is not to dismiss Epictetan meta-ethics or take a stand on the relative plausibility of one or the other account of rationality; my point is to suggest how a central point of similarity between Socrates and Epictetus comes to look like a point of fundamental difference. Yes, both of them philosophize by question and answer, and sometimes refute their interlocutors. But the natures of their elenchi differ in deep ways, which are related to deep differences in their respective conceptions of the objects of ethical knowledge, and of the nature and possibilities of rational discourse itself.

Ironies Epictetan and Socratic

Socrates is famous for his irony; Epictetus was ironical as well. When Epictetus meets a rival philosopher he begins with a flattering request for instruction, and denies that he himself is a philosopher: "It is only right that we, who are laymen, should learn by inquiring from you who are philosophers" (3.7.1). He declares that he is not a philosopher, just a lame old man (1.8.14; 1.16.20). All of these expressions are clearly instances of Epictetan irony, and can be paralleled by similar Socratic statements. But here too I believe that the differences preponderate on a closer examination.

The philosophical reasons for Socrates' irony are to be found in his assessment of his own epistemic status in relation to moral knowledge, and his assessment of the status of others. He thinks that there is a body of systematic, expert ethical knowledge to be had. He has some views about what this knowledge might look like, both in its overall shape, and in regards to some of the details. But he does not think that his grasp of the details and their interconnections comes close to constituting that knowledge. Accordingly, he does not believe that he can offer to teach anyone else, since it is a concomitant of his larger, meta-ethical and epistemological views that teaching is possible only for someone who has expert knowledge. He also never had a teacher himself; he has never been able to receive expert knowledge from someone better placed than he is. And it has been his experience, repeatedly confirmed, that people who profess to teach moral expertise do not have knowledge either, though he makes a habit of taking their professions at face value before he scrutinizes their claims to knowledge.

Philosophy in the school of Epictetus is markedly different. It is no longer early days in ethics; Socrates brought philosophy down from the heavens to the earth, but he did it 500 years ago. Epictetus is an adherent of the Stoic school, which has its established doctrines and positions, developed, codified and entrenched over four of those last five centuries. He had a teacher – he mentions Musonius with respect and affection. He has students – there is no coyness or qualification, none of the Socratic dance of disclaimers, in his institutional relation to them. He wants to teach them, and takes his role as teacher seriously (1.10.8). He sometimes expresses annoyance at his own limitations and failures (1.9.12), but it is fundamentally different from the Socratic stance of being in principle incapable of teaching, of having nothing to teach. Epictetus knows that he can teach, and knows that he has a body of doctrine to convey, namely orthodox Chrysippean Stoicism.

His ironic stance towards non-Stoic experts (see above) is grounded in their ignorance of the true Stoic way, and the need to remove people's self-conceit before they can learn anew (2.11.6, 2.17.1, 3.14.8). His ironic stance towards himself is grounded in the fact that he is not a Stoic Sage – he cannot make every one of his actions a virtuous action, and rid himself of all tendency to opine. That is not so great a failing – Stoic Sages are famously not to be found, and it had not stopped the Stoic scholarchs from teaching.

These are some of the philosophical and structural differences that give rise to differences between Socratic irony and Epictetan irony. But in addition, Socratic irony has a different emotional freighting, a sort of passive-aggressive hostility, that is generally lacking from Epictetus. For Epictetus, humility is a part of the philosopher's garb, like his beard and rough cloak; for Socrates, it is a prelude to humiliating others.

The judgment that Socratic irony is needlessly spiteful and biting – the sense that he takes a less than admirable pleasure in humiliating people, and goes out of his way to exaggerate their sense of self-importance in order to aggravate their fall – is very common among nonprofessional readers of Plato.

Some of the people whom he humiliates are moral monsters like Callicles, Alcibiades, or Thrasymachus, who perhaps in some sense deserve no better. But Socratic humiliation was not reserved for people of especial viciousness; Socrates visited it on all of his interlocutors. He tells us himself, in the *Apology*, that from his very first dialectical encounter, he provoked hatred in the people with whom he spoke. The politicians, poets, and craftsmen with whom he spoke were not all nihilists and proto-Nietzscheans like Callicles, and yet all were provoked to hatred by the treatment they received. And it is not surprising that they will have resented their humiliation, especially when Socrates tells us that it was witnessed by a crowd of his young hangers-on who enjoyed watching him examine people. They took pleasure in the spectacle, Socrates tells us, and he himself took pleasure in it. And when the young men imitated Socrates' method, they provoked the same hatred in their victims – there was something about the method, and the attitude, that had this effect. Xenophon shows us this side of Socrates, too; he begins questioning Glaucon with an air of solicitude, but Glaucon himself soon sees that Socrates is making fun of him. Xenophon's Hippias, an inoffensive sophist if there ever was one, demands that Socrates answer the question "what is justice?" for a change, saying "you are content to laugh at every one when you question and refute them, but you are never willing to submit yourself to an argument and make a declaration about anything." Socrates laughs at everyone, makes fun of them, takes pleasure in their refutation, and arouses hatred in his interlocutors.

If we professionals resist taking notice of these facts, it may be because the charge of malice is too often used as part of a reductive, nonphilosophical account of Socrates' methods and aims, which substitutes psychological speculation for the real work of understanding his views and arguments. Calling him "spiteful" or "despotic" is no substitute for understanding the structure of the dialectic, nor will it explain his interest in definitions, his use of epagogic induction, his concern with consistency and contradiction – none of the properly philosophical characteristics that make up the Socratic method.

But once we have taken account of those philosophical characteristics, in the properly philosophical way, there is still the spite left over. It does not explain the method, but the method does not explain it either. And when we want to give a full account of the similarities and differences between Socrates and Epictetus, we should be curious about this further difference in emotional tone, for which the differences in philosophical method provide no explanation. It may simply be beyond explanation, but if an explanation is to be sought, it should probably be sought exactly in the emotional positions and histories of the two individuals.

Let us first note a crucial difference in the scope of Socratic irony: he is ironical not only about wisdom and knowledge, but about beauty as well, particularly the beauty of young boys that was prized in Athens. In the *Symposium*, Plato makes Alcibiades the author of this deep insight, that Socrates' attitude towards wisdom is like his attitude towards physical beauty: he makes a great show of being impressed by the wisdom of others, only to reveal through his questions that he thinks they are not wise, and he makes a great show of being swept off his feet by the sight of beautiful men, but is in fact wholly unmoved by them. Alcibiades explicitly lists these as parallel aspects of Socratic irony:

> To begin with, he's crazy about beautiful boys: he constantly follows them around in a perpetual daze. Also, he likes to say he's ignorant and knows nothing. . . . Believe me, it couldn't matter less to him whether a boy is beautiful. You can't imagine how little he cares whether a person is beautiful. He considers all these possessions beneath contempt, and that's exactly how he considers all of us as well. In public, I tell you, his whole life is one big game – a game of irony. (216de, Woodruff and Nehamas, trans.)

Alcibiades offers his own case as an instance of this claim: Socrates at first seemed to be smitten by his youthful beauty, but later despised it and laughed at it, leaving Alcibiades deeply humiliated. And Alcibiades claims that Socrates frequently does this, with "Charmides and Euthydemus and many others" (222b), mentioning what are clearly public episodes well known to most of the people present at the symposium.

They should remind us of the other public episodes – with Protagoras, or Gorgias, or Hippias – where Socrates begins by affecting to gush over someone's wisdom, and then later leaves the claimant to wisdom publicly humiliated.

I want to suggest – though it is a step into speculation to suggest it – that this simultaneous desire for beauty and dismissal of beauty, this complicated push-and-pull, is related to Socrates' own ugliness, just as his push-and-pull attitude towards people who claim wisdom is related to his own ignorance. Plato has Socrates make this connection, or has him put it into Diotima's mouth, when she makes Eros both ignorant and ugly as a condition of his being a seeker of knowledge and beauty (*Symposium* 203–4).

But now that we are allowing ourselves to think about the source of the hostility in Socratic interactions, his ugliness takes on a different significance. It is, to be very blunt, a source of humiliation for Socrates himself. Yes, he makes jokes at his own expense (see Xenophon's *Symposium* 5.5), and seems to be at ease. But we must re-member that Socrates lived and grew up in a culture that was intensely, obsessively, conscious of male beauty and its lack, especially in young men. It is hard to imagine that the young Socrates was not made to feel his own lack of beauty, and in a way that left scars of humiliation. The grown-up accommodates and arrives at what peace he can; but that is no proof that the humiliation has entirely disappeared.

I want to take a further step into speculation by positing one particular kind of youthful humiliation. Like all speculation, it must be judged on the basis of its intrinsic plausibility, its ability to explain other facts, and its ability to make disparate data cohere.

Let us recall that young Athenian aristocrats typically came of age by attaching themselves to an older man who would teach them wisdom and virtue in exchange for

293

erotic companionship; it was an exchange of beauty for wisdom, of exactly the sort that Alcibiades offers at *Symposium* 218. Having an older suitor was a source of pride, as the *Lysis* tells us (206), and presumably it will have been a source of embarrassment to be overlooked by all the suitors, when your age-mates and companions are being courted.

In light of these facts, it is worth considering the strong likelihood that Socrates never had an *erastēs*. No man ever offered him wisdom in exchange for beauty. From the social perspective, it is not unlikely: he will have been famously ugly in his youth, too, and all the evidence about this beauty-obsessed culture suggests this would have hindered his chance of being sought after by an older man. But then from the intellectual perspective, we also have reason to believe that Socrates never had an older mentor, a trusted font of wisdom, a teacher who would take him under his wing.

That intellectual fact – that Socrates was an autodidact – is so familiar that one might wonder what is gained by rephrasing it in the social terms, replacing "untutored" with "unloved." Something is gained, however, in our understanding of the emotional roots of Socrates' ironic stance, if we see that he was publicly excluded, in his adolescence, from the marketplace in which beauty was exchanged for wisdom. Something shifts if we reconsider his familiar ironic contempt for others' beauty and for others' wisdom, his defiant expressions of untaught independence, if we consider it a reaction of lacerated pride with its origins in a boy's ordinary and understandable desire to be esteemed, included, and prized by his peers and elders. During the years when his teenage friends were being initiated into the civic and social mysteries of adult male mastery, Socrates was shunted aside, left on his own, humiliated, for reasons only too plain to see.

Again, I do not offer this speculation as an explanation for the properly philosophical aspects of Socrates' views, method, and behavior. Those aspects are best explained philosophically, not psychologically. But many other aspects of his life make better sense if we imagine him scarred by adolescent erotic rejection.

Most clear-cut in this regard are his inveterate attempts to make himself an object of erotic pursuit, instead of the pursuer. In the passage from Xenophon's *Symposium* cited before, he undertakes to prove that he is more beautiful, with his bulging eyes and snub nose, than the young and beautiful Critobolus. The scene is charming and witty; is it not, if our speculation is correct, a little sad as well? He feels a rush of lust for Charmides and thinks of a poem by Cydias on the predatory nature of pederastic desire, but then dissembles his own role by making himself the helpless fawn in the poem, and making young Charmides the ravening lion (*Charmides* 155d). Witty, indeed, and dishonest as well; and is there not still evident here the desire to be desired as an object of attraction instead of passed over as an object of indifference or loathing? Decades after his adolescence has ended, he still longs to be desirable, and manipulates others into fulfilling that frustrated wish. As Alcibiades says, "he deceives us, presenting himself as the *erastēs*, but then constituting himself as the *paidika* instead of the *erastēs*" (*Symposium* 222b). Why does he do this? Why does he maneuver young and beautiful men into playing the role of *erastēs* to his *eromenos*?

We should also revisit, in this regard, his "whispering in a corner with three or four boys" (*Gorgias* 485d) – perhaps he is not attempting to seduce them so much as attempting to return to a time when his own seducer might still appear. But no seducer is worthy of him; in his perpetual fantasy of how adolescence should have gone, a parade of great men – Protagoras, Gorgias, Hippias, and more – offer him their wisdom, and he, the *beau garçon sans merci*, spurns them all and sends them off, humiliated by his scrutiny. Here is the fantasy he must sustain: the cause of his erotic failures was not his own lack of beauty, but his suitors' lack of wisdom. It was they, not he, who came unprovisioned to the marketplace where beauty is exchanged for wisdom, and he will prove their lack of wisdom, in the marketplace, for the rest of his life. If Apollo's prophecy gave the outlines to his elenctic mission, could not his erotic disappointments have contributed the emotional overtones of gratuitous spite? He would still have philosophized no matter how his adolescence went, but with greater generosity, with less contention, with a more uniform ability to live up to the ideal of disinterested, benevolent joint inquiry that he articulates on his best days.

My proposal, then, is that we think seriously about Socrates as someone who had a youth, and whose youth partly shaped his adult behavior. And I propose that we think seriously about how strange Socrates' behavior was, even in the context of the pederastic culture of Athens – both his passive-aggressive attitude towards the beauty of young boys, and his spitefully ironical attitude towards those who claimed to be wise. I have no great confidence that my particular speculations provide the needed explanations, but it seems to me that there are facts to be explained. They are, first, the gratuitously hostile edge to Socrates' irony; second, the parallel, clearly drawn in the *Symposium*, between his irony towards beauty and his irony towards wisdom, with its push-and-pull alternation of excessive susceptibility followed by aggressive deflation; third, his tendency to cast himself in the role that society reserved for beautiful young boys, when he was no longer young and had never been beautiful. That Socrates had no teacher is an uncontroversial fact; I translate it into the controversial proposal that he had no lover, in the hope of offering some insight into these and other facts.

But at the end of the day, it still remains a highly speculative proposal. What we can assert categorically, however, is that Epictetus presents few of these complexities. There is in general a great deal less bite to Epictetus' irony, and less twist as well; it is more gentle and overt, less underhanded and sly. It is also, so far as I can see, wholly unerotic. Epictetus never ironizes beauty: he neither pretends to be overawed by the beauty of young men, nor attempts to maneuver others into acting the part of his untimely admirers. Surely the social context is partly determinative here; the elaborate system of Athenian pederastic practices is not still in force in Imperial Rome. In Musonius, Epictetus had the teacher that Socrates lacked – but there is no reason to think that he either had, or ever looked for, the complex of emotional, sexual, and social relations with Musonius that Socrates will have watched his age-mates enjoying with their *erastai*. In accounting for the differences between Socratic and Epictetan irony, these biographical differences may supplement the differences at the level of philosophical position.

Concluding Comparisons

Epictetus shows us what it meant to be Socratic, to be a follower of Socrates, in a provincial town in the second century CE, instead of fifth-century Athens. He punctures pretensions, but the pretensions that his interlocutors bring to him are more often social than intellectual. He upbraids Roman aristocrats (1.11, 2.14.18; 2.24.24), but never encounters a really clever and philosophically adept antagonist; one wonders how he would have come off against a Callicles, or even a Protagoras. He does some shadow-boxing with fictive skeptics (1.5; 2.20.28–37), and talks with an unimpressive representative of the Epicurean school (3.7), but the level of intellectual debate in Nicopolis is low – lower than that in fifth-century Athens, and lower even than the level presupposed by Cicero's dialogues. The fault lies partly in the short supply of brilliant opponents for him to argue with – Socrates was eternally lucky to be the contemporary of the sophists. But we do have one record of his meeting a pugilist in his own weight-class, and it is Epictetus who comes off bruised. A rival philosopher named Demonax heard him once extolling the virtues of marriage, and quipped that Epictetus had so thoroughly convinced him that he wished to ask Epictetus for one of his daughters' hands in marriage – this to ridicule Epictetus' own unmarried and childless state. We don't have this anecdote from Arrian, of course, but that is the problem. Plato wrote a *Protagoras* and a *Gorgias*, but Arrian did not write dialogues with titles like *Demonax* or *Favorinus*, that could have shown us Epictetus striking sparks against metal as hard as his own.

Epictetus is, for all this, a deeply admirable figure, a stirring moralist, and a captivating talker. He was convinced that so long as he tried to keep his soul virtuous, no earthly evil could undermine his happiness, and he entrusted his fate to the gods with complete confidence. He did so most often by quoting Socrates from the *Crito*, a Socrates who is notable for his sincerity, lack of irony, and tenacious reliance on a stock of convictions that, he says, have passed the test of repeated self-examination.

If we assume that Plato and Arrian both were faithful copyists, we must suppose that Socrates was incomparably greater than Epictetus, for Plato's Socrates is incomparably greater than Arrian's Epictetus. But having surveyed the evidence for Epictetus' inferiority to Socrates, we must also consider the possibility that the fault is Arrian's instead. I do not mean to suggest that Arrian recorded Epictetus inaccurately; the *Discourses* bear many traces of having been taken down verbatim and given only the lightest and least intrusive editing. No, what I mean to suggest is that Arrian may have been at fault for being too faithful, for not making Epictetus look better than he was.

Mill's methods of similarity and difference suggest that the presence or absence of Socrates does not seem to be the determinative causal factor in differences of philosophical greatness. For Xenophon's Socrates is an inferior philosopher to Plato's Socrates, and Xenophon's Socrates is only too similar to Arrian's Epictetus. It may be that Socrates was no better than Epictetus after all: it's simply that Plato was so much more brilliant than the second Xenophon.

This cannot be a popular line of speculation in a volume devoted to celebrating Socrates, but we should raise it nonetheless. Is it possible that Socrates – the historical Socrates – was really much like Epictetus – shallow and repetitive, well-versed in the opening gambits of dialectical debates but with little vision of how to construct theories or advance positive views? The author of the *Cleitophon*, whether it was Plato or not, levels this sort of charge at Socrates: that he is unsurpassed at the initial protreptic task of inspiring people to seek virtue, but then is simply unable to say anything about virtue beyond such platitudes as "just men produce something beneficial." From the *Crito* we learn that every point Socrates argues for in that dialogue is a point that he and Crito had already rehearsed many times in the past. If we had transcriptions of those earlier recitations, they might read rather like Epictetus; the same narrow ambit of ethical concerns, the same few saws and adages trotted out at every turn, the emphasis on repetition rather than exploration, the inability to progress to positive theory-construction of the kind we see in Plato's middle dialogues and later.

Although it makes me an ungracious guest, my topic requires me to raise the death's-head at the *Festschrift* – the possibility that the real Socrates may have been just as repetitive and platitudinous, just as philosophically unfruitful, as Epictetus was. Consider the extraordinary facility with which Socrates, in the Platonic dialogues, navigates his way through an interlocutor's position. Or consider the way that the themes from earlier Socratic dialogues are taken up and developed in later dialogues. Is it possible that the guiding genius here was always Plato's alone? The only god inside the Silenic exterior may have been *deus noster*, as Cicero called him, *Plato*. This, it seems to me, is the most important and far-reaching conclusion that arises from a comparison of Socrates and Epictetus.

19

Socrates and Skepticism

RICHARD BETT

Sextus Empiricus refers to the members of his Pyrrhonist school as *skeptikoi*, "inquirers." Precisely when the Pyrrhonists began to use this label for themselves is debatable, but it is clearly well entrenched by Sextus' time. The Academy during a portion of its lifetime – beginning with Arcesilaus and ending roughly with Philo of Larissa – is also regularly referred to as skeptical; the common ground between the Pyrrhonists and the Academics of this period was already noticed in the ancient world, and is sufficient to license the borrowing of the term. The crucial point of similarity between the two outlooks is a *withdrawal from definite belief*. This may take different forms in the hands of the two schools, and of different individuals within each school. But it is at the core of Sextus' explicit presentation of skepticism, and it is what is generally regarded as the hallmark of a skeptic in the ancient Greek context.

That Socrates might be a figure of special interest to skeptics, in this sense of the term, would be unsurprising. His repeated professions of ignorance in a number of the dialogues of Plato, together with his ongoing commitment to inquiry and refusal to act as if matters are resolved when they are unresolved, are clearly points on which we might expect the Greek skeptics to find Socrates congenial. In fact, however, things are not so simple. What we find is a very considerable divergence in the reactions to Socrates between the Pyrrhonists and the skeptical Academics. The picture of Socrates as a proto-skeptic is taken very seriously in the Academy; but the image of him in the Pyrrhonist tradition is rather different, even if not completely antithetical. Yet this too is unsurprising. For if we take the Socratic writings of Plato and Xenophon as a whole – to say nothing of the authors of Socratic dialogues that have not survived – there are obviously elements in their portraits of Socrates that are distinct from, and even at odds with, any outlook deserving to be called skeptical.

Socrates among the Pyrrhonists

There is no indication that the early Pyrrhonists – by which I mean Pyrrho himself, together with his disciple and biographer Timon of Phlius – saw a kindred spirit in Socrates. We have two fragments of Timon, one certainly and the other probably from his *Silloi* (*Lampoons*), in which Socrates is the subject. Both fragments allude to Socrates' concentration on ethical topics and his avoidance of physical theorizing. One of them also offers a more general sketch of Socrates' attitude and demeanor. As with many of Timon's lines, the multiple *doubles entendres* and unique coinages make adequate translation of this fragment extremely difficult, but a rough attempt might go as follows:

> But from them the sculptor, blatherer on the lawful, turned away,
> Spellbinder of the Greeks, who made them precise in language,
> Sneerer trained by rhetoricians, sub-Attic ironist.[1]

All three lines are quoted by Diogenes Laertius (*Lives of Eminent Philosophers* 2.19), but the first line is also quoted by Sextus Empiricus (*Against the Professors* 7.8) and Clement (*Miscellanies* 1.14.63.3), both of whom make clear that "them" in the first line refers to physical matters; Sextus also plausibly suggests that "blatherer on the lawful" refers to Socrates' focus on ethics. The rest of the language seems to suggest a mixture of admiration and suspicion, the latter being at least as prominent as the former. "Spellbinder" (*epaoidos*) implies powerful influence, but also danger. "Sub-Attic" suggests a merely partial attainment of the level of sophistication associated with Attic literary norms. Besides, it is far from clear that irony – or, for that matter, a focus on linguistic precision – are matters for which we are supposed to find Socrates praiseworthy; and the epithet "sneerer" (*muktēr*) is pretty clearly demeaning. Socrates does not emerge as a wholly contemptible figure, like many of Timon's literary victims. But not a single phrase in the passage is unambiguously laudatory. A few thinkers – Xenophanes, Protagoras, the Eleatics and Democritus – do receive clear commendation from Timon (albeit tempered by criticism),[2] and Socrates is not in their company. In any case, the fragment gives us no reason to think that Timon regards Socrates as sharing common ground with him philosophically.

The other fragment, quoted by Sextus (*Against the Professors* 7.10), criticizes Plato for misrepresenting Socrates as *not* solely concerned with ethics. Plato, Timon says, did not let Socrates remain a "character-depicter" (*ēthologon*); the word normally refers to a mime, but Timon is clearly playing with the etymology so as to suggest someone engaging in discourse (*logos*) *about* character (*ēthos*) – in other words, ethical discourse. This is interesting in that it shows clear recognition of a distinction between Socrates the historical figure and Socrates as represented by Plato; Timon is clearly relying on the tradition exemplified in Xenophon (*Memorabilia* 1.1.11–16) and Aristotle (*Metaphysics* 987b1–4), but reflected in only a subset of Plato's dialogues, according to which ethics was Socrates' exclusive province. But again, there is no basis for thinking that Timon himself identifies with this stance of Socrates, or views him for this reason as in any way a forerunner of his own philosophy.

That is all that survives on Socrates from the early Pyrrhonist period; there are a few other fragments of Timon about Plato, but none of them has any bearing on his depiction of Socrates. Now, when one turns to the final phase of the Pyrrhonist tradition, represented for us by the writings of Sextus Empiricus, the situation initially appears quite different. A search for the name "Socrates" in Sextus' works yields a very considerable number of "hits." The impression given by the number, however, is highly misleading; in the great majority of these cases Socrates simply occurs in examples, particularly examples in logic, standing for a generic human being (as in "Socrates is mortal," still a favorite among logic teachers). There are just 11 passages in Sextus that refer to Socrates other than in this purely exemplary way – either to the historical person or to Socrates as depicted by Plato or Xenophon. (Sextus, too, by the way, is clearly sensitive to this distinction. The skeptics' alertness to it is not unrelated to the character of their philosophy. Included in their general reluctance to make definite assertions is a reluctance to make definite attributions of views to other thinkers on the authority of some third party; hence it is important for them to distinguish "A thought that P" from "B said that A thought that P.")

Of these 11 passages, one has already been mentioned: Sextus cites Timon (and also Xenophon) in support of his own picture of Socrates as concerned solely with ethics (*Against the Professors* 7.8, 7.10, cf. 7.21). This occurs in Sextus' discussion of the parts of philosophy and the best order in which to treat them, which opens the entire sequence of books *Against the Logicians*, *Against the Physicists*, and *Against the Ethicists* (*Against the Professors* 7–11). The same point occurs again at the beginning of *Against the Ethicists* (11.2), where Socrates is also said, with some caution, to have been the *first* to engage in ethical inquiry.[3] Of the remaining nine passages several are of no philosophical significance. Sextus mentions that Socrates studied music late in life (6.13), and that he was not skilled in poetry (*mē poētikou*, 9.110). He also says, as do several other ancient authors (Diels-Kranz 60A1–3), that Archelaus of Athens was his teacher (*Against the Professors* 9.360); it is hard to know what to make of this claim, but in any case it reveals no particular attitude towards Socrates on Sextus' part. The same is true of his far more easily accepted claim (again issued cautiously with the word "seems" (*dokei*)) that the Cyrenaic school was an offshoot of Socratic discussion, as was the Platonic school (7.190). This leaves five passages of potentially greater interest, which appear to project a certain view of Socrates' thought and the skeptics' own relation to it. At first sight, these passages give a somewhat schizophrenic impression.

Two of them, relatively close to one another in the first book of *Against the Physicists*, have to do with existence of god, and show us a decidedly unskeptical Socrates. In the first (9.64) Socrates simply appears in a list of thinkers who accept the existence of god. In the second (9.92–4) Sextus paraphrases a passage of Xenophon (*Memorabilia* 1.4.2–8) in which, as he says, Socrates is portrayed as offering a *proof* of the existence of god to his interlocutor Aristodemus; the proof consists mainly in a version of the cosmological argument. In neither passage does Sextus show any special interest in specifying his own stance *vis-à-vis* Socrates; the ideas in question are simply employed as part of Sextus' general strategy of assembling opposing arguments on the topic under discussion, and for this purpose Socrates (or Xenophon's Socrates) will do as well as anyone else. In these passages, though, Socrates appears as an unambiguous dogmatist.

The same cannot be said of two parallel passages from Sextus' discussions of the criterion of truth. Sextus offers a variety of arguments suggesting that the human being (which might be regarded as in a certain sense a criterion) is impossible to conceive; and a remark attributed to Socrates is enlisted in support of this conclusion. The version in *Outlines of Pyrrhonism* (2.22) simply says that we find Plato's Socrates (*tou para Platōni Sōkratous*) openly confessing that he does not know whether he is a human being or something else. The allusion is to a passage from the *Phaedrus* (230a) in which Socrates speaks of trying to follow the Delphic maxim "know yourself," and raises the question what kind of a being he is; it is somewhat crude to interpret him as wondering whether he is a human being at all, but it is true that Socrates' remarks bear on Sextus' question of whether the human being is conceivable. In the parallel version in *Against the Logicians* (*Against the Professors* 7.264) Sextus ascribes some actual words to Socrates; again Socrates is supposed to say that he does not know whether he is a human being, but the words are clearly designed as a paraphrase of the *Phaedrus* passage. The sentence preceding the paraphrase, however, is more striking; here we are told that Socrates was in doubt (*ēporēse*), and remained in a state of inquiry (*skepsei*), about the question. These terms clearly assimilate Socrates to the skeptics themselves; Sextus explicitly lists both *aporētikos*, "doubtful," and of course *skeptikos*, "inquirer," as terms of skeptical self-description (*Outlines of Pyrrhonism* 1.7). This application to Socrates of labels normally applied to the skeptics is clearly deliberate, and shows a willingness to recognize Plato's Socrates as to some extent anticipating the skeptics' own outlook. It is noteworthy, though, that even here Sextus seems to show no special interest in specifying his relation to Socrates. He simply makes his remark about Socrates and immediately moves on; however striking the remark may be, Socrates himself is not the focus in this passage.

We have, then, a dogmatic Socrates in two passages and a skeptical Socrates in two others – all of this in the course of Sextus' broader agenda, rather than as part of any discussion in which Socrates is himself a topic of importance. The final passage differs from all these others in at least the latter respect. This is from the section of *Outlines of Pyrrhonism* where Sextus examines various philosophies that might be thought to resemble skepticism, and shows how they differ from it; and here he explicitly addresses the question whether Plato, and by extension Plato's Socrates, is a skeptic (1.221–225). He says that some people regard Plato as dogmatic, others as "doubtful" (*aporētikos*) and others as a mixture of the two. The basis given for the "doubtful" interpretation, he says, is the argumentative and nondogmatic style of discussion exhibited in certain dialogues by Plato's Socrates (221). And he seems inclined to acknowledge that there is some truth to this – that there are at least elements in Plato that conform to the "doubtful" interpretation. This is not entirely clear, since the point only ever appears as the antecedent of a conditional (223, 225).[4] But at least he never says that this antecedent is false; nor would it be surprising that he should regard it as true, given that, as we saw in the last paragraph, he in any case accepts that there is a skeptical aspect to Socrates. Nevertheless, he concludes that Plato is not a skeptic even if the antecedent is true, because there are clearly a great many positive ideas put forward in Plato (including in the mouth of Socrates) – and anyone whose writings contain *any* measure of positive doctrine does not count as "purely" (*eilikrinōs*, 222) skeptical. This is in keeping with Sextus' approach throughout: either one is a skeptic or one is not – skepticism does not come in degrees – and a true skeptic is a pure and unmitigated skeptic. On these terms it can hardly be disputed that neither Plato nor Plato's Socrates qualifies for the label.

What, then, are we to make of this seemingly scattered series of comments on Socrates? One answer might be that Sextus is drawing on a variety of sources, and simply reproduces the picture of Socrates that he finds in each; if one source has a skeptical view of Socrates and another source has a dogmatic view, then both views will find their way into Sextus' text.[5] But I think we can grant Sextus a little more autonomy and self-consciousness than that. He may indeed be indebted to varying accounts of Socrates in his sources, but his use of them need not be seen as mechanical or as precluding any conception of his own. I have already suggested that Sextus is not especially interested in the figure of Socrates in his own right. However, it is quite consistent and legitimate for him to present Socrates as dogmatic in certain respects (on matters having to do with the existence of god), as skeptical in one respect (in that he did not claim to know the nature of the human being) and perhaps in others (in his style of discussion in some dialogues), and yet, all things considered, as *not* a skeptic (since a real skeptic has to be skeptical all the time).[6] His use of the terms *aporeō* and *skepsis* in the passage from *Against the Logicians* may seem to favor a skeptical interpretation of Socrates. But he is very clear that he is talking about Socrates' position on just this one topic (the nature of the human being); no one would be tempted to think that he is marking Socrates as a skeptic *tout court*. Besides, the same usage appears in the conditional statements mentioned just now; Plato is not a skeptic, Sextus, says, "even if he is doubtful (*epaporēi*) *about some things*" (225) and "if he does express himself skeptically (*skeptikōs propheretai*) *on some points*" (223). Sextus is prepared, then, to use the terminology of skepticism of people who show skeptical tendencies, even if by his absolutist standards they are not true skeptics at all. So the overall picture is of a Socrates who shows glimmers of skepticism, but not enough to count as a genuine proponent – and hence as not deserving an exceptional level of attention.

In the passage of *Outlines of Pyrrhonism* on whether Plato and Plato's Socrates are skeptics, Sextus tells us that he has discussed this question at greater length in his *Treatises* (*Hupomnēmasi* 1.222). Does this suggest that he is actually more concerned with Socrates than the surviving works might lead us to think? Not necessarily. *Treatises* is presumably an abbreviation for *Skeptical Treatises* (*Skeptika Hupomnēmata*), a work to which Sextus refers in several other places (*Against the Professors* 1.29 [26], 2.106, 6.52; cf. Diogenes Laertius, *Lives of Eminent Philosophers* 9.116). It is clear from these references that this is the work comprising *Against the Logicians, Against the Physicists, Against the Ethicists* and, preceding all these, a lost general account of Pyrrhonism corresponding to the first book of *Outlines of Pyrrhonism*.[7] The more lengthy discussion of Plato's skepticism, or lack thereof, will therefore have occurred in the lost general account; it is not in the surviving books, and the general portion anyway is where one would expect it. Now, that Sextus should have discussed the question at greater length in this work does not show that his interest in the question was any greater than I have suggested. For the evidence suggests that *everything* in *Skeptical Treatises* was dealt with at greater length than in *Outlines of Pyrrhonism*. This is certainly true of the five surviving books, which cover essentially the same ground as the second and third books of *Outlines*; indeed, the two very lengthy books *Against the Logicians* actually cover *less* ground, in terms of the range of topics discussed, than does the corresponding second book of *Outlines* (which is little more than a quarter their length). We would therefore expect the lost general portion also to have been considerably longer than the first book of *Outlines*. Indeed, it has been persuasively argued that *Skeptical Treatises* was actually *ten* books long, in which case the lost general portion will have taken five books instead of one.[8] So for Sextus to have spent more time in this work over whether Plato was a skeptic is just what we would expect. There is no reason to think that he was more exercised over this topic *relative to other topics* than he is in *Outlines* or any other of his surviving books.

Sextus' discussion in *Outlines of Pyrrhonism* of whether Plato and Plato's Socrates were skeptics also alludes to Aenesidemus' position on this question. It was Aenesidemus who revived the figure of Pyrrho as a philosophical inspiration and started the Pyrrhonist movement of which Sextus' writings are the culmination; his view of Socrates' relation to skepticism would therefore be of considerable interest. Unfortunately Sextus' text is corrupt at the crucial point (*Outlines of Pyrrhonism* 1.222), so we cannot be sure what Aenesidemus' position was on this question. The text reads "*katapermēdoton* and Aenesidemus (for these were the most prominent adherents of this position)," and Sextus then expresses his own opposition to the idea that Plato was a skeptic. The word "these" shows that the corrupt *katapermēdoton* must conceal a second name, and most scholars have identified it as that of Menodotus, a leader of the Empiric school of medicine. The question then is whether Sextus is agreeing or disagreeing with the position of Menodotus and Aenesidemus – in other words, whether they rejected or accepted the idea that Plato was a skeptic; different reconstructions of the text yield different answers to this question. The fact that Aenesidemus was the founder of the later Pyrrhonist movement does not guarantee that Sextus would agree with him. While Sextus does follow Aenesidemus on a number of points, he also sometimes takes issue with him; the most notable case is just shortly before this passage, where he reports on a certain connection Aenesidemus claimed between the skeptical philosophy and that of Heraclitus (1.210–12), and calls this alleged connection absurd (*atopon*, 212).[9] It is also true that, as that passage illustrates, Sextus is in general strongly motivated to emphasize differences between skepticism and other philosophies that might be seen as equivalent to it – so that one would expect him to reject any claim that Plato or Socrates was a skeptic, regardless of what Aenesidemus had said on the matter. Nevertheless, I think there are a number of reasons for concluding that Aenesidemus' position, like Sextus', is that Plato was *not* a skeptic.

First, a good case has recently been made on purely textual grounds that the most plausible reconstruction is *kathaper <hoi peri> Mē<no>doton*, which would yield the sense "like those around Menodotus and Aenesidemus."[10] (The words "those around . . ." are regularly used to designate someone's school, but the term often appears to be a roundabout way of referring simply to the thinkers themselves.) In this case Sextus would be agreeing with Aenesidemus. But there are also historical and philosophical considerations pointing in the same direction. The most important surviving text describing the philosophy of Aenesidemus is a chapter from the *Bibliotheca* of Photius, a ninth-century patriarch of Constantinople (169b18–171a4). Photius refers to Aenesidemus' appeal to Pyrrho, but never mentions any appeal to Plato. Most of the passage is devoted to a summary of Aenesidemus' book *Pyrrhonist Discourses*, but at the end Photius offers a few lines of largely dismissive criticism. In the course of this criticism he specifically refers to Plato (along with "many others" who are unnamed, 170b38) as showing the worthlessness of Aenesidemus' style of argument. Given Photius' view of Plato as a preeminent antiskeptical voice, it would be very surprising, had Aenesidemus himself invoked Plato on the other side as a skeptical forerunner, if Photius had not expressed outrage about that appropriation; at any rate, one would not expect him to have remained completely silent about the issue.[11]

In addition, Aenesidemus' relation to the Academy needs to be considered. The Photius passage makes very clear that Aenesidemus developed his Pyrrhonist philosophy as a reaction against the Academy. The Academics, he says, fail to maintain any kind of skeptical outlook, and are not significantly different from Stoics (170a14–17); the point is said to apply especially to the Academics of his own day (whom we may plausibly identify as Philo of Larissa and Antiochus of Ascalon), but it has a general application as well. It would again be very surprising, given that view of even the Academics who explicitly professed a skeptical philosophy, if Aenesidemus had thought of Plato himself as a skeptical thinker. Besides, Aenesidemus was himself originally a member of the Academy.[12] If he had thought of Plato as a skeptical thinker after his own heart, one would not expect him to have made an overt break with the Academy, as Photius documents. On the contrary, one would expect him to have proclaimed himself the true torch-bearer of the Academic philosophy, as opposed to all the impostors around him. Philo and Antiochus were engaged in a dispute in this very period about which of them represented the true Academic tradition; it would have been entirely natural for Aenesidemus to insert himself into that dispute, offering a third option as to the legitimate Academy. But there is nothing of this kind, and it seems much more likely that Aenesidemus repudiated the view that Plato was a skeptic, thus allowing Sextus to agree with him. The view is anyway an implausible one, as we saw; it can only be taken seriously if one looks at Plato's Socrates in a very selective way. Aenesidemus' comments on the Academy and their Stoicizing tendencies show that his standards for counting someone as skeptical were hardly lax; for that reason alone, it is difficult to believe that he would have allowed Plato to qualify. One might put the matter in more overtly political terms: given that Aenesidemus was making a break with the Academy, it would be natural for him to distance himself from Plato and Socrates. But that cannot be the whole story, since it begs the question as to *why* he saw the need to break from the Academy. And the answer must be that he no longer saw philosophical affinities between himself and the Academics – Plato (and Socrates) included.

Socrates among the Academics

The Pyrrhonist attitude to Socrates, then, is throughout somewhat standoffish, and there are a variety of reasons for this. For the Academy, on the other hand, Socrates is a kind of proto-member of the school; one would, then, expect the relations the Academic skeptics claimed with him to be much closer – and this expectation is not disappointed.

Cicero, who himself studied in the Academy and identifies himself as an adherent of its philosophy, repeatedly connects Arcesilaus, the Academic who first took the Academy in a skeptical direction, with Socrates. First, he describes Arcesilaus as maintaining that nothing can be known – or alternatively, in terminology developed in the Hellenistic period, that nothing can be apprehended (*percipi*), either by the senses or by the mind. Cicero names Socrates, specifically Plato's Socrates, as Arcesilaus' inspiration. Arcesilaus is said to have derived this lesson from "various books and Socratic discussions of Plato" (*On the Orator* 3.67); he is also said to have arrived at this position "by the obscurity of those things that had led Socrates [and several others before him] to a confession of ignorance" (*Academics* 1.44). Socrates, of course, confesses ignorance in a number of Platonic dialogues. But the sequel to this latter passage makes clear that Arcesilaus paid particular attention to Plato's *Apology*, where the theme of Socratic ignorance receives its fullest exposition. Arcesilaus is said to have gone further than Socrates did in that dialogue. Whereas Socrates supposedly claimed to know one thing – namely, that he did not know anything (i.e., presumably, anything else) – Arcesilaus held that not even this can be known. It is far from clear that this is a fair reading of what Socrates says in the *Apology*. He talks of his lack of *wisdom*, and of his not knowing anything *important* or *valuable*, but he never suggests that he knows nothing whatsoever (with one exception); nor is it clear that this lack of wisdom or important knowledge is itself something that he claims to *know* – the closest he comes to this is *sunoida emautōi* (21b4–5), which can be understood more weakly as "I am *aware of* [not knowing anything important]." Nevertheless, it is plainly the *Apology* to which Arcesilaus is referring here, and he takes himself to be borrowing from but going beyond the Socratic position.

Arcesilaus' recognition of the unknowability of everything is said to have led to a policy of withholding assent from all definite statements (*Academics* 1.45), a policy also attested for him by Sextus (*Outlines of Pyrrhonism* 1.232–3). Cicero suggests that Plato was Arcesilaus' predecessor in this practice (1.46). But the alleged Platonic precedent has to do with the inconclusiveness of the Platonic dialogues, rather than with anything in Plato's depiction of Socrates specifically. Cicero does, however, add that Arcesilaus' practice of withholding assent was associated with a certain type of argumentative practice – namely, to invite others to argue for their own positions and then argue against them (rather than putting forward positions of his own) (*Academics* 1.45). And *this* practice, as Cicero elsewhere says several times, was again something that Arcesilaus picked up from Socrates as depicted by Plato (*On Ends* 2.2, *On the Orator* 3.67, *On the Nature of the Gods* 1.11).

Cicero, then, gives the impression that Arcesilaus' skeptical approach was in large part inspired by the figure of the Platonic Socrates; it was not just that he adopted Socrates as a sort of figurehead (as Aenesidemus perhaps adopted Pyrrho) after having already developed the skeptical approach on his own.[13] If this is correct – and there is no obvious reason for doubting Cicero's testimony – then Socrates' influence (via Plato) on the Academy's skeptical turn was very substantial. There are, however, further questions about the accuracy of Arcesilaus' reading of what Plato's Socrates was up to, and about the nature of the relation between his outlook and Socrates'.[14]

I have already mentioned that Arcesilaus' representation of Socrates' profession of ignorance in the *Apology* is to some degree distorted. More generally, to extract from Plato's portrait of Socrates in any dialogue the lesson that (virtually) nothing *can be known* seems dubious. Socrates may himself claim, in numerous dialogues, not to know a great many things; but he certainly gives the impression in the same dialogues of being a relentlessly serious *seeker* after a certain kind of ethical knowledge – which would hardly make sense if he thought this knowledge (let alone all knowledge) was impossible. And this takes us into the question whether Socrates can reasonably be seen as merely responding to the views of others, instead of proposing views of his own.

There is clearly an aspect of Socrates' procedure, in what are sometimes called the elenctic dialogues, that answers to this description. Socrates repeatedly claims not to know the answers to the questions he poses – about, say, the nature of a certain virtue – and instead asks his interlocutors to state their own views on these questions, which he subsequently subjects to scrutiny; and this scrutiny itself regularly, even if not invariably, takes the form of examining the consistency of the interlocutor's originally stated views with other views that are later elicited from him, rather than confronting the originally stated views with views for which Socrates argues in his own person. Something like this procedure is captured in the image of the midwife in the *Theaetetus*: Socrates claims to be barren of wisdom (as a midwife is no longer fertile), but capable of bringing to fruition the wisdom of others – he offers no views of his own because he has no views worth offering. The possibility of actually achieving wisdom (even if others are the ones to do this) goes against the grain of Arcesilaus' reading of Socrates. However, in the *Theaetetus* itself this does not happen; Theaetetus' various suggestions (in this case, about the nature of knowledge) are all scrutinized, and all are found wanting – which conforms rather better to Arcesilaus' reported argumentative practice than what the midwife image alone might imply. Arcesilaus' picture of Socrates, then, is certainly recognizable from Plato. But equally, as was noted in the previous section, it is a very partial picture of Plato's Socrates; scrutiny of the views of others is certainly something that Socrates does, but there is considerably more to him than that. Even those dialogues of Plato that are sometimes thought of as "Socratic" – that is, as giving us a relatively authentic picture of the historical Socrates, as opposed to putting theories of the mature Plato into Socrates' mouth – contain expressions of a number of very definite convictions on Socrates' part: for example, that the care of one's soul is the most important human task, or that it is worse for a person to do wrong than to suffer it.

Another question has to do with Arcesilaus' own philosophical approach. It is sometimes held that Arcesilaus' procedure was purely *ad hominem* or dialectical – that is, that he never put forward any views of his own; rather, he merely argued against other philosophers, and particularly the Stoics, showing them what *they* are committed to given their own premises. On this interpretation, even the claim that nothing can be known, and the resulting recommendation to withhold assent, are being foisted on the Stoics (and perhaps other non-Academics); it is they who are being told that they must, in consistency, accept this claim and follow this recommendation, while Arcesilaus himself takes no stand on these matters. If this is indeed what Arcesilaus is doing, then this raises new questions about his relation to Socrates. For Socrates' profession of ignorance, whatever its scope, is clearly not purely *ad hominem*; Socrates sincerely believes *himself* to be ignorant, not merely that this is something others should admit.[15]

But the *ad hominem* or purely dialectical reading of Arcesilaus is difficult to square with what Cicero says in the texts to which I have pointed. According to Cicero, Arcesilaus himself maintained that nothing could be known, and drew the recommendation to avoid assent as a consequence. The positive endorsement of non-assent is also apparent in Sextus (*Outlines of Pyrrhonism* 1.232–3). Cicero does not deny that Arcesilaus was largely motivated by a desire to combat the Stoics; in fact, he asserts it (*Academics* 1.44). Sextus also draws attention, in another passage, to Arcesilaus' anti-Stoic motivations (7.150–7), and the point is apparent in much of the surviving evidence. But there is no contradiction between this point and the notion that Arcesilaus himself held the view that nothing could be known, and consequently himself withheld assent.[16] Of course, the withholding of assent cannot be entirely unrestricted; it will not apply to the claim that nothing can be known – even if Arcesilaus does not claim to *know* this, he does still assert it – nor to the claim that *one ought to*, or that it is *a good thing to*, withhold assent. But there is nothing inconsistent in such "second-order dogmatism," as it has been called;[17] the recommendation to withhold assent applies to everything except a few metalevel claims that specify the skeptical outlook itself. Sextus may find this objectionable, and Cicero may not trouble to spell out the point, but it is quite comprehensible and acceptable on its own terms. In this case, Arcesilaus' claim that nothing can be known is, after all, as he says, recognizably an extension of Socrates' profession of ignorance, rather than something offered in a quite different frame of mind.

Can anything more be inferred about Arcesilaus' use of Socrates? A polemical work of Plutarch, *Against Colotes on behalf of the other philosophers*, attacks the views of the Epicurean Colotes, a contemporary of Arcesilaus, as expressed in a book with the still more unwieldy title *On the fact that it is not even possible to live in accordance with the doctrines of the other philosophers*. As we can gather from Plutarch's critique, Colotes criticized both Arcesilaus and Socrates in this work. Now, some scholars have suggested that the portrait of Socrates on which Colotes focused in his critique was the portrait of him put out by Arcesilaus.[18] And if this is correct, then the clues furnished by Plutarch will give us further information about the ways in which Arcesilaus borrowed from Socrates.

The suggestion, however, is extremely tenuous. It is true that Plutarch cites Colotes as remarking on Arcesilaus' avowed use of several predecessors, including Socrates (1121F–122A). But as regards Socrates, we have already seen enough justification for this in the points we have gleaned from Cicero. It does not follow that Colotes' critique of Socrates is a critique of Socrates *as viewed by Arcesilaus*. Plutarch does refer to denigration of the senses by Socrates, and to Colotes' criticism of this (1118A). But there is no reason to assume that Colotes took Socrates to have denigrated the senses on the basis of Arcesilaus' representation of him. Plato's Socrates has plenty to say about the inadequacy of the senses; but the grounds for this are metaphysical – they have nothing to do with the kinds of epistemological considerations deployed by Arcesilaus in his attacks on the trust placed in the senses, in certain favored circumstances, by the Stoics.[19] Indeed, Plutarch's comment, in defense of Socrates, that the senses "do not have the kind of understanding and knowledge of every thing that the philosophical soul desires to grasp" (1118B) is plainly much more reminiscent of Plato than of Arcesilaus.

In addition, it is interesting that Colotes' critique of Socrates drew attention to the same passage of the *Phaedrus*, where Socrates wonders what kind of being he is, as

Sextus refers to when he labels Socrates as in one respect skeptical (1119B). But this has no tendency to show that Arcesilaus' understanding of Socrates made appeal to the same passage. As we saw, Sextus' terminology in this context – that Socrates was in doubt (ēporēse) and remained in a state of inquiry (skepsei) – is specifically Pyrrhonist; it does not suggest an Academic borrowing. And Colotes, again, could just as well have taken the passage directly from Plato as from Plato filtered through Arcesilaus. He criticized many philosophers to whom, as far as we know, Arcesilaus made no reference at all; except for the case of Arcesilaus himself, Colotes need not be supposed to have used Arcesilaus as his source.[20]

Plutarch's attack on Colotes does not, then, give us any reliable information about the character of Arcesilaus' debt to Socrates. Nevertheless – to return from the various digressions of the last few pages – we know from Cicero that this debt was extensive, even if based on a selective and debatable conception of Plato's Socrates. And since Arcesilaus was the founder of the skeptical Academy, the debt may be said to have persisted beyond Arcesilaus to his skeptical successors.

About these successors there is much less to say. Carneades, the other major figure in the skeptical Academy, is not recorded as saying anything about Socrates; this is in keeping with his generally circumspect approach, including on matters of philosophical lineage. But Cicero makes clear that the Socratic legacy was still accepted as the skeptical Academy came to an end. Speaking on behalf of the Academy of Philo, he enthusiastically repeats the idea that Socrates (as well as Plato) should be listed among those who held that nothing could be known – again noting the one exception in Socrates' case (Academics 2.74). The point is in reply to Lucullus, who had maintained, following Antiochus, that Socrates and Plato should be removed from this list (2.15), and that Socrates' self-deprecation about his wisdom was deceptive and ironic. Lucullus had mentioned that Arcesilaus appealed to them as forerunners. But Cicero reply's makes no mention of Arcesilaus; it is delivered from the perspective of the late skeptical Academy of his own day. Besides, if the picture of Socrates as an inspiration for Academic skepticism had not continued to be congenial, it is doubtful that Cicero would have been as forthright about Arcesilaus' appeal to Socrates as he is.

Antiochus led a breakaway Academy setting itself against the skepticism that had dominated the school since Arcesilaus. Yet, despite the remark just referred to, it looks, to judge from Cicero, as if he too was not immune to the picture of Socrates as a proto-skeptic. Antiochus sought to return the Academy – his Academy – to the true doctrines of Plato, which he took to be essentially the same as those of Aristotle and the Stoics. And in another passage of the Academics (1.15–17), where Varro is Antiochus' spokesman, a conspicuous distinction is drawn between Socrates, who claimed that he knew nothing (except that very fact) and practiced a form of discourse in which definite assertions were avoided, and Plato, the originator of the one true doctrine.[21] Varro allows that Socrates was a devotee and an investigator of virtue, and this makes him less purely skeptical than he appeared in Arcesilaus' portrait. But the key elements of Arcesilaus' portrait are still there, alongside the emphasis on virtue. It is not clear how to reconcile this passage with the one in which Socrates is removed from the list of deniers of knowledge, and perhaps we should not try.[22] Still, the fact remains that even Antiochus shows some tendency to accept the conception of

308

Socrates that started with Arcesilaus. And that is one more indication of the importance of that conception in Academic circles.

Notes

1 For numerous details on the sense of this passage I am indebted to the commentary of Di Marco (1989: 165–71). A somewhat different translation, along with brief comments, can be found in Long (1988: 150–2); however, the differences do not, I think, affect the general verdict on the fragment's tone.

2 For discussion of Timon's treatment of these figures, see Bett (2000: 140–60).

3 For more on this passage, see Bett (1997: 48–9).

4 The first passage has *ei kai*, the second *k'an*; *ei kai* normally grants the truth of what follows, while *kai ei* or *k'an* does not. But this is not an inflexible rule; see Smyth (1956: sec. 2374).

5 For this kind of reading see, e.g., Ioppolo (1995: 112).

6 One could also imagine him distinguishing between, say, a dogmatic Socrates in Xenophon and a skeptical Socrates in Plato. However, there is no indication in the text of this kind of approach to rendering the overall picture consistent.

7 On the lost portion, see Janácek (1963).

8 On this see Blomqvist (1974).

9 On Aenesidemus' connection with Heraclitus, see Bett (2000: ch. 4.5).

10 See Spinelli (2000), who also documents the numerous other proposed emendations.

11 This point is made by Decleva Caizzi (1992: 187).

12 This was denied by Decleva Caizzi (1992). But a key element of her argument – that the word *sunairesiōtēs* need not mean "fellow-member," as usually thought, but could mean simply "member" – was conclusively refuted by Mansfeld (1995).

13 This point is emphasized by Long (1988: 158–9).

14 These questions are treated in much more detail, and from somewhat divergent viewpoints, in Annas (1994) and Shields (1994). Here I can offer only a few brief remarks.

15 On the sincerity of Socrates' professions of ignorance, see, e.g., Vlastos (1994: 40–2); but many have made the same point.

16 Here I am in agreement with Shields (1994) as against Annas (1994).

17 See Hankinson (1995: 85), whose reading of Arcesilaus I would generally endorse.

18 See Ioppolo (1995: sec. 3), Döring (1992: 84–5); there is also a hint of this view in Long (1988: 156), to whom Döring appeals.

19 For an overview of this issue with key texts, see Long and Sedley (1987: sec. 40).

20 Long (1988: 156) also mentions other books of Colotes against Plato's *Lysis* and *Euthydemus*. According to Long, Colotes here "maintained that Socrates ignored what is self-evident (*enarges*) and suspended judgement (*epochōs prattein*). Here Socrates . . . has been turned into a prototype of the Academic Arcesilaus." However, as I suggest in the main text, that both Socrates and Arcesilaus might be thought to cast doubt on what is self-evident does not mean that the grounds on which they might be thought to do so are the same, or even similar. As for suspending judgment, it is indeed plausible that this refers to Arcesilaus. But the passage in which these words occur is far too fragmentary for us to tell whether Colotes also associated Socrates with this stance; for the text see Mancini (1976: 66).

21 As noted by Annas (1994: 323).

22 As Burnyeat (1997: 300) suggests. Earlier, however (292–4), Burnyeat does try to reconcile them. But it seems to me that the attempted reconciliation fails to take account of the fact that the appeal to Socratic irony at 2.15 is supposed to justify the removal of Socrates from the list of deniers of knowledge.

References and Further Reading

Annas, J. (1994). Plato the skeptic. In P. Vander Waerdt (ed.), *The Socratic Movement* (pp. 309–40). Ithaca, NY: Cornell University Press. Goes as far as possible in sympathizing with ancient representations of Plato as a skeptic.

Bett, R. (1997). *Sextus Empiricus, Against the Ethicists, Translated with an Introduction and Commentary*. Oxford: Oxford University Press. Interprets the viewpoint of *Against the Ethicists*, more than Sextus' other works, as a survival of the outlook of Aenesidemus.

—— (2000). *Pyrrho, his Antecedents and his Legacy*. Oxford: Oxford University Press. Examines the philosophy of Pyrrho and earlier foreshadowings of it, and proposes a three-stage development of the Pyrrhonist tradition.

Blomqvist, J. (1974). Die Skeptika des Sextus Empiricus [Sextus Empiricus' *Skeptika*]. *Grazer Beiträge*, 2, 7–14. Analyzes the evidence for the character and structure of Sextus' most extensive, but partially lost, work.

Burnyeat, M. (1997). Antipater and self-refutation: Elusive arguments in Cicero's *Academica*. In B. Inwood and J. Mansfeld (eds.), *Assent and Argument: Studies in Cicero's Academic Books*. Leiden: Brill. Discusses the acceptability and implications of "Nothing can be known" and related statements, as treated in the *Academics*.

Decleva Caizzi, F. (1992). Aenesidemus and the Academy. *Classical Quarterly*, 42, 176–89. Examines the evidence for Aenesidemus' life and associates; argues against Aenesidemus ever having belonged to the Academy.

Di Marco, M. (1989). *Timone di Fliunte, Silli. Introduzione, edizione critica, traduzione e commento* [Timon of Phlius: Silloi. Introduction, critical edition, translation and commentary]. Rome: Edizioni dell'Ateneo. The most recent and most extensive presentation and treatment of Timon's most important work.

Döring, K. (1992). Die sog. Kleinen Sokratiker und ihre Schuken bei Sextus Empiricus. [The so-called minor Socratics and their schools in Sextus Empiricus]. *Elenchos*, 13, 81–118. Examines Sextus' treatment of and relation to Cynics, Cyrenaics and Megarians, preceded by brief remarks on Socrates and Xenophon.

Hankinson, R. J. (1995). *The Skeptics*. London: Routledge. Comprehensive survey of Greek skepticism.

Ioppolo, A. M. (1995). Socrate nelle tradizioni accademico-scettica e pirroniana [Socrates in the skeptical-Academic and Pyrrhonian traditions]. In (no eds.), *La tradizione socratica* [The Socratic tradition] (pp. 89–123). Naples: Bibliopolis. Covers much of the same ground as the present paper, from a somewhat different perspective.

Janáček, K. (1963). Der Hauptschrift des Sextus Empiricus als Torso erhalten? [Sextus Empiricus' main work surviving as a torso?]. *Philologus*, 107, 271–7. Argues that the work comprising *Against the Logicians, Against the Physicists*, and *Against the Ethicists* was preceded by a lost portion expounding skepticism in general terms.

Long, A. A. (1988). Socrates in Hellenistic philosophy. *Classical Quarterly*, 38, 150–71. Examines the influence and reception of Socrates among the various Hellenistic schools.

—— and Sedley, D. N. (1987). *The Hellenistic Philosophers*. Cambridge: Cambridge University Press. Assembles key texts relating to the philosophies of the Hellenistic period, with translation and commentary.

Mancini, A. C. (1976). Sulle opere polemiche di Colote [On Colotes' polemical works]. *Cronache Ercolanesi*, 6, 61–7. Presents and comments on papyrus fragments from Colotes' works against Plato's *Lysis* and *Euthydemus*.

Mansfeld, J. (1995). Aenesidemus and the Academics. In L. Ayres (ed.), *The Passionate Intellect: Essays on the Transformation of Classical Traditions* (pp. 235–48). New Brunswick, NJ:

Transaction Publishers. Reinstates the standard picture of Aenesidemus as having originally been a member of the Academy, challenged by Decleva Caizzi (1992).

Morrison, D. (ed.) (forthcoming). *The Cambridge Companion to Socrates*. Cambridge: Cambridge University Press. Wide-ranging collection of essays on the evidence for Socrates, the nature of his thought, and his influence.

Shields, C. (1994). Socrates among the skeptics. In P. Vander Waerdt (ed.), *The Socratic Movement* (pp. 341–66). Ithaca, NY: Cornell University Press. Examines the response to and treatment of Socrates in the skeptical Academy, partially in response to Annas (1994).

Smyth, H. W. (rev. Messing, G. M.) (1956). *Greek Grammar*. Cambridge, MA: Harvard University Press. Standard reference work on ancient Greek grammar and syntax.

Spinelli, E. (2000). Sextus Empiricus, the neighboring philosophies and the skeptical tradition (again on *Pyr.* I 220–225). In J. Sihvola (ed.), *Ancient Skepticism and the Skeptical Tradition* (pp. 35–61). Helsinki: The Philosophical Society of Finland. Examines Sextus' rejection of the claim that Plato was a skeptic, and proposes a new textual reconstruction and new arguments supporting the conclusion that Aenesidemus thought likewise.

Vlastos, G. (1994). Socrates' disavowal of knowledge. In G. Vlastos, *Socratic Studies*, ed. M. Burnyeat (pp. 39–66). Cambridge: Cambridge University Press. A classic paper (slightly revised for the volume) on a central problem in the interpretation of Plato's Socrates.

Part Two

Socrates After Antiquity

Section IV

From the Medieval Period to Modernity

20

Socrates in Arabic Philosophy

ILAI ALON

Background, Sources, and Tradition

Socrates was embraced by Arab culture in the Middle Ages as the paradigm of the moral sage rather than as a philosopher in the strict sense of the word. His image rested upon two classes of material: Plato on the one hand and subsequent authors on the other. Regarding this first source, there is written evidence for the existence of Arabic translations of some of Plato's writings, especially the *Phaedo* (Bürgel 1974: 117, 101), *Timaeus*, *Laches*, and *Meno*, which are quoted especially by al-Birūnī (d. 1034) and reported in Abū Bakr al-Rāzi's writings, as well as by those of al-Mubashshir ibn Fātik (e.g. 95, 1). Among the second class of materials there may at least be a partial contribution from the Cynic school (Rosenthal 1940: 388), perhaps transmitted to the Arab world via Indian sources. Even so, other Hellenistic works certainly found their way into Arabic tradition: Xenophon is quoted as are other authors such as Ammonius and Porphyry; Diogenes Laertius and pseudo-epigraphic writings like *Liber de Pomo* also served as direct sources for the Arabic Socrates tradition. However, in addition to complete texts it seems plausible that a certain Greek gnomic collection also existed that served the Syrians and/or the Arabs as a source for their knowledge.

As viewed from the medieval Arabic perspective, the route of the Socratic tradition went roughly as depicted in fig. 20.1. The model that Socrates provided was earnestly appreciated by the Arabs of the Middle Ages. The admiration expressed in their stories is manifest even in texts that are almost direct translations from the Greek (e.g. Ibn al-Qiftī, 205, 4) – its keenness perceptible simply from the titles of various writings. al-Kindi, usually thought of as the first Arab philosopher (d. 873 CE), wrote a number of treatises about Socrates, most of which are now lost: *On the Virtue of Socrates*; *Socrates' Pronouncements*; *On a Controversy Between Socrates and Archigenes*; *Of Socrates's Death*; *About What Took Place Between Socrates and the Harraneans* (Ibn Ibnal-Nadīm, *Fihrist* 260, 4; Ibn al-Qiftī, 374, 5). Furthermore, another early important scientific and philosophic personality, Jābir ibn Ḥayyān (d. 789), demonstrated a focused interest in the sage, composing a treatise entitled *Critical Remarks on Socrates* (in Kraus 1942–3: 64) – later, Abū Bakr al-Rāzi (d. 950) would write a work of the same name. Although not

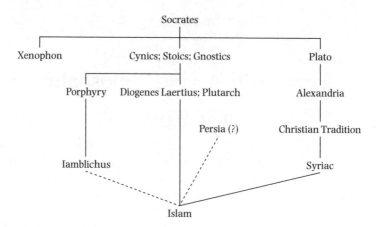

Figure 20.1   The Socratic tradition.

frequently, sayings attributed to Socrates were quoted in Arabic poetry ('Abbas 1977: 97) and were even inscribed on a public edifice in Samarqand (Shishkin 1970: 25–6). But knowledge and discussions about Socrates were not confined to written texts only; in Baghdad salons were held where the philosopher was a frequent topic of conversation (Tauḥīdī, *Ṣadāqah* 28, 15). Considering the broad range of interest that Socrates was able to capture in the medieval Arab world, the intensity of his eminence is indeed impressive. Certainly it is not surprising that philosophers, historians, and geographers would have known of him through translated texts of Plato, Aristotle, and the Neoplatonists. However, it is truly a marvel that poets, mystics, linguists, *hadith* scholars, and other nonphilosophers would also have been so well acquainted with the sage.

It seems that in medieval Arabic culture there was a stock of wise sayings that served both groups and individuals by means of its items' ascriptions to different famous personalities. We thus find sayings that are recorded as belonging to both Socrates ('Āmirī, *Sa'ādah* 84, 9) and Luqman (a Quranic non-Arab sage, appearing at *Quran* 31:12–13, for example), King David, and the Caliph 'Umar. If, indeed, beyond faithfulness to direct translations from the Greek, the historical person to whom a given saying or anecdote is secondary, the choice of Socrates for this kind of literature can perhaps be explained by didactic objectives. He was chosen because of his fame for combining philosophy and ethics, theory and practice. This combination might have struck a chord by its similarity to the Prophet's personality. However, just as plausible an explanation can be found in the considerable challenge Islam faced for quite some time after its inception – from Christianity on the one hand and from Muslims of weaker faith on the other. These groups seem to have attempted to promote their religious causes with the help of foreign sages. No wonder, therefore, that the earliest Arabic authorities who quoted and referred to Socrates were al-Kindi, the early philosopher, Mu'tazilite (Ivry 1974: ch. 3), and Ḥunain, a master translator and Christian apologist in a latent conflict with Islam (see e.g. Haddad 1975: 292–302).

Biography

Socrates was Syrian (*shami*) according to one report (Ibn al-Qiftī: 198, 10) and a northern Greek of Syrian origin (Ibn Juljul 30, 11) according to another. He was born in Athens (Fulutarkhus 141, 1) or in another town, Anisbah (perhaps a misspelling of Athens), to his father Sophroniscus (Shahrastānī: 278, 19). In the Arabic texts his name is usually written as Suqrāt, but in some cases his full name is spelt out, namely Socrates in Arabic transliteration (Ibn-al Muqaffa‘, *Manṭiq* 50, 11). According to a variety of authors, the name carries a meaning in Greek, on which they are not unanimous. However, the most commonly occurring suggestions are 'the infallibly just' (Mubashshir 82, 6), 'the holder of health' (probably a combination of the Greek *sos* and *krates*) (Ibn al-Nadīm 245, 20), and 'the one adorned with wisdom' (quoted by Rosenthal 1940: 73).

The consensus among Arab authors was that Socrates was principally a wise person, if not the wisest. As such he belonged to the Company of the Seven, the 'pillars of wisdom' (Ibn al-Qiftī 15, 5), i.e. the Greek sages (Shahrastānī 253, 14), along with Thales, Anaxagoras, Anaximenes, Empedocles, Pythagoras, and Plato – or according to another version, the Five, with Anaxagoras and Anaximenes omitted. As reported in a very traditional Arabic style, the *saj‘* (rhymed prose), Socrates was extremely savvy when it came to the hearts of men, and his influence on people's minds and intellects was like that of the purest water in the midday heat (Manṭiqī I, 557).

Several authors suggest that Socrates lived during the reign of Artaxerxes, also known in Arabic as Artashast or Long-Hands Ardashīr (Ibn al-Nadīm 245, 20). An attempt at the most precise time definition was endeavored by al-Birūnī who placed his year of birth in coincidence with the third year of that king's reign (Birūnī, al Qānūn, I.156, 3), the year 5067 from the creation of the world. Agapius preferred a span within the reign of Darius (Agapius 89, 5). In a similar way, Socrates' date of death was open to just as much speculation: according to the historians of the West, Socrates was killed at the time of Ardashīr, the son of Dara the son of Ardashīr, the son of Korresh (Cyrus), the first among the Sassanian kings; which also corresponded to the time when the Greek alphabet reached 24 letters (Birūnī, *Tahhīb*, 134, 10).

In the Arabicization of Socrates many important details were omitted from the philosopher's character, views, and activities, e.g. his political involvement, as referred to by Xenophon (*Memorabilia* 2, 7–8). In fact al-Fārābī is the only author I am aware of who explicitly mentions this aspect of the sage, allowing its inclusion in his *The Philosophy of Plato*; although another exception could be Ibn al-Suwar (d. 1017), who compares Socrates to Diogenes, Plato, and Aristotle, all the latter of whom he hails for participating in public life without compromising their respective philosophies (Lewin 1955: 283ff.). A very plausible reason for such an omission could be the Arabs' unfamiliarity with and/or lack of interest in Athenian political processes and institutions. Indeed, ignorance and apathy also go a long way in explaining some rather odd information found in the Arabic material; for instance, the fact that Socrates was reported to have been brought to trial by 'the king,' which, in reality, was simply the title of the Athenian archon in charge of the judicial system (*basileus*).

In the Arab estimation perhaps the most striking feature about Socrates as a character in narrative was his attitude and conduct at the time of his own death. It

319

'stimulated the discussion of the problem of suicide for which Islam gave an answer which apparently differed from that of Plato and Socrates' (Rosenthal 1946: 248). Thus for some like Usamah ibn Munqidh (d. 1188), Socrates symbolized civil bravery (Usamah 195, 13), and yet this never overshadowed the esteem for his mental qualities, of which wisdom undoubtedly took priority ('Āmirī, al-Amad 6r13), earning him the nickname 'The Source of Wisdom' (Manṭiqī, 14v15). His reasoning was flawless (Mubashshir 91, 2), though it was sometimes compromised by his enigmatic Pythagorean style (Mubashshir 84, 6), which often only adumbrated in the form of perplexing yet very accurate (Shahrazuri 60r10) parables (Mantiqi14v16). Altogether, Socrates was extolled as a philosopher in the original sense of the word, in that he loved wisdom to a degree that caused his followers harm (Mubashshir 82, 10).

Socrates' piety (Mubashshir 91, 1) and asceticism were hailed by almost all Arab writers, including as alien a poet to the Greek tradition as Kushajīm (d. 961) (Diwān 175). The Arab assessment of the nature of this asceticism is perhaps best apprehended within the scope of the concomitant portrayal of Socrates' attitude towards 'this world.' Contrasted with the 'world-to-come,' this term connotes passing pleasures as opposed to real happiness, a theme not alien to the historical Socrates. This contrast is particularly emphasized by Ikhwān al-Ṣafā', a politico-philosophical Isma'īlī group of the tenth century, which made a point that Socrates used to call people to the 'spiritual world' (Ikhwān IV.99). Similar reports are also made by Sufi writers, ascribing to our philosopher an interest in the improvement of the soul and a habitation in the solitude of a cave (Shahrastānī 278, 19). Nonetheless, a notable exception to this positive judgment of Socrates' piety is to be found in al-Rāzī, who, distinguishing between a young and old Socrates with respect to asceticism, presents a somewhat cynical evaluation of his motives. According to him, Socrates' inclination toward asceticism was due not to religious belief, but rather to a love of philosophy, and his abstinence from food is to be explained not by a love of God, but by a want of time (al-Rāzī 99, 19).

In conformity with the ideal of the perfect moral sage, Socrates was held as an embodiment of magnanimity, a quality that he shared with Lysandros the Just (al-Ṣalīḥ) (Ibn Sina 316, 6), and likewise he accrued a great concern for justice: he would take care of the poor and the widow rather than accumulate riches (Tauhīdī, Akhlāq, 324, 368). Fittingly for a man who claimed the counsel of a tutelary daemon, his image was argued by 'Abbas to have been a significant influence in the development the motif of the angel in poor man's guise in Arabic literature ('Abbās, Malāmih, 150). Socrates was conceived to have combined a purity of the sould with philosophy in a manner analogous to that of Suhrawardī (d. 1191) (Ḥājī I.424, 10) – yet it was understood that this virtue did not prevent him from participating in battles according to Greek custom (al-Rāzī 99, 17).

In the matter of Socrates' family life the Arabic tradition did not significantly diverge from its sources, although elements were emphasized or constructed to approximate the Athenian sage more closely to the Arab ideal. Thus one reads without protest that Socrates' ancestry was not of a high social status, but of course this did not trouble him (Mubashshir 100, 4). Yet later it is stated that Socrates was forced to wed, and as an exercise in patience and in expression of his misogyny (Anonymous, Bustān 43v7) he selected the worst available candidate (Mubashshir 82, 8). Nonetheless, Arabic tradition depicts her as a loving and caring wife, and the existence of another is only once hinted at (Ibn al-Qifṭī 204).

Straying more radically from the original account, the Arabic sources mention two motives for the arrest of Socrates by the hand of 'the king' Artaxerxes (Ibn al-Nadīm 245, 20), one religious and the other personal. According to the first, he opposed the faith of the state and its priests, against whom he created public opposition, and in fear of whom Artaxerxes had him arrested ('Āmirī, al-Amad 6r15) (a version curiously reminiscent of Jesus in the Gospels). Still elsewhere one finds him denigrating the common beliefs about the Athenian idols (Birūnī, Tahdhīb 18, 18) in a trial staged at an Eastern shrine (Shahrastānī 283, 1). Even more strangely, the second charge is posited in one place as the result of a conspiring aristocracy, vexed by Socrates' opposition to poetry (Ibn al-Qifṭī 199, 7). However, in an alternative version related in several different anecdotes, it is Artaxerxes himself who seeks vengeance, indignant after an accidental quarrel with the sage over honor (Ibn Juljul 30, 16).

The trial of Socrates, like his arrest, plays an important role in his Arabic biographies, and is frequently set down in some detail. This is surprising in view of the fact that the Athenian judicial system was very different from that of the Islamic. For instance, whereas the Athenians had civil courts (Dunlop 1962: 82, 89), the whole concept of a trial in Islam is rooted in religion (Schacht 1964: I). Furthermore not only were the Arabic authors deprived of any relevant real-life correspondences with the Athenian legal system, it is also difficult to understand where they might have obtained any textual information to remedy this deficit as the materials would necessitate. To the best of my knowledge, no book dealing with the subject was available in an Arabic translation at the time.

However accurately his trial was received, the fate of Socrates was in accord with the Quranic paradigm of persecuted prophets (e.g. 6:34) – Muhammad obviously being excluded. On the procedural side, the Arabic sources report that the court that tried Socrates was composed of 11 judges (Mubashshir 86, 5) – one version even asserts that it was they who turned the king's heart against the sage. It was also these judges who pointed out to him the possible damage ensuing from his continued life in Athens and the advantages that his death would bring (Ibn al-Qifṭī 199, 10). To substantiate the accusations 70 (Ibn Juljul 31, 8), or 11 (Ikhwān IV.99), aged witnesses were recruited.

The charges leveled against Socrates generally keep faithful to the account in the Apology, but given the philosopher's function as an ethical model, they absorb an overwhelming Islamic slant. Thus Socrates' original 'heresy' is magnified into an opposition to the astral religion and idolatry of the state (e.g. Birūnī Tahdhīb 18, 18), calling instead for the worship of the One, the Eternal, the Creator Who made the entire world, the Wise, the Omnipotent. He further propounds what moral and social values should be adopted (Mubashshir 85, 19). Denying this accusation, Socrates simply avers that he was only scrutinizing matters as best a human being could (Ibn Rushd, Parva 78, 6). The story's Islamic coloring hardly requires comment: God's attributes appear here in a purely monotheistic and Islamic conception, rather similar to al-Ghazālī's list (Ihyā' I.108) – the Creator, Omnipotent, Exclaimer of Truth, Living, Willing His Actions, Omniscient, Hearing and Seeing, Speaking, and Eternal.

Only a little later on, Socrates irrevocably secures his status as an Islamically sanctioned sage, proclaiming, 'command to do the beneficial and forbid to do evil.' This saying is one of the most important precepts in Islam (e.g. al-Ghazālī, *Iḥyā'* II 306–56) and is held to be of universal value, borne by all prophets at God's bestowal (Al-Ghazālī, *Iḥyā'* II.306, 15) – it appears in the *Quran* several times (e.g. 3:104), and also came to be one of the Mu'tazilite five principles (see al-Khayyāṭ, *Intisār* 93, 3). For his proclamation of such a vehement monotheism, Jābir Ibn Ḥayyān was led to qualify Socrates as 'having neared truth' (Jābir, *Mukhtār* 187, 16).

As for the charge of corrupting the young, it is recorded as relating to an innocent engagement in education between Socrates and a group of young princes, subsequently utilized by his opponents against him (al-Qazwīnī, *Āthār* 382). In the Arabic account there is also a suspicion of homosexuality, understood as equally false (Anonymous, *Mukhtār* 100, 7).

Perhaps the best-known part of Socrates' life concerns his death, and it enjoyed the same fame in the medieval Orient as it did in antiquity. The story is related in our tradition by two principal versions: Ibn al-Qifṭī and Mubashshir, both somehow different summaries of Plato's *Phaedo* and *Crito*, with the former being closer to the Greek original than the latter. There is no telling, however, whether the paraphrases are original Arabic or translations of unknown foreign originals. A third, considerably shorter version by Ikhwān al-Ṣafā', al-Qazwīnī, and Ibn Juljul focuses on the issue of Socrates' planned escape, and in particular on the necessity of obeying the law under all circumstances (Ikhwān IV.73, 13). The Arabic sources also disagree about Socrates' age at the time of his death: one report makes it 100 years of age (Mubashshir 91, 3); another 80 (Ibn al-Nadīm 245, 20); and yet a third, 70 (Ibn Abī Uṣaibi'ah I.47, 13).

Though relying on Plato, the principal Arabic tradition differs in several of the details of the post-trial scene. For instance, it names Rome as the offered place of refuge instead of the Greek Thessaly (Qifṭī 200), and does not refer explicitly to chance as the cause for the delay in executing Socrates. Also absent is any mention of the ship that was sent annually from Athens. On the other hand, puzzlingly, the Arab author found it necessary to name the shrine to which the ship was sent, Ir'un (Qifṭī 199, 20), whereas the Greek text only names the island of Delos as the destination of the vessel.

And yet, the Arab authors were not always so forceful in their inclination to Islamicize Socrates. In a passage which corresponds to the Greek text at 84d8ff., Socrates addresses his disciples to the effect that they should not esteem him less than they do the *ququs*, the bird of Apollo who knows the unknown. When it senses its death, it sings out of happiness and joy, rejoicing at its imminent reunion with its master. Socrates remarks that his own happiness in the same circumstances is no less than that of this bird (Birūnī, *Tahdhīb* 57, 18). Furthermore, Socrates' last words are recorded in some sources rather faithfully, and in others less so, though the discrepancies should be primarily attributed to an ignorance of Greek sacrificial customs, and perhaps only secondarily to an underestimation of its importance or a literary whitewashing. Thus, Ibn Butlan (d. 1068), a celebrated philosopher and physician clearly exempt from any suspicion of the latter motivations, remarked in our context that the cock was worshipped by the Manicheans! (Ibn Butlan 37, 27). However, more in keeping with the revisionist tendency was Ibn Riawan, who refuted this conclusion on the grounds that the fact that Muslims sacrifice lambs does not mean they worship them (Ibn Butlan 45, 3). Still further, possibly endeavoring to avoid any suggestion of pagan elements, the version of Mubashshir ends the story not with a cock, but with a quote: 'I entrust my soul to the keeper of sages' souls' (Mubashshir 90, 13).

As the paradigm of religious and ethical conduct, Socrates assumed a role in medieval Arabic literature very similar to the one he acquired in the Christian tradition. Indeed, his character expanded in accordance with his appropriation, gathering such titles as 'prophet' and 'deistic philosopher,' (or 'metaphysician' or 'theologian'), which were construed as having been earlier attributed to him by the 'Ancients' (Balkhī, *Badī'* III.8, 1). Additionally, to this 'prophethood' the Arabs also added the title of law-giver, the Arabic term used in this context connoting religious laws (Tauḥīdī, *Basa'ir* I.451, 14). This religious side of the philosopher is evinced in both circumstantial and contentual evidence – 'circumstantial' being used here to describe evidence comprising stylistic and linguistic data that attach Islamic connotations to Socrates' activities and associated matters, while 'contentual' refers to the more explicit and portrayed Islamicization of those activities and associated matters.

A good portion of the former type is demonstrated by the mere fact that many 'Socratic' sayings found in the gnomic collections are, as noted above, also ascribed to the Prophet or to other great Islamic or Islamically relevant personalities. Clearly Islamic vocabulary is unsparingly applied in this context: the words *aṣnām* (idols) and *shirk* (polytheism) suggest a likeness between Socrates and Abraham. On top of this, the expression used by Socrates' disciples for their request that he write down his wisdom, namely *qayyid 'ilmaka* (lit., 'tie down your knowledge'), is of a definite Islamic character (al-Kindī, *Alfāẓ* 28, 1; al-Darīmī, Muqaddimah, 43). Obviously, many other expressions are used which can easily be identified as bearing rich Islamic connotations, such as *dunyā* (this world), *Allāh* (God), or *zuhd* (asceticism). However, these may or may not have been chosen intentionally with Islam in mind, and the same holds for some Islamic metaphors such as the comparison of this world to a prison, which is commonly made in the *hadith* (Mubashshir 95, 1; Muslim 53, 1).

The contentual expression of Socrates' often largely religious function in Arabic literature is most pronounced in the emphasis the Arab authors placed on his model as an ascetic. Certainly this attribution in itself was not originally Islamic, as the philosopher had already been viewed as such in earlier Greek literature (Lohse 1969: 47–8; Andrae 1947: 70). And yet within the Arabic tradition this ascetic element took on a uniquely Islamic hue, permitting the Athenian philosopher's character the advantage of being regarded as more than just that of a heathen sage – he was exalted as an ideal even for Muslim holy men. Indeed, so successful was this revision that it seemed only natural to compare the celebrated al-Suhrawardi to Socrates (Haji I.424, 10). In addition, Socratic sayings and anecdotes that parallel in their contents ideas in Islamic sources also testify to this selective assimilation. Here one must also keep in mind the fact that omissions are no less evident than positive quotations, and therefore the excision of pagan expressions from Socrates' death scene or the reworking of hymns to Apollo attributed to him reveal the methods of this purgation as well.

Nonetheless, though widespread, this revision was not universal and sometimes one does come across a contrary notion of Socrates, judged not as a proto-Islamic saint but as an atheist whose example posed a menace to Islam (Abū Ḥayyān, *Imtā'* II.16, 5).

This alternative viewpoint found realization in the practice in which he, like other Greek philosophers, was used as an authority by Arab philosophers in their controversies with religious thinkers (Abū Ḥayyān, *Imtā'* II.18, 15). Called the 'apostate of his time' and 'the atheist of all time' (al-Qazwīnī, *Mufīd* 52, 19), he was accused of providing anti-Islamic thinkers with philosophical disguise and justification for their heretical views (Abū Ḥayyān, *Imtā'* II.16, 5), which included, among other things, a denial of the authority of religion on the grounds that it consisted of manmade rules and vain inventions (Ghazāli, *Tahāfut* 5, 2). As part of the 'opposition,' Socrates was even literally demonized by being counted amongst the ranks of the Djinn (Majrīṭī, *Risālah* 429, 5)!

Although Socrates' eminence in the Islamic world stemmed firstly from his conceived embodiment of ethical ideality, it should not be thought that he was largely dismissed as a theoretical philosopher, for it was the esteem in which what were believed to be his philosophical ideas were held that served as the final prop to secure him his position as the 'top and first philosopher' (Ya'qūbī, *Ta'rīkh* I.134, 1), the 'father and master of the philosophers' (Jābir, *Mukhtār* 389, 3), or the 'fountainhead of philosophy' (Shahrazuri 57r3). In fact it is reported that it was his views, as well as his leading of the Pythagorean school after the death of Pythagoras, that earned him Plato as a disciple (Qifṭī 19, 19) after the latter became disappointed with the Heraclitean school (Qifṭī 20, 4ff.).

Extracting these 'views' from the attributed sayings, one is confronted by a monotheistic Socrates, an 'enlightened thinker,' expounding a hodgepodge of Neoplatonic, mystical, alchemical, and orthodox Islamic doctrines. He was classified either as a member of the group of Anaxagoras, Pythagoras, and the dualists – in opposition to the school of Plato and Aristotle (al-Rāzī, *al-Muhassal* 84, 4), or counted amongst the 'divine philosophers' (metaphysicians), distinguished from the philosophers of nature, namely the Pre-Socratics (Stern 1960: 29; 33). According to another source, Socrates belonged to the same school as Plato and Aristotle (Qifṭī 50, 19), and metaphysics was his primary field of interest ('Āmirī, *Amad* 6r14).

He tied the world to God (Balkhi, *al-Badi* I.139, 6) (sometimes referred to as 'Intellect' [Fulutarkhus 158, 4]) from whom it emanates in Neoplatonic terms (Shahrastānī 281, 3), and proposed a world constructed of two double strata, the realm of meaning and the realm of Forms (Suhrawardī 231, 15), in which the principal components were God, Substance, and Form. Also, it must be kept in mind that in the Arab construal metaphysics was strongly connected with theology, and thus Socrates adopted this intellectual sphere as well; in fact, some of the titles of the writings ascribed to him often suggest a religious content (see below). Besides metaphysics, he was also engaged in mathematics, logic, physics, alchemy, and politics (Haji 172/1).

Yet, Socrates' most outstanding philosophical contributions were in the field of ethics (Ya'qūbī, *Ta'rīkh* I.134, 6), for he was not only considered to have been a brilliant theorist, but was also extolled for having exercised moral virtue in the form of asceticism – in order to attain final felicity – and in kind conduct towards other people and creatures (al-Tauḥīdī, *Akhlāq* 328). In an interesting divergence from accepted knowledge, Abu Bakr al-Rāzī (d. 950) presents a dynamic image of the philosopher, according to which he only reached this celebrated position in the later part of his life, preceding it with a normal life.

Renowned in his own time as much as posthumously, Socrates was said to have gathered 12,000 pupils (Mubashshir 90, 16) or, alternatively, only 70. Among his teachers were Pythagoras (Sā'id 23, 1); Archelaus (Shahrastānī 278, 19) (who only taught Socrates physics [al-Mas'udi, *al-Tanbīh* 104, 19]); Timotheus, or Timaeus (Mubashshir 82, 15), and Luqmān, whom he also met directly (Ḥājī III.91/4). If this résumé is not impressive enough, the Arab authors also numbered the majestic company of Pythagoras (Ḥājī I.72, 1), Empedocles (Suhrawardī 221, 15), Plato (Ḥājī I.72, 1), Aristotle, Leucippus, Meno (Ibn Sīnā 74, 13), Critias, Thrasymachus (Ibn Sīnā 225, 5), and Archigenes (Ibn al-Nadīm 260, 4) among his friends and associates.

Adhering to their inherited tradition, the Arabic authors claimed that Socrates refrained deliberately from writing, a stance also taken by the Prophet. Yet in spite of this conclusion, bibliographers mention a number of titles ascribed to the philosopher: *A Treatise about Politics* (perhaps Plato's *Republic*); *A Treatise about Proper Conduct* (Ibn al-Nadim 245, 21); *Law-giving* (Usāmah 437, 15) (perhaps Plato's *Laws*); *Religion (or Law – Sunnah) and Philosophy*; and *Reproof of the Soul* (Ibn abi Usaibi'ah I.49, 26).

Teachings

In his philosophical teachings Socrates's took 'the middle course,' exemplified by the argument between him and Thrasymachus in the *Republic* (Ibn Sīnā 225, 5). On the other hand another source relates that he used to 'coerce' into actuality almost everything *in potentia* (Jābir, *Muṣaḥḥahāt* fol. 1v10), a practice disliked by Plato who instead advocated treating things like 'the soul of a dead man [going] through the eye of a needle' (Jābir, ibid. 11v4). The grand expositor of a Neoplatonic metaphysics, Socrates proclaimed a First Existent from which all the other existents drew their being; a process realized through the emanation of the Good from it to them, including the perfect city and its ruler (Mas'ūdī, *Tanbīh* 101–4). Furthermore, in keeping with his Neoplatonic roots, the Arabic Socrates insisted that the principles of all things were three: Active Cause which is God; Essence which is the primary substratum for all being; and the Forms which are the elements of bodies (Ibn al-Jauzī, *Talbīs* 46, 13).

In addition to abstract considerations, Socrates gave specific directives to humans with regard to God, which are very similar to Islamic ones. For instance, he insisted that one should fear, love, and please Him (Mubashshir 85, 9), realize that He is one's protector, and avoid giving in to lusts (Ḥunain, *Nawādir* 67, 17). Besides an unswerving faith in God, Socrates advocated prophecy (Balkhī, *Bad'* III.8, 1).

In the Arabic language the word *dahr* (time), which is sometimes replaced by *zamān*, connotes along with its purely temporal meaning the sense of fate and eternity, hinting at a need for a resolution of pessimism and futility in the hopeless struggle against its flux. Thus as an 'otherworldly' metaphysician, the Arabic Socrates denounces time as constantly renewing itself (Ḥunain, *Nawādir* 70, 18) while annihilating everything else (Ḥunain, *Musrei* 18, 27), and thus never affected in its own essence (Ḥunain, *Nawādir* 71, 5). It is an intractable and invincible foe, keeping its promise to no one; it is an oppressor and an enemy, a killer and a judge, a conqueror and an insatiable dog (Ḥunain, *Nawādir Suqrat* 23r16). An intriguer (Ḥunain, *Musrei* 22, 8) full of vicissitudes

(Mubashshir 112, 3) and calamities (Mubashshir 120, 12), its only inherently positive quality is that eventually it acts equally upon all (Mubashshir 112, 11) and will finally return one to one's primal element (Ibn abī Usaibī'ah I.49, 13). Thus, the Arabic Socrates admonishes that one should regard Time negatively (Ḥunain, *Musrei* 22, 11) and mistrustfully (Ḥunain, *Musrei* 22, 4), but with perseverance (Ḥunain, *Musrei* 19, 2).

This world is depicted negatively by Socrates for its temporality, opposition to the world-to-come, transience (a characteristic also pointed out in the *Quran*, e.g. 57:20), and treachery (Mubashshir 104, 15). In its more specific relationship to the human condition it is associated with sensual pleasures and apparent advantages, namely position, wealth, and comfort (Anonymous, *Mukhtār* 112, 14). However, the seemingly desirable things of this world are, in reality, detrimental as they cause evil (Anonymous, *'Unwān* 38v6) and veil God from one. (Ḥunain, *Nawādir* 67, 19). For it is this world that diverts one from that which is incorruptible, toying with one's destiny (Ibn 'Aqnin 104, 11). Therefore one should make all effort to resist its harmful influences, since even cultivating it imparts toil while in it and, far worse, misery after having left it (Mubashshir 98, 1). To him who loves the world, it is a prison, but to him who renounces it, a paradise (Mubashshir 95, 1).

Nevertheless, Socrates assures one that there is a positive side to this world: it is a transit to the world-to-come for the road to which provisions must be prepared (Mubashshir 96, 3). Though this is hardly grounds for an unabashed optimism, one can find hope in the fact that the sufferings in this world will be rewarded in the next (Ḥunain, *Nawādir* 67, 5). And since while here one must act, proper actions are prescribed in two categories: those that will gain one entry into Paradise and those that will bring one posthumous praise (Mubashshir 98, 5). Along the way, one must be prepared for the inevitable calamities and misfortunes that this world provides (Mubashshir 117, 12), adopting a position of equanimity (Ḥunain, *Musrei* 19, 29), or at least of moderation (Mubashshir 96, 5). Yet the loftiest path during this unhappy sojourn is to suffice with the necessary little and occupy oneself with the pursuit of wisdom (Mubashshir 103, 19).

Socrates, like several other well-known Greek philosophers, was alleged to have maintained the creation of the world by God, whose existence was infinite neither in space, because it is actual rather than potential (Fārābī, *Fuṣūl* 19, 15), nor in time. God consisted of the world of meaning, further divided into the world of Divine Sovereignty and the world of the Intellects; and the world of Forms, which in turn, was divided into corporeal Forms, i.e. the world of the spheres and elements, and the spiritual Forms, also called the world of suspended images (Suhrawardī 231, 15).

On the issue of cosmology we are told that Socrates differed from his teacher Pythagoras ('Āmirī, *Amad* 8v16); and more specifically, on that of the interchangeability of the elements he held views similar to those of Anaximenes (Tauḥīdī, *Muqabasat* 271, 15). He maintained, according to an Arab author who quotes Plutarch, that there are three principles: the efficient cause or agent, which is God; Substance, which is the first substratum; and Form, which is a bodiless essence. For the Arabs Socrates' interest in cosmology was consonant with his involvement in alchemy, a discipline which he received from God and in which he voiced his views on the Balance, water, stones, and the Elixir. This first idea, the Balance, seems to have entailed a somewhat vague 'equilibrium' between the genera and nature (Jābir, *Mukhtār* 159, 10), perhaps contrived in an attempt at quantifying such diverse fields of knowledge as physics, Neoplatonism, medicine (Jābir, *Mukhtār* 263, 3), and contemporary Ismāʿīlī religious ideas. Just as mysteriously, the philosophical notion of water Socrates propounded extended beyond its traditional role, splintering into several kinds, such as 'sharp,' 'flying,' and 'the water of life,' distilled from certain stones arranged in a certain manner (Jābir, *Mukhtār* 389, 3).

The terms used in Arabic for ethics as it was exercised by Socrates were either *tahdhīb al-akhlāq* or *riyādat al-nafs* (training of the soul), both loaded with heavy Islamic connotations. Along such lines, the ethical character of Socrates was pruned and cultivated according to Islamic ethical ideals. Thus Socrates is affirmed to have taken a great interest in social justice, while opposing the amassing of property. He regarded the ability to know right from wrong as a fundamental characteristic of any human being, lacking which a person could not be fit to belong to society. The virtues incumbent upon every intelligent agent to follow and uphold (Hunain, *Nawādir* 66, 15) were serviced by innocence and culpability, through the employment of one's bodily organs (Mubashshir 85, 12). He proclaimed moral ignorance as tantamount to death (Hunain, *Mā dhakarahu* 17v4), and, therefore, preached that one ought to do what was right (Mubashshir 119, 10), even against contempt or disapproval (Mubashshir 116, 8).

Although Socrates was renowned for the nobility of his character even amongst his contemporaries, in Arabic literature this virtue is, of course, hailed in the context of its function within Islamic spiritual purification. Hence Socrates testifies that the possession of a good character absolves one from sin (Hunain, *Musrei* 22, 21) and conceals it, as well as invites a flood of other good qualities and situations, such as love, friendship (Hunain, *Musrei* 21, 16), and peace. Likewise, the justice so enthralling to Plato's Socrates in the *Republic* is poeticized by the Islamic Socrates as God's balance (Kindī, *Alfaz* 31, 8) by which He composed the world (Miskawaihi, *Hikmah* 213, 15); the most beautiful of ornaments (Usamah 432, 12), adhering to which results in salvation (Kindī, *Alfaz* 30, 6). It would seem that an integral part of this adherence was acquiescence in truth, which Socrates directly entwines with aesthetics in stating that the most beautiful person is he who knows the truth best (Mubashshir 105, 12). Any bearer of it is to be welcome, since truth raises him to its own greatness (Mubashshir 120, 7), being what distinguishes the freeman from the slave (Mubashshir 110, 12).

Very much in accordance with the Greek tradition, the Arabic Socrates praises the human intellect as identical to God (Fuluṭarkhus 163, 13), with Whom it shares simplicity, originality, and true existence (Fuluṭarkhus 159) – though he emphasizes that this lofty status is bestowed at His grace (Hunain, *Musrei* 18, 31). Quite contrarily but still in a way that is not un-Greek, Socrates elsewhere states that the intellect, obviously separate from God, is unable to describe His true essence (Sharastani 279, 4). Yet in still other places, the intellect is defined as the result of the influence of God upon the soul (Birūnī, *Tahdhīb* 65, 4), and as such, a guarantee of one's right action (Mubashshir 116, 17) as well as a safety from perdition. Not unexpectedly, the intellect's relation to the body is mostly conceived as one of opposition unless it manages to rise above it in rulership (Miskawaihi, *Hikmah* 281, 19) – such cooperation is presented as ideal (Usāmah 440, 16).

327

Following upon these assessments, the Arabs, like their Greek predecessors, had no problem creating a strong bond between the intellect and ethics. Thus Socrates' character, as presented in the full range of inherited sources, needed little tidying, merely development. In one account Socrates asserts that the intelligent person shall do nothing base, although he will not be free from self-doubts (Mubashshir 119, 16) – a core Platonic principle given further psychological qualification. Following upon this statement, then, is a list of prescriptions, proceeding in a more uniquely Islamic manner: he is oblivious to property; his demands and expectations from others do not exceed those from himself (Mubashshir 112, 19); his speech is civilized (Mubashshir 120, 5), but with the fool he should speak as a physician speaks with a patient (Mubashshir 103, 14). Conversely, the ignorant person is recognizable by his constant laughter, anger (Mubashshir 102, 1), and mistakes (Miskawaihi Ḥikmah 282, 1).

Knowledge ('ilm, ma'rifah), a central theme throughout Islamic literature, is analogous to government in a land or to the spirit presiding over the body (Anonymous, Bustān 12r12), and makes all other virtues depend from it ('Āmirī, Sa'ādah 412, 4). It trumps understanding, perception, insight, learning one's lesson, patience, reticence, and calling one's soul to account respectively (Mubashshir 119, 2); true knowledge consists in identifying the causes of things (Mubashshir 106, 20). Thus, acquiring knowledge and conducting oneself according to it is the best policy for the happy person (Usāmah 438, 14), who must gain it through experience (Ḥunain, Musrei 20, 14). However, according to one view, God is the only possible object of human knowledge (Mubashshir 85, 5).

The tool for the acquisition of knowledge is education and learning, which according to Socrates is but recollection (Ibn Sīnā 74, 13). On a purely anecdotal level, to the question of whether he was not ashamed to study at an old age, Socrates answered that being ignorant at such an age was even more shameful (Miskawaihi, Ḥikmah 211, 12). It is therefore beneficial in this quest for one to frequent the company of the knowledgeable, as they are also the guides to virtue (Mubashshir 116, 13); but the learner himself must be studious, patient, and of an understanding mind (Ḥunain, Musrei 23, 11). The process of education, Socrates argued, is like agriculture, where the teacher is the farmer, the student is the field, and study is water.

The virtue of wisdom, Socrates exhorts, has an indelible ethical efficacy in that it is essential for the soul's ascension to the Good (Kindī, Alfau 30, 7). It is inseparable from modesty, self-contempt (Ḥunain, Nawādir 54v5), and a calm indifference towards praise and blame (Sharazūrī 58v6), realizable only through a noble reticence (Ibn 'Aqnīn 80, 16). Moreover, it finds its antagonism in the degeneracy of drinking, amusement (Mubashshir 122, 1), greed (Ḥunain, Musrei 19, 21), and other self-destructive lusts (Shahrastānī 282, 13). Wisdom, as Socrates more determinately defines it, is a rational evaluation of the possible future outcomes of present events, and afterwards taking steps in accordance with one's conclusions (Ḥunain, Musrei 20, 13) while never losing sight of the long-term goal of salvation (Mubashshir 119, 5). It has a strong metaphysical aspect in that it is 'the light of nature's essence' (Mubashshir 111, 19), and the tool for escaping death (Kindī, Alfaẓ 30, 8). Psychologically speaking, wisdom is the medicine of the soul, the wise person being its healer (Sharazrī 65v12). It is pleasant (Sharazrī 58r5), better than wealth in that it is incorruptible, and exclusive of such worldly attachments ('Āmirī, Sa'ādah 60, 6).

328

Continuing, Socrates explains that the flip side of virtue, vice, is rendered by ignorantly ascribing incompatible properties to certain particulars ('Askarī, *Dīwān* II.93, 8). Further, he laments that since vice is only discernible through its consequences, it often catches one unaware (Ibn al-Mutazz 86, 11). Compounding this with the fact that vice stems from some deficiency in the soul, its detection may in some cases be possible only by the sage-psychiatrist (Mubashshir 124, 1). Indeed such a man can also help one to remove the root of all internal evils (Shahrastānī 281, 12), but, nonetheless, as long as one is evil one is to be regarded as of the living dead (Ḥunain, *Musrei* 19, 4), devoid of all goodness (Ḥunain, *Mā Dhakarahu* 17v5). Moreover, because of this state, such a man deserves no pardon, even if his sins are committed unwittingly ('Āmirī, *Sa'ādah* 84, 3).

Man's desire stands in obverse relation to his greatness (Mubashshir 113, 6), an idea Socrates inscribed on his seal: 'He whose passions overpower his intellect is disgraced' (Ibn abī, *Uṣaibī'ah* I.47, 18). Moreover he who prefers desires to his intellect is both blameworthy and regretful, in such a way that failing to overpower his body, he makes it his grave ('Āmirī, *Sa'ādah* 84, 4). Some desires, however, are laudable, although Socrates does not specify which (Mubashshir 102, 7). Still most, e.g. intoxication, greed, lying, and anger, are destructive to the soul and ought to be done away with (Mubashshir 102, 3), or, more realistically, should at least not extend beyond one's reach (Miskawaihi, *Ḥikmah* 346, 8), and there should be no exaggeration in pursuing them (Mubashshir 113, 14).

Anger is shunned by both religion and law (Mubashshir 124, 9), since it dehumanizes (Anonymous, *Bustān* 20r11) and is among the symptoms of the death of the soul (Anonymous, *Mukhtār* 106, 1). Upon analysis anger is reducible to mere self-punishment, a detriment to manly and other virtues ('Āmirī, *Sa'ādah* 131, 12) which often, unfortunately, proves intractable (Miskawaihi, *Tahdhīb* 195, 1). Nevertheless, when it is subordinated, this feat is affected by means of reticence, the panacea for desires (Kindī, *Alfaẓ* 30, 23). Free-floating anger Socrates dubs 'boldness,' and explains it as resulting from the soul's failure to consider the consequences of its actions (Usāmah 438, 15). Similarly, impropriety according to Socrates displays one's faults (Mubashshir 110, 16), disturbs one's life, and harms one's reputation (Anonymous, *Fuṣūl* 39v7). He thus urges that one govern one's manners, the most important kind of self-government (Mubashshir 124, 19).

Arabic Socrates paid much heed to social matters and in this context voiced his views on man and woman, both as a philosopher and from personal experience. He believed that women were evil (Ḥunain, *Musrei* 21, 25) and abhorred the good. Also, being the antithesis of wisdom, they desired to dominate men (Ḥunain, *Musrei* 21, 29) in assisting Satan (Ibn 'Aqnīn 130, 11). Moreover, Socrates declared that women incited revenge (Mubashshir 104, 3), and on the whole were inclined to prostitution (Ibn Kamal Basha, *Ruju'* 85, 31). For these reasons mere contact with women results either in imprisonment or death (Ibn 'Aqnīn 132, 11); Socrates himself was said to have escaped from the danger of their treacheries. Invoking metaphors to his aid, Socrates (Mubashshir 115, 6) likens woman to a fire (Mubashshir 114, 3), to the oleander tree which kills in spite of its beauty (Ḥunain, *Musrei* 22, 29), to a hunter ('Āmirī, *Sa'ādah* 84, 9) or to a trap (Mubashshir 114, 1), to a scorpion (Ibn 'Aqnīn 132, 17), a snake (Anonymous, *Bustān* 4v12), or an arrow (Ḥunain, *Musrei* 20, 5).

Threatened by such a host of dangers, Socrates urges the aspiring sage to avoid women as much as possible (Hunain, *Musrei* 22, 24) and adds further that even in exceptional moments, they should never be obeyed (Mubashshir 114, 11). Hence, more concretely, marriage is a fate worse than death (Sharazūrī 73v1), analogous to a fisherman's net wherein those outside it wish to enter and those inside to escape (Mubashshir 109, 3).

The issue of friends and friendship is salient in the Socratic teaching as it is in Arabic literature on the whole. Whereas romantic love is understood as a sort of madness (Mughulṭai 31, 11), friendship, a basic factor in human life, is defined by Socrates as a 'mutual affection of the hearts with a mutual harmony of the spirits' (Anonymous, *Fuṣūl* 39v6). More valuable than gold, it is the duty of every father to teach its value to his children (Miskawaihi, *Tahdhīb* 156, 10), so that they form friendships capable of withstanding any trial (Sharazūrī 70v1). Such constant inculcation is indeed necessary, as Socrates himself is once presented as offending the sacred bonds by accepting a disciple's gift (Mubashshir 101, 18). In choosing a candidate for one's friendship, suitability is evidenced by the prospect's conduct with his parents, brothers, and family; his personal qualities such as gratitude; his attitude toward pleasure, duty, property, and power (Miskawaihi, *Tahdhīb* 158, 9); as well as his self-appreciation (Mubashshir 119, 18).

Socrates admonishes that when building a friendship one must not act with haste or be overly zealous (Majrīṭī, *Ghāyah* 414, 18), nor should one conduct it from too close a range (Hunain, *Musrei* 18, 21). On the other hand the friend should be treated well and praised frequently, because praise is part of the foundation of friendship (Mubashshir 99, 7). Another ineluctable part is faith, and the faithful friend prevents one from erring (Hunain, *Nawādir Suqrāṭ* 44r1), points out to one one's weaknesses (Anonymous, *Mukhtār* 92, 7), and puts one before oneself for moral scrutiny (Mubashshir 113, 17). However this attitude must be reciprocal since otherwise one may be led to low-mindedness or even self-degradation (Usāmah 464, 14). Developing this point further, Socrates encourages that one exercise flexibility with one's friends (Mubashshir 118, 8) and only reproach them after one's anger subsides (Mubashshir 99, 3), if at all, as criticism might be self-damaging (Miskawaihi, *Tahdhīb* 158, 9; cf. Themistius, *On Friendship* 56). When a friendship must be put to the test, this should be done when the friend enjoys superiority and sovereignty rather than inferiority and weakness; applying this method the conclusions are thus more accurate (Isḥāq, *Nawādir* 37v18). Furthermore, once an apology is offered it must not be refused (Anonymous, *Mukhtar* 94, 1), for one can hope to overcome death by avoiding enmity ('Āmirī, *Sa'ādah* 131, 13). Summing up, Socrates insists that as a friend one must not be too tough, demanding (Shahrastānī 281, 18), or book-keepingly (Majrīṭī, *Ghāyah* 415, 4), but rather one should be trustful, as trust is the basis of being human (Majrīṭī, *Ghāyah* 415, 4). Indeed, antagonistic to the virtues of trust and faith stands betrayal, one of the five annihilators of the soul (Ghazālī, *Tibr* 111, 16).

Beyond relations between individuals, the domain of politics and society at large did not escape Socrates' notice: indeed, even in his own case, once the possibility to live within the state was withdrawn, death was preferred to the inhuman life that would follow (Ibn Rushd, *Be'ūr* 37, 31). Like the historical Socrates, his Arabic heir firmly asserts that civic life requires obedience to the law, which is universal (Mubashshir 99,

9) and beneficial to the multitude (Shahrastānī 282, 4) – religious law being to religion as medicine is to the body and psychology is to the soul (Usamah 432, 15). Further-more, as custodian of the state for whom religion and intellect are of essence (Ghazālī, *Tibr* 76, 11), it is the duty of the king to educate his subjects (Mubashshir 97, 13) and to repel injustice (Usāmah 432, 12) and evil, while promoting the reign of their opposites (Usāmah 438, 7). To competently handle such duties the king must train himself to forbear the ignorance and bad character of others ('Āmirī, *Sa'ādah* 284, 5). However, on the other side of the line of authority, Socrates urged ordinary people to avoid serving kings if they wished to adhere to truth. Along these lines he counsels that if one wants to befriend men of power one should do so before the latter assume office, for otherwise one could be viewed as a flatterer (Mubashshir 123, 5). Also, for the purely practical reason of preserving one's safety he also advises that one should beware of appearing to behave more truthfully than the king himself (Mubashshir 104, 18).

As both metaphysician and ethicist Socrates spoke broadly on issues that fall under what was referred to in both medieval Arab culture and Greek thought as 'psychology,' or the philosophical treatment of the soul. Not surprisingly he was said to have made ethics logically depend from his psychological doctrines (Miskawaihi, *Tahdhib* 87, 9), and put the relations between the soul, the body, Nature, Intellect, and God in hierarchical order ('Āmirī, *al Amad* 9a5), similar to the three Plotinian hypostases (e.g. *Enneads* IV.3, 27, 5; 12, etc.). In accordance with his above-mentioned metaphysical pessimism towards the material world, Socrates held the soul properly opposed to the body in its quest to arrive at its proper place after death (Birūnī, *Tahdhīb* 65, 2). Also, inviting a great disparity with Islamic beliefs, some Arab authors maintained that Socrates believed in the transmigration of souls (Ḥunain, *Musrei* 23, 5), which he demonstrated by his theory of recollection (Birūnī, *Tahdhīb* 43, 9). More specifically, this espousal was construed as having placed Socrates within the ranks of the pre-Islamic 'twelfth erroneous sect' of some philosophers (Al-Isfarāīnī: *Ṭabṣīr* 120, 1), who also contended that only impure souls underwent this process ('Āmirī: *al Amad* 8v20).

Socrates conceived of the soul as equivalent to the All (Mubashshir 93, l6) and sharing in a natural affinity with other souls (Mubashshir 93, 5). Despite such a regal metaphysical attribution, he nonetheless balanced this view by declaring that souls are ignorant of their futures – this was also his explanation for why they did not fly away immediately (Ḥunaln, *Nuwādir* 73, 7). As a good Neoplatonist the Arabic Socrates taught that pure souls achieve salvation for themselves and for others (Mubashshir 93, 3) and were recognizable by their acceptance of the truth (Mubashshir 92, 14), their stable goals (Tauḥīdī, *Imta'* II.47, 6), and by their being in concert with their bodies (Ḥunain, *Nawādir Suqrāṭ* 22v5). Affecting this salvation in the individual was the rational soul, crowning the microcosmic psychic hierarchy and defined as a sub-stance endowed with faculties and senses (Shahrastānī 282, 18), but not to be con-fused with the intellect (*Risālah*, in Badāwī 1974: 313, 6). In order for the rational soul to ascend to its goal, the good (Mubashshir 125, 4), it must employ the body (Tauḥīdī, *Imta'* II.34, 12): the particular object which establishes the soul's relative status through the latter's identification with it ('Āmirī, *Sa'ādah* 60, 4).

Socrates' psychology is so strongly connected with death, the afterlife, and resurrec-tion that to a certain degree it comports with Islamic teachings. He was, however, accused by some of having held unorthodox views on a portion of these issues (Sā'id 23, 6), but not on the immortality of the soul (Ibn 'Ārabī, *Bulghah* 195a3). Detailing his doctrine of the soul's perdurability, he argued that the soul was a substance different from the body, standing to be rewarded or punished for its deeds done in this world (Birūnī, *Tahdhīb* 65, 5). Alternatively Socrates proposed that the awakening of the rational soul meant the termination of its appetitive counterpart (Ḥunain, *Musrei* 18, 24).

Socrates' welcoming attitude towards death, dramatized in his cell, was shared by Islamic writers such as al-Ghazālī (*Iḥyā'* IV.496, 13); and his conception of the soul's prebirth existence was known to the Arabs (Shahrastānī 280, 17). He likened death to a prolonged sleep (Ibn Hindu 87, 14), as the closest yet most hateful thing to man (Ḥunain, *Musrei* 23, 6) but his inevitable fate (Miskawaihi, *Ḥikmah* 265, 14). Nonetheless, he did admit it a positive side as a means to the world-to-come and eternal life (Ibn 'Aqnīn 120, 7). Additionally, he hails it for liberating one from one's body (Ibn 'Aqnīn 120, 21), tiredness (Ibn 'Aqnīn 116, 7), passions, sins (Mubashshir 106, 3), and enemies (Ibn 'Aqnīn 116, 20) – from this world in general (Ibn 'Aqnīn 114, 23) – and rejoices in the thought that it rids the world of its sinners (Ibn 'Aqnīn 122, 6). In acting equally towards all, death compensates for life's unjust discriminations (Ibn 'Aqnīn 122, 14), and reconnects one with one's departed loved ones (Ibn 'Aqnīn 118, 7). In sum, death for the righteous is preferable to life in this world (Ibn 'Aqnīn 120, 18), a belief that in itself makes death easier to bear (Ibn 'Aqnin 118, 9). One's right policy towards death is, therefore, a proud despising of it rather than fear, as fear constitutes death's bitterness (Kindī, *Alcibiades* 29, 13). Furthermore, killing oneself voluntarily, which is different from prohibited suicide (Birūnī, *Tahdhīb* 481), will turn natural death into life (Kindī, *Alfaẓ* 30, 2).

Conclusions

The image of Socrates in the medieval Arab world was one of a 'super sage' and prophet, drawn in part from the fact that he addressed almost all aspects of life. This image had a positive aspect and a negative one: as a 'super sage' rather than a mere philosopher, he did not play a role in the conflict between faith and philosophy; as a 'prophet,' however, he could indeed pose a threat, and was attacked as such. He, along with other Greek philosophers, served as a weapon in the internal controversies of Islam as well as those between Muslims and Christians.

Socrates' personality and the means of portraying it prior to Islam struck more than one major chord in Islamic tradition: he conveniently served as a model person like the Prophet himself, and anecdotes and quotations like the *hadith*, rather than theoretical treatises, fit the purpose of giving authoritative meaning to doctrine within the context of such an ideal figure. This exemplary image has not ceased to date: as late as 1998 a Musical Play by Mansour Rahbani, *The Last Days of Socrates*, was staged in Beirut 'as a protest against modern tyranny and injustice'; and in a series of articles in the celebrated London newspaper *al-Sharq al-Awsaṭ*, Socrates is mentioned as a seeker of truth (Sept. 17, 2000) and a warrior for freedom (March 25, 2001).

Note

1 This chapter relies strongly on two books that I have published: *Socrates in Mediaeval Arabic Literature*, vol. X in the series *Islamic Philosophy, Theology, and Science*, eds. H. Daiber and D. Pingree (Jerusalem: Leiden, 1991) and *Socrates Arabus: Life and Teachings* (Jerusalem, 1995). In the chapter only one reference will be provided for units of information. Complete parallels can be found in the above books.

References

Primary Sources

Agapius (Mahboub) de Menbidj (1915). *K. al-'Unvān – Histoire Universelle* (ed. and tr. Franqais A. Vasiliev), in *Patrologia Orientalis*, vol. 11, Paris: Firmin-Didot.

'Āmirī Abū al-Ḥasan Muhammad b. Yūsuf (d. 992), (1982). *al-'Amad 'alā al-'Abad*, ms. Servili 179. Translated and commented upon by Rowson, Everette K., *al-'Āmirī on the afterlife*, Thesis, Yale: American Oriental Society.

—— *Kitāb al-Sa'ādah wal-Is'ād (Book on Happiness and Bringing it About)*, Facs. Mujtava Minovi, Wiesbaden: Franz Steiner, 1957–8.

Anonymous, *Fuṣūl Falsafiyah majmū'ah min Nawādir Kathīra (Philosophical Sections Collected from Various Anecdotes)*. Ms. Köprülü 1608, fols. 38r19–47v.

Birūnī, abū Raihān al- (d. 1048) (1965). *Al-Qānūn al-Mas'ūdī (The Mas'ūdī Canon)*. Cairo: al-Majlis al-A'la lil-Shu'un al-Islamiyah.

—— (1958). *Fī Taḥqīq ma lil-Hind min Maqūlah fi al-'Aql mardhūlah (Examining India)*. Haidarabad: Da'irat al-Ma'arif al-'Uthmānīyah.

—— (1862). *Risālah fi Fihrist: ist kutub Muhammad b. Zakarīy al-Rāzī (Bibliography of al-Rāzī)* (Ed. L. Krell). Leiden: E. J. Brill.

Busṭī, a. Ḥatim M. b. Ḥibbān al- (d. 354 A. H.) (1977). *Rauḍat al-'Uqalā wa-Nuzhat al-Fudala' (The Meadow of the Intelligent)* (Ed. Muḥyī al-Dīn 'Abd al-Ḥamid). Beirut: Mu'ssasat al-Rayan.

Dārimī, 'Abd Allah b. 'Abd al-Raḥmān, (d. 893) (1966/1386). *al-Sunan (Precepts)* (Ed. 'Abd Allah Háshim Yamanī al-Madanī). Al-Madinah al-Munawwarah: Silsilat Matbu'at Kutub al-Sunnah al-Nabawiyah.

Farābī, a. Nasr al- (d. 950) (1961). *Fuṣūl al-Madanī (Aphorisms of the Statesman)* (Ed. and tr. D. M. Dunlop). Cambridge: Cambridge University Press.

Fuluṭarkhus (tr. c. 900) (1954). *Fi al-Ara' al Ṭabī'yah allati taqulu biha al-Hukamā' (On Physical Theories of the Philosophers)* (ed. 'Abd al-Raḥmān Badawī). Cairo: Maktabat al-Nahdah al-Misrīyah.

Ghazālī, Abū Ḥāmid (d. 1111), *Ihya' 'Ulūm al-Dīn (The Revification of Religious Studies)*. Beirut: Dar al-Ma'rifah, n.d.

—— (1927). *Tahāfut al-Falāsifah (The Incoherence of the Philosophers)* (ed. M. Bouyges). Beirut, Imprimerie catholique.

—— (1968). *al-Tibr al-Masbūk fi Naṣīhat al-Mulūk (Cast Ore in Royal Advice)*, Cairo: Maktabat al-Kullīyāt al-Azharīyah.

Ḥunain lbn Isḥaq (d. 870), *Mā dhakarahu Ḥunain Ibn Isḥāq (Hunain's Notes)*. Ms. Köprülü 1608, fols. 12vl6–2lv10.

—— *Min Nawādir Suqrāṭ (Some Socratic Anecdotes)*. Ms. Köprülü 1608, fols. 22r19–25r12.

—— *Nawadir al-Falāsifah (Philosophical Anecdotes)*. Ms. München 651.

—— (1896). Sefer Musrei Hafilosofim, ed. A. Löwenthal, *Sittensprüche der Philosophen*. Berlin: S. Calvary.

Ibn 'Abd Rabbihi, Abū 'Umar Aḥmad b. Muḥammad (d. 940) (1952/1372). *al-'Iqd al-Farīd (Precious Necklace)* (eds. A. Amīn, A. al-Zain and I. al-Abyārī. Cairo: Matba'at Lajnat al-Ta'lif wal-Tarjamah wal-Nashr.

Ibn 'Aqnīn, Joseph be Judah (d. 1226) (1944). "Tibb al-Nafs" in: A. S. Halkin, "Classical and Arabic Material in Ibn Aqnin's 'Hygiene of the Soul,'" *Proceedings of the American Academy for Jewish Research*, 14, 25–147.

Ibn Abī Uṣaibi'ah, Muwaffaq al-Dīn (d. 1270) (1882–4). *'Uyūn al-Anbā' fi Óabaqat al-Attbbai (Fountains of Information on the Calsses of Physicians)* (ed. A. Müller). Kairo-Königsberg: i Pr., al-Maṭba'ah al-Wahbīyah.

Ibn al-Jauzī. al-Faraj (d. 1200) (1368). *Talbis Iblīs (Satan's Confusions)*. Cairo.

Ibn al-Nadīm, Abu Ya'qub Muhammad b. Ishāq (d. 987) (1871). *Kitāb al-Fihrist: ist (Bibliography)* (ed. G. Flügel). Leipzig: Vogel.

Ibn al-Qifṭī, Jamāl al-Dīn abu al-Ḥasan 'Ali b. Yūsuf (d. 1248) (1903). *Ta'rikh al Ḥukamā' (History of Physicians)* (ed. J. Lippert). Leipzig: Dieterich.

Ibn Butlān (d. 1068) (1937) in Meyerhof, M. and Schacht, J., *The Medico-Philosophical Controversy Between Ibn Butlān of Baghdad and Ibn Riḍwān of Cairo*. Cairo: al Jāmiah al-Miṣutiyah.

Ibn Hindū, Abū al-Faraj 'Ali b. al-Ḥusain (d. 1019) (1900). *Al-Kalim al-Rūhānīyah fi al-Kilam al-Yùnānīah (Greek Spiritual Precepts)* (ed. M. al-Qabbānī). Cairo.

Ibn Juljul, Sulaimān b. Ḥasan (c. 1009) (1955). *Ṭabaqāt al-Aṭibbā' wal-Ḥukamai'* (ed. F. Sayyid). Cairo: al-Ma'had al-'Ilmī al-Faransiilil-Āthar al-Sharqīyah.

Ibn Rushd, Abū al-Walīd Muhammad b. Aḥmad (d. 1180) (1969). *Be'ur Ibn Rushd le-Sefer Hanhagat Hamedinahh le-'Aflatun* (ed. E. I. J. Rosenthal). Cambridge: Cambridge University Press.

Ibn Sīnā, Abū 'Alī (d. 1037) (1960). *Kitab al-Shifa' (Book of Health)* (ed. S. Z. Qanawati). Cairo: ak-Hai'ah al-'Ammah li-Shu'un al-Maṭabi' al-Amiriyah.

Ikḥwan al-Ṣafā (c. 950) (1957). *Rasa'il (Treatises)*. Beirut: Dar Ṣadr.

Isḥāq Ibn Ḥunain, *Nawādir Falsaiyah (Philosophical Anecdotes)*. Ms. Köprülü, 1608, fols. 5r–10v.

Jābir ibn Ḥayyān (d. 780) (1354 H.). *Mukhtar Rasa'il (Selected Treatises)* (ed. P. Kraus). Cairo: Maktabat al-Khābjī.

—— *Musahhahat Aflāṭūn*, in P. Kraus, "Jabir Ibn Ḥayyan."

Jālīnūs (1951). *Jawāmi' Kitāb Timāūs fī 'Ilm al Tabī'ah*, in: *Compendium Timaei Platonis* (eds. P. Kraus & R. Wlazer). London: In aedibus Instituti Warburgiani. Also published by 'Abd al-Rahman Badawī, *Platon*, 87–119.

Kindī, Ya'qūb b. Isḥāq, al- (d. c. 870), *Fī Alcibiādes wa-Suqrāṭ (On Alcibiades and Socrates)*, Ms. Köprülü 1608, fols. 21v11–22r1.

—— (1963). Ma Naqalahu al-Kindī min Alfaẓ Suqrāṭ (Socrates's Pronouncements as Presented by al-Kindī), in: Majid Fakhrī, "Al-Kindī wa-Suqrāṭ," *al-Abḥath* 16, 23–35.

Majrīṭī, ps. (d. 1007) (1962). *Ghāyat al-Ḥakīm (Picatrix)* (eds. H. Ritter and M. Plessner). Berlin 1933–London: Warburg Institute.

al-Manṭiqī, Abu Sulaimān, *Muntakhab Ṣiwān al-Ḥikmah (Treasure of Wisdom)*, ms. British Museum, Or. 9033.

Mas'ūdī, Abū al-Ḥasan 'Alī, al- (1861–1917). *Murūj al-Dhahab (The Golden Meadows)* (ed. Barbier de Maynard). Paris: Impr. imperiale.

Māwardī, Abū al-Ḥasan 'Ali (1954). *Adab al-Dunyā wal-Dīn (Conduct of This World and Religion)*. Cairo: Muhammad 'Ala Ṣbeih wa-Awladuhū.

Miskawaihi (1952). *Al-Ḥikmah al-Khālidah (Eternal Wisdom)* (ed. 'Abd al-Raḥmān Badawī). Cairo: Maktabat al-Nahaah.

—— (1966). *Tahdhīb al-Akhlāq (Improvement of Virtues)* (ed. C. Zuraiq). Beirut: Al-Jāmi'ah al-Amirīkīyāh.

Mubashshir, Ibn Fātik (d. 1053) (1958). *Mukhtār al-Ḥikam wa-Maḥāsin al-Kilam (A Choice of Maxims)* (ed. 'Abd al-Raḥmān Badawī). Madrid: Al-Ma'had al-Maṣrī lil-Dirāsāt al-Islāmīyah.

Qazwīnī, Zakariyā al- (1842). *Āthār al-Bilād wa-Akhbār al-'Ībād (Monuments in Various Lands)*. Göttingen.

—— (1906). *Mufīd al-'Ulūm wa-Mubīd al-Humūm (Teacher of Knowledge)*. Cairo: Dar al-Taqaddum.

Rāzī, Abū Bakr al- (d. 950) (1939). Al-Sīrah al-Falsafiyah (Philosophical Way of Life), in: *Rasa'il Falsafiyah* (ed. P. Kraus). Cairo: Jámi'at Fu'ad I.

Rāzī, Fakhr al-Dīn, al- (1905). *Muḥaṣṣal Afkār al-Mutaqaddimīn wal-Muta'akhkhirin min al-'Ulamā' wal-Ḥukamā' wal-Mutakallimin (A Compendium of the Thoughts of the Ancients)*. Cairo: al-Maṭba'ah al-Ḥusaynīyah al-Miṣrīyah.

Shahrastānī, Abū al-Fatḥ (d. 1153) (1842). *Al-Milal wal-Nihal (Sects and Schools)* (ed. W. Curton). London.

Shahrazūrī, Shams al-Dīn (c. 1200), *Nuzhat al-Arwāḥ (Spiritual Promenade)*. Mss. Br. Mus. Add 23365.

Tauḥīdī, Abū Ḥayyān (d. 1023) [1965]. *Akhlāq al-Wazīrain (The Virtues of the Two Wazirs)* (ed. Muhammad b. Tāwīt al-Ṭabkhī). Damacus: Al-Majma' al-'Ilamī al-'Arabī.

—— (1964). *al Baṣā'ir wal-Dhakād'ir (Insights and Provisions)* (ed. I. al-Kīlānī). Damascus: Maṭba'at Aṭlas.

—— (1964). *Fi al-Ṣadaqah wal-Sadiq (On Frendship)* (ed. I. al-Kīlānī). Damascus: Dar Fikr.

—— (1932–44). *al-'Imtā' wal-Mu'ānasah (Pleasure and Sociability)* (eds. A. Amin, & A. al-Zain). Cairo: Lajnat al-Ta'lif wal-Tarjamah wal-Nashr.

—— (1374/1924). *Al-Muqābasāt (Things Acquired)* (ed. T. Ḥusain). Cairo.

Usāmah Ibn Munqidh (d. 1188) (1935). *Lubab al-Adab (The Core of Culture)* (ed. Ahmad Muḥāmmad Shakir). Cairo: Maktabat L. Sarkis.

Ya'qubi, Ahmad b. Abu Ya'qub (1969). *Ta'rikh (History)* (ed. M. T. Houtsma). Leiden: E. J. Brill.

Secondary Sources

'Abbas, I. (1977). *Malamih Yunaniyah fii al-Adab al-'Arabi*. Beirut: al-Muiassasah al-'Arabiyah lil-Dirasat wal-Nashr.

Andrae, T. (1947). *Islamische Mystiker* (Deutsc. Übersetz. Kanus-Crede, H.). Stuttgart: W. Kohlhammer.

Arkoun, M. (1970). *Contribution à létude de l'humanisme arabe au IV/X siécle: Miskawaihi philosophe et historien*. Paris: J. Vrin.

Badawi, 'A.-R. (1974). *Platon en pays d'Islam*. Teheran: Mu'assasat Mutala'at-i Islami-i Danishgah-i McGill, shu'bah-'i Tihran.

Berman, L. V. and I. Alon (1980). Socrates on Law and Philosophy. *Jerusalem Studies in Arabic and Islam*, 2, 163–279.

Bürgel, Ch. (1967). Adab und I'tidal in al-Ruhāwī's Adab al-Ṭabīb, *ZDMG*, 117, 101.

—— (1974). Some New Material Pertaining to the Quotation From Plato's *Phaedo* in Biruni's *India*. *Türk Tarih Kurumu Basimevi*, Ankara, 127ff.

Dunlop, D. M. (1957). Biographical Material from the Ṣiwan al-Ḥikamah. *Journal of the Royal Asiatic Society*, 82–9.

—— (1962). The Nicomachean Ethics in Arabic, Books i-vi. *Oriens*, 15, 18–34.

Haddad, R. (1975). Ḥunayn Ibn Isḥāq: apologiste chrétien. *Arabica*, 21, 292–302.

Ivry, A. (1974). *Al-Kindī's Metaphysics*. Albany: State University of New York Press.

Jardaq, G. (1910). *'Alī wa-Suqrāṭ*. Beirut.

Kraus, P. (1942–3). *Jabir Ibn Ḥayyān, contribution à l'histoire des idées scientifiques dans l'Islam. Mémoires de l'Institut d'Egypte*, vols. 44 et 45, le Caire.

Lewin, B. (1955). L'idéal antique du philosophe dans la tradition arabe. Un traité d'éthique du philosophe Baghdadien Ibn Suwaa. *Lychnos*, 261–84.

Lohse, B. (1969). *Askese und Mönchtum in der Antike und in der alten Kirche.* München und Wien: Oldenbourg.

Richter, G. (1932). *Studien zur Geschichte der altern arabischen Fürstenspiegel.* Leipzig: J. C. Hinrichs.

Rosenthal, F. (1940). On the Knowledge of Plato's Philosophy in the Islamic World. *Islamic Culture*, 14, 387–422.

—— (1946). Rosenthal, Franz. On Suicide in Islam. *Journal of the American Oriental Society*, 66, 239–59.

Shishkin, V. A. (1970). Nadpisi v. Ansemble Shakhi-Zinda, in: *Zodchestvo Uzbekistana, Materialy i isseledovaniya*, Vip. II *Ansemble Shakhi-Zinda* (ed. P. Sh. Zakhidov). Tashkent: Ministerstvo Kul'tyrii Uzbekskoi CCR.

Stern, S. M. (1960). Al-Mas'ūdī and the Philosopher al-Fārābī, in *Al-Mas'ūdī Millenary Commemoration Volume* (pp. 28–40). Aligrah: Aligarh Muslim University.

Strohmeier, G. (1974). Die arabisch Sokrateslegende und ihre Ursprünge. *Studia Coptica*, 121–37.

21

Socrates in the Italian Renaissance

JAMES HANKINS

Even after the fall of the Roman Empire in the West, it is fair to say, the life and teachings of Socrates were never entirely forgotten in the lands of Latin Christendom. The Athenian philosopher was familiar to medieval readers from the writings of early Christian writers such as Lactantius and Eusebius, as well as from the pages devoted to him in the Church Fathers, particularly Jerome and Augustine. He was known as well from pagan writers like Cicero, Seneca, Apuleius, and Valerius Maximus, all of whom were part of the medieval literary canon and were read in cathedral schools and other educational settings throughout the Middle Ages. Already in the eleventh and twelfth centuries Socrates had become a symbol of pagan virtue, as the presence of his portrait on the façade of Chartres Cathedral and other medieval decorative programs attests. With the recovery of Aristotle's writings in the twelfth century medieval scholastics were able to acquire a more sophisticated understanding of his place in Greek philosophical thought, and scholastics such as Thomas Aquinas and Henry Bate of Malines were already fumbling with the problem of distinguishing Socrates' thought from Plato's. Yet the "Socratic Problem" does not appear to have preoccupied the medieval expositors of Plato's own works. Two of Plato's dialogues – the *Phaedo* and the *Crito* – were available in Latin translation in their entirety after the twelfth century and parts of two others – the *Timaeus* and the *Parmenides* – were also known in Latin. Yet only the *Timaeus* was the subject of a developed commentary tradition, and almost all the medieval commentators, including Bernard of Chartres and William of Conches, followed the lead of Calcidius in identifying the doctrine of the *Timaeus* as Plato's own doctrine, not that of Socrates. Medieval commentators usually explained that Plato put his own doctrine in the mouth of Socrates out of humility or out of a desire to honor his teacher – both motives regarded with high approval by medieval masters (Hankins 1987; Laarmann 1995).

So it is fair to say that Latin readers in the medieval West had a reasonably good sense of who Socrates was – as encyclopedic works such as Vincent of Beauvais' *Speculum doctrinale* and *Speculum historiale* attest – though medieval accounts of his life inevitably mixed elements of myth and quasi-hagiographical elaboration.[1] But it remains the case that the richest sources for Socrates' biography – the dialogues of Plato, the works of Xenophon, Aristophanes, and Lucian, the *Lives of Eminent Philosophers* by Diogenes Laertius – were not known and exploited until the revival of learning in Quattrocento Italy. It was not until the Hellenic revival of the Italian Renaissance that Western scholars, with the help of their Byzantine teachers, were able to gain direct access to the Greek texts most useful for reconstructing the life and teachings of Socrates.[2] In the course of the fifteenth century, between 1404 and 1484 to be precise, there was a great renewal of interest in Plato and Socrates, and all the works of Plato became available in Latin, as well as the Socratic writings of Xenophon. A manuscript of Diogenes Laertius was brought to the West from Constantinople in the early 1420s and was translated into Latin by the Camaldolese monk Ambrogio Traversari before 1431 at the behest of Cosimo de'Medici. Xenophon's *Apology* was translated before 1407 by the historian Leonardo Bruni and the *Memorabilia* was translated in 1442 by Cardinal Bessarion, though the *Symposium* was only known in Latin after 1546, when it was translated by the Frankfurt Humanist Janus Cornarius (Johann Haynpul). A translation of the *Philosophical Orations* of Maximus was not made until the 1490s, nor published until 1517, but several manuscripts of the Greek text circulated and were read in Florence and Venice between 1420 and 1490 (Maximus of Tyre, *The Philosophical Orations* 66–85; Godman 1998: 194–5). The works of Aristophanes and Lucian began to be translated in the 1420s and 1430s, though knowledge of the former remained thin on the ground for a long time; with the important exception of Angelo Poliziano, it was not really until work of the sixteenth-century French Hellenists that the West had any serious engagement with Aristophanes.[3]

The case of Lucian was somewhat different. He was already being studied by the students of Manuel Chrysoloras, the Byzantine diplomat and teacher, in the first decade of the Quattrocento, and was being imitated by Leon Battista Alberti in his *Intercoenales* by the 1430s and in his comic novel *Momus*, written during the later 1440s (Marsh 1999). Alberti had a natural affinity for the kind of sarcasm and parody at which Lucian excelled, as can be seen from the following excerpt from the *Momus*. Jupiter (represented by Alberti as a vain, blundering fool), having decided to destroy the world and rebuild it again along better lines, decides to consult the philosophers to get ideas for his new design. He sends Apollo to consult Democritus and Socrates. On his return, Apollo describes his encounter with Socrates as follows:

"Now I come back to Socrates, a distinguished man universally praised for his virtue. I found him in a cobbler's shop, asking lots of questions, as is his wont. But nothing he said there concerns us." At this point Jupiter said, "Oh, the man you're talking about must be very distinguished indeed, since he associates with cobblers! But come on, Apollo, please; I want to know: what was it that Socrates was asking about? I long to hear the genuine sayings of Socrates, not things other people make up and attribute to him." – "But of course! Well then, if I remember correctly, he used these words: 'Tell me, craftsman, if you intend to make an excellent shoe, don't you decide to use the best leather?' – 'I do decide that,' said he. Then Socrates said, 'Do you take whatever leather is on offer, or do you think it makes a difference to choose the best leather from among those offered?' – 'That's what I think,' he said. – 'And how do you know the best leather? Do you do anything else but see which leather will be most fitting and suitable, and use the comparison to evaluate it and decide clearly whether it is too small or too big?' – 'That's my position,' he said. – 'Does someone who works with the best leather rely on chance or method to verify that there are no faults in it?' asked Socrates. – 'Method,' said the craftsman. – 'And what method did you use to perform the job? Did you perhaps learn it

338

from the experience and practice of preparing leather?' – 'Yup,' said the craftsman. – 'Perhaps' said Socrates, 'you used analogous procedures both to select and to prepare the leather, comparing parts with parts and the whole with the whole, so that the future leather corresponded with mathematical precision to the leather recorded in your mind and memory.' – 'Whatever you say,' replied the craftsman. – 'So what happens,' said Socrates, 'if a man has never seen leather made? Where does the description and likeness of the best kind of leather to prepare come from?' "

At this point Jupiter, who had been noting most attentively all of Socrates' questions, gave vent to his incredible admiration for Socrates, saying, "What a wonderful man! I can't keep myself any longer from shouting it out again: what a wonderful man! It goes without saying, Apollo, that although you were disguised, Socrates still knew who you were. In fact, I daresay that he knew who you were and what business you were conducting and what you wanted: in short, he knew everything. Philosophers just have that mental acuteness when it comes to secrets or subjects for investigation, as I know from experience. They take in so much of the general, the specific and the generic – more than you would believe possible. I know what I'm talking about, and I know from experience. You see how beautifully he satisfied himself once he recognized you and grasped your motives. I know where your ambiguous words are going, Socrates! Either I must restore the world in the likeness of the one I made when fashioning all the forms of beauty, or I should experiment with numerous worlds until chance happens to produce a more perfect one. But what then, what happened next?"

"Well," said Apollo, "the craftsman said that he had no idea what Socrates was talking about, so he remained silent. At that point I entered and greeted Socrates, who received me like a kind and gracious host. We talked over many things which it would take a long time to recount, but of the matters relevant to our problem, I liked particularly what he said at the conclusion of his line of micro-questions, namely, that this world, as it contains all things, is evidently such that nothing exists outside it that could be added or taken away from it by anyone. If one can't add to it, neither can one take from it, and if one can't take from it, then it can't degenerate. For how can one add something to a world outside of which nothing can exist? And how can you destroy something that can't be disaggregated?" (Alberti 2003: 253–8)

Alberti's send-up of Socratic dialogue here, as well as the other parodies of philosophic discourse scattered throughout the *Momus*, remind us that the ancient world was not always treated with reverence by Renaissance Humanists. Bloody-minded critics and outsiders like Alberti could cause trouble for the larger Humanist project of renewing Italian politics and culture on the model of the Greco-Roman past. Alberti's open admission of Socrates' appetite for male beauty (*Momus* 3.22), for example, points to an issue that would become a major exegetical problem for *bien pensant* interpreters of the ancients throughout the Renaissance.

Lucian's own picture of Socrates, of course, is by no means one well adapted to ease the reception of Socrates into a culture still deeply Christian. The case of Lucian reminds us that, along with new sources for the reconstruction of Socrates' life and teaching, the Humanists of the Renaissance also made available new sources for what might be called the anti-Socratic tradition. This included works written by the less enlightened Church Fathers such as Tertullian, Minutius Felix, Chrysostom, Theodoret of Cyr, and Jerome in his more monastic moods. Such works drew attention to the less easily assimilable aspects of Socrates' character and career. From an orthodox Christian perspective, of course, even the works of Plato – perhaps especially the works of Plato – presented problems for historians and men of letters who wished to make Socrates into a model of pagan virtue. Socrates' reputation for impiety, for pedophilia, for being possessed by a demon – his *daimonion* – were already enough to generate a vast amount of controversy in the Quattrocento, quite apart from the other rebarbative doctrines put into Socrates' mouth by Plato, most notoriously, his advocacy in the *Republic* of common ownership of women and goods, infanticide, abortion, and euthanasia (Hankins 1990, *passim*).

The significance of this issue is hard to grasp without understanding the place of Socrates in the cultural politics of Italian Humanism from Petrarch to Leonardo Bruni. In this early period, Humanism was still a militant movement, not yet a settled cultural tradition, and as such had to struggle for acceptance of its ideals and for patronage against more traditional kinds of cultural formation as well as against scholastic philosophy imported from Northern Europe. In the half-century from the 1390s to the 1440s the Humanist movement successfully convinced the elites of Italian cities that their sons and daughters would benefit from an education in the Latin and Greek classics. A prolonged exposure to the history, poetry, oratory and moral philosophy of the ancients would make them wise and eloquent, able to hold their own in the most sophisticated court settings or as citizen-magistrates in republics. Classical literature would endow them with ideal models of speech and behavior, and inspire them to acquire the nobility of character found in the best pagan soldiers, statesmen, philosophers and poets. These were the ideals that motivated Humanistic education in Renaissance Italy. It was an article of faith that the study of pagan literature would not in any way undermine Christian faith and values. Among Humanists there were disagreements about the best way to expose Christian youth to pagan literature, but few dissented from the belief that the best ancient writers would be of enormous help in reforming Christian society.

The Humanist program implied a considerable reorientation of traditional Christian modes of exploiting classical literature, those developed by the Church Fathers in late antiquity, most famously in the *De doctrina christiana* of Saint Augustine. Such works stressed the need to subordinate the study of pagan culture to the exigencies of Christian society, particularly the need for Christians to understand the Bible and to elaborate systems of theology and law. It was natural therefore that the early Humanists should encounter resistance to their ideas from cultural conservatives, typically churchmen, who feared that prolonged exposure of Christian youth to pagan literature would undermine traditional educational hierarchies. A key issue was the question whether pagans could really be models for Christians, whether there were really individuals one could describe as "virtuous pagans." In the *City of God* Augustine had ultimately denied this possibility, though he left open the possibility of a rhetorical use of the "virtuous pagan" topos, according to the formula *quanto maius*: if the pagans managed to behave with such courage or chastity or self-sacrifice, how much more should Christians be ashamed if they, aided by divine grace and the hope of salvation, do not achieve similar virtues. The *quanto maius* formula was used by a number of early Humanists such as Petrarch in his *De viris illustribus* and Boccaccio in his *De claris mulieribus* as well as Coluccio Salutati in the *De laboribus Herculis*. In their hands it became a justification for using pagan figures as moral exemplars.

In fifteenth-century Italy, however, as the Humanist movement established itself, the *quanto maius* formula was largely abandoned and the Humanists began to propose great pagan soldiers, statesmen, poets, artists and philosophers as moral models for their contemporaries in a much more straightforward way, without troubling themselves much about theological scruples. It was no longer claimed, for example, that Petrarch was a greater writer than Cicero and Virgil because he, unlike they, was in possession of Christian truth. A paradoxical result of the new situation was that it became much more important that the proposed pagan models not scandalize Christian sensibilities. While it was possible to propose Caesar as a model for contemporary generals while abstracting from his private morals, and while Vitruvius' morals were perfectly irrelevant to students of architecture, to present pagan philosophers like Plato, Aristotle, Socrates, or Seneca as models for imitation was much more difficult, thanks to the traditional association of virtue and wisdom. Wise men were expected to be virtuous. Moral *purgatio* was necessarily prior to philosophical *illuminatio* in the Christian contemplative tradition. Bad morals, on this view, inevitably led to bad doctrine. So the case of a philosopher like Socrates, who had the highest reputation as a philosopher in antiquity, and was even regarded as a kind of philosophical saint, but who also was charged with what Christians believed were severe moral failings – a case like Socrates' became a test case for the broader claims of the Humanist movement itself about the value of the pagan classical heritage.

The struggle to defend Socrates' reputation against critics of Humanism is evident from the first decade of the fifteenth century, when Leonardo Bruni undertook the earliest of the new translations that were to make the figure of Socrates well known in the Latin West. Bruni was the most important pupil of Manuel Chrysoloras and became the leading Humanist of the early fifteenth century. As apostolic secretary to four popes and later as chancellor of Florence, he was at the very heart of the movement to establish the humanities or *studia humanitatis* as the dominant educational and cultural program in Renaissance Italy. The most important early translation project Bruni undertook was designed to make available in Latin the chief sources for the life and teaching of Socrates, namely the *Apology*, *Crito*, and *Phaedo* of Plato along with the *Apology* of Xenophon. To this group of sources Bruni soon added the *Gorgias* for reasons that will emerge. The immediate motive for undertaking these translations, all completed in the first decade of the Quattrocento, was a series of attacks on Bruni's teacher, Coluccio Salutati, the chancellor of Florence and unofficial head of the Humanist movement, who was charged with promoting pagan "impiety" by clerical critics. The most considerable of Salutati's critics was the Dominican preacher Giovanni Dominici, a follower of St Catherine of Siena, later a cardinal. In sermons delivered in Florence at the church of Santa Maria Novella as well as in the *Lucula noctis*, an extended attack on the new Humanist movement, Dominici took issue with Salutati's glorification of pagan heroes and philosophers, and was particularly suspicious of Salutati's praise for Socrates and Plato (Debby 2001).

Salutati, to be sure, had been eager to avail himself of the authority of Socrates in various of his own cultural polemics. He delighted, for instance, in quoting Cicero's story of how Socrates had brought philosophy down from heaven to earth, seeing in this tale a parallel to his own efforts to redirect bright young men away from an interest in the "useless" natural philosophy of the scholastics, and towards the study of

341

literature and moral philosophy, which he believed to be more relevant to the social needs of the day. He praised the more informal style of discussion he saw in Plato's dialogues, seeing them as analogous to his own colloquies with his young disciples, and therefore also as a countermodel to the logic-chopping disputations of the scholastics. Impressed by his reading of the medieval version of the *Phaedo*, Salutati in his *De fato et fortuna* of 1396 had gone so far as to muse on the possibility that Socrates, had he been in St Peter's place, might not have denied Christ on the night before the Crucifixion (Salutati 1985: 72–4).

All this was anathema to Dominici, who himself had enjoyed a scholastic education in theology and canon law, and thought the new fashion for classical antiquity perilous for its failure to privilege Christian truth. Dominici evidently believed that an *ad hominem* attack on Socrates himself would be an effective riposte to Salutati's position. He accused Socrates of having shown contempt for public honors and magistracies, thus labeling him as exactly the sort of quietist, unengaged citizen that Salutati and Bruni criticized. Dominici repeated the charge of Socrates' skepticism and impiety towards the gods, and argued that his obedience to a "demon" showed, on the authority of canon law, that all his teachings had to be regarded *eis ipsis* as heretical. Dominici, clearly, was ready to add the sentence of the Roman Inquisition to that of the Athenian *dēmos* (Dominici 1940: 380).

Bruni's translations of Socratica, with their accompanying prefaces and arguments, were designed to show that Dominici's charges were untrue, and that in fact Socrates had been practically a Christian before Christ. The *Phaedo*, dedicated to Bruni's employer, Pope Innocent VII, demonstrated the belief of Plato and Socrates in the immortality of the soul, a doctrine regarded as the basis of all morality, and also showed Socrates' fearlessness and piety in the face of death. The *Apology* again showed Socrates' belief in survival after death and explained the true nature and function of Socrates' *daimonion*. The *Crito* contained the "Speech of the Laws," which Bruni later imitated at the end of his own tract on civic knighthood (*De militia* 1420); it showed how wrong Dominici had been in his jibe about Socrates' contempt for a citizen's duty to his country. "He is especially admirable in this section [wrote Bruni in the argument] where he treats of the citizen's duty to his country." In the *Gorgias*, translated slightly later in 1411 and dedicated to the antipope, John XXIII, he demonstrated the harmony of Platonic and Socratic doctrine with Christian thought, especially in the great myth of the afterlife at the end. As Bruni later wrote in a letter to Pope Eugene IV,

> Socrates, according to Plato in the book called the *Gorgias*, shows that it is worse to inflict than to suffer an injury. And he presses the argument to the point of saying that he has proved by the severest logic that it is far worse to inflict than to suffer injury. In the same book Socrates teaches that if someone does us an injury, we should not seek vengeance. What kind of teachings, by God, are these? Are they not divine, are they not very similar to Christian perfection? (Bruni 1987: 158; see Hankins 1990: 34–40, 51–8, 66–81)

But Bruni did not merely point out examples of Socratic virtue and doctrines harmonious with Christianity in his prefaces and arguments. He also took the more radical step of censoring, bowdlerizing and even entirely recasting works of Plato so as to prevent embarrassing aspects of Socrates' behavior from becoming known to Latin readers.

342

Already in his translation of the *Phaedo* Bruni had removed one reference to his homosexuality, and in his later translations of Plato from the 1420s, he was even more ruthless. In his translation of part of the *Phaedrus* from 1424, Bruni dropped the dispute about the type of (older male) lover a young boy should seek, dropped the passages on true and false rhetoric, and in general bowdlerized and Christianized with the greatest freedom. The passages he chose to translate had to do with the four types of divine madness and the arguments in support of the immortality of the soul. His purpose seems to have been to defend the idea that poetry and human loves were not threats to Christian morals, as conservative critics were maintaining, but could in fact serve as inspired sources of knowledge about divine things (Hankins 1990: 67–71).

Bruni was even more high-handed in his translation of "Alcibiades's Speech" from the *Symposium* (215a6–222a6), which was sent to Cosimo de'Medici in the form of a letter (1435). There had been some discussion in Florentine literary circles concerning passages of Xenophon and Plato that implied the existence of erotic attraction between Socrates and his young disciples Alcibiades and Critoboulos. Diogenes Laertius (*Lives of Eminent Philosophers* 2.19, 26) retailed reports that Socrates had been Anaxagoras' catamite and had engaged in polygamy, and though Ambrogio Travesari suppressed these passages in his translation, he may well have mentioned their gist to the dedicatee of the version. Cosimo had recently been embarrassed by receiving the dedication of Antonio Panormita's *Hermaphrodite*, a collection of obscene poetry with an accompanying letter by Poggio Bracciolini that had made reference to Plato's alleged sexual tastes (*Panormita* 1990: 152–3). This book had been burned by the public hangmen in several cities of Italy and its readers had been threatened with excommunication by Pope Eugene IV. The practice of sodomy was spreading rapidly in Florentine society (Bruni had himself condemned it in his *Isagogicon moralis disciplinae* of c. 1424) and the view that Greek philosophers were given to pedophilia was becoming something of a commonplace (Rocke 1996). Bruni's translation from the *Symposium* was designed to restore Socrates' prestige and make him once again safe for Christianity. The "translation" is a virtual *laus Socratis* in which Alcibiades confesses the powerful moral influence Socrates had upon him, extols his eloquence, chastity and integrity, and praises his military virtue. It has, however, only a very loose relationship with the Greek text. In Bruni's version, Alcibiades' account of his attempted seduction of Socrates is converted into a story of how Alcibiades pursued Socrates for his wisdom, and all references to pedophilia, flute-playing and polytheism are systematically expunged. Gratuitous moralizing with no basis in the Greek text is inserted in several places. After reading Bruni's "translation" Cosimo de' Medici, the most powerful literary patron in Florence, would have been reassured from the mouth of Plato himself that those rumors about Socrates' pederastic tendencies were nothing but the lies and slanders of his enemies (Hankins 1990: 80–1).[4]

Though Bruni's early translation activity was centrally concerned with making Plato's Socrates available in Latin, it is clear that his real affinity is with the Socrates of Xenophon: with Socrates the moral teacher and ideal citizen of Athens. In Florence Bruni had set himself up as a kind of secular preacher, teaching civic virtue by means of his translations of Greek philosophy and through his historical writings. His historical writings emphasized repeatedly the need of the *popolo*, officially the sovereign body in Florence, to accept that its will should be restrained by law and to take advice from

343

the wise and the good. Bruni would have been delighted with the famous story in Xenophon about how Socrates had, as magistrate, refused to execute the will of the *demos* when it had acted against the law (*Memorabilia* 1.1.17). He would have approved Socrates' condemnation of the uselessness of natural philosophy and its inferiority to moral philosophy (1.1.9–15), a position he had himself articulated in his *Isagogicon moralis disciplinae* of c. 1424. Bruni, like Socrates, condemned as irrational the practice of choosing magistrates by lot;[5] he too taught that reason and persuasion should be used in civil discourse and that great men needed to behave with moderation in ruling the state. Xenophon's picture of Socrates as a great moral teacher of youth and an active participant in the life of his city would certainly have appealed to Bruni; he would have heard with relief Xenophon's declarations that Socrates never engaged in pedophilic behavior; and he would have agreed enthusiastically with the Xenophontean Socrates' advice to master language and the art of speaking. Yet there is (as yet) no solid evidence that Bruni ever studied Xenophon's *Recollections of Socrates* or his *Symposium*. Deeper sympathies, perhaps, were at work.

Bruni's civic Humanist interpretation of Socrates was at length codified around 1440, in the *Life of Socrates* by Giannozzo Manetti, the first biography of Socrates written since antiquity (Manetti 2003: 176–233).[6] It was one of a pair of philosophical biographies by Manetti, the other being devoted to the Roman philosopher Seneca. As the pairing suggests, both lives were modeled formally on Plutarch. The little work was dedicated twice, first to the Spanish grandee Nugnio de Guzman, an important patron of the humanities in Italy, and again in the early 1450s to Alfonso of Aragon, who was king of Southern Italy and the Aragonese empire as well as the leading supporter of the humanities in Italy in the third quarter of the fifteenth century. In the dedicatory letter Manetti expressed the hope that by studying the lives of these two courageous philosophers, Alfonso would be stiffened up to fight the Turks, who were on the point of conquering Constantinople.

In this hope Manetti was disappointed, but he did succeed in putting together an extremely influential work of scholarship. Manetti's biographies circulated widely in manuscript and in 1470 were absorbed into the most famous edition of Plutarch's lives, that of Ulrich Han in Rome, as part of a kind of philosophical appendix to the *Lives* which also included Bruni's life of Aristotle (1429) and Guarino Veronese's life of Plato (1430). Ulrich Han's Plutarch edition was the model for almost all later editions of Plutarch in the fifteenth and early sixteenth centuries, so Manetti's life of Socrates was reprinted many times. It thus became the most important piece of biographical scholarship on Socrates in the Renaissance. Its success was no doubt due to the broad synthesis it provided of the most important ancient authorities on the life of Socrates – including Plato, Xenophon, Diogenes Laertius, Cicero, Seneca, Valerius Maximus, Apuleius, Jerome, and Augustine – and to its effectiveness as an instrument of Humanist apologetics.

Giannozzo Manetti was the most important disciple of Leonardo Bruni, so it was natural that his biography of Socrates should reflect the pains his master had taken to make Socrates acceptable to Christian readers. As Bruni was the leading republican thinker of the early Quattrocento, it is not surprising that Socrates, in Manetti's account, became a model civic Humanist and republican. Socrates lived in Athens' golden age of military and literary glory, Manetti wrote, and gave himself in youth to the study of letters. He was remarkably eloquent. He was so eager for knowledge that he became a disciple of Anaxagoras and Archelaus, but in due course he realized the uselessness of natural science and initiated the science of ethics in Greek philosophy. By so doing he became the fountainhead of the main Greek philosophical schools. Manetti indeed gives us three possible explanations for Socrates' ethical turn: either he regarded science with skepticism, or as frivolous, or – as Augustine suggested – he wanted to purify himself by the study of ethics so as to prepare himself to study theology (15).

But Manetti's real emphasis is not on the "divine Socrates," as this last alternative might suggest, but on Socrates' civic commitment to Athens. Manetti emphasizes that Socrates served bravely in the military, that he maintained a family, raised sons to help repopulate Athens after the plague, served in numerous magistracies, became rich without seeking wealth, and offered public instruction gratis. He was a model citizen and an inspiration to moral behavior. Aristotle may have treated the distinctions and definitions of virtue with scientific precision, but Socrates was more effective in instilling into young men an incredible love of virtue and a hatred for vice; his effect on morals could only be compared with the *Hortensius* of Cicero that had been so powerful in converting Augustine to the philosophical life (22). Socrates, unlike some other Greek philosophers, refused to serve tyrants and remained in Athens for most of his life, devoting himself to the education of youth.

Here, too, one might suspect the influence of Xenophon's Socrates, but as in the case of Bruni, work on Manetti's sources have so far failed to disclose any unambiguous dependence on his *Memorabilia*, *Symposium*, or *Oeconomicus*. Bessarion's translation of the *Memorabilia*, whose preface similarly stresses Socrates' example as "matching words to deeds," only became available two years later, in 1442 (Marsh 1992: 166). Once again, we appear to be dealing with elective affinities rather than direct literary influences.

Manetti's other chief emphasis in the *Vita Socratis* is apologetic: there was nothing in Socrates' life that ought to disturb the Christian reader, he maintained. Socrates was not a skeptic, as some interpreters charged: his pose of Socratic ignorance was ironic, a device to expose the ignorance of sophists and other frauds (29). In fact, Socrates had an extraordinary depth of knowledge in every science. Nor were the attacks on Socrates as "demon-possessed" on the mark. Citing Apuleius, Manetti argued that Socrates' *daimonion* was in fact a god, not a demon, and so should be interpreted as an angelic presence (48). In fact, Manetti stated, all men are attended by two angels, one good and one evil, and it was clear that Socrates had always followed the admonitions of his good angel, as his generally virtuous conduct attested (45). Finally, the stories about Socrates' erotic relations with young boys could be dismissed as malicious lies and slander. Manetti analyzes the story of the physiognomist Zopyrus, reported in Cicero and Eusebius, to show that Zopyrus had an unworthy motive in slandering Socrates (46). As Plato's *Symposium* shows – and here Manetti makes use of Bruni's bowdlerized fragment – Socrates' relations with youth were always chaste and virtuous (47). We cannot imagine that a man who made so noble a defense of himself against judicial persecutors, and who went to his death so courageously, could have yielded to vulgar bodily passions in the way his enemies alleged.

* * * *

If Manetti's *Life of Socrates* sums up the attitudes of early Italian Humanism to the figure of Socrates, we must look to Marsilio Ficino, the greatest Platonic scholar of the Renaissance, for a sense of how Socrates was seen in the Age of Lorenzo de'Medici. Ficino devoted his life to the project of orchestrating a great Platonic revival in philosophy and Christian theology, a revival that would overcome the failures of Christian Aristotelianism and provide Christian theologians, at last, with the philosophical support they needed to demonstrate central doctrines of the faith, especially the immortality of the soul. In this way the disastrous chasm that had opened up between faith and reason in the medieval period – according to Ficino – could be finally bridged. The revival of antiquity would thus come to the aid of Christian belief, and the ancient bond between Platonic philosophy and Christianity would be restored. Ficino's guides in this great project of Christian Platonism were principally St. Augustine and (pseudo-) Dionysius the Areopagite, while his principal guides to understanding the texts of Plato were Plotinus and Proclus (Hankins 1990: 267–366).

Ficino, however, was not only a writer and a thinker, but also a teacher and spiritual guide, and as such was deeply interested in the therapeutic side of Platonism and ancient philosophy. In his circle of followers, sometimes misleadingly referred to as the "Platonic Academy," he numbered over sixty of the leading noblemen of Florence as well as many prominent non-Florentines from as far away as France, Germany, and Hungary, whom Ficino counseled via his ample correspondence. It was in his capacity as a Platonic spiritual guide that Ficino made use of the example of Socrates. There is ample evidence to suggest that Ficino saw himself as the Socrates of Florence, reclaiming for piety and true religion young men exposed to the intellectual corruptions of the day, especially the godless "sophists" of the universities of Italy (Hankins 1991 and 1994). Lured by Ficino's great personal charm, his extraordinary learning, and his aristocratic circle of friends – which included Lorenzo de'Medici himself – skeptical youths would be brought through reading, informal discussion and spiritual counseling to see that the secularized philosophy of contemporary universities was inferior to the Platonism of the Church Fathers; that the superstitions and ignorance of the *fraterculi* and *mulierculae* who aroused their contempt were mere corruptions, and should not be confused with the true, ancient wisdom of Christianity.

Yet despite his new message, Ficino did not leave behind the civic Socrates of Bruni and Manetti. Ficino was himself an educator of young men, and his message of spiritual renewal through Platonism was not intended to create contemplatives alienated from society, saving their own souls by leaving "the world" behind. In fact, Ficino's followers, through the Socratic approach to teaching, would become ideal members of the commonwealth. Socratic love was no low sexual vice, as Lucian had implied, but a noble discipline intended to make virtuous adults of boys who were morally at risk.

> What is the good of Socratic Love, you ask? First, it is of great help to Socrates personally in recovering the wings to fly to heaven; secondly, it is of enormous help to his city in living honorably and blessedly. For a city is made not of stones but of men. Like trees, men must from tender years be cared for and directed towards the best fruit. The care of children is the role of parents and tutors [*paedagogi*]. But young men no sooner cross the boundaries set them by their parents and tutors than they are corrupted by the wicked habits of the vulgar. They would follow the superior rule of life they have imbibed at home were they not influenced by the company of wicked men, especially flatterers.

What then will Socrates do? Surely he will not permit youth, the seed of the future commonwealth, to be infected by shameless men? That would be unpatriotic. Socrates will then come to the aid of his country and will free its children, his own brothers, from destruction. Perhaps he will write laws preventing contact among the mischievous and the young. But we cannot all be Solons or Lycurguses: to few is it given to make the laws, and fewer still obey them. What then? Will he prevent contact among the young and their [wicked] elders by physical force? But only Hercules is said to have struggled thus with monsters; violence of this kind is most perilous for others. Perhaps he will warn, censure, rebuke the wicked? But a disorderly spirit rejects words of censure; what is worse, it turns savagely against the censor. When Socrates tried that he was kicked and cuffed.

The only way of salvation for youth is the company of Socrates. To this end that wisest of Greeks, overcome by charity, mingles everywhere and walks with a great crowd of youths accompanying him. Thus the true lover, like a shepherd, protects his flock from false lovers as from the pestilential lust of wolves. And since young people associate most easily with those their own age, Socrates makes himself young in purity of life, simplicity of language, games, jokes, and witty sallies. From a mature man he makes himself into a boy, in order, above all, to make boys into mature men through his pleasant and homely friendship. Youth, being prone to pleasure, is captivated only by pleasure; it flees strict teachers. Hence, to save his country, our tutor of youth, neglecting his own affairs, undertakes the care of his juniors and ensnares them first by the sweetness of his pleasant company. Once they are ensnared, he corrects their behavior with increasing severity until at last he is able to chastise them with a stricter censure.

In this way, he released from calamity the boy Phaedo, who had been involved with a common prostitute, and made a philosopher of him. Plato, who had been devoted to poetry, he compelled to burn his tragedies and give himself up to more valuable studies. Xenophon he led from vulgar luxury to the sobriety of the wise. Aeschines and Aristippus he changed from paupers into rich men; Phaedrus from an orator into a philosopher; Alcibiades from an ignoramus into the most learned of men. Charmides he made earnest and modest, and Theages a just and courageous citizen of the commonwealth. Euthydemus and Meno he converted from the quibbles of the Sophists to true wisdom. Thus it happened that the companionship of Socrates was still more useful than it was pleasant, and, as Alcibiades says, Socrates was loved still more ardently by young men than he loved them.[7]

Ficino believed that this "academic" style of philosophizing he found in the dialogues was admirably suited to the task of spreading Platonism among the upper ranks of Florentine society: not only the boys he dealt with in his school, but also his adult associates. Ficino's Platonic apostolate included educated professionals – doctors, lawyers, chancery officials, university teachers – as well as independently wealthy members of the political class. Dealing as he did with busy individuals, a regular cycle of university lectures (such as the Aristotelian philosophers used) was out of the question. Ficino instead tried to imitate the kinds of encounters he read about in Plato's dialogues, which seemed to offer a better model of how to make the contemplative life available to men deeply involved in the active life. So he gave few formal classes, aside from irregular evening lectures in Brunelleschi's chapel in Santa Maria degli Angeli. Instead, he tried to improvise conversations on the Socratic model, or organize banquets such as that enacted in the *Symposium*, or declamations such as Socrates gives in the *Menexenus*. Such activities did not take place in classrooms, but in private residences or churches in the city, or, as in the *Phaedrus*, in numinous places outside the city, like the Medici villa at Careggi.

347

On the evidence of the dialogues, Ficino believed that Socrates' style of teaching was informal and unhierarchical, and implied equality among the interlocutors. This provided him with an alternative pedagogical model, admirably suited to the social dynamics of his circle, and in striking contrast with the magisterial methods, the ritualized *lectio et disputatio* of the universities. Ficino and his friends believed that by developing this alternative style of intellectual debate they were reviving the true, ancient form of philosophizing which might ultimately transform their own lives and that of their city-state, bringing back the golden age when philosophers ruled and rulers were philosophers. Ficino very likely knew the passage of Plutarch's *Moralia* which sees Socrates as the antischolastic, a man who taught philosophy by his life and death, not *de haut en bas* from a professorial chair:

> Most people think that . . . those are philosophers who sit in a chair and converse and prepare their lectures over their books. . . . [But] Socrates was a philosopher, although he did not set out bleachers or seat himself in an armchair or observe a fixed hour for conversing or promenading with his pupils, but jested with them, when it so happened, and drank with them, served in the army or lounged in the market-place with some of them, and finally was imprisoned and drank the poison. He was the first to show that life at all times and in all parts, in all experiences and activities, universally admits philosophy.[8]

But whether Ficino knew this passage of Plutarch or not is hardly important; what is clear is that he understood Socrates' way of educating his fellow-citizens was something radically different from the traditional forms of scholastic education available in Europe in his day (Hankins 1994).

Though Ficino did not discard the Xenophontean Socrates, his recovery of Neoplatonic sources inevitably led him to a new interpretation of the great philosopher, which qualified in important ways the "civic" Socrates presented by Bruni and Manetti. In effect, Ficino revived the ideal of the "holy philosopher" found in late-ancient biographical literature, especially in Porphyry and Marinus. Ficino's fullest account of Socrates is given in a letter to the theologian Paolo Ferobanti, who had raised questions about Socrates' character, citing Lucian's caricature of Socrates as a pederastic simpleton. Ficino in reply said that Socrates was not only most wise, but also saintly and Christlike; his life was a kind of image or shadow of the *vita Christiana*. Like Christ, he was a prophet without honor in his own country of Athens, and underwent judicial murder for speaking the truth; he suffered hunger and nakedness, reproved sinners, turned the other cheek, hated pride and "the ambitious profession of the sciences," was gentle, humble, charitable, and chaste. Prudently using the rhetorical trope of *praeteritio*, Ficino even pointed out some typological parallels between Christ and Socrates: how at Socrates' "last supper" he took a cup, gave a blessing, performed washing, and mentioned a cock; how thirty pieces of money had been given to betray him; how he had been transfigured in contemplation; and how his disciples had gone about after his death preaching things "by which the Christian faith is confirmed" (Ficino 1563: vol. 1, 868).[9]

Ficino's reinvention of Socrates as a holy man, however, had an ironic outcome. For in the last decade of the Quattrocento Ficino's place as the "Socrates of Florence" was taken by his great rival and enemy, Girolamo Savonarola, thanks to the overheated imagination of a former student of Ficino's, Giovanni Nesi. It says something about the success of the Humanist campaign to rehabilitate and even sanctify Socrates that an ardent disciple of the Dominican preacher like Nesi was willing to identify his hero, a bitter opponent of secularism and neopaganism, with the Greek sage. In this context, Erasmus' famous remark in *The Godly Feast*, "Sancte Socrates, ora pro nobis," loses something of its irony.[10]

But to return to Ficino: as a holy man inspired by God, Socrates of course could not have been truly ignorant. Socrates' professions of ignorance could not therefore be taken literally. Ficino offered two possible interpretations. In the *Euthyphro* he is purely ironic, gently mocking "the ambitious professors of divine law."[11] But in general Socrates meant his profession of ignorance to be taken as an expression of the humility he felt when confronted with divine things. Naturally, Socrates was not truly ignorant, having been filled often and ecstatically with divine wisdom, but his pose of ignorance is adopted to make it clear that his wisdom comes from God, via the admonitory *daimonion*, and not through his own natural powers of reason. The claim that he only knew that he knew nothing was tantamount, in Ficino's view, to the following gloss, put into the mouth of Socrates:

> Abstracted from the body, seized by a *daimōn*, illuminated by God, I for my part know in the divine light this one thing, namely, that when conjoined with the body I know nothing in the natural light. By the light of nature, I say, I do not know true being through the mode of affirmation. This kind of knowledge is proper to God, who comprehends the natures themselves and the causes of natures, having himself made them. Yet I know many things through a certain way of negation, such as "that God is not a body."[12]

Socratic ignorance is thus understood in terms of Dionysian negative theology, as filtered through Thomas Aquinas. So, too, with Socratic method. For Ficino, Socratic method was essentially a purgative to free the mind of intellectual pride and false opinions, purifying it to receive divine illumination; it was a moral as well as an intellectual process. In this respect he, along with most other fifteenth-century interpreters of Socrates, follows the Xenophontean view of Socrates' teaching – that *enkrateia* must precede *sophia* – rather than the Platonic view that sees understanding as a precondition of correct moral behavior.

As Ficino writes in an argument to Book 1 of the *Republic*,

> You should know that Socrates was wont to inquire rather than to teach for many reasons. First, to admonish the arrogant that one should learn throughout life rather than [just] teach. Second to indicate that truth is straightway poured by divine means into our minds through a suitable process of questioning when separated from errors arising from the body. Third, to show that the forms of things are innate in our minds [and] through them the very truth of being sometimes glimmers when our minds are turned towards them through interrogation. Fourth, to make known that human knowledge [of the divine] consists in a kind of negation of the false rather than in affirming the true. (Ficino 1563: vol. 1, 1397)

* * * *

The Quattrocento, to sum up, presents us with two main images of Socrates: the Humanist or Xenophontean image of Socrates as a eloquent model citizen, a man of action and the fountainhead of Greek moral philosophy; and the Socrates of Ficino and the Neoplatonists, a holy man, a *theios* anēr on the model of Plotinus or of Christ himself, who despises the body and dedicates himself to religious wisdom. Both images were passed down to the sixteenth century and beyond in editions of Plutarch and in the works of Ficino. But the part of Socrates' story that was to remain the most powerful, as one might expect, was the story of his condemnation and death. In the age of religious persecution and martyrdom that lay ahead, that part of his story would become the center of his appeal both to Catholics and Protestants, eclipsing the citizen and pagan saint of the Italian Renaissance.[13]

Notes

1 Vincent of Beauvais (1964–5). See especially the *Speculum historiale* 5.56–7, 66.
2 For the revival of Greek in the Renaissance, see Hankins (2001).
3 Hankins (1990). For the translations and commentaries on Xenophon, see Marsh (1992 and 2003). The first part of the *Plutus* was translated by Leonardo Bruni in 1433/4, and a paraphrase of *Plutus* 400–626 was written by Rinuccio Aretino (under the title *Fabula Penia*), but it is not until Poliziano that we find an Italian Humanist with a broad knowledge of his comedies. The first known course on Aristophanes in the Latin West was given by the Roman Humanist Andrea Brenta in the late fifteenth century; see Brenta (1993).
4 The longer version of this paper to be published in *Images and Uses of Socrates* contains an edition and translation of this speech.
5 Xenophon, *Memorabilia* 1.2.8; compare Bruni (2001–4, 5.80–1).
6 The internal references that follow are to the paragraph numbers of this edition.
7 *De amore* 7.16; text in Ficino (2002: 245–9). See Ebbersmeyer (2002: 72–94), for Ficino's *amor socraticus*.
8 *An seni respublica gerenda sit*, 796D (H. N. Fowler, trans.) (Loeb Library; used by permission).
9 A text and translation of this letter is included in the version of this article to be published in *Images and Uses of Socrates*.
10 On Savonarola as the Socrates of Florence see Godman (1998), chapter IV. For Nesi, see Celenza (2001, pp. 41–4). For Erasmus's remark, see Erasmus (1972: 254).
11 Ficino (1563, 1983, 2: 1312). On Socratic irony in the Renaissance, see Knox (1989, part II).
12 Ibid. 2: 1389; see Hankins (1990: 321–4).
13 A longer and more fully documented version of this article will appear in the proceedings of the conference *Images and Uses of Socrates*, July 18–21, 2001, King's College, London, ed. Michael Trapp; Aldershot: Ashgate.

References and Further Reading

Alberti, L. B. (2003). *Momus*, ed. and trans. by Virginia Brown and Sarah Knight. Cambridge, MA: Harvard University Press. Contains a Lucianic parody of Socratic dialectic in Book 3.

Brenta, A. (1993). *In principio lectionis Aristophanis praeludia. La prolusione al corso su Aristofane*, ed. M. A. Pincelli. Rome: Associazione "Roma nel Rinascimento." The first known lectures on Aristophanes in the Latin West.

Bruni, L. (1741). *Epistularum libri VIII*, ed. L. Mehus. 2 vols. Florence: Paperinius. Contains the Florentine Humanist's translation into Latin of the speech of Alcibiades from the *Symposium*, in bowdlerized form.

—— (1987). *The Humanism of Leonardo Bruni: Selected Texts*, trans. G. Griffiths, J. Hankins, and D. Thompson. Binghamton, NY: Medieval and Renaissance Texts and Studies. A selection of writings by the first Latin translator of Xenophon's and Plato's Socratic works.

—— (2001–4) . *History of the Florentine People*, ed. and trans. J. Hankins. 2 vols. (to date). Cambridge, MA: Harvard University Press. The fullest expression of Bruni's civic Humanism.

Celenza, C. S. (2001). *Piety and Pythagoras in Renaissance Florence: The "Symbolum Nesianum."* Leiden: E. J. Brill. An account of the Pythagorean revival of the fifteenth century and Nesi's celebration of Savonarola as the "Socrates of Florence."

Debby, N. B. A. (2001). *Renaissance Florence in the Rhetoric of Two Popular Preachers: Giovanni Dominici (1356–1419) and Bernardino da Siena (1380–1444)*. Turnhout: Brepols. Socrates' morals denounced by Renaissance preachers.

Dominici, G. (1940). *Lucula noctis. Texte latin du XVe siècle, précedé d'une introduction*, ed. R. Coulon. Paris: A. Picard. Socrates' demon condemned by a follower of St. Catherine of Siena and a future cardinal.

Ebbersmeyer, S. (2002). *Sinnlichkeit und Vernunft: Studien zur Rezeption und Transformation der Liebestheorie Platons in der Renaissance* [Sensuality and Reason: Studies in the Reception and Transformation of Plato's Theory of Love in the Renaissance]. Munich: Wilhelm Fink. Contains a section on *amor socraticus* in the fifteenth and sixteenth centuries.

Erasmus, D. (1972). *Opera omnia Desiderii Erasmi Roterodami* [Complete Works of Desiderius Erasmus of Rotterdam]. Vol. I-3. Ed. L.-E. Halkin et al. Amsterdam: North-Holland Publishing. "Saint Socrates" encouraged to pray for our sins.

Ficino, Marsilio (1563, repr. 1983). *Opera omnia* [Complete Works]. 2 vols. Basel: Henricpetri; reprint Turin: Bottega d'Erasmo. The major works of the greatest Platonist of the Renaissance.

—— (2002). *Commentaire sur "Le Banquet" de Platon* [Commentary on the *Symposium* of Plato], ed. P. Laurens. Paris: Les Belles Lettres. Ficino's famous account of Platonic love, in the form of a dialogue-commentary on the *Symposium*.

Godman, Peter (1998). *From Poliziano to Machiavelli: Florentine Humanism in the High Renaissance*. Princeton: Princeton University Press. Overview of Florentine classical scholarship in the late fifteenth and early sixteenth centuries.

Hankins, James (1987). Plato in the Middle Ages. In J. R. Strayer (ed.), *Dictionary of the Middle Ages* (vol. 9, pp. 694–704). New York: Scribners. Overview of the medieval study of Plato.

—— (1990). *Plato in the Italian Renaissance*. 2 vols. Leiden: E. J. Brill. Overview of the Platonic revival of the fifteenth century.

—— (1991). The Myth of the Platonic Academy of Florence. *Renaissance Quarterly*, 44, 429–75. Reprinted in J. Hankins (2004). Contains discussion of Ficino as the "Socrates of Florence."

—— (1994). Marsilio Ficino as a critic of scholasticism. *Vivens homo. Rivista teologica fiorentina*, 5, 325–34. Reprinted in J. Hankins (2004). Influence of Socratic dialogue on Ficino's teaching method.

—— (2001). Lo studio del greco nell'Occidente latino. In S. Settis (ed.), *I Greci: Storia Cultura Arte Società. 3. I Greci oltre la Grecia* (pp. 1245–62). Turin: Einaudi. Original English version reprinted in J. Hankins (2003). *Humanism and Platonism in the Italian Renaissance* (vol. 1, pp. 273–92). Rome: Edizioni di Storia e Letteratura. Overview of the revival of Greek studies from the late fourteenth to the sixteenth centuries.

—— (2004). *Humanism and Platonism in the Italian Renaissance* (vol. 2, pp. 219–72). Rome: Edizioni di Storia e Letteratura.

Knox, D. (1989). *Medieval and Renaissance Ideas on Irony*. Leiden: E. J. Brill. Comprehensive discussion of Socratic irony in Renaissance literature and philosophy.

Laarmann, M. (1995). Sokrates im Mittelalter. In R. Auty et al. (eds.), *Lexikon des Mittelalters* (vol. 7.2). Munich and Zurich: Artemis-Verlag. Overview of medieval conceptions of Socrates.

351

Manetti, G. (2003). *Biographical Writings*, ed. and trans. S. U. Baldassarri and R. Bagemihl. Cambridge, MA: Harvard University Press. Contains the first and most influential biography of Socrates in Latin.

Marsh, D. (1992). Xenophon. In V. Brown et al. (eds.), *Catalogus Translationum et Commentariorum: Medieval and Renaissance Latin Translations and Commentaries: Annotated Lists and Guides* (vol. 7, pp. 75–196). Washington, DC: The Catholic University of America Press. Overview of the reception of Xenophon in the Renaissance.

—— (1999). *Lucian and the Latins: Humor and Humanism in the Early Renaissance*. Ann Arbor: University of Michigan Press. Includes remarks on the Renaissance reception of Lucian's Socrates.

Maximus of Tyre (1997). *The Philosophical Orations*, ed. M. B. Trapp. Oxford: Oxford University Press. With an account of the Renaissance reception of Maximus in the introduction.

Panormita, A. (1990). *Hermaphroditus*, ed. D. Coppini. Rome: Bulzoni. First erotic poetry of the Renaissance, with allusions to Socrates' *goûtes particulières*.

Rocke, M. (1996). *Forbidden Friendships: Homosexuality and Male Culture in Renaissance Florence*. New York: Oxford University Press. Historical background for understanding the reception of homoeroticism in Plato.

Salutati, C. (1985). *De fato et fortuna* [On Fate and Fortune], ed. C. Bianca. Florence: Olschki. Discusses parallels between Socrates and Jesus Christ.

Vincent of Beauvais (1964–5). *Speculum quadruplex sive Speculum maius* [The Fourfold Mirror or the Greater Mirror]. Graz: Akademische Druck-und Verlaganstalt. (Reprint of 1624 edition.) Compendium of medieval knowledge of Socrates.

22

The Private Life of Socrates in Early Modern France

DANIEL R. MCLEAN

Sodomite and husband of one or more shrewish wives; pagan, proto-Christian, and noble victim of an unjust death; opponent of scholastic dogma and exemplary *grand homme*. The appearances of Socrates in the literature of early modern France were organized around a series of contested and often contradictory identities, largely derived from his roles in the anecdotal tradition of antiquity and the Middle Ages and given significance in the contemporary cultural and political context. My concern in this chapter is for the reputation of Socrates in seventeenth-century France, a period in which the study of the Socratic heritage has been neglected relative to the eras that bracket it. The Socrates of Montaigne[1] or of the enlightenment humanists (for whom Socrates provided a model of political liberty in their struggles against the *Ancien Régime*[2]) has been examined in numerous studies. But the seventeenth century's Socrates has, in general, been less appreciated. In this essay, I shall concentrate on those aspects of Socrates' reception in French popular literature, and their background, that were best known to audiences of the early modern period. The image that emerges is largely inconsistent with that of the philosopher as relentless seeker of truth, the idealized dialectician to whom, as often as not, the modern imagination has reduced the figure of Socrates. What we find in the literature of this period is an amalgam of the otherworldly philosophical martyr and a more intimately realized individual whose personal life, and in particular whose erotic life, is ubiquitously discussed.

I.

"quid vetat paulisper σωκρατίζειν . . . ?"

–Petrus Ramus, *Schol. dial.* 4.13

To whatever degree the revival of Platonic studies served as a motivating force of the intellectual movement of the Renaissance – and many important studies have taught us to be cautious of generalizing away either Plato's influence in the Middle Ages or Aristotle's in the Renaissance (see especially Klibansky 1981 and Hankins 1990) – it was not through Plato that early modern France knew Socrates. For centuries after the revival of classical learning in the West, the preference is rather for the Socrates of Xenophon, Diogenes Laertius, and the Latin anecdotal tradition. This preference continues well into the modern era. Xenophon makes up by far the most frequent number of citations for the life of Socrates in Pierre Bayle's monumental *Dictionnaire historique et critique*. Even when Bayle, in a discussion of the feats of patience of the gymnosophists (1997/1734 III: 312b), notes that Socrates trained himself to stand immobile for long periods while intently focused on philosophical issues, his reference is not to Plato (from whose *Symposium* the story ultimately derives) but to Aulus Gellius.

Xenophon's newly-rediscovered Socratic texts conformed happily with and lent authoritative voice to the vibrant Latin tradition of exemplary narrative found in Cicero, Seneca, Aulus Gellius, and Valerius Maximus. The fashion for distilling the life of Socrates into edifying or mocking anecdote, for codifying and crystallizing the message of the philosopher in a series of *bons mots*, was practiced in antiquity especially by the Cynics and Stoics. As serious engagement with the figure of Socrates diminished, he became more and more a character in a type of narrative characterized especially by an obsession with the private details of his life. Plutarch reports the view of Cato the Elder that "there is nothing else to marvel at in the ancient Socrates but that he dealt reasonably and gently with his shrewish wife and senseless sons" (*vit. Caton.* 20.3). It is in this guise that he becomes the multi-valent *exemplum* of the Roman era and late antiquity. Seneca, whose own Socrates is more a source of charming moral stories than an intellectual figure, claims that Plato and Aristotle derived more from Socrates' character than from his words (*epist.* I 6.6). He advises us to approach the philosopher in the same manner:

> If you desire a model, take Socrates. That much-suffering old man was buffeted by every difficulty but still unconquered both by poverty (which his domestic burdens made more serious) and by labors (he also endured military service). He was harassed by these troubles at home, whether his wife, with her untamed character and impudent language, or his unlearned children, who were more like their mother than their father . . . (Seneca, *epist.* 104.27)

In the subsequent discussion, Socrates' troubles are expanded to include a life lived in a time of war and under the Tyrants, and his death, which his unswerving equanimity rendered a "wondrous and unparalleled object of renown" (*epist.* 104.28).

It is as this paradoxical moral exemplum – part model, part cautionary tale, a figure revolving between poles of high and low, serious and comic (McLean forthcoming) – that the legend of Socrates primarily endured. By the end of the ancient world, the story is set. Those abstract ideas and expressions of method to which his name is closely linked today – Socratic Irony, Socratic Ignorance, the Socratic Paradox, the elenchus – are not the primary terms of reference for the medieval and early modern Socrates. His name, as we shall see, is much more likely to be raised in connection with his wife's slop-bucket than with dialectic. This is not to say that Socrates did not function as a philosophical model in the Renaissance and early modern period. In France no less than in Italy, intellectuals invoked the name of Socrates in attacks on scholasticism. Petrus Ramus (Pierre de la Ramée, 1515–72), professor at the University of Paris and a member of the body that would later be called the Collège de France,[3] employed Socrates in his impassioned attacks on scholastic thought and vigorous anti-Aristotelian polemic. In one of the best-known passages of his writings, he formulates his rebellion against Aristotle biographically,[4] in terms of an encounter with the writings of Plato that led him to a new model: "What prevents me from *Socratizing* for a while and, dismissing the authority of Aristotle, seeking to discover whether this doctrine of Dialectic is true and fitting?"[5]

The accuracy of Ramus' self-characterization and the legitimacy of his rejection of Aristotelianism have been regularly called into question by scholars.[6] Nonetheless, Ramus' polemical use of Socrates – his taking the philosopher as model for his own intellectual and lived experience – followed and helped to fashion a tradition of Socratic identity as an oppositional stance. This is the Socrates employed by Denis Diderot when, imprisoned on suspicion of sedition in 1749, he used a toothpick to scratch out a translation of Plato's *Apology* in the margin of a copy of Milton's *Paradise Lost* (Seznec 1957: 1–4). In the same spirit the poet Théophile de Viau (1590–1626), while in exile on charges of atheism and obscenity that would eventually result in the first modern, state-sponsored obscenity trial (Lachèvre 1909; DeJean 2002: 29–55), composed his adaptation and translation of the *Phaedo* in a Menippean medley of prose and verse (*Tracté de l'immortalité de l'âme, ou la mort de Socrate*, 1619). In doing so, he explicitly aligned himself with the philosopher, taking on the identity of a Christianized Socrates in defense against charges of atheism. The process of identification begins in the first pages, in Théophile's adaptation of Socrates' dream, with its command to make and practice *mousikê*. The dream's admonition becomes the governing principle for the text of the poet Théophile: "*Fay Socrate, fay Socrate, fay des vers*" (Théophile 1999: 1.7.154–5). The delicately lilting command, with its syntactical ambiguity – *Socrate* functioning both intradiegetically as a vocative and programmatically as an object – initiates the apologetic alliance of author and subject. In the act of composing his new *Phaedo*, Théophile will both create and become his own Socrates, whose identity serves as a defense (however ineffectual) against the charges that would hound Théophile for years to come.

The fashion for adopting and adapting a Socratic identity, especially for turning his life into a mode of combating an entrenched political hierarchy, endured for generations. However important this style of polemical appropriation of Socrates may be, it is nonetheless not where the philosopher's reputation lies in the early modern period. Seneca had it right: it was the intimate life of Socrates that endured in the popular imagination, the often messy details of his personal behavior and familial conflicts. This latter Socrates – the erotically charged, hen-pecked *dottore* – was no less durable than the philosophical martyr. The two Socrateses had lived in close quarters since antiquity; Athenaeus (5.219b) incredulously charges the Socratics with promulgating the most outrageous stories about their master, including his dalliance with Alcibiades and his wife Xanthippe's assaulting him with the contents of a chamber-pot. A skillful polemicist could use this Socrates no less than the heroic figure; and so the Jesuit François Garasse claims in his thousand-page screed against libertinism, *La doctrine curieuse des beaux esprits de ce temps* (1623), to have penetrated Théophile's Socratic guise. Garasse notes with outraged relish that the man with whom Théophile was attempting to associate himself was, no less than Théophile himself, an atheist and sodomite (1971/1623: I, 250–4; II. 885–6, 935–6).

As we see in Garasse's response to Théophile, the literary manifestations of Socrates took place before a background informed by a concomitant and competing popular portrait. Socrates is everywhere present in the literary and cultural imagination of the early modern era; he is a popular subject in plays, operas and visual art (Brown forthcoming; Döring 2001; Lapatin, ch. 8 this volume). While he is a ubiquitous character in low literature no less than in high, there is one genre over which the Renaissance and early modern Socrates presides, where he holds sway no less than does Aristotle in the popular imagination of the Middle Ages, iconically enthroned as "the master of those who know" in Dante's *Inferno* (4.131). That genre is satire. Socrates holds the place of honor as master of ceremonies for the dinner party of the sages in the bawdy and hilarious *Le Moyen de parvenir* by Beroalde de Verville (1879/1593: 9–10); for François Rabelais he is not only "without controversy the prince of philosophers," but heralded in the first line of *Gargantua* (1970/1532: 9–10) as the very model for reading satire. Similarly, Mathurin Régnier (1573–1613) in his 1609 volume of *Satires* (1930/1609: 20) gives Socrates a programmatic place in his texts as an emblem of the genre. To understand the Socrates of early modern France, then, we must turn to works that draw upon those traditions – especially the comic and satiric traditions – by which he was most frequently presented to the popular imagination.

II.

An exemplary test-case for this process can be found in the treatment of Socrates in the writings of Mme. de Villedieu (Marie-Catherine Desjardins, 1640–83), whose light-hearted *nouvelles*, often involving imaginative reconstructions of antiquity, enjoyed a remarkable vogue in the late seventeenth century (Morrissette 1947; Cuénin 1979). Villedieu treats the life of Socrates in the second of her 1671 *Amours des grands hommes*, a series of four case studies of exemplary figures from Greco-Roman antiquity which demonstrate the power of love over even the most renowned statesmen and philosophers. Her novella on Socrates, which formed the longest and most complex narrative of the original publication[7] – a work hardly scholarly, though clearly informed by a reading of ancient sources – preserved and perpetuated the biographical accounts of Socrates then in circulation, and offers us an opportunity to review not simply her own treatment of Socrates, but the treatment of his life that would be available to and expected by readers of French popular literature in the seventeenth century. The remainder of this chapter will revolve loosely around Villedieu's text, examining its subject, sources and influence, in the expectation that this widely popular if minor work – precisely because of its rootedness in its culture and lack of ambition to transcend its time – captures better than many more significant texts the Socrates that was most often presented to French audiences of the seventeenth century.

In Villedieu's account, Socrates has received as a ward the beautiful and philosophically gifted Phrygian maiden Timandre, whose virtue he jealously and elaborately guards. His wife Myrto resents the attention her husband bestows upon his alluring pupil and chides him that his eagerness to instruct her in philosophy is merely a ruse to consort with her. Alcibiades, accidentally privileged to Myrto's boisterous complaints, is aroused by her celebration of the young ward's beauty. He sets out to conquer

Timandre, disguised as a Phrygian friend of her father's. Socrates has prudently guarded against that possibility, however, and Alcibiades is fooled into confusing Timandre's aged and foolish guardian Aglaonice with the girl herself – whose beauty he naturally dismisses as overrated. There follows a robust comedy of errors, a story of disguises successfully and falsely penetrated, of misdirected and misinterpreted letters and communications gone awry, and of love deferred and kindled. In the closing pages Socrates, learning of a planned rendezvous of the two lovers, rushes to separate them and to preserve the virtue of both. He instead finds the pair chastely devoted to one another, and himself torn by an unconscious and overwhelming love for Timandre, a love the recognition of which is forced upon him through Alcibiades' insistent argument. The incident proves the defining moment in the lives of both men:

> It was this same Timandre for whom he died shortly afterwards, as the Historian of his life witnesses; and if I can trust my satiric Memories, it was the displeasure that Socrates conceived from this adventure that made him accept death with such resolve. (Villedieu 1971/1720 II: 22–3 = V: 65–6)[8]

The four stories that make up the *Amours* are imaginative adaptations of Plutarch's *Lives*, providing intimate information to complete the gaps in his accounts. Villedieu's stated intention is to bring the heroes of antiquity – whom tradition reveres as "above mankind" – down to earth, and to demonstrate, in the words of the epistle to Louis XIV which prefaced the original publication, that they, too, were susceptible to love (*Epitre AU ROY* = Klein 1992: 181). Her narrative of Socrates takes its starting point from Plutarch's life of Alcibiades, expanding and constructing a background for Plutarch's account of Alcibiades' death in the arms of the Phrygian *hetaira* Timandra; by turning their relationship into one of courtly romance, she offers a genteel etiology that overwrites Plutarch's sordid narrative and plays upon the erotic inclinations of both her male protagonists.[9]

III.

> ". . . la beauté d'une femme & l'ame de Socrate peuvent-elles avoir quelque chose à démêler ensemble?"
>
> —Villedieu (1971/1720 II· 16 = V, 38)

To situate Socrates in an erotic narrative is already to engage with a host of intertexts with which contemporary readers would have been readily familiar. Especially provocative is the choice to triangulate Socrates and Alcibiades as competitors for the love of a young woman; the tale depends on and refigures the erotic association between the two found in the description in Plato's *Symposium* (217a–218d) of Alcibiades' heated attempts at seducing Socrates.[10] The nature of their relationship was a frequent topic in antiquity, where it is portrayed variously as pederastic (Ath. 5.219b–f; Aelian VH 4.21; Plut. *de Alex. fort.* 333a; Suda s.v. *Alcibiades*) or chaste (D.L. 2.23; Max. Tyre Or. 18.5, 32.8; Nepos *vit. Alcib.* 2). The interlocutors of the pseudo-Lucianic *Erotes*, debating the respective merits of heterosexual and pederastic love, each cites the relationship between philosopher and pupil as support for his own view of love, and finds the contact between them variously paternal (49) or pederastic (54), depending on the inclination of the speaker. Socrates' fond attention to beautiful males, an obsession both defended (e.g. Max. Tyre *Or.* 18–21) and parodied (e.g. Lucian *Dial. mort.* 6.417–8), was sufficiently well known to allow Juvenal (2.10) to refer off-handedly to *Socraticos . . . cinaedos* ("Socratic queers"). The interaction between Socrates and Alcibiades in Plato's *Symposium* is one of the primary sources of this depiction of the philosopher, and Aulus Gellius (*Noct. Attic.* I.9.9) reports Tauras' concerns that the youth of his day "itch" with erotic fervor to begin the study of Plato with Alcibiades' speech because of its capacity to titillate. Indeed, translated extracts and résumés of this speech actually found their way into medieval collections of bawdy literature (Jayne 1985: 9).

The ancient debate over the nature of their relationship was replicated in the Renaissance and early modern periods. In his 1624 *Satires* DuLorens insists that Socrates rose from Alcibiades' couch with chastity intact (1881/1624: 144), while the following year in his *Apologie pour grands hommes*, Gabriel Naudé denounces Socrates' "public declaration . . . of sodomy" (1669/1625: 224), and Jacques Abbadie's *Traité de la verité de la religion chrêtienne* (1684: 285–6) will cite the relationship between the two as proof that they were among those *monstres exécrables* who paraded that vice, prized by the Greeks, which Christianity has all but eliminated.

The mere mention of the name "Alcibiades" carried a heavy weight of indecency that some may have found distracting. His encounter with Socrates was so infamous that it made him the natural subject of Antonio Rocco's sodomitical manifesto, *L'Alcibiade fanciuollo a scola.* Printed in France in 1652,[11] *L'Alcibiade* offers a dialogue between the young Alcibiades and his schoolmaster Filotimo, in which the latter convinces his young pupil, through learned and comically embellished arguments, to submit to anal penetration. This brief dialogue gained an early reputation, in the words of an eighteenth-century bibliographer, as a text "than which no more obscene or abominable work can be imagined" (F. G. Freytag, quoted in Coci 1988: 9 n. 7). Even without direct reference to Socrates, Filotimo serves as his stand-in and brings to bear the persuasive power of Socratic dialectic.[12] Socrates makes his way into the text only in an appended ode of breathtaking obscenity, wherein he and Plato serve as classical authorization for pederastic pursuits:

> Devon fotter adunque i piú saputi
> (sentite in cortesia, non sta già bene)
> dove che fotton gl'animali brutti?
>
> Sia benedetta pur la dotta Atene,
> dove Platon e Socrate coi putti
> con gran piacer scarcavano le rene. (Coci 91)

"Socratic Love" had become code for same-sex love in Renaissance Italy (Dall'Orto 1989). The terminology was codified in eighteenth-century France when Voltaire, in a concession to the popular association, entitled the entry for pederasty in his *Dictionnaire philosophique* (1764) "So-called Socratic Love" (*Amour nommé socratique*). While Voltaire exculpated Socrates from the charge of participating in this "destructive" and "unnatural" vice (1967/1764: 18), Socrates was already at the heart of a libertine tradition that looked to the philosopher as a model for the naturalness and integrity of same-sex desire. The Marquis de Sade calls the philosopher to witness as one who, "declared by the oracle the wisest philosopher in the land, passing indifferently from the arms of Aspasia to those of Alcibiades, was none the less the glory of Greece" (1990 III: 132). And in *La Nouvelle Justine*, Sade coins the verb *socratiser*, whose meaning he presents as if widely known to his audience: "Every libertine knows that by this term one refers to the action of putting one or more fingers in the recipient's asshole" (1990 II: 416 n. 1; cf. II: 84).

What ultimately makes Socrates unsuitable for Rocco's purpose in *L'Alcibiade* is his relationship with his wife. In the nineteenth century, Xanthippe's shrewishness would serve as a misogynistic pendant to Socrates' same-sex desires, with both operating in the construction of a homosocial space exclusive of women (Blanshard, forthcoming). But in Rocco's text, the schoolmaster's arguments depend on a rejection *tout court* of sexual congress with women, and Socrates – whom popular tradition knew all too well for his disastrous marriage and wayward children – could hardly serve as a suitable example of a self-fashioned sodomitical *identity*, which *L'Alcibiade* attempted to construct (cf. Dall'Orto 1983).

IV.

"A married philosopher belongs *in comedy* . . . and as for that exception, Socrates – he malicious Socrates, it would seem, married *ironically*, just to demonstrate *this* proposition."

–Nietzsche (1969: 107)

Socrates is almost singularly inappropriate as a model for the interlocutor in Rocco's text – whose schoolmaster responds in horrified and grandiloquent disgust not only to the idea of marriage but to the suggestion that he direct his amorous attention to women. Socrates' own marriage was simply too well known. Not only was his explosive relationship with the cantankerous Xanthippe a source of innumerable anecdotes, but a common ancient tradition granted him the disastrous privilege of not one, but two shrewish wives, based on a supposed wartime decree authorizing polygamy in order to increase Athens' dwindling population. The second wife, Myrto, is no less trouble than the first. (The only other figure alleged to have taken advantage of this law is Euripides, whom ancient biography similarly credits with combative relations with women: Aulus Gellius *Noct. Att.* 15.20.6; see McLean forthcoming.) By choosing to give Socrates' wife the name "Myrto," rather than the more commonly known "Xanthippe," and by reminding us that Myrto was "perhaps the daughter of Aristides" (Villedieu 1971/1720 II: 15 = V: 35), Villedieu signals both her learned adaptation of the ancient sources and provides a tacit reminder of Socrates' erotic inclinations. While Myrto is the more obscure figure, she never entirely disappeared from Western literature in the Middle Ages, and Villedieu would have had numerous sources in French literature both for Socrates' bigamy and for the combative nature of his marriage.

Socrates' marital woes were a source not merely of amusement (as the epigraph of this section from Nietzsche insists) but of moral instruction. The story of his wife's (or wives') ill-tempered antics (*SSR* I B 7, I C 58–68 and *passim*), an especially popular subject in the Cynic *chreia* tradition, provided a cautionary lesson on the evils of marriage (Fischel 1970: 389). The story not only survived but flourished in France in the Middle Ages. Pierre Abelard (whose *Historia calamitatum* was translated into French by Jean de Meun in the thirteenth century) cites Jerome's *Adversus Iovinianum* (a primary conduit of knowledge of ancient philosophy in the Middle Ages), but gives the story a similar moral as did the Cynics: Socrates' marriage is essentially an act of self-sacrifice intended to offer an example of himself to make others more wary of reckless love-affairs (Abelard 1991: 16).

The philosopher's ill-fated marriage was a favorite topic of satirists, gaining mention in Rabelais (1970/1532: 10) and DuLorens (1869/1646: 16). It is exuberantly re-lated in Beroalde's *Moyen de parvenir* when the topic turns to hen-pecked husbands. In response to the story of a man who tamed his shrewish wife by binding her in a custom-made cradle, Aristippus is moved to exclaim:

> If the good Socrates had rocked his two wives in that way, he would have put them to sleep and he and his nurse would have had leisure to play together while his children slept! And he would not have been drenched by the piss-pot that one dumped on his head, on account of the quarrel that she had when he refused to side with her in an argument with the other wife. (1879/1593: 380)

The moralizing potential of the narrative of Socrates' dealings with his wife made it particularly popular in doxographical and didactic literature. The *Dits Moraulx des Philosophes*, Guillaume de Tignonville's popular fourteenth-century French transla-tion of an Arabic compilation of philosophical lives and sayings (whose 1477 English translation, produced by William Caxton, was among the first books printed in the vernacular in England[13]) stressed the unfortunate nature of his marriage ("he weddide the worst woman that was in alle the cuntrey," Bühler 1941: 72), but shows no knowledge of the account of his two wives. The latter story remained alive in France through the Middle Ages, however, in compilations of edifying anecdote and philo-sophic *vitae*. Socrates' intractable second wife makes tentative appearances as Myro in Vincent of Beauvais' (c. 1190–1264) *Speculum Doctrinale* (6.3 = Beauvais 1965 II: 483) and as Mirto in Walter Burley's *Liber de vita et moribus philosophorum* (cap. 30 = Burley 1886: 116–18).

Burley's influential fourteenth-century text, which survives in over one hundred manuscripts primarily preserved in France and southern Europe, was printed in Paris as late as 1530 (Stigall 1957: 44). Burley fades from prominence as the text of Diogenes Laertius becomes available, first in Traversari's fifteenth-century Latin translation and eventually in French translations by Fougerolles (1602) and Boileau (1668).[14] Diogenes offers several versions of Socrates' marital status (2.26), but his report takes the double marriage for granted, though noting that some authors considered them consecutive rather than concurrent affairs.

By far the most common and oft-reprinted source for the story of Myrto in seventeenth-century France would have been in a recently published biography of Socrates. Villedieu and her audience would have had easy access to François Charpentier's 1650 *Vie de Socrate*, whose uncritical accounts of the most outlandishly imagined details of Socrates' intimate life – his presumed legal compulsion to marry two wives, Xanthippe's befouling him with the contents of a chamber pot, her overturning a dinner table in a fit of pique – are related with an almost gleeful delight in their very sordidness. Charpentier's enormously popular volume received wide circulation, and was eventually translated into English and attached to Edward Bysshe's 1712 *Memorable Things of Xenophon*. But the greatest circulation of the philosopher's battling brides would be in Jacques Amyot's constantly republished translation of Plutarch[15] (*vit. Arist.* 27.3–4). As we shall see, Villedieu's text explicitly positions itself against the authority of this work.

V.

"quelle différence met Socrate entre l'amour et l'amitié?"
–J.-F. Marmontel, Contes Moraux (1761)

Villedieu's depiction of Socrates' benign philosophical tutelage of Alcibiades serves as a genteel pendant for contemporary stories of their amorous relationship. Her account of Socrates' efforts to preserve his pupil's honor deserve particular consideration. When Socrates intercepts a love note from Alcibiades, he rushes to rescue his friend from temptation:

> Socrates immediately recognized Alcibiades' writing and as the house where he was lay near to the Academy, he resolved to go cut short the rendezvous. He often had to impose such annoyances upon Alcibiades; he loved him tenderly, and he knew that his susceptibility to love got him into wretched situations. (Villedieu 1971/1721 II:21 = V:60)

While the details are original to Villedieu, there is ample precedent in the literature of antiquity for a rather different sort of relationship between the two men, one which stresses the moral and pedagogic influence that Socrates exerted (or failed to exert) upon the impressionable young Alcibiades. Socrates' effect on Alcibiades is generally treated by ancient authors from an apologetic standpoint that can be traced to the circumstances of his trial. Whatever Socrates' accusers may have said in court, we can be sure from Isocrates' response to Polycrates that the latter's *Accusation of Socrates* relied on Socrates' association with Alcibiades to substantiate a charge of political subversiveness (Isoc. *Bus.* 5–6; cf. Gribble 1999: 226–30; Humbert 1931.) It may also have been in response to Polycrates' charges that Xenophon offers his lengthy defense of their association (*Mem.* 1.2.12–48). For Plato the problem of Alcibiades is intimately related to the problems of Socratic education (Nehamas 1998: 63–7, 77–91) and the formation of philosophical character (Blondell 2002: 35–6, 109). The *Symposium* (215d–216d) dramatizes an Alcibiades who recognizes his full potential only while in the presence of Socrates. Later authors portray the philosopher's effect on his pupil as imposing upon the latter a forceful realization of his abjectness (Cicero *Tusc. disp.* 3.32.77; Augustine *De civ. D.* 14.8), and it becomes virtually a truism that it was not Alcibiades' association with Socrates, but rather his failure to remain in Socrates' presence and devote himself fully to his teaching, that led to political loss for Athens.[16]

Villedieu exploits simultaneously the erotic tension between the two figures and the anecdotes that only Socrates' immediate presence is sufficient to secure Alcibiades' virtue. Her particular take on their relationship, however, is both novel and influential. By imagining Socrates' hurried attempt to rescue his pupil from the dangers of erotic entanglement as one foray in his chronically recurring attempt to force virtue upon the youth, she constructs a tradition into which she fits her narrative, and creates by back-formation a pattern of interaction between master and pupil which would soon be more fully exploited.

That imaginative background, vividly if incompletely imagined in the *Amours*, is first fully illustrated by the eighteenth-century French history painter Jean-François-Pierre Peyron in his 1782 *Socrates Detaching Alcibiades from the Charms of Sensual Pleasure (Socrate détachant Alcibiade des charmes de la volupté)*. Peyron's 1782 painting is now lost, but the composition is preserved in an etching and later version by Peyron himself, and by contemporary sketches (Rosenberg and van de Sandt 1983: 102–6).[17] Socrates has entered an interior scene dominated by a priapic Herm upon whose sagging shoulders Alcibiades' shield and helmet are hung. An abashed Alcibiades is torn between the embrace of the sinuous nude females tugging imploringly at the slender fold of his cloak, and the commanding gestures of Socrates, who resolutely directs the unwilling youth from the couch that he had recently shared with the objects of his pleasure. The barely clothed Alcibiades removes his garland of flowers and steps in the direction of Socrates, who stands to the side, ushering Alcibiades out of the frame of the picture and away from both the two courtesans and the gaze of the viewer.

Beginning with Peyron, the subject of Socrates' stern imposition of chastity on the dissolute libertine became a favorite subject of French classicizing artists. Peyron's painting inspired a series of French images of the subject, including works by Regnault (1791), Garnier (1793), Perrin (1801), Gêrome (1810), and others (Rosenberg and Van de Sandt 1983: 102). The inspiration for Peyron's painting, however, has always been a mystery. There is no direct source for the story before Peyron, who, though fond of obscure subjects, is not known for originating them; when he paints topics that have no precedent in the visual arts, he is often at pains to identify explicitly their provenance.[18] Villedieu's immensely popular narrative, most recently reprinted in a collection of her complete works only a few decades before Peyron undertook his commission,[19] provides the only likely source of inspiration for the subject of Peyron's painting.[20] If Peyron adapts Villedieu's account that Socrates imposed virtue upon his dissolute friend, however, he does nonetheless tweak her genteel reevaluation of their relationship, reminding the viewer of the seamier side of Alcibiades' character. By placing the youth in the company of two courtesans, each pleadingly demanding that Alcibiades resist Socrates' admonitions, Peyron rejects Villedieu's attempt to refashion the youth's persona into that of a respectful young gallant. The artist's depiction of Alcibiades, which highlights by contrast Socrates' probity and chaste virtue, is in keeping with the view that Pierre Bayle had recently articulated in his *Dictionnaire historique et critique*: "I find, that many authors build upon the passage of Athenaeus," writes Bayle, "wherein it is said that Alcibiades was always attended by two concubines" (1997/1734 III: 703a, trans. P. Des Maizeaux). The more ribald tales, which remain under the surface of Villedieu's text, are brought back vividly in Peyron's adaptation.

362

VI.

"... il faisoit profession d'une Philosophie severe, & cependant il étoit amoureux."
–Villedieu (1971/1720 II: 14 = V: 33)

In its presentation of Socrates among those remote subjects who are brought down to earth, Villedieu's *Amours* signals Socrates' reascendance as a model of intellectual authority. Her project in the *Amours* involves rewriting the traditional narratives of exemplary individuals with the express goal of humanizing figures who have been handed down from posterity under the aspect of "awe-inspiring figures" by authors whose goal has been to depict their heroes "lacking all natural feelings" (*Epitre AU ROY* = Klein 1992: 181–2.) The narrative supposes that the most significant actions in her heroes' lives – Solon's crafting the law forbidding debt bondage of Athenian citizens, Socrates' equanimity in the face of death, Caesar's break with Pompey – are all at root motivated by love for beautiful women. And even as love conquers these heroes, so does Villedieu exert her own, uniquely feminine, authority over the ancient biographical tradition. By claiming access to "chroniques secrètes" (*Epitre AU ROY* = Klein 1992: 181) unknown to Plutarch, Villedieu can position her text as more faithful to the historical Socrates than were the writings of ancient historians. She thereby claims a narrative power particular to women: "il est permis aux Dames de chercher des endroits sensibles dans les coeurs les plus illustres" (*Epitre* = Klein 1992: 181). Just as love (a feminine and feminizing force in her account) exerts its power over the subjects of her narrative, overwhelming professor, statesman, sage and general, so does Villedieu offer her invented narrative as a demonstration of her power over the authority of Plutarch.

The same conquest of love over learning takes place within her narrative. The Socrates of her text, who claims that his philosophical detachment makes him immune to emotional attachment, is the only hero of the *Amours* who actively resists the power of love, recognition of which is belatedly and powerfully imposed upon him. In its broadest outlines, the plot replicates a common medieval pattern of the impossibility of intellectual resistance to love (Bagley 1986: 8–18) whose *locus classicus* is the thirteenth-century *Li lais d'Aristote* by the Norman poet Henri d'Andeli. Aristotle, who "knew all there was to know of wisdom," chastises his pupil Alexander for spending too much time with his mistress Phyllis; she, in turn, asserted her dominance over the philosopher by seducing him into allowing her to mount him like a horse, riding him about the grounds of the Lyceum while he held a bit in his mouth and whinnied.[21] A fourteenth-century commentator interpreted the story as a triumph over the foundation of medieval education: "In this was grammar betrayed and logic much dumb-founded" (from the fourteenth-century *Le Livre de Leesce*, quoted in Bagley 1986: 6).

The exploding popularity of the stories of Socrates' private life, and especially the celebrity of his marital afflictions (which became a staple in satiric comic sources), reflect not simply a change in Socrates' literary fortunes but a change in intellectual currents in Europe. We began by noting Aristotle's place in the medieval curriculum. As he became the dominant figure of intellectual authority in the popular imagination, the anarchic impulse that sets out to symbolically overturn hierarchies and dethrone valorized figures of authority largely focused its energies upon the Stagyrite. Socrates was not entirely ignored: the comic stories centering on his relationship with Xanthippe remain in circulation, but he is the subject of few if any new comic narratives. With the revival of classical texts in the west, however, Socrates reemerges simultaneously as a vibrant intellectual force and a figure of popular ridicule. Nine years after the publication of Villedieu's text, that anarchic and ridiculing impulse would erupt in the first of a series of comic operas that exploited Socrates' relationship with his two wives (Draghi and Minoto, 1680; G. Telemann and J. von König, 1721; G. Reutter and A. Caldara, 1731; F. A. de Almeida, 1733; cf. Döring 2001 and McLean forthcoming), and it would be present in countless stories, novels, and plays. It is not Aristotle, but Socrates whom the seventeenth and eighteenth centuries both held up as the great moral exemplar of Greco-Roman antiquity and portrayed as a paradigmatically lecherous old man. He is both a figure who serves as a model for resistance to authority and, as object of comic derision, an example of that authority. This is, as we have seen, a rather different Socrates from the one best known to us; it is a Socrates whose private life – whose love affairs, private peccadilloes and moral shortfalls – is no less (and often more) important than his intellect.[22]

Notes

1 Nehamas (1998: 101–27); Scodel (1983); McGowan (1978: 150–63); Kellerman (1954).
2 Trousson (1967); Seznec (1957: 1–22); Orwin (1998); Goulbourne (forthcoming).
3 For the life of Ramus see Waddington (1855); Ong (1958: 17–49).
4 The passage is incorporated directly into J. T. Freigius's 1575 *Petri Rami Vita*: Ramus (1969) 587.
5 Ramus (1965/1581) = *Schol. dial.* 4.13, p. 151. For Ramus' views of Socrates, see Walton (1970).
6 See especially the highly critical study of Ong (1958).
7 The 1671 edition contained novellas centering on Solon, Socrates, Cato and Caesar. Subsequent editions added several studies, likely by another hand: see Klein (1992: 120–1). The original limit of four stories is guaranteed by the dedicatory epistle to Louis XIV, for a reproduction of which see Klein (1992: 181–2).
8 Citations indicate pagination for both the 1971 folio reprint in four volumes and the twelve-volume 1720 *Oeuvres complètes* which the folio edition reproduces.
9 On the various literary account of Alcibiades' death and their significance, see Gribble (1999: 281–2) and Perrin (1906).
10 Cf. especially *Grg.* 481d; *Prot.* 309a–b; I *Alc.* 131c–d; Aesch. *Alc.* 11c (Dittmar). Despite these various testimonies of Socrates' love for Alcibiades, it is to the *Symposium* – and in particular the description of their sharing a bed – that ancient authors repeatedly return. For Alcibiades' erotic nature, see Littman (1970).
11 Of the original edition, printed in Venice in 1651, no copies survive. For text history see Coci (1985).
12 A "wise and well-read sodomite who is in fact a caricature of Socrates" (Maggi 1997: 28).
13 The first English book printed with date of publication, the *Dicts and Sayings* was once widely believed to be the first printed in English (e.g. Bühler 1941: ix), though that claim is no longer supportable; see Cox (2002).
14 The *editio princeps* is established by Frobenius in 1533; Henri Estienne's text follows in 1570. For a study of early editions of the text see Knoepfler (1991: 22–94).

15 Paris (1559, 1572, 1578, 1583, 1587, 1594, 1600, 1604, 1612, 1622, 1645, 1655), Lausanne (1571, 1574, 1578), Geneva (1567, 1613), Dijon (1583), and Lyons (1587).

16 In addition to the Plato and Xenophon passages cited above, see Maximus of Tyre 1.9, 6.6; Aelian 4.15. Plato *Tht.* 150d–151a stresses that those, like Aristeides "and many others" who depart from Socrates' presence before their moral improvement is internally generated, fail to achieve lasting philosophical progress; cf. *Theages* 130a–e. By contrast, Aelius Aristides (*De quatt.* 34) stresses Socrates' culpability in his lack of influence over Alcibiades.

17 The painting was commissioned in 1780, along with its pendant *Funeral of Miltiades*, by the Comte d'Angiviller.

18 So, for instance, a drawing for his *Funeral of Miltiades*, a subject not previously painted in France and a pendant to his Socrates and Alcibiades, includes a Latin inscription identifying its obscure source; Rosenberg and Van de Sandt (1983: 98–101). On the vogue for novelty in French historical paintings of the period, see Rosenblum (1970: 3–106), Crow (1985).

19 Editions of the *Amours* were published in Paris (1671, 1678), Amsterdam (1688, 1692, 1712) and Lyon (1679); it appeared in English (as *The Loves of Sundry Philosophers and Other Great Men*, two editions of 1673), and was reprinted in various editions of Villedieu's *Oeuvres complètes* (Paris, 1720, 1740, 1741; Geneva, 1720).

20 Rosenberg and van de Sandt (1983: 102) do briefly raise the possibility that Villedieu influenced Peyron, but dismiss the connection on the basis of too little correspondence in their accounts. My suggestion is rather that it is the back-story which Villedieu's narrative demands the reader supply which forms the basis for Peyron's subject.

21 The text of D'Andeli is edited and translated in Eichmann and DuVal (1984: 94–117). Marsilli (1984: 239–69) catalogues 218 appearances of or allusions to the story in literature and the plastic arts. On the theme of the *Aristote chevauché* see also Smith (1995: 66–102).

22 I am grateful to Kathryn Morgan, Alex Purves, Jonathan Sutton, Calvin Normore, and Brian Copenhaver for advice and encouragement; to Sam Jackson for crucially-needed assistance; and to Jon Seydl, for patiently reading and enduring drafts.

References

Abbadie, J. (1684). *Traité de la verité de la religion chrêtienne.* Rotterdam: R. Leers.

Abelard, P. (1991). *La Vie et les epistres. Pierres Abaelart et Heloys sa fame. Traduction de XIIIe siècle attribuée à Jean de Meun*, ed. E. Hicks. Paris and Geneva: Slatkin.

Bagley, A. (1986). *Study and Love. Aristotle's Fall.* Minneapolis, MN: Society of Professors of Education.

Bayle, P. (1997/1734). *The Dictionary Historical and Critical of Mr Peter Bayle*, trans. P. Des Maizeaux. London: Routledge/Thoemmes Press.

Beauvais, V. de. (1965). *Speculum quadruplex* II, *Speculum doctrinale.* Graz: Akademische Druck-u. Verlagsanstalt.

Beroalde de Verville (1879/1593). *Le Moyen de parvenir.* Paris: Garnier Frères.

Blanshard, A. (forthcoming). From *amor Socraticus* to *Socrates amoris*: Socrates and the formation of sexual identity in late Victorian Britain. In M. Trapp (ed.) (forthcoming).

Blondell, R. (2002). *The Play of Character in Plato's Dialogues.* Cambridge: Cambridge University Press.

Brown, P. M. G. (forthcoming). Socrates in Comedy. In M. Trapp (forthcoming).

Bühler, C. F. (1941). *The Dicts and Sayings of the Philosophers.* London: Oxford University Press, published for the Early English Text Society by Humphry Milford.

Burley, W. (1886). *Liber de vita et moribus philosophorum*, ed. H. Knust. Tübingen: Litterarischer Verein in Stuttgart.

Coci, L. (1985). *L'Alcibiade fanciullo a scola*: Nota bibliografica. *Studi secenteschi*, 26, 301–32.

—— (ed.) (1988). *L'Alcibiade fanciullo a scola*. Rome: Salerno.

Cox, M. (2002). *The Oxford Chronology of English Literature*. Oxford: Oxford University Press.

Crow, T. E. (1985). *Painters and Public Life in Eighteenth-Century Paris*. New Haven and London: Yale University Press.

Cuénin, M. (1979). *Madame de Villedieu (Marie-Catherine Desjardins 1640–1683)*. 2 vols. Paris: Librairie Honoré Champion.

Dall'Orto, G. (1983). Antonio Rocco and the background of his *L'Alcibiade fanciullo a scola*. In *Among Men, Among Women*. Amsterdam: University of Amsterdam Press.

—— (1989). "Socratic love" as a disguise for same-sex love in the Italian renaissance. In Kent Gerard and Gert Hekma (eds.), *The Pursuit of Sodomy: Male Homosexuality in Renaissance and Enlightenment Europe*. New York: Haworth Press, pp. 33–65.

DeJean, J. (2002). *The Reinvention of Obscenity: Sex, Lies, and Tabloids in Early Modern France*. Chicago: University of Chicago Press.

Döring, K. (2001). Socrate sur la scène de l'opera. *Philosophie Antique*, 1, 205–20.

DuLorens, J. (1881/1624). *Premieres Satires*. Paris: Librairie des Bibliophiles.

Eichmann, R. and DuVal, John (1984). *The French Fabliau*, vol. 1. New York and London: Garland.

Fischel, H. A. (1970). Studies in cynicism and the ancient near East: The transformation of a *Chria*. In Jacob Neusner (ed.), *Religions in Antiquity: Essays in Memory of Erwin Ramsdell Goodenough*. Leiden: E. J. Brill, 372–411.

Garasse, F. (1971/1623). *La doctrine curieuse des beaux esprits de ce temps*. 2 vols. Westmead: Gregg International Publishers.

Goulbourne, R. (forthcoming). Voltaire's Socrates. In M. Trapp (forthcoming).

Gribble, D. (1999). *Alcibiades and Athens*. Oxford: Oxford University Press.

Hankins, J. (1990). *Plato and the Italian Renaissance*. 2 vols. Leiden and New York: E. J. Brill.

Humbert, J. (1931). Le pamphlet de Polycratès et le *Gorgias* de Platon. *Revue de philologie*, 5, 20–77.

Jayne, S. (1985). Introduction. In Marsilio Ficino, *Commentary on Plato's* Symposium *on Love*. Woodstock, CT: Spring Publications.

Kellerman, F. (1954). Montaigne's Socrates. *Romanic Review*, 45, 170–7.

Klein, N. D. (1992). *The Female Protagonist in the* Nouvelles *of Madame de Villedieu*. New York: Peter Lang.

Klibansky, R. (1981). *The Continuity of the Platonic Tradition During the Middle Ages*. Munich: Kraus.

Knoepfler, D. (1991). *La vie de Ménédème d'Érétrie de Diogène Laërce*. Basel: Friedrich Reinhardt.

Lachèvre, F. (1909). *Le libertinage devant le parlement de Paris: Le process du poet Théophile de Viau*. 2 vols. Paris: H. Champion.

Littman, R. J. (1970). The loves of Alcibiades. *Transactions of the American Philological Association*, 101, 263–76.

Maggi, A. (1997). The discourse of Sodom in a seventeenth-century Venetian text. *Journal of Homosexuality*, 33, 25–43.

Marsilli, P. (1984). Reception et diffusion iconographique du conte de "Aristote et Phillis" en Europe depuis le moyen age. In *Amour, mariage et transgression au moyen age*. Göppingen: Kummerle Verlag, 239–69.

McGowan, M. M. (1978). *Montaigne's Deceits: The Art of Persuasion in the* Essais. Philadelphia: Temple University Press.

McLean, D. R. (forthcoming). *Refiguring Socrates: Comedy and Corporeality in the Socratic Tradition*.

Morrissette, B. (1947). The life and works of Marie-Catherine Desjardins (Mme. de Villedieu) 1632–1683. Saint Louis: Washington University Press.

Naudé, G. (1669/1625). *Apologie pour grands hommes*. Paris: F. Eschart.

Nehamas, A. (1998). *The Art of Living: Socratic Reflections from Plato to Foucault*. Berkeley and Los Angeles: University of California Press.

Nietzsche, F. (1969). *On the Genealogy of Morals*, trans. W. Kauffmann. New York: Vintage.

Ong, W. (1958). *Ramus, Method, and the Decay of Dialogue: From the Art of Discourse to the Art of Reason*. Cambridge, MA: Harvard University Press.

Orwin, C. (1998). Rousseau's Socratism. *The Journal of Politics*, 60, 174–87.

Perrin, B. (1906). The Death of Alcibiades. *Transactions of the American Philological Association*, 37, 25–37.

Rabelais, F. (1970/1532). *Gargantua*, ed. Ruth Calder. Geneva: Librairie Droz.

Ramus, P. (1965/1581). *Scholae in tres primas liberales artes. 3. Scholae Dialecticae*. Frankfurt a. M.: Minerva Press.

—— (1969). *Collectaneae Praefationes, Epistolae,Orationes*, ed. W. Ong. Hildesheim: Georg Olms.

Régnier, M. (1930/1609). *Oeuvres complètes*, ed. J. Plattard. Paris: Les Belles Lettres.

Rosenberg, P. and van de Sandt, U. (1983). *Pierre Peyron, 1744–1814*. Neuilly-sur-Seine: Arthena.

Rosenblum, R. (1970). *Transformations in Late Eighteenth Century Art*. Princeton: Princeton University Press.

Sade, Marquis de. (1990). *Oeuvres*, ed. M. Delon. 3 vols. Paris: Gallimard.

Scodel, J. (1983). The Affirmation of Paradox: A Reading of Montaigne's "De la Phisionomie." *Yale French Studies*, 64, 209–37.

Seznec, J. (1957). *Essais sur Diderot et l'Antiquité*. Oxford: Oxford University Press.

Smith, S. (1995). *The Power of Women: A Topos in Medieval Art and Literature*. Philadelphia: University of Pennsylvania Press.

Stigall, J. O. (1957). The Manuscript Tradition of the *De vita et moribus philosophorum* of Walter Burley. *Medievalia et humanistica*, 11, 44–57.

Théophile de Viau (1999). *Oeuvres complètes*, ed. G. Saba. 3 vols. Paris: Honoré Champion.

Trapp, M. (ed.) (forthcoming). *Socrates from Antiquity to the Enlightenment*. Aldershot: Ashgate.

Trousson, R. (1967). *Socrate devant Voltaire, Diderot et Rousseau*. Paris: Minard.

Villedieu, Mme de. (1971/1720). *Oeuvres complètes*. 12 vols. in 5. Geneva: Slatkine Reprints.

Voltaire [F. M. Arouet] (1967/1764). *Dictionnaire philosophique*, ed. Raymond Naves. Paris: Garnier.

Waddington, C. (1855). *Ramus (Pierre de la Ramée): Sa vie, ses écrits, et ses opinions*. Paris: Librairie de Ch. Meyrueis et Compagne.

Walton, C. (1970). Ramus and Socrates. *Proceedings of the American Philosophical Society*, 114, 119–39.

23

Socrates in Hegel And Others

NICHOLAS WHITE

A non-Hegelian philosopher considering Hegel's thoughts about Socrates is faced with a dilemma.[1] Placing those thoughts within Hegel's overall philosophical project would be a very long and difficult undertaking. That's partly because Hegel's project is an undertaking that's even longer and more difficult. On the other hand it would be uninformative and uninteresting to describe Hegel's thoughts about Socrates entirely in isolation from Hegel's other thinking. For then those thoughts would easily be taken to belong to the kind of investigation that the majority of historians of philosophy engage in. As such many of Hegel's suggestions would seem plainly indefensible.

Nevertheless Hegel's way of discussing Socrates really does do very much the same kind of thing, taken at an abstract level, as what most historians of philosophy do – including even those who work in the Anglo-American tradition of so-called "analytic" philosophy. Hegel wants to make sense of what Socrates was up to. So do most other historians of philosophy. The only thing is: Hegel's notion of what it is to "make sense of" something is special, to put it mildly. It's quite different from the notions that figure in most other attempts to describe Socratic thinking. When we abstract from these differences between Hegel's and these other respective conceptions of sense-making, the contrast between him and them fades a good deal.

This fact might serve as the basis of an irenic judgment that Hegel and non-Hegelian historians of philosophy are both basically on the right path towards understanding him. Unfortunately that's not the case. In my opinion both are on the wrong track. In my opinion they both misconstrue what Socrates was up to, and what his approach to philosophy was.

In brief, both Hegelian and analytic approaches make the mistake of regarding Socrates as a philosopher who was self-reflective and reflective, and in particular that he ascribed to himself and espoused a general method of philosophizing. Thus according to Hegel, Socrates reflected pretty explicitly about his own philosophical thinking, and his thinking therefore involved certain general philosophical ideas on which this self-reflection could be directed. Socrates had a method of doing philosophy, Hegel thought, and engaged in self-reflection on that method and his use of it.[2]

In fact, however, much evidence suggests that Socrates was a largely nonmethodical and nonreflective philosopher – perhaps even as close to being a completely non-methodical and nonreflective philosopher as one can get. At the least, it seems to me that much of Socrates' philosophical activity was carried out unreflectively and separated from general reflection on it.

It's of course controversial whether philosophy, or even thinking, can be engaged in entirely nonreflectively – that is, roughly, without thinking about how one's doing it. Nevertheless philosophers certainly differ in how reflectively they proceed. It seems to me plain that Socrates was very far over toward the nonreflective end of this scale. I also think that he seems much more interesting when he's viewed in this way.

I won't here try to demonstrate that this way of looking at Socrates fits all of the evidence smoothly. Certainly there are passages even in Xenophon (esp. in *Memorabilia* 4), not to mention Plato, that look more methodologically reflective. But the point is that since a lot of passages conspicuously don't look this way even though their content would seem to call for methodological reflection, and since the passages in Plato that do look this way fall under suspicion of being contrived by Plato to fit his own super-reflective methodological approach, the possibilities and the philosophical importance of this alternative understanding of Socrates deserve to be explored.

* * * *

For various reasons Hegel was in a poor position to appreciate a philosopher like Socrates. Hegel thought that practically everything is and should be reflective, given that the end or goal of history is "the self-awareness of freedom" (Beiser 1993: 279, 292–3). That makes any significant intellectual phenomenon, like Socrates' thought and influence, a case of the developing self-awareness of Spirit – at least, when "self-awareness" is taken in a loose enough way to fit what Hegel seems to say about it.

Hegel doesn't want to make sense only of Socrates. It seems fair to say as a first approximation that his entire approach to history is an attempt to make sense of everything that's at all important – everything that counts as falling within history, at any rate – as a progression of events and states. What Hegel counts as making sense is conditioned largely by what can be called his teleological view of things, where the *telos* is the self-awareness of freedom. This outlook makes him tend strongly to see philosophers and other thinkers as manifesting the workings in history of ideas that Hegel can treat as having a place within this teleologically shaped progression. The idea that's at work in a philosopher who's to be fitted into this scheme has to be the idea of freedom as Hegel construes it.

Moreover the way in which the philosopher manifests this idea has to involve some sort of awareness of or reflection on this idea as it is present in his own thought. Within Hegel's scheme of accounting for events as working toward the self-awareness of freedom in the world, there's no other way directly to make sense of what a significant philosopher thinks.

Thus it is that Socrates makes his appearance in Hegel's story as a highly self-reflective philosopher. The significance of Socrates – which amounts simply to his capacity to be made sense of within this scheme – can't but consist in his having reflected on ideas that figure in Hegel's teleological story. And of course it's much more natural to picture Socrates as having reflected on ideas if one also pictures him as having articulated them with at least some explicitness. As a historical figure, to be sure, Hegel can't make Socrates out to reflect too explicitly and fully on his significant ideas. If he were, he'd have to come much later in the whole story – at a point, that is, at which the idea of freedom is far more self-aware than it could have been in antiquity – and he might even have to be Hegel himself. Nevertheless, in order to fit into Hegel's story, and so to be made sense of, Socrates must reflect on some aspects of his teleologically significant thought to some extent. This is especially so in view of the fact that according to Hegel Socrates is a "great historic turning point" (*HofP* 448).

For quite different reasons, this same tendency to see Socrates' thought as self-reflective is shared by many philosophers in the analytic tradition. That tradition, almost from its beginning, has held that philosophy properly speaking should examine language. A version of such a view says, for instance, that philosophy should clear away philosophical confusions by examining everyday language. Another version maintains that philosophy should investigate the "logical syntax of language." These ways of thinking require philosophical investigation to treat the language in which it is cast and the concepts which it uses. Any attempt to treat Socrates as a kindred spirit to these ways of thinking, and thus as a truly significant philosopher, must on this view tend to regard him as engaged in an examination of his own linguistic and conceptual equipment.

Here's an example of the way in which the tendency to treat philosophy as thus reflective works itself out in Hegel's treatment of Socrates. Socrates is famous for his *daimonion*. His *daimonion* manifested itself to him as an inner voice, he said, which occasionally spoke to him when he was about to undertake some course of action, and told him not to do it. Plato says that it never urged him positively to do anything; it only warned him off. Xenophon ascribes to the *daimonion* both negative and positive advice (*Memorabilia* 1.1.2–9; 4.8.1). The idea of the *daimonion* in one form or another certainly seems to go back to the historical Socrates – one of the relatively few things that can be said confidently to do so.

Hegel appears to interpret this story – for simplicity let's just state the negative version – to say that Socrates articulated and accepted a general maxim running roughly, "I won't do what my *daimonion* says not to do," or perhaps even "No one should do what his *daimonion* says not to do." However, the story of Socrates' *daimonion* might be taken quite differently – in such a way as not to impute to him any such self-reflective use of a maxim.

Hegel seems to hold that Socrates employs, and indeed explicitly employs, some-thing like the following general test or criterion of action: "Don't do what your *daimonion* tells you not to do." This wouldn't involve merely forming a certain habit – e.g., of not doing the things that the voice of his *daimonion* forbade him to do, as one might have the habit of not going out in the rain without an umbrella. One might perfectly well have that habit without having articulated the maxim, "Take an umbrella when going out in the rain," and without even having noticed that one regularly did this – let alone being prepared to try to justify it. Rather, what Hegel ascribes to Socrates almost always suggests the explicit articulation and use of this maxim.

To be sure, observations are ascribed to Socrates that have the *daimonion* as their explicit subject matter. Xenophon's Socrates is made to claim, for instance, that his *daimonion* has never steered him falsely (Xenophon, *Apology* 13). However, the strik-ing fact about this passage is precisely that Socrates isn't made to articulate, on the basis of this observation, any general directive or policy. The positive injunctions that Xenophon speaks of, like the prohibitions stressed by Plato, are unsystematic, not methodologically articulated, and on the whole (in the current terminology) particularistic. Socrates goes on heeding his *daimonion*, but his doing so isn't backed up by a stated generalization about how to think about practical matters.

In one passage Hegel describes Socrates in the following way:

> [The] principle of subjective freedom was present to the consciousness of Socrates himself so vividly that he despised the other sciences as being empty learning and useless to mankind; he has to concern himself with his moral nature only in order to do what is best – a one-sidedness which is very characteristic of Socrates. (*HofP* 407)

This seems misleading. According to the story, the *daimonion* presented itself vividly to Socrates. It isn't at all clear that any principle was present to his consciousness – whether or not one takes a "principle" to be something that's linguistically formulated (not that Hegel here distinguishes between these two kinds of presence).

Hegel didn't think that whenever someone acts on a principle or the like, the person must have that principle articulately present to mind. Quite the contrary, Hegel believes that acting on principles doesn't require them to be present to mind. He thinks, in fact, that before the development represented by Socrates, a certain principle was present to Athenian citizens in a quite different, nonreflective way. Hegel says that at that earlier stage,

> morality, as was usually so with the ancients, consisted in the fact that the Good was present as a universal, without its having had the form of the conviction of the individual in his individual consciousness, but simply that of the immediate absolute. (ibid. 408)

This principle of living for one's country or community, Hegel holds, determined the shape of Greek political life:

> Of the Greeks in the first and genuine form of their freedom, we may assert, that they had no conscience; the habit of living for their country without further reflection, was the principle dominant among them. (*PofH* 253)[3]

Hegel thinks that the development represented by Socrates is in two ways a departure from the state of affairs that had prevailed in Athens earlier. This departure has the following two results. First, the individual is to deliberate explicitly about what to do. (Leave aside here the question what the form or the whole proper content of this deliberation; the point for now is simply that according to Hegel, Socrates introduced the idea of asking and somehow trying to answer the question, "What shall I do?") Second, the individual would no longer live "for his country." In associating these two ideas with each other in the way that he does, Hegel's downplaying, or even perhaps excluding, the possibility of unreflective practical thinking that isn't a matter of living for one's community. The important thing, though, is that these are two clearly distinguishable steps that Hegel portrays Socrates as having taken. We should ask whether they have to be taken together. I think that the answer is no.

Hegel believes that Socrates introduced the idea that an individual might, and indeed should, undertake his own deliberations about what to do and how to live:

> We now see Socrates bringing forward the opinion, that in these times every one has to look out for his own morality, and thus he looked after his through consciousness and reflection regarding himself; for he sought the universal spirit . . . in his own consciousness. (*HofP* 409)

Moreover Socrates spread this idea, Hegel thinks, among the Athenians:

> He also helped others to care for their morality, for he awakened in them this consciousness of having in their thoughts the good and the true, i.e., having the potentiality of action and of knowledge. (ibid.)

This is Hegel's interpretation of several pieces of Socratic thinking taken together. One is the Socratic injunction to care for one's soul; the other is the "theory of recollection." The former seems unquestionably Socratic. Hegel attributes the latter idea to Socrates too – whereas many scholars believe that Plato originated it – and also takes to be a further explanation of the view that a person should engage in his own deliberation about his life and action (*HofP* 410–11).

We can understand Hegel's picture of Socrates as a particular sort of philosopher if we set it alongside a picture of a philosopher of a quite different kind. Suppose that we describe Socrates in the following way. He begins by saying to himself, "What am I to do?" Then he proceeds to bring up various considerations. Then he says, "Let me, then, do such-and-such."

Hegel, on the contrary, seems to suppose that when Socrates begins deliberating, he's *eo ipso* holding the view that as a general matter one's own deliberation is the way to determine what to do. "Consciousness takes up its position as independent" (ibid. 409). It's as if, in beginning to deliberate about what to do, Socrates were already holding, "Now one should treat one's deliberation as the proper way to determine one's action." That is, in beginning to deliberate, Socrates not only is noticing that he's deliberating, but also is simultaneously saying that one should determine one's actions in this way and is as a general matter endorsing one's doing so. That is, Hegel thinks, Socrates is adopting a reflective and general view about how to think practically.

* * * *

Hegel attributes to Socrates quite a lot of explicitly adopted views about what he was doing. Hegel's picture of Socrates includes portraying him as explicitly adopting a particular kind of skeptical attitude. Ancient doxography, indeed, commonly pictures Socrates as a skeptic, and indeed as the first skeptic. Later thinkers who called themselves skeptics traced the origins of their thinking to Socrates.

In important ways Hegel follows this account. In particular he portrays Socrates as taking and encouraging a generally questioning stance toward Athenian law, of which his habit of deliberating what to do was a result. Before the sophists and Socrates made their influence felt,

> the law of the State [had] authority as the law of the gods, and thus it [had] universal destiny which [had] the form of an existent, and [was] recognized as such by all. (*HofP* 408)

372

On the other hand the kind of moral consciousness that's represented by Socrates questions this standard:

> [M]oral consciousness asks if this is actually the law in itself. This consciousness turned back within itself from everything that has the form of the existent, requires to understand, to know, that the above law is posited in truth, i.e., it demands that it should find itself therein as consciousness. (408)

Or in other words, "The immediate has no further authority but must justify itself to thought" (410).

Hegel thus ascribes to Socrates more than merely a propensity to raise questions about what one should do, and a propensity to raise questions about whether one should do things that the State has prescribed. According to Hegel's picture Socrates holds that the State should or must justify its injunctions (cf. 408–10).

Hegel's view is thus that prior to adopting a questioning attitude, a person uncritically accepts "the law of the State." Hegel thus conveys the impression that the only way to arrive at a practice of asking oneself deliberative questions in a conscious or thoroughgoing way, that is, questions about what one should do and how one should live, is to depart, in a reflectively questioning, and in that sense "skeptical" way, from an unreflective obedience to the ethical standards of one's community.

Thus the tendency often to ask, "What shall I do?," isn't distinguished from, and is tacitly presumed to amount or lead inevitably to, the open and systematic raising of certain further questions and demands. These could include the question whether community standards are in general to be trusted, and the demand that they be supported by explicit justification. (It could also include questions about how the standards are to be applied to particular cases, and demands for justification of those applications: however, these issues don't seem to make an appearance in Hegel's treatment.)

* * * *

Indeed, Hegel's imputation to Socrates of a skeptical position about community standards is somehow expanded so as to go well beyond issues concerning the law of the State. Without delineating exactly what he takes the scope of Socrates' skepticism to be, Hegel often gives the impression of believing that it's fully general. Here he links Socrates with the sophists, who (*HofP* II, 369)

> knew, as educated men, that everything could be proved. . . . The Sophists thus knew that on this basis nothing was secure, because the power of thought treated everything dialectically.

Socrates' thinking shares this outlook (though with a complexly different content, closer to what Hegel attributes to Plato; 385–6) and perpetuates it:

> Ordinary knowledge thus becomes confused, as we . . . see very clearly in Socrates, for something is held to be certain to consciousness, and then other points of view which are also present and recognized, have similarly to be allowed; hence the first has no value, or at least loses its supremacy. (370)

373

It's pertinent to remark in this connection on the undoubted historical fact that some ancient skeptical thinking subsequent to Socrates plainly seems to have been quite determinedly nonreflective. One strand in so-called "Pyrrhonian" skepticism, while raising questions about the views of "dogmatists," tries assiduously to avoid espousing any views about methods or methodology. Naturally a common strategy of opponents of this form of skepticism is to try to find in what these skeptics say and do some kind of "dogmatic" commitment to methodological assumptions that skeptics should not, *qua* skeptics, accept.

Whether this strategy succeeds is, of course, philosophically controversial. Nevertheless if we wish to see Socrates as a forerunner of those ancient philosophers who called themselves "skeptics," it seems to me that these – in this sense – nonreflective skeptics are certainly candidates for being called his successors. That ought at least to raise the possibility in our minds that Socrates' skeptical leanings might be anti- or non-reflective too.

I think in fact that Hegel's guiding assumption here – that, across the board, a questioning attitude is reflective in an intrinsically methodological way, whereas acceptance is intrinsically unreflective and naive – is utterly mistaken. The distinction, reflective/nonreflective and distinctions like skeptical/nonskeptical cut across each other. Socrates' attitude could be roughly described as nonreflectively or systematically skeptical.[4] By that I mean – more on this below – that he simply asks the questions that seem to him to arise, without espousing a position that justifies that questioning, or tries to provide either a general argument for the untrustworthiness of a particular body of beliefs, or a general demand for their justification. The asking can perfectly well be ad hoc, a response to the particular matter at hand – that's the impression that Xenophon tends to give (Plato had his own systematic agenda, and that, I believe, causes him to present Socrates' questioning, sometimes [but not always], as itself systematic and its method as reflective).

* * * *

Hegel's willingness to see Socrates as a forerunner of later Greek skeptics is connected to his adherence to the Greek doxographical practice of giving all philosophers, including Socrates, a place in a succession of teachers and pupils. Doing this fits in with Hegel's belief, already remarked on, that the development of philosophy can best be made sense of as a process of gradually progressing (though sometimes digressing) "self-awareness of freedom." This belief is exhibited in a number of other things that Hegel says about Socrates.

One extraordinary case in point is Hegel's view that Socrates is a follower of Anaxagoras' view about *nous*. Socrates, says Hegel, "adopted firstly the doctrine of Anaxagoras that thought, the understanding, is the ruling and self-determining universal" (*HofP* 385). Hegel appears to draw this connection almost solely on the basis of Socrates' willingness to examine his own life and actions and opinions. But Hegel was probably also influenced here by his tendency to regard Socrates as a generalized skeptic combined with the evidence that Anaxagoras adopted a skeptical attitude toward traditional Greek religion. Thus Socrates' relentless engagement in deliberation becomes assimilated, oddly, to physical-metaphysical theorizing.

374

Contrast this idea with the view, which many (including myself) would defend, that in spite of their spatiotemporal and social proximity, Socrates and Anaxagoras were engaged in two extremely different kinds of intellectual projects. (Hegel himself asserts flatly that Socrates disdained physical theorizing, following on this point, for better or worse, Xenophon's *Memorabilia*, esp. 4.7.2–8, without making use of the more complex story that Plato gives – perhaps accurately, or perhaps to serve his own philosophical agenda – at *Phaedo* 96ff.)

One of the kinks in the historical chain is created by the complex relationship between Socrates and the sophists – not an easy problem for any historian. On the one hand the sophists and Socrates seem to share certain tendencies and techniques of argument. On the other hand Hegel, like most people from Plato and Xenophon onwards (for their various respective reasons), wishes to place Socrates on a rather higher ethical plane. The sophists made use of the fact that "if arguments are relied upon, everything can be proved by argument" (*HofP* 368), and "knew that on this basis nothing was secure, because the power of thought treated everything dialectically" (369). Socrates falls into line too:

> Ordinary knowledge thus becomes confused, as we shall see very clearly in Socrates, for something is held to be certain to consciousness, and then other points of view which are also present and recognized, have similarly to be allowed; hence the first has no further value, or at least loses its supremacy. (370)

Both the sophists and Socrates use a way of thinking, a kind of "logic," that can be used to defend any proposition, true or false. Socrates employs it "to inspire men with distrust toward their presuppositions" (398). Thus

> when other people brought forward their principles, he, from each definite proposition, should deduce as its consequence the direct opposite of what the proposition stated, or else allow the opposite to be deduced from their own inner consciousness . . . (399)

Nevertheless Socrates' thought makes contact with the Good in a way in which the sophists' does not:

> Thus, if with Socrates, as with Protagoras, the self-conscious thought that abrogates all that is determined, was real existence, with Socrates this was the case in a way that he at the same time grasped in thought rest and security. This substance existing in and for itself, the self-retaining, has become determined as end, and further as the true and the good. (385)

The reason for this is that in spite of all of his refutations of ordinary opinions, Socrates does somehow encourage people to try to grasp the objective values that their community manifests. This mitigates his corrupting influence somewhat, though not fully.

The same chain that leads from Anaxagoras through the sophists to Socrates leads also, with a few twists and turns, from Socrates through the "later Socratics," who "laid hold of and matured . . . the standpoint to which philosophical knowledge was brought through him" (450), to the skeptics proper. Socrates constituted a turning point because he's the first one who brought people to be reflective.

375

> In Socrates, and from him onward, we thus see knowledge commencing, the world rais-
> ing itself into the region of conscious thought, and thus becoming the object. We no
> longer hear question and answer as to what Nature is, but as to what Truth is; or real
> essence has determined itself not to be the implicit, but to be what it is in knowledge.
> We hence have the question of the relationship of self-conscious thought to real essence
> coming to the front as what concerns us most. (450–1)

"With the Skeptics the dialectic side [is] further developed and brought to a higher standpoint" (464).

* * * *

Another aspect of Hegel's treatment of Socrates as a reflective philosopher leads him to attribute to Socrates a view that can in one sense be labeled "egoist." This term has to be used carefully in the present context. Nevertheless it's appropriate here, because of the connection that exists between this particular sort of egoism and the reflective character that Hegel ascribes to Socratic thinking.

If an individual undertakes to deliberate about what to do, Hegel seems to think, this undertaking brings him into a certain kind of conflict with what it is to "live for his country." This isn't the kind of conflict that appears, in many philosophers' thought, between "self-interest" and "duty," or "community" or "altruism," but it's a conflict nevertheless. For there's a way in which Hegel thinks that deliberating about what to do brings an individual into opposition to the standards of his community (if he lives in one) and brought Socrates, into opposition to the laws of Athens.

Since Kant it has been usual to describe Greek ethical thought in general as "eudaimonist." By this is meant, roughly, that according to the Greeks, it's rational to take one's happiness as one's sole or at least one's chief ultimate end. Kant regarded this as a grave mistake, and as a respect in which Christian ethics, and his own brand of ethics, are more advanced than Greek ethics was. Hegel must have been influenced by this interpretation of Greek ethics, but his understanding of Socrates is determined by other factors as well.

When "consciousness takes up its position as independent," according to Hegel, it no longer immediately acknowledges what is put before it, but requires that this should first justify itself to it, i.e., it must comprehend itself therein. Thus this return is the isolation of the individual from the universal, care for the self at the cost of the State (*HofP* 409). This is the same tendency that Hegel sees in the sophists:

> To the Sophists the satisfaction of the individual was now made ultimate, and since they
> made everything uncertain, the fixed point was in the assertion, "it is my desire, my pride,
> glory, and honor, particular subjectivity, which I make my end. (370–1)

Socrates didn't do quite this. Hegel says that in Socrates' thinking, "the good, the universal, [and] the individuality, the arbitrary will of the subject . . . [were] united" (370), so that the individual's self-conscious thought "has become determined as end, and further as the true and good" (385). The thought seems to be, roughly, that although Socrates didn't formulate his end as something so overly egoistic as "my own self-interest," the fact that he deliberated reflectively and acted on the conclusions of

376

his own deliberation, he was thereby setting himself in opposition to the State, insofar as he was not simply in unreflective accord with the standards and injunctions that it laid down.

Unlike the Sophists' outlook, Socrates' thinking isn't presented by Hegel as egoism in the most ordinary sense. As I've already said, moreover, the conflict in question isn't the usual one, which philosophers often lament, between self-interest and the good of a community. Socrates' philosophical activity has a quite broadly self-regarding character. "Socrates wished to develop himself as an individual" (469). Moreover the subjectivity that Hegel sees in Socrates is in some way closely bound up with the good of Athens and with "the true and good." As noted, Socrates "also helped others to care for their morality" (409). Hegel doesn't picture this as in any way out of keeping with the general character of Socrates' thought.

Nevertheless Hegel emphasizes the conflict between Socrates and Athens, and makes it the basis of his well-known defense of the Athenian state for putting Socrates to death. "Two opposed rights come into collision," though "it is not as though the one alone were right and the other wrong" (446).

> This [particularity of ends and interests] has, in common with the Socratic principle, the fact that what seems right and duty, good and useful to the subject in relation to himself as well as to the State, depends on his inward determination and choice, and not on the constitution and the universal. (448)

Hegel holds that already before Socrates and increasingly so after him, this "particularity of ends and interests" was a more and more important factor in Athenian life (448). In the end, says Hegel,

> [this] principle of self-determination for the individual has ... become the ruin of the Athenian people, because it was not yet identified [as Hegel thinks it was later to become in the modern state] with the constitution of the people. Thus Socrates "constitutes a great historic turning point." (448)

Hegel doesn't in his discussion of Socrates articulate the full connection that he sees between an individual's engaging in deliberation and the conflict between that fact and the constitution of the people. That's a matter for Hegel's overall treatment of the State and the way in which Spirit supposedly manifests itself in it. Hegel nevertheless thinks that the connection is sufficiently clear that one can say without embellishment that engaging in deliberation leads directly to the conflict.

Moreover the link seems to be the idea that if one deliberates and acts on one's deliberation – i.e., thinks about and thereby decides on what to do – one is making "what seems right and duty, good and useful to the subject in relation to himself as well as to the State" into something that "depends on his inward determination and choice." It seems hard to deny that as Hegel tells the story, by engaging in deliberation about what to do, an individual is brought to aim at what's "good and useful to the subject in relation to himself" (even though this was in Socrates' case also "good and useful ... to the State"). Moreover in the case of Socrates, too, Hegel seems to take this aiming to be exhibited explicitly in Socrates' discourse. In a way, deliberating is portrayed as leading automatically to aiming at one's own good or something near it, until someone – Plato, in Hegel's story, though Socrates is, we can say roughly, given part of the credit for this – explicitly makes the move of making out the Good and the Just to be "objective" (*HofP* 384–9).

In considering Hegel's view of Socrates' influence it's important to avoid certain natural mistakes. In the first place, one can easily get the impression that in Hegel's view this kind of orientation to the community was directly destroyed by the teachings of Socrates. Hegel insists, however, that the decline of the Athenian state had already begun before him, though Hegel certainly thinks that he had a deleterious influence on people's habit of living for their country.

More importantly, it's easy to gain the mistaken impression that in Hegel's view, Socrates had a corrupting influence by actually introducing the possibility of people's acting on self-interest, and did this by introducing the very concept. On this picture, Hegel thought that before Socrates had somehow generated the concept of self-interest, and had thus also generated the possibility of people's acting on self-interest, a Greek simply had no self-interest.

This, however, is after all probably the wrong way to think about Hegel's view. He says,

> the interests of the community may . . . continue to be entrusted to the will and resolve of the citizens – and this must be the basis of the Greek constitution; for no principle has as yet manifested itself, which can contravene such choice conditioned by custom, and hinder its realizing itself in action. The Democratic Constitution is here the only possible one: the citizens are still unconscious of particular interests, and therefore of a corrupting element. (*PofH* 252; cf. *HofP* 99–100, 98–9, 114)

It doesn't seem right to take this as a claim that in pre-Socratic Athens an individual citizen didn't have such a thing as his own good. Hegel may not even be saying that a citizen's good couldn't be in conflict with the good of the community. Rather, Hegel's idea appears to be that there was no explicit consciousness of such a thing as one's own good, and that it was only sophistic and Socratic ideas that articulated the idea of self-interest, and thus made it possible for self-interest to have a stronger and more important – and "corrupting" – political effect. This loosely illustrates a way in which Hegel thinks that intellectual phenomena can have an important influence.

* * * *

In all of the foregoing ways we see Hegel's interpretation tending to depict Socrates' philosophizing as methodologically reflective. By engaging in certain kinds of thinking Socrates is supposedly in effect exhibiting and even articulating certain views, and also articulating and espousing certain methods by which his thinking proceeds. Most analytic interpretations of Socrates tend strongly to see him in the same way, though usually focused more narrowly.

One of the main focuses is epistemological in a broad sense. Thus much recent such research treats the main aim of the so-called "Socratic" dialogues of Plato as the explicit exhibition of some sort of method. The assumption is taken on board, from Plato, that Socrates' effort to gain knowledge is always channeled by his search for definitions of crucially difficult terms – the chief barrier to knowledge being assumed to be our lack of clear understanding of them, which could only be provided by definitions.

One method that interpreters articulate is a "method of refutation" (elenctic), which aims to disprove theses or candidate definitions that interlocutors propose. A closely related one is the method of refutation taken as a way of showing that interlocutors hold inconsistent beliefs. A third is a combination of one of these with some extra something which will, in addition, somehow generate true theses or correct definitions that won't fall to refutations. All such interpretations have in common the ascription to Socrates, or at least to the Socratic character in these Platonic works, of a self-conscious concern with some particular method, even if the method is perhaps only hinted at (Matthews 1999: 121–5).

These interpretations present us with a Socrates who's as reflective methodo-logically as Hegel's, but in a somewhat narrower way than his. One reason for the difference is that in order to get information about his Socrates, Hegel appeals mainly to Xenophon, whereas these interpretations look mainly to Plato. When we concen-trate on Plato's Socratic dialogues, our attention tends to be caught by certain issues about definitions and counterexamples, which foreshadow the more positive philo-sophical theorizing of the mature Plato of the *Phaedo* and the *Republic*. At the least we're faced with a philosopher who's preoccupied with questions about the methods that someone might use for finding correct definitions and rejecting mistaken ones. The reflections of Xenophon's Socrates have far less definite contours. Certainly the thinking of Xenophon's Socrates strikes one as much less systematic – and Hegel does say, after all, that Socrates had nothing affirmative to say (*HofP* 407) by which he means, not that Socrates didn't have and reflect generally on his method of philoso-phizing, but that he had no "system" in the style of a pre-Socratic *physikos* (452).

Hegel's reasons for taking Socrates' philosophizing to be reflective is in a way more thoroughgoing and insistent than the reasons why these "analytic" accounts do so. These accounts discuss what they think is philosophically interesting and important in Socrates' work or in the ideas voiced by Plato's character. What these accounts find interesting and important is his method. It doesn't seem to me that they're wrong to say that his method is interesting – though other things that he treats are interesting too, and perhaps more so (Matthews 1999: 125, 127–30).

These accounts don't, however, present any reason why Socrates' philosophical activity intrinsically needed to be reflective. They don't say why, given that he was asking questions like "What is bravery?" and "Is virtue teachable?," he needed to take up questions of method. Some twentieth-century philosophy says that there can't be anything for philosophy to talk about except language and the concepts that it expresses, because everything else that there is to talk about is treated by something else – science, for instance. In addition, a fair amount of twentieth-century philosophy says that ethical philosophy has to deal with the language of ethics, because ethics has to do with values and values are a mere matter of the expression through language of emotion or the evincing of attitudes, so that they have no subject matter.

Hegel's view, on the other hand, purports to give us a reason of why Socrates' philosophizing couldn't but be reflective about the thinking that it does, or is. The reason is that all philosophy is so. And all philosophy is so, on this view, because all philosophy has to be so. The reason for that is that nothing of this kind is to be explained – that is, to be made sense of – except by viewing it as part of the movement in history toward the "self-awareness of freedom."

* * * *

We can best understand the thrust of Hegel's interpretation if we contrast it with the very different interpretation, according to which not only was Socrates' philosophizing not self-reflective, but it tended quite strongly away from being so. On this view Socrates' philosophizing didn't include an expressed or implied description of the method by which it proceeded, nor did it espouse a particular way of philosophizing.

Although I've already indicated that this way of interpreting Socrates' philosophical activity seems to me considerably more plausible than Hegel's, I present it here primarily to clarify the thrust of Hegel's interpretation by throwing that interpretation into relief. The point to be made isn't that Hegel's interpretation is wrong. If one doesn't adopt Hegel's general way of trying to make sense of the history of philosophy, his account of Socrates and of much else does appear as just obviously wrong. But quite apart from that, the point is, rather, that at least to some extent Socrates' way of philosophizing may well be one that Hegel's conception of what it is to understand the history of philosophy excludes him from taking into account, at least as philosophy.

Embodied in Socrates' activity is the possibility that someone might proceed to investigate practical questions without, or at any rate in substantial independence of, any articulation or examination of the method by which he was conducting that investigation, and might, indeed, reject all descriptions of any such method, or any claim that it's needed. That means that Socrates wouldn't, just for instance, espouse the thesis that action ought to be guided by deliberation. It's not at all easy to see how he would deal with any explicit posing of the issue of whether that's so.

Socrates' famous saying that "the unexamined life isn't worth living" leads many people to think, by a rash and unwarranted inference, that he espoused some such thesis.[5] The saying is reflective in the bare sense that it's a remark about Socrates' own activity. But Socrates' statement doesn't imply any general claim about what it is for something to be worthwhile, or even just about what makes the examination of a life worthwhile. Equally plainly it doesn't imply any theses or method about how such examination ought to proceed, or any thesis according to which it has to be general.[6] Something analogous applies to his view that the care of one's "soul" – simply meaning, of course, concern for what kind of person one is – is extremely important. Both of these are (in my opinion) true, but nevertheless they're quite restricted claims, which can be accepted without any commitment to anything about a method of thinking.

It's obvious that Plato didn't agree with this attitude. In my opinion he understood Socrates in the way that I do. He believed, though – as I think Socrates didn't, and as I think the evidence given by Plato himself shows that he didn't – that Socrates' failures to answer his own questions demonstrate that the articulation of a general method is called for. My own view is that because Plato didn't think that Socrates' approach could get anywhere, he set up the "Socratic" works in such a way as to try to show that they couldn't, and that therefore the articulation of a general method is called for. In this respect, Hegel's view of Socrates is the product of Plato's way of thinking about him and presenting him.

* * * *

Hegel's approach appears to rule out the idea of unreflectively adopting a deliberative stance, in the sense of simply always thinking about what to do – without any overarching program for such thought, but rather in the light of whatever considerations happen to appear, in the situation at hand, to be important. If we say that a person adopts a deliberative attitude about what to do, this statement certainly doesn't imply that the person must accept the thesis that a particular type of consideration should be brought to bear. (I also don't think – though this goes beyond the present issue – that this statement implies that the considerations that the person brings to bear must be of a particular type.[7]) A person can engage in deliberation without having or being committed to any particular general view at all about what sorts of considerations are relevant or will come into play, or about just how deliberation ought to issue in action.

To put the point another way, we can see that sometimes particular questions just do arise about what one proposes to do. If you want to, put it this way: they arise purely ad hoc. They don't have to arise because a certain kind of question is right or appropriate to consider, nor because it's right or appropriate to raise deliberative questions in general. A person who thinks of questions about what to do might well, if confronted with the question, "How in general do you decide how to live and what to do?," be utterly baffled as to how to begin to answer. The person might (though needn't) be inclined to think that there must exist an answer to the question but still be baffled as to what it is.

If asked to deal with the question quite generally and apart from some particular situation, the person might respond to the question by saying, "I just think of whatever considerations seem relevant, and I think about what they all, taken together, recommend." And the person might do what everyone would concede to be a very good job of that. But if it were then retorted, "Well in that case you're taking your own consciousness, or perhaps your own conscience, as your criterion," the person could rightly reply, "No, I'm not, and I don't believe that that is a good criterion for this sort of matter; deciding what to do by thinking about what to do isn't the same thing as taking the outcome of one's thinking about what to do as the criterion of what to do."

In saying this last thing, the person would be opposing (rightly, in my opinion) what Hegel seems to suppose about Socrates. Moreover it seems to me that a great deal of what's reported about Socrates suggests that he'd give a very similar reply. In addition, I think that a readiness to give such a reply to the question is – at least to go by some of the most striking evidence about Socrates – one of the most importantly characteristic and interesting features of this thinking. In many cases, Socrates attempted to address practical questions with as little reflection as possible on his own procedure.

* * * *

To help make clearer the import of this comparison between Hegel's view of Socrates and the other view that I'm contrasting with it, it's *à propos* briefly to mention some other philosophers who, though in other ways very different from Socrates, sometimes philosophize – or try to – in a similarly nonreflective way. Probably the best known of them are Moore (in some of his moods, anyway) and Wittgenstein (in much of his later period at least).

381

Moore's attempt to keep philosophy close to "common sense" is often associated in people's minds with his effort not to put points in an overtly "philosophical" way. For example, his way of combating skepticism about the external world often involves trying to express and understand claims about ordinary physical objects in such a way as to avoid conveying implications that might be open to skeptical challenge (Stroud 1984: ch. 6). Wittgenstein's way of approaching skepticism in his *On Certainty* does something similar, and the same is at least arguably true of his whole treatment of language and meaning in the *Philosophical Investigations*. It's this kind of stance that seems to me appropriately attributed to Socrates, in spite of the fact that it's excluded not only by Hegel's way of taking him but also by most analytic treatments. The examples of Moore and Wittgenstein show that "analytic" philosophers don't all have to be self-reflectively examining their method.

One of the indications that Socrates proceeded in a nonreflective way arises from the claims of ignorance that stimulate Hegel to link him to the skeptics. The meaning of Socrates' claims is of course controversial, as is their intended scope. Nevertheless their scope is clearly substantial. But what's significant is, first, precisely the fact that Socrates doesn't define their scope, as a methodologically reflective skeptic can be expected to. Second, Socrates doesn't try to justify them or give a definite idea of their point.

Rather he simply claims that he doesn't know, or that he doesn't know much, and adds, again without elaboration or justification, that he's better off for not believing that he knows than those who don't know but think they do – which is trivial, unsystematic common sense if you're trying to avoid mistakes. Then he illustrated the claim by exhibiting himself as not then being in a position to answer certain questions. That fact makes him look like the kind of skeptic – if he can be labeled a "skeptic" at all – who doesn't take a reflective stance on the character of his own thinking.

Here it is germane to reiterate the claim asserted earlier, that the distinction, reflective/nonreflective and distinctions like skeptical/nonskeptical don't coincide, notwithstanding Hegel's tendency to suppose that they do. Once again, it seems to me that with appropriate qualifications (too complex to be explored here) Socrates can be described as skeptical in a methodologically nonreflective way.

It's of course interesting that a nonself-reflective approach to philosophizing should be exhibited both by philosophers – like Moore and Wittgenstein – who attempt to extricate themselves from skeptical worries and a philosopher, Socrates, who seems to strike a skeptical pose. This, I think, is no paradox at all. It presents itself as a difficulty only to a characterization of philosophy that tends to view it as necessarily involving the kind of methodologically reflective character that Hegel ascribes to Socrates' thought.

Obviously there's a danger in thinking of a philosophical stance as nonself-reflective or nonreflective if it strikes one as being too studied as a matter of style. Partly for this reason, the act of not voicing methodological assumptions can at least seem to amount to a way of expressing methodological assumptions, or being committed to them – at least, to the assumption that there's something wrong with them. Possibly Socrates was in some such position, but I don't think so.

* * * *

Hegel's description of Socrates presents an occasion for thinking about which kinds of activities require the person engaging in them to accept some belief or other, and to think, about the way in which he is acting. As I've said, Hegel believes that in engaging in deliberation as he did, Socrates must have held certain principles concerning the fact that he was deliberating and the way in which he was doing so. To the extent that Socrates was the kind of philosopher that a lot of the evidence suggests, Hegel isn't, I think, in a position to describe him accurately or gauge his significance as a philosopher.

Following out Hegel's thinking about Socrates would seem to mean that Hegel simply shouldn't have room for the idea of an unreflective egoist. We couldn't say of someone that, to parody Hegel,

> in the first and genuine form of his freedom, he had no conscience; the habit of living for himself without further reflection, was the principle dominant in him.

I think it's evident that there are such people. If they're dreamt of at all in Hegel's philosophy, they at any rate seemingly can't count properly as "philosophers." Egoistic reasoning can be very complex and subtle, but there's no obvious reason why that kind of subtlety should require being reflective about method.

Both Hegel and recent analytic interpreters portray Socrates as an egoist of sorts – the preferred label recently being "eudaimonist," which is supposed to be free of connotations of selfishness. This is another focus for the urge to attribute to Socrates some systematic outlook – this time in ethics rather than in epistemology. I could argue that since Socrates isn't a methodologically systematic philosopher, he can't be a systematic eudaimonist. That would be a weak argument, though, since one might adopt an egoist outlook without being led to do so by methodological reflection.

However, it seems to me that it can be seen independently that Socrates in fact doesn't espouse a consistently eudaimonist or egoist position in ethics. The principles that Socrates adduces aren't systematized or self-consciously organized enough for either of these labels to fit him. I don't think that even his first systematizing interpreter, Plato, depicts him as having done so. I don't think that Socrates attempt to construct a systematic position – or "theory" – in ethics.

Plato's *Crito* presents one notorious difficulty for the interpretation of Socrates. His defense there of the thesis that he shouldn't disobey the law, though it's given a partly general basis by Plato, doesn't fit at all well with other things that Plato puts into his mouth. Plato doesn't lift a finger to explain this inconcinnity. I take it as a believable indication that Socrates' thinking didn't have an overall, worked-out architecture. I think interpreters should give up the attempt to press this work into consistency with other passages propounding his thinking.

The thesis that Socrates was a thoroughgoing eudaimonist runs up against strong evidence. In Plato's *Apology* Socrates is made to say (28b),

> you're wrong to think that a man who's worth anything will take into account the odds of living or dying, or will, when he does something, consider anything besides whether he's doing things that are just or unjust, or the acts of a good or a bad man.

This doesn't square with eudaimonism. The only way to get it to seem to do so is simply to assume that it's subordinate to an unexpressed "eudaimonist axiom," that everyone takes his own happiness as his final end (Vlastos 1991: 203, 231–2; cf. 302). But the assumption is without warrant in what Plato makes Socrates say – which directly contradicts the axiom. Better to use the text as evidence for whether Socrates accepted the axiom or not (White 2001: 173–81).

Better, too, to leave open the possibility that Socrates' philosophizing wasn't the systematic, worked out thing that one thinks of as standard. A certain kind of analytic interpreter, obeying the same impulses as Hegel, will think that if it wasn't, that would disqualify Socrates from being a great philosopher, and would – and many do – try to interpret him to give him a consistent systematic approach to eudaimonism. But those impulses seem to me misguided.

I think, for example, that if Wittgenstein didn't in fact espouse any philosophical theses or give a theory of meaning (as I think he didn't), he's no less significant a philosopher for all that. The significance of his later thought doesn't have to do with a theory or even with theses about, say, language or meaning. It has more to do with his having given examples of what to look for in thinking about the problems that are called philosophical. These examples form a pattern, to be sure. It's not, however, a pattern that Wittgenstein thinks it makes sense to try to formulate as a "theory" or even a set of theses that hang together.[8]

It seems to me that in this particular respect Socrates' philosophizing is similar to Wittgenstein's. Socrates thought a great deal about what to do, and he couldn't (as the *Apology* and *Crito* show very plainly) stand the thought of giving up thinking about what to do – without, however, thinking much at all, and certainly not much in a general systematic way, about how to think about what to do, or having a method for thinking about it.[9]

Notes

1 I write neither as a Hegel scholar nor as an admirer of Hegel, but as someone who thinks that some benefit can be derived from judicious selection of certain parts of his thinking.
2 These notions of "reflection" and "self-reflection" are not the same as Hegel's notion of "reflection" (see Burbidge 1993: 97), though they are connected to it.
3 As is well known, Hegel didn't think that the Greeks had reached the point of embodying the highest political condition fully, because they didn't fully possess the idea of the autonomous individual (see Wood 1993: 200–2).
4 Hegel's right to deny (*HofP* 388–9) that Socrates adhered automatically to ordinary opinions. Rather, Socrates' propensity to raise questions is itself characteristic of those ordinary people who don't like to accept what a *soi-disant* expert thinks unless he somehow shows that he knows what he's talking about.
5 Among many others Bernard Williams makes this mistake (Williams 1985: 1–5 and 21, e.g.). I don't think that Socrates requires the question, "How should one live?", to elicit the general methodologically reflective answers in the way that Williams assumes he does. (Being "reflective" in the relevant sense for Williams doesn't of course just mean having thoughts about oneself, but rather having thoughts, and especially general thoughts, about one's way of thinking about what to do.)
6 Williams is largely right on p. 5 to take the impersonal construction of *pōs chrē zēn* ("how one should live," *Republic* 352d) to be "noncommittal . . . about the kinds of consideration to be applied to the question." However that doesn't imply that the answer to the question

has to be "general," as Williams claims – indeed, that's one of the very things that it's "noncommittal" about.

7 *Pace*, for instance, Kantians, i.e., anyone who, holding that a properly "deliberative" attitude must be linked to rationality, infers that rationality as such requires the use of a certain type of considerations and excludes others. I'd hold that certain kinds of considerations ought to be used in the deliberation, but I certainly don't believe that this follows from its *being* ("rational") deliberation.

8 The reason is that a formulation would fall afoul of the kind of problem that he raises when he discusses rule-following and what it is "to go on in the same way as before." We should also, I think, avoid the mistake that's encouraged by Quine's suggestion that the unit of meaningful discourse is a whole "theory" – which has made people tend to think that if what they're saying makes sense, as they're inclined to do, then it must be a theory.

9 My thanks to William F. Bristow and Sara Ahbel-Rappe for very helpful suggestions.

References

Beiser, Frederick C. (ed.) (1993). *Cambridge Companion to Hegel*. Cambridge: Cambridge University Press.

Benson, Hugh (2000). *Socratic Wisdom*. New York: Oxford University Press.

Burbidge, John W. (1993). Hegel's conception of logic. In Beiser (1993: 86–101).

Hegel, G. W. F. (1892). *Lectures on the History of Philosophy*. Volume I. Trans. E. S. Haldane. London: Kegan Paul. (*HofP*)

Hegel, G. W. F. (1899). *The Philosophy of History*. Trans. J. Sibree. London: Colonial Press. (*PofH*)

Matthews, Gareth B. (1999). *Socratic Perplexity*. Oxford: Oxford University Press.

Stroud, Barry (1984). *The Significance of Philosophical Skepticism*. Oxford: Clarendon Press.

Vlastos, Gregory (1991). *Socrates: Ironist and Moral Philosopher*. Cambridge: Cambridge University Press.

White, Nicholas (2001). *Individual and Conflict in Greek Ethics*. Oxford: Clarendon Press.

Williams, Bernard (1985). *Ethics and the Limits of Philosophy*. London: Fontana Press.

Wood, Allen (1993). Hegel's ethics. In Beiser (1993: 211–33).

Section V

The Modern Period

24

Kierkegaard's Socratic Point of View

PAUL MUENCH[1]

> What our age needs ... is not a new contribution to the system but a subjective thinker who relates himself to existing *qua* Christian just as Socrates related himself to existing *qua* human being.[2]
>
> –Johannes Climacus

Shortly before he died the Danish philosopher Søren Kierkegaard (1813–1855) composed a brief essay entitled "My Task."[3] In this relatively neglected work he argues that if we want to understand him and the philosophical activities he has been engaged in then there is only one instructive object of comparison: Socrates and the role he played as philosophical gadfly in ancient Athens. In this chapter I critically discuss this text and consider in particular Kierkegaard's claim that his refusal to call himself a Christian – in a context where it was the social norm to do so – is methodologically analogous to Socrates' stance of ignorance.

Kierkegaard held a lifelong interest in Socrates and wrote about him extensively. He is perhaps best known for his 1841 *magister* dissertation, *The Concept of Irony with Continual Reference to Socrates.* Notoriously (and much to the chagrin of his dissertation committee), Kierkegaard argues in his dissertation that Socrates is not the ethical and religious figure he is usually taken to be but instead an ironist through and through. This work contains Kierkegaard's most scholarly discussion of Socrates and includes an analysis of the writings of Xenophon and Plato together with an examination of Aristophanes' *Clouds*, while also engaging the philosophical and philological scholarship of his day (primarily from Germany), including most notably the writings of Hegel.[4] Though Kierkegaard is usually represented in the history of philosophy as a great foe of Hegel's, he nevertheless inherits Hegel's philosophical vocabulary and makes use in his dissertation of a recognizably Hegelian framework.[5] Arguing that the three main depictions of Socrates that have come down to us from antiquity are each ultimately *distortions* of the truth (resulting from Xenophon's shallowness, Plato's desire to idealize his teacher, and Aristophanes' aims as a comic playwright), Kierkegaard maintains that by tracing these various distortions and their interrelationships we should be able in effect to triangulate back to their common Socratic source and so come to appreciate, on his view, the fundamentally ironic nature of Socrates' overall position.[6]

Although Kierkegaard seems to argue at times in his dissertation that none of the sources from antiquity provides an accurate depiction of Socrates, he actually allows for one exception: Plato's *Apology*. Calling the *Apology* "an historical document" that "must be assigned a preeminent place when the purely Socratic is sought," Kierkegaard holds both that "a reliable picture of the *actual* Socrates is seen in the *Apology*" and that "in this work we do have, according to the view of the great majority, a historical representation of Socrates' *actuality*."[7] As the argument of *The Concept of Irony* unfolds (proceeding from Kierkegaard's treatment of the ancient sources, to his discussion of Socrates' trial, to Socrates' significance as world-historical figure), Kierkegaard repeatedly appeals to the *Apology* and not unreasonably treats it as the final authority upon which any conception of Socrates ultimately must rest. In my view Plato's *Apology* remains the single most important text for Kierkegaard's thinking about Socrates. This is a text to which Kierkegaard returns again and again in his writings about Socrates and which dramatizes for him the Socratic ideal: a life that aims at cultivating the self while also serving as an occasion for one's fellow citizens to examine themselves more closely.

After the completion of his dissertation Kierkegaard opted not to pursue a university career and instead devoted himself to writing, publishing 31 books and numerous articles over a 14-year span before he died in 1855 at the age of 42. While he never again was to devote as many continuous pages to Socrates as he did in his dissertation, Kierkegaard frequently returns to him in his later writings and continues to refine and deepen his conception of Socrates' philosophical method.[8] Although Socrates forever remains an ironist in his eyes, Kierkegaard later comes to think that his dissertation suffers from a certain one-sidedness that neglects Socrates' significance as an ethical and religious figure.[9] In addition Kierkegaard also comes to conceive of himself as a kind of Christian Socrates who seeks by means of his various writings to make his contemporaries aware of what it is to live an authentic Christian life while simultaneously trying to draw their attention to the various respects in which their own lives may fail to live up to this Christian ideal.

Many of Kierkegaard's texts are designed to have an existential impact on the reader and involve the use of a whole host of fictional characters, including most notably Kierkegaard's so-called pseudonymous authors, each of whom is presented as the author of his respective book or books and as someone who embodies a specific outlook on life, whether this be a commitment to aesthetic detachment, ethical fortitude or religious passion. Perhaps acknowledging the difficulty that his reader may have in keeping straight all these different voices and life-outlooks, Kierkegaard also wrote several works that seek to illuminate the overall aim and purpose of his authorship as a whole.[10] "My Task" falls into this latter category of writings and represents Kierkegaard's final attempt to draw everything together for his reader and to present in as compressed and distilled a manner as possible the essence of what he takes his task to have been. As a result, despite its neglect, this text is perhaps the best single document we have for obtaining a basic picture of how Kierkegaard conceives of his own activities as a writer and thinker.[11] Over the space of just a few pages Kierkegaard eloquently sketches for us what he takes to be his contemporary situation, a situation where the authentic practice of Christianity has almost ceased to exist while it nevertheless remains the cultural norm for people (notably his fellow citizens of Copenhagen) to continue to conceive of themselves as Christians. In response to this situation Kierkegaard openly refuses to call himself a Christian and at times even denies that he is a Christian: "I do not call myself a Christian, do not say of myself that I am a Christian. . . . It is altogether true: I am not a Christian."[12] Despite the fact that he claims in "My Task" that his authorship was "at the outset stamped 'the single individual – I am not a Christian,'" this is the first time Kierkegaard has openly avowed that this is his position.[13] Furthermore, he contends that this is "the first time in 'Christendom'" that *anyone* has approached things in this particular manner:

> The point of view I have exhibited and am exhibiting is of such a distinctive nature that in eighteen hundred years of Christendom there is quite literally nothing analogous, nothing comparable that I have to appeal to. Thus, in the face of eighteen hundred years, I stand quite literally alone.[14]

As Kierkegaard clearly cannot mean by this claim that he is the first person ever to declare that he is not a Christian (since this is something atheists and people who practice other religions do as a matter of course), he must attach a special significance to the fact that he utters this phrase in a context where it has become the norm for people to declare themselves to be Christians and even to conceive of themselves as Christians while living lives that in no way reflect these supposed commitments. Kierkegaard's claim that there is no one analogous to him in eighteen hundred years of Christianity is not the only thing, however, that is extraordinary about this passage. Immediately after he claims that he stands alone in Christendom, Kierkegaard makes the perhaps even more remarkable claim that there does exist one person prior to him whose activity is analogous: "The only analogy I have before me is Socrates; my task is a Socratic task, to audit the definition of what it is to be a Christian."[15] That is, Kierkegaard claims that Socrates, a non-Christian pagan philosopher, is his one true predecessor, that Socrates' philosophical activity is the only thing analogous to his activity as a writer and thinker, such that we should conceive of his task – supposedly unique within Christianity – as a *Socratic* task. I think this is a remarkable claim. If Socrates really provides the only analogy to Kierkegaard and if Kierkegaard's task truly is as thoroughly Socratic as he seems to be suggesting, then we may be in the presence here of a thought that ultimately has the potential to revolutionize the very way we think about Kierkegaard and how we approach his texts.

Kierkegaard's Socratic Stance: "I am Not a Christian"

The idea that Kierkegaard is in some sense a Socratic figure is bound to strike most scholars of Kierkegaard as obvious. Any random selection of secondary literature is certain to include the occasional appeal to Kierkegaard's lifelong interest in Socrates and interpretations abound that seek to shore up whatever is being argued for with the thought that, after all, Kierkegaard modeled himself on Socrates, had a penchant for irony and indirection, etc., etc. But while it would be surprising to discover someone who claimed to be familiar with Kierkegaard's writings and yet who had no idea that Socrates was an important figure for him, we still lack a detailed, in-depth treatment of the matter. This is not to say that there do not exist any studies of Kierkegaard's conception of Socrates or any helpful accounts of what might be called Kierkegaard's Socratic method. But these are surprisingly few in number.[16] One reason I think "My Task" is a useful place to start is that this text is fairly compressed and schematic in nature. Kierkegaard is here not so much trying to put a Socratic method into practice as to invite us to take up a point of view that he thinks makes *intelligible* many of the activities he has been engaged in as a writer and thinker since the publication of his dissertation. This means that once the point of view at issue becomes clear we will have to turn to other parts of Kierkegaard's corpus if we want to obtain a more detailed grasp of how his task actually gets implemented in practice and what it is more specifically about this task that he thinks makes it quintessentially Socratic.[17]

Let's consider further Kierkegaard's comparison of himself to Socrates in "My Task." As readers we are invited to compare Kierkegaard's situation and the events that have unfolded in his life to the drama of Socrates' life as it is recounted by him in the *Apology*.[18] Recall that a significant portion of Socrates' defense speech consists of a more general account of how he came to practice philosophy and why he thinks such a life is worth pursuing, together with his explanation of why so many people have been slandering him over the years. Let me briefly remind you of the main cast of characters who make an appearance in Socrates' account of his life: (1) *the Sophists*, professional teachers and sometimes rivals of Socrates with whom he is often confused by the general public (19e–20a; 20d–e); (2) *the god*, who manifests himself through the oracle at Delphi (21a; 33c) and perhaps through the related phenomenon of Socrates' *daimonion* or divine sign (31d; 40a–c); (3) the broader group of *those reputed to be wise* (represented by the politicians, the poets and the craftsmen) with whom Socrates converses, along with *the public at large* which often listens to their discussions (21b–23b); (4) *the young Athenian men* who follow Socrates around and who enjoy listening to him question those reputed to be wise (23c; 33c); and (5) *Socrates himself*, who claims that the only sense in which he is wise is that he "do[es] not think [he] know[s] what [he] do[es] not know," and who believes that the god ordered him to "live the life of a philosopher, to examine [himself] and others," thereby serving as a kind of gadfly who awakens people from their ethical slumbers (21d; 28e–29a; 30e). Socrates offers this account of his life as a part of the defense speech he delivers before the jury. If we leave aside the character of Meletus and Socrates' other immediate accusers, there exist within the larger dramatic context of Socrates' defense two other significant characters worth mentioning: (6) *Socrates' jury*, a selection of his Athenian peers which also serves as a kind of literary analogue for *the readers of Plato's text*, who themselves are invited to arrive at their own judgment about Socrates' guilt or innocence;[19] and (7) *Plato*, who is represented as one of the young men in attendance at Socrates' trial (38b, 34a) and who, in turn, is also the writer and thinker who has composed the text in question.

I want to suggest that Kierkegaard models what he is doing in "My Task" – speaking more generally about his method and overall approach – on the account that Socrates develops in the *Apology* and that he invites us to treat his contemporary situation as a modern analogue to the one faced by Socrates in Athens. As the text unfolds and he develops his claim that Socrates provides his only analogy, Kierkegaard proceeds to single out a variety of characters each of whom corresponds to one of the major characters in the Socratic drama (the Sophists, the god, those reputed to be wise along with the wider public, the young Athenian men who follow Socrates, Socrates himself, Socrates' jury, Plato's readers, and Plato).[20] Simplifying a bit, the main characters discussed by Kierkegaard are the following: (1) *the pastors and theologians*, who make a profession of proclaiming what it is to be a Christian and whom Kierkegaard calls "sophists"; (2) *the public*, who conceive of themselves as Christians but who do not actually live in accord with the Christian ideal; (3) *Kierkegaard qua Socratic figure*, who denies he is a Christian and who helps to make his fellow citizens aware of a deeper sense in which they are not Christians (since they think they are Christians when they are not); (4) *the Christian God of Love*, whom Kierkegaard believes has singled him out to be the gadfly of Copenhagen; (5) *Kierkegaard's readers*, individual members of the public who are isolated as individuals by Kierkegaard's texts and whom he seeks to engage as interlocutors; and (6) *Kierkegaard qua writer and critic*, who decides how to dramatize the Socratic engagement of his audience and who offers interpretive tools for understanding his texts.

Let's start with the pastors and theologians and the larger public. Kierkegaard argues that the cultural phenomenon presenting itself as Christianity – what he calls "Christendom" (*Christendhed*) – is permeated by a kind of sophistry. In particular, he compares the pastors and theologians of his day to the Sophists battled by Socrates:

> "Christendom" lies in an abyss of sophistry that is much, much worse than when the Sophists flourished in Greece. Those legions of pastors and Christian assistant professors are all sophists. . . . who by falsifying the definition of Christian have, for the sake of the business, gained millions and millions of Christians.[21]

If the pastors and theologians correspond to the professional teachers of virtue in Socrates' day, then the larger Christian public corresponds more broadly to those in Athens who think they know what virtue is when they do not. One of Kierkegaard's main polemics is against the official Danish church and its representatives, the pastors and theologians. He contends that the church has become a business (whose main goal, then, is to make money and to perpetuate itself as an institution), and thus a body that out of self-interest obscures the true Christian message, employing a watered-down version in order for the sake of profits to maximize the total number of Christians.[22] At the same time Kierkegaard also conceives of the public itself as a distinct force to be reckoned with, as an abstract crowd or mob whose existence is predicated on the failure of people to cultivate and maintain themselves *qua* individuals. He invites us to imagine the contemporary situation of Christendom to consist of hordes of people, all running around calling themselves Christians and conceiving of themselves as Christians, often under the direct influence and guidance of the pastors and theologians, while next to no one is actually living a true, authentic Christian life. In this way he upholds a distinction between the pastors and theologians (sophists proper), who make a living advocating what it is to be a Christian, and the larger population, who more generally think they are Christians when they are not and whom Kierkegaard generically calls "the others" (*de Andre*).

Kierkegaard casts himself in the role of Socrates and, accordingly, depicts himself as someone who both seeks to reform the larger public and who combats the corrupting influence of the pastors and theologians. By making such pronouncements about his contemporary situation and by presenting himself as someone who is capable of observing such patterns of behavior and even of diagnosing what can lead to such a state of things, Kierkegaard is aware that he might appear to be setting himself up as an extraordinary Christian. But he denies that he is any such thing and suggests that his refusal to call himself a Christian at all partly helps to block such attributions:

> I do not call myself a Christian. That this is very awkward for the sophists I understand very well, and I understand very well that they would much prefer that with kettledrums and trumpets I proclaimed myself to be the only true Christian.[23]

Kierkegaard is well aware that his refusal to call himself a Christian is bound to strike his contemporaries as odd or even crazy against the backdrop of a society where everyone as a matter of course calls herself a Christian.[24] Despite this appearance of bizarreness, Kierkegaard contends that there are two significant reasons why he continues to assert this about himself. First, he ties his refusal to call himself a Christian, or in any way to modify this statement, to his desire to maintain a proper relationship with an omnipotent being, a being he later characterizes as the Christian "God of Love":

> I neither can, nor will, nor dare change my statement: otherwise perhaps another change would take place – that the power, an omnipotence [Almagt] that especially uses my powerlessness [Afmagt], would wash his hands of me and let me go my own way.[25]

At the same time, Kierkegaard ties his stance of one who does not call himself a Christian to an ability to make his contemporaries ("the others") aware of an even deeper sense in which he claims that they are not Christians:

> I am not a Christian – and unfortunately I can make it manifest that the others are not either – indeed, even less than I, since they *imagine* themselves to be that, or they falsely ascribe to themselves that they are that.

> I do not call myself a Christian (keeping the ideal free), but I can make it manifest that the others are that even less.[26]

He seems to think that adopting a position of one who refuses to call himself a Christian makes him an especially tenacious interlocutor, someone whom his contemporaries will not be able to shake off very easily:

> Just because I do not call myself a Christian it is impossible to get rid of me, having as I do the confounded characteristic that I can make it manifest – also *by means of* not calling myself a Christian – that the others are that even less.[27]

Kierkegaard conceives his task, then, to have a two-fold structure. By denying that he is a Christian in the face of his contemporaries' wont to assert the opposite, he claims to be developing and upholding some kind of religious relationship to a divine being while also acquiring a powerful means of awakening his contemporaries and making them aware of the lack of fit between how they conceive of their lives and how they actually live them.

394

Socratic Ignorance

In the process of sketching his contemporary situation and characterizing both the Sophist-like attributes of the pastors and theologians and the more general condition of his contemporaries Kierkegaard repeatedly invokes Socrates, especially in order to throw further light on his characterization of himself as a Socratic figure. He suggests that Socrates' task in Athens has the same two-fold structure as his task: Socrates is both a gadfly to his contemporaries and someone who holds that his life as a philosopher is an expression of his devotion to the god. Let's consider the image of the gadfly first. Socrates' use of this image in the *Apology* is tied to the idea of his fellow citizens' being in some sense asleep and therefore in need of being awakened. He compares their condition to that of a sluggish but noble horse who can only be stirred into life by the sting of a fly. But just as it is not uncommon for horses to kill the flies that sting them (with the quick snap of their tails), Socrates also notes that there is a certain danger involved in his being a gadfly:

> You might easily be annoyed with me as people are when they are aroused from a doze, and strike out at me; if convinced by Anytus you could easily kill me, and then you could sleep on for the rest of your days, unless the god, in his care for you, sent you someone else. (*Ap.* 31a)

Kierkegaard ties Socrates' ability to awaken his fellow citizens to his stance of ignorance, and invites us to compare this stance with his own stance of refusing to call himself a Christian.[28] He contends that Socrates' ignorance both effectively distinguishes him from the Sophists (who profess to be knowledgeable about virtue and the like and who are willing to teach this to others for a fee) while also serving as a means for making his fellow citizens aware of a different kind of ignorance that they themselves possess:

> O Socrates! If with kettledrums and trumpets you had proclaimed yourself to be the one who knew the most, the Sophists would soon have been finished with you. No, you were *the ignorant one* [*den Uvidende*]; but in addition you had the confounded characteristic that you could make it manifest (also by means of being yourself the ignorant one) that the others knew even less than you – they did not even know that they were ignorant.[29]

By likening his stance of someone who refuses to call himself a Christian to Socrates' position, Kierkegaard suggests that he shares with Socrates the ability to make people aware of a more shameful or disgraceful form of ignorance (cf. *Ap.* 29b), an ignorance that can only be counteracted through a greater attention to and cultivation of the self. The chief result of interacting with either a Socrates or a Kierkegaard is that an interlocutor comes to see that she has been self-complacent, thinking she knows things she is not able to defend under examination or thinking she lives a certain way that does not in fact square with her actual life. To be in such a condition is characterized by self-neglect and a lack of true intellectual curiosity, for if one thinks one is living as one imagines then no deeper self-examination is deemed necessary, and if one thinks one knows all about a subject then one feels no need to look into it in a more searching way. While Socrates' concern with what a person knows might on the face of it seem to be of a different order than Kierkegaard's concern with whether a person lives as a Christian, the principal focus of both of them is what we might call the practical sphere of human life, the sphere of ethics and religion, where an individual's grasp of a given ethical or religious concept is inherently tied to whether or not it plays an appropriate role in the life she leads.[30] Like Socrates, Kierkegaard focuses in particular on the tendency people have to lose track of the fundamental connection between knowing what virtue is or what it is to be a Christian and actually living a virtuous life or living an authentic Christian life.

The dangers associated with Socrates' being a gadfly include the tendency of other people to grow angry with him as well as an unwillingness to take him at his word when he claims that he himself is ignorant about what he can show that the others only think they know. In the *Apology* he says that it is not uncommon for his inter-locutors to grow angry in response to having been refuted by him and for them and the larger audience to assume that he must know, despite his claims of ignorance, what he has shown that they do not know:

> As a result of this investigation, gentlemen of the jury, I acquired much unpopularity, of a kind that is hard to deal with and is a heavy burden; many slanders came from these people and a reputation for wisdom, for in each case the bystanders thought that I myself possessed the wisdom that I proved that my interlocutor did not have. (*Ap.* 22e–23a; cf. 23c–24b; *Tht.* 151c)

The characteristic ways people have of responding to Socrates' profession of ignorance have also, according to Kierkegaard, applied with respect to his denial that he is a Christian. He claims that he often faces the same kind of anger, together with a corre-sponding presumption about his own Christian status. But he is quick to deny that it in any way follows from his having an ability to make others aware that they are not Christians that he himself is a Christian:

> But as it went with you [Socrates] (according to what you say in your "defense," as you ironically enough have called the cruelest satire on a contemporary age) – namely that you made many enemies for yourself by making it manifest that the others were ignorant and that the others held a grudge against you out of envy since they assumed that you yourself must be what you could show that they were not – so has it also gone with me. That I can make it manifest that the others are even less Christian than I has given rise to indignation against me; I who nevertheless am so engaged with Christianity that I truly perceive and acknowledge that I am not a Christian. Some want to foist on me that my saying that I am not a Christian is only a hidden form of pride, that I presumably must be what I can show that the others are not. But this is a misunderstanding; it is altogether true: I am not a Christian. And it is rash to conclude from the fact that I can show that the others are not Christians that therefore I myself must be one, just as rash as to conclude, for example, that someone who is one-fourth of a foot taller than other people is, ergo, twelve feet tall.[31]

Part of the difficulty in taking seriously Socrates' ignorance or Kierkegaard's denial that he is a Christian is an unwillingness to accept the idea that someone in that condition could nevertheless be a skilled diagnostician and able conversation partner.

We find it hard to believe that Socrates could understand his interlocutors as well as he seems to be able to (seemingly being acquainted with all the different forms that their ignorance can take) while remaining himself ignorant about the subject in question. Similarly, could Kierkegaard really be as good at depicting the various ways that a person can fall short of being a Christian while continuing to think she is a Christian if he were not himself that very thing? But this is to underestimate the power of self-knowledge. For Socrates and Kierkegaard to be good at diagnosing and treating different species of that more disgraceful kind of ignorance what is required first and foremost is that they have become acquainted in their own case with the phenomenon at issue, the tendency of a person to a kind of self-satisfaction where she imagines she knows more than she does. This tendency is a condition she is prone to that she needs to discover and – through self-examination and self-scrutiny – learn to regulate and control. While it is clearly true that a Socrates or a Kierkegaard will not make an effective conversation partner if he cannot discuss with some precision whatever it is he suspects that his interlocutor only thinks she knows, the chief qualification is that he be personally acquainted with the activity of forever being on the lookout for any such tendency in his own case. In fact, he must himself be an accomplished master of this activity (he must uphold the Delphic injunction to know thyself) if he is to be able to help others to make similar discoveries about themselves and to introduce them into the rigors of a life that seeks to avoid that more disgraceful kind of ignorance in all its various manifestations.

I suspect that a further reason that we may find it difficult to take seriously Socrates' ignorance is that it does not seem to sit well with our idea of him as a philosopher. While we may certainly applaud the manner in which he helps others to overcome their more disgraceful condition of ignorance, the fact remains that Socrates still seems to fall short of a certain philosophical ideal. The image we get of him in many of Plato's dialogues is of someone who is always approaching knowledge, perhaps gaining greater and greater conviction about what he holds to be the case but never actually arriving at knowledge itself. This picture of Socrates (upheld both by Plato and Aristotle and most of the philosophical tradition since them, including Hegel and the early Kierkegaard of *The Concept of Irony*) tends to conceptualize his philosophical activity as being only a part of a larger enterprise, as itself incomplete or preliminary in nature. While Socrates' method of engaging his interlocutors may help cleanse them of misconceptions or remove a certain kind of self-satisfaction that stands in the way of a proper philosophical engagement of a given topic, once Socrates has done what he does well (so the story goes) then other methods are required if we are actually to gain what he has shown his interlocutors to lack. Though Kierkegaard seems to endorse a version of this picture in his dissertation,[32] as his conception of Socrates develops in his later writings he more and more vehemently comes to reject this picture and instead maintains that Socrates' philosophical activity is not a mere precursor to something else but itself the human ideal (the best ethical and religious life available outside of Christianity). Socrates' life as a philosopher is thus held by Kierkegaard to be humanly complete, and ought in his view to make a claim on us and to serve as a model that we can emulate in our own lives. Socrates' activity of examining and refuting, forever on the lookout for further instances of a person's thinking she knows what she does not, becomes a life-long, ever vigilant task that he invites each of us to take part in; a task that a person will never finish, for the moment she begins to imagine that she has finished with such self-examination and self-scrutiny is the very moment when she may begin to think she knows something she does not.[33]

To motivate this picture of Socrates, Kierkegaard appeals to the religious significance that Socrates attaches to his activity as a gadfly in Athens. In the face of the reputation for wisdom that he has acquired over the years, Socrates upholds his stance of ignorance and insists that it really is the case that he lacks knowledge of the very things he tests others about. But this would then seem to leave us exactly where Socrates found himself upon first hearing of the oracle's claim that no one was wiser (*Ap.* 20e–21b). How can it truly be the case that Socrates is both ignorant (as he insists) and the wisest among human beings? Recall that in the *Apology* Socrates offers us a way out of this apparent bind and, in the process, exhibits the very modesty that is often associated with his stance of ignorance:

> What is probable, gentlemen, is that in fact the god is wise and that his oracular response meant that human wisdom is worth little or nothing, and that when he says this man, Socrates, he is using my name as an example, as if he said: "This man among you, mortals, is wisest who, like Socrates, understands that his wisdom is worthless." (*Ap.* 23a–b)

The claim that human wisdom is worth "little or nothing" can strike people in quite different ways. In the traditional picture of Socrates (in which he battles the Sophists, destroying sophistry to make room for philosophy, though himself remaining only a preliminary step in its development), one might be inclined to restrict this claim about human wisdom to prephilosophical forms of wisdom. As philosophy develops and becomes ever more sophisticated, a wisdom becomes possible that no longer is "little or nothing" but rather approaches the wisdom Socrates reserves for the god. In his later writings on Socrates Kierkegaard rejects this reading and instead takes it to be the case that Socrates means to draw a strict line *between* the human and the divine, and to ground claims of human wisdom in an individual's ability to remain aware of that distinction.[34] On this picture the difference between a wise human being and an ignorant one is that the wise person remains aware of her ignorance in relation to the wisdom of the god; the task is to develop oneself while maintaining this awareness, thereby at the same time developing a proper relationship to the god. For Kierkegaard, then, Socrates is to be taken at his word when he says that human wisdom is worth little or nothing. He does not think that Socrates' practice of philosophy is meant to begin with this little or nothing and incrementally try to bring it as close as possible to what only the god truly possesses. Rather, it is to engage in a task of self-examination and self-scrutiny of the sort that helps a person to *fortify* herself against the ever prevalent tendency to think she knows things she does not; that is, against the tendency to lose track of the difference between the human and the divine. For Kierkegaard, Socrates' life as a philosopher embodies a rigorous task of ethical self-examination that expresses in its human modesty a deeply religious commitment. Socrates' ignorance is the point from which a person shall not be moved, not the point from which a better, more developed philosophy can begin to emerge.[35]

As Kierkegaard develops the parallel between himself and Socrates, it becomes clear just how significant Socrates is for him personally. One of the ways this manifests itself stems from his claim that he stands *alone* within the Christian tradition. While under-lining yet again that he thinks that "in Christendom's eighteen hundred years there is absolutely nothing comparable, nothing analogous to [his] task," he notes that there are certain burdens associated with occupying such a unique position:

> I know what it has cost, what I have suffered, which can be expressed by a single line: I was never like the others [*de Andre*]. Ah, of all the torments in youthful days, the most dreadful, the most intense: not to be like the others. . . . With the years, this pain does decrease more and more; for as one becomes more and more spiritually developed [*Aand*], it is no longer painful that one is not like the others. To be spiritually developed is pre-cisely: not to be like the others.[36]

With such real isolation and heartfelt loneliness in view, Kierkegaard's claim that Socrates occupied an analogous position becomes all the more poignant since this in effect ensures that there is at least one person who would be in a position to under-stand the difficulties of his task. Early on in "My Task," just after he claims that Socrates provides his only analogy, Kierkegaard turns and openly addresses him:

> You, antiquity's noble simple soul, you the only *human being* I admiringly acknowledge as a thinker: there is only a little preserved about you, of all people the only true martyr of intellectuality, just as great *qua* character as *qua* thinker; but how exceedingly much this little is! How I long, far from those battalions of thinkers that "Christendom" places in the field under the name of Christian thinkers . . . how I long to be able to speak – if only for half an hour – with you![37]

In this way Socrates becomes a kind of inner companion for Kierkegaard, someone to whom he can confide and whose example he can draw upon in his darker, lonelier moments, or in those moments perhaps when he feels least understood by his contemporaries.

Kierkegaard as Writer and Thinker

In addition to characterizing his contemporary situation and his response to that situa-tion in terms of the four main figures we have been discussing thus far (the pastors and theologians, the public, the Christian God of Love, and himself *qua* Socratic figure), Kierkegaard makes clear in "My Task" that he also conceives of himself as playing a role analogous to that of Plato the writer and thinker. Just as Kierkegaard often depicts (and takes part in) Socratic exchanges within his texts, so also in his capacity as a writer does he frequently engage in a conversation with the individual readers of these texts, usually addressing them in the singular as "my dear reader."[38] Though the individual reader is frequently invited by Kierkegaard to apply what has been enacted in a given work to her own life (as a reader of one of Plato's dialogues might come to examine herself more closely in the light of certain exchanges that Plato has portrayed between Socrates and a given interlocutor), there are also cases within Kierkegaard's corpus where he engages the reader *qua* reader, seeking to instruct her on how to read his texts. Kierkegaard's activity in this case is akin to Socrates' attempt to inform his jury about his practice as a philosopher, and seeks to provide his reader with a more general understanding of his overall point of view and how he, the writer and thinker, thinks that his books should be read. Obviously the mere fact that Kierkegaard claims that his books mean thus and so, or that they ought to be read in the light of such and such, etc., does not guarantee that he is right.[39] The proof lies in how illuminating we find such orienting remarks to be. Do they reveal to us ways of approaching his texts that make those texts interesting to read, and do they help us to discern patterns of argument and literary nuance that we otherwise might not properly appreciate?

The main aim of "My Task" is to provide us with a point of view from which, according to Kierkegaard, his activities as a writer and thinker become intelligible. As should have become clear by now that point of view might be called a Socratic point of view, and it remains Kierkegaard's chief contention that Socrates is the one individual prior to him whose activity sheds any light on his task. By making such pronouncements Kierkegaard in effect presents himself as the best qualified person to offer a critical account of his authorship, and suggests that if you want to become a good reader of his texts then you should look to him and remarks of this sort for help. His claim to be the "one single person who is qualified to give a true critique of [his] work" partly rests on his belief that none of his contemporaries has properly appreciated his endeavor.[40] He contends that "there is not one single contemporary who is qualified to review [his] work" and argues that even those who sit down and try to offer a more detailed analysis only arrive at the most superficial of readings:

> Even if someone considerably better informed takes it upon himself to want to say something about me and my task, it actually does not amount to anything more than that he, after a superficial glance at my work, quickly finds some earlier something or other that he declares to be comparable.
>
> In this way it still does not amount to anything. Something on which a person with my leisure, my diligence, my talents, my education . . . has spent not only fourteen years but essentially his entire life, the only thing for which he has lived and breathed – then that some pastor, at most a professor, would not need more than a superficial glance at it in order to evaluate it, that is surely absurd.[41]

In the face of all the pastors and theologians who claim to find all sorts of things that are analogous to his task, Kierkegaard declares that "a more careful inspection" by them would reveal that there is nothing analogous within Christianity – and then adds, "but this is what [they do] not find worth the trouble."[42]

Kierkegaard wants us to be better readers than he thinks his contemporaries have been, to take the trouble to give his work that "more careful inspection" he claims it requires; and he encourages us to carry out this activity in the light of his suggestion that his task is a Socratic task. But this is not to say that we should expect such an inspection to be an easy one. If Kierkegaard is right and none of his contemporaries has understood him and his task, why should we think that it will necessarily fare any better in our own case? Kierkegaard is a strange, somewhat hybrid figure. He presents himself as a Socrates, someone skilled in the art of indirection and so seemingly forever elusive; and yet he demands that we try to understand him and offers us tools to assist us in our attempt. Anyone who embarks on such an enterprise should be warned up front that she is repeatedly likely to encounter moments of seeming clarity and a kind of shared intimacy with Kierkegaard (this most personal of philosophers), followed by moments of utter incomprehension and the anxiety that he is far too profound a character for our more limited sensibilities. Trying to bring Kierkegaard into focus can often seem akin to what it is like when one encounters irony in a text or meets face to face with an ironist herself:

> Just as irony has something deterring about it, it likewise has something extraordinarily seductive and fascinating about it. Its masquerading and mysteriousness, the telegraphic communication it prompts because an ironist always has to be understood at a distance, the infinite sympathy it presupposes, the fleeting but indescribable instant of understanding that is immediately superseded by the anxiety of misunderstanding – all this holds one prisoner in inextricable bonds.[43]

Sometimes we will feel certain we have gotten hold of Kierkegaard, only in the next moment to have the familiar experience of having him slip away yet again. Despite these difficulties, I remain convinced that there is much to be gained from taking Kierkegaard up on his suggestion that we view his activity as a writer and thinker as a Socratic task. Readers of "My Task" who share my conviction will be aware, however, that I have been operating at a fairly general level of description in this chapter. Kierkegaard's main claim is that the refusal to call himself a Christian is analogous to Socrates' stance of ignorance. He claims that so adopted, this stance gives him the ability to make his fellow citizens aware of a deeper sense in which they are not Christians, while also allowing him at the same time to pursue an authentic ethical and religious life.

With Kierkegaard's Socratic point of view now hopefully before us, the next natural step would be to turn to other texts in the corpus in order to consider further how Kierkegaard conceives of what he calls his Socratic method and where in the corpus we should look if we want to discover concrete examples of this method actually at work. But that will have to wait for another occasion.[44] Let me close by noting that there is perhaps a touch of irony in Kierkegaard's suggestion that it is only the activity of Socrates that sheds any meaningful light on his own activity. For Socrates, of all people, is about as enigmatic and elusive a character as we can find within philosophy, and is the very person whom Alcibiades claims is utterly *unlike* any other human being:

> [Socrates] is unique; he is like no one else in the past and no one in the present – this is by far the most amazing thing about him. . . . [He] is so bizarre, his ways and his ideas are so unusual, that, search as you might, you'll never find anyone else, alive or dead, who's even remotely like him. The best you can do is not to compare him to anything human, but to liken him, as I do, to Silenus and the satyrs . . . (*Smp.* 221c–d)

If Kierkegaard's claim bears out, then a proper investigation of his writings will reveal that Alcibiades was mistaken in his claim about Socrates' uniqueness by one person. When investigating further Kierkegaard's claim that Socrates provides his only analogy and that his task is a Socratic task, it's worth keeping in mind that Kierkegaard devoted the bulk of his first mature work, *The Concept of Irony with Continual Reference to Socrates*, to developing an account of who he thinks Socrates is. Despite the prominence given in the title to the concept of irony, Kierkegaard spends nearly three quarters of his discussion examining the very individual he will later model himself upon and toward whom he now points us. In this way Kierkegaard brings us full circle from his last words in "My Task" to the first words of his dissertation. His first true act as a writer and thinker was to stake his claim as the best interpreter of Socrates; in the end of his life he maintains that if we want to become interpreters of him who avoid the superficial readings he attributes to his contemporaries, then we should take his suggestion and examine his writings in the light of Socrates. In effect Kierkegaard suggests that one riddle, the riddle of Socrates (which he once thought he had solved in his dissertation and which continued to occupy him throughout his life), is the key to our trying to solve a second riddle, the riddle of Søren Kierkegaard.[45]

Notes

1 This chapter is an abridged version of a paper that originally appeared in *Kierkegaardiana* 24 (2005); I have rewritten the opening section. It is reprinted by permission of *Kierkegaardiana*. All references to Kierkegaard's published writings are to the English translations published by Princeton University Press, *Kierkegaard's Writings*; all references to Kierkegaard's unpublished writings are to the English translations published by Indiana University Press, *Søren Kierkegaard's Journals and Papers*. Citations of the English translation in question are then followed (where available) by the new scholarly edition of Kierkegaard's writings, *Søren Kierkegaards Skrifter*; otherwise I cite either *Søren Kierkegaards Samlede Værker* or *Søren Kierkegaards Papirer*. Full references to these editions and the standard abbreviations for Kierkegaard's texts can be found in the bibliography.

2 *CUP* (vol. 2) 77; *Pap.* VI B 98: 62. Cf. *JP* 2:1962 (p. 386); *Pap.* X.4 A 553.

3 *M* 340–7; *SV1* 14, 350–7. "My Task" appeared in the tenth issue of Kierkegaard's serial *The Moment* and was dated September 1, 1855 (just over two months before Kierkegaard died).

4 See especially Hegel (1995).

5 Some scholars have argued, unconvincingly in my view, that Kierkegaard's frequent appeals to Hegel in his dissertation and apparent reliance on aspects of his philosophical methodology should not be taken at face value, but rather treated as an ironic endorsement of something he means to discredit. See, e.g., Mackey (1986). For a recent reassessment of Kierkegaard's relationship to Hegel see Stewart (2003).

6 See, e.g., *CI* 154; *SKS* 1, 204–5. Cf. Olesen (2001).

7 *CI* 76; *SKS* 1, 134. *CI* 80; *SKS* 1, 138. *CI* 126; *SKS* 1, 177 (italics mine; second and third trans. modified). Kierkegaard also, however, somewhat provocatively maintains that the *Apology* "is in its entirety an ironic work" (*CI* 37; *SKS* 1, 99; trans. modified).

8 See especially the two books by Kierkegaard's pseudonymous author Johannes Climacus, *Philosophical Fragments* and *Concluding Unscientific Postscript*, and Anti-Climacus' "The Socratic Definition of Sin" (*SUD* 87–96; *SV1* 11, 199–207).

9 See, e.g., *CUP* 503; *SKS* 7, 456.

10 See especially Kierkegaard's *The Point of View for My Work as an Author*. For a discussion of the dangers of attaching too much significance to any one of these texts see Garff (1998).

11 For one recent discussion see Kirmmse (2000).

12 *M* 340; *SV1* 14, 350 (trans. modified). *M* 342–3; *SV1* 14, 353.

13 *M* 340; *SV1* 14, 350 (italics mine; trans. modified). This stance is also adopted by Kierkegaard's pseudonymous author Johannes Climacus in the *Concluding Unscientific Postscript*. See *PV* 43; *SV1* 13, 532. *PV* 8; *SV1* 13, 497.

14 M 344; *SV1* 14, 355. M 340–1; *SV1* 14, 351–2 (trans. modified). Cf. *JP* 6:6872 (p. 508); *Pap.* XI.1 A 136.

15 M 341; *SV1* 14, 352.

16 On Kierkegaard's conception of Socrates see, e.g., Himmelstrup (1924); Nagley (1980); Sarf (1983); Rubenstein (2001). On Kierkegaard's Socratic method see, e.g., Taylor (1975); Hadot (1995); Muench (2003).

17 That, however, is a much larger project which lies beyond the scope of this chapter. I've made a start on this project in Muench (2003) where I argue that Kierkegaard's pseudonymous author Johannes Climacus employs a Socratic method and represents Kierkegaard's "idealization of the Socratic within the context of nineteenth century Danish Christendom" (p. 139).

18 All references to Plato's writings are to Cooper (1997).

19 Myles Burnyeat (1997), e.g., argues that "readers are invited . . . to reach a verdict on the case before [them]" (p. 2).

20 The one exception being perhaps the young men who follow Socrates around. Kierkegaard does not present himself as someone who has had such followers, but he remains deeply interested in the youth and the problems a Socrates faces when seeking to interact with them. See, e.g., his discussion of Alcibiades at *CI* 47–52; *SKS* 1, 108–13. *CI* 187–92; *SKS* 1, 234–9. *PF* 24; *SKS* 4, 231–2. *JP* 4:4300 (p. 221); *Pap.* XI.1 A 428.

21 M 341; *SV1* 14, 352 (trans. modified). M 340; *SV1* 14, 351. It should be noted, however, that one dissimilarity between the pastors and theologians under criticism by Kierkegaard and the Sophists of Socrates' day is that while the former are part of the official establishment and as such were generally recognized as legitimate authorities, the latter were usually outsiders who traveled to Athens and who were often viewed with considerable suspicion by those in power. Cf. *M.* 91b–92c. On Socrates' relationship to the Sophists see, e.g., *CI* 201–14; *SKS* 1, 246–59.

22 Cf. *M* 347; *SV1* 14, 357.

23 M 341–2; *SV1* 14, 352 (trans. modified).

24 See *M* 340; *SV1* 14, 350–1.

25 M 345; *SV1* 14, 356. M 340; *SV1* 14, 351 (trans. modified). Thus refusing to call himself a Christian is, in part, an expression of Kierkegaard's religious convictions and may be tied to his idea that one never *is* a Christian in this life, though each person certainly can embark on the lifelong task of *becoming* a Christian.

26 M 340; *SV1* 14, 351 (italics mine; trans. modified). M 341; *SV1* 14, 352.

27 M 342; *SV1* 14, 352–3 (italics mine; trans. modified).

28 Kierkegaard, who is best known for having argued in his dissertation that Socrates is an ironist through and through, never conceives of Socrates' ignorance as incompatible with this ironic stance but neither does he think that Socrates' ignorance is feigned or merely tactical. See, e.g., *CI* 169–77; *SKS* 1, 217–24. *CI* 269–71; *SKS* 1, 306–8. Cf. Nehamas (1998), pp. 86–7.

29 M 342; *SV1* 14, 353 (underlining mine; trans. modified).

30 Cf., e.g., *Lch.* 187e–188a; *Ap.* 29e–30a.

31 M 342–3; *SV1* 14, 353 (trans. modified).

32 See, e.g., *CI* 217; *SKS* 1, 261.

33 On the idea of Socrates' activity being a kind of preliminary cleansing of the soul see *Sph.* 230b–d. By denying that Socrates' life should be understood as incomplete, Kierkegaard radicalizes this activity of cleansing the soul, insisting that this activity is never finished, never perfected but instead is of such a nature that an individual must conceive of it as a task to which she must devote her entire life.

34 Cf. *SUD* 99; *SV1* 11, 209–10.

35 Cf. *JP* 1:972 (p. 424); *Pap.* X.1 A 360. *JP* 4:3871 (p. 23); *Pap.* XI.2 A 362.
36 *M* 344; *SV1* 14, 355 (trans. modified).
37 *M* 341; *SV1* 14, 352 (trans. modified).
38 *M* 345; *SV1* 14, 356.
39 Kierkegaard would not dispute this. See, e.g., *PV* 33; *SV1* 13, 524.
40 *M* 343; *SV1* 14, 353.
41 *M* 343–4; *SV1* 14, 354 (trans. modified).
42 *M* 344; *SV1* 14, 354–5.
43 *CI* 48–9; *SKS* 1, 109.
44 See note 17.
45 Thanks to Bridget Clarke, Ben Eggleston, Robert Haraldsson, Brian Söderquist, and Jon Stewart for helpful comments on an earlier draft of this chapter, and to Sara Ahbel-Rappe for suggestions on how to shorten this paper for the present collection.

References

Works by Kierkegaard (Danish)

SV1 *Søren Kierkegaards Samlede Vaerker* [Søren Kierkegaard's Collected Works], 14 Volumes. Edited by A. B. Drachmann and others. Copenhagen: Gyldendalske Boghandels Forlag, 19016.

Pap. *Søren Kierkegaards Papirer* [Søren Kierkegaard's Papers], Second edition, 16 Volumes. Edited by Niels Thulstrup and Niels Jørgen Cappelørn. Copenhagen: Gyldendal Forlag, 1968–78.

SKS *Søren Kierkegaards Skrifter* [Søren Kierkegaard's Writings], 55 Volumes. Edited by Niels Jørgen Cappelørn and others. Copenhagen: Gads Forlag, 1997–.

Works by Kierkegaard (English Translation)

JP *Søren Kierkegaard's Journals and Papers*, 7 Volumes. Translated by Howard Hong and Edna Hong. Bloomington: Indiana University Press, 1967–78.

KW *Kierkegaard's Writings*, 26 Volumes. Edited by Howard Hong and Edna Hong. Princeton: Princeton University Press, 1978–2000.

CI *The Concept of Irony with Continual Reference to Socrates* (*Kierkegaard's Writings*, Vol. 2). Translated by Howard Hong and Edna Hong. Princeton: Princeton University Press, 1989 (original work published 1841).

PF *Philosophical Fragments* (*Kierkegaard's Writings*, Vol. 7). Translated by Howard Hong and Edna Hong. Princeton: Princeton University Press, 1985 (original work published 1844).

CUP *Concluding Unscientific Postscript to Philosophical Fragments* (*Kierkegaard's Writings*, Vol. 12). Translated by Howard Hong and Edna Hong. Princeton: Princeton University Press, 1992 (original work published 1846).

SUD *The Sickness Unto Death* (*Kierkegaard's Writings*, Vol. 19). Translated by Howard Hong and Edna Hong. Princeton: Princeton University Press, 1980 (original work published 1849).

M *The Moment and Late Writings* (*Kierkegaard's Writings*, Vol. 23). Translated by Howard Hong and Edna Hong. Princeton: Princeton University Press, 1998 (original work published 1854–5).

PV *The Point of View for My Work as an Author* (*Kierkegaard's Writings*, Vol. 22). Translated by Howard Hong and Edna Hong. Princeton: Princeton University Press, 1998 (original work published 1859).

Other Sources

Burnyeat, Myles (1997). The Impiety of Socrates. *Ancient Philosophy*, 17, 1–12.

Cooper, John M. (ed.) (1997). *Plato's Complete Works*. Indianapolis: Hackett Publishing.

Garff, Joakim (1998). The Eyes of Argus: *The Point of View* and Points of View on Kierkegaard's Work as an Author. In J. Ree and J. Chamberlain (eds.), *Kierkegaard: A Reader* (pp. 75–102). Oxford: Blackwell Publishers.

Hadot, Pierre (1995). The Figure of Socrates. In *Philosophy as a Way of Life* (pp. 147–78). Trans. Michael Chase, ed. Arnold I. Davidson. Oxford: Blackwell Publishers.

Hegel, G. W. F. (1995). Socrates. In *Lectures on the History of Philosophy*, Vol. 1: 384–448. Trans. E. S. Haldane. Lincoln: University of Nebraska Press (reprinted from the 1892 translation published by Kegan Paul; original work published 1840).

Himmelstrup, Jens (1924). *Søren Kierkegaards Opfattelse Af Socrates [Søren Kierkegaard's Conception of Socrates]*. Copenhagen: Arnold Busck.

Kirmmse, Bruce (2000). 'I am not a Christian' – A 'Sublime Lie'? Or: 'Without Authority,' Playing Desdemona to Christendom's Othello. In P. Houe, G. D. Marino, and S. H. Rossel (eds.), *Anthropology and Authority: Essays on Søren Kierkegaard* (pp. 129–36). Amsterdam: Rodopi.

Mackey, Louis (1986). Starting From Scratch: Kierkegaard Unfair to Hegel. In *Points of View: Readings of Kierkegaard* (pp. 1–22). Tallahassee: Florida State University Press.

Muench, Paul (2003). The Socratic Method of Kierkegaard's Pseudonym Johannes Climacus: Indirect Communication and the Art of 'Taking Away.' In P. Houe and G. D. Marino (eds.), *Søren Kierkegaard and the Word(s)* (pp. 139–50). Copenhagen: C. A. Reitzel.

—— (2005). Kierkegaard's Socratic Point of View. *Kierkegaardiana* 24.

Nagley, Winfield (1980). Kierkegaard's Early and Later View of Socratic Irony. *Thought*, 55, 271–82.

Nehamas, Alexander (1998). *The Art of Living: Socratic Reflections from Plato to Foucault*. Berkeley: University of California Press.

Olesen, Tonny Aagaard (2001). Kierkegaard's Socratic Hermeneutic in *The Concept of Irony*. In R. L. Perkins (ed.), *International Kierkegaard Commentary: The Concept of Irony* (pp. 101–22). Macon, GA: Mercer University Press.

Rubenstein, Mary-Jane (2001). Kierkegaard's Socrates: A Venture in Evolutionary Theory. *Modern Theology*, 17, 442–73.

Sarf, Harold (1983). Reflections on Kierkegaard's Socrates. *Journal of the History of Ideas*, 44(2), 255–76.

Stewart, Jon (2003). *Kierkegaard's Relations to Hegel Reconsidered*. Cambridge: Cambridge University Press.

Taylor, Mark C. (1975). Socratic Midwifery: Method and Intention of the Authorship. In *Kierkegaard's Pseudonymous Authorship: A Study of Time and the Self* (pp. 51–62). Princeton: Princeton University Press.

25

Nietzsche and "The Problem of Socrates"

JAMES I. PORTER

Nietzsche's engagement with Socrates was a lifelong adventure. References and allusions to the charismatic teacher of Plato and inadvertent founder of the Socratic school are rife in Nietzsche's published and unpublished materials from their earliest traces (1856 is the first detectable mention) to the bitter end of his productive life (the last mention is in a notebook entry from late 1888). One could easily say that Nietzsche made a career of descanting on Socrates (though at times *vilifying* would seem more apt), were it not for the fact that Socrates is only one of a series of philosophers, thinkers, artists, and other public presences who are spotlighted by Nietzsche throughout the bulk of his writings. In effect, Socrates has to compete for attention on Nietzsche's stage with the likes of Plato, Epicurus, Christ, St. Paul, Luther, Goethe, Schopenhauer, Wagner, and Dühring.

The qualification is important, as it puts into perspective what might otherwise appear to be a unique obsession with Socrates. Of equal importance is the fact that when all is said and done Socrates is the unequivocal object of neither Nietzsche's hatred nor his admiration, whatever his momentary outbursts may suggest. Categorical claims one way or the other would be too crude to capture the complexity of Nietzsche's views of Socrates, a fact that is also true of his views of Plato and Epicurus, as it is also true of most of the targets of his praise and criticism (though as a rule Greeks tend to fare better in this regard than do their modern counterparts). Thus, if we can say that Socrates has a special place in Nietzsche's heart, he is not alone in being there. Nor was Socrates Nietzsche's longest-held intellectual rival: the palm here goes to Plato by at least a few years, if we look back to the time when Nietzsche was championing the philosophical atomism of Democritus against Plato and Platonism during the late 1860s, and Socrates was an irrelevancy.

Still, the sheer duration of Nietzsche's encounter with Socrates and the intensity of that relationship bespeak a fraught interchange that needs to be unpacked. Various attempts to get at the question why Nietzsche was so invested in Socrates have been made, from articles and book chapters to entire monographs devoted to the topic. Invariably, scholars point to Nietzsche's exasperated confession (if that is what it is) from a note jotted down in 1875: "Socrates . . . stands so close to me that I am practically always waging a battle with him" (KSA 8.97, 6[3]). But the confession explains less than it can be made to seem to do, in part simply by begging the twofold question, Who is "Socrates," and what does Nietzsche mean by him? The first half of the question was a long-standing issue known as "the Socratic problem" at least since the early nineteenth century (see Montuori 1981, 1992; Patzer 1987: 1–40; Murray 2002), although the problem (expressed as a disputed legacy) first arose soon after Socrates' death (Xenophon, *Recollections of Socrates* 1.4.1; Aristotle, *Metaphysics* M 1078b27–31). The second half of the question, *Nietzsche's* Socratic problem as it were, has had its own troubled history. Despite the tantalizing glimpse of a fraternal struggle motivated by profound psychological ambivalence, and even if some like Kaufmann (1974) have sought to palliate this view, scholarly common sense has been hard to quash and, psychodramas aside, the net results have all tended to look predictably alike: if the similarities between the two thinkers are striking, so are the differences.[1] But even this is to assume a clearer idea of what is being weighed and compared than the case warrants.

The problem with "the problem of Socrates" in Nietzsche has to do with the range of meanings that the name *Socrates* has for Nietzsche at any given point in his career. These are not reducible to a single compact entity, and least of all the much-disputed entity, the "historical Socrates," of which the Nietzschean half of the problem is a reflex. Ambivalence is a poor index to this latter problem or its solution precisely because of the ambiguity of the target. It won't do to saddle Nietzsche with simultaneously loving and hating Socrates out of an ambivalent self-regard (Bertram 1965 [1st ed. 1918]; Nehamas 1985: 30), or with competing with Socrates for philosophical distinction, however this comes to be understood (Dannhauser 1974; Nehamas 1998: 5), if "Socrates" is not a fixed entity in Nietzsche's eyes but is a constantly moving and changing target. "Nietzsche's ambivalence towards Socrates" is for all of these reasons, and also because of the very ambiguity of "ambivalence," an empty phrase. As we shall see, Nietzsche inherits several different versions of Socrates, he interprets these creatively, and he adds a few of his own. What is more, his writings, being the fluid and dynamic medium they are, pick freely from among this range depending upon his momentary polemical and rhetorical requirements. As a consequence, any attempt to pin down Nietzsche's presumed view of Socrates and to attach it to a singular fixed meaning, or to anything other than his ever-changing use and multiply layered understanding of Socrates, is bound to come up hopelessly short.

What follows is less an attempt to propose a new solution to Nietzsche's Socratic problem than an effort at clarification. My intention is to outline some of the ways in which any approach to the problem of Socrates in Nietzsche must be made. These will include approaches to the problem made to date as well as some approaches that have not yet to my knowledge been attempted. The result ought to yield a richer and less reductive picture of Socrates in the writings of Nietzsche. To return to our starting point, where Socrates does perhaps have a unique claim to distinction among Nietzsche's pantheon of great names in the history of thought is in his counting as Nietzsche's most *variously imagined* rival. A good deal of this variety will, I hope, emerge over the course of this chapter.

A Divided Socrates: Ambiguity or Ambivalence?

One of the chief problems in assessing Nietzsche's attitude towards Socrates is going to be the question whether Nietzsche's view of Socrates is divided or whether Socrates is merely divided in Nietzsche's view of him. The problem may come down to question of deciding between ambivalence and ambiguity, in other words. A brief survey of the evolution of Socrates' role in Nietzsche's thought can help clarify the issue.

Nietzsche's most concerted and memorable confrontation with Socrates took place in his first and most spectacular publication, *The Birth of Tragedy* (1872), a work in which Socrates is tarred for hastening the demise of Greek culture and for ushering in the modern world of rational decadence. But Nietzsche's encounters with Socrates predate even the studies that lead up to *The Birth of Tragedy*, for example, the lecture "Socrates and Greek Tragedy," which was published privately in 1871, and their associated notes, which reach back to 1869. Prior to that Nietzsche's interests are for the most part tamely philological and historical: his efforts are aimed at slotting Socrates in the succession of ancient philosophers and their schools, tracked according to their innovations and their evolving literary output (or lack thereof, as in Socrates' case), a project to which he would return after 1872, at least in the notebooks and in the classroom, and which he would pursue to the end of his teaching days at Basel in 1879. Only, in the latter phase Nietzsche's historiography carries the burden of the animus against Socrates that Nietzsche had cultivated in the run-up to *The Birth of Tragedy*; and Socrates suddenly assumes a position of central and inestimable importance that he had never enjoyed in the earlier studies in the history of philosophy from the 1860s.

It is here, after 1872, that Nietzsche develops his famous contrast between "pre-Socratic" and "post-Socratic" philosophers (a break named by Cicero, *Tusculan Disposi-tions* 5.10 and understood among earlier philosophers, including Aristotle; see Laks 2002), or rather a series of contrasts in which Socrates marks a watershed in the history of philosophy and a turn for the worse – the beginning of the end, or else the start of philosophy and reflection as we know it today. Earlier, Nietzsche was content to see in Socrates a minor innovator who did not invent ethical philosophy *per se* but merely introduced the practice of ethical definition (BAW 4.81; 1867/68) – a picture Nietzsche modified considerably in his lectures on the Platonic dialogues from 1871 to 1872 (KGW 2, pt. 4, pp. 1–188, esp. 152–63) and in the final lecture on the "Preplatonic Philosophers" delivered over the course of three or four semesters (1869–70[?], 1872, 1875/6, 1876). Now, and henceforth, Socrates takes on world-historical importance, as do his predecessors. The whole picture is inflated and steeped in high drama. And Socrates is drawn as the major impediment to the evolution of human thought and practical achievement.

The Socratic moment is no longer characterized in terms of the contrast, made famous in *The Birth of Tragedy*, between Apollo and Dionysus, which has lost its relevance as an organizing device, but is instead viewed as an event internal to the history of philosophy itself: "I conceive of [the Presocratics] as *precursors to a reforma-tion* of the Greeks: but not of Socrates"; "with Empedocles and Democritus the Greeks were well on their way towards taking the correct measure of human existence, its unreason, its suffering; they never reached this goal, thanks to Socrates"; "the earlier Greek world displayed its powers in a series of philosophers. With Socrates this display comes to a sudden halt: he attempts to produce himself and to reject all traditions"; the Presocratics don't have "'the loathsome pretension to happiness,' as philosophers do from Socrates on. Not everything revolves around the condition of their souls"; and, finally, "[the Greeks] never found their philosophers and reformers; one need only compare Plato: he was diverted by Socrates" (KSA 8.102, 104, 105, 107; 6[14], 6[17], 6[18], 6[25]; 1875). Clearly, in this phase Nietzsche has abandoned the apparatus of *The Birth of Tragedy* and resumed his earlier study of the history of ancient philosophy. But this is only a temporary adjustment, and all will change once Nietzsche leaves his university post in 1879.

From this point on, Nietzsche's picture of Socrates broadens. The focus is less technical, less historical and philological (as is only to be expected with the change of audience) and more cultural-historical and more inflected with world-historical importance. At the same time, Nietzsche returns to the intense psychological analysis he had given to Socrates in *The Birth of Tragedy*, even if that analysis was never really aimed at Socrates as a person so much as at Socrates as an event, or (better yet) an *idea*. And although Socrates never again retains Nietzsche's undivided attention that he had enjoyed during the 1870s, apart from one section of *The Twilight of the Idols* (1887) titled, aptly enough, "The Problem of Socrates," Socrates' name continues to dot the published and unpublished writings, functioning as a mnemonic and a chiffre or shorthand (a "semiotic," as Nietzsche would say) for any number of themes. But despite his low profile in the later writings, in point of fact Socrates can be said to come into his own once again – albeit this time as an idea, as a role and a posture, and as a voice. But before explaining this new conceptualization and especially this new *deployment* of Socrates by Nietzsche, it will be useful to outline some of the ramifications in Nietzsche's later presentations of Socrates the person, and not least of all his multiple stances towards this philosopher.

The following note from 1888 captures well Nietzsche's view(s) of Socrates at the time, as well as sounding many of the themes that run through Nietzsche's different versions of Socrates, early and late. It also captures one of the central puzzles of the Socratic problem in Nietzsche mentioned at the start of this section, namely, whether for Nietzsche Socrates is divided in himself or whether Nietzsche's view of him is. Although familiar from *The Will to Power* (§432), what follows preserves the original layout of Nietzsche's notebook entry:

The problem of Socrates.
  The two antitheses:

      the *tragic* disposition   ⎫
                        ⎬   measured against the law of life
      the *Socratic* disposition ⎭

: to what extent the Socratic attitude is a phenomenon of *décadence*
: to what extent, however, there is nonetheless a robust health and strength (*eine starke Gesundheit und Kraft*) in the whole *habitus*, in the dialectics, efficiency, and self-discipline of the scientific man (– the health of the *plebeian*; his wickedness,

esprit frondeur, his cunning, his *canaille au fond* are held in check by *shrewdness*; "ugly").

> *Making ugly*:
>> self-mockery
>> dialectical dryness
>> shrewdness as *tyrant* in opposition to "the tyrant" (the instinct).

Everything about Socrates is exaggerated, eccentric, caricature, a *buffo* with the embodied instincts of Voltaire;

> — he discovers a new form of *agon* [contest] –
> — he is the first fencing master to the leading circles of Athens
> — he represents nothing but the *highest form of shrewdness*; he calls it "virtue"
> (– he guessed it was *deliverance*: he was not by choice *shrewd*, he was this *de rigueur*
> — to have oneself under control, so as to enter into battle with reason and *not* with affects – the *cunning* of Spinoza – the unraveling of the errors caused by affects . . . to discover how one can capture anyone in whom one produces affects, that affects proceed illogically . . . practice in self-mockery so as to damage the *feeling of rancor* at its roots.

I try to understand from what partial and idiosyncratic states the Socratic problem is to be derived: his equation of reason = virtue = happiness. It was with this absurdity of a doctrine of identity that he *fascinated*: ancient philosophy never again freed itself <from this fascination> . . .

(KSA 13.268; 14[92] = WP 432; trans. corrected and adapted)

The picture given here is fundamental to understanding not only the variety of roles played by Socrates in Nietzsche (which is even more important, I believe, than determining Nietzsche's view or views of Socrates), but also the dynamic roots of Nietzsche's philosophy in its maturest phases. The point is not just that Socrates can be said to be ambivalently admired or detested by Nietzsche – say, that he is admired for some reasons and detested for others. It is that Nietzsche constructs Socrates as despicable and admirable here *for the very same reasons*. And it is this last consideration which plays serious havoc with any readings that would try too hard either to underscore Nietzsche's enmity or to eliminate his revulsion to Socrates (Kaufmann 1974: 13, is an example of the latter, counteracting the former tendency, exemplified by Brinton 1941: 83).[2] For it is plain that the very characteristics that make Socrates an exemplary and indeed a *potent* decadent are what make him both powerful and magnificent and, as Nietzsche says of him in *The Birth of Tragedy*, one of "the very greatest instinctive forces" ever known (§13). And yet even there, in the same section, this very endowment earns Socrates the label of "monstrosity" – "a monstrosity *per defectum*."

This phenomenon of double-voiced reading is in fact common in Nietzsche, although it is rarely noted as such. It is also an ineluctable consequence of the way in which Nietzsche configures his moral universe. Such is the case with "the maggot 'man'" of *On the Genealogy of Morals*, First Essay, sec. 11: "the 'tame man,' the hopelessly mediocre and insipid man, [who] has already learned to feel himself as the goal and zenith, as the meaning of history, as 'higher man',," and whom Nietzsche accordingly both reviles and (willy-nilly) admires "as something at least relatively well-constituted, at least still capable of living, *at least affirming life*" (italics added) – and, it needs to be stressed, of living a life equipped with all the signs of an "active," assertive consciousness of the ascendant spirits, capable of despising the sprawling masses, though the lowly entity ought, by all rights, to represent the antithesis of these hyperactive creatures. Nor is this the only instance in which *les extrêmes se touchent* in Nietzsche's gallery of rogues and heroes. Indeed, such approximations of seemingly opposite "moralities" are everyday occurrences (see Porter 1998).

Robust health, strength, efficiency, self-mastery, wicked cunning, shrewd dialectics, plebeian *habitus*, the capacity to seduce and fascinate, all the while under the delusion of an ethics and a set of principles gone (in Nietzsche's view) awry – all of these attributes of Socrates attest to an extraordinary strength of mind, will, and character. But they also attest to a primal *optimism* towards life and its possibilities that would lead Nietzsche, in his seventeenth lecture on the Preplatonics (KGW 2, pt. 4.354), to proclaim Socrates the first "philosopher of life" (*Lebensphilosoph*) in the Greek tradition, and in his notebooks from 1875 (KSA 8.104, 6[17]) to dub Socrates the first of the "virtuosos of life" (*Lebensvirtuosen*) – a risky breed, primarily owing to their terrible fragility, and very much resembling Nietzsche's own later-developed category of "free spirits" (Socrates is in fact labeled a "free spirit" in *Human, All Too Human* I, §§433 and 437).

Instinctually driven to ward off the instincts, rational but flawed and absurdly so, shrewdly damping down, or simply masking, his own and others' reactivity (*Rancune* – rancor and vengefulness), Socrates is a heady mix of contrasts, inconsistent to the core and yet somehow whole. To affirm him is *eo ipso* to affirm a jumble of contradictions. As Nietzsche's portrait suggests, the question is not whether Nietzsche was drawn to Socrates, but how anyone could *fail* to be drawn to him. But Nietzsche's portrait of Socrates is also shot through with ironies that remain to be explored. The note from 1888 above adumbrates all of this, and it points to some of the other ways in which Socrates comes to be figured in Nietzsche's corpus. For the sake of clarity and emphasis, I will simply list these, before going on to comment on them.

Socratic Constructions

On a comprehensive view of Nietzsche's writings, we can say that Socrates is constructed in a variety of ways, whether as:

- the last of the Preplatonics
- the first Socratic and the beginning of post-Socratic philosophy
- an expression of "Socratism" (a "tendency" that preexisted Socrates and that flourished long after him)
- a proto-Cynic
- an ethical innovator (the first dialectician, seeker of ethical concepts and definitions, the inventor of the *elenchus*, or cross-examination mode of philosophical inquiry)
- claiming knowledge of moral truth
- claiming ignorance of moral truth
- a supreme ironist

- the first philosopher of life, and a true lover of life
- robust, powerful, vital, and erotic
- a sworn enemy of sensuality and the senses, of instincts and the unconscious, and of life, as well as of myth, music, culture, and science
- an exemplar of Greek optimism, rationalism, etc., restlessly and instinctually *driven* to rationalism
- a pessimist towards life who sought to "correct" being and reality
- the first self-producing and self-fashioning philosopher, who turned his focus exclusively inward, to the soul (more than to his "subjectivity," as Hegel would have it, and Kierkegaard as well); and an ascetic, who arrived at his ethical substance by denials and deprivations
- the first modern, viz., non-Greek, ugly, diseased and decadent, proto-"Alexandrian," but also proto-Christian, rational, scientific, weak and epigonal, a living "caricature" of what came before; hence also a major "turning-point" in world-history
- a literary fiction, a "fluid" literary "caricature," indeed a "myth"
- a conversationalist and nonwriter, dwelling entirely in speech (including his inner "acoustic hallucinations," those of his *daemon*); virtually a *voice* (Nietzsche notices, dilating on an ancient testimonium, how one of the seductive lures of Socrates lay in his "extremely captivating voice," which could enslave his interlocutors), and at the extreme, a pastiche of voices and of voicings
- a Platonic invention (as "the Platonic Socrates" of the Platonic dialogues)
- a Platonic Idea (and hence, Apolline)
- Plato's creator
- Plato's corruptor
- "a semiotic for Plato"
- demonic, mad ("Socrates *mainomenos*"), Dionysian, music-making
- historically unascertainable
- seductively and essentially inscrutable, insoluble, a "problem," a *mysterium*.

This list is not meant to be exhaustive, but it is fairly representative and it should suffice to bring home the essentials of Nietzsche's varied constructions of Socrates – nor should we imagine that they all owe their origin to Nietzsche, who inherited a tradition rich in Socratic images and cheerfully made use of the whole of it. As a quick glance suggests, while some of these attributes are mutually reinforcing, a good many of them are irreconcilably at odds. By comprehending the entirety of the Socratic tradition and activating so many of its registers at any given time, Nietzsche's representations of Socrates achieve a maximal plurality and fluidity of their own. As a result, they collectively render the name *Socrates* in his own writings referentially unstable and nearly opaque – in short, a "problem."

This instability is Nietzsche's way of reflecting the traditional "problem of Socrates" mentioned at the start of this chapter. Socrates left no writings, and his teachings and his identity necessarily come filtered through ancient sources, many of them contemporary, but often conflicting or competing in their perspectives. After his death in 399, a veritable "Socratic literature" (known as *Sokratikoi logoi*) sprang up, as Xenophon, Aeschines of Sphettos (the Socratic), Antisthenes, Phaedo of Elis, and others sought to lay claim to the legacy of Socrates, as it were in an apostolic succession. Plato's project was the most ambitious attempt at hijacking this legacy, and he largely succeeded in displacing the other fourth-century contenders – and, in the process, in assimilating Socrates to his own project, and ultimately to himself. As Nietzsche writes in a note captioned "Plato's jealousy" from 1875, "[Plato] wants to monopolize Socrates *for himself*. He penetrates him with himself, thinking to beautify him, καλὸς Σωκράτης ["beautiful Socrates"], to wrest him away from all the Socratics, to depict himself [*sic*; a possible slip for "him"?] as continuing to exist [even after his death]. But he presents him in an entirely unhistorical light, dangerously heading down a slippery slope (as Wagner does with Beethoven and Shakespeare)" (KSA 8.499, 27[75]).

Nietzsche the philologist is careful to highlight this process of assimilation at work in Plato when he chooses to, or to contrast it with the known alternative perspectives on the historical Socrates, some of them of more recent vintage, whether philological like Zeller's or philosophical like Hegel's. But in the final analysis, Nietzsche's Socrates, or rather the composite effect of his various imaginings of Socrates, attests to the irrecuperability of the historical Socrates just by leaving him in the unresolved condition of a "problem" that he has occupied since his memory was first recorded. To return to the question of Nietzsche's stance towards Socrates, to suppose that Nietzsche stood one way or another towards Socrates, whether hostilely, admiringly, or ambivalently, is to erase the very knowledge that Socrates is a variously transmitted idea. It is to assume that Nietzsche somehow forgot what he knew and what was foundational (or rather, fatal) to his basic imagination of "Socrates." How, after all, can one compete with a fictionalized and fetishized historical construct?

The "Socratic Question" thus has more or less the same status for Nietzsche that the "Homeric Question" had for him, the question of Homer's identity which Nietzsche inherited from the philological tradition and dealt with in detail alongside his philosophical studies at Basel (Porter 2000b: ch. 1; Porter 2004).[3] In each case, at issue is not a person or individual so much as the transmission, projection, and construction of one – with Nietzsche's own version or versions occupying the most recent link(s) in the chain. *Socrates*, in Nietzsche's writings, represents the tradition that claims to represent Socrates. None of this need prevent Nietzsche from ever having imagined himself standing in close proximity to Socrates, whether as his rival or thrall. Ideas can be strangely compelling – witness Plato on Nietzsche's reading of him, compelled by the "*ideal*" and "*image*" of "*the dying Socrates*" to burn his own poetry and to sit at the feet of the master (*The Birth of Tragedy* §13; first two italics added). Nor is Socrates a random assemblage of ideas, as Nietzsche construes him: there is a coherence to the attributes listed above, which is both historical and conceptual, even if these attributes are often shot through with difficulty and aporia. But what all of this does go to show is that Nietzsche's proximity to Socrates can no longer be taken at face value. His proximity is not in the first instance to a personality who modeled a way of being in the world but, precisely, to an assemblage of effects – a "Socrates-effect" – the net effect (which is not to say consistent sum) of the ways in which Socrates' image has ramified in the philosophical and cultural traditions since the end of the Athenian fifth century down to the contemporary present (see Schmidt 1969: 370).

Let us run through some of these attributes a little more closely, if also in a somewhat abbreviated form, starting at one of their central points of intersection, which is also one of their central points of aporia, namely, the circular problem that Socrates

413

is as much an invention of literary tradition, and in particular of Plato, as he is the (unlocatable, unascertainable, unknowable) source of inspiration for that tradition. Something of the same paradox governs Kierkegaard's reading of the Socratic problem in his dissertation, *The Concept of Irony with Continual Reference to Socrates* (1841). There, Kierkegaard had essentially turned the insoluble problem of the historical Socrates back on itself by reducing Socrates to a chiffre of his own uncertain identity, an enigma not only to us, but also *to himself* – hence, literally "knowing nothing," "infinitely ambiguous," empty, a mask concealing nothing, a pure abstraction of a self, and ultimately a soundless, expressionless (unvoiced, unutterable) idea of pure nega- tion (whence, ironic in the highest philosophical sense) – in more recent parlance, a "vanishing mediator" (Jameson 1973), though Kierkegaard would add, one "vanishing at every moment" (Kierkegaard 1989: 258), en route to the development of modern subjectivity and a fuller spirituality. In a word, if Socrates could not be known after his death, this was because he could not even know himself while he was alive: the search for his identity began with the Socratic mission itself.

Similarly, though less abstractly, Nietzsche's Socrates embodies the contradictions of his own historically elusive construction in his very conception. But he also stands for far more than the individual who lived from c. 469–399 BCE. As with Kierkegaard, Nietzsche's Socrates, from 1872 on, is the personification of an idea: he embodies a refinement in the development of the Western self, and as a consequence he is a cultural icon, larger than life. A telling notebook entry from 1885 reads:

> I believe that the magic of Socrates was this: that he had one soul, and behind that another, and behind that another. Xenophon lay down to sleep in the foremost one, Plato in the second, and then again in the third, only here Plato went to bed with his own, second soul. Plato is himself somebody with many recesses and foregrounds. (KSA 11.440; 34[66])

"Socrates" here is both the site of construction (interpretation, projection) by his clos- est contemporaries, and he is the cave-like personality whose complex inner construc- tion – he is "hidden, reserved, subterranean" (*Twilight of the Idols*, "The Problem of Socrates," 4) – allows for and literally invites these multiple interventions (this is his "magic"). The formal identity of the two functions, inner and outer, is complete. Is Socrates anything other than this identity? Doubtfully. And to acknowledge this fact about Socrates is to deny him an identity in the usual sense of the word.

The kernel of this curious logic of (non)identity was developed already in *The Birth of Tragedy* (see Porter 2000a). We have already seen how "*the dying Socrates* became the new ideal, never seen before, of noble Greek youths: above all, the typical Hellenic youth, Plato, prostrated himself before this image with all the ardent devotion of his enthusiastic soul" (§13; trans. Kaufmann). In one sense then, Socrates, transformed into an image and an idea, fulfilled all the prerequisites of a full-blooded Platonic ideal, which it only remained for Plato to flesh out in his own philosophical writings by fashioning his philosophy in the Socratic image. And so one can indeed say, along with Nietzsche and inverting the standard intuition, that "Plato is a Socratic work of art" (KSA 7.224, 8[13]). But in another sense the opposite continues to be the case: surely it is *Socrates* who is Plato's work of art, at least the Socrates of the Platonic dialogues, "the dialectical hero of the Platonic drama" (*The Birth of Tragedy* §14). Nietzsche will have it both ways, not depending on how the mood strikes him, but in his core conception of Socrates.

On the other hand, to focus on what is specifically Socratic in Socrates, to worry about his core identity, whether this is felt to be obscured or simply lost and irrecuperable, is to get at the problem from the wrong end. For in another respect, Socrates is, we can only say, a most *un*-Socratic creature even on Nietzsche's apparent schema from around 1872: with his lips puffed up and his baggy paunch and bulging eyes, he bears a direct resemblance to Silenus, the companion of Dionysus, as was noticed in antiquity starting with Plato himself in the *Symposium*, long before Nietzsche underscored the fact again, explicitly in "The Dionysian Worldview" (KSA 7.544), and implicitly in the whole of *The Birth of Tragedy* (Hadot 1995: ch. 5 ["The Figure of Socrates"]; Porter 2000a). The connection is disconcerting, indeed disabling, given the way Nietzsche bills Dionysianism (standing for ecstasy, disorderliness, music, dance, orgy, the unconscious, and a contempt for appearances and existence) and Socratism as irreconcilable polar opposites. Until, that is, one realizes that the two share quite a lot in common, starting with the last-named feature: the belief, which both the god and the philosopher are more than happy to propagate, in "the essential perversity and reprehensibility of what exists" (*The Birth of Tragedy* §13). But what they share is not Dionysianism, but its myth and ideal – in other words, *Platonism*. In Nietzsche's revised Greek mythology, Dionysus and Dionysianism are in fact rooted in the same phenomenon as Socratism, what Nietzsche glosses as a prototypical Greek "idealism" (KSA 7.72, 3[43]; 7.75, 3[53]), which he conceives as a kind of Platonism before Plato; and the tutelary gods Apollo and Dionysus are in fact exemplifications of this idealizing tendency. Indeed, as puzzling as it may sound to us, Nietzsche is perfectly content to describe these two divinities, both in *The Birth of Tragedy* and elsewhere, as *Platonic Forms*, the one being "*the Idea of appearance* itself," the other "*the Idea that alone has true reality* . . . , [i.e.,] in the Platonic sense" (KGW 3, pt. 5.1, pp. 172–3 with Porter 2000a: 99–100; second italics added).

Seen in this broader light, Socrates is anything but an aberration of Greek culture. Quite the contrary, he is its inevitable product, a view that Nietzsche would continue to espouse even in the later works (e.g., *Twilight of the Idols*, "The Problem of Socrates," 9). Indeed, all the relevant features of Socrates' innovations can be seen to have been well underway generations before Socrates arrived on the scene to crystallize them, with the notable assistance of his contemporary and kinsman, Euripides. In this respect, Socrates is to all intents and purposes *irrelevant* to the story that unfolds around him. At the very least a catalyst for the final chain reactions that occur at the end of the fifth century in Athens, at most he is the sign of a cultural vector with a force all its own, that of the sinking fate of an ideal Greece, doomed to decline from its first origins: its strong tendency to idealism, to narcosis, to denial of reality, and so on (Porter 2000a: 101–5 and *passim*). Or so the story goes. Whether "ideal Greece" is in fact anything other than a fantasy of the Western imagination is a fair question to ask. If it is such a fantasy-object, then it has to be confessed that Greece never suffered a real decline, but only an imaginary, ideal one. Nietzsche's deepest ironies towards Socrates and the antiquity he comes to represent owe everything, I believe, to the knowledge that this is the case.

Socratic Voices

The single man (*der Einzelne*), the "individual" (*das Individuum*), as people and philosophers have hitherto understood this, is an error: he does not constitute a separate entity all by himself (*er ist nichts für sich*), an atom, a "link in the chain," something merely inherited from the past – he constitutes the entire single line of mankind up to and including himself. (*Twilight of the Idols*, "Expeditions of an Untimely Man," 33; trans. Hollingdale, adapted)

If we take Nietzsche at his word, whether in the foregoing analysis or in the passage just quoted, Socrates cannot be a self-standing individual who emblematizes the art of how to become an individual. And the recent trend that follows Greenblatt or Foucault and would see in Nietzsche's Socrates a model of a self-fashioning subject, an individual who styles himself into an idiosyncratic and unique work of art, while it can draw comfort in some of Nietzsche's pronouncements, will have to face embarrassment at other pronouncements by him. To take this line is also to assume that Nietzsche was modeling his own personality – rather naively, I think – on one particular strand within the assemblage of Socratic constructions that he had at his disposal thanks to the tradition – namely, the image of a "classically" balanced and harmonious Socrates in control of his instincts and mastering himself in good Apollonian fashion (Nehamas 1998: 138–9) – as opposed to modeling himself on the plurality of Socrateses that the same tradition records, the many-layered and many-faceted figure of "Socrates" that Nietzsche's writings trace from start to finish.

Why assume that Nietzsche identified with a reductive reading of Socrates and not with a generative and more explosive one? Why not assume, in other words, that Nietzsche was drawn to the very *source* of the enigma of Socrates – not to Socrates as a clichéd superficiality, which the image of the statues of the Sileni from Alcibiades' speech in Plato's *Symposium* (216e–17a) in any case shatters ("I believe that it matters that [Socrates] was the son of a sculptor. If these plastic arts were ever to speak, they would appear superficial to us; in Socrates, the son of a sculptor, *their superficiality surfaced*," KSA 8.107, 6[23]; italics added), but to Socrates as a difficult because unlocatable identity, a personality that refuses identification in the ways we have been witnessing throughout this chapter, or as in the following tribute to Socrates from *Human, All Too Human*, written during Nietzsche's so-called middle period:

If all goes well, the time will come when one will take up the memorabilia of Socrates rather than the Bible as a guide to morals and reason. . . . *The pathways of the most various philosophical modes of life lead back to him*; at bottom they are the modes of life of the various temperaments confirmed and established by reason and habit and all of them directed towards joy in living and in one's own self; *from which one might conclude that Socrates' most personal characteristic was a participation in every temperament.* ("The Wanderer and his Shadow," §86; trans. Hollingdale; italics added)

It is this extraordinary availability, not to say generative productivity, of character and spirit that is arguably Socrates' most compelling "feature" in Nietzsche's eyes, and, again arguably, the single most characteristic feature of Nietzsche's *own* personality – or rather persona – in his own writings as well. Socrates' defining trait is paradoxically his lack of any defining identity, owing to his participation in every identity, his availability to being "voiced" by a dialogically formed tradition. His style is to have no style in particular but to participate in every style, not least of all in the way he weaves in and out of engagement with others in a public arena – which is, after all, how he constitutes his self: for this is Socrates' defining *praxis*. Similarly, surely one way of reading Nietzsche's writings is to hear in them a polyphony and often cacophony of enacted and staged voices, frequently borrowed (or better yet, "sampled") from a vast cultural repertoire, or else imagined as props, but in any event mingling with one another, theatricalized and hyperbolized, in all registers and tonalities, and at all decibels, from shrill and deafening to barely audible. His frequent use of inverted commas – quotation of (fictive) voices stolen from the registers of culture at large – is only the most conspicuous example of this kind of mimetism. Leaving out these marks is by far the more common practice. Nietzsche is a self-conscious poser and a poseur (the tonality of his voice is everywhere that of a *falsetto*). He is constantly performing in the presence of an audience, as before a camera, but slyly so (often pretending that nobody is watching). All of which makes locating Nietzsche's voice in his writings supremely difficult.

A contemporary reviewer of *Beyond Good and Evil*, encountering the work for the first time, was struck by this very fact: "Nor is this any new philosophy that he is offering up for us, but rather a prelude, an overture. Manifold voices and melodies can be heard to ring and sing, sometimes barely hinted at, at other times more elaborated . . ." (Michaelis 1886). The disintegration of Nietzsche's name and voice in his twilight letters following his mental collapse in 1889 is but a further manifestation of this same penchant: "Though this is unpleasant and goes against my modesty, I am basically every name in history" (letter to Jacob Burckhardt from January 6, 1889). But Nietzsche's voice is *already* disintegrative in his earlier writings, never "properly" his. Indeed, this propensity, this *style* of thinking and writing, is detectable from its very first traces. As he notes in *Ecce Homo*, "considering that *the multiplicity of inner states is in my case extraordinary*, there exists in my case the possibility of *many* styles – altogether *the most manifold (vielfachste) art of style* any man has ever had at his disposal" ("Why I Write Such Good Books," 4; italics added). Nietzsche's voice is forever a projection of others' voices. Occasionally, Socrates is one of these other voices. But the very feature of this style is in itself Socratic, as the passage from "The Wanderer and its Shadow," written a decade earlier, suffices to show.

Although Socrates is the ultimate inspiration, nonetheless Nietzsche nearest literary and philosophical kin might well be Rameau's nephew in Diderot's dialogue of that name (*Le Neveu de Rameau*, dating from 1761–74). Like the hysterical actings-out of Diderot's pantomimist, who totters between (among other things) being a latter-day Socrates and a Cynic (see Jauss 1983), part-sage and part-*buffo*, when he is not basically every name in history and then some ("at such times I recall everything others have said, everything I have read, and add everything I can get from my own resources, which in this respect are amazingly productive," Diderot 1966: 83), Nietzsche's texts are a "dialogization" in the sense that he is continuously exploring the inner voices and poses – the self-projections – of emblematic agencies (nobles or slaves, artists or priests), who are in fact complex psychological and conceptual portraits – imaginary projections – drawn from a repertoire of public discourses and fantasies, and most often giving voice to their repressed incoherence. The sheer hyperbole of this extroverted acting-out is part of its subversiveness, as is the lure to identification, which leads into an incoherence that mimics that which his voices echo. Nietzsche's texts tend to activate all of these registers all at once, in a theater of voices – which is why his texts are so attractive, so vulnerable to conflicting interpretations, and ultimately so hard to "read aloud" (*Beyond Good and Evil*, §247), let alone to describe.

Nietzsche, I believe, cultivated this manner of self-presentation, and he seems to suggest that *mutatis mutandis* Socrates did so too, before the tradition took over this function for him – most immediately and powerfully of all starting with Plato. Whence the uncanny *fluidity* of Socrates, both in antiquity and in Nietzsche's uses of him. Compare the following note from 1876: "The Platonic Socrates is properly speaking a caricature, for he is overloaded with characteristics that could never coexist in a single person. Plato is not enough of a dramatist to capture (*festzuhalten*) the image of Socrates in even a single dialogue. [His Socrates] is therefore not only a caricature, but a *fluid* one" (KSA 8.327, 18[47]; italics added). The term *caricature* is intelligible in literary terms, but what are we to make of its reoccurrence in Nietzsche's description of the presumed historical Socrates in the passage quoted earlier?: "Everything is exaggerated, eccentric, caricature, in Socrates, a *buffo* with the embodied instincts of Voltaire" – assuming, that is, that "Socrates" is meant to stand for the historical and not the historically contaminated philosopher (a distinction that Nietzsche, most of the time, is unwilling to press after, perhaps wisely so). On the other hand, it is not inconceivable that Socrates was in real life a caricature of his environment, or that Nietzsche imagined him to be this – this shape-shifting eccentricity, this excess of vitality with its foolish and at times cruel edge – or that this is just the image that Socrates, or Nietzsche's imagined version of him, sought in practice to cultivate and project, theatrically performing extroversions of himself – playful, dramatic roles much like those worn and discarded in a happy, endless succession by Rameau's Socratic-Cynic nephew – as he attempted "to produce himself." At any rate, Socrates so conceived is only tenuously "one," and hardly the image of a classical harmonized self.

The most recent full-length study of Plato's philosophical art suits these readings well. It finds a plurality of "Socrateses" in the Platonic corpus (limiting the count to three, although the second of these, the "aporetic" Socrates, is in itself indeterminate enough). It makes the interesting speculation, previously mooted by Gilbert Ryle (Ryle 1966: ch. 2; see Usener 1994: 189, 207–12), that Plato's dialogues were meant to be read aloud and thus "performed" and enacted for pedagogical reasons. And it casts the philosophical implications of the dialogue form in terms of a tension between embodiedness and particularity (or if one prefers, the plural materialities of the voice) on the one hand, and the "disembodied" quality of the "philosophical ideal" on the other (Blondell 2002: 9–11, 23–7, and 48–52). One need only add the historical link to Cynic role-playing, understood as a moral provocation and ethical practice in its own right aimed at engaging the audience in a radical questioning of conventions and comfortable beliefs, to complete the picture (see Branham and Goulet-Cazé 1996). None of these implications will have been lost on Nietzsche, who was keenly interested in precisely these sorts of issues. Needless to say, Plato frowned on all such polymorphous perversity and any Protean multiplicity of forms, as he makes especially clear in the *Ion*, *Gorgias*, and *Republic*, even as he found these to be an ineluctable element of all

418

representation and human perception. And so to Nietzsche's images of Socrates we would need to add two further traits: as a fluid caricature of an identity he is profoundly un-Platonic (though perhaps on a revised or expanded notion of Platonism he would be Platonic after all); and he is equally, or to that same extent, a profoundly *human* creature.

Thematizations

As we've seen, Socrates in Nietzsche's corpus oscillates back and forth between an embodied and disembodied presence, between being a flesh-and-blood character with a definite historical location on the one hand, and a voice, idea, or posture that can be resurrected at will on the other. These two functions can, of course, overlap: ideas can refer to Socratic doctrines (such as questions of moral knowledge), or they can vaguely gesture at Socrates across a transhistorical divide (as does the very idea of Socrates). Either way, "Socrates" lends himself to an extended use or application, which might be called *thematization*, whereby his presence can be evoked through abstract allusions even where he is not explicitly named. And as such he can be called upon to lend coherence to an argument or structural unity to a series of arguments, or else, at the limit, to an entire work.

Thus Spoke Zarathustra (1883–5) has been read through this kind of interpretative lens, for instance as an extended parody of Socrates and critique of Socratic irony, or simply as an outbidding of Socrates through the figure of the cave-dwelling sage dispensing a new, Nietzschean wisdom (Conway 1988; Gerhardt 2001: 315–16, 317–19).[4] Similarly, the entirety of *Ecce Homo* (1888) parodies the Socratic *voice* and *posture* through hyperbole and distortion – the first two full sections are titled "Why I am So Wise" and "Why I am So Clever" (Kaufmann 1974: 408–9 notices the allusions to Socrates) – and through an impossible (because Platonic) contrast – the next section is titled "Why I Write Such Good Books." Taken as a whole, the image that comes to mind is of a Nietzsche dressed up in Socratic garb, ranting against German mores (and Socratic philosophy) – much in the manner of Rembrandt or Cindy Sherman, two agile performance artists (of roles and identities) and semi-transparent impersonators – and then switching roles at the turn of a page to become Socrates' successor, or inventor, or else his amanuensis, namely Plato, the consummate stylist who *could* boast to have written such good books, at least in Nietzsche's estimation (*The Birth of Tragedy* §14; "Introduction to the Study of the Platonic Dialogue," KGW 2, pt. 4, pp. 8–9; "History of Greek Literature" [1874–6], KGW 2, pt. 5, pp. 197–8, 321; *Human, All Too Human* II, §214). *Beyond Good and Evil* (published in 1886) could similarly be read through a Socratic filter. Only here, in the place of parody, outbidding, or theatrical mimicry and histrionics, what one finds is a curious mixture of explicit critique and implicit cooption. In closing, let us consider how Nietzsche can extend his uses of Socrates in often inexplicit ways, taking *Beyond Good and Evil* as our final case-study.

The work opens with a salvo of Socrates-bashing and persiflage, albeit this time *in defense of Plato*, whom Nietzsche describes, rather uncharacteristically, as "the most magnificent growth of antiquity": "Did the wicked Socrates corrupt him after all? . . . And did he deserve his hemlock?" (Preface). Reversing his lifelong prejudice against

419

Plato, Nietzsche in this work reads Plato as a "noble" spirit – a misguided spirit perhaps, and the source of the most "dangerous" and detestable of the dogmatists' errors known to mankind ("namely, Plato's invention of the pure spirit and the good as such," ibid.), but admirable and powerful nonetheless. (The very fact that "free spirits" borrow a kind of spirituality at all already suggests an irony and a tainting, an embarrassing coincidence of opposites, one that normally is overlooked.) Indeed, what is admirable and seductively powerful in Plato (Nietzsche speaks of his *Zauber*, or "charm") lies precisely in the willful audacity of his dogmatism, for instance his repudiation of the senses. Rejecting these, Plato managed to "overcom[e] the world" through sheer self-assertion and a will to interpretation, notwithstanding the deliverances of common sense and everyday intuition (§14; cf. §191). Needless to say, Nietzsche's own reevaluation of Plato reflects another striking will to reinterpret appearances, here his own prior utterances against Plato and his occasional applaudings of Socrates, though not his earlier attacks against the "plebeian" Socrates.

The revaluation of Plato in *Beyond Good and Evil* makes sense in a few different ways, once the larger aims of that work are taken into account. These are, roughly speaking, its exposition of two doctrines: "the will to truth" as it stands in relation to "the problem of the value of truth" (§1; trans. Kaufmann), and the theory of the will to power that looms larger in this work than in any other published work from Nietzsche's later period. Accordingly, Plato is an object-lesson, first in the way in which truth is a function of willing a value, and then in the ethical corollary of the will to truth, namely that "every morality is . . . a bit of tyranny against 'nature'; also against 'reason'," in other words, that morality is a willful imposition of untruth in the name of truth (§188). Second, what emerges from *Beyond Good and Evil* even more clearly than from other late works by Nietzsche is his apparent belief that *every* assertion from *any* quarter whatsoever is value-creating, and that such assertions also secretly harbor hidden complexities, disavowals, recesses, and masked truths or untruths. That they do flows from the claim (which is in fact adduced merely as a hypothesis) that there are no opposites but "only provisional perspectives" (or "frog perspectives," possibly an allusion to *Phaedo* 109b) which "are insidiously related, tied to and involved with these wicked, seemingly opposite things – maybe even one with them in essence" (§2). Nietzsche's view of things in *Beyond Good and Evil*, in other words, is generous and all-embracing, and vulnerable to endless complications. This is to be sure true of all of his writings, but the present case is an extreme and express case.

Third, and most important of all, Nietzsche's goal in this book is to arrive at an observation about human action that puts the preceding, seemingly metaphysical claim about the world to work in the realm of human action: "Our actions shine alternately in different colors, they are rarely univocal – and there are cases enough in which we perform actions *of many colors*" (§215; elsewhere we find equivalent claims: our actions are "rich in marvels and monstrosities" or "variations," §262; they are "manifold," §291). Indeed, the pattern of *Beyond Good and Evil* as a whole is to move from without to within, from questions about the truth of what is (ontology) to questions about the truth of the soul (psychology), its drives and passions and complex willings, by passing through the middle term of morality ("moral prejudice"), which for Nietzsche binds the two realms together (§34). It is for this reason, I would suggest, that the work changes focus and passes from Plato to Socrates.

As the focus of the work shifts from metaphysics to ethics, and Nietzsche adopts the perspective of a connoisseur of the soul committed to its proper science ("For psychology is now again the path to the fundamental problems," §23 – thus the closing statement to Part One), Socrates comes increasingly to the fore. And understandably so, for Socrates was the uncontested master in the art of divining souls. Or at least that is how Nietzsche chooses to remember him in the present work. It was Socrates, Nietzsche says, who first developed a mechanism for assessing the quality of actions by posing the simple question, "Why?" In other words, Socrates' philosophical achievement was to bring questions of value to bear on actions by inquiring into the relative worth of reason or the instincts in relation to those actions. Even if Nietzsche disagrees with Socrates' final devaluation of the instinctive impulses of action, he nevertheless acknowledges that Socrates was at the very least the first to identify *both* the irrational and rational mainsprings of action.

Thus Nietzsche can say, with complete justification, that what is of interest to him "is the same old moral problem that first emerged in the person of Socrates, . . . [who] at bottom . . . had seen through the irrational element in moral judgments" (§191; trans. adapted).[5] Whence, too, Nietzsche's claims about a resurgence of psychology today: "psychology is *now again* the path to the fundamental problems," for Nietzsche wants us to see himself as a present-day maieutic force carrying out a Socratic mission as the times require it of him today: "Anyone to whose task and practice it belongs to search souls will employ this very art *in many forms* in order to determine the ultimate value of a soul and the unalterable, innate order of rank to which it belongs" (§263; trans. adapted; italics added). To search through souls is no easy task. It is to look for "something that goes its way unmarked, undiscovered, tempting, perhaps capriciously concealed and disguised, like a living touchstone" (ibid.). It is to be a "genius of the heart . . . and born pied piper of consciences whose voice knows how to descend into the netherworld of every soul," who can induce others, charismatically, to embark on the same search,

> to press ever closer to him in order to follow him ever more inwardly and thoroughly, . . . the genius of the heart from whose touch everyone walks away richer . . . in himself, newer to himself than before, broken open, blown at and sounded out by a thawing wind, perhaps more unsure, tenderer, more fragile, more broken, but full of hopes that as yet have no name, full of new will and currents, full of new dissatisfaction and undertows. (§295; see Kaufmann's apposite note to this passage)

The mission is in a deep sense Socratic. Is it noble? The Socratic approach to the question would be to pose another question, which is also Nietzsche's: "What is Noble?" (This is the title to the last book of *Beyond Good and Evil*, although the question-mark is oddly missing from Kaufmann's English version: the title is emphatically a *question*, not a proposition. Cf. also §227.) Thus, what began to all appearances as an ode to nobility (albeit a paradoxical one, for recall that its recipient was Plato) here ends on a note of Socratic uncertainty – but also, for the same reason, one of unimagined possibilities. The noble, free spirit is no longer the caricature of the rapacious blood-curdling voluntarist all too familiar from other parts of Nietzsche's corpus (and even more so from the frequent two-dimensional readings of him). On the contrary, such a spirit is marked by profound suffering; his certainty is of a "shuddering" sort; it carries a negative knowledge, the knowledge, which is "*more* than the wisest and cleverest could possibly know," that others "know nothing" (§270). But it is also no more than this negative knowledge, and it is assuredly not premised on any wealth of self-knowledge, for "what ultimately do we know of ourselves?" (§227) Even Dionysus, the titular god if not pseudonym of the free-spirited soul, practices the art of philosophical "dialogue" (§295). Such a spirit is in the final analysis profoundly Socratic – but then it is this only to the extent that it is also uncompromisingly human and humane.[6]

To appreciate how Nietzsche's stance in *Beyond Good and Evil* fits into what might be called "the radical humanism" of his mature writings would take us well beyond the limits of the present chapter. But it would not necessarily take us much beyond Nietzsche's views and uses of Socrates.[7]

Notes

1 Dannhauser (1974) is typical: "All these similarities (sc., between Socrates and Nietzsche) may be less significant than the kinship – amidst great difference, of course" (270).

2 When Kaufmann charges his adversaries (ibid.: 397) with overlooking the evidence of "the fragments of that period" (viz., the early to mid-1870s), which "reiterate the same profound admiration" as the last of the lectures on the Preplatonic philosophers (a dubious claim in itself), he is himself guilty of overlooking the evidence of the very fragments he claims to cite (some of which was presented above).

3 It is no coincidence that F. A. Wolf, whose *Prolegomena to Homer* from 1795 raised the modern specter of the Homeric Question from within classical studies, was also one of the first modern classicists to address the Socratic Problem (Wolf 1811, Preface), three years before his colleague in Berlin, Schleiermacher, famously attacked the same problem by doubting the testimony of Xenophon.

4 Gerhardt compares the final scenes in the cave to the jail scene of the *Phaedo* (with obvious reminiscences to the cave-analogy of Book 7 of the *Republic*). But Zarathustra's exit from the cave arguably recalls the close of the *Symposium*, Nietzsche's "*Lieblingsdichtung*" from his school days at Pforte (BAW 2:420–4 [1864]): "Well then, they still sleep, these higher men, while *I* am awake: *these* are not my proper companions. It is not for them that I wait here in my mountains. I want to go to my work, to my day: but they do not understand the signs of my morning. . . . They still sleep in my cave, their dream still drinks of my drunken songs" (*Thus Spoke Zarathustra*, IV ["The Sign"], §20; Kaufmann, trans.).

5 The same honor is awarded to Euripides in *The Birth of Tragedy* §11, whose fundamental diagnosis of the irrational motives of prior tragedy is shown to have been essentially *correct*: "he observed something incommensurable in every feature and in every line, a certain deceptive distinctness and at the same time an enigmatic depth, indeed an infinitude, in the background. . . . And how dubious the solution of the ethical problems remained to him! How questionable the treatment of the myths!" Time and again the Socrates of antiquity draws out to the surface unconscious, disavowed, and thus – at least by Nietzsche's criteria (see *BGE* §263, to be quoted momentarily) – irrational beliefs in his interlocutors, as at *Gorgias* 492d: "You make a brave attack, Callicles, with so frank an outburst, for clearly you are now saying what others may think but are reluctant to express" (Zeyl, trans.).

6 Nietzsche's later view is consistent with his earlier, "middle" view. Cf. *Human, All Too Human* II.2 ("The Wanderer and his Shadow") §6, railing against "priests and teachers, and . . .

idealists of every description," who divert attention away from the "smallest and closest things" in favor of various attainments: "the salvation of the soul, the service of the state, the advancement of science, or the accumulation of reputation and possessions, . . . while the requirements of the individual, his great and small needs within the twenty-four hours of the day, are to be regarded as something contemptible or a matter of indifference" – to which Nietzsche adds: "Already in ancient Greece Socrates was defending himself with all his might against this arrogant neglect of the human for the benefit of the human race, and loved to indicate the true compass and content of all reflection and concern with an expression of Homer's: it comprises, he said, nothing other than 'that which I encounter of good and ill in my own house'" (trans. Hollingdale).

7   I hope to develop this project in a book-length study (in progress), provisionally entitled *Nietzsche and the Seductions of Metaphysics: Nietzsche's Final "Philosophy."*

Abbreviations

BAW   *Friedrich Nietzsche. Werke und Briefe. Historisch-Kritische Gesamtausgabe. Werke.* 5 vols. H. J. Mette, K. Schlechta and C. Koch (eds.) (1933–42). Munich: C. H. Beck

KGW   *Friedrich Nietzsche. Kritische Gesamtausgabe, Werke.* G. Colli and M. Montinari (eds.) (1967–). Berlin: W. de Gruyter.

KSA   *Friedrich Nietzsche. Sämtliche Werke. Kritische Studienausgabe in 15 Einzelbänden.* G. Colli and M. Montinari (eds.) (1988). 15 vols. 2nd ed. Berlin: W. de Gruyter.

References

Bertram, E. (1965). *Nietzsche: Versuch einer Mythologie* [Nietzsche: Attempt at a Mythology]. 8th ed. Bonn: H. Bouvier u. Co. Verlag (1st ed. 1918).

Blondell, R. (2002). *The Play of Character in Plato's Dialogues.* Cambridge: Cambridge University Press.

Branham, R. B. and Goulet-Cazé, M.-O. (1996). *The Cynics: The Cynic Movement in Antiquity and its Legacy.* Berkeley: University of California Press.

Brinton, C. (1941). *Nietzsche.* Cambridge, MA: Harvard University Press.

Conway, D. W. (1988). Solving the problem of Socrates: Nietzsche's *Zarathustra* as political irony. *Political Theory,* 16(2), 257–80.

Dannhauser, W. J. (1974). *Nietzsche's Image of Socrates.* Ithaca: Cornell University Press.

Diderot, D. (1966). *Rameau's Nephew and D'Alembert's Dream,* trans. L. Tancock. Harmondsworth and New York: Penguin.

Foucault, M. (1985). *The Use of Pleasure: Volume 2 of The History of Sexuality,* trans. Robert Hurley. New York: Vintage Books.

—— (1986). *The Care of the Self. Volume 3 of The History of Sexuality,* trans. Robert Hurley. New York: Pantheon Books.

Gerhardt, V. (2001). Nietzsches alter-ego: Über die Wiederkehr des Sokrates. *Nietzscheforschung: Jahrbuch der Nietzsche-Gesellschaft,* 8, 315–32.

Greenblatt, S. J. (1980). *Renaissance Self-Fashioning: From More to Shakespeare.* Chicago: University of Chicago Press.

Hadot, P. (1995). *Philosophy as a Way of Life: Spiritual Exercises from Socrates to Foucault,* ed. A. I. Davidson. Malden, MA: Blackwell.

Hegel, Georg Wilhelm Friedrich (1971). *Vorlesungen über die Geschichte der Philosophie.* In *Werke,* vols. 18–20, ed. Eva Moldenhauer, Karl Markus Michel, and Helmut Reinicke. Frankfurt am Main: Suhrkamp. (1st ed. 1833–6.)

Jameson, F. (1973). The vanishing mediator: narrative structure in Max Weber. *New German Critique*, 1 (Winter), 52–89.

Jauss, H. R. (1983). *The Dialogical and the Dialectical Neveu de Rameau: How Diderot Adopted Socrates and Hegel Adopted Diderot. Protocol of the Forty-Fifth Colloquy, 27 February 1983*, ed. William R. Herzog II. Berkeley, CA: Center for Hermeneutical Studies in Hellenistic and Modern Culture.

Kaufmann, W. (1974). *Nietzsche: Philosopher, Psychologist, Antichrist.* 4th ed. Princeton: Princeton University Press. (1st ed. 1950.)

Kierkegaard, S. (1989). *The Concept of Irony, with Continual Reference to Socrates, together with Notes of Schelling's Berlin Lectures*, trans. H. V. Hong and E. H. Hong. Princeton: Princeton University Press.

Laks, A. (2002). "Philosophes Présocratiques": Remarques sur la construction d'une catégorie de l'historiographie philosophique. In A. Laks and C. Louguet (eds.), *Qu'est-ce que la philosophie présocratique? What is Presocratic Philosophy?* Cahiers de philologie. Série Apparat critique, v. 20. Villeneuve-d'Ascq: Presses universitaires du septentrion.

Michaelis, P. (1886). rev. of F. Nietzsche, *Jenseits von Gut und Böse* [Beyond Good and Evil]. *Berlin National-Zeitung*, December 4.

Montuori, M. (1981). *De Socrate iuste damnato: The Rise of the Socratic Problem in the Eighteenth Century.* London studies in Classical Philology, 7. Amsterdam: J. C. Gieben.

—— (1992). *The Socratic Problem: The History, The Solutions. From the 18th Century to the Present Time. 61 Extracts from 54 Authors in their Historical Context.* Amsterdam: J. C. Gieben.

Murray, O. (2002). Burckhardt, Nietzsche and Socrates. In M. Ghelardi and M. Seidel (eds.), *Jacob Burckhardt: Storia della Cultura, Storia dell'Arte* (pp. 55–61). Collana del Kunsthistorisches Institut in Florenz, Max-Planck-Institut, 6. Venice: Marsilio.

Nehamas, A. (1985). *Nietzsche, Life as Literature.* Cambridge, MA: Harvard University Press.

—— (1998). *The Art of Living: Socratic Reflections from Plato to Foucault.* Berkeley: University of California Press.

Patzer, A. (ed.) (1987). *Der Historische Sokrates.* Wege der Forschung, vol. 585. Darmstadt: Wissenschaftliche Buchgesellschaft.

Porter, J. I. (1998). Unconscious agency in Nietzsche. *Nietzsche-Studien*, 27, 153–95.

—— (2000a). *The Invention of Dionysus: An Essay on "The Birth of Tragedy."* Stanford: Stanford University Press.

—— (2000b). *Nietzsche and the Philology of the Future.* Stanford: Stanford University Press.

—— (2004). Nietzsche, Homer, and the classical tradition. In P. Bishop (ed.), *Nietzsche and Antiquity: His Reaction and Response to the Classical Tradition* (pp. 7–26). Rochester, NY: Camden House.

Ryle, G. (1966). *Plato's Progress.* Cambridge: Cambridge University Press.

Schmidt, H. J. (1969). *Nietzsche und Sokrates: Philosophische Untersuchungen zu Nietzsches Sokratesbild* [Nietzsche and Socrates: Philosophical Investigations on Nietzsche's Image of Socrates]. Monographien zur philosophischen Forschung, Bd. 59. Meisenheim am Glan: Hain.

Usener, S. (1994). *Isokrates, Platon und ihr Publikum: Hörer und Leser von Literatur im 4. Jahrhundert v. Chr.* Tübingen: Gunter Narr Verlag.

Wolf, F. A. (ed.) (1811). *Aristophanes' Wolken: Eine Komödie, griechisch und deutsch.* Berlin: G. C. Nauck.

Zeller, Eduard (1856–68). *Die Philosophie der Griechen in ihrer geschichtlichen Entwicklung.* 2nd ed. 3 vols. in 5. Tübingen: L. F. Fues. (1st ed. 1844–52.)

Further Reading

K. Hildebrandt's *Nietzsches Wettkampf mit Sokrates und Plato* (2nd ed. 1922, Dresden: Sibyllen-Verlag) attempts to moderate Bertrand's conclusions from 1918, but complicates without displacing Bertram's view that Socrates is Nietzsche's ambivalent *Doppelgänger*. S. Kofman, *Socrate(s)* (Paris: Editions Galilée, 1989; English translation: *Socrates: Fictions of a Philosopher*, Cornell University Press, 1998) has a short chapter and a half on Nietzsche. For all her sophistication, Kofman nonetheless psychologizes Nietzsche's relationship to Socrates, likewise à la Bertram. For background on Nietzsche's views of antiquity, see M. S. Silk and J. P. Stern, *Nietzsche on Tragedy* (Cambridge: Cambridge University Press, 1981); H. Cancik, *Nietzsches Antike: Vorlesung*, 2nd ed. (Stuttgart: Metzler, 2000); and Paul Bishop (ed.), *Nietzsche and Antiquity: His Reaction and Response to the Classical Tradition* (Rochester, NY: Camden House, 2004). Further, V. Gerhardt, Die Moderne beginnt mit Sokrates, in F. Grunert and F. Vollhardt (eds.), *Aufklärung als praktische Philosophie. W. Schneiders zum 65. Geburtstag* (pp. 2–20) (Tübingen: Max Niemyer Verlag, 1998); D. M. McNeill, On the relationship of Alcibiades' speech to Nietzsche's "problem of Socrates," in Bishop (2004, pp. 260–75). An excellent annotated online guide to Nietzsche is published by the New York Public Library (www.nypl.org/research/chss/grd/resguides/nietzsche/).

26

The Socratic Hermeneutics of Heidegger and Gadamer

FRANCISCO J. GONZALEZ

It should be no surprise that two thinkers who sought to redefine philosophy at the end of metaphysics should have confronted Socrates along the way. Socrates has become practically synonymous with the philosophical enterprise, so that not only his immediate followers, but all philosophers, including self-proclaimed anti-Socratics, have fought for his legacy. To rethink the nature and task of philosophy is thus always in some measure to rethink and reappropriate the eternally enigmatic figure of Socrates. The result, perhaps, is as many portraits of Socrates as there are conceptions of philosophy. The focus of the present chapter, however, is on two German philosophers who, in rethinking the nature of philosophy in an especially radical and fundamental way, also carry out an especially radical and fundamental appropriation of the figure of Socrates.

Heidegger's Socrates: Being on the Way

This claim might be counterintuitive in the case of Heidegger, given how rarely Socrates, as distinct from Plato, appears in his texts. However, the few references to Socrates indicate significant ways in which Heidegger sees himself as a "Socratic." One affinity is the central importance both grant to *method* in philosophy. In a course from 1919/1920 entitled *Fundamental Problems of Phenomenology*, Heidegger characterizes philosophy as "a struggle for method" (ein Ringen um die Methode) and observes: "What is distinctive of philosophical method itself is that it cannot be technicized" (Heidegger 1993a: 136).[1] This means that for Heidegger method in philosophy is not a mere instrument for producing results, to be discarded once these results are achieved, but rather itself contains and exhibits the truth philosophy seeks. If philosophy is both a struggle for truth and a struggle for method, this is because truth and method are inseparable for it.

Such a conception of philosophy is precisely what Heidegger, in the 1926 course, *Fundamental Concepts of Ancient Philosophy*, characterizes as Socrates' historical contribution:

> No new contents or areas, no philosophical movement . . . The significance of the *methodological* determination was demonstrated here once and for all in the history of

knowing and investigating. Method is not technique, but rather looking to the ground of things and the possibility of grasping and determining them [auf den Grund der Sachen sehen und die Möglichkeit ihrer Erfassung und Bestimmung]. (1993b: 92)

Thus what Heidegger finds in Socrates is his own conviction that the truth of philosophy lies not in new discoveries or new areas of research, but rather in a certain way of seeing things and thus in *method*. If we can identify the truth of the sciences with a certain body of knowledge produced by their distinct methods, the truth of philosophy is its method.

Is Heidegger justified in seeing Socrates as a model for such a conception of philosophy? It is certainly at least plausible to suggest that Socrates' greatest contribution to philosophy was not any new discovery but rather a method; even the so-called Socratic paradoxes can be seen as more provocations to reflection than "doctrines." Furthermore, one could argue that Socrates himself, at least as depicted in Plato, places much more emphasis on method than on results, not only because his discussions are often aporetic but also, and more importantly, because he appears to value more the process of dialectic and dialogue than any outcome of this process. Perhaps the most striking expression of such an attitude is to be found at *Apology* 38a1–7:

> And when I say that the greatest good for human beings is to spend every day discussing virtue and the other topics about which you hear me conversing and examining both myself and others, and that the life without examination is not worth living for human beings, you believe what I say even less.

What makes this characterization of the greatest human good so strange is that it identifies it not with the possession of correct doctrines about virtue and other topics, but rather with the process of examining and discussing these topics; in other words, it identifies the highest good not with a result but with a method. Yet only this strange characterization of the human good can justify Socrates' conviction that his own life of ceaseless examination is the greatest benefit the city of Athens has ever received (*Apology* 30a) and is capable of making its citizens happy (36d).

It would of course be absurd to suggest that Socrates is interested only in talking about virtue and not in knowing the truth about virtue. If both Socrates and Heidegger do not regard method as a mere instrument, neither do they make it an absolute end-in-itself divorced from the truth. Rather, the view that Heidegger himself identifies with Socrates is that the truth of the matter in question shows itself, not in some definition or teaching that would conclude philosophical questioning, but rather in the very carrying out of this questioning. This is the aspect of Socratic method which Heidegger emphasizes in his 1924–5 course on Plato's *Sophist*. A central thesis of Heidegger's reading of this dialogue is that it had no planned sequel entitled *The Philosopher* but instead itself "accomplishes the task of clarifying what the philosopher is, and indeed it does so not in the primitive way, by our being told what the philosopher is, but precisely Socratically" (Heidegger 1997: 169). The meaning of the adverb "Socratically" is clarified at a later point in the course when, while again maintaining that the *Sophist* reveals the nature of the philosopher, Heidegger observes: "This entirely accords with the *Socratic bearing of Platonic philosophy, which provides the positive only in actually carrying it out* and not by making it the direct theme of reflection" (Heidegger

1997: 368; with slight modification). Thus what Heidegger considers "Socratic" is not mere questioning, refutation and aporia, but rather revealing the positive, the truth, by in some sense performing it in and through the very process of philosophical examination.

This conception of the "Socratic" seems closely tied to the notion of productive negation which Heidegger finds in the dialogue: "it becomes clear that negation, understood in this way, as possessing a disclosive character [*Erschließungscharakter*], can have, within the concrete uncovering of beings, a *purifying* function, so that negation itself acquires a *productive character*" (Heidegger 1997: 388; italics in the German). Heidegger appears to understand Socratic method as itself such a productive negation: it can disclose the positive in the very process of questioning, refuting and thus negating what stands opposed to it. This is not hard to see in the case of disclosing the nature of the philosopher through a critique of the sophist. But this understanding of the "Socratic" can arguably be applied more broadly. If, in the words from the *Apology* cited above, the highest human good is discussing and examining virtue everyday, then there is a sense in which Socrates, in examining and refuting inadequate conceptions of virtue, is positively manifesting and enacting the human good in question. The suggestion again is that the truth is to be found more in what Socrates does than in what, if anything, he concludes.

Heidegger's understanding and even emulation of Socrates in the 1920s anticipates the most important and famous reference to Socrates in his work, namely, that found in the series of lectures Heidegger delivered in 1951–2 under the title *What is called Thinking?*:

> Once we are so related and drawn into what withdraws, we are drawing into what withdraws, into the enigmatic and therefore mutable nearness of its appeal. . . . All through his life and right into his death, Socrates did nothing else than place himself into this draft, this current, and maintain himself in it. This is why he is the purest thinker of the West. This is why he wrote nothing. For anyone who begins to write out of thoughtfulness must inevitably be like those people who run to seek refuge from any draft too strong for them. An as yet hidden history still keeps the secret why all great Western thinkers after Socrates, with all their greatness, had to be such fugitives. Thinking has entered into literature. . . . (Heidegger 1968: 17–18)

The Socrates described here is in essence the same as the Socrates who inspired Heidegger three decades earlier: a Socrates who persists in questioning, who remains always underway, who endures in the draft of that which withdraws without every taking refuge in that pretense of having arrived called writing. If Socrates is the purest thinker of the West despite not being the greatest philosopher, i.e., not making the greatest contribution to philosophical knowledge (see p. 26), this is because, as Heidegger asserts in his own person later in the course, "Thinking itself is a way. We respond to the way only by remaining underway" (168–9). If thinking is thus understood, then writing, with its apparently inevitable finality, cannot help but be a betrayal of thinking. Thus Socrates, as the only philosopher to have avoided writing altogether, must be seen as the purest thinker, as the one who most truly remained underway in the chilling draft of thought.

428

THE SOCRATIC HERMENEUTICS OF HEIDEGGER AND GADAMER

Judged by this standard, Heidegger is himself as impure as any other post-Socratic thinker. Yet even here the "Socratic" tendency in Heidegger is unmistakable. While he did indeed write, he wrote remarkably little for publication, and often, as in the case of *Being and Time*, only under external pressures. While the published *Gesamtausgabe* of his works is already very large and will continue to grow for many years to come, it consists mostly of courses and lectures which Heidegger delivered orally and which are preserved in student transcripts and/or lecture notes. That Heidegger shared Socrates' preference, as expressed in the *Phaedrus*, for oral discourse over written discourse is made explicit in a letter to Elisabeth Blochmann on October 12, 1968. In reference to seminars he had just conducted in Provence, Heidegger writes:

> On the other hand, against the rigid teaching and learning system of the French, my way of conducting a seminar (Socratic, as it were) was completely new and stimulating. Perhaps something new can develop here. In the end, living conversation is more potent than the written word, which is in every way vulnerable to misinterpretation. But Plato already knew that at the end of his *Phaedrus* dialogue. (Storck 1989: 117)[2]

Therefore, if Heidegger does write, he, like Plato, tries to make his writing as compatible as possible with the Socratic refusal to write, whether it be by writing predominantly in the context of courses to be delivered orally or by composing a text such as the *Contributions to Philosophy* which, as a text not published during the author's lifetime and consisting largely of fragments and questions, seems deliberately to sabotage everything that normally defines a "text."

Significant in this regard is Heidegger's insistence that the texts published in the *Gesamtausgabe* be called *Wege* rather than *Werke*, as well as his choice of the titles *Wegmarken* and *Holzwege* for two collections of his essays and lectures. What Heidegger is insisting on here is that his writings be considered not "literature," i.e., not ends-in-themselves, goals and destinations, but rather ways or signposts along a way: where the ways in question do not themselves *lead anywhere* (thus the French translation of *Holzwege* as *Chemins qui ne mène nulle part*). But this is also to insist that his writings are "Socratic," that to the extent possible they do not betray what for Heidegger made Socrates the purest thinker of the West: that determination to remain underway towards a destination that continually withdraws and is thus "nowhere." In *What is Called Thinking?* Heidegger himself suggests the possibility of a kind of writing that remains a way of thinking: "The burden of thought is swallowed up in the written script, unless the writing is capable of remaining, even in the script itself, a progress of thinking, a way" (1968: 49). Later in the course Heidegger appears to find such a form of writing in the Platonic dialogue. Claiming that Plato's dialogues admit many different interpretations, Heidegger insists that this multiplicity of meanings is a virtue rather than a defect, for "multiplicity of meanings is the element in which all thought must move in order to be strict thought" (71). He then proceeds to observe that "not a single one of Plato's dialogues arrives at a palpable, unequivocal result which common sense could, as the saying goes, hold on to" (71). Though Heidegger, for reasons to be considered below, does not himself choose the dialogue as his form of writing, his goal is apparently the same as Plato's: to find a way of writing that does not betray the purity of Socratic thinking.

If Heidegger finds in Socrates his own emphasis on being underway, on "method," he also finds in him his own single-minded focus on one matter: the being of beings. If Heidegger's way is always devoted to the question of being, so is Socrates' way a continual asking of the question of what something *is*. Thus, in *What is a Thing?* Heidegger writes:

> Socrates had no other topic than what things are. "Are you still standing there," asked condescendingly the much traveled Sophist of Socrates, "and still saying the same thing about the same thing?" "Yes," answered Socrates, "that I am. But you who are so very clever, you *never* say the same thing about the same thing" (1967: 74; with slight modification)[3]

If Heidegger cites this anecdote, this is because it mirrors his own conviction that thinking, far from being a complex process of inference and synthesis, is characterized by the simplicity of saying the same of the same, a simplicity that is by no means simple in the sense of "easy." In a number of later texts, especially the *Contributions to Philosophy*, *On Time and Being* and the *Zähringen* seminars, Heidegger characterizes his own attempt to think Being/Ereignis as an attempt to say the same of the same.[4] What in the end can be said and thought of being except being? This "tautology" is for Heidegger not an empty identity statement that predicates A of A, but rather an attempt to get beyond predication (and thus logic) in a silent meditation that allows being to show itself in its selfsameness.

While this characterization of thought as "tautologies" certainly goes well beyond what Socrates meant by "saying the same of the same," a certain affinity can nevertheless be detected if one considers Socrates' well-known words at *Phaedo* 100c10–d8:

> I no longer understand nor can I recognize those other clever reasons; but if anyone gives me as the reason why a given thing is beautiful either its having a blooming color, or its shape, or something else like that, I dismiss those other things – because all others confuse me – but in a plain, artless, and possibly simple-minded way, I hold this close to myself: nothing else makes it beautiful except that beautiful itself, whether by its presence or communion or whatever the manner and nature of the relation may be; as I don't go so far as to affirm that, but only that it is by the beautiful that all beautiful things are beautiful. (Gallop, trans.)

If both Socrates and Heidegger remain always underway in thinking, this is perhaps because both refuse to characterize a thing's being as anything other than itself. To "know" the being of beauty or of anything else is not to assert propositions about it – precisely the kind of writing both Socrates and Heidegger reject – but to persist in a questioning relation to it that preserves its mysterious and irreducible sameness.

The noted affinities between Socrates and Heidegger can perhaps be best summarized by citing the following words with which Walter Jens has remembered Heidegger:

> I cannot imagine that there is anyone, a single person, who could say of himself that his life did not become more earnest, his thinking more alive, his questions more relevant after having learned with this man, this German Socrates (for thus he worked in the seminar: not instructing, but questioning and probing) . . . after having learned with Martin

Heidegger what it means to be insistently called upon by a subject matter, what it means to put oneself on the way and thereby assume the risk that one's thinking, under the influence of the thing itself, will be transformed underway. "Therefore it is advisable," in the words of the text "Identity and Difference," "to pay attention to the way and less to the content." (Neske 1977: 152)

This thinking that is always underway and yet so in touch with the being of the matter in question as to be continually changed by it, this thinking that pays more attention to the way than to the content without becoming contentless, this thinking that transforms without instructing: here lies the true kinship between Heidegger and Socrates. Here alone can calling Heidegger the "German Socrates" find any justification.

But if the affinity runs as deeply as this, why is Socrates relatively neglected in Heidegger's texts, especially in comparison with the Presocratics?[5] If we find tempting the simple answer that Socrates wrote nothing, that his thought cannot be discussed precisely because he was the purest thinker of the West, then we can reformulate our question as follows: why does Heidegger neglect what he himself characterizes as "the Socratic bearing" of Plato's dialogues? Why is the Plato who appears very frequently in Heidegger's writings a Plato without Socrates, indeed, a Plato without the Socratic dialogues?[6] For the figure who normally bears the name "Plato" in Heidegger's texts is a dogmatic metaphysician and thus the complete antithesis to the figure Heidegger himself names "Socrates." It seems that, apart from the enigmatic appearance in *What is called Thinking?*, Socrates simply drops out of Heidegger's history of Western philosophy. Why is this so?

Apparently, and perhaps surprisingly, what Heidegger finds alien in Socrates is *dialectic*, not in its dimension of radical questioning and saying the same of the same but rather in its dimension of *conversation*, of the *give-and-take of question and answer*. Already in the 1924 course, *Fundamental Concepts of Aristotelian Philosophy*, one finds an implied critique of Socrates' method. Citing a passage in which Aristotle criticizes those who take refuge in λόγος, Heidegger translates λόγος as "Geschwätz" ("chatter") and insists both that the Socratic method is the target here and that Aristotle has correctly understood Socrates (Heidegger 2002b: 184). What explains this surprising identification of Socratic conversation with chatter is Heidegger's belief that such conversation obstructs the seeing of the things themselves. The 1924/5 course on the *Sophist* develops this critique. While Heidegger there grants that dialectic can to an extent "break through and control idle talk," he insists that it can never fully transcend idle talk and attain its goal because it "does not purely and simply disclose beings, as long as it remains in λέγειν . . ." (Heidegger 1997: 136). This opposition between dialectic and "phenomenology" persists in Heidegger's thought to the very end: when in the last seminar at Zähringen he identifies phenomenological intuition with saying the same of the same, i.e., "tautology," he explicitly opposes this to dialectic (2003a: 81). It could thus be said that for Heidegger Socrates did not remain true to the demand to say the same of the same because his commitment to conversation dispersed his thought into the multiplicity of *logoi* expressed by his interlocutors. He remained too caught up in the give-and-take of conversation to penetrate to a vision of the being itself of what is in question. If dialectic is a philosophical embarrassment, as Heidegger asserts in *Being and Time* (Heidegger 1996: 22), then so is Socrates.[7]

Once this opposition is noted, the apparent similarities between Socrates and Heidegger begin to betray differences. A text such as the *Contributions to Philosophy* might seem "Socratic" in its emphasis on questioning as the end of philosophy, rather than only the beginning: Heidegger there defends questioning and the wonder of questioning against the charge that such a comportment is a renunciation of knowledge in favor of the undecided and undecidable (Heidegger 1999a: 8). With regard to the question of the essence of truth in particular he asserts: "And yet questioning here is no mere *prelude* in order to display something that is without question, as though that had been achieved. Questioning is here beginning and end" (242). He even goes so far as to identify questioning and knowledge in the notion of "inquiring knowledge" (247; see also 258).[8] Yet other passages make clear how distinct this questioning is from Socratic questioning. Heidegger's questioning is not a questioning of the views and presuppositions people already have, not an examination of others in conversation with the goal of arriving together at the truth, but rather a *silent openness to the truth of being.* "Seeking as questioning *and nevertheless reticence in silencing* [Erschweigen]" (56; my emphasis). This silent questioning is an openness to the self-concealing, self-withdrawing of being.[9] Contrasted with such silent questioning, Socratic questioning must appear distracting chatter.

Accordingly, while Heidegger in *What is Called Thinking?* indeed claims dialogue to be essential to all interpretation, he does so only with the surprising qualification that genuine dialogue is *not conversation*:

> Every interpretation is a dialogue [Gespräch] with the work, and with the saying. However, every dialogue becomes halting and fruitless if it confines itself obdurately to nothing but what is directly said – rather than that the speakers in the dialogue involve each other in *that* realm and abode about which they are speaking, and lead each other to it. Such involvement is the soul of dialogue. It leads the speakers into the unspoken. The term "conversation" ["Konversation"] does, of course, express the fact that the speakers are turning to one another. Every conversation is a kind of dialogue. But true dialogue is never a conversation. (Heidegger 1968: 178)

True dialogue, far from involving the verbal give-and-take of conversation, is at its core *silent*. It would in this case appear inaccessible to that garrulous and passionate lover of *logoi* named Socrates (*Phaedrus* 228 c1–2). But then what exactly is this true dialogue? As a letting-oneself-into-the-unspoken, it is presumably a *letting-be-seen* of the matter itself in what is unsaid. Understood thus, genuine dialogue is not an exchange of *logoi*, not communication or conversation at all.[10]

In another text in which Heidegger suggests that dialogue is essential to philosophy, *What is Philosophy?*, the qualification is that such dialogue need not be dialectic:

> When do we philosophize? Obviously only when we enter into a discussion [Gespräch] with philosophers. This implies that we talk through with them precisely that about which they speak. This mutual talking-through of what always anew peculiarly concerns philosophers as being the Same, that is talking, *legein* in the sense of *dialegesthai* [conversing], is talking as dialogue [Dialog]. If and when dialogue is necessarily dialectic, we leave open. (Heidegger 1958: 67)

432

Here we get an indication of how for Heidegger genuine dialogue is paradoxically a saying of the same. But what is the "dialectic" potentially to be distinguished from this dialogue? Unfortunately Heidegger does not explain, but presumably he means here what he means elsewhere by dialectic: the attempt to overcome the limitations of *logos* by confronting *logos* with *logos* without transcending *logos*.[11] Yet it is precisely such a dialectic that appears essential to Socratic dialogue. Socrates cannot "see" what virtue is except in confronting one logos about virtue with another in conversation with others. It is this discursive, intersubjective, social, and ethical dimension of Socratic philosophy that appears to be left out of Heidegger's appropriation of Socrates. In this appropriation one finds the emphasis on questioning, the emphasis on being underway, the emphasis on being, and even the emphasis on "dialogue": what is absent is the element in which alone all of this lives for Socrates. The "German Socrates" is a Socrates without an agora.

Gadamer's Socrates: The Dialectic of Question and Answer

If Socrates is given little opportunity to speak in Heidegger's texts, he speaks frequently, and with significant impact, in the texts of the other German Socrates. At least part of the reason is that Gadamer appears to emphasize precisely that dimension of the Socratic conception of philosophy which Heidegger rejects. Before turning to these differences, however, it is important to note that Gadamer's Socrates is nevertheless in important ways strikingly similar to Heidegger's.

Like Heidegger, Gadamer finds in Socrates the priority of the question over the answer. He indeed counts among the greatest insights of the Platonic dialogues – and he has the "Socratic dialogues" especially in mind here – the recognition that questioning is harder than answering (Gadamer 1989: 362). More significantly, he grounds this priority of the question in a priority of negation understood as productive. In *Plato's Dialectical Ethics*, the dissertation Gadamer wrote under Heidegger's direction, the negative and positive dimensions of dialectic are succinctly expressed as follows: "On the one hand, Socrates conducts the conversation as a process of refutation; but, at the same time, through this refutation, that which is sought is laid bare. It becomes possible to see what that to which the refuted accounts laid claim must be" (Gadamer 1991a: 55; see also 59). In *Truth and Method* Gadamer grounds the negative dimension of dialectic, and thus the priority of the question, in what he claims to be the negativity of experience itself. This means that experience is not the gradual articulation of generalities but instead a process of contradicting false generalizations. But, like the negativity that characterizes Socratic dialectic, "the negativity of experience has a curiously productive meaning" (Gadamer 1989: 353). The negation produced by the experience provides a better understanding both of what is experienced and of what one earlier presumed to know. It is clearly this productive negation characteristic of experience as such which Gadamer takes to be the heart of dialectic.

Heidegger's influence is even more evident in Gadamer's attribution to Socrates and Plato of a nontechnical conception of method. In the following passage from *Plato's Dialectical Ethics*, Gadamer even echoes Heidegger's words in the passage from the course on the *Sophist* cited above:

> Plato's philosophy is a dialectic not only because in conceiving and comprehending (*im Begreifen*) it keeps itself on the way to the concept (*zum Begriff*) but also because, as a philosophy that conceives and comprehends in that way, it knows man as a creature that is thus "on the way" and "between." It is precisely this that is Socratic in this dialectic: that it carries out, itself, what it sees human existence as. (Gadamer 1991a: 3–4)

Like Heidegger, therefore, Gadamer finds in Plato's Socrates a conception of philosophical method according to which it is not a mere instrument or tool applied to a foreign content, but rather is itself the manifestation and performance of this content.[12] Thus in *Truth and Method* Gadamer sees an affinity between his hermeneutics and ancient dialectic to the extent that the latter is not a method *applied* to the subject matter, but rather an action of the thing itself [das Tun der Sache selbst] (see Gadamer 1989: 464, 474). The title of Gadamer's *Truth and Method* expresses an opposition only if "method" is understood in the modern sense; if "method" is understood in the ancient sense, the title expresses more an identity. For Gadamer, as well as for the ancients on his interpretation, method is truth and truth is method in philosophy. What Gadamer is attempting to overcome in returning to the ancients, and to Plato's Socrates in particular, is what Heidegger characterizes as the "technicization" of method: a technicization that, in turning method into nothing but a tool for arriving at the truth, alienates it from the truth.

Another similarity between Gadamer's appropriation of Socrates and Heidegger's is that Gadamer too finds in Socrates a conception of philosophy as essentially *underway*. This dimension of Gadamer's interpretation is most evident in the essay with the suggestive title of "Socrates' Piety of Not-knowing" ["Sokrates" Frömmigkeit des Nichtwissens"]. Here Gadamer interprets Socratic conversation as "protreptic" in the true sense of an "'epogoge,' a conducting [Hinführung], one that indeed will conduct one not to a conclusive knowledge, but rather to a persistence in the search for true knowledge [zu einem Bestehen auf der Suche nach wirklichem Wissen]" (Gadamer 1991b: 106). The language here cannot help but recall Heidegger's characterization of Socrates in the passage from *What is Called Thinking?* cited above. Significantly, however, Gadamer does not follow Heidegger in stressing Socrates' refusal to write as evidence of the purity of his thinking. On the contrary, in *Truth and Method* Gadamer dismisses the critique of writing in the *Phaedrus* as "an ironic exaggeration" (eine ironische Übertreibung) contradicted by Plato's own literary art (1989: 393). If Gadamer refuses to make a sharp distinction between the spoken word and the written word,[13] this is because he wishes to model the interpretation of texts, and thus hermeneutics in general, on conversation (see, e.g., 331).

This is where the differences between Gadamer and Heidegger, both as philosophers and as interpreters of Socrates/Plato, begin to emerge. If Heidegger stresses Socrates' refusal to write, this is not because he wishes to model his philosophy on Socratic conversation. On the contrary, his goal is a type of "intuition" or, if one prefers, a "saying the same of the same," that transcends both conversation and writing. Of course, Heidegger's attempts to overcome the inherited language still had to take place within this language, his attempts to say the same of the same still had to take the form of predicating something of something else, his most radical intuitions still needed to make themselves *understood* in conversation with others. The result is what Gadamer

434

repeatedly diagnoses as Heidegger's "Sprachnot": "For Heidegger thinking was a suffering on account of its own linguistic hardship [Sprachnot], which is what drove him to such a thing [as doing great violence to language]" (Gadamer 1987: 374). While Gadamer sees Heidegger's "Sprachnot" as evidence of the power of his thinking (369), he also makes clear, in the essay "Destruktion und Dekonstruktion," that Heidegger's way is in this respect not his own way: a way which he characterizes as a way "from dialectic back to dialogue and conversation" (Gadamer 1993: 367–8), back, in other words, to Socrates![14]

A reexamination of Gadamer's characterization of dialectic in *Plato's Dialectical Ethics* can help clarify the nature of this parting of ways. There Gadamer describes the negative dimension of dialectic as being that it

> does not present the reality itself but seeks out what speaks for it and what speaks against it; which is to say that it takes up its position not by explicating the seen object by progressively moving closer to it, while keeping it always in view, but rather by developing in itself all the sides of the explications (*Ausgelegtheiten*) through which it encounters the object and by embroiling them in contradictions, so that its distance from the object comes to the fore . . . (Gadamer 1991a: 18)

While Heidegger, like Gadamer, sees a positive and productive dimension to this negative dialectic, i.e., its ability in some sense to disclose the thing itself, he criticizes dialectic precisely for its failure to encounter the thing itself except in *logoi* about it, i.e., precisely for its failure to achieve the phenomenological standpoint of interpreting the thing itself *as seen* (what Heidegger in the 1920s calls "hermeneutical intuition"[15]). In contrast, Gadamer makes dialectic as described in the cited passage his model for hermeneutics in *Truth and Method* and thereby rejects the phenomenology of his teacher. Thus Gadamer describes as follows the similarity between dialectic and hermeneutics: "The hermeneutical experience also has its own rigor: that of uninterrupted listening [des unbeirrbaren Hörens]. Here too a thing does not present itself to the hermeneutical experience without an effort special to it, namely, that of 'being negative toward itself' ['negativ gegen sich selbst zu sein']" (Gadamer 1989: 465; with slight modification). Note how here the consequence of hermeneutical experience as of dialectic is not a seeing, but a *listening*. Indeed, for Gadamer, the matter itself in both cases is not seen but offers itself only through negation. The positive, productive, disclosive dimension of both dialectic and hermeneutics cannot, in other words, be separated from the negative dimension. Later in *Truth and Method* Gadamer considers the following kinship between dialectic and hermeneutics: "As philosophical dialectic presents the whole truth by superceding all partial propositions, bringing contradictions to a head and overcoming them (*Aufhebung*), so also hermeneutics has the task of revealing a totality of meaning in all its relations" (1989: 471).

Yet here we appear to have left Socratic dialogue behind in favor of Hegelian dialectic. This is why Gadamer immediately qualifies that hermeneutical dialectic differs from the mentioned philosophical dialectic through its recognition of radical finitude (472). This is also why Gadamer describes his way, in the passage cited above, as a way *from dialectic* (and it is the metaphysical dialectic of Hegel that is primarily intended here) *back to dialogue and conversation*. But what exactly does this mean? Like Heidegger,

435

Gadamer resists the hegemony of propositional logic in modern philosophy. His alternative to this logic, however, is not an attempt to get beyond *logos* altogether, is not Heideggerian silence ("Sigetik"),[16] but rather what he calls "a logic of question and answer." The essence of this logic is the following principle stated in the essay "Was ist Wahrheit?":

> There is no proposition that does not represent a type of answer. Therefore, there can be no understanding of any proposition which does not receive its sole standard (Maßtab) from an understanding of the question which the proposition answers. (Gadamer 1993: 52)

Thus we return to the priority of the question, but now in the context of conversation. Only in the exchange of question and answer can understanding take place, whether we are conversing with another or reading a text. For even to understand a text we must discover the question to which it is an answer and we must allow it to become a question to us (1989: 373–4). Furthermore, if every assertion is an answer motivated by a question, so is every question in its turn motivated and thus itself an answer (Gadamer 1993: 52). It is the impossibility of an absolute beginning here that constitutes what Gadamer sees as the radical finitude of the hermeneutical situation. The only thing that is really prior is the open-ended dialogical situation itself. Thus Gadamer at one point writes: *"Thus the dialectic of question and answer has always already preceded the dialectic of interpretation. It is what determines understanding as an event"* (1989: 472; with some modifications). This is why Gadamer, in an essay entitled, "Die Universalität des hermeneutischen Problems," calls the principle cited above "das hermeneutische Urphänomen" (Gadamer 1993: 226).

Yet this is not the whole story. If Gadamer returns to Socratic conversation, this is because he takes conversation to be not only the site of understanding, but also the site of *truth*. In other words, for Gadamer truth can emerge or show itself only in conversation with another, and it is precisely on this point that he appeals to Plato's Socratic conversations:

> Already Plato communicated his philosophy only in written dialogues and did not do so solely out of piety towards that master of conversation who was Socrates. He saw a principle of truth in the fact that the word finds its confirmation [Bewährung] only through its reception in another and the agreement of another and that the outcome of a thinking that is not at the same time a going-along of the other person with the thoughts of the first person remains without the power to compel. (Gadamer 1993: 210)[17]

Here one sees again how for Gadamer, as for Plato's Socrates on his interpretation, truth is inseparable from method, as long as "method" is not understood as it is by the natural sciences but rather as the dialectic of question and answer. If the truth could be "seen," "demonstrated" or in any way "had" independently of conversation, e.g., through some sort of phenomenological intuition, then the link Gadamer forges between hermeneutics and conversation would be broken. Here, therefore, we have the explanation of why Gadamer's return to Socrates goes as far as retrieving the priority of dialogue as conversation, whereas Heidegger's does not.

436

That Gadamer's hermeneutics is in the respects mentioned genuinely "Socratic" is certainly a defensible proposition. If Socrates sees dialogue with others as indispensable to philosophy, is this not because he can appeal to no criterion of truth beyond the agreement of his interlocutors, where this means genuine agreement produced by repeated examination rather than simply verbal agreement or agreement with ulterior motives?[18] Thus in the *Gorgias* Socrates says to Callicles, under the erroneous assumption that Callicles is honest and good-willed: "I know well that if you concur with what my soul believes, then that is the very truth" (486e–487a; Zeyl trans). Later in a well-known passage, Socrates, after claiming that the positions he has been defending are "held down and bound by arguments of iron and adamant," immediately qualifies: "And yet for my part, my account is ever the same: I don't know how these things are, but no one I've ever met, as in this case, can say anything else without being ridiculous. So once more I set it down that these things are so" (509a–b). Truth not only emerges from the give and take of question and answer, but also has its proper place there, i.e., can never be possessed as a final result. If Gadamer with Heidegger rejects traditional logic's characterization of truth as the property of a proposition, what he puts in its place is not simply a characterization of truth as a prelogical unconcealment, but a characterization of truth as the property of *dialogue*.

Gadamer's return to the priority of conversation also enables him to retrieve another dimension of Socrates entirely neglected by Heidegger: the ethical. This is because, as Gadamer sees, Socratic conversation is not only *about* ethics but rather is itself an ethical comportment. The passage from the *Apology* 38a cited above makes this especially clear: discussing and examining virtue everyday *is itself good*, is indeed the greatest human good. The essay by Gadamer referred to above, "Socrates' Piety of Not-knowing," is particularly successful in bringing out the ethical dimension of Socratic examination. There, after himself citing *Apology* 38a, Gadamer writes: "One can express that as follows: the readiness to give an account of the good [Die Bereitschaft zur Rechenschaftsgabe über das Gute] is itself the way in which one knows about the good" (Gadamer 1991b: 106). This means that one knows about the good not in some final account of the good but rather in the readiness to discuss and explain it, i.e., in the very process of examining oneself and others about it. This implies, of course, that our knowing about the good is also a not-knowing, and that is indeed how Gadamer interprets Socratic ignorance. "The Socratic question remains standing as the challenge, which is true human wisdom (ἀνθρωπίνη σοφία), to be aware of one's not-knowing in having-to-know the good [des Nichtwissens im Wissenmüssen des Guten]" (108). For Gadamer, Socrates' self-aware not-knowing, as the taking of a stand between ignorance and wisdom, is not ignorance but a type of knowing. Thus, on Gadamer's interpretation, the *Euthyphro* depicts Socrates as knowing what piety is (117), despite his lack of the expert knowledge Euthyphro for his part claims to have. Indeed, it is precisely in disclaiming an expert knowledge of piety and refuting the pretensions to such knowledge in Euthyphro that Socrates emerges as both knowing and exhibiting piety. Paradoxically, Socrates' not-knowing piety and the good *is* his piety and goodness: thus the title of Gadamer's essay. Here we see more specifically how the Socratic method enacts what it is about or, in Gadamer's words, is a doing of the thing itself. If what Gadamer finds in Socrates here is what Heidegger calls "inquiring knowledge," then Gadamer has returned this "inquiring knowledge" to the dialogical and ethical context from which Heidegger abstracted it.

One final and important difference remains to be noted between Gadamer's appropriation of Socrates and Heidegger's. While Heidegger was seen to introduce a strong dichotomy between Socrates the radical questioner and Plato the dogmatic metaphysician, with the result that the latter in the end eclipses the former in Heidegger's history of metaphysics, Gadamer's emphasis on dialogue allows him to bring Socrates and Plato much closer together. Gadamer explicitly rejects Heidegger's characterization of Plato's thought in terms of the Aristotelian conception of metaphysics (1991b: 273, 280); he asserts, for example, that the ontological *chorismos* between Forms and particulars is Aristotle's invention, not Plato's (1991b: 281).[19] Furthermore, Gadamer denies that Socratic dialogue is abandoned in "later" dialogues in favor of a nondialogical and systematic dialectic: as he asserts succinctly in an essay on Plato's *Sophist*, "In Platonic dialectic Socratic dialogue lives on" (1991b: 340; see also 1993: 12). In short, Gadamer rejects, at least to the extent indicated, the existence of either a non-Socratic metaphysics or a non-Socratic method in Plato. If his Socrates is always the Platonic Socrates, his Plato is always the Socratic Plato. Thus he can even claim that "In the end, [Plato's] entire collection of dialogues is an apology of Socrates [eine Apologie des Sokrates] . . ." (Gadamer 1976: 8). A book on Gadamer's "Platonic hermeneutics" is therefore appropriately entitled: *The Resocratization of Plato* (Renaud 1999). For anyone who questions such a reading of Plato, Gadamer and his hermeneutics would have to be judged more "Socratic" than "Platonic."

None of the above is meant to suggest that Gadamer simply is a faithful Platonist or Socratic. Towards the very end of *Truth and Method*, Gadamer attempts to distance his hermeneutics from the dialectic of both Plato and Hegel (1989: 465ff.). However, since most of Gadamer's criticisms appear directed at Hegel and since he is not very careful to distinguish between Hegel and Plato in this context, it is very difficult to extract from the text his reasons for distancing himself from Plato in particular. When he criticizes not only Hegel, but also Plato, for subordinating language to the statement (Aussage) (468), one must be puzzled; has Gadamer forgotten that he is indebted to Plato for his "logic of question and answer"? Gadamer's critique of Plato (and Socrates?), in particular the suggestion that Plato's dialectic seeks to free itself from the power of language, appears to go back to his interpretation of the *Cratylus* (406–18), but this is a highly debatable interpretation of a difficult dialogue. An adequate exposition of Gadamer's thought, which is clearly beyond the scope of the present essay, would need to clarify and evaluate this critique as well as show more subtle ways in which he distances himself from the "ancient dialectic."[20]

What should be evident from this account of two similar and yet significantly different receptions of Socrates is how important the legacy of Socrates remains for a school of thought that might on the surface appear anti-Platonist and anti-Socratic. Both Heidegger and Gadamer can be called "Socratic" in a strong and determinate sense. Where they can be said to part ways is precisely on the question of whether or not philosophy is in essence dialectic and dialogic and thus "Socratic" *in this sense*. This remains an open question even, or especially, among those who agree that the task of philosophy is interpretation (hermeneutics) rather than proof. And the question amounts to this: Is the way back to Socrates also the way forward for thinking?

Notes

1 All translations are my own unless otherwise indicated.

2 See also Heidegger's approving citation and interpretation of Plato's critique of writing in the 1957 lecture series *Grundsätze des Denkens*, in Heidegger (1994: 130–2).

3 Heidegger tells the same anecdote in a Zollikon seminar from 1964: Heidegger (2001: 24; see also 133 and 296). Heidegger in neither context cites a source for the anecdote, but the source is presumably the exchange between Hippias and Socrates reported in Xenophon's *Memorabilia* 4.4.6, though a similar exchange occurs between Callicles and Socrates at *Gorgias* 490e–491b.

4 In the Zollikon seminar, immediately after the recounting of the Socrates anecdote, we have the comment: "We will also endeavor to say the same thing about the same thing here" (Heidegger 2001: 24). In the lecture *On Time and Being*, which is professedly an attempt to think and say Being/*Ereignis*, Heidegger near the end observes: "What remains to be said? Only this: Appropriation appropriates [das Ereignis ereignet]. Saying this, we say the Same in terms of the Same about the Same" (Heidegger 2002a: 24). See also Heidegger (1999a: 333); and Heidegger (2003a: 80).

5 Though, given the texts cited above, one can no longer say with Arendt that *What is Called Thinking?* is "the only point in his work where he speaks directly of Socrates" (1978: 174).

6 Even Boutot, who otherwise defends Heidegger's critique of Plato, must grant: "Il ne nous dit rien ou presque rien sur la dialectique, par example, pourtant fondamentale chez Platon, sur les conceptions morales et politiques de Platon, sur la structure des *Dialogues*, sur l'ironie socratique, sur la signification des mythes, etc." (1987: 323).

7 Martens concludes that Heidegger is "un semi-socratico. Egli rispetta solo una parte di Socrate, quella a-razionale e non riconosce l'altra, la razionalista, come parte necessaria della terza via ricercata" (1995: 68). For a detailed treatment of Heidegger's critique of dialectic, see Gonzalez (2002).

8 Recall also the seemingly very Socratic statement with which *The Question Concerning Technology* comes to a close: "For questioning is the piety of thought" (Heidegger 1977: 35).

9 Thus, while Heidegger asserts that his questioning, on account of its very primordiality, is subject to fundamental transformations and even reversals [Umstürze] (1999a: 59), he denies that such changes (and he is clearly referring to changes in his own thought) are caused from objections coming from the outside; objections are not even *possible* since the *question* has still to be grasped (59).

10 In a recently published text, what Heidegger opposes to Platonic dialogue is the "dialogue of being" (*Gespräch des Seins*), which he proceeds to characterize as a *remaining silent* with regard to what must remain unspoken (Heidegger 2003b: 14, 24–6).

11 See Heidegger (1968:156–7). The discussion there concludes: "In dialectic, too, thinking is defined in terms of the proposition, the *logos*" (157).

12 Here is an obvious contrast with the reception of Socrates in the "analytical" tradition, where much of the debate has focused on the effectiveness of Socrates' method as a tool for producing constructive philosophical results.

13 "In fact, writing and speech are in the same plight" (1989: 393).

14 It is important to note, however, that in a letter to Medard Boss dated November 25, 1950, Heidegger recognizes that "the question of communication (the way and manner, the right moment, the hearer and the reader) is of the greatest importance here and in all essential matters. . . . Socrates knew about that better than anyone else up to the present. But we hardly know anything of what he knew" (Heidegger 2001: 240).

15 See, for example, Heidegger (1999b: 117). For an attempt to demonstrate that some form of the priority of intuition within understanding persists throughout Heidegger's work, see Gonzalez (2002: 368–71).

16 For the notion of "sigetics" as a "logic" of philosophy in which silence (σιγή) replaces *logos*, see Heidegger (1999a: 55).

17 See also Gadamer (1993: 52–6). For very helpful accounts of Gadamer's conception of truth as having its locus in dialogue, see Grondin (1994: esp. 14–15 and 20); and Wachterhauser (1999: 181).

18 For an excellent defense of such a conception of truth in Plato's dialogues, see Trabattoni (1994: esp. 75–6 and 338).

19 Contrast Heidegger (1968: 227).

20 For some help here, see Grondin (1994: 21–4).

References

Arendt, H. (1978). *The Life of the Mind*. New York: Harcourt Brace.

Boutot, A. (1987). *Heidegger et Platon: le problème du nihilisme* [Heidegger and Plato: the Problem of Nihilism]. Paris: PUF.

Gadamer, H.-G. (1976). *Plato: Texte zur Ideenlehre* [Plato: Texts Regarding the Theory of Ideas]. Frankfurt am Main.

—— (1980). *Dialectic and Dialogue: Eight hermeneutical studies on Plato*, trans. P. Christopher. New Haven: Yale University Press.

—— (1987). *Hegel–Husserl–Heidegger. Gesammelte Werke*. Vol. 3. Tübingen: J. C. B. Mohr [Paul Siebeck].

—— (1989). *Truth and Method*, trans. W. Glen-Doepel, D. G. Marshall, and J. Weinsheimer. New York: Crossroad (original Work Published 1960).

—— (1991a). *Plato's Dialectical Ethics: Phenomenological Interpretations relating to the* Philebus, trans. R. M. Wallace. Yale University Press (original work published 1931).

—— (1991b). *Plato im Dialog. Gesammelte Werke*. Vol. 7. Tübingen: J. C. B. Mohr [Paul Siebeck].

—— (1993). *Wahrheit und Methode: Ergänzungen, Register. Gesammelte Werke*. Vol. 2. Tübingen: J. C. B. Mohr [Paul Siebeck].

Gonzalez, F. J. (2002). Dialectic as "philosophical embarrassment": Heidegger's critique of Plato's method. *Journal of the History of Philosophy*, 40, 361–89.

Grondin, Jean (1994). *Hermeneutische Wahrheit? Zum Wahrheitsbegriff Hans-Georg Gadamers*. 2d ed. [Hermeneutical truth? On the concept of truth in Hans-Georg Gadamer]. Weinheim: Beltz Athenäum Verlag.

Heidegger, M. (1958). *What is Philosophy?*, trans. W. Kluback and J. T. Wilde. Twayne Publishers (original work published 1956).

—— (1967). *What is a Thing?*, trans. W. B. Barton, Jr. and V. Deutsch. Chicago: Henry Regnery Company (original work published 1962).

—— (1968). *What is Called Thinking?*, trans. J. G. Gray. New York: Harper & Row (original work published 1954).

—— (1977). *The Question Concerning Technology*, trans. W. Lovitt. New York: Harper & Row.

—— (1993a). *Grundprobleme der Phänomenologie (1919/20). Gesamtausgabe*. Vol. 58. Frankfurt am Main: Vittorio Klostermann.

—— (1993b). *Grundbegriffe der antiken Philosophie Gesamtausgabe*. Vol. 22. Frankfurt am Main: Vittorio Klostermann.

—— (1994). *Bremer und Freiburger Vorträge, Gesamtausgabe*. Vol. 79. Frankfurt am Main: Vittorio Klostermann.

—— (1996). *Being and Time*, trans. J. Stambaugh. Albany, NY: SUNY Press (original work published 1927).

—— (1997). *Plato's* Sophist, trans. R. Rojcewicz and A. Schuwer. Indiana University Press (original work published 1992).

—— (1999a). *Contributions to Philosophy (From Enowning)*, trans. P. Emad and K. Maly. Indiana University Press (original work published 1989).

—— (1999b). *Zur Bestimmung der Philosophie. Gesamtausgabe.* Vol. 56/57. 2d ed. Frankfurt am Main: Vittorio Klostermann.

—— (2001). *Zollikon Seminars: Protocols–Conversations–Letters*, trans. F. Mayr and R. Askay. Evanston, IL: Northwestern University Press.

—— (2002). *On Time and Being*, trans. J. Stambaugh. Chicago: University of Chicago Press (original published 1969).

—— (2002b). *Grundbegriffe der aristotelischen Philosophie. Gesamtausgabe.* Vol. 18 Frankfurt am Main: Vittorio Klostermann.

—— (2002c). *The Essence of Truth: On Plato's Cave Allegory and Theaetetus*, trans. T. Sadler. London: Continuum Books (original work published 1988). This course Heidegger delivered in 1931 is of central importance to his, and arguably our, understanding of Plato, though it has little to say about Socrates, treating him as nothing but Plato's mouthpiece.

—— (2003a). *Four Seminars*, trans. A. Mitchell and F. Raffoul. Bloomington: Indiana University Press (original work published 1977).

—— (2003b). "Die Dichtung." *Heidegger Studies*, 19, 13–28.

Martens, Ekkehard (1995). Heidegger un Socratico? In G. Giannantoni (ed.), *La Tradizione Socratica* (pp. 57–69). Naples: Bibliopolis.

Neske, Günther (ed.) (1977). *Errinerung an Martin Heidegger*. Pfullingen: Neske.

Renaud, François (1999). *Die Resokratisierung Platons: Die Platonische Hermeneutik Hans-Georg Gadamers* [The Resocratization of Plato: The Platonic Hermeneutics of Hans-Georg Gadamer]. Sankt Augustin: Akademia Verlag.

Storck, J. W. (ed.) (1989). *Martin Heidegger – Elisabeth Blochmann: Briefwechsel 1918–1969*. Marbach am Neckar: Deutsche Schillergesellschaft.

Trabattoni, Franco (1994). *Scrivere nell'anima: verità, dialettica e persuasione in Platone* [Writing in the soul: truth, dialectic and persuasion in Plato]. Firenze: La Nouva Italia Editrice.

Wachterhauser, Brice R. (1999). *Beyond Being: Gadamer's Post-Platonic Hermeneutical Ontology.* Evanston, IL: Northwestern University Press.

441

27

The Socratic Method and Psychoanalysis

JONATHAN LEAR

I can't as yet know myself as the inscription at Delphi enjoins; and so long as that ignorance remains it seems to me ridiculous to inquire into extraneous matters. So, saying goodbye to all that . . . I direct my inquiries to myself, to discover whether I really am a more complex creature and more puffed up than the monster Typhon, or a simpler, gentler being whom heaven has blessed with a quiet, un-Typhonic nature.[1]

–Socrates in Plato's *Phaedrus*

In its origin, function and relation to sexual love, the "Eros" of the philosopher Plato coincides exactly with the love-force, the libido of psychoanalysis.[2]

–Freud

1.

Can conversation make a fundamental difference to how people live? Socrates is thought to have been trying to improve the lives of those he talked to, through his peculiar form of conversation. As he said in his own defense, "I go around doing nothing but persuading young and old among you not to care for your body or your wealth in preference to or as strongly as for the best possible state of your soul."[3] But his aim was not merely to convince someone of this as though it were the conclusion of an argument. That would be compatible with indolence – a person might believe that it is better to care for his soul than his body or wealth, but leave it at that. It is also compatible with a person becoming passionately concerned with his soul, but going off in cockeyed directions. Socrates' conversation was meant to motivate a person to care about his soul, and to help him take steps to improve it. That is, Socratic conversation had a therapeutic intent.

But when one asks what method Socrates used, the answer that typically comes to mind – the famous method of cross-examination, the elenchus – seems unsatisfying. First, if one looks at the dialogues in which the elenchus is used, there is no evidence that any of the interlocutors are improved by the conversation. Indeed, they often seem irritated, fed up, anxious to leave. Second, the Socrates of the *Republic* seems to give us an account of why elenchus on its own won't work. There he famously divides the soul into three parts – appetite, spirit, and reason. And he argues that personalities can be formed by any one of the parts gaining dominance over the other two. So, an honor-loving person is one in which spirit rules. This is a person who organizes his life to gain recognition and admiration. His reason is subjugated to the task of figuring out how to get it; and his appetites are prevented from getting in the way. It would seem that such a person will not be improved by a straightforward cross-examination. For if a proud man is shown in a public space to have contradictory beliefs – and just at the moment when he is showing off – it is most likely he will feel embarrassed and angry. And, in any case, once one has a theory of psychic structure, the primary issue can no longer be changing a person's beliefs; it must be a matter of changing the structure of his soul. It is not clear how the elenchus could do that. And it is a notable feature of the Platonic dialogues that when Socrates discusses psychic structure – notably in the *Republic* and *Phaedrus* – the elenchus disappears.

But what then is Socrates' method? One typical answer is to insist that the Socratic method just is the elenchus. Then when Socrates departs from the elenchus in the Platonic dialogues – so this answer goes – it is not really Socrates speaking, but Plato. This answer is, I think, unsatisfying: both because it fails to think deeply enough about what elenchus is and because it thereby fails to see a unity in Socrates' method that transcends the issue of whether he is or is not using elenchus. I can give my answer in a nutshell, but I warn you that in that nutshell the answer will most likely be mis-understood: Socratic method is irony. But to see why this answer is correct we need to abandon much of what we mean in general by irony; and much of what we have assumed Socratic irony to be.

My method of argument will be roundabout and unusual. In the bulk of this essay, I shall look carefully at how psychoanalysis works. Psychoanalysis commends itself to our attention because it takes seriously the idea that the soul has structure. Indeed, it is a peculiar form of conversation that aims to bring about a structural change in the soul. How could any conversation do that? Philosophers have long been interested in psychoanalysis – and they have long been interested in its similarities to Socratic method – but they have tended to focus on psychoanalytic *theory* – what one can get out of reading Freud – and have ignored how that theory is instantiated in psychoana-lytic practice. If we look to that, I think we can find a Socratic practice that might otherwise escape our notice. And we can discover in convincing detail how psycho-analytic conversation might genuinely promote structural change. Having done that, I shall return to the Platonic dialogues and show that there is a Socratic method that includes elenchus but transcends it. That method is irony.

2.

If we want to understand the Socratic method in psychoanalysis, the method of cross-examination, the elenchus, is the wrong place to look. In a paradigm case of elenchus, an interlocutor will put forward a belief about what, say, piety is. Socrates will then elicit other beliefs, draw inferences that the interlocutor agrees to, and finally bring out a contradiction.[4] If the interlocutor wants to avoid contradiction, he must change some of his beliefs. But psychoanalysis is not particularly concerned with changing anyone's beliefs about anything. In the course of a therapy, analysands may change their beliefs in all sorts of ways; but analysis does not aim for this as an outcome. Psychoanalysis is a peculiar conversation that aims to change, not a person's beliefs, but the structure and function of her soul. Moreover, it aims to do so by means that are transparent, fair and noncoercive. It promotes the development of a certain kind of psychic freedom. But what does this mean?

To understand the distinctive contribution psychoanalytic therapy can make, we need to understand the difference between changes the psyche undergoes as part of its normal functioning and changes in the way the psyche itself functions. When people's psyches are functioning normally, they typically change their beliefs and emotions on the basis of their experiences. Sometimes those experiences may bring about massive changes. You might say something that hurts my feelings terribly, and changes the way I lead my life. Someone else might say something that causes massive changes in beliefs. Imagine that you are living through a scientific revolution: you are in a class-room and Galileo (or Newton or Darwin or Einstein) is your teacher. It may well be that by the end of the semester basically everything you ever believed about the world has changed. And it may well be that these changes in cognitive state are accompanied by thrilling emotional changes: the marvel of it all. Still, this is just what the psyche does. So too with the simpler case of changes in one's beliefs in response to an acknowledged contradiction. That kind of change is just what a normally functioning psyche will do. The psyche is in the business of metabolizing experience: changing cognitive and emotional states in response to experience.

But what might it be to change the forms of metabolization themselves? Imagine a fellow student in your Galileo class who began the semester with the same beliefs about the natural world as you had and, as the semester proceeded, he changed his beliefs just as you did. But for him, it was all flat, dull, *lifeless*. It is as though he were looking at life through plate glass. One might speculate whether he was depressed; but what certainly seems true is that his capacity to process beliefs is cut off from his capacity to react emotionally to his experiences. Now imagine that he enters a peculiar conversation whose outcome is that a new vibrancy enters his life. He believes the same things, but he believes them differently: there is a newfound sense of wonder that humans could have thought this, amazement that the world could be *here* rather than *there* – a sense of joy and dread that it is no longer clear what "*here*" could mean.[5] This does seem to be a change in how his psyche functions. His emotional life now seems connected to his cognitive life. This is an example of the kind of a difference psychoanalysis can make.

3.

Freud developed psychoanalysis to alleviate a particular form of human suffering which he called neurosis. If we look just below the surface of human life, we will see that people regularly sabotage their own attempts at happiness or freedom – often in ways that they do not understand. A person may know she should break up with her boyfriend, but she can't quite do it. She cares for him, but not *that* much; she doesn't think they have *that* much in common; but she will marry him rather than break up.

She may have no idea why – just a sense that she *can't* break up. A student may actually want to do his homework and yet somehow he can't quite get around to it. He puts it off and puts it off; and by the time he finally does get around to it, it is a mad rush where he does much less well than he would otherwise have done. It makes him unhappy and exhausts him. Yet it is somehow also OK with him; it is the way he lives. Another might find himself blurting things out in class that sound stupid – almost as if he were out to humiliate himself. Another might find herself drinking too much, even though she told herself she wouldn't, and then doing things she regrets. Some people are lonely and would like so much to talk to others, but they just can't. Others talk so much the intimacy they crave becomes impossible. There are some who are successful in their professional lives, but get no pleasure out of it; and others who look as though they are in a happy marriage, but feel empty inside. The list is endless. Some cases are complex; others are bizarre. But in each case the people are disrupting themselves – and in a strange way they are *motivated* to do so – even though there is no straight-forward sense in which they want to make themselves unhappy.

Freud explained neurosis in terms of psychological conflict, but his account of the conflict shifted over time. At the beginning of his career, he thought the conflict was basically between a person's wishes, beliefs, emotions and judgments. So, for instance, a person's erotic wishes may come into conflict with her sense of what is proper. Instead of making a reasoned judgment of what to do on the basis of this conflict, the erotic wish is simply repressed. It disappears from the person's conscious awareness, but not from her mind. It lives on in the unconscious, pressuring the person in weird and incomprehensible ways.[6] This is a conflict between items that are in the mind.

But in his maturity, Freud came to think that the psyche could come into conflict with itself. The psyche was not a mere container of conflicting atoms, but had a struc-ture of its own. Like Plato, Freud divided the mind into three parts. Freud's division into parts is significantly different from Plato's, but the principles by which the division is made are remarkably similar.[7] Both are concerned with a peculiarly human vulner-ability: to be subject to conflicts between fundamentally different types of desires, aspirations or inhibitions. Freud famously partitioned the psyche into an id, ego, and superego.[8] The id is a reservoir of wishes and fantasies, largely unconscious; it bears a striking similarity to what Plato called appetite. The ego is largely concerned with reality and functioning in the world. Our conscious sense of who we are, our capacity for monitoring our own beliefs and emotions, our sense of what the world is like – all of these are ego-functions. The superego is a repository of our ideals and hopes – and it can also exercise a cruel, punishing function when we don't live up to them.[9]

Freud now thought that neurotic suffering was an expression of a *structural* conflict inside the mind. So, for instance, if someone had a punishing superego, the superego would be set over against the ego, judging it remorselessly. This structural conflict might manifest itself in all sorts of ways. Most obviously, I might hear myself saying, "Jonathan you idiot! Why can't you just . . . ?" Here I am addressing myself in the second person – I am virtually treating myself as though I were someone else – and from this distanced position I unleash a barrage of criticism – onto myself! This is one instance of what it is to take up a superego position.[10] Other examples are less obvious. A person may just feel depressed. (But when the depression is analyzed, it turns out that the person is depressed because she feels nothing she could do would ever measure up.) Another person may have an amorphous sense of guilt. (When analyzed it turns out there is a harsh voice saying everything is his fault.) Another person may continually write and then rip up copies of his screenplay. Another person may suffer writer's block and not be able to write a single word. Another person may be wildly critical *of others* – but in therapy it emerges that he is deflecting outwards criticisms he really holds against himself. And so on.

But if neurosis is an expression of a structural conflict inside the psyche, a cure must involve a structural change. It is difficult to see how any conversation could bring that about. Certainly, a standard Socratic cross-examination won't work: for while facing a contradiction in one's beliefs might cause some discomfort in the interlocutor, neurotic structures are too stubbornly stable to be undone so easily. Even Plato seems to have recognized that. For, in the *Republic*, not only does Socrates develop a tripartite division of the soul, he gives a sophisticated account of how particular forms of human suffering are the outcomes of structural conflict between the different parts. He doesn't use the word "neurosis," but he does have an account of neurotic conflict. So, for example, the oligarchic personality will tend to hold down his appetites by brute force – and this will have all sorts of unfortunate consequences, both in his own soul and in his family environment.[11] It is a striking fact that by the time the Socrates of the *Republic* spells out his theory of psychic structure, he is not using the elenchus. And though the limitation of elenchus is not explicitly discussed, it is dramatized. Socrates engages in a famous examination of Thrasymachus in *Republic* I; but at the beginning of Book II Glaucon asks him, politely but firmly, whether, in addition to his virtuoso performance, he would actually like to convince anyone.[12] For the next nine books, the investigation into the nature of justice, soul and polis proceeds in the absence of elenchic argument. It remains a fascinating question what Socratic method could be once the soul is discovered to be structured. I shall return to this question at the end of the paper.

4.

We are looking for the Socratic spirit alive in psychoanalytic practice. How it got there is not our business. The point is not that Freud was a Plato scholar and self-consciously introduced a Socratic method; nor that psychoanalysis has been shaped by any explicit interpretation of Socrates. (In my experience, when Socrates is invoked to explain a practice, he is regularly misapplied. Is there anything more un-Socratic than the so-called "Socratic method" in law schools?) Socrates is, of course, part of the air we breathe in Western culture; and there is no doubt that Freud breathed deeply. Thus there may well be circuitous and complex influences that proceed from Socratic to psychoanalytic practice. To trace them would be the job of an intellectual historian. For the purposes of this paper, I am just as happy with the thought that psychoanalysts, like Socrates, came up against something very remarkable about the human soul and responded to it in similar ways. The important causal influence is not of Socrates upon Freud, but of the human soul upon both Socrates and psychoanalysts. Moreover, I am concerned with capturing the Socratic spirit in *contemporary* psychoanalytic practice – when that practice is well done. I am not concerned here with Freud's actual practice

– which could be intrusive, cajoling, even bullying. There were occasions where Freud cross-examined his patients as though he was a prosecuting attorney trying to wrest a confession out of a hostile witness.[13] Whether there is anything "Socratic" about such awful therapeutic technique is not the subject of this inquiry.

If we wish to find Socrates alive in psychoanalytic practice, the place to look is in the use of irony to address the question of how to live. This claim requires two important qualifications: one about what it is to "address the question," the other about what is meant by irony.

It is not any question we are dealing with, Socrates tells us, but *how should one live?*[14] But there is a serious *practical* question of how one might succeed in raising this question. If, for example, one examines Socrates' conversation with Phaedrus, it is not clear that anything in the conversation has made any difference to Phaedrus. The entire dialogue is given over to the question of how to live – whether it is better to be loved by a lover than a nonlover, what is the power and proper use of speech and writing, what is it about the nature of our souls that pulls us away from living well – and yet, looking at Phaedrus, it is arguable that he never seriously faces the question. Phaedrus is someone who, as Socrates puts it, *feasts* on speeches.[15] He is smitten with the sounds and sights of speech – so much so that there is little evidence that the truth or falsity of what is being said matters to him. He takes a kind of sensuous delight in speech: consuming it with appetitive hunger. It is hard to see, then, how anything Socrates says could get to Phaedrus in the right sort of way. For Phaedrus is metabolizing speech in the wrong sort of way. Socrates might try to show Phaedrus that Lysias' speech praising the nonlover is in fact misleading and dangerous – but for Phaedrus this is one more delicious speech which he can bring back to Lysias in the hopes of eliciting from him yet another marvelous speech to consume.[16] What a banquet! They may talk about how one should live, but in an important sense the conversation has not yet begun – and it is precisely the "conversation about how to live" that is getting in the way.

In psychoanalysis, similar problems arise all the time. When analysands start to talk explicitly about how to live, they are often using their capacity for intellectual thought to maintain a distance from what is really on their minds. When they talk about some psychological trait they have – "I have this obsessive need to . . ." – it is usually in the service of staying with pat formulations, and thereby avoiding any genuine insight into what they are like. It may even be that the content of what they are saying is true; the problem is that it does not connect to their lives in a living sort of a way. Psychoanalysts call these *resistances* to genuine analysis. In short, "raising the question of how to live" can be a way of avoiding the question of how to live. It is a serious technical question in psychoanalysis how to allow the question of how to live emerge in ways that genuinely engage the soul. From the dramatization of a number of the dialogues, it looks like this was a serious issue for Plato too. For example, if one looks for signs of progress or development in the reactions of the interlocutors in *Phaedrus*, *Euthyphro*, and *Symposium* it is not clear that anyone has developed as a result of the conversation. And Socrates' famous worry that writing philosophy down may be a form of forgetting it rather than remembering is, among other things, a worry that the use of stock phrases can mislead people into thinking they are doing philosophy when in fact they are engaged in an empty exercise.

Now if irony were only what it is commonly taken to be in contemporary culture, it would be no more than another resistance to analysis. There might be a technical question about how to deal with such questionable "humor" in an analytic context, but irony would not be any more significant than that. So, for example, in "Irony in psychoanalysis" the psychoanalyst-author gives this example:

Analyst: I have your bill ready.
Patient: Fantastic!

This, of course, is an example of irony as we popularly know it. The author comments:

My remark, "I have your bill ready," was literal and straightforward, allowing of no other meaning. My patient's reply, "Fantastic!" was clearly ironic, and would be so understood by any person familiar with analysis. The speaker did not imply that he was thrilled at being presented with a bill – quite the contrary; he intended that I should understand him in a sense opposite to the literal expression.[17]

From a psychoanalytic point of view, what is strange about this account is the claim that the analyst's remark "was literal and straightforward, allowing of no other meaning." For it is virtually constitutive of psychoanalysis that no statement is so literal and straightforward that it allows of no other meaning. Indeed, it is my hunch that, even when he wrote this, the author didn't really believe it. Rather, he was in the grip of a popular theory about irony, in which the ironic person achieves his effect by saying the opposite of what he means.[18] And he is certainly supported by many authorities, including for example the *Oxford English Dictionary* which defines irony as "a figure of speech in which the intended meaning is the opposite as that expressed by the words used; usually taking the form of sarcasm or ridicule in which laudatory expressions are used to express condemnation or contempt."[19] And, of course, if this is what a billion English speakers mean by irony, then this is what "irony" means.

Still, perhaps the dictionary only gives us, as it were, the ego of the concept. Perhaps there is a deeper meaning, a deeper use, of the concept of irony that escapes everyday awareness. I think there is; and I think this deeper use is significant for understanding how psychoanalysis works; and I think one can find this deeper use of irony in Socrates' practice. But to discover this deeper use, we need to abandon the assumption that we already know what irony is: namely, a somewhat sarcastic saying the opposite of what one means. Obviously, the issue of Socratic irony is, and will remain, a debatable topic – and it is not the purpose of this article to work through that debate.[20] Rather, I simply want to pick out one strain of what Socratic irony might be and show how fruitful it is to understanding how psychoanalysis works.

But to do that, I have to go against an interpretive assumption that has governed much of the debate about Socratic irony. In a number of passages, Socrates' interlocutors – notably Thrasymachus, Alcibiades and Callicles – accuse Socrates of being ironic.[21] They are frustrated by him – even fed up – and they do seem to mean that he is shamming, saying the opposite of what he really means. (The Greek words *eirōneia*, *eirōn*, and *eirōneuomai* did suggest an attempt to deceive.) But Thrasymachus, Callicles and Alcibiades all have distorted characters – twisted out of shape by narcissistic (*thumos*-driven) longing for recognition, honor, or seduction. Obviously, there is a question whether their pride has distorted their perceptions of Socrates. Perhaps he is not shamming as they – in their frustration and wounded pride – imply. But, less obviously, there is a deeper question whether, for all their distorted perceptions, they are also speaking beyond themselves: uttering a truth that they themselves do not understand. Let "irony" serve as an enigmatic name that picks out Socrates' distinctive activity – however that is properly to be understood. Then Socrates is being "ironic" even though his accusers are confused about what his irony consists in.

5.

My understanding of Socratic irony is indebted to Søren Kierkegaard. Consider this entry from his diary:

> What did Socrates' irony actually consist of? Could it be certain terms and turns of speech or such? No, these are mere trifles; maybe virtuosity in speaking ironically. Such things do not constitute a Socrates. No, his entire life was irony and consists of this: while the whole contemporary population . . . were absolutely sure that they were human beings and knew what it meant to be a human being, Socrates probed in depth (ironically) and busied himself with the problem: *what does it mean to be a human being?* By doing so he really expressed that all the bustle of these thousands was an illusion . . . Socrates doubted that a person was a human being at birth; it doesn't come so easy, and neither does the knowledge of what it means to be a human being.[22]

For Kierkegaard, Socratic irony is not a turn of phrase but a way of life. It is made possible by a peculiar gap between pretense and aspiration that is embedded in our lives. In this example, human life is not merely participation in a biological species, but involves some understanding of what it is to be human. Thus the whole contemporary population can be sure they are human. In their lives, their professions, their social roles they put themselves forward *as* human. Call this the *pretense* of the concept in the literal, nonpejorative sense of "the putting forth of a claim"[23] There need be no hypocrisy involved. The members of the contemporary population in the very living of their lives *put forward a claim* that this is what is involved in living a human life. But the concept also has an aspiration that typically transcends the social practice. We glimpse this when we ask, of a particular act, was that a *humane* thing to do? The question is not about whether the act was perpetrated by a member of the human species. Or if, at university, we consider the division of the *humanities*: by and large the division teaches remarkable aspects of the human spirit. (It leaves the study of our everyday, mediocre habits to the social sciences!)

Socrates investigates what it is to be human by considering various ways humans try to live up to something. So, he considers the virtues or human excellences and asks, What is it to be pious? What is it to be courageous? What is it to be just? He also considers various professions – the human effort to profess oneself to be something. What is it to be a politician? What is it to be a sophist (one who knows)? What is it to be a rhetorician? What is it to be a doctor? He also asks about social formations: What is it to be a city?

In each case, Socrates is able to isolate an aspiration that escapes the practices which express the current social understanding of the category. So, for instance, if doctors are those who promote health in their patients, the current social group that puts themselves forward as doctors are, Socrates argues, failing to do this. Instead, they provide drugs that may alleviate pain, but allow people to maintain their dissolute lives. In the name of promoting health, they in fact promote the diseased status quo. They need not be doing this hypocritically or cynically. They may sincerely be trying to promote health. The *pretense* of medicine is simply the socially accepted practices in which people put forward the claim that they promote health, that they legitimately occupy their position, that, in short, they are doctors. But once the claim is made, there is room for the (ironic) question:

> Among all the doctors, is there a doctor?

And it is a stunning fact about us that we can immediately sense that there is a real question here. It is as though our ears are attuned to something which transcends our current social understanding. If, by contrast, we should ask,

> Among all the ducks, is there a duck?

we have no idea what this purported question could mean.[24] But in the former case, we intuitively detect that a genuine question is being asked about how well or badly our current social understanding of doctoring – the pretense – fits with our aspirations of what is truly involved in doctoring.

This kind of question provides a test for Socratic irony – at least, the type of irony that is most relevant to Socrates. Consider these questions, and what I take to be Plato's answers:

- Among all the sophists, is there a sophist (one who knows)? –Yes, there is one: Socrates – for he is the one who knows that he doesn't know.
- Among all the rhetoricians, is there a rhetorician? –Yes, there is one: Socrates – for he is the one who is trying to lead the souls of those with whom he speaks towards what is true.
- Among all the politicians is there a politician? –Yes there is one: Socrates – for he is the one using the political art to try to shape Athens into a true polis.
- Among all the citizens of Athens is there a citizen? –Well, there was one: he was put to death by a majority vote.

Note that there are two features of this Socratic irony which go against the grain of the popular understanding of what irony is. First, in asking these questions one can mean exactly what one is saying, not the opposite. Second, being ironic in this sense is compatible with being earnest at the same time. In asking, for example,

> Among all the politicians in America, is there a politician?

we may be asking the most serious question imaginable about the future well-being of the country. As one of Kierkegaard's pseudonyms put it,

From the fact that irony is present it does not follow that earnestness is excluded. That is something only assistant professors assume.[25]

6.

With this understanding of Socratic irony in hand, we can now see two distinct but related ways it is present in psychoanalysis. One is more general, the other more technical. I shall deal with them in that order.

Freud once wrote that the aim of psychoanalysis is to help people to love and to work. Some critics interpret this as meaning that the aim of psychoanalysis is to help people put up with their flawed marriages and boring jobs. Call it adjustment![26] But a deeper reading is possible: in their attempts to work out a life for themselves, people experience a profound need for intimacy and for creativity. The forms of these aspirations will vary enormously: they need not be grand or conform to any established ideal. Typically people will formulate very specific problems for themselves, but if one listens long enough, one can often hear a large-scale ironic question:

- As a friend, am I a friend?
- As a lover, am I a lover?
- As a beloved, do I allow myself to be loved?
- In my life, am I living?

And so on. These are all questions of how pretense and aspiration fit together. Often people will have an inchoate sense that in their efforts to put themselves forward in a certain way, they somehow sabotage their own aspirations. To take a paradigm example, a person might come for psychoanalytic therapy after the second or third break-up of a serious relationship. She may experience the break-up as something that happened to her, but has a vague intuition that perhaps she is somehow implicated in ways she doesn't understand. Above all, she is sick of it, sick of herself. And she wants to know in a pressing, urgent way: is this her fate? Is this as far as it is ever going to go for her in terms of human intimacy? Or might it just be possible, between now and death, to have a more meaningful human relationship?

Sometimes the analysand's official problem – the symptom – will look bizarre. And it will certainly seem as though it has nothing to do with these large-scale ironic problems. I had a patient who sought analysis because he could not urinate or defecate in a public toilet. If anyone came into the bathroom his sphincter muscles would clamp shut. And he became so upset by this that, even when no one was present, his muscles would remain rigid. What could this have to do with high-minded questions about intimacy and creativity? As it turns out, a lot. A symptom is never an isolated atom, even though it often presents itself as one. In this case, the patient organized his life around the symptom. For example, he organized his diet – lots of coffee at night – so that he would be sure to feel the urge to urinate and defecate while at home. He would not eat or drink anything during the day for fear that he would feel the need to go to the bathroom. Of course, he stayed away from the place others had lunch for he didn't want them to notice anything was odd. He had to turn down all lunch invitations. But then he also started to turn down dinner invitations – what if he had to go to the bathroom. And he turned down requests from his boss to travel. And he then he stopped traveling altogether. The fact that airplanes and trains have single-person toilets no longer seemed to register with him. It all became impossible. The analysis did uncover specific links to bathrooms, to being overheard, to urinating and defecating – but it also uncovered how, unbeknownst to himself, this patient also used this symptom to isolate himself from his friends and colleagues. Living with the symptom became his life. And it was held in place by tremendous anxiety triggered by his aspirations for friendship, love, and creative expression in the workplace. His personal version of the question – What is it to be a friend? – was "answered" with an urgent need to urinate followed by a muscle-bound sense that urinating was forbidden, impossible.

While this case may at first look strange, when we consider more general difficulties – like nervous tummies, irritable bowels, impulsive eating and bingeing, anxiety attacks, etc. – we can see that the overall structure is not that uncommon.

7.

Freud came to think that neurotic suffering was the outcome of conflict between different parts of the soul. On this view, problems we see on the surface of life – for example, repeated difficulty in writing papers for class – will be a manifestation of intrapsychic conflict between warring parts of the soul. In this case, there might be a nit-picking "parental" superego that "says" that *nothing* the person does could ever measure up. Or there might be an ego that is fearful of its own ambition and aggression: writing a paper means progressing in the generational process, becoming an adult, *taking over* from the parents and assigning them to old age.[27] Instead of being able to negotiate these conflicting feelings, the parts of the soul are set over against each other in a kind of intrapsychic civil war. The outcome is writer's block and suffering in school – though the student has no idea why.

If a conversation were to make a significant difference it would have to bring about a structural change in the psyche. It is not enough simply to talk about one's fears of success, one's feelings that one never measures up, and so on: for while the conversation may be of some value in expanding one's psychological awareness, it will most likely get caught up in the very problem it is trying to solve. The person will begin to feel that he isn't quite measuring up *in the therapy*; that his insights really aren't that good, that he can't really take a step forward, that all this talking isn't really doing much good in terms of writing papers – and this must be his fault! If he genuinely has a fear of success, he may be able to talk about it – but that needn't stop him from sabotaging the therapy for fear of success.[28] Neurotic structures are wily – and they are extraordinarily durable. So how could any conversation bring about a structural change? Somehow the conversation would have to undo a neurotic structure and bring about healthy relations between what had hitherto been warring parts.

It is here that Socratic irony plays a crucial role. For it is possible to think of each of the parts of the soul in terms of aspiration and pretense. The id is a primitive and archaic source of wishes and appetites – but in its own way it is also a voice of aspiration. Think of Cookie Monster, on the US children's program *Sesame Street*: "Me Want

Cookie!" In effect, the id is "saying" things like "Me want Mommy!" It is left vague whether the aim is to *have* Mommy or to *be* Mommy – or, in having Mommy to be her. The point is that these wishful, appetitive impulses are not simply desires for a distinct object: they express aspirations in their own id-like way.[29] It goes to the heart of the psychoanalytic conception of eros that – from the most elemental bodily appetites to the highest ideals – humans are aspiring animals.

The superego is much more obviously a voice of aspiration. It expresses a person's ideals and ambitions. And it also has a cruel punishing voice for any failure to live up to them. The cruel superego is – in its own superego-like way – a voice of aspiration.

And, of course, the ego is the voice of pretense. Stretched between wishful impulses one side and criticizing voices on the other, I *put myself forward*: as Jonathan Lear, a teacher, professor, someone who has trained as a philosopher and psychoanalyst, someone capable of writing this essay, and so on. To repeat: the voice of pretense need not be hypocritical. Of course, it may be.

Once we conceptualize the parts of the soul this way, we can see that in neurotic conflict there will necessarily be a gap between aspiration and pretense. It is constitutive of neurotic conflict that the parts are cut off from each other, and that real communication between them is impossible. The aim of psychoanalysis is to overcome this structural impasse. One way to think of the therapeutic process is in terms of *bringing out the irony*. For it is precisely by making the gap between aspiration and pretense explicit that one starts to draw the different parts of the soul into communicative relations.

Let me give a brief example. At the time he sought analysis, Mr. A was single, middle-aged, and successful in his professional occupation. But in spite of his outward professional success, inwardly he felt anxious and inhibited. He saw himself as "wearing a nice mask to hide the real, ugly, nasty me."[30] He was anxious about aggressive impulses and angry feelings, particularly towards those in positions of authority. This became prominent in his relations with his analyst – in what analysts call the transference.[31] He experienced his analyst as a controlling authority who inhibited him and kept him in line.

Overall, Mr. A had a successful analysis – he was able to open up in all sorts of ways to others and to himself – and there is much to be said about how these changes came about. But I want to focus on one moment towards the end of the analysis, in the so-called termination phase. In the fourth year of his treatment, Mr. A began to talk about bringing the analysis to a close, but he used noticeably aggressive language. He talked of "quitting" the analysis; he began to "warn" his analyst about it; and he insisted this was his decision, not the analyst's, because he didn't want to take the decision "lying down." He felt joy when he finally proposed that they end the analysis, but then quickly felt hurt, angry, and abandoned when the analyst agreed to his proposal. It was as though their roles had switched: Mr. A experienced the doctor as the aggressive one who was rejecting him.

Mr. A then switched to gratitude. He began to speak of all the gains he had made in the analysis. He was much happier than he had been, he felt freer and more relaxed. He had been able to make life-changes that gave him real pleasure: he was now happily married, together they were buying a house, his wife was pregnant and they were both looking forward to having a baby. And he said that these external changes were

453

manifestations of significant internal changes. He was now a more confident person; and he felt that he could thus take on commitments with others in a more trusting and genuinely intimate way. He expressed his heartfelt gratitude to the analyst. And Mr. A's remarks did fit the analyst's sense that Mr. A had indeed used the analysis to make some far-reaching changes. "On the surface, at least, it seemed that this taking stock of what had been accomplished in his analysis was part of a 'rebuilding' or synthesizing process appropriate to termination."[32]

And yet. Mr. A also had a lingering cough. It began as part of infectious illness, but it never quite went away. And it seemed that Mr. A would start coughing more vigorously in the analytic session at times when he was talking about hostile feelings. Might the cough be a symptom? And might it be expressing some neurotic conflict that was being covered over by all the sincerely meant testimonials? Mr. A was, by now, an old hand at analysis, and he began to wonder about the meaning of his own cough. However, he didn't recognize the connection between his cough and his angry feelings "until an extended fit of coughing occurred when he suddenly became very angry with me, saying 'Do I want to tell you to fuck off!' "

> He then began coughing uncontrollably for several minutes, finally leaving the office for a minute to go to the bathroom for a drink of water. Returning to the couch, he asked, "Why would I want to tell you to fuck off? You haven't done anything but been here."
> I said, "Maybe that's why."
> "Yes, you're the doctor," he replied. "Why haven't you cured me? I've been waiting for you to fix me."
> This was the moment when Mr. A experienced the full intensity of his hostility toward me in the waning months of the analysis.[33]

Of course, this is no more than a snapshot of a brief moment in a long and complex analysis. But if we look carefully, there is a lot we can learn from it. Let us first consider the intrapsychic configuration that led up to this outburst. In terms of aspirations, there are id-like wishes for a magical cure: somehow the analysis was supposed to turn him into a completely different person – wonderfully handsome and powerful, effort-lessly successful. *Superman!* As the analysis is coming to an end, there is a dawning sense that these infantile wishes will never be gratified. And so there arise angry id-like feelings of disappointment. These too express a voice of aspiration in that they are directly linked to the wishes. Then there is a punishing superego which issues an aspiration-filled command: *You shall not be angry! If you get angry, you are a bad person and will be punished! You ungrateful wretch!* What emerges between these conflicting forces is the pretense: Mr. A, who puts himself forward as, say, "a mild mannered reporter," who nevertheless feels he is somehow living behind a mask. This is the ego. And yet, the pretense doesn't quite work: Mr. A finds himself blurting out angry thoughts; acting impulsively in spastic angry outbursts. This is what brought him into analysis: an inchoate sense that his pretense was breaking down.

What is striking about neurotic conflict is that it makes thoughtful evaluation all but impossible. Mr. A is disappointed he has not received a magical cure; and he is angry at his analyst for not giving him one. But he would also be embarrassed to recognize those wishes. And he is also afraid of his own anger – indeed, he is angry at himself about his own anger. On top of that, he is genuinely grateful to his analyst for all the help he has received. He has grown in many ways and he is proud of that. Nevertheless, instead of being able to take up all these conflicting and ambivalent feelings and think about what he wants do with them all, he develops a cough. The cough becomes a kind of nucleus of the conflict – expressing his angry feelings while also keeping them under cover. This is what makes Mr. A's conflict neurotic: the aspiring and pretending parts of the soul cannot find any genuine way to communicate; and lacking this, they conflict in ways that have bizarre and often unwelcome manifestations.

What is striking – and beautiful – about the analyst's response is that he confines himself to bringing out the irony. He does not offer Mr. A any content; no fact is presented for Mr. A to accept. If the analyst had said something like, "Your problem is that you are suffering from a conflict between your wish to blah blah blah and your ambition to blah blah blah," Mr. A's compliant self would have accepted the "insight" with gratitude. He might then tell others of his "inner needs" – and what he is saying might be true. But it would have made no real difference to the underlying structural conflict. Rather, the pretending part of Mr. A's soul – the ego – would have taken it up as part its role of "self-understanding." The analyst's "interpretation" would then be used as one part of the neurotic conflict, rather than as anything that might resolve it.

Instead, the analyst invites the analysand back to his own just-spoken words.

"You haven't done anything but been here."

This is the sincere, heartfelt voice of pretense. Mr. A is expressing genuine puzzlement over his angry outburst. The analyst invites Mr. A to see that the very same words might also express a complaint: "I've been coming four days a week for four years, and what have you done? You've just sat there! And now I have to leave, and I have all these unsatisfied wishes, and what have you done? Nothing! You've just been here. That's it!" This is the voice of complaint – which is the voice of aspiration denied.

It is constitutive of neurotic conflict that Mr. A cannot hear both voices at the same time. This is because, in neurosis, the id, ego, and superego are all split off from each other. In the ego-position, Mr. A is all sincerity and puzzlement: he feels genuine gratitude and cannot understand his angry outburst. So as he says, "You haven't done anything but been here," he can only hear the voice of pretense. His angry feelings are right there in the room – he has just had a furious outburst – yet they are weirdly cut off from his feelings of gratitude and puzzlement. In the moment of speech, gratitude and puzzlement is *all* Mr. A feels.

The analyst's remark – "Maybe that's why" – brings Mr. A back to his own words – and thus back to the feelings of gratitude and puzzlement he has just been experiencing – and invites him to listen to another voice that may also be getting expressed in the here and now. What is important about this example is not simply that the same words can be used to express the voices of pretense and aspiration; it is, rather, that these words can be used as a *point of attachment* between different parts of the soul. That is, Mr. A can now use his own words to go back and forth between his genuine feelings of gratitude and his equally genuine feelings of disappointment and anger. This is just what he could not do when he was in a state of neurotic conflict. In effect, the analyst's remark invites Mr. A to use his own words to perform a bridging function between the aspiring and pretending parts of his soul. He can now actually consider his conflicting feelings, and think about how he feels overall. He may learn simply to live with conflicting feelings. There may be no overall resolution. Still, this is a better way to deal with one's wishes and feelings than having a persistent cough, spastic outbursts, and mad dashes to the toilet.

It is important that by "maybe" the analyst means *maybe*. The analyst, like Socrates, genuinely does not know. Instead of offering an answer, the analyst extends an invitation to the analysand *to bring out the irony for himself.* Ultimately, bringing out the irony is the analysand's task, not the analyst's. And the invitation might not have worked – for various reasons. It might be that the analysand's hunch was wrong; it might be that the analysand was still in such neurotic conflict that he could not tolerate hearing any other voices than the one he was putting forward. One should keep in mind that this vignette occurs towards the end of a successful analysis, so Mr. A was ready to make connections that would likely have been impossible for him earlier on. Although in the moment of utterance, he could only hear his voice of pretense, as soon as the invitation is extended, he is ready to make the connection:

> "Yes you're the doctor . . . Why haven't you cured me? I've been waiting for you to fix me."

It is by making a thousand such connections that bridges of communication are established between the aspiring and pretending parts of the soul. And it is these bridges that both constitute and facilitate structural change. Irony – used gently, carefully, but firmly – is essential to this therapeutic process. And it is in the use of irony that we shall find the Socratic method alive and well in the practice of psychoanalysis.[34]

8.

Throughout this essay I have used the expression "Socratic method" ironically. For there is a widespread assumption that the Socratic method just is the method of cross-examination, the elenchus. Let us call this the *pretense* of the Socratic method. That is, it is what scholars have put forward as a claim about what constitutes Socrates' method. It is well known that in the various Platonic dialogues the figure of Socrates espouses differing beliefs and uses different methods of inquiry. So much so, that it has led one distinguished ancient philosopher to claim that in the Platonic dialogues there are two Socrates:

> I have been speaking of a "Socrates" in Plato. There are two of them. In different segments of Plato's corpus two philosophers bear that name. The individual remains the same. But in different sets of dialogues he pursues philosophies so different that they could not have been depicted as cohabiting in the same brain throughout unless it had been the brain of a schizophrenic. They are so diverse in content and method that they contrast as sharply with one another as with any third philosophy you care to mention, beginning with Aristotle's.[35]

It is then assumed that the dialogues which employ the elenchus are "earlier" and that they provide insight into the historical Socrates. The dialogues that forego elenchus and use demonstrative argument to put forward theses about the nature of the soul and world are said to come later; and in them "Socrates" is just a spokesman for Plato. "The metamorphosis of Plato's teacher into Plato's mouthpiece is complete."[36]

This is not the place to offer a detailed critique of this picture, though it is worth noting in passing how tightly woven its interpretive principles are: Socrates is revealed by his method, which is the elenchus, which provides a basis for dating the dialogues into earlier and later (on the grounds that the younger Plato would be more loyally reflecting his teacher). Every inference here is open to challenge. But, for the purposes of this essay, I simply want to put forward a different interpretive principle: if we take Socratic method to be irony, and if we understand irony broadly – not in terms of saying the opposite of what one means or shamming – but as bringing out the gap between aspiration and pretense, then we can see a unity of method that spans the supposed division of the two Socrates. The aim is not to recover the historical Socrates, but to find a larger unity among specific differences.

First, Socrates' paradigmatic *use* of elenchus can be seen as a type of irony. Here I am not particularly concerned with the formal marks and features of elenchus, but with the distinctive ways Socrates deploys it. Socrates' major interlocutors have it in common that they *put themselves forward* as having knowledge of what they are talking about. Euthyphro, for example, takes himself to be an expert on piety.[37] Laches, as a successful general, takes himself to have some insight into what courage is. Protagoras puts himself forward as someone who can teach virtue, and thus who knows that virtue is teachable. Thrasymachus puts himself forward as someone who knows what justice really is. Socrates' interlocutors are paradigmatically men of pretense. And so, when Socrates deploys elenchus *on them*, he not only elicits contradictory beliefs – as befits the formal structure of elenchus – he also elicits from them an aspiration buried in their own understanding of the relevant virtue which outstrips their pretense to know. There is something about piety or courage or justice that transcends the claim put forward by the interlocutor. Thus Socrates' actual use of elenchus can be seen as a species of irony. Of course, if we think of elenchus merely as a method of cross-examination, as eliciting a contradiction in an interlocutor's beliefs, there is no reason to think of elenchus as a form of irony. But when we attend to the particular ways Socrates deploys elenchus – especially in the paradigm cases – we see that he is putting elenchus to ironic use. Irony is the *how* not the *what* of Socratic elenchus. (One will not be able to see this if one concentrates exclusively on the formal structure of elenchus. Nor will one see it if one focuses solely on the interlocutor's propositional attitudes; e.g. "X believes that p. But he also believes q and r which imply not-p." One also needs to see how those propositional attitudes fit into the interlocutor's pretense and his ultimate ability to recognize aspirations built into the virtue he pretends to know.)

Second, it is a commonplace of Platonic scholarship that by the time Socrates discovers the tripartite soul, he has abandoned elenchic method. And, as we saw in sections 1 and 2 above, there are good reasons for doing so: if a person's belief system is dominated by appetites or desire for honor, it is not clear that merely drawing out a contradiction in his beliefs will make much difference to him. So far, so good. But this has led commentators to assume that Book I of the *Republic* – which is largely given over to an elenchic examination of Thrasymachus – must be significantly earlier than, even tacked onto the later books, in which the soul is divided and the elenchus is not used. Supposedly this shows that Socrates is in Book I, and his Platonically altered namesake is in Books II–X. But if we think in terms of irony, a unity will emerge amidst the differences. I do not know to what extent Plato was aware of this unity. However, the claim that Book I is simply tacked onto the *Republic* arises largely from a failure to see such unity.

Socrates divides the soul into three parts. Appetite desires sex and food (and money which can be used to gratify appetites). Spirit (or *thumos*) desires recognition and honor. Reason desires truth. He also argues that human personalities can be understood in terms of one of the parts gaining dominance over the others. So, for instance, in an honor-loving person like Thrasymachus, the desire for admiration will have the upper hand, and his reason will largely be subjugated to the calculative function of figuring out how to get more. He will have subjugated his appetites as well, for he wouldn't want to do anything that looked base. Similarly, in an appetitive personality like the oligarch, reason will be subjugated to figuring out how to acquire large amounts of wealth. And to the oligarch it will appear that wealth is worthy of honor. Socrates argues that there is only one stable, harmonious and happy personality-formation: that of the just person. In this person reason rules: it lets spirit feed on what is truly honorable; and allows the appetites to be gratified only in healthy ways. All other personality-formations are unstable and disharmonious to some degree: one should expect division and strife among the parts. In Freudian terms, all other personalities are to some extent neurotic.

Let us now return to Thrasymachus. We are now in a position to see that irony is occurring both in the macrocosm of elenchic debate and in the microcosm of Thrasymachus' soul. In the macrocosm, Thrasymachus is an ideal candidate for irony. He puts himself forward as someone who knows what justice really is. And, in putting himself forward, he gives an official account, the pretense of justice. Socrates' distinctive use of elenchus consists in forcing Thrasymachus to acknowledge that justice also has aspirations which transcend his official account.

But now that we have a theory of Thrasymachus' intrapsychic make-up we can also give a more nuanced account of what is going on within him during the elenchus. Thrasymachus is a spirited, honor-loving personality. That means that his soul is organized around *thumos*. Not only does *thumos* shape his understanding of justice, it motivates him to put himself forward as someone who deserves recognition for knowing what justice really is. Thus, in Thrasymachus' personality-organization, *thumos* is functioning as a pretending part of his soul. In an honor-loving personality, reason will be subjugated to figuring out ways to acquire honor – as understood by *thumos*. Still, Socrates has argued that every such personality-organization is unstable. Socratic elenchus takes advantage of this instability. While Thrasymachus' reason is crippled and distorted by *thumos*, there is some aspect of it which aspires to truth. Even Thrasymachus – or part of him – aspires to truth; and this helps to explain why the elenchus comes to be such an ordeal for him. After all, why not just laugh it off? He cannot because his soul is genuinely conflicted. The elenchus awakens the aspiring part of his soul and brings it into close proximity to his pretended understanding.

The outcome of this juxtaposition is – preserved and remembered through the millennia – a blush:

Thrasymachus agreed to all this, not easily as I'm telling it, but reluctantly, with toil, trouble and – since it was summer – a quantity of sweat that was a wonder to behold. And then I saw something I'd never seen before – Thrasymachus blushing.[38]

If we consider only the macrocosm of public debate, it is natural to think that Thrasymachus is blushing *before others*: he had wanted to show off, and he is getting his comeuppance instead. But if we think of the microcosm, we can see that the elenchus awakens the aspiring part of Thrasymachus' soul and, at least temporarily, partially frees it from its domination by *thumos*. In the moment, Thrasymachus can feel how far his pretence to knowledge has fallen short of his own aspiration to truth. We can now see that Thrasymachus is also blushing *before himself*. At least in the moment, Socrates has disrupted the unhealthy configuration of an honor-loving soul. And the aspiring and pretending parts of Thrasymachus' soul have been brought into a different relation with each other.[39] Thrasymachus' blush is the blush of psychic upheaval. And perhaps that upheaval will lead to more lasting psychic change. (In this context, consider Socrates' later remark that he and Thrasymachus have become friends [VI: 498c–d]; and Thrasymachus' joining in with the rest of the group [at V.450a].)

Obviously, the Socrates of the *Republic* is not particularly concerned with individual talking cures, or with the psychic transformation of adults. He is concerned with political formations which through education will properly shape the souls of children and young adults. And even if elenchus did succeed in disrupting the configuration of Thrasymachus' soul, there is no reason to think it is a particularly good method for effecting lasting psychic change in a divided soul. Thus once one discovers the tripartite soul, and the personality-structures based on it, there is reason to abandon elenchus as a therapeutic method. Nevertheless, it is not implausible to conjecture that the philosopher who thought through the tripartite theory of the soul might then wonder what effect, if any, the elenchus could have on such a soul. And he might dramatize that effect in a sophist's blush.

Finally, let us consider Socrates' famous profession of his own ignorance. In the *Apology*, Socrates says that it is precisely because he has spent his life exposing the pretenses of others to know, that he has generated widespread resentment against him.[40] Thus it is the practice of irony – as it is interpreted in this paper – that, Socrates thinks, will be responsible for people voting to condemn him. In contrast with others, Socrates is, famously, the wisest of men because he is the one who knows that he doesn't know. In particular, Socrates claims that he knows that he does not know how to give an adequate account of the virtues or human excellences. In terms of the structure of irony we have been investigating, Socrates "puts himself forward" as the person who is not in a position to put himself forward. That is, when it comes to knowledge of the virtues, Socrates is the man without pretense. He makes no claim to know. *He is all aspiration and no pretense.*[41] And thus, ironically, while Socrates can bring out the irony in others – that is his Socratic irony – there is nothing *about him* that is ironic at all. At one point Phaedrus and, at another point, Alcibiades say that Socrates is the most unique, the strangest person who has ever lived.[42] The Greek word is "*atopōtatos*": literally, the person most lacking a *topos* – a place, position, or location. But think of *topos* in terms of pretense: the putting forth of a claim is precisely taking up a position in argumentative space. It is saying, for example, "When it comes

459

to justice, I have a position; I know what it is." Socrates has no such position – he is *atopos* – and this turns out to be the quintessence of human wisdom.

There are readers of Plato who agree with Thrasymachus that Socrates' profession of ignorance is a sham – a pretense in the *pejorative* sense of pretending to be something other than one is. These readers take Socratic irony to be his saying the opposite of what he means. And thus, for them, it is only a pretense that Socrates has no pretenses. For these readers too there must be *another Socrates*. This time the other Socrates isn't Plato's mouthpiece, it is the real Socrates hidden behind his masks. I don't think there is any knock-down proof that will show that this interpretation is wrong. And if a latter-day Thrasymachus wants to hold onto it tenaciously, so be it. But, for the rest of us, I hope this essay will contribute to a different outlook. The true power of Socrates to reach out across the millennia – and *grab us* – lies in the fact that, in his irony, he is also intensely earnest. He is saying precisely what he means. It is a question for us and about us why this has been so difficult to accept.[43]

Notes

1 *Phaedrus* 229e–230a.
2 Freud, *Group Psychology and the Analysis of the Ego* (*Standard Edition of the Complete Psychological Works of Sigmund Freud* (London: Hogarth Press, 1981) (hereafter SE) XVIII: 91. See also *Three Essays on the Theory of Sexuality*, SE VII: 134; "Resistances to psychoanalysis" SE XIX: 218; and *Beyond the Pleasure Principle*, SE XVIII: 50;
3 Plato, *Apology* 30a–b.
4 See, e.g., Gregory Vlastos, "The Socratic elenchus: method is all," in *Socratic Studies*, (Cambridge and New York: Cambridge University Press, 1994), pp. 1–37.
5 See my *Therapeutic Action: An Earnest Plea for Irony* (New York: Other Press, 2003), pp. 1–27.
6 See, e.g., *Studies on Hysteria*, SE II: 3–305, especially the case history of Elizabeth von R. And cf. my *Freud* (London and New York: Routledge, 2005), ch. 2.
7 See *Republic* IV.436b–441a.
8 Freud, *The Ego and the Id*, SE XIX: 1–66. For Plato's method of division of the soul, see *Republic* IV: 434d–445a.
9 See Freud, *Civilization and its Discontents*, SE XXI: 57–145.
10 For an example of a Platonic figure taking up what Freud would call a superego position, see the discussion of Leontius at *Republic* IV: 439e–440a.
11 Plato, *Republic* VIII: 554a–555a, 556b–c, 559d. See also C. D. C. Reeve, *Philosopher-Kings: The Argument of Plato's Republic* (Princeton: Princeton University Press, 1988); and my "Inside and outside the *Republic*," in *Open Minded: Working Out the Logic of the Soul* (Cambridge, MA: Harvard University Press, 1998), pp. 219–46.
12 *Republic* II: 357a–b.
13 See Freud, *Fragment of an Analysis of a Case of Hysteria*, SE VII: 7–122; and my *Freud* (London and New York: Routledge, 2005), ch. 4; and "Give Dora a break!," in *Erotikon: Essays on Eros, Ancient and Modern*, eds. T. Bartscherer and S. Bartsch (Chicago: University of Chicago Press, 2005).
14 *Republic* I: 352d.
15 Plato, *Phaedrus* 227b7–8.

16   See, for instance, Phaedrus' response to Socrates' impassioned palinode at *Phaedrus* 257c; and G. R. F. Ferrari, *Listening to the Cicadas: A Study in Plato's Phaedrus* (Cambridge and New York: Cambridge University Press, 1987), pp. 86–112.

17   Martin H. Stein, "Irony in psychoanalysis," *Journal of the American Psychoanalytic Association* 33 (1985): 35–57.

18   It is possible to be *pleased* that one is receiving a bill: one might be proud that one can afford to pay for it. "Fantastic" would then, unironically, mean fantastic.

19   *Oxford English Dictionary*, online, 2nd ed., 1989.

20   For good introductions (with which I disagree) see Gregory Vlastos, *Socrates: Ironist and Moral Philosopher* (Cambridge: Cambridge University Press, 1991); and Alexander Nehamas, *The Art of Living: Socratic Reflections from Plato to Foucault* (Berkeley and Los Angeles, University of California Press, 1998), pp. 19–98.

21   For Thrasymachus, see *Republic* I. 337a; for Alcibiades, *Symposium* 216e4, for Callicles, *Gorgias* 489d–e.

22   Søren Kierkegaard, *The Diary of Søren Kierkegaard*, trans. P. Rhode (New York: Citadel Press, 1993), §163, pp. 128–9.

23   *Oxford English Dictionary*, online, 2nd ed.

24   In the diary entry just quoted above, Kierkegaard says: "Going to South America descending into subterranean caverns to dig up remains of vanished animal fossils: there is nothing ironical about that, for the animals one comes across today living in such places do not, after all, pretend to be the same as the ancient ones. But plumb the middle of Christendom to want to excavate the foundation of what it means to be a Christian, which bears almost the same relation to our contemporary Christians as the bones of the ancient animals to those now living: that is the most intense irony. The irony is that while Christianity is supposed to exist there are at the same time thousands of prelates in velvet, silks and broadcloth, millions of Christian's begetting Christians, etc."

25   The pseudonym is Johannes Climacus, *Concluding Unscientific Postscript*, trans. D. F. Swenson and W. Lowrie (Princeton: Princeton University Press, 1941), p. 246n. Both Vlastos and Nehamas misunderstand what Kierkegaardian irony is. While they disagree with each other, they both assume that the Kierkegaardian ironist must be saying the opposite of what he means. For Vlastos, this flows from a misreading of what Kierkegaard means by "negativity." (See *Socrates: Ironist and Moral Philosopher*, op. cit., p. 43.) Nehamas quotes a more compelling passage from Kierkegaard: "one can deceive a person into the truth. Indeed when a person is under an illusion, it is only by deceiving him that he can be brought into the truth." (Nehamas, p. 52; quoting from Kierkegaard, *The Point of View of My Work as an Author*, trans. W. Lowrie; New York: Harper and Row, 1962, pp. 39–40.) Nehamas has, I think, misunderstood this passage. The point is not strictly about the need to dissemble to those under illusion; it is to recognize that *anything* one says will be systematically distorted by someone in the grip of illusion. Even an earnest, truthful communication will be misunderstood. The task then is to find a form of communication that will disrupt the illusion. This is a problem that Socrates, Kierkegaard and psychoanalysts have confronted. But the answer to the problem need not involve saying the opposite of what one believes.

26   See Jacques Lacan, "The direction of the treatment and the principles of its power," in *Ecrits: A Selection*, trans. Bruce Fink (New York: W. W. Norton, 1999), pp. 215–70. But see also Paul Gray, *The Ego and Analysis of Defense* (Northvale, NJ and London: Jason Aronson, 1994).

27   See Hans Loewald, "The waning of the Oedipus complex," in *The Essential Loewald* (Hagerstown, MD: University Publishing Group, 2000), pp. 384–404.

28 For an introduction to transference, see Freud, *Fragment of an Analysis of a Case of Hysteria*, SE VII: 112–22; "Remembering, repeating and working-through," SE XII: 147–56. See my *Freud*, op. cit., ch. 4; *Therapeutic Action: An Earnest Plea for Irony*, op. cit., ch. 5, pp. 181–211; and "An interpretation of transference," in *Open Minded: Working Out the Logic of the Soul* (Cambridge, MA: Harvard University Press, 1998), pp. 56–79. The classic psychoanalytic essays on transference are collected in *Essential Papers on Transference*, ed. A. Esman (New York: NYU Press, 1990).

29 Even when a grown person is bingeing on ice cream, aspiration is there. For an introduction to the psychoanalytic understanding of eating disorders, see L. Reiser, "Love, work and bulimia," in *Bulimia: Psychoanalytic Treatment and Theory*, ed. H. J. Schwartz (Madison, CT: International Universities Press, 1988), pp. 373–97; S. Ritvo, "Mothers, daughters and eating disorders," in *Fantasy, Myth and Reality: Essays in Honor of Jacob A. Arlow, M.D.*, eds. H. Blum et al. (Madison, CT: International Universities Press, 1988), pp. 423–34; S. Ritvo, "The image and uses of the body in psychic conflict – with special reference to eating disorders in adolescence," *Psychoanalytic Study of the Child*, 39 (1984), pp. 449–69.

30 I take this case from Lawrence Levenson, "Superego defense analysis in the termination phase," *Journal of the American Psychoanalytic Association*, 46 (1998), pp. 847–66. I discuss this case in *Therapeutic Action: An Earnest Plea for Irony*, pp. 121–33, 176–8, 207–11.

31 See note 29 above.

32 Levenson, "Superego Defense," p. 858.

33 Ibid.

34 For simplicity, this chapter concentrates on Freud's structural model, but the same overall technique will apply to any model – for example, the models of self-psychology – in which there are aspiring and pretending aspects to the psyche. See, for example, Heinz Kohut, *The Analysis of the Self: A Systematic Approach to the Psychoanalytic Treatment of Narcissistic Personality Disorders* (Madison, CT: International Universities Press, 1987).

35 Gregory Vlastos, "Socrates 'contra' Socrates in Plato," in *Socrates: Ironist and Moral Philosopher*, p. 46.

36 Vlastos, *Socratic Studies*, p. 37.

37 *Euthyphro* 3c, 4b,e.

38 *Republic* I, 350c–d.

39 Of course, it is also possible to conceptualize *thumos* as aspiring to honor. The point is not that there is only one proper characterization of the psychic parts; it is, rather, that there is one accurate characterization that at the same time shows how irony is possible.

40 *Apology* 21b–c.

41 See Apology 29a–b: "And surely it is the most blameworthy ignorance to believe that one knows what one does not know." That is, it is blameworthy to have a pretense to know that cannot live up to the aspirations of the concept.

42 *Phaedrus* 230c; *Symposium* 221c.

43 I would like to thank Gabriel Lear, Karin Ahbel-Rappe, Sara Ahbel-Rappe, Iakovos Vasilious, and Joan Wellman for valuable comments on a previous draft.

28

Lacan and Socrates

MARK BUCHAN

"The Freudian world isn't a world of things, it isn't a world of being, it is a world of desire as such."

–Lacan (1991a: 222)

"There is an entire thematic area concerning the status of the subject when Socrates declares that he does not place desire in a position of original subjectivity, but in the position of an object. Well! Freud, too, is concerned with desire as an object."

–Lacan (1978: 13)

Let me begin with a story from Plato that illustrates the complexity of the relationship between knowledge and desire, a relationship that is at the center of both the psycho-analytic and Socratic discourse. At the opening of the *Greater Hippias*, Hippias tells Socrates that he can speak on any subject well, educate the youth of any community on that topic, and accordingly get his sophist's fee. Yet despite this ability, he is strangely unable to gain money from the Spartans, and this despite the fact that he is welcomed by them, and that they enjoy listening to his discourses. How can this be? The Spartans, Hippias claims, are not allowed by law to turn over the education of their children to any outsider, and thus keep themselves immune to external knowledge. Yet how can they enjoy listening to Hippias and his knowledge? The melancholy punch-line comes when Socrates finds out exactly what Hippias has been teaching the Spartans. They ask him to tell them more about their own genealogies, and he goes to great lengths to find out about, and offer up to them, antiquarian details of their own past. Now this knowledge, far from opening them up to outsiders, merely hardens their own social and cultural conservatism. Thus they love his words, but only insofar as they are not "foreign," and thus do not disrupt their own cultural laws, which buttress the rule of father over son. So why should they give a sophist an educator's fee?

Someone speaks quite knowledgeably, but is unable to get what he wants. If this remains an amusing puzzle for Hippias, it need not for us. For it is easy enough to diagnose his error. When he reacts to their offer, he reads only what they say, "tell us about our genealogies," but not what they seem to want. He acts as if knowledge could be removed from desire, as if it is possible to give a "straight" command without taking into account not only the content of the desires of those of who give the

463

command, but also the strategy behind that desire. He duplicates the errors of many a Herodotean character who seeks a similar kind of objective knowledge from the Delphic oracle, only to find out that what is at stake is not objective truth, but rather the way a subject is caught up in that game of knowledge, and that knowledge is framed by his own desires. But one should not also necessarily read this as a victory for the Spartans and their ongoing ability to delight in their self-image. For that, perhaps, would give too much consistency to what we believe their desire is. Is it really to have their self-knowledge affirmed? Or were they hoping against hope that this sophist would teach them something new, a desire implied by the very invitation to speak in the first place? As Lacan puts it, not everyone wants you to give them the thing they ask for. Is not Hippias' very presence in Sparta symptomatic of a flaw in their supposed desire for self-withdrawal from the world into their closed community? At all events, what is missed out for here, and which the dialogue itself will try to open up, is the possibility of a dialogue between people who recognize their own desires less as fixed than inde-terminate, ongoing enigmas rather than puzzles with a simple solution. In this case, we have one person who knows, but remains puzzled by his inability to get what he desires, and another culture that seems to "know itself" well enough to deflate the fee-hungry sophist, but only at the price of hinting at a desire for something beyond this sterile self-knowledge, a something that the sophist is quite unable to provide.

Both the Socrates of Plato's dialogues and Lacanian psychoanalysis are unusually sensitive to the problems of knowledge that this story opens up, and both seek forms of communication that can get beyond its impasse. This chapter will be little more than an attempt to outline this, and in three parts. First, I give a basic overview of some of Lacan's contributions to psychoanalytic theory, and the force of his "return to Freud." In doing so, I want to begin to sketch out some of the overlap between the concerns of psychoanalysis and the Socratic process of question and answer, the elenchus – and not just as a coincidence, but because of the explicit debt owed by psychoanalysis to Socrates. Second, I suggest ways in which Lacan can help us approach some central Platonic texts, and the kinds of questions Socrates raises in them. For to read Socrates via Lacan is to ask a series of questions about the relationship between knowledge and desire that are not commonly asked of the Platonic texts. Finally, I want to provide a brief overview of some of Lacan's own thoughts on Socrates, with particular reference to some of his observations on Socrates in the *Meno* and the *Symposium*. The goal is to be suggestive rather than exhaustive.

The Origins of Psychoanalysis

In 1954, in a speech given to an audience of psychoanalysts in Rome that remains one of Lacan's most accessible and fundamental texts, *The Function and Field of Speech and Language in Psychoanalysis* (Lacan 2002: 31ff.), he announced the need of a return to the essence of the Freudian discovery. The epigones of Freud had gradually come to forget what was most interesting and revolutionary in his teaching – the discovery of the unconscious, the significance of human sexuality, the precarious nature of our subjectivity, and the assorted forms of self-illusion that we turn to in order to avoid this precariousness. Instead, they had turned to the relatively therapeutic safety of Freud's so-called second topography, his division of the self into ego, superego and id. Working from this model, ego-psychology, the dominant form of psychotherapy in the United States at the time, outlined a form of therapeutic practice whose goal was to strengthen the ego, equated with the analysand's self, against the hostile forces of superego and id. The hostility of the superego lay in the ongoing pressures of paternal commands, demands to live up to impossible ideals, while the id consisted of the unconscious reservoir of repressed impulses that threatened to overpower it.

For Lacan, this strengthening of the ego could only end up in strengthening the illusions that surround a subject, and in resulting in an authoritarian form of psycho-analytic practice. For insofar as Freud took the goal of psychoanalysis to be the uncov-ering of unconscious desire, it in part did so because of the contrast between a kind of subjective truth revealed by slips of tongue, dreams, etc., and the relative falsity of our conscious desires, the discourse of the *ego*. For the Freudian discovery shows that our egos are themselves *not* us, but only a part of us, and an alienated version of ourselves at that, a kind of sedimentation of all the ways we have identified with others. The ego, as Lacan puts it, is not an agency but an object, created out of all those temporary, externally derived masks we have worn.

This is not to suggest that the unconscious itself is authentically who we are. Quite the reverse is the case. It is central to Lacan's most famous claim, "the unconscious is structured like a language," that there is no subjective "freedom" in these kinds of disturbance in and of themselves, but rather the unconscious obeys a logic that looks very much like a language; the kind of "unconscious thought" Freud discovered in the processes of condensation and displacement in dreams now translated by Lacan into the linguistic processes of metaphor and metonymy. Nevertheless, it is at least a wit-ness to the way that we are more than our ego-identifications. For all that it suggests something alien, hidden from ourselves, an alien voice within us, the agency heard in our slips of the tongue at least shows that the we have some space for a subjectivity at a distance from the objectifying discourse of the ego. Indeed, ultimately, psychoana-lytic practice is less about finding an authentic kind of subjectivity or self, but rather about a peculiar conversation that allows us both to take stock of, and responsibility for, the alien discourses that make each of us who we are. The point is never to pick the "truest" or most real part of the divided self (whether ego, superego, id, or even the elusive subject of the unconscious), for we are necessarily all of them. Indeed, for Lacan, if there is a need for the notion of an authentic subject, it is no more, or less, than a necessary ethical hypothesis, a presumption without which psychoanalytic inquiry would have no meaning. In terms of the unconscious, the goal of psychoana-lytic practice is not to reject the forms of unconscious thought in the name of a more socially acceptable or rational self, but rather to let it speak, and to allow the subject time to work through its significance. There is a lurking authoritarianism in ego-psychology that Lacan also isolated. To speak of bolstering an ego can only mean a culturally specific ego – that is, it can only endorse a particular ideology. Less a goal of self-exploration, this kind of therapy becomes a social quietism, using the power of the analyst to foster a particular version of the self on the analysand. It is as if, to translate into the terms of Plato's Socrates, Socrates' early dialogues were not to end in *aporia*, but a series of social injunctions: "Be like this!" "Do this!," rather than "Examine your soul." In the terms of the anecdote from the *Greater Hippias*, Hippias acts out the role of ego-psychologist to the Spartans, who buttress their own doubt about themselves *via* his status as external authority figure, whereas Socrates seeks a quite different kind of dialogue.

The comparison to Socrates here is not lightly chosen. For in specifying a return to Freud, we could just as easily argue that Lacan was demanding a return to Socrates and the Socratic roots of psychoanalysis. Psychoanalysis came into being at the moment it realized the power of speech itself, not only negatively – in that the signifiers registered by a subject in the discourse of others around him/her could create symptoms – but positively, in the creative use of language in the analytic situation to help dissolve those symptoms. Freud had initially found that hypnosis could be used to trace forgotten memories, and thus opened up aspects of the past to his patients. But to know the past is in no way a guarantee that it has lost its hold. It has to be worked through. To take a basic example, I might very well discover, through hypnosis, a repressed moment in my childhood when I awoke to find my mother staring at me with piercing blue eyes; that I can't stop being attracted by some specific, repeated characteristic in my love objects that is somehow attached to this moment. But re-membering this moment in the past does not mean that I will change my behavior, or that the power of the blueness of a gaze will loosen its grip on me. But why did Freud turn to language in the first place? If the answer in part lies in his observation of the power of language in his interaction with his patients, it also lies in his interest in Socrates. For at the very beginnings of psychoanalysis, Freud had recently finished translating the Victorian classicist George Grote's book on Socrates into German, and had found a model there for something akin to "the talking cure" (Burgoyne 2000). Psychoanalysis joins itself to Socrates at its very beginning.

Let us take an obvious parallel from Plato to this therapeutic situation, which can perhaps suggest why. At the end of the *Symposium*, Alcibiades talks of the power Socrates has over him:

> He makes me admit that while I'm spending my time on politics I am neglecting all the things that are crying for attention in myself. So I just refuse to listen to him – as if he were one of those Sirens, you know – and get out of earshot as quick as I can, for fear he keep me sitting listening until I'm positively senile. (216a3ff.)

Alcibiades knows, on some level, that he ignores his soul when he leaves Socrates behind, and yet he goes ahead and does this all the same (though it is indeed doubtful whether Socrates would consider the word "knowledge" rightly applied in such a case). Thus, in both psychoanalysis and the Socratic elenchus a certain kind of self-hindered knowledge comes up against the greater power of what some unclear source of the self wants, and the goal of both procedures, will be not only to recognize this, but to rectify it.

There are also crucial differences between the elenchus and talking cure. In an elenctic exchange, the primary commandment is that the interlocutor must say what he believes, that his soul is involved, and this is in response to pressing a moral ques-tion: what is justice, piety, etc. The fundamental principle of psychoanalysis is "free association," of articulating words that immediately come into one's head without any rationalizing cover, which is in turn part of the effort to free the analysand from the constrictions of ego-talk. But for all this, perhaps we underestimate how much theoretical common ground they share. For are they not both engaged in showing that humans are much more victims of language than we believe? In the case of psychoanalysis, we are caught between the Scylla of the automatic functioning of the unconscious, and the straitjacket of our conscious selves that are modeled on ego-identifications with others. What of the Socratic elenchus?

Let us turn again to Alcibiades, but this time to the Alcibiades of the eponymous dialogue, the *Greater Alcibiades*. In this dialogue, Alcibiades, an ambitious youngster on the way to political power and fame, finally converses with Socrates. Alcibiades is about to become an adult, and embark on the project of ruling the world. Socrates, as always, tries to trump him. When you go to advise the Athenians, to prove yourself, what will you be advising them about? The young Alcibiades isn't sure. He must be knowledgeable about the subject. After all, if he does not have a kind of craft knowledge, then he can't demand power in a democracy – he would be the run-of-the-mill Athenian citizen that has every right to speak because of his collective ignorance. But before the argument progresses – and, as one might expect, it leaves Alcibiades in a strangely perplexed state – Socrates makes further specifications about his knowledge. It is not enough that he has undermined the arrogance of Alcibiades' presumed knowledge; rather, Socrates also offers up an explanation for why he cannot find it. For either he has learnt what he knows from somewhere (in which case Socrates must know where, as he has followed him his whole life, carefully spying upon his educational process just as he has carefully stalked the beautiful young Alcibiades himself, above and beyond his other lovers, who have come and gone, their suits rejected by reason of his arrogance). And if he hasn't learnt it from a teacher, he must have discovered it himself.

What is of interest here, especially from a psychoanalytic perspective, is the lurking premise that Alcibiades holds that leads to the ongoing debate. Later, Socrates returns to the moment when Alcibiades fought over the rules of games at school. He *knew* he was being cheated. But, as Socrates has just proved, he seems to be unaware of justice now. Could he not have known he was cheated then? What Alcibiades desperately seems to believe in, and yet rationally cannot, is the possibility of intuitive knowledge – that he might know something to be the case without having learnt it from others. But it is this that Socrates will force him to fight against. He knows very well – in his more rational moments – that this cannot be true, since he has no access to this knowledge and therefore cannot put it to use. And yet, he cannot help acting *as if he knows*. The source of all his dilemmas lies here. When with Socrates, he is not allowed to go along acting in this kind of way – he is not allowed *not* to confront his ignorance. But this ignorance, or so it seems, is tied to powerful forms of self-deception.

Now let us take something of a Socratic test case of this difficulty, the doctrine of knowledge as recollection in the *Meno*. Is not the controversial thesis of this Socratic dialogue the answer to this apparent *aporia* in the *Greater Alcibiades*? That is, the theory of recollection or *anamnēsis* – the possibility that all knowledge is somehow already present in our souls at birth from where it is recollected – does seem to offer up a theory of why Alcibiades might intuitively know something. This would further widen the gap between psychoanalysis and Socrates, and, as it happens, this very point is made by a fellow analyst, Octave Mannoni, to Lacan, in an exchange during Lacan's

Second Seminar (Lacan 1991a: 15ff.). Mannoni tries to resist any easy conflation of psychoanalysis and Socratic thought by emphasizing the different kind of knowledge involved in each case. In psychoanalysis, the aim is to discover a historical truth that happens to an individual subject, one that he is unable to integrate into his conscious worldview. In the *Meno*, what is remembered is a truth about the objective world, a truth of natural science. In response to this point, and quite typically, Lacan does not disagree with him – indeed, a decade later he will make exactly the same point himself – but nevertheless offers up very different lessons from the dialogue, which narrow the gap. He suggests that what is at stake for Socrates is not just a knowledge based on latent information that is hidden in the soul, and thus can be awakened in us by Socrates' questions, but rather the distinction between this kind of knowledge and a different form of knowing entirely, one that Lacan calls truth, and what he links to what Socrates calls "*orthē doxa*," true opinion, in the *Meno*. Let us follow Lacan's argument here.

Lacan provides a commentary on the central scene of the dialogue, when Socrates first draws out a 2 by 2 square in the sand, and tries to get the slave to produce a square twice as large in area. Lacan's first point is that, in showing Meno that a slave can "recollect" information about the area of squares, that the kind of knowledge Meno seeks can be voiced in and through the person of someone who is *a nonperson*. "Take this human life, this one here, the slave, and you will see that he knows everything. All that is needed is to awaken it" (Lacan 1991a: 17). Meno's initial attempt to seek knowledge was through what he thought he could remember from others, and in particular, the lessons of the sophists, though he could not articulate it himself. Indeed, the problem is not simply that he listens to the sophists, but that he does not understand their essential message: "He doesn't understand what the Sophists have to teach him, which isn't a doctrine which explains everything, but the use of discourse, which is really quite different. You can see how bad a pupil he is when he says – If Gorgias were here, he would explain all this to us. You would be knocked over by what Gorgias said. The system is always in the other" (Lacan 1991a: 16). Here, unlike the normal Socratic procedure of confronting the internal inconsistencies of his interlocutors, and thus undermining any sense they have of rational, moral consistency, he acts in reverse: the kind of knowledge that Meno seeks, from a specialized knowledge to be found in others, is available to every human. An authoritative, alluring absent authority – the sophist Gorgias – is replaced by the child-slave.

Lacan's second observation depends on paying close attention to the process the slave goes through. When asked to double the square, he intuitively tries to do so by doubling the square's side in order to double the area. "Well, the slave may be in possession of all the sciences in the book, as accumulated in his previous life, it won't change the fact that he will start by making a mistake. He goes astray by quite properly employing what we use as a starting-point in the standard intelligence test – he employs the relation of equivalence $A/B = C/D$" (Lacan 1991a: 17). In order for the slave to see how to double the square, a "neat trick" of Socrates is required. He cuts off the corners of the larger square, thus halving its size, and produces a square double the original size. Now Lacan's point is not simply that the knowledge of the slave requires the intervention of the master, Socrates, but rather that the experiment traces out two kinds of knowledge: "Don't you see there is a fault line between the intuitive element and the symbolic element? One reaches a solution using our idea of numbers, that 8 is half of 16. What one obtains isn't 8 square units. At the centre we have surface units, and one irrational element, $\sqrt{2}$, which isn't given by intuition. Here, then, is a shift from the plane of the intuitive bond to a plane of symbolic bond" (Lacan 1991a: 18). Socrates, without quite making it explicit, finds a relationship between things that are intuitively incommensurable. He replaces squares with triangles, and we are left with a relationship that is not the same as that of whole numbers to each other, that twice 2 is 4, but of the relationship of the side of the original square to its diagonal, 2 to the square root of 2.

The intervention is symbolic in that it goes beyond the intuitive knowledge of the slave, and forces its way into his reality. This is vastly different from *a priori* forms of intuitive knowledge, which Lacan suggests are linked to the theory of the Forms. To remember the unchanging forms is to have this kind of intuition, but the relation of the human subject to knowledge cannot be reduced to this; and this is in part why Socrates' intervention seems so violent; it is because it is, quite simply, *new*. Now this possibility of a symbolic intervention is what Lacan calls "true opinion," *orthē doxa*, and he sees the role of the psychoanalyst overlapping with both Socrates himself, and the interventions of statesmen such as Pericles and Themistocles. For what is puzzling to Meno about both these figures is that they seem to have been virtuous, political actors, and yet could not systematize their knowledge in any way in order to pass it on to their children. For Lacan the answer is that they acted like analysts. They intervened in response to a contingent situation in such a way as to bring about a truth that, until that moment, remained concealed. They demonstrated a kind of knowledge that was beyond any intuitive knowledge of Forms.

Let us try to sketch out what Lacan means here by teasing out the example of Themistocles. When offered an oracle that suggested Athens build a wooden wall, he offered an interpretation. He suggested that the Athenians build a navy, not defend themselves with a real wall. The intuitive understanding of walls, and indeed of self-protection in general, is replaced by an intervention that will both work – building ships will save Athens – but only by changing the conception Athenians have of themselves, and their identity. It will set in motion a great deal of historical events that will transcend this particular need for Athenian safety, and this discourse of Athens-and-ships will have its own symbolic autonomy and logic. But it cannot be measured by the formal terms of coherence that would constitute a field of knowledge because it is an intervention that changes the very parameters that constitute what "knowledge" is. Now it might be tempting to argue that this "interpretation" was already latent in the double meaning of "wooden wall," and that we are dealing with an oracle that does have access to some kind of truth of the world as it is eternally constituted. But from a Lacanian perspective, what this misses out on is the way, from the outside, a properly symbolic intervention retroactively changes the past in line with its own insight; for we only see the double meaning *after* the success of the intervention. This is why Lacan can say that "for Socrates, the good statesman is a psychoanalyst," because it is this kind of interpretation that psychoanalysis seeks to offer to those who offer themselves up to its services.

It is worth lingering over the possible significance of this. For Lacan, the point of the exchange with Meno, and the rest of his interlocutors, is to undermine a knowledge that was the knowledge of masters, knowledge that we can call personal, and which Socrates' form of argument in the elenchus depersonalizes. It is surely for this reason that Lacan implicitly offers us an interpretation of why Socrates was so shocking. The ancients, both in Plato's reconstruction of their motives in the *Apology*, and in other accounts, had their own indictments of Socrates, their own culturally specific way of sending him to his death – corrupting the youth, bringing in new gods to the city. Socrates himself had his own version; that those around him were unable to stop pretending that they had knowledge, so as a consequence he was needed as a constant reminder to them of their ignorance, a gadfly sent by the god to wake them from their comatose condition. But Lacanian psychoanalysis adds something to this. Not only did he emphasize ignorance, he emphasized this to a culture of masters, for whom know-ledge was essentially a personal matter. If there was a dictum or taboo of the ancient world that Socratic elenchus challenged, it was quite simply: no *knowledge* without a *person-who-knows*. In the place of such a subject, Socrates offered us something rather different: the omnipotence not of a master, but of a someone who was believed by others to be a master but to have rejected the title, and who offered up instead a conversation. Truth, in Socratic terms, belongs not to a person, but rather to some-thing outside the person.

Consider two cardinal features of the elenchus; first, his interlocutors should say what they believe, but also there is a need to follow the consistency of the argument, the *logos*. For, as Socrates will keep reminding them, it is the argument that convicts them, not Socrates. In short, the kind of learning Socrates offers is not a competition, because at bottom it is not about the person of his interlocutors. Rather, in Socrates' terms, it is about the good of their souls. As with psychoanalysis, there is the convic-tion that language has extraordinary power over who one is, that words are danger-ous and go straight to the soul. And yet, this does not mean that we should not talk, but quite the opposite: we must talk all the more. This is exactly the lesson the young Hippocrates must learn in the *Protagoras*. At first, he seems naively unaware of the power of words, and is willing to turn his soul over to the sophist Protagoras, without any knowledge of the possible harm Protagoras' words might do. It is worse, as this harm is irrevocable, since words that have made their way into his soul can never be unsaid. But after explaining this, far from turning away from this alien discourse of the sophists, Socrates leads Hippocrates straight to Callias' house, where they are gathered. For if Socrates' scorn for some of the sophists is well known, his scorn for those who ignore the challenges of what it means to be human in the face of discourse itself, the working premise of so much of sophistic theory, is far greater. The only way we have of making some kind of progress in terms of self-knowledge is through this ongoing form of subjective destitution, of turning ourselves over to an argument that in one way will involve us extremely intimately, forcing us in the process to give up long-cherished, narcissistic beliefs about ourselves. But if it does so, it is because the argument has nothing to do with us. It is impossible to find an answer to our questions that will not also be a story, not about us, but a story of how we got it. Knowledge of the self is extrinsic to the self.

Socrates as Interpreter and Socrates' Desire

Now according to Lacan, the psychoanalyst himself is "subject-supposed-to-know," and this supposition that the analyst knows is the mainspring of the transference. Freud was quick to realize that the emotions that were being aimed at him within therapeutic sessions were transferred from other relationships onto him. For Lacan, that could only happen in a scenario where the analysand believed in the knowledge of the analyst, his/her ability to solve her problems. Now the role of the Lacanian analyst is not to foster the illusion that this external person *does* have some kind of answer, an answer akin to the Socratic knowledge of, say, one of the virtues, but to resist any such position. The situation of transference can be useful because it opens up the possibility, for the analyst, of intervening not in order to prop up the analysand's self-illusions, but to think through where their desires come from and why they exert so much power over them.

Here, Lacan and Socrates join one another once more. For Lacan chose to interrogate the importance of the psychoanalytic concept of transference by devoting a seminar to Plato's *Symposium*, and, crucially, the interchanges between the drunken Alcibiades and Socrates at the end of the text (Lacan 1991b: 179ff.). For there, we not only have an example of Socrates acting as the "subject-supposed-to-know" for Alcibiades, we also find Socrates acting as a proto-analyst, refusing to authenticate Alcibiades' belief in his knowledge, and instead offering him an interpretation about his own desire.

When the drunken Alcibiades enters the party, he claims he will tell the truth about Socrates. But he talks not of Socrates' desires, or even his person, but of the precious objects, *agalmata*, that are inside Socrates. These *agalmata*, according to Alcibiades, belie his external ugliness, and are far more precious than any ordinary goods. Because of this, Alcibiades offers his own sexual services in the hope of an exchange. Socrates' response is instructive. First, he rejects the exchange not from his own beliefs about their value, but on Alcibiades terms. For him to give himself over to him would be to give "gold for bronze." But he also appends a qualification, asking if Alcibiades might not have made a crucial error, and that he has misrecognized Socrates, who far from full of precious objects is really a nothing, a void (218e–219). Now this seems to relate to Socrates' well-known claim, earlier in the dialogue and elsewhere, that he only knows of desire, and that for him this desire is correlative to a lack in the self, this "being nothing." Now this, for Lacan, is the essence of the problem of Socrates' desire. For Socrates does too *know* about desire, but because he knows his own desire he remains something of an enigma. But rather than offering an interpretation of this enigma, Lacan instead puts it to use as a model for how the analyst should manipulate the transference. This being of nothing, this man who can avoid his own need for narcissistic props to the self, can act both as a cipher for his partner, but also as a reader of the inconsistencies of the other's discourse, precisely because he has acquired a certain distance from his own desires. In the case of the *Symposium*, Lacan argues, Socrates first manipulates Alcibiades' desire by refusing to give him a sign of any reciprocal desire from him (he sleeps with him, but is not sexually aroused). That is, he remains an enigmatic object for Alcibiades by refusing to speak of what he wants, but that object is fascinating because it seems to signify a desirousness that captivates him.

This is what Lacan means when he says that Socrates places desire in the position of the object, not an original subjectivity. Alcibiades desires not Socrates, but an object *in* Socrates that is believed to be far more valuable than Socrates himself. And Socrates' response is not to confirm this desire, but rather to become even more of a puzzling, paradoxical object for Alcibiades. Desire here is not internal to the subject, but *caused* by something outside of himself. Of course, the everyday sense of subject and object are being complicated here. The objects in Socrates cannot be described or evaluated in any straightforward way; when Alcibiades makes this effort, he falls into inconsistencies that Socrates preys upon. But nor are these objects mere illusions, because they set Alcibiades' desire in motion. So the object ends up having a paradoxical kind of agency, and the subjective desire ends up being less a constituent of the subject than something that is forced upon him from without. But what this leads to in the dialogue is what Lacan will simply call an interpretation, a symbolic intervention of the analyst akin to the interpretation of the statesman Themistocles, but this time concerning the meaning of Alcibiades' desire. For Socrates suggests that his drunken satyr-play is staged not for him, but entirely for Agathon. Here, Lacan notes, he does not demand that he look to his soul, but rather interprets what he desires.

Socrates' Desire

What does this leave us of Socrates himself, or at least the Socrates of "the Platonic comedy," as Lacan refers to the dialogues? Perhaps we can do no more than try to analyze the way Socrates himself responds to others' tales of him, and tells his own philosophical life story. Consider the opening of the *Apology*. The defense speech begins with Socrates resisting the arguments that he heard, even as he recognizes their power.

> What you have suffered from my accusers, Athenian gentlemen, I don't know. But I for my part nearly forgot myself, so persuasively they were speaking.

They spoke so persuasively, I nearly *forgot myself*. An alien version of himself is quite simply the sum of the stories of everyone else about him, his social resume, or sum total of his fame. Now, he says, the problem is that none of this is true, and he goes on to tell what he says is the truth. What is Socrates up to here? At first, it seems as if he wants to replace one concrete version of Socrates (that of rumor, popular opinion, the comic stage) with another, that of the real Socrates. But the first complication lies in the way Socrates famously replaces a positive thesis with a negative one: rather than a sophist who transmits knowledge, he affirms that he does not know. Rather than a caricature, we have instead a cipher, constituted by little more than his resistance to the stories of others. Finally, rather than a repository of valuable knowledge, we have once more a void, the kind of void Socrates acknowledged himself to be to Alcibiades. But if he is nothing, he is a nothing that is determined to cling to that status, and thus resists other people's stories. If Socrates himself is anywhere to be found, it is the minimal resistance to the discourse of others in the word "oligou," I "almost" forgot myself.

472

Now let us follow the *Apology* a little further. When he says he will speak the truth, it is, he claims, because he is not the sort of person to dress up words.

> Nor would it be fitting for me, at this time of my life, like a youth to come before you, making up stories.

The initial difficulty might lie in the typically paradoxical rhetorical gesture of claiming to be ignorant of rhetoric while making use of one of its clichés. But we should also pay attention to the signifier itself here. The Socrates of the *Apology*, and not any but *Plato*'s – itself one of many attempts to tell the story of Socrates' defense speech – after speaking of the alien, untrue version of himself that exists in the words of others, mumbles out the name of the very person who is writing him up even as he claims his own authenticity: "It is not fitting for a man of my age to come before you 'making up stories'" (*plattonti logous*). What to do with this pun?

At the moment he expresses his authenticity, he blurts out the very words that suggest that this is not him – but a Platonic version of him. The only way to Socrates is surely through someone's words – but, it turns out, his own words advertise that they are not his own. Is this a kind of Platonic slip? Is it a proleptic Socratic resistance, if we believe these are the real words of Socrates, to Plato's attempt to make him his? The pun opens up a dilemma for the reader, or, perhaps, an opening. If the first thought was, quite simply, that there is something of the self that cannot be reduced to other people's versions of it, this suggests the opposite; that there is *no* way of getting at the self accept through what other people say about it. In Lacanian terms, it suggests that to speak is to speak in a system that is not yours, alienating by its very nature. And yet, this can't be all. To identify with Socrates, it is as if he were saying "I'm not the sort of person who can be Aristophanized, or vulgarized, *or Platonized*." To take the side of Plato, it's as if he is saying: "I can only ever be part of the many discourses that try to dress up Socrates, for there is no way to tell the whole story." He was a figure who produced the desire for stories, not one who could be reduced to them.

With this problematic communicative exchange at the forefront, we can turn to the central enigma in the life of Socrates, his relationship to the oracle. If, so far, I have placed too much weight on a possible pun on Plato's name, we will try to lighten it by offering up a couple more. Socrates tells us of a man Chaerephon, a good democrat, who asked the oracle at Delphi a shocking question. Who is wisest? The answer, of course, is Socrates. Now Socrates' own response to this oracle will concern us soon enough. But let us first pay attention to how we know of this story. For we find out that the story is not guaranteed by Chaerephon himself, who is dead, but only via his brother:

> You know the kind of man Chaerephon was, how eagerly he went after things. And so once, having gone to Delphi, he dared to ask the oracle the following. Don't, I ask you, get too upset, gentlemen. For he asked if anyone was wiser than I. The Pythia replied that no one was wiser. And his brother here will bear witness to you about these things, since that man is dead.

The knowledge of Delphi promises an immediate truth, a truth from the womb, as the etymology of Delphi as "womb" suggests. Yet its truth is at a clear distance from us, not only because it is filtered through the language of the Pythia, but because even this message comes to us via an inherited human discourse, via a brother, an *adelphos*, who preserves the story of one who is dead. For this reason, it is perhaps doubly appropriate that the name of the person who sets Socrates' quest in motion, and whose own words appear only in the words of his brother, had "goodbye," *chaire*, written into his name. He speaks only to disappear forever.

Nevertheless, for all that we have a story from a past that we have every reason to doubt, it will set in motion a process of doubt and belief that will constitute the life of Socrates. For what does Socrates do in response to this information? He rejects it, but in the kind of way that suggests there is some kind of desire to believe it. He tries to prove it is wrong, and thus acts "impiously," questioning a divine authority by his actions, only to find out that it is only by the attempt to prove it wrong that he is able to prove it true. That is, the "knowledge" of Socrates appears only when he believes he does not have it, and disappears the moment it tries to reify itself, turn itself into a systematic, coded form of truth. One could say that, as is the case with psychoanalysis, knowledge is not a matter of content, but rather of form, dependent not on what Socrates knows but the method he uses to pursue his self-knowledge. The stupidity of others lies in this: that they do not appreciate the full nature of this paradox. Self-knowledge is not possible because the self is not an entity that is "knowable," but rather a process of negotiating the paradox that anything you know is never enough, is never really yours, and is set in motion by the desires of others that occurred before you were born and are never entirely recuperable, but nevertheless leave their traces. Lacan suggests that psychoanalysis exists because of something left unanalyzed in Freud, in the ongoing problem of his desire. In Socrates' case, it is in the desire of Chaerephon. But what both offer is a way *out* of our selves and their blockages, and out of the impasses of the pseudo-autonomy of a Hippias.

References

Bozovic, M. (2004). Auto-iconicity and its vicissitudes. In Buchan and Porter (2004).

Buchan, Mark and Porter, J. I. (eds.) (2004). Before subjectivity? Lacan and the classics. *Helios*, 31, 1–2.

Burgoyne, B. (2000). Freud's Socrates. *The European Journal of Psychotherapy, Counselling and Health*, 4, 1.

Dolar, M. (2004). In *Parmenidem* parvi commentarii. In Buchan & Porter (2004).

Fink, B. (1995). *The Lacanian Subject.* Princeton: Princeton University Press.

—— (1997). *A Clinical Introduction to Lacanian Psychoanalysis.* Cambridge: Cambridge University Press.

Lacan, J. (1978). *The Four Fundamental Concepts of Psychoanalysis.* New York: W. W. Norton & Co.

—— (1991a). *The Seminar of Jacques Lacan. Book II: The Ego in Freud's Theory and in the Technique of Psychoanalysis 1954–55*, trans. John Forrester, ed. Jacques-Alain Miller. New York: W. W. Norton & Co.

—— (1991b). *Seminar VIII: Le Transfert* [The Transference]. Paris: Editions du Seuil.

—— (2002). *Ecrits: A Selection*, trans. Bruce Fink. New York: W. W. Norton & Co.

Leader, Darian (1996). *Why Do Women Write More Letters Than They Post?* London: Faber and Faber.

—— (1997). *Promises Lovers Make When It Gets Late*. London: Faber and Faber.

—— (2002). Lacan's myths. In Rabate (2002).

Rabate, J. M. (ed.) (2002). *The Cambridge Companion to Lacan*. Cambridge: Cambridge University Press.

Zizek, S. (1994). *The Metastases of Enjoyment: Six Essays on Woman and Causality*. London & New York: Verso.

Further Reading

Though he is notoriously difficult and provocative, the best entry to Lacan is through his *Seminars*, written transcripts of what were weekly oral presentations. Lacan discusses Socrates at greatest length in the eighth *Seminar*, published in French, and soon to be translated into English by Bruce Fink. The first half of this seminar takes the form of an extended oral commentary on Plato's *Symposium*. It is full of fascinating and original remarks on each section of this text, and thus can be usefully read as a kind of extended psychoanalytic commentary on it. The Socrates of the Platonic dialogues lurks in the background of all Lacan's work, but most extensively in the second and eleventh *Seminars* (on the Ego, and "The Four Fundamental Concepts of Psychoanalysis"). Within Lacan's published writings, the encounter between Alcibiades and Socrates is discussed at the end of "Subversion of the Subject" in *Ecrits*.

There are now a host of general introductions to Lacan's thought. Perhaps most reliable and clearly written are the books of Bruce Fink, the most entertaining by Darian Leader. Leader's essay on Lacan's use of myth in the *Cambridge Companion to Lacan* (in general a good overview of Lacan's thought) is worth consulting for further possible parallels with Plato's well-known use of myth. The most sustained effort to think through Lacan as a philosopher is in the numerous works of Slavoj Zizek; if I single out *Metastases of Enjoyment*, it is because of the book's appendix, which, in the form of a self-interview, tries to answer the major questions that Lacanian psychoanalysis has to confront, including its relationship to Socrates.

Lacan continues to cause some interest among professional classicists. For an attempt to come to terms with this, and an example of it, there is now the edited collection of Buchan and Porter. The essays by Mladen Dolar and Miran Bozovic deal directly with Socrates.

29

From Grade School to Law School: Socrates' Legacy in Education

AVI MINTZ

Socrates is a towering figure in Western culture and has come to represent the consummate philosopher. He practiced philosophy by questioning people. The Socratic practice of questioning others in order to make them examine their beliefs, has led many to view Socrates as a teacher *par excellence*. There are references to Socratic education, Socratic teaching, Socratic practice, and Socratic seminars at all levels of contemporary schooling, from elementary schools to schools of higher education. The word "Socratic" is so prevalent in certain types of schooling that there are people who have never heard of Socrates' most famous student, Plato, who can nevertheless give an informal account of a pedagogical technique called the Socratic method.

In this chapter, I show that there are two distinct versions of Socratic education currently practiced, one based specifically in law schools and one based mostly in elementary, middle, and secondary schools. (For the remainder of this essay, I will use "Socratic method" only to refer to Socratic education in law schools and "Socratic teaching" to refer to Socratic education in elementary schools through high schools. "Socratic education" will serve as a general term which encompasses both the Socratic method and Socratic teaching.) Although both versions of Socratic education cite Socrates as their inspiration, the two versions of Socratic education have emerged from different sources and are actually practiced in quite different ways. Following a brief account of the history of the Socratic method and Socratic teaching, I discuss how teaching through questions, for many, is synonymous with Socratic education. I then show that this broad understanding of Socratic education is generally based on Socrates' discussion with the slave-boy in *Meno*, a discussion which is not representative of Socrates' educational conversations. I then discuss four features of Socratic education – the classroom setting, the role of the teacher, the community of inquiry and the subject matter – to illustrate how Socratic education is practiced when it goes beyond mere questioning. I compare each of these four features of Socratic education to the surviving portraits of Socrates.

A Brief History of Socratic Method and Socratic Teaching

The literature on the Socratic method, also known as the case method, in legal education is unanimous in dating its roots to the pedagogical practices of Christopher

Columbus Langdell, dean of the Harvard Law School from 1870 to 1895. In 1870, Langdell began teaching his contracts class by providing students with cases (reasoned judicial opinions about particular law suits) which they were to study before class. Instead of lecturing on rules of law or legal theory, Langdell called upon students to summarize the cases and answer hypothetical questions about the judicial reasoning in the case. Langdell and his students called his case method Socratic for two reasons. First, the cases were taught through a series of questions to extract their legal content. Second, the teacher and pupils had to work together to elucidate the principles of the law which are revealed through cases (Redlich 1914: 12–13).

Within 40 years of its inception, the Socratic method became the standard pedagogical practice in many law schools (Patterson 1951: 1). However, even early in its history there was much criticism of the Socratic method, ranging from its inability to convey information quickly to the method's failure to address issues which were not subject to litigation (Patterson 1951: 22–3). In the latter half of the twentieth century, critique of the Socratic method took place not only in legal journals but in the public sphere as well. In 1971, John Jay Osborn, Jr., a Harvard Law School graduate, published *The Paper Chase*, a novel depicting Professor Kingsfield, whose cruel use of the Socratic method terrorized his students. Professor Kingsfield became the popular face of the Socratic method as *The Paper Chase* was made into a film, a television series, and a theatrical play. Scott Turow published an autobiographical account of his first year at the Harvard Law School in 1977 entitled *One L: The Turbulent True Story of a First Year at Harvard Law School*. Turow's book painted a harsh picture of the competitive culture of law school, which was partly a result of intimidation in Socratic classrooms. The critiques of the Socratic method are varied and I shall explore a few of them in some detail below. In most cases, as soon as critiques have arisen, there have been people who have come forward either to defend Socrates' name from impious invocations or to defend the Socratic method from its misuses.

Despite widespread critiques of the Socratic method, and several reports that its use is declining, Steven Friedland's survey of teaching in American law schools revealed that the Socratic method remains a pillar of legal education. Friedland's survey showed that 97 percent of professors use the Socratic method in their first-year classes, which encompasses on average 59 percent of class instruction. In second- and third-year classes, the percentages drop to 93 and 47 percent, respectively (Friedland 1996: 27).

In contrast to the Socratic method of legal education, which has been the subject of much criticism, Socratic teaching in primary and secondary education has received almost unanimous praise. Engaging students through questioning is generally accepted as sound pedagogy. There have been many advocates for educational reform who have called for the incorporation of Socratic teaching into schooling, most of whom do not cite a particular educational theorist. Instead they refer directly to the Socrates of Plato, especially Plato's *aporetic* Socratic dialogues (the dialogues which end with Socrates' inducing some perplexity about an issue and which fail to arrive at any conclusion). Mortimer Adler's *The Paideia Proposal: An Educational Manifesto* (1982) is but one of the many examples, and perhaps the most influential, of the calls for Socratic teaching. Teachers, principals, and administrators who want to implement Socratic teaching in their schools have several resources available to them including a *How To Teach Through Socratic Questioning* video series (Paul 2001) and books such as

Wanda Ball and Pam Brewer's *Socratic Seminars in the Block* (2000)[1] and Michael Strong's *The Habit of Thought: From Socratic Seminars to Socratic Practice* (1997).

In contrast to the commonly agreed upon history of the Socratic method in law schools, the history of Socratic teaching in other types of schooling has not been the subject of much attention. Michael Strong is one of very few people who offer a history of Socratic teaching. He identifies the discussion classes on "Great Books," usually at the undergraduate level, as the root of Socratic Practice.[2] These discussion seminars were "Developed between 1910 and 1940 by Alexander Meiklejohn at Amherst College, John Erskine at Columbia University, Stringfellow Barr and Scott Buchanan at the University of Virginia and Mortimer Adler and Robert Hutchins at the University of Chicago" (Strong 1997: 6). Strong dates the first use of the term "Socratic Seminars" to Saint John's College in 1937, where Scott Buchanan coined the term (Strong 1997: 5).

As Strong points out, Socratic teaching's roots clearly lie in undergraduate college education. Socratic discussions may frequently be found in colleges today. In addition, proposed reforms to college education are often based on Socrates' educational practices. Evidently, Socratic education is not limited to primary and secondary education and law schools. As many medical students can attest, their schooling too is Socratic (at least insofar as some of it is conducted through questions and answers). However, most of the literature on and the resources for Socratic teaching focus on primary and secondary education. Given this fact, Socratic teaching in this essay shall refer to Socratic education which occurs in elementary, middle, and high schools.

Before I examine Socratic education in greater depth, I must note that I embark upon this project with caution. Classes that feature Socratic teaching or the Socratic method will necessarily differ depending on how each teacher or professor understands Socratic education. As Steven Friedland points out in his report on teaching in law schools "the phrase 'Socratic method' has perhaps as many definitions as there are law schools or even professors" (Friedland 1996: 15). Friedland's caution undoubtedly holds true for Socratic teaching in primary and secondary education as well. One must be careful not to make a caricature of the professor who uses the Socratic method or the classroom featuring Socratic teaching. (If one wants a caricature, all one has to do is consult Osborn's Professor Kingsfield!) Although there may be discrepancies among various practices of Socratic education, there are some significant features which are common to most versions of Socratic method and to most versions of Socratic teaching. I look to these generally common features to illuminate how Socrates has been appropriated in different educational contexts.

Furthermore, because of space limitations, in this chapter I refer to only a few of the books and articles on Socratic education to highlight aspects of this mode of educating. Also, in order to focus on the contemporary appropriation of Socrates in education, I do not address any of the contemporary debate among academic philosophers and classicists about Socrates as educator.[3] Thus, this chapter does no justice to the wealth of fine scholarship produced by philosophers, classicists, legal theorists, and educational theorists on this topic. However, by contrasting two distinct practices of Socratic education, I hope that this chapter demonstrates that several elements of Socrates' educational practices remain vital to contemporary education.

Teaching Through Questions

Common to both contemporary versions of Socratic education is the active engagement of students through questioning. To understand what is involved in contemporary Socratic education it may be useful to point out the educational practice to which it is opposed. Socratic education is directly opposed to lecturing; that is, to a teacher standing in front of his class and speaking at length about a subject. During lectures, students are expected to passively sit and absorb the information to which they are exposed; or, as Socrates says in Plato's *Republic*, some believe that education consists in "putting knowledge into souls that lack it, like putting sight into blind eyes" (*R*. 518bc).[4] While this type of education certainly still occurs in various forms, especially in post-secondary education, it has largely been challenged in primary and secondary education. In its place, practices and techniques which actively engage the student have come to be standard in education. Edwin W. Patterson noted that precisely this point was one of the presuppositions of the early supporters of the Socratic method in legal education: "the chief pedagogical presupposition of the case method was that students learn better when they participate in the teaching process through problem-solving than when they are merely passive recipients of the teacher's solutions" (1951: 5).

Engaging students through questions clearly has its roots in the figure of Socrates. The Platonic dialogue *Alcibiades* features Socrates' confrontation of young Alcibiades about his political ambition. Socrates says that he can help Alcibiades by providing him the "influence that [he] craves" (*Alc*. 105e). Alcibiades asks Socrates, "But supposing I really do have these ambitions, how will you help me achieve them? What makes you indispensable? Have you got something to say?" To these questions Socrates makes explicit that he can only respond to Alcibiades through a conversation of questions and answers: "Are you asking if I can say some long speech like the ones you're used to hearing? No, that sort of thing's not for me. But I do think I'd be able to show you that what I said is true," – that he will be the most beneficial influence for young Alcibiades – "if only you were willing to grant me just one little favor" (*Alc*. 106b). That favor, of course, is answering Socrates' questions.

In Plato's *Protagoras*, Socrates converses with the great sophist Protagoras and insists that Protagoras confine himself to a question and answer discussion (*Prt*. 334d). Protagoras initially resists this demand and claims that the length of his responses to Socrates' questions ought to depend on the nature of the question, but he finally acquiesces. In *Theaetetus*, Protagoras' position on the method of debate is presented as even more flexible: "If you feel prepared to go back to the beginning, and make a case against this theory, let us hear your objections set out in a connected argument. Or, if you prefer the method of question and answer, do it that way; there is no reason to try to evade that method either, indeed an intelligent person might well prefer it to any other" (*Tht*. 167d). Clearly Protagoras was comfortable with either debating through speeches or through questions and answers.

Likewise, in *Gorgias* Socrates insists that Gorgias confine himself to brief questions and answers (*Grg*. 449b–d). Gorgias responds to Socrates' stipulation with a remark which is substantially the same as Protagoras': "There are some answers, Socrates, that must be given by way of long speeches" (*Grg.* 449b). However, Gorgias then claims that he would be happy to answer Socrates' questions briefly and boasts, "There's no one who can say the same things more briefly than I" (*Grg.* 449c). Additionally, the sophists Hippias and Prodicus are noted in Plato's *Phaedrus* to believe, like Protagoras and Gorgias, that they are adept at answering questions by either long speeches or short answers (*Phdr.* 267a–b). What emerges from these passages is that the Sophists were generally willing to debate by offering presentations (long speeches) or by questions and answers. Socrates, on the other hand, insisted on the exclusive use of the question and answer method. Therefore, that Socratic education is now synonymous with teaching through questioning is quite reasonable based on the ancient depictions of Socrates. Socrates conversed through questions, and refused to conduct joint investigations in any other way.

The use of questions has often been taken as the necessary and sufficient condition for a pedagogical technique to be deemed Socratic. Consider "teaching machines," a pedagogical device that grew in use in the middle of the twentieth century. Teaching machines are textbooks that have a series of questions which claim to build a knowledge base. On a separate page following the questions, students can find the correct answers against which they can check their own. The following example shows the explicit link made between teaching machines and Socratic teaching. "One can consider the communication process between the teaching machine and learner as analogous to that taking place when a student is taught with the Socratic method by a live teacher. The learner, through answering a sequence of questions, is led from one state of knowledge or skill to another" (cited in Jordan 1963: 97; from *Teaching by Machine*, published by the US Department of Health, Education, and Welfare in 1961).

The claim that teaching machines are Socratic is analogous to the use of Socratic method in legal education for randomly "cold-calling" upon students to recite specific facts of a case. Like the teaching machine, the law-school professor sometimes uses a sequence of direct questions to draw out *correct* answers. Teaching machines and eliciting factual information through cold-calling are appropriations of Socrates in education at the broadest level; that is, for those who call teaching machines and cold-calling Socratic, Socratic education means only that teachers use questions to solicit information from their students.

There have been many who have risen to defend Socratic education from either teaching machines or the above type of cold-calling. James Jordan contrasts teaching machines with the method that Socrates uses in Plato's *Euthyphro*, and notes that unlike a teaching machine, Socrates was genuinely an open-minded inquirer who did not have a correct answer in mind towards which he sought to lead his interlocutors (1963: 102). In a similar vein, Phillip Areeda, in a lecture on the Socratic method that was published after his death in the *Harvard Law Review*, argues that the Socratic method is not intended to have students recite facts and, hence, recitation of facts through cold-calling is not Socratic: "The essence of the [Socratic method] is not recitation but reasoning and analysis that forces the student to use what he knows (or supposes that he knows) from the assigned judicial opinion (or statute or other materials)" (Areeda 1996: 915). Areeda does note that recitation is part of the questioning that occurs in the Socratic method but argues that recitation serves only as a propaedeutic for the Socratic method in legal education; questions which require recitation of facts merely establish that there is a concrete foundation from which the Socratic method can draw.

Jordan's point that teaching machines fail to be Socratic because the questions are not open-ended and Areeda's argument that the Socratic method is about reasoning based on what the student "knows (or supposes that he knows)" enable us to refine our understanding of Socratic education. Jordan's and Areeda's points are sound. Socrates was, in most instances, dealing with complex subjects that did not permit simple, factual answers (such as easily mastered historical facts). Whether or not we accept the claim that Jordan and others have made that Socrates was genuinely an inquirer with no answers of his own, the subjects of Socrates' discussions always demanded deep probing and substantial engagement.

The claim that education is Socratic if the teacher merely uses questioning is quite prevalent and is based on a frequently cited example of Socratic education, the conversation that Socrates has with a slave-boy in Plato's *Meno*. In this dialogue, Meno and Socrates investigate the question, "what is virtue?" One-third of the way into the dialogue, Socrates tells Meno that he can prove to him that what we call learning is really recollection. Socrates demonstrates the doctrine of recollection, or *anamnēsis*, by having one of Meno's slaves come forward to answer some of his questions. Socrates shows that through questions the slave recollects geometrical principles. The conversation begins as follows:

SOCRATES: Tell me now, boy, you know that a square figure is like this?
SLAVE-BOY: I do.
SOCRATES: A square then is a figure in which all these four sides are equal?
SLAVE-BOY: Yes indeed.
SOCRATES: And it also has these lines through the middle equal?
SLAVE-BOY: Yes. (*M.* 82bc)

The interrogation continues in this way and eventually Meno is satisfied that the slave has not learned anything but must have recollected his geometrical knowledge (*M.* 86b). After this aside with the slave ends, Meno agrees with Socrates that the slave recollected knowledge that must have already been in his soul, and Meno and Socrates return to their investigation of virtue.

If one accepts the slave-boy portion of *Meno* to be the paramount example of Socratic education, then it is clear how teaching machines or recitation have been confused with Socratic education. There are three reasons why the slave-boy conversation is anomalous in the ancient depictions of Socrates' educational conversations.

First, there are clearly correct answers to his questions about geometry while, as I noted above, there are no clear answers expected or elicited from interlocutors in conversations about piety, justice, courage, friendship, virtue, or the other subjects that Socrates investigates. Ironically, *Meno*, the very same dialogue from which people have extracted the slave-boy conversation, contains a torpedo fish metaphor that represents the common outcomes of Socrates' conversations about complex issues. Socrates' examinations of others' ideas often resulted in *aporia*, or perplexity. When Meno is reduced to this state of perplexity he says,

481

> Socrates, before I even met you I used to hear that you are always in a state of perplexity and you bring others to the same state, and now I think you are bewitching and beguiling me, simply putting me under a spell, so that I am quite perplexed. Indeed, if a joke is in order, you seem, in appearance and in every other way, to be like the broad torpedo fish, for it too makes anyone who comes close and touches it feel numb, and you now seem to have had that kind of effect on me, for both my mind and my tongue are numb, and I have no answer to give you. Yet I have made many speeches about virtue before large audiences on a thousand occasions, very good speeches as I thought, but now I cannot even say what it is. (*M*. 80ab)

The torpedo fish metaphor in *Meno*, and Socrates' probing questions of Meno's views about virtue which preceded it, capture a feature of Socrates' educational conversations that is absent from the aside with the slave-boy. Socrates encounters people who believe that they know about some particular issue and Socrates questions them until they find that several of their implicit assumptions are inconsistent, and they end up feeling stunned. In contrast, the slave-boy is questioned by Socrates not to examine and challenge his beliefs but rather to demonstrate that such knowledge exists in his soul. While the slave-boy tells Socrates at some point that he does not know the answer to Socrates' question, which could be read as an experience of *aporia* (84ab), the slave-boy's perplexity regarding geometry is not similar to the profound, numbing effect that Meno, like most of Socrates' interlocutors, experiences when Socrates' questions cast doubt upon dearly held beliefs.

Second, Socrates was not a teacher of specialized types of knowledge, such as reading, writing, arithmetic, or geometry. In *Memoirs of Socrates* 4.7,[5] Xenophon writes that Socrates believed geometry to be a somewhat useful subject of study. However, "he deprecated taking the learning of geometry as far as figures which are difficult to comprehend. He said that he didn't see the use of them – and he said that these studies were capable of wasting a man's life and keeping him from learning many other useful things" (*Mem*. 4.7.3). Thus, according to Xenophon, Socrates' teachings focused on the "useful things," which included some knowledge of geometry. However, imparting factual information or developing mathematical skills were not typically the objects of his investigations. While Socrates may have thought that it was important to learn some geometry, nowhere, with the exception of Meno, can he be found as teaching such types of knowledge.

Third, one must look at the relationship, or lack thereof, that Socrates had with the slave-boy. The slave-boy is a mere instrument to Socrates in the *Meno*. Peter Cicchino, in "Love and the Socratic Method," argues that "for the purposes of contemporary teachers of law, the locus classicus of the Socratic Method – Plato's dialogue Meno – is singularly unhelpful, indeed almost guarantees pedagogical failure" (2001: 533–4). Cicchino contends that law professors should look at Socrates' conversations where "an understanding of community, of a learning context of genuine affection and concern . . . fairly called 'friendship' or a kind of 'civic love' among interlocutors" exists (2001: 534). Below I will return to the idea of community in Socratic education. For now, it is important to note that the lack of any kind of relationship between Socrates and the slave-boy make that conversation quite problematic as a paradigm example of Socratic teaching. The slave-boy is very obviously not a part of Socrates' community of inquiry, and Plato does not even deem him worthy of being identified by name.

482

Socrates makes no attempt to get to know him or develop a rapport with him, as he does with most of his interlocutors. Nor is there any indication that Socrates is concerned with the slave-boy's fate after their conversation.

In summary, the slave-boy discussion has been identified by many as the classic example of Socratic education. The discussion is certainly consistent with some fundamental Socratic insights (e.g. that learning occurs within a person and that one can use questions to stimulate such learning). However, Socrates' education of the slave-boy, especially when contrasted with that of Meno, did not genuinely induce *aporia* by challenging the consistency of his beliefs. Also, Socrates did not genuinely engage the slave-boy as a partner in inquiry, for he did not make any attempt to create a personal connection with him. For these reasons, the slave-boy is an atypical Socratic interlocutor and the discussion of geometry is an atypical topic for a Socratic discussion. Merely asking questions to elicit facts or cold-calling on people in class, while similar to the slave-boy discussion insofar as Socrates helped the slave-boy learn geometry after randomly selecting him from a nearby crowd, lacks several of the most important features of Socratic education as portrayed in the Socratic dialogues.

The Features of Contemporary Socratic Education

Thus far, I have shown that questioning serves as the foundation for both the Socratic method in legal education and Socratic teaching. In both traditions, there have been scholars who have noted that Socratic education does not merely solicit simple, factual information. The differences between the Socratic method and Socratic teaching emerge as one considers how each is practiced. There are four features of the Socratic method and Socratic teaching which I will now compare to create a picture of what is currently known as Socratic education.

The Socratic classroom

If one walked into a Socratic classroom, one would immediately notice some differences between the Socratic method and Socratic teaching. In law schools, Socratic classrooms are large, often with well over 100 students in the class. Given this large number of students, the classroom is usually set up with the professor standing at the front of the room facing rows of students. In elementary schools through high schools, Socratic classrooms are small and, according to Strong, ideally have only 10–15 students (Strong 1997: 23–4). The students usually sit facing each other in a circle, of which the teacher is a part.

Of course, Socrates did not hold formal classes. He is most famous for holding his conversations in the *agora*, the marketplace, where he was available to all passers-by. In this sense, Socratic teaching in primary and secondary education may approach the informality of Socrates' conversations because students have an informal class setting rather than the more traditional lecture structure.

While Socratic teaching makes an attempt to have students feel as though they are in a less formal environment, there are much less often attempts to make the Socratic method of legal education less formal.[6] If one considers the fact that the Socratic method

483

is explicitly supposed to help students think quickly on their feet and to speak publicly, as they will be required to do in the strict formality of a courtroom, the idea of an informal classroom could be viewed as antithetical to sound legal education. In "Not Socrates, But Protagoras: The Sophistic Basis of Legal Education," William Heffernan (1980) points out that the people in Greece who trained young men to speak persuasively to juries, the legal educators of their day, were the Sophists, not Socrates. Heffernan offers an overview of the Protagorean *paideia*, or education, to argue that the case method approach to education would better be described as Protagorean than Socratic. He contends that Protagoras trained his students to seek victory in argument, in contrast to Socrates, who sought truth. The modern legal system holds that everyone has a right to a fair trial, which necessarily implies that everyone has the right to be represented by a lawyer who can argue her side of the case. Heffernan states,

> For Protagoras, as for law professors, the aim of instruction is not to expose students to substantive points of knowledge (although this is a byproduct of their training) but instead to equip them with the technique by which instruction is carried out. This is the feature of Sophistic and legal education which has provoked qualms in outside observers, but it is also the one that distinguishes both systems from Socrates' method of moral instruction. (Heffernan 1980: 420–1)

To the extent the Socratic method retains the formality of professional training for lawyers, one must side with Heffernan that such a classroom more closely resembles that Sophists' formal schooling than the informal conversations of Socrates.

The role of the teacher in Socratic education

In the large classrooms in law schools, the professor is the "Socrates" of the conversation. That is, the professor is the one who asks the questions and directs the conversations. Additionally, the students are sometimes randomly selected to respond to the questions. When a student is selected she may be the focus of a prolonged, focused exchange with the professor.

In Socratic teaching in elementary, middle, and high schools, the teacher's role is quite different. The teacher will usually start the conversation by raising a question but he will then let the students engage each other in dialogue. As Bell and Brewer claim, in Socratic seminars students speak 97 percent of the time; "Students are responsible for talking primarily with each other, not with the teacher, who facilitates and clarifies through questions, but who never contributes to the discussion" (2000: 1). In Adler's words, "The teacher is first among equals. All must have the sense that they are participating as equals, as is the case in a genuine conversation" (1982: 54). That the conversation takes place among students most of the time in Socratic teaching is enabled through the face-to-face, circular classroom seating. When students face each other, the students' ideas become central to the dialogue. When the students face only the professor, as they do in law schools, the professor's questions serve as the foundation of the dialogue.

Both Socratic teaching and the Socratic method could point to particular instances in the Socratic dialogues which resemble their own practice of Socratic education. In the dialogues featuring Socrates, Socrates almost always dominates the conversations, and he sometimes converses with several people in a single dialogue. In this sense, Socrates closely resembles the law professor who dominates the class discussion, following most comments in class with her own question or comment.

It is extremely rare that Socrates does something akin to the practice of Socratic teaching in classroom circles; Socrates rarely raises a topic and then remains a silent observer while others probe the issue through questions and answers. Yet, there is one dialogue, *Sophist*, which does outwardly resemble the Socratic classroom. In *Sophist*, a visitor from Elea is present, and Socrates asks him how the people from Elea distinguish sophists, statesmen and philosophers (*Sph.* 216d–217a).[7] The visitor agrees to answer Socrates' question, and chooses to do so by question and answer with Theaetetus. Since the visitor becomes the "Socrates" of the discussion in *Sophist*, by leading the question and answer session with Theaetetus, one could argue that this dialogue merely reinforces the fact that Socratic education occurs when someone takes the reins of the conversation, as Socrates usually does, and poses questions.

Hypothetically, if one were to insist that Socratic teaching in primary and secondary education is not Socratic because it fails to have a single, dominant questioner misunderstands one of its fundamental objectives. This is possibly because, to the best of my knowledge, Socratic teaching has never explicitly articulated its objective in the following way. Socratic teaching does not invoke Socrates' name because Socrates serves as the model for a teacher, but rather because *it holds Socrates as a model for its students*. By maintaining that the teacher should be silent much of the time in a Socratic seminar, Socratic teaching hopes to create an environment where students speak directly to one another, probe each other's comments as Socrates would have, and create an understanding of the topic by communally building upon agreed premises.

Community in Socratic education

Due to the large size of law-school classes, it is difficult to overcome an individualistic ethos and create a community of students within the classroom. In fact, many have argued that the Socratic method not only fails to foster the growth of a community but actually creates an egoistic and competitive atmosphere which hinders learning instead of facilitating it. This criticism of the Socratic method has been particularly prevalent in the feminist critiques of legal education. In *Becoming Gentlemen: Women, Law School, and Institutional Change*, a critique of legal education based on studies conducted at the University of Pennsylvania Law School, Lani Guinier, Michelle Fine, and Jane Balin write that, for many women,

> the first year of law schools is experienced as the construction of the law school hierarchy; for them it is the most emotionally draining and intellectually debilitating year . . . One's place in the law school hierarchy is orchestrated by a mandatory grading curve, large Socratic classrooms, skewed presentations of professional identity, and fierce competition brewing uninterrupted within peer culture. *The Socratic classroom itself becomes the idealized representation of a system of legal education in which there are few winners and many losers.* (1997: 60; emphasis added)

485

According to this critique and others, the Socratic classroom is to be condemned for creating an environment in which students sit in fear of being called on by professors who expose their answers as incorrect or insufficient and who intimidate and sometimes mock students in the process. The surveys of Guinier et al. and others have showed that, although such reactions to the Socratic method are common to both sexes, women are more likely to suffer from intimidation in Socratic classrooms.

In contrast, studies of Socratic teaching in primary and secondary education have shown that females fare quite well. Michael Strong reports on two empirical studies which were conducted on the effectiveness of Socratic teaching, using the Watson–Glaser Critical Thinking Appraisal. One study showed comparable improvements in test scores for male and female students who had spent the year learning through Socratic Practice. The test results for the other study are quite provocative, especially when they are juxtaposed with the surveys conducted in law schools. The second study showed far greater test score improvements among minority females, and females generally, compared to males. The collaborative, engaging communal inquiry of Socratic teaching may be the source of the females' gains (Strong 1997: 133). Researchers seem to suggest that Socratic teaching in primary and secondary education is a deviation from modes of learning which would disproportionately benefit males while the Socratic method in law schools is a male-oriented mode of instruction. Furthermore, in the anecdotal evidence that Strong and others present there is often broad student support (and even enthusiasm) for Socratic teaching. The student support for Socratic teaching is a rather stark contrast to legal education, in which students are less supportive of the Socratic method, although some acknowledge it as a powerful teaching technique.

The rules of the discussion in Socratic teaching also differ from those of the Socratic method. Socratic teaching in primary and secondary education seeks to have students take their peers' comments seriously in respectful interactions. Ball and Brewer cite the claim that "learning is facilitated by the absence of fear, risk, and judgment" and contend that the practice of Socratic teaching is consistent with this fact (2000: 3). They add that Socratic teaching allows students to "clarify positions and learn the language of civil disagreement" (2000: 4).

With respect to a community of inquiry in Socratic education, there is a wide gulf between the Socratic method's emphasis on publicly asserting one's views and exposing them to the scrutiny of others, regardless of how that scrutiny may make the student feel, and Socratic teaching's emphasis on gentle, respectful engagement of ideas by a community of inquirers. I believe that one can find the roots of both of these divergent claims in the metaphor that Plato provides for Socrates' teaching method, the midwife metaphor.

In *Theaetetus*, Socrates claims to be a midwife of young men in the midst of a conversation with Theaetetus concerning the question, "what is knowledge?" When Theaetetus grows frustrated that he cannot provide Socrates with a single account of knowledge, Socrates tells him that he is having pains of labor (*Tht.* 148e). Socrates says that his mother, Phaenarete, was a midwife and that he is a midwife as well. "The difference" says Socrates, "is that I attend men and not women, and that I watch over the labor of their souls, not their bodies" (*Tht.* 150b).

For Socratic teaching, the midwife metaphor seems to embody everything that is to be celebrated about creating a respectful and nurturing community of inquirers, wherein the teacher watches over the labor of his students' souls. After all, what would represent this tender care for students' souls more than the support that is given to a woman at the moment of childbirth? Yet within the midwife metaphor there also rests an aspect of Socratic midwifery that lends itself to the harsh, unforgiving interactions which have traditionally been associated with the Socratic method.

Socrates tells Theaetetus "that there is not in midwifery the further complication, that the patients are sometimes delivered of phantoms and sometimes of realities, and the two are hard to distinguish" (*Tht.* 150ab). Socrates explains that, as a midwife for the brain-children of young men, it is his duty to test the brain-children of their worthiness to live; "the most important thing about my art is the ability to apply all possible tests to the offspring, to determine whether the young mind is being delivered of a phantom, that is, an error, or a fertile truth" (*Tht.* 150c). Socrates tells Theaetetus, "when I examine what you say, I may perhaps think it is a phantom and not truth, and proceed to take it from you and abandon it" (*Tht.* 151c). And later in the dialogue, when Theaetetus has produced his first brain-child for testing, Socrates reiterates, "Is it your opinion that your child ought in any case to brought up and not exposed to die? Can you bear to see it found fault with, and not get into a rage if your first-born is stolen away from you?" (*Tht.* 161a).

In the midwife analogy, Socrates is clearly aware of the embarrassment and pain that are involved in the exposure of one's ideas as inconsistent or unsound. Socrates recognizes that when one has an idea, one feels a deep, personal attachment to it – an attachment so deep that it is akin to a mother's attachment to her child. Socrates warns Theaetetus, "you mustn't get savage with me, like a mother over her first-born child. Do you know people have often before now got into such a state with me as to be literally ready to bite when I take away some nonsense or other from them. . . . I don't do this thing out of malice, but because it is not permitted to me to accept a lie and put away truth" (*Tht.* 151cd).

There are numerous examples from the Socratic dialogues of people who become so angry with Socrates that he feared for his physical safety. Perhaps the most famous example is Socrates' discussion with Thrasymachus in *Republic*, in which Socrates admits to being quite afraid (*R.* 336b–d). Although in the works of Xenophon and Plato there is never any physical violence done to Socrates because of his questioning (at least prior to his execution), the same is not true in another source on Socrates. Diogenes Laertius' *Lives of Eminent Philosophers*, probably written 700 years after Socrates' death, reports that Demetrius of Byzantium claimed that Socrates was often physically abused for his inquisitive endeavors: "frequently, owing to his vehemence in argument, men set upon him with their fists or tore his hair out" (1972: II.21). In *Theaetetus*, Socrates admits that his passion for inquiry occasionally makes him neglect the feelings of others. When nobody comes forward to answer his request to put into words what knowledge is, Socrates says, "I hope my love of argument is not making me forget my manners – just because I'm so anxious to start a discussion and get us all friendly and talkative together" (*Tht.* 146a).

I have suggested that the midwife metaphor contains the roots of both the caring and nurturing aspect of engaging students, emphasized in Socratic teaching in primary and secondary education, and the harsh, uncompromising exposure of the students' ideas, central to the Socratic method in legal education. However, there is more to be said about the matter of the learning environment that Socrates created. Although Socrates may have sometimes "forgotten his manners" and acted rudely, he is sometimes portrayed as being acutely aware of the emotions of his interlocutors. Furthermore, Socrates seems to have manipulated emotions freely, as he deemed it pedagogically appropriate. He often used his questions to embarrass his interlocutors into recognizing their own ignorance, especially when they were politically ambitious young men like Theages (see *Thg.* 125e; where Theages recognizes that Socrates has been teasing him) or Alcibiades (see *Alc. I* 116e; where Alcibiades admits his confusion after Socrates' exposes his lack of political knowledge). However, Socrates also used flattery to make his interlocutors let down their guard so they could be refuted. To further reflect on the Socratic learning environment I will now turn to three of Xenophon's stories.

In *Memoirs of Socrates*, 4.2, Xenophon describes Socrates' interaction with Euthydemus, another politically ambitious young man, who believed that he was wise because he accumulated and read many books. Xenophon writes that this story reveals Socrates' "attitude towards those who thought that they had received the best education and prided themselves on their wisdom" (*Mem.* 4.2.1). When Socrates saw that Euthydemus was listening to his conversation with others, he broached the subject of political rule by young men who lack experience. Socrates proposes a speech that Euthydemus might give if he were applying for a public medical post: "Gentlemen of Athens, I have never learned medicine from anyone, nor have I tried to secure any doctor as a teacher. I have consistently avoided not only learning any-thing from medical men, but even giving the impression of having learned this art. However, I ask you to give me this medical post. I shall try to learn by experimenting on you" (*Mem.* 4.2.5). Xenophon records that this speech "made everyone present laugh" (*Mem.* 4.2.5).

Euthydemus' public embarrassment appears to have been tactically employed by Socrates to get Euthydemus to open himself up to Socrates' questions. Socrates fol-lowed this public embarrassment by going to the saddler's shop to confront Euthydemus away from his peers (*Mem.* 4.2.8). After the public embarrassment, Socrates approached Euthydemus with flattery: "I really do admire you for preferring to stockpile wisdom rather than silver and gold" Socrates tells him, referring to Euthydemus' large collec-tion of books (*Mem.* 4.2.9). When Socrates won his trust, he challenged Euthydemus' idea of political leadership. The end result of Socrates' examination was Euthydemus' comment, "Evidently the fault lies in my own incompetence; and I am considering whether it may be best to keep my mouth shut. It looks as though I know absolutely nothing" (*Mem.* 4.2.39). Xenophon then writes that Euthydemus "went away, very much dejected because he had come to despise himself and felt that he really was slavish. Many of those who were treated in this way by Socrates stopped going to see him; these he considered to show a lack of resolution" (*Mem.* 4.2.40). The further embarrassment of Socrates' forced intellectual disrobing through questions was too much to bear for many. Xenophon notes that, unlike Euthydemus who decided to return to Socrates after leaving dejected, others did not return. Withstanding the em-barrassment of having one's ideas exposed as false serves as a litmus test of whether someone could suppress his personal feelings and ambitions enough to join the Socratic community of inquiry.

Socrates clearly varied his educative interactions depending on the personality of his interlocutor, as Xenophon says explicitly in *Memoirs of Socrates* (*Mem.* 4.1.3). Consider two stories that Xenophon places consecutively in *Memoirs of Socrates* to illustrate this point. In *Memoirs of Socrates* 3.6, Socrates confronts Glaucon, who is young (not yet 20) but has bold political aspirations. Xenophon reports that Glaucon was so impervious to criticism that his ambitions were not dampened even though he was frequently laughed at and dragged off the stage when he made political speeches (*Mem.* 3.6.1). Socrates successfully intervened, but he did so in a different way than he did with Euthydemus. With Euthydemus, public embarrassment served to make him receptive to Socrates' examination. In contrast, Glaucon seemed to be immune to public embarrassment, so Socrates' initial approach was different; instead of embarrassing Glaucon, Socrates flattered him by telling him what a fine thing it is to lead people and gain a reputation (*Mem.* 3.6.2). After Socrates captured Glaucon's attention through flattery, he proceeded to question him about his knowledge of various aspects of governing. Glaucon's answers revealed that he had not sufficiently tended to the details of governing and the conversation ends with Glaucon's political ambition tempered. Socrates told him that instead of worrying about ruling all the households of the city, Glaucon should start by ensuring that he can at least manage a single one. Glaucon's last line in this conversation is a concession; "Well . . . I might do something for my uncle's household, if he were to follow my advice" (*Mem.* 3.6.15).

Xenophon clearly wants us to appreciate the range of Socrates' pedagogical skills by juxtaposing Glaucon's story with a story about Charmides (*Mem.* 3.7). Charmides was very much the opposite of young Glaucon. Xenophon says that Charmides, "though a person of influence and much more capable than the active politicians of that time, was hesitant to enter public life and handle his country's affairs" (*Mem.* 3.7.1). Socrates attempts to convince Charmides that he would make a good politician because whenever Charmides is approached by politicians for advice, his advice and critiques are good. Charmides protests that it is different to say such things in public and in private. Socrates replies that Charmides should examine himself to note his strengths and use them to benefit the city. Though Xenophon does not report how Charmides responds to Socrates' prodding, what is clear from the two accounts is that Socrates had a very different approach with a modest conversation partner and with an arrogant one. Unlike the flattery of Glaucon, which was used to create an opening for refutation, Socrates' flattery of Charmides genuinely serves to bolster his self-esteem.

Thus, to the extent that Socrates would anger the people with whom he conversed by asking them questions which publicly exposed their ignorance, Socrates' questioning resembled the intimidating intellectual disrobing that occurs as part of the Socratic method. Furthermore, Socrates seems to have believed that embarrassment could be pedagogically effective. Yet, Socrates usually made some effort to flatter his interlocutors (and was quite aware that he needed to be more sensitive with modest men) ensuring that there existed a personal rapport between them. Socrates sometimes took care to make his conversation partners comfortable enough through flattery to withstand his examinations. Insofar as Socratic teaching attempts to establish a comfortable, caring environment in the classroom, it resembles many Socratic conversations.

Subject matter

In Socratic teaching in primary and secondary education, the subject matter of the class is broadly conceived. According to Adler, the subject matter of Socratic teaching is of two types. First, "books of every kind – historical, scientific, philosophical, poems, stories, essays" but "*not* textbooks." Second, "products of human artistry [which] include individual pieces of music, of visual art, plays, and productions in dance, film, or television" (1982: 28–9).

The texts which are the center of the Socratic method in law schools are cases (which is why the Socratic method is often used as a synonym for the case method). However, as Heffernan points out, using a text for study was quite common to the Sophists but was not a pedagogical technique often used by Socrates. Heffernan's criticism applies to Socratic teaching because Socratic teaching tends to be text-based as well, although Adler defines "text" broadly. Heffernan notes a prominent example in *Protagoras* of a sophist using poetry as part of his lesson. Protagoras claims that poetry is vital to a person's education and proceeds to analyze a poem with Socrates (*Prt.* 338e–348a). Particularly relevant for the critique of contemporary Socratic education is Socrates' statement, "When a poet is brought up in a discussion, almost everyone has a different opinion about what he means, and they wind up arguing about something they can never finally decide . . . We should put the poets aside and converse directly with each other, testing the truth and our own ideas" (*Prt.* 347e–348a). Socrates is quite clear that the subject matter of his conversations should be the beliefs that a person holds. Socrates' conversations do not center on texts but on the beliefs that one holds about issues that are relevant to one's life. As James Jordan notes, "The experience of every rational adult supplies sufficient data for the inquiry. It is not an inquiry into things that have not yet been experienced but an inquiry into the meanings of experience as it is presently held" (Jordan 1963: 102).[8]

There is a distinction that can be made between the texts of Socratic teaching and those of the Socratic method. The Socratic method uses cases which simultaneously teach the law and provide an opportunity to engage in the kind of reasoning about these cases that is necessary for the practice of law (i.e. the case method can make students "think like a lawyer"). In contrast, Socratic teaching does not use texts as instruments of knowledge. Rather, Socratic teaching often uses rich, complex works which serve to enlarge the students' experiences, as well as to improve their thinking processes. As Strong says, Socratic teaching "involves an obligation to make sense of the disparate phenomena which make up experience" (Strong 1997: 147). However, the fact remains that insofar as many manifestations of Socratic teaching rely on texts, they fail to resemble the kind of conversations that Socrates had with his associates, in which one's ideas served as the only starting point for the discussion.

Conclusion

The ancient depictions of Socrates provide a complex and rich portrait of a man as educator. In this chapter, I distinguished two contemporary appropriations of Socrates in education and I compared these to ancient depictions of Socrates. Although one can argue whether particular invocations of Socrates are well-rooted in the ancient stories, as I have done throughout this paper, that argument may ultimately miss one of the key reasons that Socrates' name is so frequently mentioned in education. It is not only that he happened to practice a pedagogical technique which, understood broadly as engaging students through questioning, is tantamount to sound pedagogy. Socrates was a man who made education his life's mission. Responding to the charges of corrupting the youth of Athens in Xenophon's *Socrates' Defense* (*Apologia*), Socrates says "at least where education is concerned; people know that I have made a special study of the matter" (*Ap.* 20). He was an ideal teacher for he genuinely embraced inquiry, which simultaneously made him an ideal student as well. He was a teacher so revered by his own students, that several of them joined Plato and Xenophon in writing Socratic dialogues. Furthermore, he was a man who could never be accused of educating merely as a means to financial well-being, for he refused fees. Socrates not only filled his days with his project of inquiry but he ultimately staked his life on his educational project, and was executed for doing so. Given these facts, one should not be surprised that educators will continue to christen their pedagogical theories Socratic. Such theories may not be inspired by Socrates' pedagogical methods so much as by his life and reputation as an educator.[9]

Notes

1 "Block" refers to the fixed class periods which divide up each school day in most high schools and middle schools.

2 Strong uses the term "Socratic Practice" to specifically refer to his version of Socratic teaching.

3 For readers who wish to explore the debate about the historical figure of Socrates as educator, Werner Jaeger's *Paideia: The Ideals of Greek Culture* (1943) remains the most comprehensive account. Gary Alan Scott's *Plato's Socrates as Educator* (2000) is a recent nuanced, provocative work which, in addition to offering a good bibliography, may serve as a good introduction to many of the key contemporary discussions among academic philosophers and classicists about Socrates as teacher.

4 All translations of works from the Platonic corpus in this chapter are from *Plato: Complete Works*, ed. John M. Cooper (1997).

5 All quotations from Xenophon in this chapter are the translations of Hugh Tredennick and Robin Waterfield, *Conversations of Socrates* (1990).

6 However, the articles on legal education over the last 20 years have increasingly called for and reported on attempts to make law-school classes less formal and intimidating.

7 This conversation is continued in *Statesman* in which Socrates (a young man who is a friend of Theaetetus) replaces Theaetetus in the discussion with the visitor.

8 Jordan's claim that Socrates only had conversations with rational adults is debatable, unless "rational adult" would include people possibly as young as 12 years old, the age which many scholars date Socrates' youngest interlocutors, Lysis and Menexenus.

9 I would like to thank Michael Brent, David Hansen, Robbie McClintock, Karen Mintz, and Dror Posta for their comments on this chapter. I am above all indebted to D. S. Hutchinson's conscientious and enthusiastic support of this project.

References

Adler, Mortimer (1982). *The Paideia Proposal: An Educational Manifesto*. New York: Macmillan.

Areeda, Phillip (1996). The Socratic method (SM) (lecture at Puget Sound, 1/31/90). *Harvard Law Review*, 109, 911–22.

Ball, Wanda and Brewer, Pam (2000). *Socratic Seminars in the Block*. Larchmont, NY: Eye on Education.

Cicchino, Peter M. (2001). Love and the Socratic method. *American University Law Review*, 50, 533–50.

Diogenes Laertius (1972). *Lives of Eminent Philosophers*, trans. R. D. Hicks. Cambridge, MA: Harvard University Press.

Friedland, Steven (1996). How we teach: A survey of teaching techniques in American law schools. *Seattle University Law Review*, 20, 1–44.

Guinier, Lani, Fine, Michelle, and Balin, Jane (1997). *Becoming Gentlemen: Women, Law School, and Institutional Change*. Boston: Beacon Press.

Heffernan, William C. (1980). Protagoras, not Socrates: The sophistic basis of legal education. *Buffalo Law Review*, 29, 399–424.

Jaeger, Werner (1943). *Paideia: The Ideals of Greek Culture*. 3 volumes. Trans. Gilbert Highet. New York: Oxford University Press.

Jordan, James (1963). Socratic teaching? *Harvard Educational Review*, 33(1), 96–104.

Osborn, John Jay, Jr. (1971). *The Paper Chase*. Boston: Houghton Mifflin.

Patterson, Edwin W. (1951). The case method in American legal education: Its origins and objectives. *Journal of Legal Education*, 4(1), 1–14.

Paul, Richard W. (2001). *How to Teach Through Socratic Questioning*. Video series. The Foundation for Critical Thinking.

Plato (1997). *Plato: Complete Works*, ed. John M. Cooper. Indianapolis, IN: Hackett Publishing.

Redlich, Josef (1914). *The Common Law and the Case Method in American University Law Schools: A Report to the Carnegie Foundation for the Advancement of Teaching*. Bulletin Number 8. New York.

Scott, Gary Alan (2000). *Plato's Socrates as Educator*. Albany, NY: State University of New York Press.

Strong, Michael (1997). *The Habit of Thought: From Socratic Seminars to Socratic Practice*. Chapel Hill, NC: New View.

Turow, Scott (1977). *One L: The Turbulent True Story of a First Year at Harvard Law School*. New York: Putnam.

Xenophon (1990). *Conversations of Socrates*, trans. Hugh Tredennick and Robin Waterfield, ed. Robin Waterfield. London: Penguin Books.

30

Socrates' Definitional Inquiries and the History of Philosophy

HAYDEN W. AUSLAND

"There is little or nothing under the sun that is entirely new in Platonic Scholarship."
–Harold Cherniss

The problem of Socrates is at least twofold. The question of the relative merits of Plato, Xenophon, and Aristophanes as contemporary sources is but ancillary to a more fundamental problem of the worth of the Socratic teaching (see Strauss 1966: 6f.). Both arose together almost two centuries ago out of a third issue – the paradox of Socrates – which at the time was felt to consist in the strangeness of a figure who had apparently produced no philosophically interesting doctrines, but had been generally accorded a pivotal a role in the history of philosophy. This problem was solved initially by ignoring Aristophanes and generating some recognizably philosophical doctrines for Socrates out of Plato and Xenophon, reinterpreted in the light of some scattered statements of Aristotle. This picture lacked universal appeal, but dominated the field for almost a century, after which systematic doubts about it were raised. These were countered with some effect. Two wars subsequent, a new enigma emerged: a literary figure in a definite group of Platonic dialogues – presumptively the same as the historical Socrates – who claimed to know nothing whatever except things erotic. This figure also appeared committed to several remarkable philosophical positions at the same time as conspicuously failing in the duty of love for his fellow man. Today, this picture of Socrates is increasingly subject to question, while a restoration is underway of the more politically oriented Socrates of Xenophon and Plato seen against the background of Aristophanes.

The postwar enigma differs from Xenophon's Socrates and the Socrates in Plato's other dialogues in various interesting ways, as in his aversion for the usual responsibilities of public life. He touches on politics only in the context of specific ethical inquiries, since the regnant canons of interpretation generally forbid him political discourse (cf. Xenophon, *Memorabilia* 1.2.37). Thus, when in the *Republic*, the conversation turns from justice to politics, this Socrates, like Cephalus before him, is obliged to withdraw in order to make way for a more Platonic Socrates. At an extreme, he is allowed to speak in his own defense on the ethics of obedience vs. disobedience to political authority in its various forms, but only in order to contradict himself in a way giving rise to an engaging mini-paradox. He is for similar reasons suffered to make an enigmatic claim to a singular political expertise. But in general, this Socrates is held *ex hypothesi* incompetent to offer a political teaching as such, unless it should emerge as an epiphenomenon of his properly ethical inquiries pursued with multiple interlocutors he may wish to benefit individually. On a methodical level, he is similarly permitted a dialectical search for moral definition pursued through questions of the form, "What is X?" (see Xenophon, *Memoribilia* 4.6.1), so long as he does not thereby appear to be introducing novel metaphysical entities. This study aims to explain this methodical restriction historically in the light of the political limitations placed on Socrates during the past two centuries.

Socrates' Place in a Critical History of Philosophy

Until the nineteenth century modern treatments of the philosophy of Socrates were eclectic in their use of sources, making little distinction between statements in Xenophon or Plato and evidence scattered though the works of later writers. In the first history of philosophy of the modern era, Jacob Brucker described Socrates' method in rhetorical terms as consisting in irony and induction, citing as testimonies statements of Quintilian and Cicero, respectively (Brucker 1742: I.532, in Enfield 1819: 1.168).

By the nineteenth century, a new critical philology had emerged in Germany, as had the Romantic movement and an idealistic conception of philosophy and its history. In 1799, the theologian Friedrich Schleiermacher began translating the Platonic dialogues. His versions began appearing in 1804 and ended in 1828, with each dialogue preceded by a critical introduction. The first volume contained a general introduction, in which Schleiermacher set forth his theory of an orderly method by which Plato himself had planned and written his dialogues. Since neither the historical record nor Plato himself mentions such an ordering, Schleiermacher made inferences drawn mainly from evidence within the dialogues. The modern practice of athetizing numerous dialogues deemed un-Platonic had begun already with Tennemann's attempt to reduce Plato's philosophy to a quasi-Kantian "system" in the early 1790s. Schleiermacher now also arranged those he held genuine into three main groups. First comes a series of "elementary" dialogues (*Phaedrus*, *Protagoras*, and *Parmenides*, along with other related pieces) containing a preliminary methodological inquiry into the logical character of ideas as the condition for knowledge. A second, intermediate group (*Theaetetus*, then *Sophist* and *Politicus*, finally *Phaedo* and *Philebus*, again with several lesser partners) represents an epistemological phase in which ideas are related problematically to real things. This group is designed to bring into greater connection the theoretical and practical aspects left sharply divided in the elementary dialogues. These aspects are wholly unified in the focal point of the entire series, the *Republic*, *Timaeus* and *Critias* (with the *Laws* as a kind of appendix), which finally offer a direct exposition in accordance with the categories of ethical and physical science. Plato's dialogues so ordered reveal a philosophical plan guided by the single leitmotiv of science, or *Wissenschaft* (Schleiermacher 1836: 41–7).

Times were turbulent and Germany's national identity in suspense. After spending 1796–1802 in the midst of Berlin's Romantic circle, Schleiermacher held the position of University Preacher at Halle from 1803 until 1806, when it was overrun by Napoleon's troops. In 1809 Wilhelm von Humbolt established the University of Berlin. Schleiermacher was Secretary of the Founding Committee, remaining until his death in 1834 as a Professor of Theology and a member of the Philosophical-Historical section of the Academy of Sciences. By 1812, he was developing a new view of Socrates in his lectures on the history of philosophy, and on July 27, 1815, Schleiermacher delivered a lecture entitled, "The Value of Socrates as a Philosopher," later published as one of the proceedings of the Academy for that year, and destined to influence profoundly the subsequent study of Socrates.

Schleiermacher poses as a problem the fact that the amiable preceptor we encounter in Xenophon and many later sources has been traditionally accorded so pivotal a role in reorienting the history of philosophy. Since Plato shows us a more philosophically conversant Socrates, Schleiermacher comes to grips with the problem by mediating the choice between Plato and Xenophon as sources for the historical Socrates. His subsequently canonical formulation runs as follows:

> What can Socrates still have been, beside what Xenophon informs us about him, yet without contradicting the character-lines and practical maxims that Xenophon definitely establishes as Socratic, and what must he have been in order to have given Plato the inducement and right to exhibit him in his dialogues as he has done? (Schleiermacher 1818: 59)

Schleiermacher arrives at a compromise that allows Xenophon his ethical preceptor but understands his teacher's quest for moral clarity as directed first and foremost at scientific definition and as concerned with practice for the purpose of illustration. Schleiermacher himself formulated a dialectical method for scientific purposes, and he understands Socratic dialectic accordingly: once a scientific focus is admitted as central to the character of Socrates, Xenophon's homely depiction of his teacher can be reconciled with Plato's comparatively philosophical portrait, and Socrates' own historical position can be understood. Almost all the conversations reported by Xenophon take the same basic form as those he describes as intended to make Socrates' interlocutors more dialectical (*Memorabilia* 4.6), a method confirmed as Socratic in Plato's *Phaedrus*; Schleiermacher concludes that what is common to both writers is a dialectician who uses a determinate method for the sake of securing knowledge. In support of this estimate, he appeals in passing to the testimony of Aristotle, who while describing Plato's ideas in the *Metaphysics* notes that Socrates concerned himself with moral questions, thereby pioneering induction and general definition as significant contributions to theoretical philosophy (*Metaphysics* 1.6 987a29–b9 and 13.4 1087b9–32). Schleiermacher is skeptical of a later claim that Socrates pursued definition with a view to "the ideas" (Aristocles in Eusebius, *A Preparation for the Gospel* 11.3) and observes that Plato sometimes uses poetic license to depict Socrates partaking in subsequent philosophical developments he inspired.

A decade or so later, Schleiermacher's student Christian Brandis published an article entitled "Outlines of the Teaching of Socrates," in which he modified, while building on Schleiermacher's beginning. Criticizing earlier accounts and dubbing his teacher's approach path-breaking, Brandis sets out to reassess the traditional account even of

Socrates' moral philosophy by tracing it first through various Aristotelian testimonies, which he then employs as his touchstone for detecting Xenophon's misunderstandings, and Plato's extensions, of the historical Socrates' fundamental viewpoint. Brandis sees Socrates' ethical concerns as fundamental, but again appeals to Aristotle's characterization in the *Metaphysics* (adding *On the Parts of Animals* 1.1). He adduces some more logically tinged descriptions of induction from Quintilian and Cicero and restates Socrates' method in the terms of Aristotelian logic, allowing that it is difficult to establish the extent to which Socrates was himself conscious of this dimension. Brandis then argues that Xenophon and Plato both show Socrates using such a method for scientific purposes (Brandis 1827: 141).

Schleiermacher and Brandis' general account of Socrates soon appeared in a history of ancient philosophy written by Heinrich Ritter (1830: 9–11 and 17–86), another student who would later edit Schleiermacher's own lectures on the subject. Meanwhile, G. W. F. Hegel had been holding to a different account of Socratic method as consisting in irony, midwifery, and perplexity, while identifying Socrates with a "subjectivity" opposed in principle to the "substantial morality" represented by the Athenian state (Hegel 1892: I 384 and 397–406). His lectures on the history of philosophy were published only in the 1840s, and his interpretation of Socrates became generally known first in 1827 through H. Rötscher's study of Aristophanes, which contained an appendix critical of Brandis, who responded the following year. Their two antagonistic approaches would eventually be synthesized by Eduard Zeller.

Plato's Genetic Development

Ritter's account was criticized by Karl Friedrich Hermann, who had recently formulated the influential hypothesis that Plato's own thought went through a development. Hermann conceived the relationship of the sophists to Socrates and Plato in the light of the relation of the Enlightenment *philosophes* to thinkers of the Restoration. Hermann corrects Ritter accordingly by moving the sophists from the end of the first period of Greek philosophy to a primary position in the second period, alongside of Socrates. But the Platonic Socrates' teaching on knowledge and ideas was presented as only one among a variety of responses on the part of other Socratics; Socrates himself had made no claim to ideas as things' essences. Hermann finds Ritter too dependent on Schleiermacher in assuming an immediate relation between Socrates and Plato, attributing this oversight to his neglect of the "genetic development" of Plato's philosophical system (1833: 24–39).

Hermann follows Schleiermacher in viewing the dialogues as constituting a series. But he follows Friedrich Schlegel in holding that Plato's development was natural rather than deliberate, and G. W. F. Hegel in seeing it as necessary rather than random. Plato came under various influences, but his (paradigmatically Greek) spirit developed in accordance with definite historical "moments." There is thus an essential relation between Plato's philosophy and a crucial turning point in history, which presented an impasse both practical and theoretical to which he offered his philosophy as a solution. Using Fichte's category of "national cosmopolitanism," Hermann holds that Periclean Athens uniquely embodied "the idea of the state." He understands

Plato's politically conservative response to her demise accordingly. On the theoretical side, earlier philosophies had mistaken what were only "moments of the concept" for "the absolute itself," pointing to the need for a common principle as a defense against the "antinomies" to which each was individually subject. Plato succeeded in finding this, but his measures were again preservative rather than explorative of new solutions. His dialogues are the record of the process by which the Greek philosophical spirit came to be realized as a unity within Plato's own mind, and thereby also document the final and absolute stage of the Greek people's national spirit, with its paradigmatic human value, as well as its particular limitations (1839: 13–37, 132–7, and 345f.).

Plato's philosophy is essentially historical in nature, according to Hermann, and his dialogues are developmental in a sense in accord with this fact. This is the idealistic side of Hermann's interpretation. But the Romantic influence also has important consequences for the way Hermann interprets the relationship of a given dialogue to the entire series. The "inconclusive" Socratic dialogues of ethical search are not to be regarded as "purposely" preparatory as part of a pedagogic scheme, but rather as signs that Plato was himself at a tentative stage in his philosophical development; a constructive dialogue like the *Timaeus* shows the mature results of its author's researches.

The complex structure of the *Republic* had already posed a problem for Schleiermacher (1836: 351–4). Explaining the "Socratic" Book 1 poses an even greater problem for Hermann, since what Schleiermacher understood to be a view's preparation followed by its articulation, Hermann sees as two distinct views – so distinct that there can be no question of a gradual development (1839: 537–9). Since antiquity, a question about the principal aim of the *Republic* had been resolved by recognizing it as embodying a complex teaching for individuals and communities alike. Hermann sees this compromise as itself posing another problem: if the right political order is formally identical with the justice of the individual, and with the cosmos, then why does Plato establish his social organization on the scale of a single city rather than extending it to encompass the entirety of mankind? (Hermann 1849: 134–7). Again recalling Fichte's vision of German national destiny, Hermann holds that Plato envisages a mankind articulated into cities related via the subjection of the lesser to the greater in the same way as the different parts of the soul of a man, or the cosmos.

In stark contrast, Socrates' ideal of wisdom and virtue in principle excluded no one and was concerned with the laws of the city only insofar as necessary to living the life of a "world-citizen." Plato, however, saw class distinctions as the only means by which partners with a lesser share in wisdom might participate at least indirectly, and so institutionalized this wisdom within the restricted compass of the traditional Greek polis (1849: 140f.). Plato's preference for conservative, Spartan institutions amounts to his insistence upon forcing the science developed through historical necessity back into the illiberal container of a moribund Hellenic provincialism. The city is thus fundamental to his project because he resists the cosmopolitan historical trends of his times. The *Republic* is not merely unrealistic, moreover, it is incoherent, since it seeks to subordinate a scientific development intertwined with a historical movement toward cosmopolitan individuality (represented by Socrates and the sophists) to Plato's own nostalgia for the aristocratic order of the traditional Greek polis. The work as a whole is a monument to the inevitable end of the Greek way of life under the pressures of scientific and historical progress. Hermann arrives at an ambiguous evaluation of

497

Plato's political teaching. His endeavor was vitiated in principle by its futile resistance to the progress of history, but it also embodied a magnificent first step toward realizing the free and autonomous spirit that is the goal of that progress. In this Hermann is viewing the *Republic* from the perspective of Hegelian Idealism, according to which the shortcomings of what comes earlier in a historical sense are seen to be nullified by means of their assimilation as moments into a subsequent and more perfect whole (1839: 542f.; cf. Hegel 1892: II. 90–9 and 113f.)

Hermann sees the relation between Socrates' and Plato's practical teachings in the light of the theoretical difference between the Socratic "conceptualism" and the Platonic "doctrine of ideas." Socrates' conceptual activity points historically forward, while Plato's metaphysical speculation represents a regression following it. Plato's idealism is the theoretical analogue of his narrowly nationalistic, and aristocratic, political bias, and Socrates' empiricism correspondingly answers to his openness in practical questions. Plato's ideas are the deductive basis for his reactionary institutional measures, as Socrates' inductive method of conceptual formation had been the foundation of his cosmopolitan life-style. The figure restoring the historically appropriate movement is then Aristotle, whose method proceeds deductively from axioms first established by inductive means: his politics are likewise liberal in character, representing the practical application of principles arrived at through experience (1839: 132f.). According to Hermann, then, the difference between the Socratic "concept" of justice in Book 1 of the *Republic* and the Platonic "ideal" based upon the hierarchical division of the body politic into differing strata in Book 4 is no less than the difference between distinct moments in a political and philosophical *Geistesgeschichte*. The Socratic determination of justice leaves its acquisition open to anyone, thus accounting for its primarily ethical orientation; the Platonic comparison of the well-organized individual (or world-) soul with the closed society of the traditionally constituted Greek *polis* is historically conservative, limiting the breadth of the concept's application in all its spheres, most significantly in the ecumenic. This is why the Socratic view cannot properly prepare for the Platonic: their true relation as historically revealed shows them to be opposed to each other.

Socrates Logico-Philosophicus

In 1844, Brandis incorporated his views about Socrates into the first of two histories of ancient philosophy he would eventually write. Two years later, Eduard Zeller combined Schleiermacher's and Hegel's approaches in the first edition of his history of Greek philosophy. By the time a revised second edition appeared in 1856, the idea was entrenched that the significance of Socrates' method consisted in his having introduced a kind of *Begriffsbildung* (formation of concepts), but that he (a) began from the Delphic injunction to self-knowledge as an erotic motivation, (b) employed irony as a critical and dialectical tool for exposing ignorance, and (c) attempted to create real knowledge by taking the first step toward it by forming concepts (see Zeller 1877: 109–14 and 121–34). In 1862, Brandis produced a second, shorter history of philosophy along similarly developmental lines, where his account of Socrates remained substantially as before.

Heinrich Ritter had earlier followed Schleiermacher in doubting that Socrates had introduced definition for the sake of the ideas, but allowed that the relation he found between concepts and what things are must have spurred investigations apt to invite the theory (1830: 58f. cf. 262–6). For such a view, certain passages in Plato's "Socratic" dialogues of definition posed a problem. For instance, the *Euthyphro* features Socrates trying to define piety by an inductive method, but more than once has him refer to his definiendum as the specific character (*eidos*) or the form (*idea*) of piety:

> What kind of thing do you say the holy and the unholy are, both with regard to murder and with regard to the rest? Or is not the pious the same in all action, itself to itself; and the impious, in turn, while opposite of all the pious, itself similar to itself and possessing a single form (*idea*) in its entirety – whatever may be going to be impious? – Entirely, Socrates. (5c9–d6)

And again, after Euthyphro's answer has been found inadequate:

> Do you recall then that this I did not ask you – to teach me one or two of the many pious things, but that specific character (*eidos*) itself, by which all pious things are pious? For you acknowledged that it is by a single form (*idea*) that both impious things are impious and pious things pious? Or do you not remember? – I do. – Well, then teach me what that very form (*idea*) itself is . . . (6d9–e4)

Nineteenth-century conceptualism postulated fine distinctions between such terms' supposed denotations (cf. Ross 1951: 14f.), but with Hermann's hypothesis of a Platonic development, the problem could be recast as the question whether such passages "already" imply ideas of the kind Socrates speaks of in the *Phaedo* or *Republic*. In a book summing up the past half century's scholarship, Franz Susemihl saw the *Euthyphro* as advanced beyond the *Meno*, since it "hypostatizes" the subjective *Begriff* (*eidos*), giving it an individual personality and elevating it to the status of an objective *Grundgestalt* (*idea*) (1855: 122).

The early nineteenth century witnessed important developments in logic. In England, J. S. Mill's Baconian approach influenced George Grote's account of Socrates in his *History of Greece*. On the continent, Adolf Trendelenburg established a system on Aristotle's model intermediate between the subjective-formalism represented by Kant and Herbart, and the metaphysical logic of Hegel. In 1855 Carl Prantl produced the first modern history of logic, in which the dialectic of Plato's dialogues is explained as preliminary to Aristotle. In 1857 Friedrich Überweg's jointly historical and systematic *System der Logik* premised an Aristotelian view of conceptual formation. This entailed categorizing "the pious" or the "form" or "specific character" of things pious as referring to items to be predicated of a subject, rather than to such a subject itself. Plato's Socrates does not always speak in ways congenial to this assumption, however, so that Überweg shortly found grounds for athetizing the *Euthyphro* in a logical confusion in the way Socrates at 5d applies the predicate "having an idea" to "the pious" (which Überweg holds is itself an idea), rather than saying it of a particular pious action (Überweg 1861: 251). Some scholars agreed this posed a problem, while others held the theory of ideas was "not yet" present in the *Euthyphro* or that Socrates' statement concerned only the idea's domain. Beginning in 1862, the problems and available interpretations of such phenomena were set out in Überweg's own *Grundriss der Geschichte der Philosophie*, eleven further editions of which continued influential well into the twentieth century. By century's end, Socrates' seminal role in the history of *Begriffsbildung* had become the subject of detailed research, as well as of strong skepticism. Whether a dialogue like the *Euthyphro* was best viewed as advanced Socratic, primitive Platonic, or simply spurious remained in suspense.

A Later, Self-Critical Plato

After Überweg reassessed some of Plato's dialogues on grounds of their logic viewed from an Aristotelian perspective, Lewis Campbell fundamentally reconsidered the basic groupings that had been authoritative since the days of Schleiermacher. In preparing an edition of the *Sophist* and *Statesman* that appeared in 1867, Campbell concluded that stylistic peculiarities they exhibited in common with the *Laws* argued for their rather later dating (as too for the *Philebus*, *Timaeus*, and *Critias*, but not for the *Republic*). Campbell saw Plato's development as more than merely stylistic, as he sought to show him becoming also more Aristotelian. He held, specifically,

> (1) That side by side with the poetical and metaphysical there grew up in Plato's mind a logical mode of conceiving the ideas; (2) That as he viewed them in this two-fold aspect, and saw the latter of the two more clearly, he became conscious of the difficulties which the theory involves; and (3) That he was led, partly through the consideration of these difficulties, to alter considerably his theory of Knowledge and Being: passing from the bare assertion of an absolute object of mind, to which he had been led by interpreting Socrates through Parmenides, towards the Aristotelian conception of logical categories and of Being as composed of Matter and Form by an efficient Cause. (1867: lxxi)

During the early 1880s, Henry Jackson wrote a series of articles in which he sought to identify a "later" theory of forms, with the *Theaetetus* as introductory to this "more exact teaching of later years" (Jackson 1885: 242–4). On the continent a new interest had meanwhile sprung up for locating certain dialogues relative to a supposed feud between Plato and Isocrates, which led to parallel attempts on the continent at dating several such dialogues, and eventually all dialogues, by stylistic criteria. Before the end of the nineteenth century, such "scientific" datings of the dialogues had for the most part tended to look for confirmation of Hermann's general ordering, which still granted the *Republic* a place with the *Timaeus* and *Critias* near the end of the series, with "critical" works like the *Sophist*, *Politicus*, and *Philebus* coming earlier. But in 1896 the Polish scholar Wincenty Lutoslawski made Campbell's earlier work for the first time generally known on the continent. There was some resistance to the new paradigm, but in short order most Platonic scholars had reconsidered Schleiermacher's ordering, reclassified the *Republic* as a dialogue of Plato's middle years, and promoted the *Sophist* et al. to a more sophisticated, late period in Plato's supposed philosophical development.

The apparently unified picture represented a complex of elements, with the earlier account extended to include a later Plato moving away from a metaphysical realism now confined to his middle years and back toward a sensible position like that first adopted by Socrates and later embodied in Aristotle. Campbell saw this cycle as but one aspect of the author's broader psychological maturation. Thus

> A deepening religious consciousness is associated with a clearer perception of the distance between man and God, and of the feebleness and dependence of mankind. But the feeling is accompanied with a firm determination to face and cope with the burden and the mystery of the actual world – to provide support for human weakness, alleviations of inevitable misery. The presence of Necessity in the universe and in life is acknowledged, in order that it may be partially overcome. The change here implied is not one of creed, but of mental attitude, induced, as we may gather from indications that are not obscure, by a large acquaintance with the contemporary world, and by the writer's own experience in wrestling with intellectual and practical difficulties. (Campbell 1889 [1894: 60f.])

Campbell and others' stylistic studies had laid claim to a scientific objectivity, but quickly moved beyond this. A number of derivative attempts to connect a progress in certain dialogues' "Socratic" style with one hypothesized as present in their "early" contents likewise tended to remain, as they began, an application of romanticizing theories of "natural" personal and stylistic development.

The Unity of the Platonic Socrates' Thought

While Brandis was drawing his picture of Socrates from the testimonies of Aristotle, J. W. Süvern published a study of Aristophanes in which he concluded that the target of the *Clouds* was a comic type modeled on fifth-century sophists generally, having no resemblance to the historical Socrates. Aristophanes' professor would experience a recrudescence in Nietzsche's attack on behalf of tragedy, but was effectively suppressed as a factor in philological treatments of Socrates into the following century. Three depictions remained to be weighed against one another, however. Controversy grew, and by the century's last decade energetic combatants for the claims of both Aristotle (Joël 1893) and Xenophon (Döring 1895) had emerged on the continent. Joël's radicalization of Brandis' approach was adopted in Theodor Gomperz's (and later incorporated into Joël's own) history of Greek philosophy.

Plato too found capable defenders as a reaction against the past century's separatism set in. Lutoslawski's "science" of stylometry had been unable to find any reliable test by which to distinguish the supposedly early, Socratic dialogues from those of what would henceforth become Plato's middle period, and Aristotle's testimony offered no suitable corroboration for a more exact theory in a later set of dialogues. A. E. Taylor developed a suggestion deriving from Zeller, arguing that Aristotle was so far from offering valuable testimony that his remarks were but confused derivations from Plato's dialogues themselves, in which the terms *idea* and *eidos* are generally used of primary substances not unlike those of the Presocratic philosophers (Taylor 1911: 40–90 and 178–267). John Burnet argued that the theory of ideas explained in the *Phaedo* was Socrates' own, and moreover that understanding the forms as thoughts or concepts makes interpretation of the doctrine impossible (Burnet 1914 [1964: 125f.]). Their conclusions ran directly counter the approach of the previous century.

501

But this had just fundamentally altered its suppositions about Plato's later develop-ment, and Taylor's skepticism about Aristotle was shortly seconded in a lengthy study of Socrates by Heinrich Maier, who saw Socrates as on a kind of mission. Maier care-fully considers and rejects the view that Socrates was a philosophical conceptualist (1913: 262–95). Socrates' philosophy was a search for a personally moral life, and his dialectic aimed at waking others from their sleep to a life worthy of mankind. Maier does not shrink from entitling a chapter in his book "The Socratic Gospel" (296).

Taylor and Burnet's undermining of Aristotle's testimony came under criticism in England, notably by W. D. Ross, editor of Aristotle's *Metaphysics* (1924: xxxiii–xlviii; cf. 1933). Ross later wrote *Plato's Theory of Ideas*, a book in which he examined appearances of the ideas in the dialogues developmentally in accordance with their newer ordering. The views of Burnet and Taylor had won some acceptance (for in-stance, in E. Brehier's history of philosophy of 1938) but were less popular in England, so that Ross could in reasonable comfort make Aristotle's account fundamental once more, finding a gradual movement away from language suggesting "immanence" in the early dialogues toward language of "transcendence" in later ones (1951: 154–64; cf. 21 and 230f.). He was unable to confirm Jackson's thesis of a later period in which Plato significantly altered the theory of forms, but another such view, more akin to Campbell's of 1867, had meanwhile arisen from another source.

Socrates Oxoniensis

As Campell had anticipated German scholars in stylistic dating, so Gottlob Frege pioneered what became British analytic philosophy. Under the influence of Russell and Wittgenstein, a new movement took form in England during the first half of the twentieth century, with ramifications affecting the interpretation of Plato's dialogues. A second generation of analysts busy with ancient texts for the sake of "doing philo-sophy" discovered a soulmate in the author of the *Parmenides, Sophist, Statesman,* and *Philebus,* whose passages concerning the interrelations between forms were now seen as anticipating Russell's theory of types, or Wittgenstein's theory of logical syntax. Since the movement tended to regard "Platonism" – the theory that universal charac-ters correspond to real entities – simply as an error, it found Campbell's theory of a less idealistic late Plato congenial. Plato's decisive turn away from metaphysics was located in the *Parmenides,* which features the eponymous philosopher criticizing the theory of forms of a youthful Socrates. Around mid-century a number of such treatments of Plato appeared, several of which were reprinted under the title *Studies in Plato's Metaphysics.* As R. E. Allen explains in the editor's preface, the collection asks the question how Plato viewed his own theory of forms later in life. Allen observes that the answer one gives to this historical question is liable to be influenced by one's philosophical preferences. Relevant here are the century's "extraordinary advances in formal logic and logical theory," as well as those of the "revolution" constituted by Anglo-Saxon "conceptual or non-formal linguistic analysis." These have both directed attention toward, and complicated debate concerning, "the classical problem of universals – the ancient issues of realism, nominalism and conceptualism . . . the nature and the viability of the Theory of Forms." What is philosophically interesting about Plato's forms is thus their role as ancient precursors to the *universalia realia* put forward in medieval scholastic controversies over the status of universals. A Latin tradition opposing Plato to Aristotle in these terms is traceable to Boethius' *Commentary on Porphyry's Isagoge* 1 (86 col. 2b, Migne), but the question for Allen's collection is instead whether Plato himself came to reconsider his own "Theory of Forms" in the light of his "developing and increasingly sophisticated interests" (viz., the interests constituting a precursor to the above-mentioned present century's "extraordinary advances in formal logic and logical theory"). What Hermann had seen as the development of Plato's *Geist* now became his abandonment of metaphysics for conceptual analysis.

> The critic of Plato who shares this temper of mind is liable to view the Theory of Forms as a simple mistake, and to suppose that Plato himself came to think it so. If he did, then the development of his thought in some measure recapitulated, or perhaps better, precapitulated, the development of philosophy in this century . . . At the end of his life, Plato had begun to ask the questions that many philosophers ask today; speculative ontology had largely given place to logic – not formal logic, but the informal logic of concepts in ordinary use. The founder of the *ancien régime* had himself become a revolutionary. (Allen 1965: xf.)

The *Timaeus* was a thorn in the side of this approach, since it was late stylistically, but also reliant on the ideas. The 1950s had witnessed a debate about its exact dating, in the course of which Harold Cherniss called the revolutionaries' entire interpretive approach into question, comparing it to religiously colored medieval commentary.

> Platonic interpretation . . . has been . . . largely a series of insistently charitable efforts on the part of Western philosophers and their acolytes, each to baptize Plato in his particular faith – having shriven him first, of course, by interpreting the heresies out of his works. Now, the Analysts of Oxford have succeeded to their own satisfaction in reading the dialogues that they call "critical" as primitive essays in their own philosophical method. The author of *these* works, they feel, they could adopt as their worthy precursor, if only he could be absolved of the embarrassing doctrine of ideas that he elaborated in all its metaphysical and epistemological absurdity in the *Phaedo*, the *Symposium*, the *Republic*, and the *Phaedrus*. (Cherniss in Allen 1965: 347)

Allen seems to have Cherniss in mind when he mentions counter-revolutionary "conservative critics" (xi). But charitable interpretation was already the method of Ockham, and the previous century had come to question not only the application of modern terminology and categories to Plato's "doctrine of ideas," but even the very notion that Plato really had such a doctrine (cf. Jowett 1892: 13–19).

The new picture of a late Plato divested of the ideas had its natural counterpart in a philosophically interesting Socrates assumed innocent of them. The analytical approach to the ancients converged with Ross' Aristotelian account of Plato's development out of Socrates to yield an English treatment of Socrates as one who made historical "contributions to philosophical method and to ethics" (Gulley 1968: 2). At Cambridge, W. K. C. Guthrie duly absorbed the approach into his treatment of Socrates in a new history of Greek philosophy.

503

Socrates' "Failure in Love"

The vogue the analytical revolution enjoyed for a few decades occasioned a curiously tenacious version in America in the postwar writings of Gregory Vlastos, with consequences for the study of Socrates. Vlastos' activity falls into three distinguishable periods. An interest in ancient philosophy appears first in his middle period, where it can be seen to grow out of social interests he had earlier as a participant in a Protestant "Christian Revolution." After the war, Vlastos combined the analysts' picture of a late Plato with Campbell's *Bildungsroman*. According to Vlastos, Plato could have refuted the regressive argument against the theory of ideas in the *Parmenides*, but the theory served Plato as a kind of philosophical security-blanket, so that this dialogue's inclusion of objections to it are "the expression of his acknowledged but unresolved puzzlement" (Vlastos in Allen 1965: 255). Three years later he correspondingly reconfigured Schleiermacher's question of Socrates as the problem of finding a unitary account for both Maier's evangelistic preacher and the relentlessly methodical dialectician in Plato's dialogues. Vlastos resolved his own paradox by delineating a new, less ironic Socrates, a frank searcher, "always pursuing his own search and seeking his fellow seekers." This Socrates "enrich[ed] the common life of humanity," was "a reformer of the conscience which in the very long run has the power to make or break social institutions," and rejected the contemporary class-morality that Plato would not. Vlastos nonetheless regards Socrates as having failed, and not only by expecting too much of knowledge where something "akin to religious faith" is required. Behind this, according to Vlastos, "lay a failure in love":

> If men's souls are to be saved, they must be saved his way. And when he sees they cannot, he watches them go down the road to perdition with regret but without anguish. Jesus wept for Jerusalem. Socrates warns Athens, scolds, exhorts it, condemns it. But he has no tears for it. One wonders if Plato, who raged against Athens, did not love it more in his rage and hate than ever did Socrates in his sad and good-tempered rebukes. One feels there is a last zone of frigidity in the soul of the great erotic; had he loved his fellows more, he could hardly have laid on them the burdens of his "despotic logic," impossible to be borne. (1957: 512)

The Socrates of Vlastos' middle period is potentially a man of faith, but one who tragically mistakes mere knowledge for that faith. What Socrates lacked is not simple altruism, as distinct from either the *eros* or the *philia* of the Greeks, but a "cooperative mutuality" that asks for justice while demanding protest against all inequality (cf. Vlastos 1935: 120f. and 131). Vlastos' closing allusion to Nietzsche suggests a complex antipathy running deeper than the sufficiency characteristic of analytic circles. His treatment of Socrates' method of moral inquiry is correspondingly ambivalent. On the one hand, it is his "greatest contribution . . . because it makes moral inquiry a common human enterprise, open to every man. Its practice calls for no adherence to a philosophical system . . ." Socrates' definitional method emerges as an expression of his "vision of human freedom." But this necessitates its close restriction, since only the Aristotelizing interpretation of it as a logical procedure free of any metaphysical commitment secures its claim to a humanistic breadth (Vlastos 1957: 515f.).

Late in life, Vlastos resumed his study of Socrates, arguing for his thesis and spreading the word through publicly-funded NEH seminars. He now reversed Brandis' method of reading Plato in the light of Aristotle's testimony. Premising a distinction between two Socratic figures in different sets of dialogues, he constructs several features he holds characteristic of the Socrates of the "early" dialogues, and then discovers most of these confirmed in Aristotle, whom he concludes to have had reason to think these dialogues, and no others, represented Socrates as he really was (1988: 108). Vlastos in this way manufactures a Socrates whose characteristics include his complete lack of a metaphysical theory of forms. But where Ross had found a gradual development away from the "immanence" of the early toward "transcendence" in the middle and even the late dialogues, Vlastos resembles Hermann in postulating a sharp break between Plato's "daringly inventive metaphysics" and his teacher's "radically different philosophy" (103). The Socrates of the early dialogues has forms only in the sense that "the objects of his definitional inquiries were universals, stable objects of knowledge exempt from flux" – "unseparated universals he sought to define," and not "separate from particulars," like Plato's ideas (104f.). Where Hermann saw a contrast in terms of his opposition of Socrates' cosmopolitanism to Plato's reactionary politics, the Late Vlastos hopes for an unmystical Socrates' repudiation of the Platonic "presumption of superhuman knowledge," admitting, however, that this aspect fails altogether of corroboration in Aristotle (109, 97, and 100; cf. a similar statement in Hermann 1833: 24f.).

With so much at stake, Vlastos was in his final book at extraordinary pains to maintain and defend the complex position mentioned above: a passage like *Euthyphro* 5d had at the same time to be of universal value but also cleansed of the autopredication Überweg had noticed and that Vlastos held Plato himself later in life half-recognized as the great mistake of his middle years. Illustrative is the way Vlastos translates away this particular problem:

> Is not the pious the same as itself in every [pious] action? And the impious, in turn, is it not opposite to all that is pious but similar to itself, everything which is to be pious having a certain single character (*idean*) with respect to impiety? (Vlastos 1991: 57)

Where Plato's Greek concludes with a circumstantial participial construction ἔχον ἰδέαν ("having . . . a form") modifying the universally quantified substantive expression τὸ ἀνόσιον πᾶν ("all . . . the impious"), Vlastos particularizes the closing expression by translating with a fresh grammatical subject in uninflected English suitable rather for rendering an originally absolute construction.

Vlastos spent his last years refining such means of reconciling Maier's evangelist with the analysts' logician, while maintaining the resulting amalgam an erotic failure. One result has been exponential growth in a kind of scholasticism about problems having to do with "separation," "immanence," and related themes. Another is that Schleiermacher's problem of the moral preceptor strangely credited with transforming the history of philosophy has for many been replaced by Vlastos' paradox of an earnest preacher so lamentably deficient in human compassion.

Both effects are evident in a plethora of works imitative of Vlastos' methods, but the second is given an interesting twist in a more radical criticism according to which

Socrates' flaw is his failure to be tragic in Nietzsche's sense (cf. Nussbaum 1986: 122–35 with Vlastos 1957: 512 n. 3). In *The Fragility of Goodness*, Martha Nussbaum likewise modifies Campbell's Victorian framework. According to Hermann, it was Plato who separated the forms, which Socrates had treated only as concepts, but then Aristotle brought things back down to empirical reality. According to Campbell, signs could also be made out of a late, more reflective Plato. Vlastos had followed Hermann in associating Socrates' conceptualism with his humanism, and adapted the second part of Campbell's *Bildungsroman* to an ostensibly analytical treatment of the *Parmenides*, reinterpreting it as Plato's own "record of honest perplexity." Nussbaum's history of classical Greek ethics is designed along the same lines (see 1986: 8), except that, since the hard-hearted rationalist Socrates will no longer do as foil to Plato's excesses, the Tragedians are awarded this role. Nussbaum selects new representative texts: the *Protagoras* instead of the definitional dialogues, different aspects of the ideal dialogues, and the erotic indulgence of the *Phaedrus* in place of the self-criticism of the *Parmenides* (all construed in the terms of Aristotle's *Nicomachean Ethics*, which now play the part of the *Metaphysics*). These changes in detail are required by the ethical subject matter, but the general form remains:

Basic sequence	Logical application	Ethical application
(i) Primitive Naturalism:	Socratic Definition	Tragic Vision
(ii) Platonic Extravagance:	Theory of Forms	Masculine Asceticism
(iii) Platonic Crisis:	Third Man Reductio	Bathos of Passion
(iv) Aristotelian Resolution:	Immanent Universals	Fragility of Goodness

Socrates becomes part of the problem, rather than Plato's antecedent, more sober, paradigm.

Cherniss thought that the account of a logical development was adopted in analytic circles in order to expropriate the ancient evidence on behalf of one side of the twentieth-century version of the debate on universals. Nussbaum does something of the kind on behalf of an ideologically feminist reinterpretation of Greek ethics, designing her story to appeal to an audience schooled in a particular history of Greek metaphysics (cf. Nussbaum 1986: 20 and 228). This offers at least the benefit of reminding a forgetful modernity how closely intertwined these two realms of philosophy are. Nussbaum brings out more clearly than Vlastos himself ever did key assumptions motivating his peculiar interpretation of Socrates.

Socrates Politicus Redivivus

Vlastos' contrast between Socrates' attitude toward Athens and Jesus' tears for Jerusalem sentimentalizes a subtler remark of Thomas More noting the lack of any record of Jesus' having ever laughed (cf. Strauss 1964: 60f.). During the same years Vlastos was developing his interpretation, Leo Strauss forged a complementary approach to the problem of Socrates, taking his departure from the ancient tradition that Socrates originated political philosophy. In a series of lectures given at the University of Chicago in 1958 but published only in 1989, Strauss examined anew the four main ancient sources, further rehabilitating Aristophanes, and carefully reconsidering the testimony of Xenophon. Strauss concluded that Aristophanes' portrayal of Socrates contained serious charges of the same general kind found later in Nietzsche, which both

> Xenophon and Plato sought to answer in their portrayals of Socrates. By Aristophanes' account, Socrates is unpolitical because he lacks self-knowledge. He does not understand the political context within which philosophy exists. He is unaware of the essential difference between philosophy and the polis. He does not understand the political in its specific character. This is because he is unmusical and unerotic. To this accusation Xenophon and Plato give one and the same reply. Socrates is political and erotic. He understands the political in its nonrational character. He realizes the critical importance of *thymos*, of spiritedness, as the bond between the philosophers and the multitude. He understands the political in its specific character. In fact, no one before him has done so. For he is the first to grasp the significance of the *idea*, of the fact that the whole is characterized by articulation into classes or kinds, whose character can be understood only by thought, and not by sense-perception. (1989: 169)

In another context, Strauss makes it clear that, whatever difference there may be between Socrates' and Plato's ideas, one ground for "separating" ideas lies in the problem of the realizability of a perfectly just order (1964: 119–21). His linking of these themes may be taken as a criticism not only of contemporary liberalism such as Vlastos', but also of antecedent presuppositions underlying Hermann's earlier formulations. In commenting on Xenophon, *Memorabilia of Socrates* IV.6 (a chapter devoted to showing how Socrates made his companions more dialectical), he further undercuts Schleiermacher by contrasting the "What is X" question pursued throughout that chapter with the conversational method of the bulk of the *Memorabilia* (1972: 116f.)

Strauss influenced a number of treatments of Socrates that have tended to break free of the scholarly conventions originating in nineteenth-century Germany. Central is the tendency to regard even Socrates as devoted to political philosophy, in the sense of philosophy pursued with methodical regard to the limitations placed upon philosophizing as such by politics. A number of scholars following Strauss' precedent have once more viewed Socrates' moral inquiries against the background of Cicero's statement that he brought philosophy down from heaven into the cities of men, or in the light of the interconnection between ethics and politics. These same scholars have accordingly tended to pursue ironic readings of both Xenophon's and Plato's Socrates. On a parallel track, Strauss' fellow student Jacob Klein developed Julius Stenzel's account to Plato's dialectic so as to make better sense of Aristotle's association of the theory of ideas with Pythagorean number-theory. Klein's students have pursued Taylor and Burnet's attempts to understand Plato's ideas independently of an Aristotelian logical framework, but there exists within the terms of this interpretation as yet no detailed account of Socrates' definitional method. To judge from a recent move away from the developmental interpretation of Plato's dialogues, a wholesale treatment of the question may not be necessary before scholars reconsider a habitual reliance upon some scanty later and likely derivative statements of Aristotle in preference to the fuller pictures Xenophon and Plato give us of Socrates. What this may leave is a field on which a few will seek to understand his worth in its appropriate political context, some will for a time still long for an ancient Wittgenstein, and most will doubtless continue to look upon Socrates as they always have.

References

Allen, R. E. (1965). *Studies in Plato's Metaphysics*, ed. R. E. Allen. London: Routledge & Kegan Paul.

Brandis, C. A. (1827). Grundlinien der Lehre des Sokrates. *Rheinisches Museum für Philologie*, 1, 118–50.

Brucker, J. (1742). *Historia critica philosophiae* [A Critical History of Philosophy]. Leipzig: Breitkopf. (Abbreviated Eng. version in Enfield, W. [1819]. *The History of Philosophy*. London: J. F. Dore.)

Burnet, J. (1914). *Greek Philosophy, Thales to Plato*. London: MacMillan. (Reset and reprinted with new pagination 1964.)

Campbell, L. (1867). *The Sophistes and Politicus of Plato*. Oxford: Clarendon.

—— (1889). On the position of the *Sophistes, Politicus*, and *Philebus* in the order of the Platonic dialogues and on some characteristics of Plato's latest writings. *Transactions of the Oxford Philological Society*, 25–42. (Reprinted in B. Jowett and L. Campbell [eds.] [1894]. *Plato's Republic*, II [pp. 46–66] Oxford: Clarendon.)

Döring, A. (1895). *Die Lehre des Sokrates als sociales Reformsystem* [The Teaching of Socrates as a System for Social Reform]. München: Beck.

Gulley, N. (1968). *The Philosophy of Socrates*. New York: St. Martin's Press.

Hegel, G. W. F. (1892). *Hegel's Lectures on the History of Philosophy*, trans. E. S. Haldane. London: Kegan Paul. (Original work published 1840–3.)

Hermann, K. F. (1833). *Über Herrn Professor Heinrich Ritter's Darstellung der sokratische System in den neusten Bänden seiner Geschichte der Philosophie alter Zeit* [On Prof. Ritter's Account of the Socratic System in the Most Recent Volumes of his History of Philosophy of Ancient Times]. Heidelberg: Winter.

—— (1839). *Geschichte und System der Platonischen Philosophie*. Vol. 1 [History and System of the Platonic Philosophy]. Heidelberg: Winter.

—— (1849). Die historischen Elemente des platonischen Staatsideals [The Historical Elements of the Platonic Ideal State]. In *Gesammelte Abhandlungen und Beiträge zur classischen Litteratur und Alterhumskunde*. Göttingen: Dietrich. (A later expansion of elements of Hermann's review of Stallbaum's edition of the *Republic* in the *Allgemeine Schulzeitung* from the year 1831, section ii, numbers 81 and 149.)

Jackson, H. (1881–5). Plato's later theory of ideas. *Journal of Philology*, 10, 253–98; 11, 287–331; 13, 1–40 and 242–72; and 14, 173–230.

Joël, K. (1893). *Der echte und der xenophontische Sokrates*, Vol. 1 [The Genuine and the Xenophontean Socrates]. Berlin: R. Gaertner.

Jowett, B. (1892). *The Dialogues of Plato*. Vol. 2, 3rd. ed. Oxford: Clarendon.

Maier, H. (1913). *Sokrates* [Socrates]. Tübingen: J. C. B. Mohr.

Nussbaum, M. (1986). *The Fragility of Goodness. Luck and Ethics in Greek Tragedy and Philosophy*. Cambridge: Cambridge University Press.

Ritter, H. (1830). *Geschichte der Philosophie alter Zeit*, Vol. 2 [A History of the Philosophy of Ancient Times]. Hamburg: Friedrich Perthes. (Eng. version from the third edition of 1837, in *The History of Ancient Philosophy*, trans. A. J. W. Morrison. Oxford: D. A. Talboys 1838.)

Ross, W. D. (1924). *Aristotle's Metaphysics*. Oxford: Clarendon Press.

—— (1932). The Socratic problem. *Proceedings of the Classical Association*, 30, 7–24. (Reprinted in Patzer, A. [ed.], *Der Historische Sokrates* [The Historical Socrates] [pp. 225–39]. Darmstadt: Wissenschaftliche Buchgesellschaft.)

—— (1951). *Plato's Theory of Ideas*. Oxford: Clarendon.

Schleiermacher, F. (1818). Über den Werth des Sokrates als Philosophen [On the Value of Socrates as a Philosopher]. *Abhandlungen der Berl. Akad. der Wiss.* (philosophisch-historische Klasse) 1818, 50–68. (Reprinted in *Werke*. Vol. II. Abteilung 3; or *Sämmtliche Werke* III.2, 287–308; also reprinted in Patzer, A. [ed.], *Der Historische Sokrates*. Darmstadt: Wissenschaftliche Buchgesellschaft [pp. 41–58]; Eng. trans. by C. Thirlwall [1832–3] in the *Philological Museum* Cambridge, and repr. in *A Life of Socrates* [1840] by Dr. G. Wiggers, trans. from the German with notes, London: Taylor & Walton, cxxix–clv, and again in *Xenophon's Memorabilia of Socrates* [1883], ed. C. Anthon. New York: Harper & Bros [pp. 442–8].)

—— (1836). *Schleiermacher's Introductions to the Dialogues of Plato*, trans. W. Dobson. Cambridge: Pitt. (Original work published 1804–28.)

Strauss, L. (1964). *The City and Man*. Chicago: Rand McNally.

—— (1966). *Socrates and Aristophanes*. New York & London: Basic Books.

—— (1972). *Xenophon's Socrates*. Ithaca, NY: Cornell University Press.

—— (1989). The problem of Socrates. In T. Pangle (ed.), *The Rebirth of Classical Political Rationalism: Essays and Lectures by Leo Strauss* (pp. 103–83). Chicago: University of Chicago Press.

Susemihl, F. (1855). *Die genetische Entwicklung der platonischen Philosophie*, Vol. 1 [The Genetic Development of the Platonic Philosophy]. Leipzig: B. G. Teubner.

Taylor, A. E. (1911). *Varia Socratica*. First Series. Oxford: J. Parker & Co.

Überweg, F. (1861). *Untersuchungen über die Echtheit und Zeitfolge Platonischer Schriften und über die Hauptmomente aus Plato's Leben* [Investigations Concerning the Authenticity and Temporal Sequence of the Platonic Writings and the Principal Events in Plato's Life]. Wien: Carl Gerold.

Vlastos, G. (1935). What is Love? *Christendom*, 1, 117–31.

—— (1957). The Paradox of Socrates. *Queen's Quarterly*, 64, 496–516. (Reprinted with modifications in Vlastos [ed.] [1971]. *The Philosophy of Socrates* [pp. 1–21]. Garden City: Doubleday & Co. Also in Vlastos, *Studies in Greek Philosophy*, Vol. 2 [pp. 3–18]. Princeton: Princeton University Press.)

—— (1988). Socrates. *Proceedings of the British Academy*, 74, 89–111.

—— (1991). *Socrates: Ironist and Moral Philosopher*. Ithaca, NY: Cornell University Press.

Zeller, E. (1877). *Socrates and the Socratic Schools*, trans. O. J. Reichel. London: Longmans, Green, & Co. (2nd. Eng. ed. revised from the 3rd German edition of *Die Philosophie der Griechen in ihrer geschichtleiche Entwicklung* [The Philosophy of the Greeks in Its Historical Development]. Leipzig: Fues 1875. The first edition was published under a different title. Tübingen: Fues 1846.)

Further Reading

Cherniss, H. (1935). *Aristotle's Criticism of Presocratic Philosophy*. Baltimore: Johns Hopkins University Press. Examines in detail how Aristotle interprets all earlier thinkers as his own "lisping precursors."

Deman, T. (1942). *Le témoignage d'Aristote sur Socrate*. Paris: Les belles letters. A still standard collection and treatment of Aristotle's statements about Socrates.

Gigon, O. (1959). Die Sokratesdoxographie bei Aristoteles [The Doxography of Socrates in Aristotle]. *Museum Helveticum*, 16, 174–212. An independent reexamination of the Aristotelian testimony.

Klein, J. (1968). *Greek Mathematical Thought and the Origin of Algebra*, trans. E. Brann. Cambridge, MA: MIT Press. (Original work published 1934–6.) Chapter 7 makes the mathematical case for Plato's "separation" of the ideas.

Magalhães-Vilhena, V. de. (1952). *Le problème de Socrate. Le Socrate historique et le Socrate de Platon* [The Problem of Socrates. The Historical Socrates and the Socrates of Plato]. Paris:

Presses Universitaires de France. An exhaustive review of earlier scholarship, sympathetic with Taylor and Burnet.

Montuori, M. (1992). *The Socratic Problem: The History – The Solutions. From the 18th Century to the Present Time. 61 Extracts from 54 Authors in their Historical Context.* Amsterdam: J. C. Gieben. A source-collection keyed to several related studies by the same author.

Sachs, J. (1993). What is a what-is question? *The St. John's Review*, 42, 41–56. An exploration of the theoretical and political context for Socratic inquiries.

Scholtz, G. (1979). Zur Darstellung der griechische Philosophie bei den Schülern Hegels und Schleiermachers [On the Representation of Greek Philosophy in the Epigones of Hegel and Schleiermacher]. In H. Flashar, K. Gründer, and A. Horstmann (eds.), *Philologie und Hermeneutik im 19. Jahrhundert* (pp. 289–311). Göttingen: Vandenhoeck und Ruprecht. A study of the influence of Schleiermacher and Hegel on several histories of philosophy.

Wiggers, G. (1807). *Sokrates als Mensch, als Bürger und als Philosoph, oder Versuch einer Charakteristik des Sokrates* [Socrates as Man, Citizen, and Philosopher, or an Attempt at a Characterization of Socrates]. Rostock: Adlers Erben. (English version from the 2nd. ed. of 1811 in *A Life of Socrates by Dr. G. Wiggers*, trans. C. Thirlwall. London: Taylor & Walton, 1840; and again in C. Anthon [ed.] [1883]. *Xenophon's Memorabilia of Socrates* [pp. 371–440]. New York: Harper & Bros.) A treatment of Socrates from the perspective traditional before Schleiermacher.

Zuckert, C. (2004). The Socratic turn. *History of Political Thought*, 25, 189–219. A study of Socrates' development by his own account as found in the dialogues of Plato.

Index

Note: Numbers in *italics* signify illustrations.